ISBN 978-0-260-45016-6
PIBN 10948970

FB &c Ltd, Dalton House, 60 Windsor Avenue, London, SW19 2RR.
Company number 08720141. Registered in England and Wales.

SEVENTY-FIRST ANNUAL REPORT

OF THE

SUPERINTENDENT OF PUBLIC INSTRUCTION

OF THE

STATE OF MICHIGAN

WITH

ACCOMPANYING DOCUMENTS

FOR

THE YEAR 1907

BY AUTHORITY

LANSING, MICHIGAN
WYNKOOP HALLENBECK CRAWFORD CO., STATE PRINTE.
1908

LETTER OF TRANSMITTAL.

STATE OF MICHIGAN,
DEPARTMENT OF PUBLIC INSTRUCTION,
Lansing, December 31, 1907.

To His Excellency, FRED M. WARNER,
Governor of the State of Michigan:

SIR—In compliance with the provisions of law, I have the honor herewith to transmit through you to the Legislature, the annual report of the Superintendent of Public Instruction, together with the accompanying documents for the year 1907.

Very respectfully,
Your obedient servant,

L. L. Wright

Superintendent of Public Instruction.

TABLE OF CONTENTS.

	Page.
Superintendent's report (introduction)	1
New legislation	1
Teachers' institutes	2
Summer schools	2
County schools of agriculture	2
Rural high schools	3
Investigation of school records	3
School officers' meeting	3
Work of county normal training classes	4
Compulsory attendance	4
School savings banks	5
Bulletins published	5
Special educational institutions	5
Reforms needed	5
Summary of statistics for 1907	6
Needed Legislation	7
General state supervision	7
Proposed legislation	7
School System of Michigan	8
Rural schools	8
Graded Schools	8
Township unit system	9
City schools	9
Normal schools	9
Relation between normal and public schools	9
Agricultural college	9
State University	9
List of high schools on accredited list of the University	10
Needed reform in school curriculum	11
Rural Schools	11
The rural school problem	11
The solution	12
Consolidation	12
Special conditions	12
Limitations	13
Rearrangement on township basis	13
Larger Consolidation	14
Economy of the child's time	14
Reform courses	14
Administration	15
Economy of expense	15
Economy of buildings	15
Graded and City Schools	16
Number of graded schools	16
High school course of study	16
Weak points	16
Normal Schools	17
University of Michigan	19
Taxes	19
Income	19
Purpose of higher education	19

	Page.
The Rural High School	20
Bulletin No. 25	21
An Act to provide for the establishment, and maintenance of rural high schools	22
Organization	23
Equipment	24
Course of Study	27
Library	33
County Schools of Agriculture, Bulletin No. 24	35
An Act to provide for the establishment of county schools of agriculture, manual training, and domestic economy	36
Organization	37
Course of Study for County Schools of Agriculture	39
Library and Reference Books	40
County Normal Training Classes	42
Teachers' Institutes	44
Teachers' Examinations	44
Bulletin No. 16	46
Kindergarten, Music, and Drawing Certificates	48
School Officers' Meetings	50
School Moneys	51
Uses of School Funds	51
Report on Auditing District Accounts	53
Agriculture in the Public Schools	58
Bulletin No. 26	59
An Elementary Laboratory Study in Crops	60
Industrial Education	78
Trade Schools	79
The Day Schools for the Deaf	81
Patrick Henry Kelley	82
Supreme Court Decisions:	
Board of education—Power to contract	87
Schools and school districts—Organization of districts—Certiorari—Propriety	87
Examination questions:	
State examinations	91
County examinations	107
Eighth grade examinations	140
Educational funds	147
University of Michigan, financial report of	148
Statistical tables:	
Comparative summary of statistics	157
Apportionment of the primary school interest fund	164
General school statistics	166
Employment of teachers	169
Resources of school districts	172
Expenditures of school districts	175
Miscellaneous financial statistics	178
Cost per capita of public schools	180
Statistics of township and district libraries	182
Branches of instruction	185
Private or parochial schools	187
Examination and certification of teachers	188
Miscellaneous statistics as reported by county commissioners	191
Condition of schools and school houses	193
Instruction in physiology	195
Graded school statistics	196
Census, enrollment, attendance, etc., in city and graded village schools	216
Miscellaneous statistics of city and graded village schools	232
Financial statistics of city and graded village schools	248
Special report of the superintendents of city schools	261
Receipts and disbursements at teachers' institutes	264
Local committees, conductors, etc., at teachers' institutes for 1907	268

Page.
Enrollment at teachers' institutes for 1907 272
County boards of school examiners 276
General statistics of educational institutions 281
Financial statistics of educational institutions 284
Special statistics compiled from commissioners' reports:
Parochial schools 286
Commercial schools 288
Private schools 289
Special report of day schools for the deaf 290
Special report of the county normal training classes 291
Summary of children blind or with defective vision 292
Index 295

STATE OF MICHIGAN.

DEPARTMENT OF PUBLIC INSTRUCTION.

1907.

LUTHER L. WRIGHT,	State Superintendent.
WALTER H. FRENCH,	Deputy Superintendent.
A. HAMLIN SMITH,	Chief Clerk.
NORA B. SHARPSTEEN,	Statistician.
GRACE B. WALLACE,	Assistant Statistician.
LYDIA M. OLSON,	Editor.
ETTA H. GARDINE,	Stenographer.
NETTIE GARDNER,	Assistant Stenographer.
HARRY A. WILSON,	Shipping Clerk.
JOHN G. BOHNETT,	Janitor and Messenger.

STATE BOARD OF EDUCATION.

1907.

DEXTER M. FERRY, JR.,	President.
W. A. COTTON,	Vice-President.
WM. J. McKONE,	Treasurer.
LUTHER L. WRIGHT,	Secretary.

SUPERINTENDENTS OF PUBLIC INSTRUCTION.

APPOINTED.	
JOHN D. PIERCE,	1836–1841
FRANKLIN SAWYER, JR.,	1841–1843
OLIVER C. COMSTOCK,	1843–1845
IRA MAYHEW,	1845–1849
FRANCIS W. SHEARMAN,	1849–1851
ELECTED.	
FRANCIS W. SHEARMAN,	1851–1855
IRA MAYHEW,	1855–1859
JOHN M. GREGORY,	1859–1865
ORAMEL HOSFORD,	1865–1873
DANIEL B. BRIGGS,	1873–1877
HORACE S. TARBELL,	1877–1878
CORNELIUS A. GOWER,	1878–1881
VARNUM B. COCHRAN,	1881–1883
HERSCHEL R. GASS,	1883–1885
THEODORE NELSON,	1885–1887
JOSEPH ESTABROOK,	1887–1891
FERRIS S. FITCH,	1891–1893
HENRY R. PATTENGILL,	1893–1897
JASON E. HAMMOND,	1897–1901
DELOS FALL,	1901–1905
PATRICK H. KELLEY,	1905–1907
LUTHER L. WRIGHT,	1907——

DEPUTY SUPERINTENDENTS OF PUBLIC INSTRUCTION.

CORTLAND B. STEBBINS,	1859–1878
WILLIAM L. SMITH,	1878–1883
DAVID PARSONS,	1883–1885
WILLIAM L. SMITH,	1885 ——
W. F. CLARKE,*	1885–1891
HUGH BROWN,	1891–1893
JASON E. HAMMOND,	1893–1897
DANIEL E. McCLURE,	1897–1901
WALTER H. FRENCH,	1901–1905
WALTER H. FRENCH,	1905–1907
WALTER H. FRENCH,	1907——

* In place of W. L. Smith, resigned.

SUPERINTENDENT'S REPORT.

This is the seventy-first annual report of the Superintendent of Public Instruction. It is my duty to record the work of public education during the year nineteen hundred seven.

Under the constitution, the legislature was given full power to establish a school system for the State; this was done early in the year 1837. At that time the settlements in Michigan were comparatively few and scattered. Only a few hundred school districts were organized during that year, but the early settlers of our great State realized the value of educational privileges and set about the organization of a school system with commendable zeal.

During the past seventy-one years we have built up a system of public education second to none in the great union of commonwealths, and while this system has not reached a state of perfection, yet in the main it provides a good common school education for every boy and girl and the means whereby the child may pass through the several stages of the public schools and enter higher institutions of learning.

There have been no marked changes in our educational policy during the past year, but there has been a steady growth in the professional spirit manifested by public school teachers and instructors in state institutions.

The work of the Department is largely executive, in that it makes plans and directs the work of county commissioners of schools and suggests to school officers better means and methods of accomplishing the real purpose of education. New legislation has brought new duties and thus increased the amount of work falling within the province of the Department. This has necessitated a slight increase in the clerical force and a more careful division of labor.

I am pleased to record the hearty co-operation of city superintendents, commissioners of schools, and school officers generally, without which the Department could be of very little value to the State. In fact, the real work of public education must necessarily be done by those who have immediate charge of the public schools, and it is the duty of the legislature and of this Department to so legislate and interpret our laws that the greatest possible degree of effectiveness may be given to the work of those who have the immediate charge of instructing the children of the State.

New legislation.

The legislature of 1907 enacted several laws which should increase the effectiveness of our school work. The mose important of these were the following:

Act 247, amending the general graded school law of the State, making it easier to organize such districts and providing for a superintendent of schools.

Act 74, amending the truancy law in particulars where the original law had been found defective, and in addition to this act, a new law providing for the compulsory education of blind children and of deaf children.

Act 35, a new law, providing for the establishment of county schools of agriculture.

Act 256, amending the law in regard to school districts issuing bonds by providing that any school district may bond itself by a majority vote of the taxpayers.

Several other minor amendments were made, and already the wisdom of this new legislation has been demonstrated.

In the following pages of this report the various phases of the educational system of Michigan will be treated more specifically, and the following outline merely covers in a general way the work done under the immediate supervision of the Department.

During the year two day schools for the deaf have been discontinued and permission given for the establishment of one new day school for the deaf at Marquette.

Permission has also been given for the establishment of five new county normal training classes in the following counties: Cheboygan, Genesee, Menominee, Montcalm, and Tuscola, making the whole number of county normal training classes at present in operation thirty-seven.

Teachers' institutes.

One hundred twenty-four teachers' institutes have been held during the year 1907, classified as follows:

One general state institute in connection with the State Teachers' Association;

Four six-weeks institutes in connection with the summer sessions of the State normal schools;

Ten two-weeks' institutes in connection with summer sessions of county normal training classes;

Seven three-weeks institutes;

Eighty-four short term institutes of from one to three days;

Eighteen traveling institutes, or institutes extending through one week, in which the instructors travel through the county and meet the teachers and patrons at different points.

Summer schools.

The policy of the State Board of Education in providing a summer session at each of our State normal schools is to be commended, because in this way opportunity is given to a large number of those who are actually engaged in the work of teaching for receiving such special instruction as will enable them to return a better value to the districts in which they are employed. During the past summer more than three thousand persons were enrolled in the four State normal schools and the plan of having a teachers' institute in connection with these summer schools gives additional privileges and adds a better professional spirit to the rank and file of our teaching force.

County schools of agriculture.

Under the law authorizing the establishment of county schools of agriculture, Menominee county is the first to inaugurate this system. $20,000 was voted for the establishment of such a school and the city of Menominee gave to the county a tract of land of one hundred fifteen acres. Thus we have established a new system of education in our state, the purpose being to provide elementary training in agriculture, manual training and domestic science. This school is really preparatory to the more extensive work of our State Agricultural College, and it is to be hoped that other counties will soon follow the lead taken by Menominee.

The legislature of 1901 provided for the establishment of rural high schools in townships where no graded school districts existed. During the current year one rural high school has been established in Excelsior township, Kalkaska county, this being the first township to take advantage of this law. Three townships in Genesee county have voted to establish rural high schools for the ensuing year, and other townships are giving serious consideration to this important question.

Rural high schools.

The Department has been frequently called upon to assist school district officers in adjusting the records and accounts of their districts. The records and accounts of about fourteen hundred districts have been investigated by a personal representative of the Department, and in about five hundred additional districts the records have been investigated and adjusted by the county commissioners of schools, under the direction of the Department. In all these cases the main difficulty has been that there is no uniform system of keeping the books and accounts of the districts. In many instances all funds have been mixed together in such a way that it was impossible for the treasurers to know what funds were on hand or what orders could be legally paid. In a few cases we found that no books or records were kept by the treasurer, and in others it was found that the treasurer had misappropriated school funds. The need for a uniform system of school records is very apparent and it is very apparent, also, that school officers are not familiar with the law governing their powers and duties.

Investigation of school records.

The purpose of these investigations is to assist school officers in the performance of their duties and set them right with reference to the uses and care of public money. The school officers of the state taken together are an honest, conscientious body of men, and they desire to do what will be for the best interests of their schools; but many school districts do not appreciate, evidently, the services of their officers, as they refuse to give them any compensation for the time spent in the performance of their duties, and this injustice has in part been the cause of the carelessness with which the public business has been performed.

In order to arouse an interest in school matters and instruct officers in their powers and duties I have inaugurated the policy of holding school officers' meetings in the several counties of the State, and up to December 31 meetings have been held in the following counties: Iosco, Bay, Huron. Allegan, Calhoun, Oakland, Macomb, and Saginaw. The attendance at these meetings has been large, in some cases every district in the county being represented. The interest manifested has been intense and already the value of such meetings has been demonstrated. It is my opinion that the Department should hold these meetings annually in every county of the state, if possible, but it should be remembered that Michigan is a large state, and there are many duties for the State Superintendent to perform, so that it may not be possible to reach every county. But if this policy inaugurated in 1907 is continued it will ultimately prove of inestimable value to the school officers and through them to the schools of the State. In every instance a permanent organization has been effected, so that hereafter the officers will be prepared for a vigorous program.

School officers' meeting.

In addition to these meetings, I desire to repeat the recommendation of my predecessor that the several Granges and Farmers' Clubs of the State should institute in the several school districts and townships, school improvement clubs, the function of such clubs being the welfare of the local school in the way of improving school grounds, school houses and appurtenances and increasing the attention of the patrons to their schools. The people of the State of Michigan can have just as good schools as they desire, but they will never have better schools than they desire, no matter how much work the Department and the school officers of the State may do. It remains for the people in each locality to provide the funds and to see that local conditions are made the best possible. In this connection the county commissioner of schools can be an effective factor in the organization of these clubs and in directing the local Granges and Farmers' Clubs towards a better school status.

Work of county normal training classes.

In the work of improving the rural schools the county normal training class is proving an important factor. Through this institution we have increased the percentage of trained teachers in the rural schools from two per cent to twenty per cent during the past four years, and reports from the county commissioners of schools where the classes are located show clearly that the professional spirit and the effectiveness of all the teachers of the county have been improved materially through this agency. During the current year thirty-six of these training classes were in operation and about six hundred young people in attendance. To this number we should add those who are pursuing the rural school courses at our State normal schools, so that during the ensuing year our effective rural teaching force will be increased by about one thousand trained teachers. Thus it will be seen that the day is not far distant when every rural school in the State will be taught by a trained teacher. And when we can unite with this an increased public spirit on the part of the patrons in our rural schools, we shall have come very near to solving the rural school problem so far as instruction is concerned. But it must be remembered that even trained teachers can do little under such unfavorable conditions as are found in some rural school districts. Place a trained teacher in a poorly equipped schoolroom where no adequate heating, ventilating, or lighting is found and where the sanitary conditions are of the poorest, where the school property is unattractive and untidy, and we cannot expect proper educational results therefrom. Hence I say that our people can have as good schools as they demand, but it requires effort on the part of every school patron in order to place the public school on a plane where it properly belongs.

Compulsory attendance.

The enforcement of the truancy law has increased the regular attendance by about twenty-five per cent, and has increased the number of those who complete the rural school course and secure eighth grade diplomas by the same percentage. On the whole, the new truancy law is working well, and yet we find that even this law and our child labor laws are being violated in some quarters. Statistics show us that forty-two persons in every one thousand of the population of Michigan are illiterates. This is a startling showing when we consider all that has been done in Michigan for public education. The child labor law is not well enforced in all our cities and there is need for such a law in our rural communities. Truant officers report that it is more difficult to secure regular and continuous attendance of children up to the time they are sixteen years of age in the country districts than it is in the cities. This condition of things is a menace to the welfare of the State, and our people should demand the enforcement of both the truancy and child labor laws.

In order to inculcate habits of thrift and economy, school savings banks have been established in about fifty villages and cities of the State, and reports from these schools show that the plan is working well. It is really a part of the child's education, and I would recommend that the superintendents of schools in all the villages and cities should give the matter of establishing school savings banks very careful attention.

School savings banks.

During the year two meetings of the county school commissioners of the State have been held. These meetings were well attended and have resulted in unifying the work of these officers and reducing it more nearly to an established system.

I call attention to the publications that have been prepared by the Department during the year and distributed to the teachers and patrons:

(a) Institute bulletins Nos. 1, 17, and 18, outlining the work of teachers' institutes in counties, county normals and State normals.

Bulletins published.

(b) Bulletin 16, outlining the teachers' examinations for the year.

(c) Bulletin 15, giving the compulsory attendance law in full with forms for the officers to use in enforcing the law.

(d) Bulletin 20, giving a tabulated statement in regard to the distribution and use of primary school moneys.

(e) Bulletin 21, giving the papers and discussions of the county normal training class teachers at their annual meeting in March.

(f) Bulletin 22, prepared by Professor Calkins of the Mt. Pleasant normal school on the subject of teaching geography.

(g) Bulletin 23, on the new laws passed by the legislature of 1907.

(h) Bulletin 24, outlining the course of study for county schools of agriculture and general regulations for their management.

(i) Bulletin 25, outlining the course of study for rural high schools and rules and regulations for their management.

(j) Bulletin 26, prepared by Joseph A. Jeffery of the Michigan Agricultural College, outlining a course of study in agriculture on the subject of farm crops. This bulletin will be followed by others of similar nature during the ensuing year.

In addition to these bulletins the Department has prepared in Circular No. 10 a careful statement of the division of school moneys, showing the several funds to be accounted for and used by school districts organized under the general school laws. Any of these bulletins can be had by making application to this Department.

In addition to the foregoing brief review of educational matters in the State I desire to call attention to the excellence of educational institutions not directly connected with the public schools of the State. This includes the seven denominational colleges of the State, the School for the Blind, the School for the Deaf, the State Public School and the State Industrial Schools. These institutions, each in its proper sphere, are performing an important work in connection with public education and the attention of our people should be frequently called to the work they are doing.

Special educational institutions.

During recent years there has been a very evident awakening among our people in connection with educational interests and I predict that in the near future some important changes will take place in connection with the organization of our public

Reforms needed.

school system. There are several matters which will be mentioned in the following pages of this report to which I desire to call the serious attention of the people of Michigan, and among these are the county normal training class, the rural high school, county school of agriculture and the re-arrangement or re-organization of the school district system of the lower peninsula.

SUMMARY OF STATISTICS FOR 1907.

1. School census	743,030
2. Total enrollment	523.969
3. Enrollment in graded schools	305,531
4. Enrollment in ungraded schools	218,438
5. Percentage of attendance	.69
6. Total number of teachers	17,286
7. Number employed in graded schools	8,526
8. Number employed in ungraded schools	8,760
9. Total teachers' wages	$7,087,589.56
10. Average wages for men per year	$550.70
11. Average wages for women per year	$386.21
12. Non-resident tuition	$120,112.81
13. Average number of months school in graded and city districts	9.4
14. Average number of months in ungraded districts	8.4
15. Primary money apportioned	$8,803,647.51
16. One mill tax	$1,058,866.43
17. District taxes	$4,223,343.58
18. Library money, fines, etc	$144,622.40
19. Loans	$1,071,897.84
20. Other sources	$909,154.75
21. Cash	$6,334,603.14
22. Per capita cost per year by school census	$16.27
23. Per capita cost per year by enrollment	$23.07
24. Expense for several State educational institutions for the fiscal year ending June 30, 1907:	
University of Michigan:	
(a) Paid from State funds	$434,819.59
(b) Paid from other sources—tuition, productive funds, etc	396,070.82
Michigan State Normal College:	
(a) Paid from State funds	120,342.95
(b) Paid from other sources	17,364.08
Central Michigan Normal School:	
(a) Paid from State funds	71,565.00
(b) Paid from other sources	6,570.90
Northern State Normal School:	
(a) Paid from State funds	98,538.89
(b) Paid from other sources	2,782.10
Western State Normal School:	
(a) Paid from State funds	50,000.00
(b) Paid from other sources	2,959.85

Michigan Agricultural College:	
(a) Paid from State funds	$316,155.22
(b) Paid from other sources	98,029.26
Michigan College of Mines:	
(a) Paid from State funds	71,000.00
(b) Paid from other sources	38,906.99
School for the Blind:	
(a) Paid from State funds	34,489.78
(b) Paid from other sources	823.98
School for the Deaf:	
(a) Paid from State funds	89,672 00
(b) Paid from other sources	18,309.12
Industrial School for Boys:	
(a) Paid from State funds	86,100.00
(b) Paid from other sources	8,999.90
Industrial School for Girls:	
(a) Paid from State funds	74,250.00
(b) Paid from other sources	4,173.15
State Public School:	
(a) Paid from State funds	48,000.00
(b) Paid from other sources	6,624.99
Total	$2,096,548.57

NEEDED LEGISLATION.

During the past ten years many changes have been made by the legislature in the School Laws of the State, but most of these are in connection with administrative work or with the minor affairs of the schools. I desire to suggest to the legislature several points of needed legislation which in my judgment are of the greatest importance.

General state supervision.

Under the statute the State Superintendent has general supervision of the schools of the State, but this language is so general and the range of his effective work is so limited that any definite supervision has not been possible. Several years ago the Department prepared and published a course of study which gave the recommended minimum amount of work to be done in the high schools of the State. Inspection of the work done in the graded and city schools shows that there is no uniformity in the courses of study and requirements for graduation from our high schools. This results from a lack of general State supervision. There is no one whose duty it is to visit these high schools and inspect the work. The recognition by our State institutions of the work done in the public schools is not satisfactory in all cases to either party, and there should be not only more uniformity in the work of the public schools, but there should be thorough understanding as to the relations existing between the public schools and the State institutions.

Proposed legislation.

The subject of industrial training is one that is being agitated in all parts of our land and must be met. The matter of economic administration of the rural schools is one that should receive the most careful attention of our legislature. I desire, therefore, to recommend without further comment, the following genera

ation which in my judgment if enacted into law and put into operation would materially advance all the educational interests of the State.

1. Legislation authorizing the appointment of a State high school inspector who shall have authority to fix the educational relations between high schools and State institutions.

2. Authority to appoint an inspector of rural schools who shall have general supervision over county normal training classes, teachers' institutes, teachers' examinations, the course of study, school officers' meetings, and in general all that relates to rural schools.

3. In order to advance the cause of industrial education the legislature should authorize an appropriation for State aid to be given in limited amounts to schools that introduce courses in elementary agriculture, manual training and domestic science.

4. A law requiring all school districts to furnish free text books.

5. Authority should be given for the organization of school officers' associations.

6. The legislature should extend to the whole State the statute governing the schools of the upper peninsula.

7. A law should be enacted providing for the equitable distribution of the primary school interest fund.

SCHOOL SYSTEM OF MICHIGAN.

The school system of this State at the present time, so far as it relates to public education, is organized as follows: Rural schools, graded schools, township schools, city schools, normal schools, Agricultural College, State University.

Rural schools.

The rural schools are for the most part under the primary district system. The school inspectors are authorized to divide their township into school districts and number them consecutively, but after the township has once been organized in this way the inspectors cannot thereafter either divide or consolidate districts without the consent of a majority of the resident taxpayers of the districts interested. As a result of this plan the number of school districts in townships varies from five to twenty. This means that there are from five to twenty single room schools and the taxing area divided accordingly. The number of pupils in these districts varies from one to twenty on the school census. The course of study pursued covers practically the first eight grades, though in a few instances advanced branches are taught. The school board consists of three members.

Graded schools.

The graded schools are organized under general law, and any district having one hundred or more pupils of school age may organize as such. There are 578 graded school districts at present in the State, and of this number about 450 have a twelve-grade course of study. The remainder of these districts have courses of study varying from nine to eleven grades. The board of education consists of five members.

The township districts are organized by general law for the upper peninsula and by special act for certain parts of the lower peninsula. Nearly the whole upper peninsula is organized under the general law, and each township constitutes a school district. The board of education has authority to locate schoolhouses and provide a sufficient number of schools and teachers. In nearly all cases in the upper peninsula there are village schools or graded schools organized within the township, but under the general township control, and in such schools the superintendent is superintendent of all the schools of the township. In the township system all children have the privileges of at least an eight-grade course of study, and in most cases a full twelve-grade course. The board of education consists of five members elected at large.

Township unit system.

City school districts comprise those organized under the fourth class city act, and all other cities organized by special acts of the legislature. In all these schools a twelve-grade course of study is provided and the work is supervised by a superintendent of schools.

City schools.

There are four State normal schools whose special function is to train teachers for the work of the public schools. These are under the supervision of the State Board of Education, consisting of three members, with the Superintendent of Public Instruction *ex officio* a member. The relation between the public schools and the normal schools is expressed in the following quotation from the records of the State Board of Education:

Normal schools.

"Resolved that the pupils regularly graduated from twelve years of public school systems in which four years are devoted to high school work with not less than two teachers employed in distinctively high school work, and whose term is not less than thirty-six weeks, be accepted in the regular two-year life certificate course without examination."

Students for other courses of the State normal schools are admitted from high schools with less preparation than above indicated, in fact all students who enter the normal school for any course less than the life certificate course are received from all the graded schools of the State. This means that there is no specially accredited list of schools for our State normals and no inspector is sent out by the normal schools to visit high schools and approve or reject their work. The relation, therefore, between the public schools and State normal schools is very close. In another place we shall make a special report upon the work of the normal schools.

Relation between normal and public schools.

The Agricultural College is organized for the special purpose of giving technical instruction in the subject of agriculture and has under its direction the experiment stations. Courses are also given in mathematics and all the sciences. The Agricultural College is under the direction of the State Board of Agriculture, consisting of six members. This institution has an accredited list of high schools which is the same as the University list with the addition of ten or twelve of the larger graded schools. No high school inspector is employed, and all the schools on the list are entitled to the same privileges in the institution.

Agricultural College.

At the top of our educational system is the University of Michigan, which is the largest State university in the United States. This institution has a wide range in its work and is under the control of a board of eight regents elected by the people. The University employs a high school inspector whose duty it is to visit high schools, examine their course of study and make such requirements as are

State University.

necessary in order that graduates from the high schools may be admitted to the University without examination. The following is the list of 138 city and graded schools in Michigan that are at present on the accredited list, and graduates from these schools may enter the University without examination and are given credit on one or more courses.

LIST OF HIGH SCHOOLS ON THE ACCREDITED LIST OF THE UNIVERSITY.

- Adrian
- Albion
- Allegan
- Alma
- Ann Arbor
- Bangor
- Battle Creek
- Bay City, E. S.
- Bay City, W. S.
- Beacon
- Belding
- Benton Harbor
- Bessemer
- Big Rapids
- Birmingham
- Buchanan
- Cadillac
- Calumet
- Caro
- Cass City
- Cassopolis
- Champion
- Charlevoix
- Charlotte
- Cheboygan
- Chelsea
- Chesaning
- Clare
- Coldwater
- Constantine
- Corunna
- Crystal Falls.
- Decatur
- Delray
- Detroit { Central, Eastern, Western
- Dexter
- Dollar Bay
- Dowagiac
- Durand
- East Jordan
- Eaton Rapids
- Elk Rapids
- Escanaba
- Evart
- Fenton
- Flint
- Fremont
- Gaylord
- Gladstone
- Grand Haven
- Grand Rapids { Central, Union
- Greenville
- Hart
- Hancock
- Harbor Springs
- Hastings
- Hillsdale
- Holland
- Holly
- Houghton
- Howard City
- Howell
- Hudson
- Ionia
- Iron Mountain
- Ironwood
- Ispheming
- Ithaca
- Jackson
- Kalamazoo
- Lake Linden
- Lansing
- Lapeer
- Lowell
- Ludington
- Manchester
- Manistee
- Manistique
- Marine City
- Marquette
- Marshall
- Mason
- Menominee
- Midland
- Milan
- Monroe
- Mt. Clemens
- Mt. Pleasant
- Muskegon
- Nashville
- Negaunee
- Newberry
- Niles
- Northville
- Norway
- Olivet
- Ontonagon
- Otsego
- Ovid
- Owosso
- Oxford
- Paw Paw
- Petoskey
- Plainwell
- Plymouth
- Pontiac
- Port Huron
- Portland
- Quincy
- Reed City
- Reading
- Republic
- Romeo
- Saginaw
- Saginaw, W. S.
- St. Clair
- St. Johns
- St. Joseph
- St. Louis
- Saline
- Sault Ste. Marie
- Schoolcraft
- Shelby
- South Haven
- Sturgis
- Tecumseh
- Three Rivers
- Traverse City
- Union City
- Vassar
- Vicksburg
- Wayne
- Williamston
- Wyandotte
- Woodmere
- Yale
- Ypsilanti

It will be seen from this sketch of our school system that there is supposed to be a close articulation between the several schools from the rural school to the University. The courses of study followed in all the public schools are mainly prepared with the view that young people shall go through the public schools and enter higher institutions of learning. At least this side of public education has been strongly emphasized, and while our entire system of education theoretically seems to be nearly perfect, practically it does not meet the real needs of the great majority of our young people. The training offered in our educational institutions practically leads only to the professions, and as a result too small a number of our young people pass even through the public schools. We find that of a stated number of students entering the public schools in the first grade nearly fifty per cent of them have disappeared by the time that group has reached the eighth grade, and when the same group has finally arrived at the twelfth grade we find only about ten per cent of the original number still in attendance. This leads us to the conclusion that there should be a reform in the curriculum of the public schools, and that said public schools shall be made to meet more nearly the problems of actual life as they are.

Needed reform in school curriculum.

RURAL SCHOOLS.

The foregoing discussion of the school system of Michigan makes it clear to my mind that the establishment of a proper course of study with work for the first eight grades of the public schools is at the basis of all public education. The work of our secondary schools, or the graded and city schools, is not closely related to the life of rural communities, and the problem of adjusting the courses of study and the instructors for these schools has so nearly been solved that it is unnecessary to discuss the subject at great length.

The only real school problem in Michigan at the present time is the rural school problem, and this subject has been discussed by all my predecessors from various standpoints. In the light of the increased attention given public schools and the investigations that have been instituted, it is my desire to contribute to the solution of this great problem.

At the outset the people in Michigan were thinly scattered over the lower part of the State. They were poor and the support of public education was limited. Michigan inherited practically the New York district system and the necessities of the case caused the construction of small, one-room school buildings, and these were furnished and equipped to give instruction in a limited number of subjects and on a very narrow scale. The subjects of reading, writing and arithmetic covered nearly the whole course. The increase of population and the increase of wealth caused the number of these schools to increase while their character remained nearly the same, and it is only in very recent years that the course of study now pursued has been practically followed in all the rural schools. The introduction of such subjects as language, history, civics, physiology, drawing, nature study, has been slowly accomplished, and at the present time the course of study covers many subjects, and yet the equipment of the room and the number of teachers employed has remained about the same as in former times. Very few school buildings have even yet been erected having more than one room, and practically none have been constructed with basements which may be finished off for workshops, kitchen and play-room use. The plot of ground selected as the school site has not averaged over one-half an acre, and thus the means for observation work in nature study and for experimental work in agriculture which is now being talked about has not been possible. Because of all these things and

The rural school problem.

because of the pressure now being brought to bear upon the rural schools in the way of increasing the course of study by the introduction of some forms of manual training and a study of agriculture, and because of the construction of our buildings and the training of our teachers, I repeat the state ment that the real school problem before the people of Michigan today is the rural school problem.

The solution. Various remedies have been suggested from time to time, and most prominent among those of recent times is the consolidation of school districts, which means the increase of the taxing area set apart for the purpose of a single school or for a group of people in a particular community. This remedy to my mind is one of the best. But the simple increase of area in the school district will not solve the problem; there must come with it a complete reformation and reconstruction of our school buildings and grounds, also the production of an adequate, trained teaching force. These will come, I believe, with the township unit district, which means, each township to constitute one district, with one board of education, a central high school with twelve grades, as many primary schools as are needed at properly located points in the township, expert supervision, and better school conditions.

CONSOLIDATION.

The subject of consolidation of school districts has been agitated now for several years and some very decided results have already been secured. Enough has been done to establish beyond cavil the idea that increasing the size of the school district even to the point when transportation of pupils is necessary and the construction of a modern, well equipped building and the employment of an adequate teaching force will produce something like the educational results that our people desire.

As mentioned in the report of my predecessor, the consolidated school at the village of Martin, the consolidation by legislation in Charlevoix county, the consolidation of schools in Genesee county at Grand Blanc and Mt. Morris, at Comstock in Kalamazoo county, and in a large number of other places where consolidations have taken place with and without transportation of pupils, has given an object lesson which may be studied by our people without great difficulty, and I find that the subject is receiving an increasing amount of attention by people in various parts of the state. People in certain parts of Isabella county, Kent county, Berrien county, St. Joseph county, are giving the matter very serious attention, and doubtless results will be seen in the very near future. It is not necessary at this point to give statistics in regard to these places, but the school authorities there will be pleased to give information to anyone who may desire it.

The consolidation of districts in isolated instances is of some value, but if we are to get adequate results the consolidation should go far enough to rearrange the entire township in which they are located. In the township of Orleans in Ionia county there are ten school districts with something over 350 pupils on the school census. Of this number ninety are between the ages of fourteen and eighteen, or high school age, and out of these ninety only forty are attending high school. The others are either pursuing an indifferent course in their own rural schools or not attending a school at all. This condition of things in Orleans township is simply a type, and the most pitiable part of it is that while the parents of the forty are able to send their children away from

Special conditions.

home to school, the lack of ability on the part of the parents of the other fifty, who are equally bright and should have equal privileges, closes the door of opportunity to them. And thus, while the theory of our public educational system is that every boy and girl may go by successive steps through the rural schools and higher institutions of learning, the practical working out of the system fails entirely to meet this theory.

The course of study as pursued in our rural schools is practically identical with the course pursued in the lower grades of the graded schools, and this course of study points almost solely to the professional side of life and not to the solution of the everyday bread and butter problem. Thus the boys and girls who are enabled to secure only such education as the rural school affords, practically go out with the ability merely to read and write.

Public education should be suited, so far as possible, to the conditions of the people and to their future aspirations, and while it is a laudable ambition for every boy and girl to plan to take a college or university course, this should in no way prevent the securing of practical training in the problems of their own neighborhood as a foundation for such advanced work. That is to say, the rural school should teach the academic subjects and to them there should be added instruction in music, drawing, manual training, domestic science and agriculture. These latter subjects cannot be classed as academic because they deal with the practical problems of life. A knowledge of the use of tools is a valuable asset for any and every boy. A knowledge of housekeeping and home economy is equally valuable for every girl, and a knowledge of agriculture, that is, the study and practice in the management and use of soils, crops, machinery, fertilizers, together with their relation to the commercial world, is bound to prove valuable to both young men and women.

The present arrangement of our rural schools makes it impossible to give all this instruction. The present course of study provides for full eight grades with an average of four subjects in each. Thus the teacher of the ordinary rural school is bound to have from twenty-four to thirty classes per day. At the same time she is the superintendent of schools, the kindergarten teacher, and too often the janitor and the truant officer, and with all these problems before her and with the very short time she can possibly give to each subject, the children leave the school at the close of the eight grades with simply a smattering of the subjects presented. Instead of opportunity for thorough drill and practice, absolutely no time can be given to these things.

Limitations.

The problem of securing trained teachers, that is, persons who are skillful in their work, for the rural schools is being slowly solved in Michigan by the establishment of county normal training classes and special courses in our State normal schools. It remains, therefore, for the people to so adjust their schools that the teacher shall be given an opportunity to do what is best for the welfare of the children now and hereafter. The course of study pursued should be preparatory for higher education and at the same time should include the practical instruction herein mentioned. I repeat that the present organization of the rural schools absolutely precludes the accomplishment of the thing that our people all desire.

Rearrangement on township basis.

Therefore, one remedy is first—Unite small school districts or consolidate them, and instead of one-room buildings, the construction of two or three-room buildings with basement under the entire building and the putting together into one school of the children who now are found in three or more separate schools. Second—Readjust the course of study. Third—Introduce such apparatus, tools and materials as is necessary to give instruction in branches not now included in our course of study. This plan will increase the efficiency of the teaching force by providing a community of interests and opportunity for consultation and advice, and by creating the spirit of emulation among the young people.

Referring again to the township of Orleans, the remedy for the conditions now existing there, it seems to me, is to unite all the territory of that township into one school district, and establish at or near the center of the township, a school for the lower grades and also a high school for the instruction of all children above the sixth grade, and construct an adequate building. Then discontinue the use of all of the present school buildings except four, which are conveniently located towards the corners of the township, and in these the instruction of the younger children, or those below the sixth grade, could be given by one teacher, and these pupils when they have passed the sixth grade would go to the central school. This plan would reduce the problem of transportation to the minimum, and through consolidation, not simply of territory but of the interest of the people and of the product of taxation, the people of that township could accomplish the thorough, practical training of all the children of the township almost at their own door.

LARGER CONSOLIDATION.

The discussion thus far has related to the consolidation of two, three, or four districts, as may be most convenient, and the establishment of at least two-room schools in the place of the present one-room school. This is an age of centralization, an age of economy and of the solution of economic problems. In the schools as at present organized the reports from the several school districts of the State prove conclusively that we are extravagant in the following items: (a) The child's time; (b) the administration of school affairs; (c) the expense connected therewith.

Economy of the child's time.

Under the first item, or the child's time, I call attention to the following points: We teach arithmetic for nine years, language and grammar for six years, geography for five years, history three years, and other subjects accordingly. This is an extravagant waste of time of the child. Teachers are continually complaining that they have not time enough to teach the various subjects, while the main trouble is that they use too much time in teaching. Yet the teacher herself cannot be blamed because our courses of study have been practically machine made all these years. All of arithmetic can be learned, and learned well, in the years from the seventh to the ninth grades. All of geography that is really essential and that needs to be learned from books can be secured in a half year. All of the technical grammar that is really essential, either for actual life or for advanced work, can be secured in a year, if the work is introduced at the proper time. What the child needs is to learn to speak and write the English language, and he will get this ability by speaking and writing, not through the study of technical construction.

Reform courses.

The first reform, therefore, in connection with the larger consolidation of our schools is a consolidation of our course of study, thus giving ample time to introduce before the high school the foundational work necessary in manual training, domestic science, agriculture, nature study, that will meet the needs of the individual should his educational opportunities be limited, and which will give him a proper foundation for the continuation of this work as well as the academic work of the high school and college.

Under the second head, or administration, we have in the average township ten school districts, each having a board of education of three members, thus making thirty men essential to the management of ten schools. Every business man knows that this is an absolute waste of administrative powers. Under the statute school officers are given the power to look after the business affairs of the district, and if instead of having thirty men to care for ten schools, the people of the township could indicate and select five men, it would increase the efficiency of the administration many fold.

Administration.

The third item, or expense, is one where the greatest study along the line of economy is needed. The administration as indicated above is unwieldly and expensive. Every school officer should be paid something for his services, and if we suppose that they are paid even a small amount the compensation given to thirty men in a township will not adequately pay any of them for the time he must necessarily use, and yet if the same amount of money could be used in paying one or two executive officers of a board of five we would have secured the maximum of efficiency at the minimum of expense.

Economy of expense.

To provide apparatus such as maps, globes, dictionaries, libraries, stoves and other material for ten schools in a township where only five schools are needed, and when five would produce much bétter educational results, is an absolute waste of money. The amount of money that has been used by the school officers in the purchase of useless charts and apparatus, in the purchase of fuel which has been allowed to go to waste, in improper construction or improper repairs of school property, and particularly in the employment of unskilled and untrained teachers, amounts to an immense sum. Close estimates show that the amount of money expended for these items and wasted during a year amounts to nearly a million dollars in the State of Michigan.

My plea, then, is for absolute economy in the time of the children, in the matter of administration of the schools, and particularly in the expense connected therewith. A careful study of these conditions will lead the student to the clear conclusion that instead of thirty officers in a township there should not be more than five. In the place of ten school buildings there should not be more than five. In the arrangement of the course of study we should secure the broadest possible course that will give us the maximum result. This conclusion will lead us, first, to the consolidation of the schools of each township into one school district, the election in each township of one school board, the organization in each township of not more than five primary schools and not less than one high school.

Economy of buildings.

I have not exaggerated in any of these statements and I call the attention of the people of the state to these matters because in my judgment it is high time that the grange, the farmers' clubs and the school officers' organizations should take hold of this problem of the readjustment of the rural schools with a firm hand, with clear and definite aims in mind and with a resolute purpose to solve the greatest school problem of our age, the rural school problem, in a manner that shall bring to the children of the present generation the greatest and best possible preparation for those duties of life which they will be called upon to discharge in the next generation.

GRADED AND CITY SCHOOLS.

The legislature of 1859 enacted a law that any school district having one hundred or more pupils of school age might organize as a graded district, elect a board of education of five members and establish high schools. Prior to this enactment there were a number of so-called union schools and private academies in the State, this idea having been brought to Michigan from New York. The enactment of the graded school law, however, provided for free education in the advanced subjects, through the establishment of high schools, and the system grew rapidly. The private schools and academies were replaced by the public high school. At the present time there are 578 graded school districts in the State, and of this number 100 may be classed as city districts. Of the entire number of graded school districts about 450 maintain twelve-grade courses of study, and all of the cities maintain such courses. The balance of the graded school districts have courses varying from nine to eleven grades.

Number of graded schools.

Under the Michigan system it has been the aim of all these high schools to secure recognition by the University, and the courses of study have been to a large degree shaped and controlled by University authorities. Until recent years the courses in high schools have been purely academic, and the training which the children were required to receive was controlled by the idea of higher education.

High school course of study.

The result of this has not been all that could be desired. Within the last few years a demand has come that our courses of study be made more practical, and three years ago a committee of the State Teachers' Association reported to the State Superintendent a uniform course of study for high schools. This course of study represents the minimum amount of work required for recognition by the University. It provides for several elective subjects, also for the introduction of music, drawing, manual training, domestic science, and commercial branches. In many of the city schools some or all of these special subjects had been introduced before this general course of study was prepared. The course of study here mentioned has been adopted by a large number of the city and village schools, and thus the work of these schools is becoming more nearly uniform. At the present time, however, there is great diversity in the work done in the graded school districts, and there seems to be a necessity for some radical reforms along the line of public education in high schools.

Weak points.

The number of students who after completing a high school course enter the colleges and University has been variously estimated from two to ten per cent of the graduating classes. The records of the past show that we have been compelling the ninety per cent of our students to conform to the special courses that meet the needs of the ten per cent. As a result of this, large numbers of students have found public school work irksome and the necessities of the bread and butter problem have caused them to drop out of school. The unfortunate part of this condition is the fact that the young people who do not complete the high school courses leave the public school with little more than a smattering of the common branches. Nothing has been done in the graded and city schools by way of giving them special instruction for particular lines of work. Thus they are prevented from entering immediately into the activities of life upon leaving school.

It is my opinion that within the scope of public education we may properly include such lines of special instruction as will in a measure fit young people to take up particular vocations upon leaving school. While it may not be possible to attach to our public school system such departments or trade schools as will turn out skilled workmen, yet we can give to our young men the rudiments at least of vocational training. It appears to me that the problem of the next ten years in the public schools of our State is the revolutionizing of our courses of study along these lines.

Special reports to this Department give the following results as to the introduction of special courses:

I. Cities.	
Number of cities reporting	97
Number having kindergarten departments	45
Number teaching music	68
Number teaching drawing	66
Number teaching manual training	35
Number teaching domestic science	20
Number teaching special commercial branches	57
II. Graded or Village Schools.	
Number of schools reporting	292
Number reporting kindergarten departments	77
Number reporting music courses	51
Number teaching drawing	40
Number teaching manual training	3
Number teaching domestic science	1
Number teaching commercial branches	70

From this statement of fact it will appear that a considerable start has been made along the line of special instruction, and the attention of our superintendents and boards of education is earnestly directed to this particular phase of education.

NORMAL SCHOOLS.

The normal school system consists of four institutions, the State Normal College at Ypsilanti, the Central Michigan Normal School at Mt. Pleasant, the Northern State Normal School at Marquette, and the Western State Normal School at Kalamazoo. The actual head of each of these institutions is as follows:

President L. H. Jones of the State Normal College.
Principal C. T. Grawn of the Central Normal School.
Principal James H. Kaye of the Northern Normal School.
Principal D. B. Waldo of the Western Normal School.

Executive Council.

These gentlemen constitute the Normal Executive Council, and the function of this Council is to recommend to the State Board of Education courses of study, instructors for each of the schools, recommendations as to buildings, and needed appropriations. These gentlemen act in harmony in all these matters and thus produce uniformity in the work of the normal schools and simplify the labors of the State Board of Education.

The State Board of Education under the statute is the controlling body of the normal school system and has full power under the constitution to regulate the work and decide upon the conditions of graduation, also the character of the certificates that shall be granted. The following is a summary of the attendance during the current year:

(a) Total number of different students enrolled during the entire year, July 1, 1906, to July 1, 1907:

State Normal College	2472
Central Michigan Normal School	968
Northern State Normal School	441
Western State Normal School	313
Total	4694

(b) The attendance at the summer session:

State Normal College	1387
Central Michigan Normal School	618
Northern State Normal School	296
Western State Normal School	557
Total	2858

(c) The number of graduates from each of the institutions for the year, July 1, 1906, to July 1, 1907, in the several courses as follows:

	Life certificate.	Graded.	Rural.
State Normal College	326	96	17
Central Michigan Normal School	65	32	66
Northern State Normal School	90	25	....
Western State Normal School	58	15	19
	539	168	102

This summary shows that the product of our normal schools for the current year is 800 graduates who are at once added to the available teaching force of the State. As will be seen, a large majority of these graduates are prepared for the work in the graded and city schools.

It should always be remembered that the excellence in quality of work done should be the real merit of an educational institution as of any other institution, and Michigan may take pride in the announcement that our normal schools rank high when compared with similar institutions in other states.

In addition to the work of our normal schools and the number of graduates therefrom it is proper to report that the State Board of Education has granted 91 four-year certificates to graduates of denominational colleges and the Agricultural College during the year. Also, 33 college life certificates were issued to those who had previously received the regular college certificate and had complied with the statute in regard to experience in teaching.

Under the law authorizing the State Board of Education to conduct teachers' examinations, the State Board has held two State examinations, the first during the last week of March, the second during the second week of August. From these examinations five State life certificates were granted.

The State board has also recognized and indorsed seventeen normal school diplomas or State certificates granted in other states and brought into Michigan by persons who desire to teach here.

UNIVERSITY OF MICHIGAN.

Taxes.

The founders of the State of Michigan were wise enough to look into the future and see the necessity for an institution which should provide special training for the various professions, and our State University has grown to be one of the largest in the United States. The land grants set apart for the founding of a University were wise provisions for a permanent fund, and the legislature from time to time has made large appropriations for its support. At the present time a tax of three-eighths of a mill upon the valuation of the State is set apart for the support of the University and to this is added special legislative appropriations from time to time, and even these resources are not sufficient to provide buildings and equipment suitable for such a great institution. At the present time the attendance is in round numbers five thousand students, coming from all parts of the world. The reputation of this great University is not confined to our own State, but it is known the world over. Under the wise administration of President Angell it has moved steadily forward, doing its great work.

The library consists of about 225,000 volumes, and has special departments as follows: Law, medical, dental, homeopathic, engineering, and architectural.

Income.

The income from the three-eighths of a mill tax produces something over $300,000; the interest on land grants $38,524; legislative appropriations and special sources increase the receipts to $916,542.70. The expenditures during the past year have been about $350,000.

For the year ending September, 1907, the number of degrees conferred is as follows:

Bachelor's degrees	794
Master's degrees	33
Doctor's degrees	8
Honorary degrees	9

Of these the degree of bachelor of arts was conferred upon 297; bachelor of laws upon 206; bachelor of science, including all engineering courses, 149; medical degrees, 68.

Thus it will be seen that from this great institution a large number of men and women who are fitted for special work and special professions are annually being added to the intellectual wealth of the country.

Purpose of higher education.

The purpose of a great educational institution is to add to the productive power of the country by increasing the number of those who through special training are fitted to become leaders in business, art, literature, and science, as well as to furnish a stimulus to the great body of people who cannot secure University training.

One of the prominent ideas presented in our common schools in the last

that the University doors are open wide to all who may desire to enter them and who are willing to prepare themselves by taking a thorough course in the public schools. The general educational system of the State is indebted greatly to the work of the University, and the institution stands at the head of our educational system.

The law authorizing the board of regents to issue teachers' certificates to certain graduates of the literary department has been the means of providing specially trained teachers for the larger high schools of the State, and in this way we are continually strengthening the general teaching force. The State has always taken a great pride in its University and our citizens should stand ready to provide the necessary money to enable the University to retain its present proud position.

THE RURAL HIGH SCHOOL.

The legislature of 1901 authorized the establishment and maintenance of rural high schools in townships where no graded schools were already established. This law has been practically a dead letter until the year 1907. During this year the township of Excelsior in Kalkaska county voted for and established a rural high school. For the current year the pupils of the township from the sixth, seventh, eighth, and ninth grades are admitted, and as these pass on through the grades, the higher grades will be organized and established. Three townships in Genesee county have voted to establish rural high schools, and these will be organized for the next school year. In many townships of the State there are no graded school districts and therefore no high schools. If the plan suggested under the previous head of reorganizing the schools of a township were followed out the high school would be provided under general statute, and the rural high school law by itself would become useless, but the law is valuable and will meet those cases where the people do not deem it advisable to disorganize and consolidate their school districts. It is unnecessary in this day to argue that all school children should have high school privileges. This is an accepted fact by everybody, and therefore I will enter into no discussion of the subject.

I give herewith the contents of a bulletin published this year containing the general plan of organization, the course of study and the suggested reference library for the use of rural high schools. It will be seen that the course of study does not follow the course usually provided for graded school districts, but seeks to introduce those things that are vital in the life of our boys and girls. For instance, the subjects of the common branches together with careful work in business correspondence, arithmetic, bookkeeping, and commercial geography, a careful course in literature which should be a mine of wealth intellectually for all our children, and added to this is a carefully prepared course in agriculture, domestic science and manual training.

I most earnestly urge that every township shall take up the consideration of the question of the establishment of a high school for the especial benefit of our rural people.

BULLETIN NO. 25.

STATE OF MICHIGAN.

DEPARTMENT OF PUBLIC INSTRUCTION.

LANSING, September 20, 1907.

To County Commissioners and all interested in rural high schools:

The legislature of 1901, by Act 144 of the Public Acts, authorized the establishment and maintenance of rural high schools in townships where no graded schools are already established. The reason for such a statute is that in many of our townships there are no opportunities for advanced instruction for children, and parents if they desire that their children receive such instruction must send them to some school miles away from home and pay their board and tuition. As a result, many of our bright young people who have completed the eighth grade are unable to attend high school because their parents are not in position to bear the extra expense. This makes an unfair discrimination in favor of the children of wealthy parents. But by the establishment of a rural high school in a township, all boys and girls will have equal educational privileges so far as the public schools are concerned. This is my idea of free public schools.

I most earnestly urge upon county commissioners and all interested in schools that rural high schools shall be established in every township where no graded school already exists, and it is my opinion that the law should be so amended that, even in townships where there are graded school districts, rural high schools may be established for the benefit of the rural communities.

I give in this bulletin the law governing rural high schools, together with a course of study, list of reference books, and some suggestions in regard to their organization and equipment. This course of study it seems to me will meet the needs of our rural young people.

Very respectfully,

L. L. Wright

Superintendent of Public Instruction.

[Act 144, 1901]

An Act to provide for the establishment and maintenance of rural high schools.

The People of the State of Michigan enact:

(297). SECTION 1. The township board of any township, not having within its limits an incorporated village or city, upon the petition of not less than one-third of the taxpayers of such township for the establishment of a rural high school, shall submit such question to a vote of the qualified electors of said township at a special election called for that purpose within sixty days from date of receipt of said petition.

(298). SEC. 2. All elections ordered by any township board in pursuance of section one of this act shall be held at the usual place or places of holding township elections, and notice shall be given and the election conducted in all respects as provided by law for the election of township officers and the ballots shall have printed thereon, "For rural high school—yes." "For rural high school—no."

(299). SEC. 3. If more votes are cast in favor of such high school than against it at such election, the qualified electors of said township shall elect at their next annual election of township officers a board of trustees of three members, one for one year, one for two years, and one for three years, and on the expiration of their terms of office and regularly thereafter their several successors shall be elected in like manner for a term of three years each. The township clerk shall be ex officio member and the clerk of the board, and the township treasurer shall be ex officio member and treasurer of the board with the same power as other members of the board.

(300). SEC. 4. Said board of trustees shall meet on the third Monday in April of each year and organize by electing one of the trustees as president. Regular meetings of the board shall be held on the second Mondays of May, August, November, and February, in each year. Special meetings may be called upon five days' notice by the president or secretary. The board shall have power:

(a) To supervise and visit the school;

(b) To admit all children of the township above the sixth grade and to admit and provide rates of tuition for non-resident pupils if they so elect;

(c) To select and adopt text books;

(d) To appoint legally qualified teachers;

(e) To fix wages, make general rules and regulations for the control of the school, suspend or expel pupils, fix the time of school, which shall not be more than ten months nor less than seven in any one year;

(f) To rent or to purchase and hold real estate for such high school, build and furnish township schoolhouses, determine location of grounds and buildings, which shall be as near the center of the township as practicable, according to sanitary conditions, and to receive and hold bequests and gifts for the benefit of the school, and to dispose of property belonging to the district subject to the provisions hereinafter named;

(g) To provide a course of study which shall be approved by the superintendent of public instruction and the president of the Michigan Agricultural College, and shall not consist of more than four years' work. Said course of study may include instruction in manual training, domestic science, nature study and the elements of agriculture.

(h) To estimate and vote the amount of tax necessary to support the school at a meeting previous to October first in each year and report the same to the supervisors, which amount shall be spread upon the tax roll the same as other district taxes, and in their discretion borrow money for current expenses, which amount shall not exceed fifty per cent of the amount of tax voted.

(i) To publish annually in one newspaper of the township or county a statement of the proceedings of the board meetings and an itemized account of all receipts and expenses, and file a copy of the same in the office of the county school commissioner and State superintendent of public instruction within sixty days of the date of publication of the same.

(301). SEC. 5. The secretary of the board shall receive not to exceed fifty dollars per annum for his services. It shall be his duty to keep the records, provide supplies, visit the school and make annual reports to the school board, the county school commissioner and the State superintendent of public instruction, in such form as the superintendent of public instruction shall direct.

(302). SEC. 6. All orders on the treasurer for moneys shall be ordered by the board and signed by the secretary and president.

(303). SEC. 7. A majority of the taxpayers of the township shall determine the amount to be expended in the grounds and building of said school and may bond the township for such amount: Provided, That the amount of said bonds shall not exceed five thousand dollars, and that the period of such bonds shall not continue beyond ten years.

(304). SEC. 8. The high schools established under the provisions of this act shall be under the supervision of the county commissioner of schools, and all questions of management, support, and control arising under the provisions of this act and not expressly provided for therein shall be subject to the provisions of the general school laws of this State.

ORGANIZATION.

1. The township board of any township not having within its limits a high school is required, upon the petition of not less than one-third of the taxpayers of such township, to call a special election within sixty days from the receipt of said petition.

2. At such special election the question of the establishment of a rural high school will be voted upon. The election is to be held at the usual place or places of holding township elections.

3. If a majority of the votes cast are in favor of the establishment of a rural high school, the qualified electors of the township at the next annual meeting shall elect a board of trustees of three members who, with the township clerk and township treasurer, shall constitute the township board of education.

4. This board of trustees must meet on the third Monday of April of each year and organize by electing a president. The township clerk is ex officio clerk of the board and the township treasurer is ex officio treasurer of the board.

5. Regular meetings of the board are to be held on the second Mondays of May, August, November and February, and special meetings may be called upon five days' notice.

6. Section four of the original Act was amended by the legislature of 1907 in clause (b) by providing that all children above the sixth grade may be admitted if their parents desire to send them.

7. The powers and duties of the board of education are specified in the statute, and among them the board is authorized to purchase and hold such real estate as may be necessary, to determine the location of grounds and buildings, and to build and furnish a school house when authorized by the voters of the township.

8. They are to provide a course of study which must be approved by the Superintendent of Public Instruction and the President of the Michigan Agricultural College, the course to consist of not more than four years.

9. They are to estimate and vote the necessary tax to support the school and report this tax before October first in each year. They may also borrow money for current expenses for an amount not to exceed fifty per cent of the tax.

10. The board is required to publish in a newspaper an annual statement of all receipts and expenses and make all necessary reports to the Superintendent of Public Instruction and county commissioner of schools.

11. The taxpayers of the township are authorized to determine and vote the amount of money to be expended in grounds and buildings and they may bond the township if they desire, the limit of the bond to be five thousand dollars.

12. High schools established under this Act are under the supervision of the county commissioner and the Superintendent of Public Instruction.

SUGGESTIONS.

(a) It should be noted that the special election provided for in this Act may be held at any time during the year, but that the trustees or board of *education can be elected* only at the time of the annual township meeting

(b) Frequently the town hall or some other public building may be rented, or a part of it rented, and fitted up for temporary school use.

(c) The course of study given herewith has been approved by the President of the Agricultural College. The industrial side of education is emphasized in this course together with such academic high school training as will give a liberal English education to our young people. In case students below the ninth grade are admitted they will pursue the usual subjects for seventh and eighth grades.

(d) It is not necessary that the course of study for a township high school shall conform to the usual course of study in city high schools, but it will train our young people for admission to the Agricultural College and normal schools if they desire to attend such institutions.

(e) The building constructed for the use of a rural high school should be large enough for two assembly rooms with superintendent's office and two or three recitation rooms on the first floor, and basement under the entire building. The basement should be constructed mostly above ground, extending not over two or three feet below the surface. It should be divided into three rooms, one for a furnace and fuel room, another for the girls for domestic science, and the third for the boys for manual training work.

(f) There should be at least three recitation rooms which may be used as class rooms. One of these should be fitted up as a physical laboratory for simple experiments in botany, physics and agriculture. The others should be fitted up as chemical laboratories for experimental work in agriculture and chemistry.

(g) The lot selected for the school should contain not less than two acres and it would be better if it contain five acres. This would give ample room for a play ground and a good sized plot for experimental purposes in agriculture.

(h) The pupils themselves, having been supplied with proper material by the board of education, should, under the direction of their instructors, do the work of decorating the school grounds, that is, planting trees, shrubbery, flower gardens, etc.

(i) The rural high school should be closely affiliated with the Agricultural College, and arrangements can be made with several professors of said College to appear before the rural high school and give lectures on various subjects.

EQUIPMENT.

The equipment necessary for teaching the different subjects will depend entirely upon the location of the school, the number of students and the character of instructors. The following is only suggestive and in all cases the material should be purchased as the need arises.

AGRICULTURE.

½ doz. hoes.
½ doz. garden rakes.
¼ doz. spades.
¼ doz. earth forks.
1 doz. garden trowels.
1 doz. pruning knives.
½ doz. pruning shears.
1 hand cultivator.
1 hand weeder.
A supply of whatever seeds, grains, plants or bulbs that are to be planted.

MANUAL TRAINING.

The equipment for this work may be made as extensive as required and much instruction can be given with a small amount of material. The following is given as a suggestive list which may be purchased entire or in part. Usually these can be purchased from local dealers but the regular school supply houses also handle the articles.

Six single benches with rapid acting vise, costing $8 to $15 each.

Double bench with rapid acting vises, $10 to $18 each.

TOOLS.

Set for each individual.

1 No. 5 iron plane.
1 10 in. Atkins back saw.
1 13 oz. adz eye hammer.
1 6 in. Stanley graduated all iron try square.
1 Stanley patent boxwood brass faced marking gauge.
1 each ½ in. and 1 in. firmer tang chisels, handled and sharpened (Buck Bros.)
1 Swedish sloyd knife.
1 hickory mallet.
1 9 oz. all bristle bench brush.
1 4 in. Champion screw driver.
1 6 in. winged divider.
Approximate cost, $5.00.

Set of general tools sufficient for six pupils, which should be duplicated for each six additional pupils in the class, except in bit sets which should be added to in assorted sizes as required.

1 8 in. ratchet brace.
1 Buck Bros. rosehead countersink.
1 Buck Bros. screw driver bit.
1 Buck Bros. 8 in. draw knife.
1 Stanley spoke stave.
1 26 in. rip saw, Atkins No. 53.
1 22 in. cross cut saw, Atkins No. 53.
1 6 in. coping saw with 1 doz. extra blades.
3 cabinet scrapers.
3 10 in. ½ round cabinet files.
1 steel 24 in. x 16 in. framing square.
6 6 in. malleable iron clamps.
6 36 in. Sheldon patent malleable cabinet clamps.
1 2 in. x 6 in. combination oil stone.
1 3 in. bronzed oil can.
Approximate cost, $20.00.

In addition to the foregoing it would probably be well to have one large work bench equipped with a vise. A supply of lumber including 2 inch, inch and one-half inch stuff, can be provided at small expense.

Whenever desired or convenient a small gas engine may be installed to furnish power for turning lathe and small circular saw.

If any blacksmithing is to be done, one or two blacksmith's forges with proper supply of tools, hammer, chisel, etc., can be installed.

DOMESTIC SCIENCE.

The domestic science tables are usually in two forms, one with a case or cupboard attached, another a plain table with drawers underneath. These tables can be purchased at from $3.50 to $6 each and will accommodate from two to four pupils. There should be a half dozen of these tables with the necessary dishes for the use of students, one range with usual cooking utensils and one scale or balance.

DOMESTIC ART.

½ doz. sewing tables.
2 doz. small scissors.
½ doz. large shears.
1 sewing machine.
1 large flat topped table.
Suitable supply of cloth, thread, needles, etc.

SCIENCE.

The usual laboratory material and apparatus for experiments in physics, chemistry, and botany.

COURSE OF STUDY.

	First year, 9th grade.	Second year, 10th grade.	Third year, 11th grade.	Fourth year, 12th grade.
English.	Grammar, Reading, Spelling.	English classics. Business correspondence.	English literature. American literature.	(Boys) Building contracts and specifications, orations, business law. (Girls) Essays.
Mathematics.	Algebra.	(Boys) Business arithmetic, bookkeeping, farm economics. (Girls) Household economics.	Advanced and mental arithmetic.	(Boys) Elements of geometry. (Girls.) Mental arithmetic.
Geography and Science.	Physical, Commercial.		Elementary chemistry.	Elementary physics.
Agriculture.	Botany.	(Boys) Elementary agriculture.	(Boys) Elementary agriculture.	(Boys) Elementary agriculture.
Domestic Science.		(Girls) Domestic science.	(Girls) Domestic science.	(Girls) Domestic science.
History and civics		American history.	English history ½ yr. Civics, ½ yr.	Political economy. General history.
Manual training.	(Boys) Shop work. (Girls) Sewing.	(Boys) Projects, farm utensils, etc. (Girls) Sewing.	(Boys) Farm machinery, care, repairs. Roads. (Girls) Hygiene, nursing.	
Drawing and music.	Freehand. Voice, Rote singing.	(Boys) Models for shop work. (Girls) Freehand—Plants, designs of wall papers, etc. Voice, Elementary music.	(Boys) Same as 10th. Designing in architecture. (Girls) House furnishing and decorating. Chart and song book.	(Boys) Building plans, blue prints, etc. Pattern drafting. (Girls) Millinery, etc. Costumes. Chorus and song book.

SUGGESTIONS FOR WORK IN AGRICULTURE.

The following is an outline covering in a general way things that may be done and subjects that may be studied under the head of agriculture. This will include the subjects of farm economy and the application of physics and chemistry.

I. Soil:
  1. Origin—
  2. Formation—
    a. Glaciers.
    b. Winds.
    c. Water.
    d. Frost.
    e. Plants.
    f. Animals.
    g. Gases in the air.
  3. Kinds—
    a. Sandy—locality in which it is found.
    b. Clayey—locality in which it is found.
  4. Modification of forms—
    a. Clayey loam.
    b. Sandy loam.
    c. How modifications are produced. (Experiments).
  5. Foods furnished to plants by soil.—
    a. Lime.
    b. Soda.
    c. Iron rust.
    d. Nitrogen.
    e. Sand.
    f. Magnesia.
    g. Potash.
    h. Phosphoric acid. (Effect of absence of any of these elements and how detected).
  6. How soil is exhausted—
    a. Planting same crop year after year without fertilizing.
    b. Planting crops that root at same depth.
    c. Planting crops that require similar foods.
  7. How soil is improved—
    a. Rotation of crops—
    b. Tillage—
      (1). Shallow *versus* deep plowing.
      (2). Harrowing.
    c. Effects of tillage—
      (1). Coarse soil broken up.
      (2). Fine and coarse soil mixed.
      (3). Air gets into soil.
      (4). Insects and their eggs destroyed.
      (5). Soil protected from drought.
    d. Drainage.
      (1). Open ditches *versus* tile drainage.
      (2). Importance of following natural waterways.
      (3). Kind of soil generally in need of drainage.

[illegible]

II. [illegible]

III. [illegible]

(3). Hoeing.
(4). Topping.
(5). Harvesting.
(6). Amount of sugar in beet.
(7). How amount of sugar may be increased.
(8). Value to the soil of beet pulp.
(9). Value of beet pulp as stock food.

c. Special study of potato. (Determined by locality.)
(1). Early potatoes *versus* late potatoes.
(2). Commercial value of red potatoes and white potatoes.
(3). Common diseases and how treated—blight, scab.
(4). Insect enemies and how treated—potato beetle.

d. Special study of onions. (Determined by locality.)

3. Leaf crops. (Determined by locality.)
a. Tobacco.
b. Cabbage.
c. Clover hay.
d. Timothy hay.

IV. Weeds.
1. Rye in wheat field.
2. Classes—
a. Annual.
b. Biennial.
c. Perennial.
3. Best means of destroying various classes.
4. Recognize common weeds at sight.

V. Stock on the farm.
1. Horses—
a. Draft horse—
(1). Breed, muscle, weight, wind.
(2). Blemishes.
(3). Common diseases and how treated—heaves.
(4). Insect enemies and how treated—bot fly.
(5). Care, shelter, pasture, food, salt.

b. Carriage horse—
(1). Same outline as above.

c. Best general purpose horse.

NOTE.—Have pupils select and describe examples in accordance with above outline—correlate with work in language and composition.

2. Cows—
a. Milch cows.
(1). Breed, disposition, general build.
(2). Care, shelter, pasture, food, salt.
(3). Regularity in milking.
(4). Care of milk.

b. Beef cows.
(1). Same outline as above.

NOTE.—Correlate with language and drawing.

3. Sheep. (Determined by locality.)
    a. Meat producers.
    b. Wool producers.
    c. Shearing.
    d. Same outline as above.
4. Swine. (Determined by locality.)
    a. Same outline as for horses and cattle.

VI. Bees.

1. Kinds.
2. Care, swarming, shelter.
3. Grades of honey.
4. Commercial value of wax.

VII. Poultry.

1. Hens—
    a. Egg producers.
    b. Meat producers.
    c. Best general hen.
    d. Care, food, shelter.
    e. Why variety of food is desirable.
    f. Green food, bone food.
    g. Common diseases.
    h. Insect enemies.
2. Care of turkeys.
3. Care of ducks and geese.

VIII. Orchard.

1. Kinds of fruit as determined by soil and climate.
2. Planting, cultivating, pruning, budding, grafting.
3. Common insect enemies and how treated.
4. Common diseases and how treated.

IX. Small fruits.

1. How cultivated.
2. How propagated.
3. Preservation for winter use—canning, drying, etc.

X. Forestry.

1. Care of the wood lot.
2. Reforesting.

NOTE.—Correlate with nature study.

XI. Kitchen garden.

1. Location, care, variety of vegetables.
2. Storage—Cellars, pits.

XII. Value of diversified farming.

XIII. Value of good water on a farm.

XIV. Farm buildings.

1. Location, drainage, etc.
2. Relative location.
3. Importance of implement shed and tool house.

XV. Things that will improve appearance of farm.
1. Paint.
2. Good fences.
3. Well-kept lawns.
4. Trees.
5. Flowers.

SUGGESTIONS.

Some use may be made of geology, botany, and chemistry, but scientific phraseology should be avoided and teachers should remember that agriculture is the science taught.

Correlation: This subject should be correlated with language, geography, arithmetic and drawing.

Make the work practical.

Sources of information: James' Practical Agriculture, Hatch and Hazelwood's Elementary Agriculture, George's Plan Books, Bulletins of Agriculture, Michigan Farmer, Teachers' Journal, conversation of practical farmers and men of affairs.

SUGGESTIONS FOR MANUAL TRAINING.

This course will principally cover instruction in the use of wood-working tools, their names, parts, uses and care. It will include exercises with pencil, knife, gauge, try-square and T-bevel; the making of the plain joint, the mortise, the tennon; splicing and dove-tailing, with some wood carving. It is unnecessary to state here the different articles that may be made.

Blacksmithing. This will include the proper tending of forge, how to clean, start fire, hold heat; welding, annealing, tempering, twisting and soldering.

Drawing. The drawing will cover general freehand work, mechanical drawing, ornamental lettering, geometric construction, simple projection, drawing to square, geometric solids, perspective, architectural drawing—including plans, elevations, details, working drawings and blue prints.

Domestic Science and Art. This work will include basting, stitching, gathering, buttonholing, darning, patching, feather stitching, and applications of these on small garments and other useful articles, such as kimonos, aprons, sewing bags, etc. The eye must be trained to accuracy. In the latter part of the work of sewing we may include measuring, drafting of fitted linings, waists and skirts, and cutting from drafts and patterns.

In the work of cooking we should include building and care of the fire, oven temperature, sources and composition of foods, food values and classifications of foods, chemical changes in the process of cooking, and for practical work a study of marketing, cuts of meats and carving. To this will be added laboratory work in which each student will prepare representative foods, such as beverages, cereals, eggs, meats, soups, vegetables, breads, cakes, etc.

LIBRARY.

It will not be possible to supply at the beginning a full working library, but each year should find additions until the school is well equipped. It should contain sets of works in literature, history, science and art, such as are proper for any private or public library, and in addtion the following books should be secured as early as possible, as they deal particularly with some of the special subjects to be taught in the rural high schools.

GENERAL REFERENCES.

Adams,
Commercial geography..................D. Appleton & Co.
Bender,
The teacher at work....................Educational Publishing Co.
Hinsdale,
Teaching the language arts.............D. Appleton & Co.
Hodge,
Nature study...........................Ginn & Co.
Kratz, H. E.,
Studies and observations in the schoolroom.Educational Publishing Co.
Painter,
History of education.
Redway,
Commercial geography..................Charles Scribner's Sons.
Seidell, R.,
Industrial education....................D. C. Heath & Co.

AGRICULTURE.

Armsby, H. P.,
Manual of cattle feeding ....Wiley & Sons.
Bailey, L. H.,
Types of farming....................
Principles of agriculture..............
Principles of fruit growing............ } The Macmillan Co.
Beal, W. J.,
Grasses of North America..............Henry Holt & Company.
Coburn, F. D.,
Swine Husbandry......................Orange Judd Company.
Collins,
New agriculture.
Felch, I. K.,
Poultry culture........................Donohue.
Goff & Mayne.
First principles of agriculture...........American Book Co.
Goodrich, Charles L.,
The first book of farming..............Doubleday, Page & Co.
Gurler, H. B.,
American dairying.....................Breeder's Gazette.

Hatch & Hazelwood,
Elementary agriculture .... R. K. Row & Co.
James,
Practical agriculture.................. D. Appleton & Co.
Johnson, S. W.,
How crops grow....................... Orange Judd Co.
King, F. H.,
Irrigation and drainage............... } The Macmillan Co.
Physics of agriculture................ }
Stevens, Burkett & Hill,
Agriculture for beginners............... Ginn & Co.
Weed, C. F.,
Insects and insecticides................ Orange Judd Co.
Wilcox & Smith,
Farmer's cyclopedia of agriculture.

AGRICULTURAL CHEMISTRY.

Gatterman,
Organic Chemistry..................... The Macmillan Co.
Holleman,
Laboratory manual of organic chemistry. Wiley & Sons.
Sadtler,
Industrial organic chemistry............ Lippincott.
Storer, F. H.,
Agriculture in some of its relations with chemistry, 3 volumes................ Charles Scribner's Sons.
Voorhees,
Chemistry of soil and fertilizers......... The Macmillan Co.

SOILS.

Campbell,
Soil culture.
Hall,
The soil.
Hilgard, E. W.,
Soils.................................. The Macmillan Co.
Roberts, I. P.,
The fertility of the land............... } The Macmillan Co.
The farmstead......................... }
Voorhees, E. B.,
Fertilizers............................ The Macmillan Co.

MANUAL TRAINING.

Bowker,
Busy hands.......................... A. Flanagan Co.
Channing and Whittaker,
Working tools and how to use them.... D. C. Heath & Co.
Dopp, Katherine,
Industries in elementary education...... University of Chicago Press.
Ham, Charles H.,
Mind and hand....................... American Book Co.

Rouillion,
Economics of manual training.
Summers,
First lessons in handicraft.
Woodward, C. M.,
The manual training school............D. C. Heath & Co.
Teachers' handbook of manual training...The Macmillan Co.

DOMESTIC SCIENCE.

Lush,
Domestic economy....................The Macmillan Co.
Salmon, L. M.,
Progress in the household..............Houghton, Mifflin & Co.
Sheppard,
Handbook of household science.........Webb Publishing Co.
Wilson,
Handbook of domestic science..........The Macmillan Co.

HOME DECORATION.

Burrage and Bailey,
School and home sanitation and decoration.D. C. Heath & Co.
French,
Homes and their decoration............Dodd, Mead & Co.
Wharton and Coddman,
Decoration of houses..................Charles Scribner's Sons.
Wheeler,
Principles of home decoration...........Doubleday, Page & Co.

COUNTY SCHOOLS OF AGRICULTURE.

I give herewith a bulletin prepared during the current year giving the plan of organization, the course of study and a reference library list for county schools of agriculture. These schools were authoized by the legislature of 1907 and Menominee county at once began preparations for the establishment of such a school. The county voted $20,000 for building and equipment. The city of Menominee gave a tract of land containing one hundred fifteen acres. The board of education was elected and organized and the work begun. The building has been constructed and the school will open early in the first of the year 1908.

Course of study.

It will be noted that the course of study covers two years, its aim being to take up the work at the close of the eighth grade and to combine in the succeeding two years a practical business course together with elementary work in the subjects pursued in schools of agriculture.

It is too early to pass any positive opinion as to the value and results of the organization of such schools, and I shall watch the progress of the institution at Menominee with great interest. The purpose of this article in this report is to call the attention of our people to the institution in order that they may carefully study it and investigate it in all the phases of its work.

BULLETIN NO. 24.

STATE OF MICHIGAN,

DEPARTMENT OF PUBLIC INSTRUCTION.

Lansing, Michigan, August 12, 1907.

To County School Boards and Instructors in County Schools of Agriculture:

The legislature of 1907 by Act 38 of the Public Acts of 1907 made it possible to establish county schools of agriculture, manual training and domestic economy.

These institutions are to be established for the special purpose of training the farmers and farmers' wives of the future and thus improve the social conditions of rural communities in general and uplift the farm home.

I give herewith the Act in full and some general suggestions in regard to the organization of these schools, the course of study and list of reference books. It is to be hoped that the people of the several counties of the State will avail themselves of this great educational opportunity and that many schools of this kind will be established in the comparatively near future.

Very respectfully,

L. L. Wright

Superintendent of Public Instruction.

[ACT NO. 38 OF 1907.]

AN ACT to provide for the establishment of county schools of agriculture, manual training and domestic economy.

The People of the State of Michigan enact:

SECTION 1. The board of supervisors of any county is hereby authorized to appropriate money for the organization, equipment and maintenance of a county school of agriculture and domestic economy. The board of supervisors of two or more counties may unite in establishing such a school, and may appropriate money for its organization, equipment and maintenance: *Provided*, That whenever the board of supervisors of the county shall by a two-thirds vote of all members elect, resolve to contract indebtedness or issue bonds to raise money for the organization, equipment and maintenance of such school, the question shall be submitted to the vote of the electors of the county at a general or special election to be called for that purpose. Notice of the submission of such resolution to the vote of the electors and in case a special election is called, notice of the calling of such special election shall be given in the same manner and for the same length of time as is now prescribed by law for general elections. If a majority of the electors of each county, voting on such resolution, shall vote in favor thereof it shall be deemed to have carried. The returns of the election herein provided for shall be canvassed and the results declared in the same manner and by the same officers as is provided by general law for canvassing the returns of and declaring the results in city, county and district elections. The manner of stating the question upon the ballots shall be prescribed by the resolution of the board of supervisors.

SEC. 2. A board to be known as the county school board is hereby created, which shall have charge and control of all matters pertaining to the organization, equipment and maintenance of such schools, except as otherwise provided by law. Said board shall consist of five members, one of whom shall be the county commissioner of schools of the county or district in which the school is located. The other members of the board shall be elected by the board of supervisors, one for one year, one for two years, one for three years and one for four years, and thereafter one member of the board shall be elected annually for the full term of four years from the date of the expiration of the term about to become vacant, but no member of the board of supervisors shall be eligible. Vacancies existing in the board from whatever cause, except in the case of the county commissioner, shall be filled by appointment made by the chairman of the board of supervisors, if the board of supervisors is not in session when such vacancy occurs. If the board of supervisors is in session, vacancies should be filled by election by said board for the unexpired term. Appointments made by the chairman of the board of supervisors, as hereinbefore specified, shall be for the period of time until the next regular meeting of the board of supervisors. Each person appointed or created a member of the county school board shall, within ten days after the notice of such appointment, take and subscribe an oath to support the constitution of the United States and the constitution of Michigan, and honestly, faithfully and impartially to discharge his duties as a member of said board, to the best of his ability, which oath shall be filed in the office of the county clerk. He shall also, within the same time, file a bond in such sum as may be fixed by the board of supervisors, which bond shall be filed in the office of the county clerk. Within fifteen days, after the appointment of said board, the members thereof shall meet and organize by electing one of their number as president. The county commissioner of schools shall be ex officio secretary of the said board. The board hereafter created shall prescribe the duties of the several officers except as fixed by law.

SEC. 3. Whenever two or more counties unite in establishing such a school, the provisions of section two of this act shall apply to the organization of the county school board, and to filling vacancies therein: *Provided*, That the county commissioner of the county in which the school is located shall be a member of the board and ex officio its secretary; and two members shall also be elected from each county by the board of supervisors thereof, one for one year and one for two years, and thereafter one member of the board shall be elected annually in each county for the full term of two years, but no member of the county board of supervisors shall be eligible.

SEC. 4. Whenever two or more counties shall unite in establishing and maintaining a school under the provisions of this act, the county school board herein provided shall, on or before the first day of October in each year, determine the amount of money necessary for the equipment and maintenance of said school for the ensuing year, which said amount they shall apportion among the counties in proportion to the assessed valuation of each county as last fixed by the State Board of Equalization, and shall report their estimate and apportionment to the county clerk of each county, who shall lay said report before the board of supervisors at its annual meeting. The amount so apportioned to each county shall be levied by the board of supervisors of such county, as a portion of the county tax for the ensuing year, for the support of the said school.

SEC. 5. The county treasurer of the county in which said school is located shall be ex officio treasurer of said board; all moneys appropriated and expended under the provisions of this act shall be expended by the county school board and shall be paid by the said county treasurer on orders issued by said board or in counties having a board of county auditors, by such auditors, and all moneys received by said board shall be paid to the said county treasurer for the fund of the county school board.

SEC. 6. In the county schools of agriculture and domestic science organized under the provisions of this act, instruction shall be given in the elements of agriculture including instruction concerning the soil, the plant life, and the animal life of the farm; a system of farm accounts shall also be taught; instruction shall also be given in manual training and domestic economy and such other related subjects as may be prescribed.

SEC. 7. Each such school shall have connected with it a tract of land suitable for purposes of experiment and demonstration, of not less than ten acres in area.

SEC. 8. The schools organized under the provisons of this act shall be free to the inhabitants of the county or counties contributing to their support, who shall be qualified to pursue the course of study as prescribed by the school board. Whenever students of advanced age desire admission to the school during the winter months in sufficient number to warrant the organization of special classes for their instruction, such classes shall be organized and continued for such time as their attendance may make necessary.

SEC. 9. The State Superintendent of Public Instruction shall give such information and assistance and establish such requirements as may seem necessary for the proper organization and maintenance of such schools, and with the advice of the president of the Michigan State Agricultural College determine the qualifications required of teachers employed in such schools: *Provided*, That no person shall be eligible to a position as superintendent of any school established under this act who is not a graduate of a state college of agriculture. The State Superintendent of Public Instruction shall have the general supervision of all schools established under this act; shall from time to time inspect the same, make such recommendations relating to their management as he may deem necessary, and make such report thereon to said schools as shall give full information concerning their number, character and efficiency.

ORGANIZATION.

1. County schools of agriculture are under the direct control of a board known as the county school board, consisting of five members, four of whom are appointed by the board of supervisors, and the county commissioner of schools is ex officio member and secretary with the same powers as other members.

2. Each member of the board is required within ten days after notice of appointment to take the usual constitutional oath of office and file a bond with the county clerk in such sum as the board of supervisors may direct and within fifteen days thereafter the board shall organize by electing one of their own number as president.

3. The board has authority to prescribe the duties of its officers

as fixed by law, and to have immediate supervision and control over the school.

4. The county treasurer is ex officio treasurer of the board, but is not a member of the board and has no vote.

5. All funds voted by the board of supervisors shall be kept separate and distinct from all other county funds and known as the fund of the county school board.

6. All orders drawn on this fund must be drawn and signed by the secretary of the board and countersigned by the president.

7. The county treasurer should keep a special set of books for the record of the county school fund, and he should pay no orders except such as are drawn on the county school fund for purposes specified by law and signed as above stated.

8. The secretary of the board should provide and keep suitable records of all meeting and transactions of the board, also a record of all orders drawn.

9. The secretary should prepare and have printed proper receipts, orders and vouchers necessary for the proper accounting of all moneys expended for the county school of agriculture and domestic science.

10. The school year should consist of not less than thirty-six weeks.

11. The minimum qualification of students for entrance will be the completion of the first eight grades in the public schools or other schools. Holders of eighth grade diplomas should be admitted and those who are not holders of such diplomas may be admitted upon examination.

12. The course of study as arranged covers a period of two years.

13. Upon completion of this course of study the county school board should issue to the graduates a suitable diploma signed by the superintendent of the school and the members of the county school board.

14. Instructors in manual training, domestic science, agriculture, and the specified academic subjects should be provided.

QUALIFICATIONS OF INSTRUCTORS.

1. The minimum qualifications of the superintendent of the school, as fixed by law, is that he must be at least a graduate of a state college of agriculture.

2. The instructors in manual training, domestic science and agriculture must be graduates of at least reputable institutions giving special instruction in these subjects. The teacher of the academic subjects should be a graduate of a university, college or normal school and have had experience in teaching.

3. It is possible that suitable instructors can be found who can teach two or more of these lines of work. This matter will be left to the discretion of the county school board.

COURSE OF STUDY FOR COUNTY SCHOOLS OF AGRICULTURE.

For Boys.

FIRST YEAR.

First semester...	English—grammar, writing, spelling. Arithmetic. Plants—elementary botany. Carpentry. Drawing.
Second semester.	English—composition and business correspondance. Business arithmetic and farm bookkeeping. Soils and fertilizers. Vegetable, flower and fruit gardening. Poultry.

SECOND YEAR.

First semester...	American histo.y. Plant life, vegetation, crops. Animal husbandry. Farm economics, 3 days; reading, 2 days. Chemistry.
Second semester.	Civics. Literature. Blacksmithing, shop work, harness and tool repairing. Rural architecture, 3 days; gardening, 2 days. Commerce and commercial geography.

For Girls.

FIRST YEAR.

First semester...	English—grammar, writing, spelling. Arithmetic. Cooking and sewing. Domestic hygiene. Drawing.
Second semester.	English—composition and business correspondence. Business arithmetic and farm bookkeeping. Cooking and sewing. Domestic economy. Vegetable, flower and fruit gardening.

SECOND YEAR.

First semester.	American history. Cooking and sewing. Laundry, 2 days; art work, 3 days. Home decorations, 3 days; reading, 2 days. Domestic economy.
Second semester.	Civics. Literature. Chemistry in foods. Millinery, 2 days; nursing, 3 days Dressmaking, 3 days; gardening,

SHORT COURSES.

Under the provisions of Section eight of the Act it is provided that short courses may be given during the winter months for students of advanced age and for farmers of the county. These courses should be continued from four to six weeks and should cover such subjects as dairying, stock feeding, stock raising, the sugar beet, rotation of crops, gardening, fruit raising, and such other subjects as may be suitable for the locality. I believe these short courses may be made a most important factor in the agricultural advancement of the county.

LIBRARY AND REFERENCE BOOKS.

The following books should be placed in the library of the county school of agriculture as soon as possible. If they cannot all be purchased at the start the list should be made complete at the earliest possible date.

GENERAL REFERENCES.

Adams,
Commercial geography.................D. Appleton & Co.
Bender,
The teacher at work...................Educational Publishing Co.
Hinsdale,
Teaching the language arts.............D. Appleton & Co.
Hodge,
Nature study..........................Ginn & Co.
Kratz, H. E.,
Studies and observations in the schoolroom.Educational Publishing Co.
Painter,
History of education.
Redway,
Commercial geography.................Charles Scribner's Sons.
Seidell, R.,
Industrial education....................D. C. Heath & Co.

AGRICULTURE.

Armsby, H. P.,
Manual of cattle feeding...............Wiley & Sons.
Bailey, L. H.,
Types of farming....................} The Macmillan Company.
Principles of agriculture..............}
Principles of fruit growing............}
Beal, W. J.,
Grasses of North America..............Henry Holt & Company.
Coburn, F. D.,
Swine husbandry.......................Orange Judd Company.
Collins,
New agriculture.
Felch, I. K.,
Poultry culture.......................Donohue.

Goff & Mayne,
First principles of agriculture...........American Book Co.
Goodrich, Charles L.,
The first book of farming..............Doubleday, Page & Co.
Gurler, H. B.,
American dairying......................Breeders' Gazette.
Hatch & Hazelwood,
Elementary agriculture.................R. K. Row & Co.
James,
Practical agriculture....................D. Appleton & Co.
Johnson, S. W.,
How crops grow.......................Orange Judd Co.
King, F. H.,
Irrigation and drainage............... } The Macmillan Company.
Physics of agriculture............... }
Stevens, Burkett & Hill,
Agriculture for beginners...............Ginn & Co.
Weed, C. F.,
Insects and insecticides.................Orange Judd Co.
Wilcox & Smith,
Farmers' cyclopedia of agriculture.

AGRICULTURAL CHEMISTRY.

Gatterman,
Organic chemistry.....................The Macmillan Co.
Holleman,
Laboratory manual of organic chemistry.Wiley & Sons.
Sadtler,
Industrial organic chemistry............Lippincott.
Storer, F. H.,
Agriculture in some of its relations with chemistry, 3 volumes................Charles Scribner's Sons.
Voorhees,
Chemistry of soil and fertilizers.........The Macmillan Co.

SOILS.

Campbell,
Soil culture.
Hall,
The soil.
Hilgard, E. W.,
Soils................................The Macmillan Co.
Roberts, I. P.,
The fertility of the land............. } The Macmillan Co.
The farmstead....................... }
Voorhees, E. B.,
Fertilizers............................The Macmillan Co.

MANUAL TRAINING.

Bowker,
Busy hands...........................A. Flanagan Co.
Channing and Whittaker,
Working tools and how to use them....D. C. Heath & Co.

Dopp. Katherine,
Industries in elementary education......University of Chicago Press.
Ham, Charles H.,
Mind and hand........................American Book Co.
Rouillion,
Economics of manual training.
Summers,
First lessons in handicraft.
Woodward, C. M.,
The manual training school.............D. C. Heath & Co.
Teachers' handbook of manual training..The Macmillan Co.

DOMESTIC SCIENCE.

Lush,
Domestic economy.....................The Macmillan Co.
Salmon, L. M.,
Progress in the household..............Houghton, Mifflin & Co
Shepperd,
Handbook of household science.........Webb Publishing Co.
Wilson,
Handbook of domestic science..........The Macmillan Co.

HOME DECORATION.

Burrage and Bailey,
School and home sanitation and decoration.D. C. Heath & Co.
French,
Homes and their decoration. ....Dodd, Mead & Co.
Wharton & Coddman,
Decoration of houses.. ....Chas. Scribner's Sons.
Wheeler,
Principles of home decoration...........Doubleday, Page & Co.

COUNTY NORMAL TRAINING CLASSES.

During the year thirty-two county normal training classes have been in operation in the following counties: Arenac, Antrim, Charlevoix, Clinton, Gratiot, Kalkaska, Oakland, Osceola, St. Clair, Wexford, Barry, Ionia, Ingham, Iosco, Macomb, Mason, Mecosta, Midland, Oceana, Shiawassee, Calhoun, Cass, Manistee, Newaygo, Otsego, Allegan, Branch, Lapeer, Lenawee, Ottawa, Saginaw, Van Buren.

Permission has been given for the establishment of five additional training classes in the following counties: Cheboygan, Genesee, Montcalm, Menominee, Tuscola.

Graduates. Four hundred students were graduated in June, 1907, making an average of twelve students for each class. This number added to those who had already graduated and were teaching, together with those graduated from the rural courses of the State normal schools, has provided sufficient trained teachers to supply twenty per cent of the rural schools of the State. For the school year opening in September,

1907, thirty-six classes were in operation with an attendance of about six hundred students.

On the first of March, 1907, a meeting was held in Lansing of all the training class teachers, superintendents and commissioners. At this meeting subjects directly connected with the work of the training classes and the rural schools were discussed; among others the subject of agriculture in the rural schools, geography, language work were given especial attention. All but two of the teachers were present at this meeting and it was most excellent in its results.

We find that the spirit of the students in the training classes is excellent. They are imbued with the proper teacher's spirit and are anxious to devote their services to the improvement of the rural schools of the State.

We have been very fortunate in securing suitable persons to give instruction in these classes and it is to be hoped that the tenure of office of these persons will be permanent. It is not advisable that the teachers in these classes be changed about as frequently as teachers are changed in the public schools. They should remain in the county where they locate long enough to gain the confidence of the teachers and of the people and thus become of real service to the public schools of the county.

Visitations.

The State Superintendent has general supervision of county normal training classes, and a representative of the Department has made one or more visits to each of these classes during the year. In these visits the Department desires to see the actual work done and to make such suggestions as may be helpful and as will improve the character of the product of the training classes.

It is not necessary to give herewith the plan of organization and course of study, as we have been pursuing the same as was used during the year 1906.

When we consider that at the time the law was enacted authorizing the establishment of these classes less than two per cent of the teachers employed in the rural schools of the State had ever received any special training to fit them for their work and at the present time twenty per cent of the rural schools are employng trained teachers, it is very apparent that the establishment of these classes was a wise measure on the part of the legislature, and that our people may look forward confidently to the time in the near future when all our rural schools will be taught by persons who have had special training to fit them for their work.

Summer sessions.

In fourteen of the county normals, summer sessions of from two to four weeks were held, thus giving additional opportunity for study and training to the general teaching force of the county. We are very much pleased at the reports received from the county commissioners and school officers in regard to the work of the graduates of the training classes. Almost without exception these report [illegible] show that the young people appreciate their opportunities and resp[illegible]ies, and show a decided improvement in the work over teachers wh[illegible] had this training. It should always be borne in mind that expe[illegible] the equivalent of training, as training should always precede [illegible] basis upon which a proper experience may be secured. The one [illegible] upon experience may go along for years [illegible] errors and [illegible] knowing that he has done so.

So far as the instruction in rural [illegible]ned, all our [illegible] take courage at the thought that we [illegible] give to our [illegible] such instruction as will enable them [illegible] of their [illegible]

It cannot be said that any institution is perfect, and the training class movement has its weak points, but on the whole we have only words of praise and congratulation.

TEACHERS' INSTITUTES.

The plan pursued during the year 1907 in regard to teachers' institutes has been a continuation of that inaugurated in the preceding year. The counties adjoining those in which State normal schools are located were united with said normal schools for an institute to be continued during the summer session of six weeks. More than three thousand teachers were enrolled in the four normal schools for this special institute work. In many cases they requested and received credit on regular normal school courses for the work done. In other cases they received credit only for institute instruction. These summer sessions together with the special session of the county normal training classes afforded an opportunity for special training and instruction to nearly five thousand teachers.

It is probable that no single plan of conducting teachers' institutes would secure the best results for all, but experience up to date shows that the plan of having these summer sessions, followed during the year by short institutes in the several counties, is productive of most excellent results. It is safe to say that we are nearer the solution of the teachers' institute problem in Michigan today than we have ever been before, and that they are being conducted so as to produce the greatest possible good to the greatest possible number of teachers.

For the work in the summer sessions and for the short institutes to be held during the year a special list of persons was selected by the State Superintendent, and these persons were supplied with full instructions in regard to the work expected, such instructions being incorporated in bulletins Nos. 1, 17 and 18. The persons so selected were requested to give special attention to the suggestions of the Department and to carry out as far as possible a uniform policy in the matter of instruction and management of teachers' institutes.

TEACHERS' EXAMINATIONS.

Reports to this office show that the number of persons who take teachers' examinations has been steadily diminishing during the past fifteen years. At the same time the character of the personnel of the teaching force has been steadily improving.

As the Department is authorized to fix the list of subjects in which teachers shall be examined, and prepare examination questions, the plan has been adopted of announcing in advance special subjects for the study of the teachers as a preparation for the examinations. This plan seems to be working well, and in order that the work of the past year may become a matter of permanent record, I give herewith an outline of the special work that has been pursued by the teachers. The first statement gives a list of selections that have been studied by the teachers in preparation for the examination in reading, followed by a list of special subjects for the eighth grade examinations. The Department has been very much pleased with the results secured along literary lines as an outgrowth of this plan of making a special study of literary selections. As a result we have increased the knowledge of the teachers of literary subjects, increased their liking for literature and their power to interest children in it, and have greatly improved the quality of the instruction in the subject of reading in the public schools.

MASTERPIECES FOR TEACHERS' EXAMINATIONS.

March,	1901	To a Waterfowl. Bryant.
June,	1901	Evangeline (selections from). Longfellow.
August,	1901	Enoch Arden. Tennyson.
October,	1901	Elegy. Gray.
March,	1902	Vision of Sir Launfal. Lowell.
June,	1902	The Courtship of Miles Standish. Longfellow.
August,	1902	Merchant of Venice. Shakespeare.
October,	1902	Deserted Village. Goldsmith.
March,	1903	Vision of Sir Launfal. Lowell.
June,	1903	Sesame. Ruskin.
August,	1903	American Scholar. Emerson.
October,	1903	A Rill from the Town Pump. Hawthorne.
March,	1904	Canto V, Lady of the Lake. Scott.
June,	1904	Cotter's Saturday Night. Burns.
August,	1904	Act III, Julius Caesar. Shakespeare.
October,	1904	Thanatopsis. Bryant.
March,	1905	Silas Marner. Eliot.
June,	1905	Legend of Sleepy Hollow. Irving.
August,	1905	Elegy. Gray.
October,	1905	Oration at Laying the Corner Stone of the Bunker Hill Monument. Webster.
June,	1906	Act III, Hamlet. Shakespeare.
August,	1906	Intimations of Immortality. Wordsworth.
October,	1906	Gray Champion. Hawthorne.
June,	1907	Speech on Conciliation of American Colonies. Burke.
August,	1907	Princess. Tennyson.
October,	1907	Ode to a Skylark. Shelley.

MASTERPIECES FOR EIGHTH GRADE EXAMINATIONS.

May,	1901	Concord Hymn. Emerson.
February,	1902	Snow-Bound. Whittier.
May,	1902	Planting of the Apple Tree. Bryant.
May,	1903	Great Stone Face. Hawthorne.
May,	1904	Paul Revere's Ride. Longfellow.
May,	1905	Barefoot Boy. Whittier.
May,	1906	Landing of the Pilgrims. Hemans.
May,	1907	Rip Van Winkle. Irving.

BULLETIN NO. 16.

STATE OF MICHIGAN,

DEPARTMENT OF PUBLIC INSTRUCTION.

LANSING, January 2, 1907.

To Commissioners, Examiners and Teachers:

The commissioners present at the annual meeting at Battle Creek expressed their approval of the plan pursued last year for conducting teachers' examinations. I therefore submit the plan and special subjects for 1907. Attention is called to the change in rule 9 governing two trials for second and first grade certificates. Applicants must write all the third grade subjects for all certificates at one examination.

The special topics given herewith apply to third grade only.

Commissioners should see that these circulars are sent to all teachers, prospective teachers and graduating classes.

DATES.

June 20–21.
August 8–9.
October 17–18.

ARITHMETIC.

June. Percentage with its various applications.
Mensuration: surfaces, solids, square root, cube root.
Mental analysis; commercial forms.

August. Fractions, common and decimal; denominate numbers; short methods of multiplying and dividing integers and fractions.
Mental analysis.
Business arithmetic including commercial forms and business problems.

October. Fundamental processes; factoring and its applications; analysis of difficult problems in fractions and percentage; proportion; occupations.

GRAMMAR.

June. Nouns and their inflections.
Adverbs, comparison, and all forms and uses.
Verbs and all their modifications.
Sentence study; syntax and analysis.
Infinitives, participles, gerunds.

August. Pronouns and their inflections.
Adjectives, comparison, and all forms and uses.
Prepositions and conjunctions, forms and uses.
Sentence analysis.
Infinitives, participles, gerunds.
Construction of words.

October. Paragraphing and punctuation.
Verbs and their modifications.
Construction of words.
Idiomatic constructions.
Parsing.

GEOGRAPHY.

June. Mathematical geography—circles, zones, latitudes, longitude causes of seasons day and night, etc.
Physical features—mountains, plains, plateaus, divides.

Europe—divisions, physiography, resources, transportation, cities, commerce, education, forms of government, mining.
United States—same as Europe.

August. World's drainage systems.
Asia—same as Europe.
Similar study of all continental and oceanic islands.
Michigan—same as Europe, adding history.
Canada—same as Europe.

October. Climate and distribution of life.
General study of continents, formation and physiography.
South America—same as Europe.
Africa—same as Europe.
Mexico—same as Europe.

CIVIL GOVERNMENT.

June. United States Constitution.
- Powers of Congress.
- Consular service.
- Ambassadors.

August. The executive and judicial branches of national government.
National prohibitions and state prohibitions.

October. State government.
Officers—duties and powers.
School system.

UNITED STATES HISTORY.

June. A study of the Declaration of Independence and its effects.
A study of the Constitution.
A study of the Monroe Doctrine and its effects.
The establishment of banks, and the subsequent history of banking.
Legislation since the civil war.
Features of present progress.
Michigan history.

August. The Revolution and the Critical Period.
The Civil War and reconstruction.
The Spanish-American War, its causes and results.
The Mexican War and its results.
War of 1812.
Michigan history.

October. The colonial period.
- a. Old world conditions.
- b. Discovery and settlement.
- c. Governments.
- d. The wars of this period.

Current events, including:
- a. Biographies of present day statesmen.
- b. Problems of the nation.
- c. Investigations and their effects.
- d. National projects.
- e. Other events.

*Michigan history, including:
- a. French occupancy.
- b. Jesuits in Michigan.
- c. Conspiracy of Pontiac.
- d. Michigan under four flags: French, English, Spanish, United States.
- e. Territorial government.
- f. Toledo war.
- g. Biographies of Cadillac, Mason, Pingree, Alger, Chandler, Blair, Pierce Marquette, La Salle, Peter White.
- h. Location of the capital.
- i. The "Soo" and its importance.
- j. Michigan as a part of northwest territory.
- k. Ordinance of 1787.

KINDERGARTEN, MUSIC AND DRAWING CERTIFICATES.

The subjects of music, drawing and kindergarten instruction have become recognized parts of the course of study of nearly all our graded and city schools. The first of these to be introduced was the kindergarten, the law authorizing it being passed in 1891. In 1901 the legislature provided the means for recognizing kindergarten, music, and drawing teachers and granting certificates to the same. The statute placed this power in the hands of the State Superintendent, and he is also given power to approve institutions where special courses are given in these subjects. During the year 1907 the State Superintendent has issued 71 kindergarten certificates, 59 music certificates and 49 drawing certificates. These certificates are based upon the completion of the required course of study as provided in the statute and upon the approval of the State Superintendent of the institutions where the instruction was secured, and they qualify the holders to teach these subjects for life in the public schools of the State. For the information of superintendents and teachers I give herewith a list of the institutions whose courses of study have been approved by the State Superintendent and whose graduates are recognized in Michigan. The following is the lists:

Certificates issued.

KINDERGARTEN.

Alma College.
Benton Harbor College.
Buffalo Free Kindergarten Association.
California State Normal School (Los Angeles).
Central Michigan Normal School (Mt. Pleasant).
Chicago Free Kindergarten School.
Chicago Froebel Kindergarten.
Chicago Kindergarten College.
Cleveland Kindergarten Training School.
Detroit Kindergarten Normal School.
Ferris Institute.
Grand Rapids Kindergarten Training School.
Indiana Kindergarten and Primary Normal School.
Indianapolis Kindergarten Training School.
Keble Kindergarten School (Syracuse, N. Y.).
Lucy Webb Hayes National Training School (Washington, D. C.).
Michigan State Normal College (Ypsilanti).
Milwaukee Mission Kindergarten School.
Milwaukee State Normal School.
Minneapolis Kindergarten Association.
Northern Indiana Normal School (Valparaiso, Ind.).
Northern State Normal School (Marquette).

Oberlin College Kindergarten Training School.
Oswego Normal School (New York.)
Phoebe A. Hearst Kindergarten Training School (Washington, D. C.).
Ruth Avery Kindergarten Training School.
Stout Kindergarten Training School (Menomonie, Wis.).
Superior (Wisconsin) Normal School.
Thomas Normal Training School (Detroit).
University of Chicago (School of Education Kindergarten).
Western State Normal School (Kalamazoo).

MUSIC.

Albion College.
Alma College.
Central Michigan Normal School (Mt. Pleasant).
Chicago Auditorium Conservatory of Music.
Chicago Musical College.
Chicago New School of Methods.
Cottey College (Nevada, Mo.)
Crane Normal Institute of Music (Potsdam, N. Y.).
Detroit Conservatory of Music.
Lawrence University (Appleton, Wis.).
Michigan State Normal College (Ypsilanti).
New England Conservatory of Music (Boston).
Northern State Normal School (Marquette).
Olivet College.
Tomlin's School of Music (Chicago).
Thomas Normal Training School (Detroit).
University of Michigan Conservatory of Music.
Western State Normal School (Kalamazoo).

DRAWING.

Art Institute (Chicago).
Central Michigan Normal School (Mt. Pleasant.)
Massachusetts Normal Art School.
Michigan State Normal College (Ypsilanti).
Northern State Normal School (Marquette).
Olivet College.
Pratt Institute (Brooklyn, N. Y.)
Thomas Normal Training School (Detroit)
University of Michigan Conservatory.
Western State Normal School (Kalamazoo).

SCHOOL OFFICERS' MEETINGS.

In order that the Department may come into closer touch with the people of the State, and particularly with school officers, the plan of holding in each county annually a school officers' meeting has been inaugurated, and during the fall of 1907 meetings have been held in the following counties: Iosco, Bay, Huron, Saginaw, Allegan, Calhoun, Oakland, and Macomb, and during the following year this plan will be continued until meetings have been held in every county of the State.

Plan of organization.

It is unsatisfactory to attempt to reach those in charge of the public schools by means of reports or circulars. Greater and better results will certainly be secured through a personal acquaintance and contact. The meetings thus far held have been very largely attended, and in some of the counties practically every school officer was present. The plan pursued thus far has been to take up matters of school law and the business administration of school affairs, giving particular attention to the use and care of school moneys and the duties and limitations of the officers who were elected as representatives of the people. Full and frank discussions have been given in regard to all these matters, and in each county a permanent organization of the officers has been effected. The purpose of this permanent organization is that there shall be at least an annual meeting of all the school officers of the county under the general direction of the Department, but under the specific direction of the county commissioner of schools, who is elected by the people to be the actual head of the school system of the county. It is believed that through this organization all the officers of the county will become acquainted with one another, and a bond of confidence will be established which will very greatly promote the welfare of the schools of the county. Teachers institutes are valuable for teachers, but if we are ever to improve our schools we must begin at the bottom, and here we find the board of education elected by the people with large powers and duties and even larger responsibilities in regard to the public welfare. No school can be efficient where the officers are indifferent or ignorant of their powers and responsibilities, or where the officers elected assume to interfere with matters that do not belong to them. We find both extremes. In some cases school boards are absolutely indifferent and give no attention to school affairs. In other cases they are extremely attentive, and by constant interference with the work of the teacher and the work of the school they hamper the teacher and retard school progress.

There is a proper field of usefulness for the board of education, but it is not found in the schoolroom. Their duties pertain exclusively to school administration, and the rules and regulations which they may make have to do only with the external management of the school. The purposes of these meetings is therefore not only to promote an acquaintance among the officers themselves, but to distinguish carefully the line of demarcation between the functions of the Department of Public Instruction, the school board, and the teaching force.

Purpose of meetings.

There is great need for economy in all lines of school administration. There is still greater need for an active interest and earnest and hearty co-operation on the part of the people with the officials whom they elect to represent them and do business for them. All of these results it is believed will come from the careful management and continuation of school officers' meetings in the several counties of the State.

SCHOOL MONEYS.

Under the provisions of section 1197 of the Compiled Laws it is provided that all moneys coming into the hands of any officer of the State, county, township, or school district, pursuant to any provision of law shall be denominated public moneys.

The sources of revenue for the public schools of Michigan are as follows: Primary school interest fund, one mill tax, fine moneys, dog tax, tuition, and voted taxes.

The officers elected by the people to receive and disburse public money are required to keep such money separate and apart from their own and not mix it with their own money nor with that of any other person, firm or corporation. Further, such officers shall not under any circumstances use or allow this money to be used for any purpose other than that in accordance with the provisions of law. They cannot use it for their own purposes nor loan it to other persons, and such officers with the sureties on their bonds are absolutely liable to the school district or other public corporation which they represent for the safe-keeping of all moneys coming into their hands.

Care of money.

The treasurer of each school district is required to keep the school money separate and distinct from his own money, and under the statute it is separated into five different funds as follows: (a) building sites and permanent repairs; (b) teachers' wages; (c) library; (d) general; (e) incidental.

These funds are derived as follows:

(a) Building sites and permanent repairs from taxes voted by the people.

(b) Teachers' wages from primary school interest fund, one mill tax, and voted tax.

(c) Library, from fine moneys derived from the penal fines levied in the county and voted taxes.

(d) General fund, from taxes, interest on deposited funds, dog tax, delinquent tax and tuition.

(e) Incidental fund, from voted taxes, together with any surplus mill tax properly transferred to this fund.

USES OF SCHOOL FUNDS.

1. All moneys voted by the people as taxes for the purpose of buildings, sites and permanent repairs must be used for these purposes, and if any surplus remains after such matters have been completed, this surplus may be continued in that fund for future contingencies, or may by a two-thirds vote of the taxpayers of the district be transferred to other funds.

Teachers' wages. 2. The primary school interest fund can be used for teachers' wages only and cannot be borrowed and used for other purposes, nor can it be transferred to any other account. The one mill tax must be used for teachers' wages only until the district has had eight months of school, when any surplus remaining may by a majority vote of the taxpayers present and voting be transferred to the general or incidental fund.

Library fund. 3. All fines assessed in any courts of a county for violations of the penal laws must be paid over from the court assessing the fine to the county treasurer, who will place these funds under the library account. The county treasurer annually, on the first of June is required to distribute this money under the direction of the Superintendent of Public Instruction to the several school districts of the county which maintain libraries and this money can be used by boards of education for library purposes only. No school board has authority to transfer library funds to other accounts or use them for other purposes. Any moneys voted by the people as a tax for library purposes must also be added to this library fund and used for library purposes.

4. The following is a statement of the taxes voted *by the people, not the board,* which constitute the *general fund,* and the items which may be purchased out of this fund:

Under clause 7 of section 4665 (43) the people should vote stated sums for additional appendages, apparatus, library, debts, services of officers, transportation of pupils and indemnity bonds; the total of these sums together with the interest, dog tax, and delinquent tax and tuition, if any, will constitute the general fund, which may be used as follows: To pay for outhouses, fences, care and grading of grounds, taking of census, books for indigent children, furniture, apparatus not mentioned in section 4686 (64), transportation of pupils, officer's salaries in districts having more than fifty pupils, for bonds of the treasurer and for insurance. In paying for any of these items the director may draw an order on the general fund and the treasurer will charge the amount to this fund. It should be noted that the people at the annual meeting, if they need *money for any of these items,* should vote specific taxes for *each* of the items mentioned in said clause 7, for if they fail to vote money for each of these purposes then there would be no money in the general fund with which to pay for such omitted item.

5. Under section 4674 (52) the board is authorizd to vote a tax for incidentals and this is construed to include all such items or articles as are essential to the maintenance of the school. A school may be conducted without a library, transportation of pupils, etc., but the essential items mentioned in Sec. 4672 (50), 4686 (64), 4679 (57), 4778 (156) are to be purchased by the director and paid for out of the incidental fund and are as follows: Record books and blanks for officers, janitor's services, certain maps, glo[illegible], dictionary, library case, reading chart, looking glass, comb, towel, w[illegible]er pail, cup, ash pail, poker, shovel, broom, dust pan, duster, wash b[illegible]sin, soap, chalk, erasers, as noted in said section 4686, also minor repairs such as window glass, door knobs, locks, etc., and free text books. The board is also required to provide fuel and a water supply (see sec. 4679), and as this may mean the renting of a well or the putting down of a [illegible]ell, the pay for such water supply would come from the incidental fund. The director in drawing orders for any of these items will draw such orders on [illegible] incidental fund and the treasurer will pay for them out of that fund.

***The investigation of* the accounts and records of [illegible]chool districts has brought**

to light the fact that in the great majority of school districts, especially of rural school districts, the treasurer does not keep separate accounts of these funds, and there is great irregularity on the part of school officers in the drawing and cashing of school orders. School funds are mixed all together and no separate account kept of each, consequently school boards are unable to make out accurate reports of receipts and expenditures at the end of each year as the law requires. The purpose of the statute in defining school funds and their uses was clearly the protection of the people who pay the taxes, and all public officials who handle public money should be held to strict account for every penny coming into their hands and every penny they pay out. Such looseness and carelessness on the part of school officers as has been discovered is absolutely inexcusable, and results in many instances not only in the loss of public money but in the misappropriation and misuse of funds to the detriment of school interests. It is to be hoped that in the future school district officers will be more particular in their care and use of school funds, and that the plain provisions of the statute shall be strictly observed in every case.

School accounts.

Circulars have been printed by this department at various times and distributed to the school officers of the State calling their attention to their duties in this connection and every officer is supposed to have a copy of the statute which he can consult at all times and determine his powers, duties, privileges and limitations.

REPORT ON AUDITING DISTRICT ACCOUNTS.

The law authorizing the superintendent of Public Instruction to audit accounts of school districts is of recent date. It has, however, already justified itself. Before it had become operative there were requests for an auditor from several districts, and as it has become more generally known that such a law exists, the calls have increased far beyond our ability to respond, there being no one in this department who can give the matter his whole attention. The many requests show however that there is much dissatisfaction with the present method of accounting for public funds.

Need of an auditor.

The carelessness and negligence, disregard and ignorance of the plain letter of the law with reference to accounting for public moneys is surprising and altogether too common. Sometimes officers do not so much as read the laws under which they are supposed to be operating, to say nothing of following such laws, nor is this condition confined to the school districts. In many cases it has been necessary to consult the books of the township before the district accounts could be audited. Oftentimes the data needed could not be found in the township officers' books until these books had been audited and proper corrections and additions made. Sometimes it has been necessary even to go to the books of the county treasurer for data that should be found in the township treasurer's books. This would not be the condition if the township books were kept in accordance with the forms which they contain, i. e., if each account was kept under its proper fund or head. In some cases the various columns for the proper data are ignored and the whole of the moneys

Condition of records.

"bunched" and paid out in a hap-hazard manner, some funds thus becoming over paid while others are made to suffer a shortage of money in some special use for which it was voted.

It is the clear intent of the law that the people shall know how the money paid by them in taxes is used. To this end it provides that a report of all township expenditures shall be made in writing and filed with the township clerk and open to the inspection of any inhabitant of the township or any outside taxpayer, and further that it shall be read at the annual township meeting if so requested. The law also provides that the district board shall at the annual meeting of the district give a full report of all receipts and expenditures. The above district report must be in writing and contain a statement of all taxes assessed upon the property of the district during the preceding year, the purposes for which such taxes were assessed and the amount for each particular purpose, and the report become a permanent record of the district. Seldom is the last part of the above law followed. Indeed I have not found a single case in which the annual report was copied in the minutes and had been made a permanent record.

Reports to township and districts.

This neglect is generally because of ignorance of the law, but in some cases it is to cover up the illegal use of the funds that have been diverted to some purpose not voted by the people, or in a few cases used in the private business of the officer, or stolen. Oftentimes the "statements" made cover a misuse of funds in plain violation of the expressed prohibitions of the statutes. The ordinary tax payer, unless he is willing to stand as a "knocker," and besides being somewhat ignorant of his rights in the case, sits silent and goes away from the annual meeting dissatisfied with matters.

In some cases the district board take it upon themselves to make the repairs voted by the district, and allow themselves such wages as they choose, and in some cases they have gone so far as to build a schoolhouse because "the district had voted that the district build a schoolhouse," all in direct violation of the provisions of the law. And sometimes the term "incidentals" covers an actual embezzlement of district funds.

Rights of the people.

The people have the right to know for what purpose every dollar of taxes has been used. They have, also, the power to recover moneys illegally used by district officers, and officers who have assumed powers not authorized by law should be made to account for the assumption of such powers. The tax payers alone can divert money voted for one purpose to another purpose, and this they can do only by a vote of two-thirds of all the tax payers in the district.

The same may be said of the moneys voted by a township. In the township records that I have been obliged to audit I have found different cases where the moneys have not been correctly accounted for. In some cases the school district had not received the moneys due it, but such moneys had been deliberately used for township purposes or for private business; in some cases the township books have been destroyed or were purposely secreted; in one case the township board voted money to build a town hall, and built the same, doing a large share of the work and paying themselves out of the moneys not voted for such purpose.

Frequently all warrants, orders and receipts are destroyed after a settlement is made with the proper officers, leaving the treasurer and the clerk without any original documents of defense in case of an investigation into the financial affairs of the township or district; the books may be produced but they are not conclusive. It is the indorsed warrants and orders, and the receipts that really show how money has been expended. Treasurers of both school districts and townships should forbid the destruction of any of the original documents of their administrations.

From the above facts and the experience gained in auditing district accounts it is my opinion that each county should have an auditor whose duty it should be to audit the books of townships and school districts annually; also that the laws should be so amended that one of the qualifications for holding the office of treasurer should be the ability to read the English language and write it legibly.

County auditor.

The violations of the laws in handling school funds and accounting for the same are usually along some of the following lines:

First. School moneys are not kept separate from all other moneys. This is in violation of section 1198 of the general school laws.

Second. The school moneys are often used by the treasurer and sometimes by the other members of the board for their own purposes. These officers have no thought of defrauding the district, but it is very convenient when some ready money is needed to use some of the school money which will not be needed for school purposes. As many districts have a large amount of money on hand which cannot be used for school purposes, the money is not returned to the treasury; instead more is used. Again and again this happens until the officer finds it quite impossible to reimburse the district when he is called upon to do so. The result in several districts has been criminal proceedings against the officers.

Section 1199 of the general school laws provides as follows: "No such officer shall, under any pretext, use nor allow to be used any such moneys for any purpose other than in accordance with the provisions of law; nor shall he use the same for his private use, nor loan the same to any person, firm or corporation without legal authority to do so." The penalty for violating this law is fine or imprisonment or both.

Third. The money is sometimes loaned to some friend or corporation; sometimes the district votes to loan its surplus funds on a real estate mortgage. In both of the above cases the law is violated. The district cannot go into the loaning business, even if it has a large surplus of cash on hand.

Fourth. The money is sometimes used for other purposes than those prescribed by law; the primary school interest fund which can legally be used for teachers' wages only, has in many districts been used for all purposes; the one-mill tax money has also been used contrary to the express provisions of law. In no case can the primary money be diverted legally from the teachers' wages fund; the one-mill tax can, however, by a vote of the district, be used for other purposes after a district has had in any school year eight months of school. In no other way can any of this fund be used for other purposes than teachers' wages. Occasionally money voted for a certain purpose has been diverted to some other purpose and so covered in the accounting that the ordinary person cannot discover the discrepancy; again interest that has been paid by banks has been kept by the officers contrary to law, such interest being the property of the district; and again, money has been voted by the district board for purposes not authorized by law, and the district kept in ignorance of the fact.

Fifth. In a few cases officers have deliberately defrauded the district, using the money of the district for private business, making no attempt to replace the same, and deliberately falsifying the district accounts and the annual report to this department. A common method of defrauding the district is for two persons of the same family or the same ilk to secure the offices of director and treasurer of the district board. Then these officers present bills for real or fancied services. Two of the officers being of the same family they pass upon the bills favorably and. have them allowed, an order is drawn for the payment of the same and when presented to the moderator for his signature is signed by him rather than have any trouble about the matter; quite likely he is bribed by being allowed to do some work about the school grounds or by furnishing some wood or "supplies," real or fancied, at an extravagant price, another illegal act.

Sixth. Often the cause for errors is the failure to understand the various funds as designated by law. To make this matter clear a bulletin has been prepared by this department and distributed among school officers. This appears herewith under head of school moneys and classifies the funds, gives their sources and the purposes for which each fund may be used.

Seventh. Another cause for errors in accounting for school funds is a misunderstanding of the powers and duties of the school officers and taxpayers. Certain taxes are voted by the district and certain others by the school board. Officers have sometimes taken advantage of their right to vote taxes by voting a much larger amount than will be needed and then diverting the surplus to some other use than that for which the money was assessed.

A district has full power as to the amount of money to be raised for permanent repairs on buildings and for constructing new buildings. It has also the power to choose its building committee, but it has not the power to instruct the district board to construct or repair a building. The district board cannot be interested in any contract, neither can an officer receive pay for working on a building for the district either in repairing or constructing the same. If a district wishes any member of the board to do any work on a building for the district, it must first secure the resignation of such officer.

It will be evident from the above that the opportunities for errors in the handling of district funds are many, and officers who are elected to the responsibilities should study carefully their powers and duties. They should also give special attention to some system of accounting that will apply to district accounting as laid down in the school laws. I append some suggestions that should be observed in the keeping of school accounts.

First. The director and treasurer should keep the same form of accounts.

Second. All moneys received by the treasurer should be charged on Dr. side of the proper fund; all orders paid credited on the Cr. side.

Third. All warrants drawn upon the township treasurer should state the exact amount, and not read "All moneys in your hands belonging to said district." To insure this the statement of the township clerk to the director giving the moneys due the district in the township treasurer's hands should be carefully preserved by the director.

Fourth. All warrants drawn upon the township treasurer should be cashed by the district treasurer before the annual settlement with the school director.

Fifth. The stubs of orders drawn upon the district treasurer should give the items for which the order is drawn. Such stub should be filled out before the order is detached.

Sixth. Never omit placing number, date and fund upon both order and stub. The number is as important in accounting as is the date, and should not begin with number *one* each year but go on indefinitely.

Seventh. Never tear out a stub nor destroy an order. All spoiled orders have an explanation made upon the stub.

Eighth. When money is hired by the district the director should charge the district treasurer with the same when the notes or bonds properly signed are placed in the treasurer's hands, explaining the matter in the entry.

Ninth. The director of a fractional school district can draw warrants on the township treasurer only of the township in which the schoolhouse is situated, and such treasurer must apply to each township treasurer of any other townships in which any part of the district is situated for any money in his hands belonging to such district, according to section 4713 of the general school laws.

Lest there be a misunderstanding of this report, I wish to say in conclusion that there are not many cases in which there is the least appearance of dishonesty among school officers. A few there have been and they have answered to the law for their malfeasance, but the ordinary school officer is a philanthropist. He does a large amount of work for the good of the schools, receiving no pay therefor, but instead the abuse of those people who have little or no interest in education, and the better officer he is, usually the more of the criticisms he receives.

I wish here to thank the school officers whose accounts have been audited for their uniformly courteous treatment of my representative. Indeed the officers have seemed as desirous that the financial matters of the district be straightened out as is this department and have rendered every assistance possible. The same may be said of the township officers.

SUMMARY OF ACCOUNTING.

The financial reports of district officers have been corrected in 1342 districts, scattered through over seventy counties of the State. These corrections were as follows:

1. For incorrect report of primary money received..............	653
2. For incorrect report of primary money on hand, generally because illegally used..	261
3. Incorrect report of cash on hand..........................	279
4. For incorrect accounts for various other reasons among which are—lack of items of receipts and expenditures, incorrect report of wages paid, amounts due the district, failure to account for all the funds in the treasurer's hands..................	337
Total corrections in the above 1342 districts...............	1530

In addition to the above there have been many cases in which primary interest money and one-mill tax money have been used illegally, also many cases of officers being paid for services which they could not legally perform for pay, such as labor on the buildings and grounds, furnishing fuel, etc.

There have been a few cases of defalcation which are at present being prosecuted by the Attorney General.

In nearly every case in which money has been illegally use[d] ... suc-ceeded in having it replaced in the district treasury. Thes[e] ... ry from a few dollars in some districts to over $1400 in others.

There are many district accounts yet to audit, but the b[...]

is done. I believe that when once the accounts are correct and officers realize that their accounts are subject to audit, greater care will be exercised in safeguarding the people's money, chief among which will be ample and secure bonds of the district treasurer and a systematic method of keeping school district accounts.

AGRICULTURE IN THE PUBLIC SCHOOLS.

At a national meeting of the presidents and instructors of agricultural schools in the United States, held two years ago, the subject of agriculture in the public schools received a large amount of attention. With the introduction of manual training, domestic science, and commercial courses into the public schools, has come a demand also for instruction in agriculture. Agriculture is at the foundation of our national prosperity and it is probable that no business or profession has received so little attention at the hands of educators as this most important one. In several states laws have been enacted providing that agriculture shall be taught in the public schools, but as yet the reports show that little has been done to carry out the spirit of such legislation.

Courses of study. There is a great diversity of opinion among educators as to the field that shall be covered in agricultural instruction. No one has yet evolved a course of study that seems exactly adapted to the needs of farmers. Special courses are given in our agricultural colleges and other colleges for the benefit of the farmers of the State. The so-called short courses given in the winter at our Agricultural College provide a small amount of special instruction along certain special lines, but the attendance at these classes is so small that the results when applied to the State at large make very little impression.

It seems clear, therefore, that if we are to spread the benefits of agricultural instruction over the state it must be done through the medium of the public schools. As stated before, no one has yet decided exactly what can or ought to be taught. All agree upon the advisability of such work. This Department, in order to furnish a foundation upon which agricultural instruction may be given has requested members of the faculty of our State Agricultural College to prepare certain material along agricultural lines which shall be elementary and fundamental and which can be used to some degree of advantage by teachers who have not had special courses in agriculture. The subjects selected by the Department are as follows: soils, crops, horticulture, nature study, animal husbandry. Joseph A. Jeffery, Professor of Agronomy of the Agricultural College, has prepared a bulletin on the subject of crops along the lines above indicated, and this bulletin has been distributed to the several normal schools and county normal training classes to be used by the students in these institutions in their course in agriculture. This bulletin will be followed during the ensuing year by the following bulletins:

A Study in Soils.
A Study in Horticulture.
A Study in Animal Husbandry.
A Study in Elementary Botany and Nature Study.

All these will be placed in the hands of instructors in our normal schools and county normal training classes in order that the young people who are going out to teach may have had some specific instruction along agricultural lines and be able to give to the children the elementary ideas of agricultural pursuits. These bulletins are not intended to be textbooks exactly, but are to be used as the basis of simple experimentation and to supplement the use of certain text books that are now on the market.

The bulletin on crops I give herewith in order that it may become a matter of public record.

BULLETIN NO. 26.

STATE OF MICHIGAN,

DEPARTMENT OF PUBLIC INSTRUCTION.

LANSING, November 15, 1907.

To Commissioners, Superintendents and Teachers:

The subject of nature study has been discussed for a number of years and has been taught in our public schools with such a degree of success that there is a general demand among those interested in agriculture that the subject of elementary agriculture shall also be taught. The president and faculty of the Agricultural College have given much time and thought to determine just what is meant by elementary agriculture and how much of agriculture can profitably be taught in the rural and village schools.

At the request of this Department, Joseph A. Jeffery, Professor of Agronomy in the Michigan Agricultural College, has prepared the material presented in the following pages as an elementary study in crops, and this bulletin is published for the purpose of putting into the hands of our teachers some simple and definite work in the subject of agriculture. We submit it to the schools and teachers of the State in the hope that it will be of material assistance in presenting this important subject to our students, and that ultimately we may be able to introduce into our courses of study a concise and profitable course in the subject of elementary agriculture.

Very respectfully,

L. L. Wright

Superintendent of Public Instruction.

AN ELEMENTARY LABORATORY STUDY IN CROPS.

TABLE OF CONTENTS.

		Page.	Hrs.
Introduction		7	
Laboratory equipment		7	8
Collecting grains		7	8
Experiments:			
I.	A study in seed germination—beans	8	10
II.	A study in seed germination—corn	9	4
III.	How the young plants appear above ground—beans	9	6
IV.	How the young plants appear above ground—corn	10	6
V.	How the young plants appear above ground—other seeds	10	6
VI.	The quantity of food stored in seeds	10	3
VII.	The depth to which seeds should be planted	11	3
VIII.	Effect of age upon the vitality of seeds	12	3
IX.	The vitality of bin grains	13	3
X.	The vitality of sprouted grains	14	4
XI.	The vitality of kernels from different parts of the ear of corn	15	2
XII.	The effect of freezing upon the vitality of seed corn	17	3
XIII.	Necessity for air in the germination of seeds	17	3
XIV.	The effect of temperature on the germination of seeds	19	3
XV.	Corn seed testing	20	
	The importance of early saving and drying of seed corn	16	
	Corn judging	22	
	The ideal or perfect ear	22	
	Score card—corn	27	
	Outline for scoring dent corn	28	

INTRODUCTION.

The farmer should understand the nature of a seed, its relation to the future plant, the importance of vitality in the seed, the conditions lessening its vitality, and the conditions requisite to preserve its vitality. He should understand also the conditions outside the seed upon which depends the production of vigorous plants. Upon such knowledge depends all rational practice in crop production.

The following course of laboratory exercises has been outlined with a view to giving the pupil the opportunity of demonstrating for himself by actual experiment the importance of such knowledge.

It is expected that some textbook will be studied in conjunction with this work.

LABORATORY EQUIPMENT.

The following apparatus will be needed:

Two doz. dinner plates or pie tins.

Two doz. discs of Canton flannel (or a like number of filter papers) of a diameter one inch less than that of the plates or pie tins.

One doz. 600 *c. c.* lipped beakers.

Two doz. one-quart bean pans (graniteware preferable).

One doz. shallow four-quart pans (graniteware preferable).

One doz. deep gallon jars.

One doz. one-pint graniteware or porcelain dishes.

Two doz. wooden boxes 18 inches long, 10 inches wide and 2 inches deep.

Two hundred pounds of fine quartz sand. (This sand can be procured of the Wausau Quartz Co., of Wausau, Wis.)

Two bushels of air-dry fine sand or fine sandy soil for germinating seed.

A collection of seeds and grains for illustrative purposes and for experimental work.

Tight boxes with covers should be provided to hold the sands and soil.

Glass receptacles should be provided to hold the seeds and grains. Pint, quart, and two-quart Mason fruit jars make inexpensive and convenient receptacles.

A SHORT COURSE IN SEEDS AND GRAINS.

Make a collection of seeds and grains commonly grown on the farm. This collection should include beans, peas, clover, timothy, beets, wheat, oats, barley, corn, buckwheat, etc. Different varieties of each should be brought in so far as possible.

Samples of each should be placed in 4 oz. screw-cap vials for later examination and reference, while larger quantities should be kept in bulk for study and experiment. Samples of many of these should be gathered in the pod, head, and ear, with portions or all of the plant. The extent to which this is done, beyond the study needs of the class, must depend upon the storage facilities of the laboratory or museum. The pupils should be required to help or indeed to do all the work of making the collection.

THE STUDY OF THE SEED.

The pupil should be made to understand that a seed or a kernel of grain consists of (a) a young plant, or embryo; (2) a supply of food prepared and stored for the use of the young plant until it can send out its roots and leaves; and (3) a coat inclosing both young plant and nourishment. That all this may be clear to the pupils, the following experiments should be perfor also observing the development of the plant from the seed:

EXPERIMENT I.

A Study in Seed Germination.

Apparatus and material needed:

Two ordinary dinner plates or two eight-inch pie tins.

Two pieces of blotting or filter paper, or Canton flannel of proper size to rest in the plate or pan used.

A beaker or cup of water.

Ten beans of any variety.

The experiment:

1. Place one of the pieces of paper or cloth in the bottom of a plate or tin. If the cloth is used, thoroughly wet and wring out before placing it in the bottom of the plate or tin. If the paper is used, wet thoroughly after it is set in place.
2. Distribute the ten beans over the paper or cloth.
3. Place the remaining paper or cloth over the beans, wetting the cloth before putting in place (or the paper afterwards).
4. Add water to the bottom of the plate or tin, but not enough to stand deeper than the paper or cloth lying on the bottom.
5. Cover the plate or tin by placing the remaining one, inverted, over it, and set in a warm room.
6. See, each day, that water enough is added to keep the moist condition of plate and paper, or cloth, about as it was the first day.
7. Examine the beans each day and (a) notice and record any changes that take place. (b) Open one bean each day for three days, and examine the embryo or young plant.
8. Set apart one particular bean and make a drawing of it each day for ten days, to show the changes that take place.

EXPERIMENT II.

A Study in Seed Germination.

Apparatus and material needed:

One dinner plate or eight inch pie tin.

Two pieces of filter paper or two pieces Canton flannel of proper size to lie in bottom of plate or tin.

Ten kernels of good seed corn.

The experiment:

1. Place a piece of filter paper in a plate or tin and wet, or wet a piece of cloth and place in bottom of plate or tin.
2. Distribute the ten kernels of corn over the paper or cloth.
3. Place the remaining paper or cloth over the corn, properly wetting the paper after, or the cloth before, so placing.
4. Add water enough to just cover the bottom of the plate.
5. Cover the plate or tin by placing the remaining one, inverted, over it and set in a warm room.
6. See, each day, that the moist condition in the plate is kept about as it was the first day.
7. Examine the corn each day and note how the young plant makes its appearance and whether it is alike in all cases.
8. Set apart one particular kernel of corn and make a drawing of it each day for eight days to show the changes that take place.

EXPERIMENT III.

How the Young Plants Appear Above Ground.

Apparatus and material needed:
One one-quart pudding or bean pan.
One quart of air-dry sandy soil.
Ten beans.

The experiment:
1. Fill the pan three-fourths full of the sandy soil, shake down, and smooth over.
2. Add water until the soil is thoroughly wet and the water begins to glisten in the surface of the soil.
3. Place the ten beans upon the soil in the pan—two on their sides, two on one end, two on the other end, two with the scar down, and two with the scar up. *Make a chart of the planting.*
4. Cover these beans to the depth of one-half inch with the air-dry soil.
5. If on the next day the soil is not all moist, add just water enough to moisten.
6. Examine from day to day. Add water sufficient to keep surface from drying. Note (1) the manner and (2) the order in which the plants come up, and make a record of the same.
7. When the young plants have all appeared above the surface, carefully pull up one of them, examine, and make a drawing of it. Before pulling it may be necessary to loosen the soil.
8. Did the positions in which the beans were planted affect the order in which the young plants appeared?
   Did it affect the manner in which they came up?

EXPERIMENT IV.

How the Young Plants Appear Above Ground.

Repeat Experiment III, using corn instead of beans.

EXPERIMENT V.

How the Young Plants Appear Above Ground.

Repeat Experiment III using other seeds and grains, all together or separately, in order that the pupils may observe the manner in which the young plants appear above ground.

EXPERIMENT VI.

Quantity of Food Stored in Seed.

Apparatus and material needed:
One four-quart pan.
One gallon of well-washed, pure quartz sand, or the same amount of good clean building sand, which has stood for some time in strong hydrochloric acid and then has been thoroughly washed.
Four large and four very small kernels of the following: corn, wheat, oats, beans, and peas.

The experiment:

1. Fill the pan three-fourths full of the sand.
2. Moisten until thoroughly wet.
3. Distribute the several four seed lots over the surface of the sand with the different lots sufficiently separated that when they start to grow they will still be distinguishable as groups. Carefully make a chart on paper of the distribution of the lots to help later in locating the young plants.
4. Cover the grain and seed with a half-inch layer of the sand.
5. Set in a room having a temperature ranging from 70° to 85° F., and water just enough from time to time to keep the surface from becoming dry.
6. Observe each day until all plants cease to grow, and record observations.
7. Do you discover any difference—

   1st. In the time required for the plants from the small and the large seeds or kernels to appear above ground?

   2nd. In the size of plants from the small and the large seeds or kernels when they have ceased to grow?

   If there is an observable difference, account for it if possible.
8. Do the results in this experiment suggest a rule for practice on the farm? If so, formulate it.

EXPERIMENT VII.

The Depth to Which Seed Should be Planted.

Apparatus and material needed:

Four deep one-gallon jars.

Enough well-moistened, well-crumbled loam soil or sandy soil, to fill these jars.

Sixteen good kernels each of corn, oats and wheat.

Twenty good seeds of red clover.

The experiment:

1. Fill the jars with the soil.
2. In one of the jars of soil plant four kernels of corn six inches deep, four kernels four inches deep, four kernels two inches deep, and four kernels one inch deep.

   Note: To plant the kernels of corn use a round stick with a square end. With the stick make a hole for each kernel. Introduce the kernels into the holes and fill the holes with the crumbled soil.
3. In the same way plant the sixteen kernels of oats in another jar.
4. In the same way, plant the sixteen kernels of wheat in the third jar.
5. In the remaining jar plant the twenty seeds of June clover—four seeds six inches deep, four seeds four inches deep, four seeds two inches deep, four seeds one inch deep, and four seeds one-half inch deep.

   Note: Use a smaller stick to make the holes for the clover seed.
6. It would be well to make a chart of the plantings in each jar.
7. Place all the jars in a room with a temperature ranging from 70° to 85° F.
8. Moisten enough to keep surface from drying, but do not moisten heavily.

Note—Pure quartz sand can be had of the Wausau Quartz Co., Wausau, Wisconsin.

9. Make a record of the rate and number of germinations.
10. If after three weeks any of the kernels or seeds have failed to send plants to the surface, carefully remove the soil, making reference to the proper chart, if necessary, and discover and record why the young plant has failed to reach the surface.

Use a table like the following for each jar.

Germination of Seeds at Various Depths.

Depth of planting.	Number of germinations to the day indicated.																	
	3	4	5	6	7	8	9	10	11	12	13	14	15	16	17	18	19	20
1 inch....................	...	...	...	...	...	...	...	...	...	...	...	...	...	...	...	...	...	...
2 inches..................	...	...	...	...	...	...	...	...	...	...	...	...	...	...	...	...	...	...
4 inches..................	...	...	...	...	...	...	...	...	...	...	...	...	...	...	...	...	...	...
6 inches..................	...	...	...	...	...	...	...	...	...	...	...	...	...	...	...	...	...	...

Combine what you learn from this experiment with what you learned in experiment No. XX in soils and what you may learn later in experiment No. XIV of this series, and make a rule for the depth of planting seed.

Experiment VIII.

Effect of Age Upon the Vitality of Seed.

Apparatus and material needed:

One wooden box, 10 inches x 18 inches x 2 inches deep.

Lots of seed corn 1, 2, 3, 4, and 5 years old respectively and a sample also of the last preceding crop.

Enough well-crumbled, air-dry, sandy soil to fill the box.

A straight-edge.

The experiment:

1. Fill the box rounding full with the soil, tap lightly, and strike off the surface.
2. Lay off six lines two inches apart and running the width of the box.
3. Count out ten kernels from each lot of corn.
4. Plant these six lots of corn in order of age—one lot on each line marked on the soil in the box. Plant to the depth of one inch.
5. Cover the kernels and place the box where the temperature will range from 70 to 90 degrees. See that the soil is kept moist but not too much so.
6. Observe and record the rate and vigor of germination.

Use a table like this:

Vitality of Old Seed Corn.

Age of seed.	Total germination up to and including the day indicated.											Order of germination.	Order of vigor.	No. to plant in each hill.
	3	4	5	6	7	8	9	10	11	12	13			
New														
1 year														
2 years														
3 years														
4 years														
5 years														

7. How old should seed corn be to give best germination according to results obtained in this experiment?
8. Are you sure that the lots of seed used in this experiment were saved with equal care?

The above experiment should be repeated, using different grains and seeds common to field and garden. Assign one kind of seed or grain to one pupil and another to another.

Plant corn, beans, and peas one inch deep in the boxes; wheat, oats, barley, flax, etc., one-half inch deep; and clover, timothy, and the like one-fourth inch deep. Have pupils compare results and conclusions.

It may not be possible to procure at once seeds and grains of different ages or those originally saved with uniform care and judgment. Each year a stock of the best fresh seed should be collected and saved for future study.

The Vitality of Bin Grains.

If pupils have access to grain bins on the farm, have them bring in gallon samples of grain that have molded or musted in the bin because of excessive dampness. Keep the lots so brought in separate.

If the pupils can procure, at the time of threshing, grains that have molded in the shock from being "shocked" too green, or that have molded or rotted in the shock or stack from wetting, have them bring in gallon samples.

These samples should be preserved in glass or metallic receptacles with close-fitting covers, and should be carefully and completely labeled.

There should be gathered, also, bin grains that have not suffered from mold, and these should be preserved and labeled.

EXPERIMENT IX.

Apparatus and material needed:

A number of 100-kernel lots of molded oats.

One 100-kernel lots of good seed oats.

One wooden box, 10 inches x 18 inches x 2 inches deep, for every three lots of grain.

Sufficient air-dry, fine, sandy soil to fill the boxes.

The experiment:

1. Fill the box or boxes with soil, rounding full, settle by tapping, and strike off with a straight edge.
2. Divide the surface of the soil in each box into three areas—10 inches by 6 inches each.
3. Plant in each of these areas one 100-kernel lot of oats, carefully labeling each area. Plant to the depth of one-half inch.
4. Thoroughly wet down the soil in the boxes.
5. Set the box or boxes where the temperature will range from 70° to 85° F. and see to it that the soil is kept moist, but not too much so —never so moist as after the first wetting.
6. Observe and record the rate and number of germinations, using table like the one below:

Germination of Poor and of Good Seed Oats.

Description.	Total germination on day indicated.												Order of total germinations.	Vigor of young plants.
	3	4	5	6	7	8	9	10	11	12	13	14		
Good seed..........	.....	.....	.....	.....		.....	.....		.....	.....	.....	.....	.....	.....
Moldy seed from, etc...	.....	.....	.....	.....		.....	.....		.....	.....	.....	.....	.....	.....
Moldy seed from, etc...	.....	.....	.....	.....		.....	.....		.....	.....	.....	.....	.....	.....
Moldy seed, from etc...	.....	.....	.....	.....		.....	.....		.....	.....	.....	.....	.....	.....
Moldy seed from, etc...	.....	.....	.....	.....		.....	.....		.....	.....	.....	.....	.....	.....

7. Observe and record the vigor of the young plants.
8. Do the results suggest any new ideas concerning the saving of seed oats? Do they confirm any old ideas? Do they suggest any warnings against methods now in use?

It would be well to repeat this experiment by using other grains and seeds. Or each pupil might be assigned a certain kind of seed or grain to experiment with. Then have pupil bring together the results obtained and compare and discuss results and conclusions. This experiment has a most important bearing upon crop yields.

EXPERIMENT X.

Vitality of Sprouted Grain.

Apparatus and material needed:

One-fourth pint of wheat, home grown preferable.
One pint dish.
One wooden box, 10 x 18 x 2 inches deep.
Enough air-dry, well crumbled sandy soil to fill the box.

The experiment:

1. Place one-eighth pint of wheat in the bottom of the pint dish; cover with water and keep covered for a few days. Keep in a room with temperature ranging from 70° to 85° F. The wheat will soon begin to sprout.

2. As rapidly as the kernels acquire sprouts one-sixteenth inch long, remove the kernels and place on a piece of blotting paper and dry in warm room. In this way pick out and dry at least 200 kernels and allow to dry for one week.
3. Fill the box with the soil as described in experiment seven and divide the surface into three divisions—10 inches by 6 inches each.
4. Count out two 100-kernel lots of the dry sprouted kernels, and also one 100-kernel lot of the unsprouted wheat—that which was not covered with water.
5. Plant the two sprouted lots of wheat in the end areas of the box and plant the lot of unsprouted wheat in the middle area. Plant one-half inch deep.
6. Wet down the soil in the box and set the box in a room having a temperature ranging from 70° to 85° F. Water from time to time, but not excessively.
7. Observe and record the number and rate of germinations. Use a table something like the one below:

Germination of Sprouted and Unsprouted Seeds.

Description.	Total germinations on day indicated.												Vigor of young plants.	Per cent of germination.
	3	4	5	6	7	8	9	10	11	12	13	14		
Good seed	....	....	....	....	....	....	....	....	....	....	....	....	......	......
Sprouted seed	....	....	....	....	....	....	....	....	....	....	....	....	......	......
Sprouted seed	....	....	....	....	....	....	....	....	....	....	....	....	......	......
Average of sprouted.	....	....	....	....	....	....	....	....	....	....	....	....	......	......
Difference between sp't'd and unsprouted......	....	....	....	....	....	....	....	....	....	....	....	....	......	......

8. How do the results agree with your previous notion concerning the vitality of sprouted grains?
9. Would you advise the practice of using sprouted grains for seed?

This experiment may well be repeated, using other grains and seeds.

Vitality of Kernels from Different Parts of the Ear of Corn.

The question is often asked whether the kernels from different parts of the ear of corn are equally good for seed, or whether some should be discarded, and if so, why?

EXPERIMENT XI.

Apparatus and materials needed:

Three wooden boxes 10 x 18 x 2 inches.
Enough air-dry light, sandy soil to fill the boxes.
Three well-filled, carefully saved ears of seed corn.

The experiment:

1. Fill the boxes with soil as in the previous experiments.
2. From one of the ears shell off carefully 50 kernels from the extreme tip of the ear, 50 kernels from around the middle of the ear, and 50 kernels from the extreme butt of the ear.
3. Divide the surface of one of the boxes of soil into three areas 10 inches x 6 inches each.
4. In the middle area plant the 50 middle kernels, in one of the end areas plant the 50 tip kernels, and in the remaining one, the 50 butt kernels.
5. In like manner shell off from another ear 50 each of tip, middle and butt kernels and plant in one of the other boxes.
6. In like manner plant 50 each of tip, middle and butt kernels from the third ear in the remaining box.
7. Carefully label the boxes and the areas in which tip, middle and butt kernels are planted.
8. Thoroughly moisten the soil in the boxes and keep just moist enough to prevent the surface from getting dry.
9. Place the boxes in a room with temperature ranging from 70° to 85° F.
10. Observe and record the number, rate, and vigor of germinations, using a table like the following:

Germination of Tip, Middle and Butt Kernels of Corn.

Description of kernels.	No. of box.	Total number of germinations on day indicated.												Average height on 14th day.	Quality of stalk.
		3	4	5	6	7	8	9	10	11	12	13	14		
Tips...........	1	....	....	....	....	....	....	....	....	....	....	....	....	......	......
	2	....	....	....	....	....	....	....	....	....	....	....	....	......	......
	3	....	....	....	....	....	....	....	....	....	....	....	....	......	......
Middles.........	1	....	....	....	....	....	....	....	....	....	....	....	....	......	......
	2	....	....	....	....	....	....	....	....	....	....	....	....	......	......
	3	....	....	....	....	....	....	....	....	....	....	....	....	......	......
Butts..........	1	....	....	....	....	....	....	....	....	....	....	....	....	......	......
	2	....	....	....	....	....	....	....	....	....	....	....	....	......	......
	3	....	....	....	....	....	....	....	....	....	....	....	....	......	......

11. On the fourteenth day or when germination is complete, determine the average height of each lot of corn plants and record.
12. Shall the farmer shell off tip and butt kernels from ears when preparing his seed corn? Give reasons for your answer.
13. Compare and discuss results.
14. Ask your farmer friends whether they discard tip and butt kernels, and if they do, why?

If there are more than three pupils in the class, furnish one ear of corn and germinating box for each.

The Importance of Early Saving and Drying of Seed Corn.

For this work the teacher or some very trustworthy person should prepare the corn to be used or direct the pupils in the preparation.

1. He should select a number of good ears before the first severe frost. These ears should be carefully dried at a temperature ranging from 70° to 80° F., stored, and later shelled for class use.

2. He should as late in the season as possible select an equal number of ears as good as the first lot of ears selected. These ears should be hung where the opportunity for drying is not good and where later they will freeze. An open corn crib or shed would be a good place to hang the corn. Later, dry, shell, and store for class use.

3. Select an equal number of ears from the corn crib when winter weather has thoroughly set in. Place in pail or other vessel of water and let stand until they are well soaked. Then place them where they will freeze solid. After a week, dry, and later shell and store for class use.

EXPERIMENT XII.

Effect of Freezing Upon the Vitality of Seed Corn.

Apparatus and material needed:

One wooden box 10 x 18 x 2 inches deep.
Enough air-dry fine sandy soil to fill the box.
Fifty kernels each of the three lots of corn described above.

The experiment:

1. Fill the box with the soil as in previous experiments.
2. Divide the surface of soil in box into three areas, 10 inches x 6 inches each.
3. Plant in these three areas respectively the three lots of corn.
4. Carefully label the areas.
5. Thoroughly moisten the soil and thereafter moisten just enough to keep surface from drying out.
6. Place box in a room with temperature ranging from 70° to 85° F.
7. Observe and record the number, rate, and vigor of germinations, using a table like the following:

Germination of Frozen Corn.

Description of corn.	Total number of germinations on day indicated.												Relative vigor of plants.
	3	4	5	6	7	8	9	10	11	12	13	14	
(1) Carefully saved and dried ..	....	....	....	....	....	....	....	....	....	....	....	....	......
(2) Carefully saved but not dried	....	....	....	....	....	....	....	....	....	....	....	....	......
(3) Crib corn wet and frozen...	....	....	....	....	....	....	....	....	....	....	....	....	......
Difference between lots 1 and 2 .	....	....	....	....	....	....	....	....	....	....	....	....	......
Difference between lots 1 and 3..	....	....	....	....	....	....	....	....	....	....	....	....	......

8. Do you discover any differences in the number, rate, and vigor of germinations? Account for any such differences.
9. Does the experiment suggest an important practice in saving seed corn?

EXPERIMENT XIII.

Necessity for Air in the Germination of Seeds.

Apparatus and material needed:

Six one-quart pudding or bean pans.
Two quarts finely crumbled air-dry clay soil.
Two quarts finely-crumbled air-dry loamy soil.
Two quarts finely-crumbled air-dry fine sandy soil.
Six 25 kernel lots of *good* seed corn, all from the same lot of bulk seed.

The experiment:

1. Fill one pan half-full of the clay soil, weigh the pan and contents and introduce into another pan enough of the clay soil to bring its weight to that of the first pan.
2. Smooth down the soil in each pan to bring to uniform depth, and tap the sides of the pans to settle the soil.
3. Over the surface of the soil in each pan distribute a 25-kernel lot of corn, and then add to one of the pans one-half inch of the clay soil. Weigh the pan and contents, and add enough soil to the other pan to make the weights of the pans equal again. Number these pans 1 and 2.
4. Fill two other pans with the loam soil. Place 25-kernel lots of corn in each, and cover with half-inch layers of the loamy soils, following the directions given in paragraphs 1, 2, and 3 above. Number these pans 3 and 4.
5. In like manner, fill two pans with fine sandy soil. Introduce 25-kernel lots of corn and add a half-inch layer of fine sandy soil. Number these pans 5 and 6.
6. To pans 1, 3, and 5 add water enough to thoroughly moisten, and thereafter just enough to keep the surface from getting dry, but not enough to prevent the clay from cracking. (In applying water, lay a piece of paper upon the surface of the soil and pour the water lightly upon the paper. The water thus spreads from the paper over the soil without tearing up the soil.)
7. To pans 2, 4, and 6 add water till it stands one-fourth inch deep over the surface after the soil has been thoroughly saturated, and thereafter enough to keep the surface covered at all times. (Use a piece of paper in applying water as described above).
8. Set the pans in a room where the temperature ranges from 70° to 85° F.
9. Observe and record the number, rate and vigor of germinations, using a table like the following:

Germination of Corn in Different Soils.

Moisture condition.	Kind of soil.	Total number of germinations on the day indicated.												Order of vigor.	Germinations after removal of excess of water.			
		3	4	5	6	7	8	9	10	11	12	13	14		11	12	13	14
Good	Clay																	
	Loam																	
	Sandy																	
Excessive	Clay																	
	Loam																	
	Sandy																	

10. Account for any differences in the rate and number of germinations.
11. Have you ever noticed a similar difference in germinations, and for apparently similar reasons in fields of corn?
12. Does this experiment suggest to you a lesson in field management? If so, what is it?

This experiment may be varied as follows:

13. At the close of the tenth day carefully remove with a pipette or glass tube as much of the excess of water as you can conveniently. Allow the remaining excess to evaporate until the soil begins to crack, after which add just water enough to keep the soil moist.
14. Observe and record any further germinations.
15. If more germinations do occur, account for them.
16. Observe also whether these new germinations are as vigorous as the earlier. Account for differences.

This experiment might be repeated, using other grains and seeds.

EXPERIMENT XIV.

Effect of Temperature on the Germination of Seed.

Apparatus and materials needed:

Three one-quart pans.
Three quarts of air-dry fine sandy soil.
Three 25-kernel lots of good seed corn, all obtained from the same bulk lot.

The experiment:

1. Fill the three pans one-half full of the sandy soil, even off to uniform thickness, and tap pans to settle soil.
2. In each pan distribute evenly over the surface of the soil one of the 25-kernel lots of corn and cover with a half-inch layer of the sandy soil.
3. Add water to each pan to thoroughly moisten the soil, and add water thereafter just sufficient to keep surface from becoming dry.
4. Place one of these pans where it will take on a temperature of 50° F. or less, but not less, if possible, than 38° F.
5. Place another of the pans where it will take on a temperature of *from 65° to 75° F.*—ordinary room temperature.

6. Place the third pan where it will be subjected to a temperature ranging from 85° to 95° F.
7. Observe and record the rate, number, and vigor of germinations, using a table like the following:

Germinations of Corn at Different Temperatures.

Number.	Temperature.	Total number of germinations on day indicated.								Vigor of plants on 10th day	Total number of germinations on day indicated.						Vigor of plants on 16th day
		3	4	5	6	7	8	9	10		11	12	13	14	15	16	
1	85° to 95°.......									......							......
2	65° to 75°.......									......							......
3	38° to 50°.......									......							......
Differences between 1 and 2............										......							......
Differences between 1 and 3............										......							......

8. After ten days place plants together in a room, temperature ranging from 65° to 75° F. and keep properly moistened.
9. Observe and record germinations as before.
10. On the sixteenth day observe and record the average height and vigor of plants.
11. What do the results in this experiment teach?
12. Can the farmer control the temperature of his soil?
13. Can he modify the temperature of his soil?
14. Give reasons for both answers.

EXPERIMENT XV.

Practical Seed Corn Testing.

Apparatus and materials needed:

One wooden box 10 x 18 x 2 inches.
Twenty-five feet of store wrapping twine.
Enough air-dry light sandy soil to fill box.
Forty-two to 140 ears of seed corn.
Fifty tacks or three quarter inch brads.
A straight edge.

The experiment:

1. On the sides and ends of the box, one-fourth inch below the edge, drive tacks or brads one and one-fourth inches apart, allowing the heads to stand out one-eight to one-fourth inch.
2. Fill the box with the soil, tap lightly, and strike off.
3. Tie or loop one end of the string to one of the corner tacks or brads and stretch back and forth over the surface and under the tack or brad heads.
(This divides the surface of the box of soil into eight rows of squares with fourteen squares in each row, and each square on fourth inches on a side.)

4. On the ends number the rows, and on the sides number the squares in the rows.
5. Place the seed corn in rows on tables, shelves or floor, 14 ears per row, and number the rows to correspond with the rows of squares in box of soil.
6. Remove four kernels of corn from each ear of row one and plant each four kernels so removed in the corresponding square of row one of the squares. Remove the four kernels from as many separate points on the ear. Plant the kernels tips down and deep enough to have the back of the kernels about one-eighth of an inch below the surface.
7. In like manner plant four kernels from each of the ears of the other rows. Keep all rows in order.
8. Moisten the soil and keep properly moistened.
9. Place box and contents in room where temperature ranges from 75° to 85° F.
10. On the seventh day examine carefully and if in any square there fails to occur four vigorous germinations, discard the ear from which the four kernels were taken.
11. Read in connection with this experiment, Corn Improvement, p. 293, Report of Michigan Board of Agriculture for 1906.
12. What per cent of ears are you required to discard?

CORN JUDGING.

Much attention is given in corn growing sections of the country to the study of the ear of corn. This study brings us ultimately to *corn judging*. Many texts in agriculture now take up a discussion of this important subject. An exercise in corn judging is here offered, including a description of a perfect ear of corn and directions for scoring in accordance with the rules of the Michigan Corn Improvement Association. The description and directions are copied from special bulletin No. 34, Michigan Experiment Station. See p. 293, Report of Michigan Board of Agriculture for 1906.

THE IDEAL OR PERFECT EAR.

It is not often found. It must possess certain physical qualities or characteristics:

1. Shape. In shape it should be cylindrical, or only slightly tapering. The very tapering ear is being bred away from. The rows should be straight, extending completely from butt to tip.

2. Color. The cobs should be red for yellow corn, white for white corn, and red or white for the white caps as now bred, but all red or all white.

There should be no kernels present indicating by color or shape that cross polinating from another breed has taken place.

3. Tips. The tips should be well covered with kernels of uniform size, the rows remaining unbroken to the end. The question as to whether the cob may not protrude slightly is an open one.

4. Butts. The butts should be well rounded The shank or ear stalk should equal about one-third the total diameter of the ear.

5. Kernels. The kernels should be wedge-shaped, so that they shall fill completely all space between the circumference of the ear and the circumference of the cob. To examine kernels, remove two kernels side by side from the cob, one third or one-half the distance from butt to tip, and lay them on some flat surface, germs up in the same relative position they occupied on the cob.

6. Length and circumference. At the present time the standards of the Michigan Corn Improvement Association are 9 inches for length and 7 inches for circumference. The circumference is measured one-third the distance from butt to tip.

It is thought by many that it would be better not to have definite arbitrary standards for length and circumference, but that it would be better to require a definite relation between length and circumference, with a stated definite minimum length of each.

7. Spaces. (a) The outer spaces between rows should be small. With very rare exceptions ears have even numbers of rows, and the rows are in pairs. This distinctness of pairing of rows is considered one of the evidences of good breeding. The space between the rows in the pairs is smaller than the spaces between the pairs. (b) There should be no spaces between kernels as they stand in the rows.

8. Per cent of grain to ear. The M. C. I. A. requires that 100 pounds of ears shall shell out 88 pounds of grain, and individual ears shall shell in that proportion.

In corn judging the following additional points are considered:

9. Trueness to type. It is not sufficient that the ears shall be properly shaped, etc.; they must have also the special characteristics of the breed to which they belong—the roughness or smoothness of kernel, the style of dimple, general outline of kernel, etc.

10. Uniformity. Ears may show that they belong to a particular breed, and yet lack in uniformity of appearance, just as a group of cows may leave no doubt as to what breed they belong, and yet may not be uniform in appearance in the group.

11. Market condition. This takes into account whether the corn is ripe, sound, free from disease and injury, bright in color, and of apparently good vitality.

12. Uniformity of kernels. Two kernels are removed from each ear as described above and the pairs placed in rows for comparison. Every pair should look like every other pair in shape and size.

Apparatus and materials needed.

Several ten-ear lots of the best dent corn that can be had.
One thirty-six inch tape.

CORN JUDGING OR SCORING.

In judging corn, 10 ears are studied, their defects determined and charged against them. The score card is a convenient form for use in this work.

CORN.

SCORE CARD.

Scale of Points.	Standard.	Student's score.	Corrected score.
1 Uniformity:			
(a) Trueness to type	5		
(b) Uniformity of exhibit	5		
2 Shape of ear	5		
3 Color	10		
4 Market condition	10		
5 Tips	5		
6 Butts	5		
7 Kernels:			
(a) Uniformity	5		
(b) Shape	5		
8 Length of ear	10		
9 Circumference of ear	5		
10 Space:			
(a) Between rows	5		
(b) Between kernels at cob	5		
11 Proportion of grain to ear	20		
Total			

Date..........

Variety..........

Weight of five ears..........

Weight of grain from these five ears..........

Proportion of grain to ear..........

The following outline of things considered and rules for cuts is found convenient for beginners in corn judging:

OUTLINE FOR SCORING DENT CORN.

Department of Practical Agriculture, M. A. C.

	Things to Consider.	Rule for Cuts.
1 (a)	Nearness of approach to type as to general form of kernel, indentation, etc.	1/3 point off for each variation from type.
(b)	Likeness between ears exhibited.	1/2 point off for each odd ear.
2	Shape of ear. Arrangement and character of rows.	1/2 point off for each poorly shaped ear.
3	Freedom from cross-breeding. Trueness to variety color of kernel and cob.	10 points off for { red cob in white ear or white cob in yellow ear. 1-10 point off for each mixed kernel.‡
4	*Ripeness, soundness, freedom from injury, brightness of color and vitality.	1 point off for every diseased, injured, chaffy, or immature ear.
5	Uniformity of kernels, regularity of rows, completeness of covering. †	1/4 point off for every badly covered tip. 1/2 point off for every inch of exposed tip. 1/8 point off for every 1/4 inch exposed tip.
6	Manner of rounding out and quality of kernels.	1/2 point off for every uncovered butt. 3-10 point off when butt is covered but kernels are flat.
7 (a)	Likeness in shape and conformity to type.	1/2 point off for each set of kernels lacking in general uniformity.
(b)	Approach to ideal wedge shape.	1/3 point off for each set of poorly shaped kernels.
8	Variation from standard length.	1 point off for every inch of excess or deficiency in length of ear.
9	Variation from standard circumference.	1 point off for every 2 inches of excess or deficiency in circumference of ear.
10 (a)	Outer space.	No cut for less than 1-32 inch between rows. 1/4 point off for 1-32 to 1-16 inch between rows. 1/2 point off for 1-16 inch between rows.
(b)	Inner space.	1/4 to 1/2 point off for each marked case of space between near points of rows.
11	Per cent of grain to ear.	1 point off for each per cent short in weight of corn.

*Indicated by firmness of kernel on cob. †Does not have reference to length of cob.
‡Kernels missing count as mixed kernels.
For Dent Corn ears should have length of 9 inches, circumference of 7 inches, and shell 88% grain.

INDUSTRIAL EDUCATION.

The question is frequently asked in teachers' associations and educational gatherings, "Why do so many young people drop out of the public school between the sixth and tenth grades?" and the answer has been given by some that it is because the public schools are purely academic, and that the instruction given therein is not adapted to all classes of people, that is to say, that the course of study in the public school being academic is adapted to those who are intellectually keen and who desire to gain a livelihood in future years through the exercise of the intellectual faculties. Statistics show us that from the first grade to the sixth, inclusive, the number of children entering school and those in the sixth grade is not materially different, that is, that not many drop out before the the sixth grade, but from the sixth grade to the twelfth, which practically includes the years twelve to eighteen, the number of pupils in the public schools rapidly decreases. This condition exists in all public schools, and the means of closing this gap between twelve and eighteen years has been the source of a large amount of discussion. Experience shows that the introduction of manual training and the domestic arts has increased the number of pupils who remain in school, and it has been argued on this basis that if we can introduce these subjects, or industrial subjects, into the work of the public schools then we shall be able to retain in school the maximum number of children until the course of study is completed.

Why pupils leave school.

No doubt this claim is well founded, but when we enter upon the discussion of industrial education we have an exceedingly large problem to meet. In the German system of education "continuation schools" have been introduced, also trade schools, and in the regular public schools the subjects of manual training, domestic science and allied subjects had already been introduced. The continuation school and trade school has followed the introduction of the industrial subjects in the regular grades. The "continuation school," is an institution designed to meet the needs of young men and women who are obliged to drop out of the regular school course early and enter some active occupation. This continuation school may be either a night school or a school conducted on certain days for employed boys and girls in order that they may secure the largest possible amount of practical academic instruction. At the same time they may be employed in some active work. In some cities of Germany attendance at such schools is compulsory up to the eighteenth year.

Continuation school.

The trade school is what its name implies, a school in which actual vocational work is done, thus fitting the student upon completion of the course to enter directly into some trade. The magnitude of this phase of education may be more readily understood when we know that there are more than three thousand vocations or trades open to men and women to-day that were unknown fifty years ago. In other words, our industrial development has so multiplied the avenues into which men and women enter in order to secure a livelihood, that the attempt to teach in a trade school such things as will enable young men and women to enter all trades is practically an impossibility. Those who dis-

Trade school.

cuss trade schools seem to think that shop work and mechanics constitute the chief trades. This is evidently untrue. If we are to establish a school to train the carpenter or the mechanic, why not include courses in painting, paper hanging, stone cutting, brick laying, designing, and other three thousand trades that may be followed?

If we are to give training at public expense for any trade, the logic of the case will compel us to give training for all trades. This phase of the case would seem to preclude the possibility of introducing into our public schools the idea of trade schools.

If we are to teach any trade, the one most vital to the welfare of our country and of our people is the trade of agriculture, consequently any system of trade schools that does not include this subject will not touch the greatest need of our land.

In these days the ideal university is that institution that can supply the best instruction in *any study*, yet the work of our colleges and of our universities in special lines aims at the production of managers, superintendents and foremen, and not the production of men for the bench, the sledge, the plane and the saw. There is nothing in the general public school course which leads to craftsmanship, yet the industrial future of our country depends upon the trained craftsman, and again the question arises in view of the fact of the great burden already resting upon our public schools, "Can we add to that burden a department or an institution which will produce the artisan?" It appears to me that it is a hopeless task, yet I am thoroughly convinced that the introduction of commercial branches, manual training, domestic science, music, art, and elementary agriculture will to a large degree meet the problem above stated of closing up the gap between the ages of twelve and eighteen and give an opportunity to the public schools to discover the latent abilities of the child. Practically all there is in education is to present such objects of knowledge as will enable the learner to discover himself, and the introduction of the subjects just stated will in a large measure afford the opportunity while not aiming at specific instruction or specific skill in any particular line or vocation.

Subjects to be taught.

TRADE SCHOOLS.

I am convinced that if trade schools are to be a success in this country they must be under public auspices instead of private, and there is no more appropriate public authority than the school authority for their control. It certainly is possible to introduce trade schools to a limited extent in which certain trades may be taught successfully and fit the student for actual vocations. It is true that good citizenship and the morals of our country are quite as dependent upon the mass being trained to skilled work as upon a class being advanced in scientific or professional accomplishments. The greatness of our nation is dependent upon the proper development of the masses. It may be that our schools have caused an over-production of highly educated people, yet to my mind we have none too much specific education nor too many well educated people, but the great need of our citizenship is the extension of wider educational facilities to all classes of people.

Work of corporations. To meet the need of vocational training many public corporations have established trado schools in connection with their business. The Baldwin Locomotive Works has a special school of its own. The Westinghouse Company, New York Central Railway Company, and many others have done the same thing. All this is good, but I return to my previous statement that trade schools under the control of the people and for all the people will produce the greatest good to the greatest number. It must be remembered that America is republican and not monarchical, and therefore a system of education which may work well in Germany is not necessarily well adapted to the needs of this country. We may learn wisdom from the experience of Germany, but we cannot hope to engraft upon our public system of education the system in vogue in that empire. The establishment of trade schools means a large increase in the expense for education. The trade school in order to be successful must be conducted as a shop, that is, a building which has the appearance and management of a shop or a factory. To get the highest results we must get away from the school atmosphere. The instruction must be given by practical workmen, not by theoretical instructors. In many of our manual training schools we have women for instructors. The effect of this upon the boy will not produce the vocational instinct. The trade school therefore must be under the control of a real boss or a foreman. The course of study must contain instruction in those trades which have the greatest number of workmen in them, and added to this the trades selected must be such as can be most easily converted or adapted to other lines.

Vocations to-day. It is not my purpose to state the specific courses that can be undertaken as the industries of the locality will have a very large bearing upon the character of the trade school. Trade schools must be for both men and women, and the following are some of the more important trades from which selections may be made or which may be included in the entirety:

Carpenters, blacksmiths, braziers, book binders, cabinet makers, carvers, cooks, confectioners, dressmakers, artificial flower makers, bakers, barbers, basket makers, dyers, engravers, gardeners, glaziers, horse shoers, leather workers, locksmiths, masons, milliners, paper hangers, painters, photographers, potters, printers, rug makers, sadlers, stone cutters, tin smiths, tailors, trunk makers, watch makers, wagon makers, wheelwrights, iron workers, foundrymen, electrical machinists, general machinists, farmers.

This list is only a beginning in the entire number of vocations which may be followed in these days.

The purpose of education is to make good citizens. The good citizen is the worker and the one who is law abiding. The product of the public schools should be a person who is resourceful and who not only can see an opportunity, but can adapt himself to it so as to secure from life the highest possible results to himself and to his fellows.

THE DAY SCHOOLS FOR THE DEAF.

The day schools for the deaf evidently have become a permanent part of the public school system of Michigan. They will continue to be such as long as conditions make them helpful to the children afflicted with total or partial deafness. Experience will enable the day schools for the deaf and the State School for the Deaf at Flint to find their proper relations.

Teaching trades.

It is my opinion that no attempt should be made to teach the oral method to totally deaf children fourteen or more years of age. Such children should attend the Flint school for at least two years. Such attendance should be for the purpose of permitting every boy and girl to learn some of the trades and arts there so well taught. Moreover, pupils of such ages who have attended the oral schools should be sent to Flint for the same reason. In these cases where there is a well equipped manual training school it is possible that one year at Flint would be sufficient. It should, however, be one of the purposes of these schools to so educate that its pupils may be able to take their places as self-supporting citizens.

Home relations.

On the other hand, younger pupils should be sent to the day schools situated near enough for the children to reach home each night, and so that they will have the benefits of the home. For no public institution can fill the place of the home, no other relation compare with the family relation, no other heart throb with the love and tenderness of the mother heart, and these unfortunates who must live and enjoy within narrow limits should not be deprived of any portion of their inheritance.

Again I am more and more convinced that the lives of the deaf may be broadened and their usefulness and power to enjoy increased by the oral method of teaching. Speech and lip-reading, even if imperfect, gives enjoyment and a sense of individuality to the pupil. It does more; the intense attention necessary to achieve even a small degree of success develops power of concentration, perseverance and self control. These in turn enable the pupil to accomplish more in all lines of study and labor. It is my belief that in all schools for the deaf, at least two years should be given to this method of instruction to the total exclusion of sign work. If after two years of such work the pupil fails to make a reasonable advance in lip-reading and speech, he should be taught the sign language, whether he be in the day schools or in the State School at Flint.

Day schools and State institutions.

It is time, in my opinion, that the advocates of the two standard methods of teaching the deaf found some common ground, and that all strife and criticism be buried by a wave of earnestness and sympathy for these unfortunate children. A long step in this direction was taken last October when at the annual meeting of the State Teachers' Association a special section of the teachers of the deaf was arranged. At this meeting representatives from nearly all the cities having the day schools, and the teacher of the oral method in the Flint school were present. Excellent papers were read and discussed. Pupils from Flint were used to exemplify the work under Miss Billings in the Flint school. A very c mendable exhibit of manual training work was also made. Methods, des and school work were discussed and much good accomplished along these lines. An organization of the teachers of the deaf was perfected, and hereafter there will be arrangements for a section for them at the annual meeting of the State Teachers' Association. This is a step in the right direction.

Two day schools for the deaf have been discontinued, the one in Jackson and the one in Muskegon. During the past year one was established at Marquette, and the year previous one at Sault Ste. Marie.

Location of schools.

Below are the names of the cities now having schools for the deaf and the teachers employed: Bay City, Caroline Shaw, teacher; Calumet, Frances Dewar, teacher; Detroit, Gertrude Van Adestine, principal, Charlotte Willits, Anna Akins, Lucie Dumon, Margaret Daly, Urda Voight, Elizabeth Blondin, assistants; Grand Rapids, Martha Hill, principal, Henrietta E. Allen, Anna M. Condon, assistants; Ironwood, Tillie Walden, teacher; Iron Mountain, Anna Troudson, teacher; Ishpeming, Jessie Banford, teacher; Kalamazoo, Alice Roby, teacher; Marquette, Marie Paine Templeton, teacher; Manistee, Harriet Sanford, teacher; Menominee, May Howlet, teacher; Saginaw, Etta MacFarlane, teacher; Sault Ste. Marie, Jessie L. Thaw, teacher; Traverse City, Margaret Maybury, teacher.

These teachers, either through good fortune of the State, or because of the enrichment which always accompanies work among the unfortunate, are remarkably successful in their various positions, and while here and there may be seen weaknesses, it would be difficult to imagine a more conscientious, sympathetic and enthusiastic class of teachers. As long as these unfortunate children can have such teachers just so long will the State continue to benefit in its citizenship, having instead of entirely helpless deaf, a class of self helpful, self reliant and happy citizens.

PATRICK HENRY KELLEY.

Patrick Henry Kelly was born at Silver Creek, Cass County, Michigan, October 7, 1867. His early education was acquired in the rural schools of Cass and Berrien counties and later in the high school at Watervliet. After completing the high school course he taught in the rural schools of Berrien and Van Buren counties for a number of years and then spent two years at the Northern Indiana Normal and Business University at Valparaiso, Indiana. After leaving school he re-entered the teaching profession and acted as superintendent of schools at Galien and Hartford. In 1891 and 1892 he attended the State Normal College at Ypsilanti, and then was superintendent of schools at Mt. Pleasant for five years.

Mr. Kelley had always been interested in matters of law, and early determined that he would prepare for this profession at the first opportunity. He began this study while yet in school work, and after leaving Mt. Pleasant he completed his law studies at the University of Michigan, graduating from the law department of that institution in 1900. Upon graduation Mr. Kelley moved to the City of Detroit and entered upon the practice of his profession.

In 1901 Mr. Kelley was appointed as a member of the State Board of Education to fill a vacancy, and the next year was regularly elected by the people and served on the Board until December 31, 1904. In November, 1904, Mr. Kelley was elected Superintendent of Public Instruction and served the State in this capacity for two years. During his administration and under his direction important changes were made in school laws and in many other matters pertaining to the management of the schools. He conducted an investigation of the school treasurers of the State to determine whether they had complied with the statute and had given proper bonds to protect the public money. This was a new field of work for the Department, and it proved valuable in that school boards were required to properly protect public funds.

During Mr. Kelley's administration he published a number of pamphlets and pushed forward the work his predecessor began in the matter of the consolidation and improvement of rural schools. Among the most important pamphlets published were the Pioneer Day Program, in 1906, Suggestions for Manual Training, 1905, A Uniform Course of Study for the High Schools of the State, and a revision of the State Course of Study for Rural Schools.

Another important work undertaken by Mr. Kelley was the revision of the teachers' institute work of the State. It was his idea that it would be preferable to consolidate as many county institutes as possible with the summer sessions of the State normal schools, thus giving the teachers of the counties thus united the benefit of a six weeks' professional course and the advantages of the normal school libraries, conservatory, gymnasium and training school. This plan proved to be so profitable to the teachers that it has been continued ever since as the settled institute policy of the Department.

Mr. Kelley gave a large part of his personal attention to the work of the Department. He had been a popular speaker in the State for a number of years, and this no doubt attracted the politicians of the State, for in November, 1906, he was selected by the people as lieutenant governor of the State. I am pleased to testify to the energy and ability of Mr. Kelley, and to thus record a summary of the labors which he performed for the people of Michigan while at the head of its educational system.

L. L. Wright

Superintendent of Public Instruction.

SUPREME COURT DECISIONS

IN MATTERS OF

EDUCATIONAL INTEREST.

TARSNEY V. BOARD OF EDUCATION OF CITY OF DETROIT.

BOARD OF EDUCATION—POWER TO CONTRACT.

Certiorari to Wayne; Murphy, Brooke and Hosmer, JJ. Submitted February 19, 1907. (Calendar No. 21,998.) Decided March 5, 1907.

Mandamus by Timothy E. Tarsney to compel the board of education of the city of Detroit to audit a claim for services rendered. There was an order denying the writ, and relator brings certiorari. Affirmed.

"We next come to consider the question of the legal power of the board of education to enter into the contract upon which the relator relies. It will be remembered that the suits in which the relator's services were engaged were suits brought against the auditor general of the state, and were defended by the State through its proper officer, the attorney general. There is statutory provision empowering the State to employ further counsel if necessity arises; but nowhere is there any authority which permits an individual or a corporate body within the State to interfere in litigation wherein the State is a defendant. It is true, as argued by relator, that the citizens of Detroit (not the board of education) were vitally interested in the maintenance of the validity of the act in question in that case. The interest of the citizens of Detroit was not as residents of a particular school district, but as taxpayers having property liable to taxation within the corporate limits of the city of Detroit, which happened to be co-extensive with the limits of the school district under the control of the board of education. Should the validity of the act be sustained, the tax for school purposes within the city of Detroit would be less. Should the act be held invalid the taxes would be more. The board of education as such had absolutely no interest in the question at all. If it, as a board, had had an interest in, directly, still in our opinion it would not have the power to expend public moneys for the purposes indicated by the resolution, but, as we have pointed out, we believe the interest, indirect as it was, was not the interest of the board of education, but of the taxpayers of the city of Detroit."

The decision of the court below was clearly right, and stands affirmed.

SILVER V. HAMILTON TOWNSHIP BOARD.

SCHOOLS AND SCHOOL DISTRICTS—ORGANIZATION OF DISTRICTS—CERTIORARI—PROPRIETY.

The issuance of a writ of certiorari being largely discretionary, and not permissible to accomplish a palpable injustice, a writ issued to review the setting aside of the organization of a school district out of the territory of two others will be dismissed, where each of the three districts as so organized would be financially unable to support a school without imposing upon their residents a greater burden than they are able to bear.

Certiorari by Warren S. Silver, Joseph W. Allen and Robert Fisch, school board of district No. 5 of Hamilton township, to review an order of the township board of Hamilton, setting aside the action of the board of school inspectors in organizing said school district. Submitted October 29, 1906. (Calendar No. 21,889.) Writ dismissed November 13, 1906.

George J. Cummins, for appellants.

John Quinn, for Appellee.

Per Curiam. A writ of certiorari brings before us for review the proceedings of defendant, setting aside the organization of the plaintiff school district. That district was organized June 9, 1906, by the school inspectors of Hamilton township, Clare county. It was composed of four sections, two of which were taken from district No. 2, and two from district No. 3 of Hamilton township. It appears from the return of defendant, which must be taken as true, that the property of the new district has an assessed valuation of $14,610, and that the effect of its organization will be to reduce the property in school district No. 2 from an assessed valuation of $29,760 to $24,020, and that of district No. 3 from $27,110 to $19,360. The organization was set aside by defendant because:

"With this territory detached, said districts (2 and 3) will be unable to maintain their schools as they should be, without imposing a greater burden upon the residents than they are able to bear, and the new district proposed to be formed . . . will be in the same condition, so that two good school districts are sacrificed for the sake of having three poor ones."

Plaintiff in certiorari asks us to reverse the action of the township board because of various irregularities in its proceedings. If plaintiff had a legal right to have a court review those proceedings, it is possible that its claim of error would be allowed. But it has no such right. At least, it has not that right in this case. As heretofore stated, this case is brought before us by writ of certiorari. That writ, the issuance of which is largely discretionary, will not be permitted to accomplish a palpable injustice. (West v. Parkinson, 130 Mich. 401, and authorities there cited), and it is clear for the reason stated by respondent that injustice would be accomplished by setting aside the order under consideration, and sustaining the organization of the plaintiff school district.

The writ of certiorari is dismissed.

EXAMINATION QUESTIONS

FOR

STATE AND COUNTY CERTIFICATES

AND

EIGHTH GRADE DIPLOMAS.

1907.

STATE EXAMINATIONS: MARCH AND AUGUST.
COUNTY EXAMINATIONS: JUNE, AUGUST, AND OCTOBER.
EIGHTH GRADE EXAMINATION: MAY.

STATE EXAMINATIONS.

I. Questions prepared by the State Board of Education for the State examination held at Lansing and Marquette, March 25–29, 1907.

ALGEBRA.

1. Discuss algebra under the following heads:
   (a) Its relation to mathematics.
   (b) Its value as a factor in mental development.
   (c) Its practical utility.
2. Discuss factoring, giving illustrations of the various cases.
3. Give a graphic illustration of
   (a) $a^2 + 2ab + b^2$ as the square of $(a + b)$.
   (b) $a^2 - b^2$ as equal to $(a + b)(a - b)$.
4. Show that in a series of equal ratios the sum of the antecedents is to the sum of the consequents as any one antecedent is to its consequent.
5. (a) Prove that $(ab)^n = a^n b^n$.
   (b) Discuss the Binomial Theorem.
6. Solve for value of x: $\begin{cases} x^4 + y^4 = 82. \\ x - y = 2. \end{cases}$
7. If the product of two numbers be added to their difference, the result is 26; and the sum of their squares exceeds their difference by 50. What are the numbers?
8. What is the length of that rectangular field of $2\frac{1}{4}$ acres whose area would be diminished one acre by decreasing its length 10 rods and its width 2 rods?
9. Two cubical vessels have together a capacity of 1,072 cubic inches, and the sum of their heights is 16 inches. What is the capacity of each?
10. A man rents a farm for $200. He retains 5 acres for his own use and sublets the rest at $1 an acre more than he gave, gaining thereby $10 on his entire rental. How many acres does he rent?

ARITHMETIC.

1. Discuss the educational value of arithmetic, with reference to its effect upon (a) reason, (b) memory, (c) imagination, (d) judgment.
2. (a) Show why the difference between 1234 and 6725 may be found by adding the complement of 1234 to 6725 and then subtracting 10,000.
   (b) $25^2 = 20 \times 30 + 5^2$.
   Explain *why* this is true.
3. (a) Prove that the product of any three consecutive numbers is divisible by 6.
   (b) Show that the product of the L. C. M. and H. C. D. of two numbers is always the product of the numbers.
4. How much pure alcohol must be added to a mixture of $\frac{3}{4}$ alcohol and $\frac{1}{4}$ water, so that $\frac{9}{10}$ of the mixture shall be pure alcohol? Solve by analysis.
5. (a) Express on a Fahrenheit scale the following temperatures:
   $+ 40°$ C., $- 5°$ R. Explain.
   (b) The surface of a pyramid one foot high is made up of equilateral triangles. Find the surface of its sides.
6. Explain standard time, illustrating by examples.
7. A sphere and a cube have the same volume; find the ratio of their surfaces.

8. (a) Which is better for the purchaser and how much? 30%, 15%, 10% off or one discount of 47%?
   (b) At what price above cost must goods be marked that r% may be deducted and still s% profit be made?

BOTANY.

1. State and describe the several stages or epochs in the life history of a plant.
2. Name the chemical elements of plants which may be discovered by the use of reagents. Name several of the reagents you would use in such work.
3. Name the essential material and apparatus for a well-equipped botanical laboratory for a high school.
4. What subjects should be introduced in a course in elementary agriculture? Why?
5. Name five kinds of roots and describe each.
6. (a) Describe dormant bud, accessory bud, terminal bud.
   (b) Describe several kinds of estivation.
7. (a) Describe osmosis in roots and root hairs.
   (b) What is meant by root pressure?
8. Explain how plants obtain food from the air and from the soil. What foods are secured from each source?
9. Describe three types of bundles found in fibro vascular tissue.
10. (a) Name and describe five flower clusters.
    (b) Describe the process of pollination.

CHEMISTRY.

1. Define and illustrate acid, salt, base, alkali, neutralization.
2. Write the formulæ and give brief description of each: glycerin, chloroform, methyl, alcohol, glucose, phenol.
3. (a) Where and in what forms is nitrogen found in nature?
   (b) Name several compounds with nitrogen.
4. (a) Describe the preparation of hydrochloric acid.
   ( ) Name and give formulæ for the several compounds of chlorine, hydrogen, and oxygen.
5. Outline a method for the sanitary analysis of water; of vinegar.
6. Give a few simple tests to detect the presence of iodine, silver, and sulphuric acid in a solution.
7. (a) What are hydro carbons? Name several.
   (b) Give a test for carbon dioxide in the air.
8. Give the chemical significance of the terminations ate, ic, and ite.
9. Describe gunpowder chemically. Write the reaction caused by the explosion.
10. (a) Name and describe four compounds of iron.
    (b) Give Avogadro's law.

CIVIL GOVERNMENT.

1. How can civil government be correlated with United States history?
2. What are the sources of revenue for the national government? How may such revenues be increased? State the reasons for and against your answer.
3. Explain fully, using concrete illustrations, what is meant by the 59th Congress.
4. What steps have been taken to revise the constitution of Michigan? What remains to be done? What are some of the weaknesses of the present document?
5. What are the Michigan methods of controlling the sale of liquor? Are they effective? If not, why not?
6. Describe a trial in a justice court in detail? What is the jurisdiction of the justice court?
7. Give and explain several new ideas in methods of government—national, state, or local.

8–10. Give a full account of the Michigan system of taxation.

GENERAL HISTORY.

1. (a) Mention three elements of civilization transmitted by the ancients. Trace the transmission.
   (b) Characterize the first century A. D. as to politics and religion.

2–3. (a) What reference works (not regular text-books) do you use for the study of English history? What books on general history has your school library? Name a short, comprehensive list of histories (not less than ten) which should be used for studying the history of France, Greece, Rome, Germany.
(b) How should reference work in general history be assigned? What is its purpose?
4. What is the condition of Germany (a) politically, (b) commercially? Account for each.
5. (a) What is a concordat?
(b) What was the famous concordat of Bonaparte in 1801, and how is it affecting the history of France at the present time?
(c) What seems to be the social spirit of the French people and what is your opinion of this?
6. Discuss the present relations between the United States and Japan.
7. Trace in outline the struggle between France and England. What are their relations at the present time?
8. Mention some of the great problems which the English people are facing. Name some of her statesmen and state what solutions of these problems they advocate.
9. When and how were England and Scotland united?
10. What was the Holy Alliance, its purpose, and its effects?

GEOGRAPHY.

1. What mathematical geography should be taught in the grades?
2. What nations of Europe have interests in Africa and where? Which one has recently come into unpleasant notoriety over the rubber industry? How and why?
3. Name some geographical material and state what use you have made of the same.
4. Describe the physical features of Michigan (both peninsulas).
5. What would you aim to bring out and enforce in the study of a single foreign country, say Italy?
6. Name ten products of any kind and the state or country that stands pre-eminent in the production of each.
7. Describe the government of Canada in detail.
8–10. South America.
(a) *Countries:* Capitals; government.
(b) *People:* Nationality; language; religion; character.
(c) Leading imports (not less than ten).
(d) Leading exports (not less than ten).
(e) Largest and smallest country. Two largest cities.
(f) Speak of the production of (*a*) coffee, (*b*) rubber, (*c*) "jerked beef," (*d*) Paraguay tea, (*e*) nitrates, (*f*) wool, (*g*) vegetable ivory, (*h*) frozen mutton, (*i*) coca, (*j*) cocoa.
(g) Why do we send missionaries to this continent?
(h) Why is not South America as progressive as North America?
(i) What are our trade relations with that continent?

GEOLOGY.

1. (a) Give proofs of the theory of the origin of soils.
(b) Define disintegration and give factors of same.
2. Describe the formation of water falls, ravines, gorges, and give examples.
3. Describe glaciers. Name several noted glaciers. What is drift?
4. (a) Name organic agencies which have operated to change geographic and geologic conditions.
(b) Give notable examples.
5. What is the theory of the internal condition of the earth. Give proofs.
6. Describe the formation of coal beds, petroleum beds, salt beds and lakes.
7. Name and describe the stratified rocks.
8. Explain the terms fault, dip, strike, syncline, cleavage.
9. (a) Describe igneous rocks.
(b) Describe and name the granitic group or forms.
(c) Describe and name the volcanic group or forms.
10. (a) Explain the origin of mineral and metal veins.
(b) Explain the formation of mountain ranges and systems.

GEOMETRY.

1. (a) Give your method of distinguishing and illustrating the following geometrical terms: axiom, corollary, scholium.
   (b) Give what you consider the three most important axioms of geometry.
2. Discuss
   (a) Loci.
   (b) Theory of limits, giving such illustrations as you would use before a class.
3. (a) In how many cases are two triangles identically equal?
   (b) Give four cases.
4. Discuss concurrency of lines as related to triangles, illustrating one case by a theorem with proof.
5. (a) Draw a figure to prove the square upon the hypotenuse equal to the sum of the squares on the other two sides of a right triangle.
   (b) Mention in their logical order the points to prove in making the demonstration of the above from the figure.
6. Prove that if two line segments intersect so as to make the product of the segments of one equal to the product of the segments of the other, their four extremities are concyclic, i. e., in a circumference.
7. Compute the area of a triangle in terms of its sides. Demonstrate.
8. (a) What is the volume of a truncated triangular prism? Demonstrate.
   (b) A cistern is 8 ft. square at the top, 6 ft. square at the bottom, and 8 ft. deep. How many gallons of water will it hold?
9. The area of a regular tetrahedron is 16 inches. Find the edge of a similar tetrahèdron having twice the volume.
10. The area of a zone is equal to the product of its altitude and the circumference of a great circle. Demonstrate.

GERMAN.

1. (a) Decline a masculine, a feminine, and a neuter noun of the strong declension together with an article and a qualifying adjective.
   (b) What nouns are declined in the weak declension?
2. Give the principal parts of brennen, senden, rufen, finden, bitten, sprechen, preisen, wissen, loben.
3. (a) What prepositions govern either the dative or the accusative case? When the dative and when the accusative?
   (b) What is the use of the passive voice in German? How is it formed? Conjugate finden in the present, past, and perfect subjunctive, passive voice.
   (c) What idioms are used in German as a substitute for the passive voice?
4. (a) When is von used in place of the genitive?
   (b) When do als, wenn, and wie each introduce adverbial clauses?
   (c) What adjectives require the dative? Illustrate.
5. Translate:
   (a) He is the father of three children.
   (b) How many sacks of potatoes did the farmer bring?
   (c) Be welcome to us.
   (d) He begged that he might be allowed to go. (Express in active voice.)
   (e) The gentleman whose house I bought has gone away.

6–7. Translate and give constructions of italicized words:

Draussen auf *der Strasse* war es tiefe Dämmerung; er fühlte die frische Winterlust an seiner heissen Stirn. Hie und da fiel der helle Schein eines brennenden Tannenbaums aus *den Fenstern*, dann und wann hörte man von drinnen das Geräusch von kleinen Pfeifen und Blechtrompeten und dazwischen jubelnde Kinderstimmen. Scharen von Bettelkindern gingen *von Haus zu Haus*, oder stiegen auf die Treppengeländer und suchten durch *die Fenster* einen Blick in die Versagte Herrlichkeit *zu gewinnen*. Mitunter wurde auch eine Thür plötzlich aufgerissen, und scheltende Stimmen trieben einen ganzen Schwarm solcher kleinen Gäste aus dem hellen Hause auf die dunkle Gasse hinaus; anderswo wurde auf den Hausflur ein altes Weihnachtslied gesungen; es waren klare Mädchenstimmen *darunter*. Reinhardt hörte sie nicht, er ging rasch an allem vorüber, aus einer Strasse in die andere. Als er an seine Wohnung gekommen, *war* es fast völlig dunkel *geworden;* er stolperte die Treppe hinauf und trat in seine Stube. Ein süsser Duft schlug *ihm* entgegen; *das heimelte ihn an,* das roch wie zu Haus der Mutter Weihnachtsstube. Mit *zitternder Hand* zündete er sein Licht an; da *lag* ein mächtiges Paket auf *dem*

Tisch, und als er es öffnete, fielen die wohlbekannten braunen Festkuchen heraus; auf einigen waren die Anfangsbuchstaben seines Namens in Zucker ausgestreut; das konnte niemand anders als Elisabeth gethan haben. Dann kam ein Päckchen mit feiner, gestickter Wäsche zum Vorschein, Tücher und Manschetten, zuletzt Briefe von der Mutter und von Elisabeth.

8. Quote a German poem.

9–10. Translate:

Ich lebte still und harmlos—das Geschosz
War auf des Waldes Tiere nur gerichtet,
Meine Gedanken waren rein von Mord—
Du hast aus meinem Frieden mich heraus
Geschreckt; in gährend Drachengift hast du
Die Milch der frommen Denkart mir verwandelt,
Zum Ungeheuren hast du mich gewöhnt—
Wer sich des Kindes Haupt zum Ziele setzte,
Der kann auch treffen in das Herz des Feinds.

GRAMMAR.

1. Discuss, under not more than three heads, the educational value of grammar study.
2. Give accurate and complete definitions of the following: verb, infinitive, preposition, relative pronoun, case, conjugation.
3. Illustrate the various uses of the infinitive.
4. Define and illustrate the factitive, adverbial objective, dative object, objective subject.
5. Use like in four different contructions and parse it in each.
6. Criticise the following, correcting if wrong, and give reasons:
   He who made the mistake you should talk to, not me.
   They who do well, I will reward.
   Let's you and I go.
   Neither she or I is invited.
   The band have bought their instruments.
7. Discuss mode, giving outline.
8. Give outline of the verb.
9. Show four grammatical uses of the word *as;* four of the word *but;* three of the word *so;* three of the word *that.*
10. Analyze the following and parse the italicized words:
    He *looked as though* the speed of thought *were* in his limbs.

LATIN.

1-2. Translate:

Erant hae difficultates belli gerendi, quas supra ostendimus, sed multa Cæsarem tamen ad id bellum incitabant: iniuriae retentorum equitum Romanorum, rebellio facta post deditionem, defectio datis obsidibus, tot civitatum coniuratio, imprimis ne, hac parte neglecta, reliquae nationes sibi idem licere arbitrarentur. Itaque cum intellegeret, omnes fere Gallos novis rebus studere et ad bellum mobiliter celeriterque excitari, omnes autem homines natura libertati studere et condicionem servitutis odisse, priusquam plures civitates conspirarent, partiendum sibi ac latius distribuendum exercitum putavit.

3. Decline liber, natio, nomen, acer, plus, relative qui.
4. (a) Distinguish between the use of posse and licet.
   (b) Give the outline for formation of tenses for verbs of the third conjugation, passive voice, indicative and imperative modes.
5. Give constructions for all verbal forms in 1–2.
6. Name five uses of the dative case, seven of the ablative.
7. How is condition expressed in Latin?
8. What cases are used in relative clauses and when?
9. (a) Name the causal conjunctions.
   (b) What verbs take the infinitive construction?
10. Translate:
    (a) Even if Cæsar had come, yet we should have been conquered.
    (b) If your brother says this, it is true.
    (c) You can easily bear this hardship.

LITERATURE.

1. (a) What is a drama?
   (b) Name three English and three American dramatists and a work of each.
   (c) What is the condition of American drama at present?
2. Give a sketch of the life of Chaucer, tell what influences affected his productions, and the importance of his works.
3. (a) Name the comedies which Shakespeare wrote.
   (b) In any one of his comedies outline the mental and moral qualities of five of the chief characters.
   (c) Give a brief statement of Shakespeare's influence upon his immediate successors.
4. What are the chief characteristics of the literature of the Victorian period?
5. Compare the novels of Sir Walter Scott with those of a present day novelist.
6. (a) Name five good magazines and the editor of each.
   (b) Discuss "yellow journalism" and its influence.
7. Who is William Dean Howells and what does American literature owe to him?
8. How has the West and Middle West influenced American literature? Name ten of the best writers whose productions show this influence.
9. (a) What is a realist? a humanitarian?
   (b) Name ten authors whose productions have one of these qualities.
   (c) hat can you say of these qualities in the literature preceding the Elizabethan period?
10. (a) Give a biography of Longfellow.
    (b) What are the chief qualities of his productions?
    (c) How is he regarded in (*a*) America, (*b*) England?

ORTHOGRAPHY.

1. Do you teach written or oral spelling? Give the arguments for each.
2. How do you account for poor spelling?
3. Do you teach diacritical marks? Where?
4. How do you teach pronunciation?
5. What use do you make of spelling in other subjects?

LIST OF WORDS.

1. recede
2. stalwart
3. surly
4. languor
5. inertia
6. heinous
7. malign
8. soliloquy
9. ravel
10. veil
11. censor
12. erase
13. furlough
14. ellipsis
15. poultice
16. treatise
17. emery
18. judiciary
19. coral
20. rinsing
21. flourish
22. smolder
23. bivouac
24. falcon
25. lyceum
26. museum
27. sycamore
28. correspondent
29. tympanum
30. waive
31. razo
32. clique
33. Houghton
34. reservoir
35. ptomaine
36. arguing
37. conscience
38. truly
39. hoeing
40. Roosevelt
41. changeable
42. separate
43. hemorrhage
44. Sault Ste. Marie
45. scepter
46. syncline
47. frieze
48. steppe
49. abridgment
50. Sebewaing

PHYSICS.

1. What is the momentum of a battleship of ten thousand tons steaming 18 knots per hour?
2. (a) Explain the terms foot pound, kilogrammeter, foot-poundal, erg.
   (b) Give laws of falling bodies.
3. (a) Give Boyle's law.
   (b) If the barometer stands at 28½ inches, what is the elastic tension of the air in dynes per square centimeter?
4. Explain musical interval, scale, gamut, fundamental and overtones, covibration, coincident waves, resonance.
5. A mass of air at 0°, and under an atmospheric pressure of 30 inches, measures 100 cubic inches; what will be its volume at 40°, under a pressure of 28 inches?
6. Define radiant energy, a ray, a shadow, an image, photometry.
7. Draw figure to illustrate spherical aberration of light. Give effects of same.
8. How should 50 cells each with a resistance of 3 ohms be arranged so as to secure the greatest current through a circuit of 30 ohms external resistance? What current strength may be obtained in the foregoing circuit if each cell is of two volts force?
9. (a) Give Ampere's theory of magnetism.
   (b) Give Ohm's law.
10. Explain construction and use or uses of transformer, induction coil, Crookes tubes, Wheatstone bridge.

PHYSIOLOGY.

1. What benefits have been derived from the teaching of scientific temperance? (Do not theorize.)
2. Is the medical inspection of schools feasible in small towns? Is it advisable?
3. What can a teacher do in looking after the health of children?
4. What is the difference between contagious and infectious diseases? Give examples.
5. Name some of the common means by which communicable diseases are spread.
6. Name some of the common disinfectants and tell how they are used.
7. Tell some of the things you teach relative to "first aid to the injured."
8. Explain the art of cooking and the part it plays in health.
9. Give some good rules as to the use and care of clothing.
10. What are some of the common insanitary conditions and sources of disease and what may be done to correct these?

RHETORIC.

1. What styles of composition, oral and written, should be required in high school work? Give the chief characteristics of each.
2. How do you correct manuscripts in work in English and what work do you require on the part of pupils after the return of papers?
3. Discuss force, illustrating by reference to standard authors.

4-5. Write a complete description of some picture which appealed to you.

6. Discuss the development and the relative importance of thought and expression.
7. (a) What matters of form should be taught in regard to the paragraph?
   (b) What things should be taught regarding the devolopment of the paragraph?
8. (a) Name five persons of the present time whom you consider "masters of English".
   (b) Criticise the current papers and magazines from a rhetorical standpoint.
9. (a) Define scansion, metre, poetry, rhyme, couplet.
   (b) Define solecism, idiom, figure of speech, climax, syllogism.
   (c) What qualities of composition are derived from word study?
10. (a) Write the essential form for a business letter, a formal letter of introduction, a friendly letter.
    (b) What are the chief rhetorical requisites for a good conversationalist?

SCHOOL LAW.

1. How many regents of the University, when elected, and for how long?
2. Under what conditions may corporal punishment be inflicted?
3. Give the law in regard to holidays, and in regard to loss of time when school is closed on account of contagious diseases.

4. What is the legal procedure in hiring a teacher? When must the contract be executed? Who are parties to it?
5. Give the chief provisions of the compulsory attendance law.
6. (a) How may a school district library be established?
   (b) What funds are distributed for the support of libraries?
7. Who fixes the length of the school year and when?
8. What are the powers and duties of the township board of school inspectors?
9. Give powers and duties of the county commissioner of schools.
10. (a) Under what conditions may a graded school district be organized?
    (b) Give the substance of the law governing the issuing of bonds by a school district.

THEORY AND ART.

1. Name a text in psychology, one in school management with which you are familiar.
2. Discuss school sanitation from the standpoint of the teacher.
3. (a) What constitutes professional ethics in the teacher?
   (b) In what ways do many teachers violate these principles?
4. "A class recitation is a business proposition." Explain fully the foregoing statement.
5. Give three laws of mind and the three corresponding laws of teaching.
6. Can pupils be taught to study? If so, how?
7. How should reading classes be conducted? Give pedagogical reasons.
8. (a) Give five characteristics of a good course of study.
   (b) What subjects taught in the public schools do you consider practical?
9. (a) Define education.
   (b) What do you consider the most important work of the teacher?
10. Give the laws of association and illustrate each.

UNITED STATES HISTORY.

1. What is the present status of the Panama canal? What is the "canal zone?" How did we secure the right to build this canal on foreign territory? What are the chief difficulties that have developed?
2. Give an outline of history work for the first eight grades.
3. How much use can be made of outside reading in connection with the United States history work? Name some books you have used successfully for collateral reading.
4. What would you say concerning the teaching of dates? Name the dates that you consider pivotal.
5. Trace the origin and development of the two leading political parties of to-day.
6. What is source material? What source material have you used?
7. Make an outline for teaching the causes of the Civil War.
8. What are national banks? What is their place in our government?
9. Discuss "The United States as a World Power."
10. Give an estimate (not over 200 words) of the life, character, and service of Theodore Roosevelt.

ZOOLOGY.

1. Give apparatus necessary in a zoological laboratory. Where have you studied this subject? Under what method?
2. What specimens may be secured as typical of each of the following branches: mollusca, vertebrata, orthropoda?
3. If you have examined specimens of the foregoing name them and give your findings.
4. Give the branch to which each of the following belongs: snail, fly, sponge, crayfish, frog.
5. The animal kingdom is divided into protozoa and metazoa. Explain this.
6. Describe the circulatory and digestive systems of the cow.
7. Give the method and history of the development of the butterfly, frog, oyster.
8. Describe the habits, skeleton, plumage of the robin, hawk, quail.
9. Name the injurious insects common in Michigan. Name the insects that are beneficial.
10. Describe as briefly as possible the development of the nervous system in the vertebrates.

II. Questions prepared by the State Board of Education for the State examination held at Lansing and Marquette, August 12–16, 1907.

ALGEBRA.

1. (a) If a man walks s miles in r hours, at what rate does he walk? (b) If a man can do a piece of work in m days, how much of the work can he do in r days?
   (c) If a thermometer at 1 o'clock p. m. indicates s degrees below zero and at 7 p. m. c degrees below zero, express the difference in temperature of the two hours. (d) How many times is m a factor of $(2m)(3m^4)$?
2. (a) Given $5x^2+21x=62$. Solve.
   (b) What name is given to this equation from the fact that it contains both x^2 and x?
3. (a) Reduce to simplest form the complex fraction $\dfrac{1+\dfrac{a}{1-a}}{\dfrac{1+a}{1-a}}$

   (b) $\dfrac{x^2+3}{x-3}\times\dfrac{1}{x+3} - \dfrac{x-3}{x+3}=?$
4. Prove, giving the fundamental principles of fractions, that the expression $\dfrac{m}{a-b}+\dfrac{n}{b-a}$ is equal to the expression $\dfrac{m}{a-b} - \dfrac{n}{a-b}$
5. Three towns are at the three angles of a triangle. From the first to the second through the third is 82 miles; from the first to the third through the second is 97 miles; from the second to the third through the first is 89 miles. Find the direct distance between the towns.
6. (a) Simplify the expression $4^{-\frac{5}{2}}$. (b) Divide $3\sqrt{7}$ by $2\sqrt{8}$ and express the result in its simplest form.
   (c) Simplify the expression $\left\{\dfrac{\dfrac{1}{a^{m+1}}}{b^{m}}\right\}^{m^2-1}$
7. Two persons, A and B, can do a piece of work in 16 days. They work together 4 days; after which B finishes the work in 36 days more. In what time can each do it separately?
8. (a) State an axiom which gives authority for changing the signs of all the terms of an equation.
   (b) Define elimination. (c) Define and give illustration of like, or similar terms.
9. Solve without clearing of fractions: $\begin{cases} \dfrac{10}{x} - \dfrac{9}{7}=8 \\ \dfrac{8}{x} + \dfrac{15}{7}=-1. \end{cases}$
10. Two cubical vessels have together a capacity of 1072 cubic inches, and the sum of their heights is 16 inches. What is the capacity of each?

NOTE—What is your preparation in this subject? Where obtained?

ARITHMETIC.

All solutions of problems must be explained by analysis. Solutions by algebra will not be accepted.

1. An article was sold at 50% above cost. Had the cost been 50% less, the gain would have been $120. What did it cost?
2. Which is the better investment—$4,752 in a real estate mortgage at 5% or 4% R. R. bonds at 1.10 brokerage 1-8%, the mortgage being taxed 1¼% per annum?
3. Write a 90 day note payable to your bank, drawing the legal rate of interest, such that discounted at a bank at 8% it will produce $5,000.

4. How far apart are two cities, one being 200 miles south of the other and whose time is 20 min. 19 sec. slower?
5. When ¾ of an article is sold at the cost of ⅞ of it, what is the rate of gain or loss?
6. Explain the effect upon the value of a fraction when the same thing is added to both terms.
7. (a) Explain as to a class, standard time.
   (b) From what geographical line is standard time taken for your locality?
8. (a) Mention the "checks" you would teach in arithmetic.
   (b) Why does the product of the L. C. M. and the H. C. D. of two numbers equal the product of the numbers?
9. A ladder 45 feet long stands against a building, the top reaching to a window 30 feet high. How far is the foot of the ladder from the house?
10. At what time in the study of arithmetic would you introduce the equation? Geometrical demonstrations? Business arithmetic?

BOTANY.

1. (a) Where have you studied botany, how long, and from what texts?
   (b) How much time have you given to laboratory work?
2. Discuss the important characteristics of protoplasm.
3. Describe in detail the origin and development of the root, and give its functions.
4. Describe the various devices by which nature prevents self-pollination.
5. Give the botanical name of the edible part of the following plants: potato, bean, celery, strawberry, cabbage, apple, rhubarb, peanut, beet, walnut.
6. Describe three types of bundles found in fibro-vascular tissue.
7. Name three legumes and state their commercial and fertilizing value.
8. (a) Explain photo-synthesis.
   (b) Describe osmosis in roots and root hairs.
9. Describe cell contents and multiplication of cells.
10. Name ten plant families with a type under each.

CHEMISTRY.

1. Define alotrophy; endothermic and exothermic compounds.
2. Write the formulae and briefly describe each of the following: alcohol, sugar, lime, gypsum, iron rust, potassium nitrate.
3. What experimental facts led to Avogadro's hypothesis? Prove it to be a theory and not a law.
4. Give the main assumptions made by the dissociation theory. Define ion, anion, kation.
5. State in full the process for making Le Blanc soda.
6. What is the basis of the classification of the elements?
7. What salts may be formed from sulphuric acid and a monivalent metal?
8. State the laws of "definite proportions," "multiple proportions," and give the law of "equivalent combining proportions of compounds."
9. Give a few tests to detect the presence of chlorine, arsenic, potash.
10. Outline an approved method for the sanitary analysis of water and milk.

CIVIL GOVERNMENT.

1. Outline the work of a course in civics for the public schools.
2. What is meant by a "city of the fourth class"?
3. How may a village be incorporated in Michigan? A city?
4. What is the work of the board of supervisors?
5. How are the following selected: justice court jury, coroner's jury, grand jury, circuit court jury?
6. What is an inheritance tax, a game law, the "third house"?
7. How is the coming constitutional convention to be organized?
8. What was done by the last legislature?
9. Describe the United States diplomatic service.
10. *Name some points of* difference between the Michigan legislature and Congress *of the United States.*

GENERAL HISTORY.

1. Discuss the rise and fall of the temporal power of the popes.
2. How and when did the Carolingian Dynasty come into power? Name four of its most important members.
3. What were the causes and results of the Thirty Years' War?
4. What is the present ruling house in England? How and when did it come into power?
5. Discuss the rise of the English power in India.
6. Discuss the events which brought about the unification of Italy.
7. What were the conditions in France at the time when Louis XVI came to the throne?
8. Name the four leading powers in Europe during the sixteenth century; how do you account for the supremacy of each during this period?
9. What was the feudal system? What were its effects?
10. Discuss the Revival of Learning in England.

GEOGRAPHY.

1. Discuss the correlation of geography and history.
2. Give a complete description of the following points on Canada: (a) physical features; (b) principal industries and products; (c) people, manners and customs; (d) language and religion.
3. Give five uses of the globe and three of maps in the schoolroom.
4. Give the physiographic reasons which account for the growth and influence of Seattle, Chicago, Hamburg, Calcutta, Liverpool.
5. What is a topographic map? Describe the topography of Europe.
6. Why should water ways and railroads be given much attention in the teaching of geography?
7. Locate New Guinea, Borneo, Formosa, Isle of Pines, Madagascar, and state to which class of islands each belongs.
8. Sketch a map of modern Africa locating the possessions of foreign nations.
9. State where each of the following is produced and its commercial use and value: glucose, jute, marl, chocolate, cottolene, resin, hemp, quinine, camphor, cork, eucalyptus oil, platinum.
10. Give some methods of doing field work in geography and proper results to be secured.

GEOLOGY.

1. (a) Define dynamic and structural geology.
   (b) Name three famous geologists.
2. What is the relation of geography to geology?
3. Define erosion. Name three eroding agencies and give examples.
4. (a) Describe sandstone, granite, quartz, marble.
   (b) State as to a class how these classes of rocks are distinguished or recognized.
5. What is a terminal moraine. Locate one in Michigan.
6. Locate the drift line in North America. Give general statement as to glacial action.
7. Define dikes, veins, fissures.
8. Give the origin, extent, and classification of igneous rocks.
9. (a) In what classes of rocks do we find fossils. Why?
   (b) Describe three fossils found in the United States.
10. Account for the natural wonders of Yellowstone Park.

GEOMETRY.

1. Outline a *complete* demonstration to prove that the square constructed on the hypothenuse of a right triangle is equal to the sum of the squares constructed on the other two sides.
2. Explain dividing a line in extreme and mean ratio.
3. Give an original demonstration of some theorem in solid geometry, not found in this examination.

4. Give your method of illustrating to pupils in seventh or eighth grades some of the simple practical theorems of geometry.
5. The area of a circle is 1; what is the side of an inscribed equilateral triangle? square? pentagon? hexagon?
6. If the opposite sides of an inscribed quadrilateral are produced until they meet the bisectors, the angles produced are perpendicular to each other.
7. Represent by a drawing a five-sided truncated pyramid and find its volume. Give proof.
8. The sum of the angles of a spherical triangle is more than two right angles and less than six right angles. Demonstrate.
9. The surface of a sphere is equal to the product of its diameter by the circumference of a great circle. Demonstrate.
10. Demonstrate: What is the volume of a spherical segment?

GERMAN.

1. Decline in German: the rich man; a whole year; this good woman; the little child; a long day.
2. How are adjectives compared? Compare *mild, schön, alt, gross, gut, hoch, viel, nah.*
3. (a) Give a list of the prepositions which govern the dative case.
   (b) Give a list of the prepositions which govern the accusative case.
   (c) Give four prepositions which govern the genitive case.
4. (a) Distinguish as to the use of *als, wenn,* and *wann.*
   (b) Distinguish as to the use of *aber, allein,* and *sondern.*
5. Give the principal parts of the following verbs: *helfen, sein, anerkennen, leiden, hauen, schliessen, wachsen, werfen, zwingen, leihen.*
6. (a) Give the synopsis of the verb *schlagen* in the third person, singular, active.
   (b) Give the synopsis of the verb *loben,* in the first person, singular, passive.
7. Translate:

"Und ich ein Muselmann.
Der Christ ist zwischen *uns.*—Von diesen drei
Religionen kann doch eine nur
Die wahre sein.—Ein Mann, wie du, bleibt da
Nicht stehen, wo der *Zufall* der Geburt
Ihn hingeworfen: oder wenn er bleibt,
Bleibt er aus Einsicht, Gründen, Wahl des Bessern.
Wohlan! so teile deine Einsicht mir
Denn mit. Lass mich die Gründe hören, *denen*
Ich selber nachzugrübeln, nicht die *Zeit*
Gehabt. Lass mich die Wahl, die diese Gründe
Bestimmt,—versteht sich, im Vertrauen—wissen,
Damit ich sie zu meiner *mache.*—Wie?
Du stutzest? wägst mich mit dem Auge?—Kann
Wohl sein, dass ich der erste Sultan bin,
Der eine solche Grille hat; die *mich*
Doch eines *Sultans* eben nicht so ganz
Unwürdig *dünkt.*—Nicht wahr?—So rede doch!
Sprich!—Oder willst du einen Augenblick,
Dich zu bedenken? Gut; ich geb' ihn dir.—Denk' nach!
Geschwind denk' nach! Ich säume nicht, zurück
Zu kommen."

From Lessing's Nathan der Weise.

8. Give constructions of italicized words in above.
9. Give a sketch of the life of Goethe and name eight of his most important works.
10. Translate:
    (a) We were helped.
    (b) I shall take my first German lesson today.
    (c) When it struck four o'clock he stepped out of the house.
    (d) At what o'clock? At half past five.
    (e) He said that he would go.
    (f) He walked along the street.

GRAMMAR.

1. Discuss the formation of the possessive case, and give illustrations of the common errors in its formation.
2. Give a complete outline of the pronoun as you teach it.
3. In the sentence "John is here," discuss the word *here* according to its different constructions by various authors.
4. (a) Illustrate the various uses of the infinitive and parse each.
   (b) Mention two authors that do not agree in their disposition of infinitives, and state wherein they disagree, giving illustrations.
5. Give an illustration of what some authors call "the subjective predicate adjective," and also "the objective predicate adjective."
6. Discuss the uses of *shall* and *will, should, would* and *could.*
7. How would you have a class dispose of the following expressions: "they ran away crying;" "he was laughed at;" "two and two are (is) four;" "four times five are (is) twenty"?
8. Analyze the following sentences and parse the italicized words: "Whom say *ye me to be*"? "*To think that* he should be so foolish!" "Oh, *that* I had wings *like* a dove!"

9-10. Explain and analyze the following:

"If it were done when 'tis done, then 't were well
It were done quickly: if the assassination
Could trammel upon the consequence, and catch
With his surcease success; that but this blow
Might be the bė-all and the end-all here,
But here, upon this bank and shoal of time,
We 'ld jump the life to come."

LATIN.

1. Discuss the law of sequence of tenses.
2. Decline rex, urbs, opus, mare, vis, spes.
3. (a) Give a full synopsis of the verb *capio* in the second person, singular, active voice.
   (b) Give a full synopsis of the verb *video* in the first person, singular, passive voice.
4. Translate:

   Video duas adhuc *esse* sententias; *unam* D. Silani, qui censet eos, qui haec delere *conati sunt, morte esse multandos;* alteram C. Caesaris, qui mortis poenam *removet,* ceterorum suppliciorum omnis acerbitates *amplectitur.* Uterque et pro sua dignitate et pro rerum magnitudine in summa severitate *versatur.* Alter eos, qui nos omnis *vita privare* conati sunt, qui *delere* imperium, qui populi Romani nomen *extinguere,* punctum temporis *frui vita* et hoc *communi spiritu* non putat *oportere,* atque hoc genus poenae saepe in improbos civis in hac re publica ésse usurpatum *recordatur.* Alter intellegit mortem ab *dis* immortalibus non esse supplici causa *constitutam,* sed aut necessitatem naturae aut laborum ac miseriarum *quietem.* Itaque eam sapientes numquam inviti, fortes saepe etiam libenter *oppetiverunt.* Vincula vero, et ea sempiterna, certe ad singularem poenam nefarii sceleris inventa sunt. (Cicero IV-4.)
5. Give the constructions of all the italicized nouns and adjectives in the above.
6. Give the construction of all the italicized verbs in the above and conjugate them in the tenses used here.
7. Discuss the use of the periphrastic conjugation and illustrate.
8. Write and translate into Latin sentences illustrating the following:
   (a) Subjunctive of purpose.
   (b) Subjunctive of result.
   (c) Dative of possession.
   (d) Accusative of duration of time.
   (e) Dative of agent.
9. Give a sketch of the life of Cicero.
10. Define the gerund, supine, gerundive, deponent verbs, ablative absolute, predicate genitive, ethical dative.

LITERATURE.

1. What standard English works have you read?
2. Give your method of conducting a class in the reading of an English masterpiece.
3. What makes a piece of literature classic?
4. Name five authors that have made American literature famous and the masterpiece of each.
5. Give a brief character sketch of Longfellow, Whittier, Bryant.
6. What constitutes the greatness of Shakespeare's work?
7. What is an epic poem? What are the great epics?
8. Characterize the Bible as literature.
9. How much attention should be given to the mechanics of a classic? How much to thought? How much to style?
10. How may young people be taught to love literature?

ORTHOGRAPHY.

1. (a) What is an elementary sound?
   (b) What is the value of the study of elementary sounds?
2. What are the chief essentials of good articulation, and how is it to be secured?
3. What benefits are derived from the study of word analysis?
4. Discuss the growth of the English language.
5. Give the rules for spelling the following words: wrapping, singeing, fencing, essays, berries.

LIST OF WORDS.

1. alliteration
2. reminiscence
3. dyspepsia
4. sacrilege
5. appall
6. battalion
7. accede
8. eligible
9. acquittal
10. parallelogram
11. instill
12. privilege
13. serviceable
14. admissible
15. solstice
16. precision
17. vermilion
18. connoisseur
19. completeness
20. playwright
21. consensus
22. achieve
23. measurable
24. emaciated
25. garrulous
26. croquet
27. gazetteer
28. cartoon
29. abridgment
30. colloquial
31. scepter
32. assimilate
33. larynx
34. vestige
35. euchre
36. amateur
37. antecedent
38. colossal
39. artillery
40. amanuensis
41. complaisance
42. satellite
43. equinoctial
44. anathema
45. immaculate
46. imagine
47. punctilious
48. erroneous
49. synonymous
50. territories.

PHYSICS.

1. What is the principal difference between the structure of the lamp producing the arc light and that producing the incandescent light.
2. Illustrate a dynamo having a field magnet that is shunt wound, series wound, compound wound. Give the special advantages of each.
3. Describe the condenser method of measuring battery resistance.
4. *Tell how to determine* the power of an engine.

5. If a cable weighing 8 pounds per yard sags 12 inches in a span of 200 feet, what is the maximum tension per square inch in it?
6. Give the laws of falling bodies. Explain the law of acceleration.
7. Explain what is meant by the production of cold by absorption; by dispersion; by interference. Give examples of each.
8. Define a foot poundal in terms of units of length, mass, and time.
9. Explain Archimedes' principle as to a class.
10. Explain and illustrate composition of forces.

PHYSIOLOGY.

1. Discriminate as to the meaning of the following: anatomy, physiology, and hygiene; and speak of their relative importance in public school teaching.
2. Mention some good results from the work of the State Board of Health.
3. What is the germ theory of disease? What diseases are so classified? How treated?
4. What progress has been made in pure food legislation? Give some illustrations of the necessity for them.
5. How does the work of the schools injure childrens' eyes?
6. Give several useful suggestions for "first aid to the injured."
7. What are the physiological arguments for and against recess in school?
8. Give three useful hints for bathing, care of the eyes, eating.
9. Describe the nervous system.
10. What reasons can be given why a boy should not use tobacco, especially cigarettes?

RHETORIC.

1. Define rhetoric and tell what purpose is to be held in mind in the study.
2. What is the relation of grammar and rhetoric?
3. What is the relation of rhetoric and literature?
4. What is diction? How may one secure a good vocabulary?
5. How will the reading of a classic aid in the rhetoric work?
6. Apply the doctrine "We learn to do by doing" in rhetoric.
7. Can you give a successful plan for conducting rhetoricals?
8. Give an outline for the preparation of an essay.
9. Give your plan for conducting ninth grade English composition.
10. (a) Give ten suitable subjects for paragraph writing and (b) ten suitable themes for ninth grade composition.

SCHOOL LAW.

1. How many members of the State Board of Education? When elected and for what term?
2. Give the general provisions of law governing the care and use of public money.
3. Give the procedure for organizing graded school districts.
4. Give the permissive powers, and the mandatory duties of boards of education.
5. What are included in necessary school appendages?
6. Name the boards governing the following institutions: university, normal schools, agricultural college, school for the blind, school for the deaf, and state how many constitute each board.
7. Give the legal qualifications for the office of commissioner of schools, for members of boards of examiners.
8. Who are voters in a school meeting?
9. Give the substance of the laws governing the following: display of flag, teaching communicable diseases, the effects of alcohol and narcotics.
10. Do you own a copy of the school law? Give three reasons why you should thoroughly know this subject.

THEORY AND ART.

1. (a) What is the value of the study of psychology?
   (b) In your study of psychology what benefits have you received for the practical work of the schoolroom?
2. Discuss the three most important requisites of a teacher.
3. Define the following: (a) envy, (b) jealousy, (c) malice, (d) revenge.
4. Mention two of the world's greatest educators and explain the essential differences in their views.
5. Discuss the "Batavia Method."
6. What is the justification from a psychological point of view for teaching drawing and music in the public schools?
7. Discuss under classified heads one of the following topics:
   (a) Discipline, (b) the recitation, (c) waste in the schoolroom.
8. (a) What is the educational value of a definition?
   (b) When should a definition be taught?
9. Give five laws of mental growth and a principle of teaching founded upon each.
10. Define: (a) consciousness, (b) imagination, (c) attention, (d) judgment, and (e) discuss attention.

UNITED STATES HISTORY.

1. Upon what did the following nations base their claims to territory in the New World: England, Spain, France?
2. Give an account of the organization and work of the London and Plymouth companies.
3. Sketch the work of the constitutional convention of 1787.
4. What events led up to the election of Jefferson, Lincoln and Cleveland?
5. What results followed the Alien and Sedition laws, Dred Scott decision?
6. Locate in history the following: James G. Blaine, Henry Clay, William H. Seward, Lewis Cass, John C. Fremont, John Hay, Cyrus Field, Edward Everett Hale, Washington Irving, Rufus Choate.
7. Speak of the social conditions in the "South" at the present time.
8. What is the origin of the present difficulties between the United States and Japan?
9. What was the function of the first National Bank? What of the present National Banks?
10. What is the present status of railroad rate regulation?

ZOOLOGY.

1. Where have you studied zoology? How much time have you given to laboratory work? What specimens have you examined?
2. Give a careful statement of observations made on one specimen.
3. Name five men prominent because of their researches in zoology and biology.
4. Describe the structure and habitat of the coral, oyster, sponge.
5. Describe the anatomy of the infusoria.
6. Give the history and method of development of the codling moth.
7. Name the different classes under Arthropoda and give general characteristics of each.
8. Compare plants and animals as to origin, development, composition, and propagation.
9. Give general statement of circulatory systems of invertebrates.
10. Define branch, class, order, genus, species.

COUNTY EXAMINATIONS.

I. Questions prepared by the Superintendent of Public Instruction for the regular examination, June 20–22, 1907.

ALGEBRA.

First Grade.

1. Find the H. C. D. of $6x^2 + 13x - 5$, $3x^3 + 2x^2 + 2x - 1$, $6x^3 + 19x^2 + 8x - 5$.
2. Reduce to simplest form

$$\left(\frac{a+b}{a-b} + \frac{a^2+b^2}{a^2-b^2}\right) \div \left(\frac{a-b}{a+b} - \frac{a^3-b^3}{a^3+b^3}\right)$$

3. Discuss simple equations under two of the following heads: (a) Impossible, (b) negative results, (c) variables, (d) limits, (e) inequalities.
4. Deduce the formula for the cube of a number and apply the same in extracting the cube root of a number.
5. Factor $x^3 - y^3 - 3xy(x-y)$; $(a^2 + a - 4)^2 - 4$; $x^2 + xy - 6y^2 + x + 13y - 6$.
6. What is a logarithm? What advantage in the use of logarithms?
7. The sum of the terms of a fraction is 17. If the numerator is increased by 5, and the denominator diminished by 5, the product of the resulting fraction and the original fraction is 4-21. Required the fraction.
8. A man rows down stream 12 miles in 4 hours less than it takes him to return. Should he row twice as fast, he would go down stream 10 miles an hour. Find his rate in still water.
9. Find three quantities in arithmetical progression such that the sum of the squares of the first and third exceeds the second by 123, and the second exceeds one-third the first by 6.
10. Given a, n and l in a geometrical progression, to find the formula for r and S.

Second Grade.

1-2. Discuss the following: (a) the signs plus and minus in algebra, (b) change of sign, (c) "Like signs produce plus, unlike signs minus."

3. Divide $a^2 - b^2$ by $a^{\frac{1}{2}} - b^{\frac{1}{2}}$.
4. Factor $x^{10} - y^4$; $27x^3 - \frac{1}{8}y^3$; $3x^2 - xy - 4y^2$.
5. Discuss exponents.
6. Difference between A's and B's ages is 24. Eight years ago A's age was 4 times the age of B. How old is each?
7. In a number of three digits the units' figure is 3 times the hundreds' figure and the tens' figure equals the difference between the hundreds' figure and the units' figure. If 18 be added to the number the tens' and units' figures will change places. What is the number?
8. Divide 36 into two such parts that their product will be 320.
9. The number of dollars A has multiplied by the number B has is 96; but if A gives B $4 their money will be equal. How much has each?
10. The sum of three numbers is 100. The first plus its one-half equals the second, and the second is 9-10 of the third. What are the numbers?

ARITHMETIC.

First and Second Grades.

Second grade answer first ten; first grade the last ten.

1. At 16% premium what will be the income on U. S. 6's which can be bought with $464.50, brokerage ⅛%?

2. Find the L. C. M. of $2\frac{1}{2}$, $\frac{3}{4}$, $\frac{5}{8}$.
3. How many cords of stove wood in a pile 35 ft. long, 6½ ft. high at one end, increasing in height to 8½ ft. high at the other end?
4. Draw a negotiable 60-day note due Jan. 30, 1908, and compute the interest on the same at legal rate.
5. Find the surface of a block that is square on the end and three times as long as wide, containing 81 cu. ft.
6. The longitude of Paris is 2° 20′ 22″ E. When Omaha time is 11 min. 57½ sec. p. m. on Tuesday, what is the longitude of Omaha, if it is 45 min. past 3 a. m. Wednesday in Paris at the same instant?
7. A man succeeded in insuring a house worth $7,900 at such a price as to cover both the value and the insurance at a rate of 1¼%. What was the face of the policy?
8. A horse was sold for $175 at a loss of 12½%. What would have been the selling price had there been a gain of 12½%?
9. How thick a shell must be taken from a ball 10 in. in diameter to get one-third of the ball?
10. What is the diagonal of a cube of silver weighing 8 lbs.?
11. A sphere and a cube have the same solid contents, 10 ft. What is the ratio of their surfaces?
12. Commission on buying is 5%, on selling is 3%. I send my broker cash to use for me in buying and selling. He buys stock and sells it at 10% advance, sending me $17 net profit. For how much did he sell, and how much did I send him?
13. Draw a negotiable 90-day note drawing 6%, such that discounted the same day at 10% it will produce $1,000.

Class B.

Third Grade.

1. Give your method of teaching pupils to write decimals.
2. Give a model lesson on some topic in percentage.
3. A man owns a farm of 120 acres which he rents at $500 per annum. He pays annually $75 taxes and $50 repairs. How much will his net income be changed if he sells the farm at $60 an acre and invests in 6% non-taxable stock at 20% premium?
4. Which is better 4% stock at 10% discount or 6% stock at 20% premium, and how much?

5-6. At $20 per thousand what will the lumber cost to cover the roof of a 30x40 foot barn, the ridge being 20 ft. above the plate and the eaves projecting 2 ft.?

7. The space necessary to store 1,000,000 silver dollars is 250 cu. ft. On April 30, 1901, there were $436,485,494 silver dollars in the U. S. Treasury. How much space was required to store it?
8. Make out in proper form a receipted bill for 10 articles bought at a general store.
9. A boy 150 ft. from a tree flies his kite into the top, using 250 ft. of string in so doing. If his hand holding the string is 6 ft. from the ground, how high is the tree.
10. Find the diagonal of a cube containing 1,331,000 cu. in.

Class A.

1. Give your method of writing decimals.
2. Give a model lesson in fourth grade work.
3. Make a problem that will be solved by the following indicated operations: (4×$16) ÷ ($3×4).
4. Explain, as to a class, substracting when a figure of the subtrahend is greater than the corresponding figure of the minuend.

5-6. At $20 per thousand what will the lumber cost to cover the roof of a 30x40 foot barn, the ridge being 20 ft. above the plate and the eaves projecting 2 ft.?

7. The space necessary to store 1,000,000 silver dollars is 250 cu. ft. On April 30, 1901, there were $436,485,494 silver dollars in the U. S. Treasury. How much space was required to store it?

8. Make out in proper form a receipted bill for 10 articles bought at a general store.
9. Sold ¼ of my farm at $20 an acre and invested ⅜ of the proceeds in 25 cows at $36 each. How much had I at first?
10. ⅔ of ⅚ of 12 is ½ of 2 times what?

MENTAL ARITHMETIC.

All grades.

Second and third grade applicants analyze fully without algebraic equations, the first five; first grade applicants the last five. Twenty-five credits for this work.

1. What part of ¾ of 60 is ⅔ of 30?
2. If ¾ of a farm at $40 an acre costs $2,400, how many acres in the farm?
3. Sold a horse and cow for $270, receiving 2-7 as much for the cow as for the horse. What did I receive for each?
4. Divide 12 apples among three boys so that the first shall have ½ as many as the second and ⅓ as many as the third.
5. A can do ⅔ as much as B. Together they can build a fence in 144 days. How long for each to build it alone?
6. A train passes a telephone pole every 4 seconds. If the poles are 66 feet apart, how many miles per hour is the train going?
7. A boy can pick up twice as many potatoes as his father but can dig only one-half as many. They together can dig 12 bushels in an hour and pick them up in 20 minutes. How many bushels can they dig and pick up in 2 hours?
8. The men in a factory struck for a raise of 12½%. The proprietor compromised by reducing the 10-hour day instead. What was the length of the new day?
9. I bought two lots for $600 and $900 respectively. I sold them both at the same price, gaining the same per cent on one that I lost on the other. What was my real gain or loss per cent?
10. B sold goods costing $300 to C; C sold them to D for $432. Both men made the same gain per cent. What was the gain per cent?

BOTANY.

First Grade.

1. Upon what bases are plants divided into classes and families?
2. What phases of botany do you emphasize in your teaching? Why?
3. Describe the pistil of a flower, giving the function of each part.
4. Give the morphology of the floral parts of a plant.
5. Describe the processes leading to the formation of seeds.
6. Explain the terms perianth, perigynous, gamopetalous. Describe the different methods of attachment of the anther.
7. Name the important plant foods and state how and where the plant obtains them.
8. Describe the structure of wood, bast fibers and grit cells.
9. Explain the word tissue as used in botany.
10. Describe plant circulation, transpiration, storage of plant food.

Second Grade.

1. Describe the process of germination of seeds.
2. Name the parts of a complete flower and describe each.
3. Describe in full the method of propagation, growth and fruit of the strawberry.
4. Name four root forms and name plants having them.
5. Define panicle, cyme, raceme, umbel, spike.
6. Describe the general structure of a herbaceous stem.
7. Name ten early spring flowers. What is the habitat of each?
8. Name several plants suitable for window gardens.
9. Describe the berry, the pome, the drupe.
10. Why do plants wilt and corn leaves roll in a dry time?

CIVIL GOVERNMENT.

First and Second Grades.

Applicants for second grade answer the first ten; for first grade, the last ten.

1. What are the qualifications for Congress?
2. Discuss Gerrymandering, and illustrate, as to a class, its workings.
3. Give the Constitutional provisions with reference to the adjournment of either house of Congress.
4. In what ways has the Speaker of the House special influence upon legislation?
5. (a) State the Constitutional provision under which Congress can raise money to carry on the government.
   (b) How was this applied in the recent war with Spain?
6. Filibustering. What is it? Illustrate its workings.
7. How does the United States borrow money? Give illustration.
8. How many senatorial districts are there in Michigan? In which do you live?
9. Give the method of pardoning criminals in Michigan.
10. Discuss the power of Congress over commerce.
11. What are the prohibitions of the Constitution?
12. Give the principal duties of the Auditor General of Michigan.
13. Outline the Federal Judiciary.

Third Grade. Both Classes.

1. (a) What are the three general departments of government?
   (b) Briefly outline one of these departments of the United States government.
2. Give the powers and duties of the President as outlined in the constitution.
3. When do the following take place: The convening of Congress; of the State legislature; inauguration of the President; election of United States senator?
4. What are the qualifications for voting in Michigan?
5. Why are senators in Congress chosen for a longer period than are the representatives?
7. (a) How does an alien become a voter? (b) Why should he do this before being given the right to vote? (c) Would you change the length of time?
8. Where must bills for raising revenue originate? Give a reason for this.
9. Give five parallels between the United States constitution and the Michigan State constitution.
10. How may the State Constitution be amended?

COURSE OF STUDY.

All Grades.

1. Outline the fifth grade.
2. In general, what is the difference between the teaching of first or second grade pupils and that of seventh grade pupils?
3. Name four of the poems given for memorizing.
4. What is recommended with reference to "checks" upon arithmetic work?
5. In what grades is spelling from a text-book recommended or implied?
6. Explain the plan of "alternation" suggested.
7. What topics are treated in commercial geography?
8. Outline the plan of teaching history.

9-10. Criticize the Course of Study under the following heads: (a) Methods, (b) omissions, (c) changes needed.

GENERAL HISTORY.

First Grade.

1. Discuss the temperament and religion of the Greeks. Were they influenced by their environment? If so, how?
2. (a) Give results of the Battle of Arbela.
   (b) What became of Alexander's empire after his death?
3. (a) Discuss the conspiracy of Catiline.
   (b) What was the First Triumvirate and what did it do?

4. (a) What events led up to the Council at Nicaea?
   (b) What was the religious policy of Constantine the Great?
5. (a) When and by whom was the Empire in the West restored?
   (b) Give the points in the Treaty of Verdun.
6. Discuss the rise of Chivalry. Why did this institution decline, and what were its influences?
7. (a) What was the Great Schism?
   (b) How was it settled?
8. What was the Act of Supremacy? What was its significance?
9. (a) Give the causes that led to the rise of Cromwell.
   (b) Give the causes and events of the Restoration.
10. (a) Give a sketch of the present political situation in Russia.
   (b) In the United States.
   (c) What two expositions are being held at present? Why?

Second Grade.

1. (a) What was the religion of the Greeks?
   (b) Name five deities and explain their significance.
2. Who was the hero of Marathon? What were the results of the battle? Why is it considered one of the decisive battles of the world?
3. Who said "Carthage must be destroyed!"? Why did he say it? How were these words carried into effect?
4. Give causes of the fall of the Roman Empire in the West. When did it fall? Who was ruler at the time? Who succeeded him?
5. (a) Who were Peter the Hermit, Saladin, Richard Coeur de Lion? In what great religious expeditions did they take part?
   (b) What were the results of these expeditions?
6. What was the Hanseatic League? Why organized?
7. Give a sketch of Joan of Arc.
8. (a) When and where did the name "Protestant" arise?
   (b) What was the Diet of Worms?
   (c) What was the Diet of Augsburg?
   (d) Who were Calvin, Zwingle?
9. (a) What events led up to the Thirty Years' War? What powers were involved?
   (b) Give results of the war.
10. Name five European monarchs at the present time, and give a brief statement regarding some present day matter of interest in the country of each.

GEOGRAPHY.

First and Second Grades.

Applicants for second grade answer first ten; for first grade, last ten.

1. Name the zones and give the width of each in degrees.
2. (a) Why are the tropics located 23½ degrees from the equator?
   (b) Compare the north and south temperate zones as to land area.
3. Name the plateaus and the plains of South America. Describe the climate, vegetation and productions of each.
4. What are the chief commercial exchanges between South America and the United States?
5. Compare the mountain systems of Asia with those of N. America.
6. Name the industries of Massachusetts, Georgia, Texas, Michigan.
7. Name the natural resources of the United States, the means of transportation, the chief cities of the southern states.
8. What "raw materials" are shipped from the United States to Europe? What "raw materials" do we import?
9. Name and locate ten cities of Europe, and indicate their pronunciation.
10. What important commercial, political and educational results are expected from the recent conference between England's home officials and the heads of the Colonial governments?
11. Describe in detail the topography of Europe.

12. If as some claim the gulf stream is not the cause of the modified climate of Western Europe, how do you account for it?
13. Describe the progress of China during the past 25 years.
14. State briefly the present status of the Philippines as to government, education, commerce.
15. How do the mines of Michigan compare in value with agricultural products?

Third Grade.

Class B.

1. Define great circle, zone, longitude, latitude.
2. Give causes of change of seasons as to a class.
3. Define divide, plain, mountain chain.
4. Locate the chief divides of the United States.
5. Name the political divisions of Europe. Capitals of each.
6. For Russia give the following: Physiography, resources, cities, education.
7. Name twenty cities of the United States, in order of importance if possible.
8. How does the educational system of South Carolina compare with that of Michigan? Give points of difference.
9. In what states is mining the most important industry? Agriculture?
10. Name five great trunk line railroads of the United States and state what parts of the country are reached by each.

Class A.

1. Outline a lesson on rivers for the fourth grade.
2. Outline a lesson on trees for the fourth grade.
3. Explain the causes of day and night as to a third grade.
4. What work should the fourth grade do in map making?
5. What would you teach in regard to Michigan, below the fifth grade?
6. For Germany give the following: Physiography, resources, cities, education.

7, 8, 9, 10. Explain the term "oral geography" as applied in primary grades.

GEOMETRY.

First Grade.

Notes.—Demonstrate all theorems. All constructions must be by lines and explained.

1. Give three fundamental theorems of plane geometry.
2. Show by two demonstrations what the sum of the interior angles of a triangle is.
3. If in a triangle the angles are as 1; 2; 3, the sides are as 1; $\sqrt{3}$; 2.
4. The three perpendiculars from the vertices of a triangle meet in a common point.
5. The sum of the three lines from any point within a triangle to the three vertices is less than the sum of the three sides, but greater than half their sum.
6. Show how the height of a standing tree may be ascertained by geometrical processes.
7. Construct a square and an equilateral triangle having equivalent areas.
8. Having the following conditions construct the triangle: one angle 30°, side opposite 1 in., difference between the other two sides ½ in.
9. Prove the ratio of the areas of the regular inscribed and circumscribed triangles.
10. Give and demonstrate a theorem relating to circles.

GRAMMAR.

First and Second Grades.

Applicants for second grade answer first ten; for first grade, last ten.

1. What are the divisions of grammar and of what does each treat?
2. Give four rules for the use of the possessive sign and illustrate each.
3. Define inflection. What parts of speech are not inflected?

4. Define and explain the different classes of nouns, also verbs.
5. How many forms has the participle? State what each expresses.
6. Explain the difference between a conjunctive adverb and a conjunctive pronoun. Illustrate.
7. Analyze—I know him to be a scoundrel but the burden of proving it is yours.
8. Give the construction of him, scoundrel, but, proving, yours, in the foregoing sentence.
9. Explain the infinitive mode, gerunds, passive voice.
10. In the following sentences state whether the verbs are transitive or intransitive, and why, also give the voice:
    (a) The driver walked his horse.
    (b) The man walked.
    (c) The sea broke the ship to pieces.
    (d) The sea broke on the rocks.
    (e) The butcher cuts the meat.
    (f) The meat cuts tough.
    (g) He laughed heartily.
    (h) He laughed at me.
11. Explain factitive verbs and the constructions following them. Give examples.
12. Define and illustrate paragraph, loose sentence, compound complex sentence.
13. Discuss the propriety of using the potential mode.
14. (a) Some authors name five kinds of pronouns. Classify them and give examples.
    (b) Classify adjectives and adverbs.
15. What is the essential thing to be taught in sentence analysis? In parsing?

Third Grade.

Class B.

1. Name the parts of speech. Define two of them.
2. Classify sentences as to form. Give examples.
3. Give four rules for forming the plural, and three for forming the possessive.
4. Define case. Name the cases. State in how many and what ways a noun may be in the objective case.
5. What properties have verbs? Define two.
6. Give the principal parts of lay, see, go, sit.
7. Write a sentence containing a predicate adjective, a conjunctive adverb, a verb in the subjunctive mode.
8. Name the classes of pronouns. Select a pronoun and decline it.
9. Classify adjectives. Select an adjective and compare it.
10. Analyze—"Sirrah," replied the spider, "if it were not for breaking an old custom, I should come to teach you better manners."

Class A.

1 and 2. Outline a course in language for the first four grades.
3. Show how language and nature study may be correlated.
4. When and with what material do you begin written language work?
5. Why must oral work be emphasized in the primary grades? What points must have special care?
6. Classify pronouns, adjectives, adverbs.
7, 8, 9, 10. Write an essay on "Technical grammar as related to language work."

ORTHOGRAPHY.

All Grades.

Applicants for second grade, answer first five; for first grade, last five; for third grade any five.

1. Define orthography, etymology, philology, root, prefix, suffix.
2. (a) Give the meanings of the following abbreviations: P. M., C. O. D., Jr., Hon., Messrs.
   (b) Give five other abbreviations and their meanings.
3. Illustrate the correct use of the following words in sentences: pr wait, weight; pare, pear, pair; lie, lye; oar, ore.

4. (a) What is syllabication?
   (b) What is a primitive word? Example.
   (c) What is a derivative word? Example.
   (d) What is an idiom? Example.
5. Give the present participles of the following verbs, and give the rules for spelling these participles: drop, ride, die, spin, dye.
6. After indicating the pronunciation of the following words, write the names of the diacritical marks used: nations, machinery, err, recipe, lawsuit, crises, judge, merchandise, canon (a gorge), burglar.
7. (a) How many syllables has a word?
   (b) Classify words as to syllables.
8. What devices or methods would you use in order to interest your pupils in written and oral spelling?
9. Give:
   (a) Three English prefixes with meanings, and illustrate.
   (b) Three Latin prefixes with meanings, and illustrate.
   (c) Five suffixes with meanings, and illustrate.
10. Why do we teach elementary sounds, and when should such study begin? How would you proceed?

LIST OF WORDS.

All Grades.

1. consensus
2. pneumatic
3. seizing
4. occasion
5. counterfeit
6. Massachusetts
7. judgment
8. usury
9. quinine
10. Presque Isle
11. ammonia
12. paralysis
13. catarrhal
14. freight
15. gossiping
16. diagnosis
17. percentage
18. presidential
19. hydrangea
20. participle
21. turquoise
22. practicing
23. believe
24. morocco
25. pleurisy
26. disappoint
27. admissible
28. infinite
29. separate
30. consular
31. ellipse
32. receipt
33. vermilion
34. Milwaukee
35. mattress
36. Illinois
37. vengeance
38. miscellaneous
39. magnanimity
40. menacing
41. preamble
42. conciliation
43. applicable
44. symbol
45. scrupulously
46. minimum
47. daffodil
48. acknowledge
49. Great Britain
50. parliamentary.

PHYSICS.

First Grade.

1. Give the law of weight. Illustrate.
2. Give the general law of machines. Explain the *efficiency* of a machine.
3. Give the rules for liquid pressure. Make and solve a problem under one rule.
4. Give the laws of vibrations of air columns. Explain the position of nodes in an open and closed pipe sounding its fundamental tone.
5. (a) Define heat, temperature, heat unit.
   (b) Explain the graduation of a Fahrenheit thermometer.
6. (a) Explain real, virtual and multiple images.
   (b) Explain focus, conjugate foci.
7. Give the causes of refraction of light. Illustrate.
8. Give the laws of spectra. Of what use is the spectroscope?
9. Give the process of constructing an electroscope, a Leyden Jar, a battery.
10. Explain the uses of a transformer, induction coil, volt-meter, microphone.

Second Grade.

1. (a) Give formula for distance a body will fall in a given time.
   (b) A body is thrown upward with a velocity of 240 feet per second. How long and how far will it rise?

2. Give and illustrate the three conditions of equilibrium.
3. Define hydrostatics, pneumatics, prism, induction.
4. Illustrate and explain the operation of the hydraulic press.
5. Make and solve a problem involving the wheel and axle.
6. Give the theory of light. Define ray, image, refraction.
7. Illustrate and explain the construction of a refracting telescope.
8. What is color? Name some complementary colors.
9. State two differences between frictional and galvanic electricity. Define conductor, ohm, volt.
10. What results are obtained by grouping several cells in series? In parallel?

PHYSIOLOGY.

First and Second Grades.

Applicants for second grade answer first ten; for first grade, last ten.

1. What is the epidermis? What important work does it do for the body?
2. Explain the importance of reflex action.
3. (a) What is respiration? Name the organs of respiration.
   (b) What is the purpose of perspiration?
4. (a) What is meant by the "blind spot"? What is the function of tears?
   (b) Discuss the care of the eye.
5. Name the parts of the brain and describe each as to structure and function.
6. How would you teach the evil effects of alcohol upon the nervous system?
7. What should a teacher know in regard to communicable diseases, and what are her duties in regard to them?

8-9. Name the organs of digestion in their order, and state what changes the food undergoes in each. Explain fully.

10. What is lymph? Of what use is the lymphatic system?
11. Name some of the elements that are needed in our food supply, and show how these may be obtained.
12. (a) What is the difference between an artery and a vein structurally?
    (b) What changes does the blood undergo in the lungs?
13. What organs constitute the nervous system, and what is the function of each?
14. (a) What is the osseous system? Its functions?
    (b) What is the composition of bone?

Third Grade.

Both Classes.

1. (a) What are the functions of bone?
   (b) Contrast the bones of a youth with those of an older person.
2. Locate the following bones: clavicle, scapula, humerus, radius, ulna.
3. (a) What is cartilage? How does it differ from bone?
   (b) Give its chief uses.
4. (a) How do we classify muscles as to structure?
   (b) What are the uses and functions of muscles?
5. (a) Trace the circulation of the blood.
   (b) What are the capillaries and why are they so important?
6. Where in the body are the following fluids secreted and what service does each render—bile, gastric juice, saliva, tears? Explain fully.
7. Name and describe the different parts of the eye.
8. (a) Of what does the nervous system consist?
   (b) State fully the effects of alcohol upon the capillaries.
9. (a) What is a narcotic?
   (b) Mention three common opiates and explain their effects.
10. Mention two emergencies that may occur in the schoolroom. What would you do in each case?

READING.

Burk 's Speech on Conciliation with America.

All Grades.

Answer ten questions including those marked *.

*1. Give a sketch of the life of Burke.
2. When and where was this speech delivered? Why was it so important?
*3. (a) Discuss the then existing conditions in England and in America.
(b) Show the commercial relation between the colonies and the mother country.
4. Name several of the most prominent men at the head of affairs in both countries. Who was king of England?
5. What plan had previously been submitted for settling the difficulty, and by whom?
*6. (a) What did Burke advise Parliament to do, and why did he believe that England should take the initiative?
(b) What precedents did he cite?
*7. (a) What, in one sentence, is the theme of the speech?
(b) Along what two lines does he develop it?
8. On what facts and characteristics of the American colonists does he base his plea?
*9. Give the actual concessions proposed by Burke.
10. How were his resolutions received? What was the effect of this speech?
*11-12. Write a brief sketch discussing Burke's literary style. What method or methods of reasoning does he use? Judging from this speech what would you say regarding the man's personal qualities? His knowledge of literature?

SCHOOL LAW.

All Grades.

Answer any five.

1. Name the duties of a school director.
2. What duties of a school board must be performed at a board meeting.
3. Give the powers of boards of education in township districts.
4. Give the duties required of a teacher by law.
5. What are the duties of a board of school inspectors? Who compose this board?
6. How are fractional school districts formed or changed in boundaries?
7. Give the chief provisions of the law governing county normal training classes.
8. Give date of the annual school meeting. When must the school census be taken?

THEORY AND ART.

All Grades.

Applicants for second and third grade answer first ten; first grade, last ten.

1. Define study, learning, teaching.
2. Name the books on teaching you have read during the past year.
3. Should a teacher ever "break in" when a pupil is reciting and help or explain? Why?
4. Describe your method of teaching long division. Are you sure your method is based upon pedagogical principles?
5. Name five indispensable requisites in a teacher.
6. Give your plan or method of calling and dismissing classes. Do your pupils *observe strictly* your plan?
7. What are the two chief factors in attention? How do you secure or produce them?
8. Explain what you understand by local geography.
9. What is your idea of the proper results to be secured in the teaching of (a) language, (b) grammar.
10. Define perception, consciousness, conception, memory.
11. Give the laws of association and illustrate their application in teaching.
12. Explain the mental process by which we arrive at a judgment.

13. Define motive, incentive, desire.
14. What have ideals to do with successful teaching?
15. Classify the emotions. What have they to do with education?

UNITED STATES HISTORY.

First and Second Grades.

Applicants for second grade answer first ten questions; for first grade, last ten.

1. Give the character of the Jamestown colony. How did it affect the later history of Virginia?
2. Give the cause and effect of the French and Indian War. What treaty closed this war and what were its chief provisions?
3. How were funds provided for the Revolutionary War?
4. What controversies were settled by the Ordinance of 1787?
5. Give an account of the "Toledo War" and results of same.
6. (a) Why has the President a right to suspend the writ of habeas corpus during the time of war?
   (b) State whether this has ever been done; when and by whom?
7. What was the Critical Period in American history? Why so called?
8. Give the chief events of the first year of the Civil War.
9. Under what theory of constitutional authority did the United States begin the Mexican War?
10. State the compromises that were made by the convention which framed the constitution.
11. Give the history of tariff legislation from 1820 to 1892.
12. What powers has the Interstate Commerce Commission?
13. Give the process by which a territory becomes a state. What has been done by Oklahoma and New Mexico toward becoming states?
14. Give the chief events of Roosevelt's administration.
15. Give the causes and effects of the panics of 1837 and 1873.

Third Grade.

Both Classes.

1. What is a revolution? An insurrection? A rebellion?
2. What was the political situation in the colonies at the time of the Declaration of Independence?
3. (a) By whom and when was the Declaration of Independence drawn up?
   (b) What were its effects at home? Abroad?
4. (a) Give the preamble to the Constitution of the United States.
   (b) What are the divisions of government under the Constitution?
5. (a) Name ten powers of Congress.
   (b) Which of these is most important to the people? Why?
6. (a) What is the Monroe Doctrine?
   (b) When and under what conditions has this doctrine been invoked since the time of President Monroe?
7. (a) When and how was the first Bank of the United States established?
   (b) What was Hamilton's plan for paying the debts of Congress?
8. What legislation encouraged the development of the Great West?
9. Give a brief sketch of any three of the following:
   (a) Peter White.
   (b) Austin Blair.
   (c) The Conspiracy of Pontiac.
   (d) The founding of Detroit.
10. Discuss the importance of the "Soo."

II. Questions prepared by the Superintendent of Public Instruction for the regular examination, August 8–10, 1907.

ALGEBRA.

First Grade.

1. Explain as to a class the algebraic significance of the signs plus and minus in the four fundamental operations.
2. Show that the difference of any equal positive powers of two quantities is divisible by the difference of the quantities.
3. Show that the sum of any equal positive powers of two quantities is divisible by the sum of the quantities only when the exponents are odd.
4. Solve by factoring $\frac{x + 3}{2x - 7} = \frac{2x - 1}{x - 3}$
5. Prove, (a) that if four quantities are in proportion, they are in proportion by inversion, alternation, composition, and division; (b) that in a series of equal ratios the sum of the antecedents is to the sum of the consequents as any one antecedent is to its consequent.
6. If y varies inversely as x, and $y = 7$ when $x = 3$; what is y when $x = 2\frac{1}{3}$?
7. Develop the Binomial formula for the sixth term and apply the same in writing the sixth term of $(x^2 - 6\,\frac{1}{2}) - \frac{1}{2}$.
8. A man has a 64 gallon cask full of wine. He draws three times the same number of gallons of the liquid, each time filling up the cask with water when there are 27 gallons of wine in the cask. How many gallons of the liquid did he draw each time?
9. A man bought a number of $20 shares for $1,500 at a certain discount. He sold all but 60 for $1,000 at the same rate of premium as the rate of discount when he purchased them. How many shares did he buy and at what price?
10. A sets out to walk to a town 7 miles away; 20 minutes afterwards B traveling at a 4-mile rate sets out with a message for A which he delivers and at once returns to his starting point, reaching it at the same time that A reaches his destination. What was A's rate per hour?

Second Grade.

1. What principles or axioms are involved in the following operations or equations: (a) transposing terms, (b) clearing of fractions, (c) dividing by coefficient of the unknown.
2. Explain as to a class the algebraic significance of the signs plus and minus in addition, subtraction, multiplication and division.
3. Simplify the following expressions: $17 - [45 - (9 - \overline{23 - 32})]$, $\frac{a^{\frac{3}{2}} - b^{\frac{3}{2}}}{a^{\frac{1}{2}} - b^{\frac{1}{2}}}$ $(a + b + c) \cdot (-a + b + c)(a - b + c)(a + b - c.)$
4. Factor $(a^2 + 9)^2 - 36a^2$, $a^6 - a^4 - a^2 + 1$, $a^{10} - 1$.
5. Reduce to simplest form $\frac{\frac{1 - x^2}{1 + x^2} - \frac{1 + x^2}{1 - x^2}}{\frac{1 - x}{1 + x} - \frac{1 + x}{1 - x}}$
6. Solve for equations $\begin{Bmatrix} u + x + y = 6 \\ x + y + z = 7 \\ y + z + u = 8 \\ z + u + x = 9 \end{Bmatrix}$
7. Solve for value of x, $\sqrt{x + 6} + \sqrt{x + 9} = \sqrt{4x + 29}$.
8. If the product of two numbers be added to their difference the result is 23; and the sum of their squares exceeds their difference by 50. What are the numbers?
9. If the product of three consecutive numbers be divided by each of them in turn, the sum of the three quotients is 74. What are the numbers?
10. Write the Binominal formula for $(a + x)n$ to the sixth term and apply the same in expanding $(x + 2y)^8$.

ARITHMETIC.

First and Second Grades.

Second grade applicants answer the first ten· first grade applicants the last ten.

1. Formulate and solve problems to illustrate three cases in percentage.
2. Show how the principles of division apply in the operations on fractions.
3. Show the relation of division, of fractions, and of ratio to one another.
4. If 25 hills of corn produce a basket of ears of corn, how many baskets will a square 40-acre field produce, the hills being 2½ ft, apart and the outside rows 5 ft. from the fence around the field?
5. Explain the effect of the following: (a) annexing two ciphers to a whole number, (b) to a decimal, (c) annexing two ciphers to a whole number then multiplying by 4 and dividing by 3, (d) cutting off 2 figures and multiplying by 4.
6. If 6% bonds pay annually 4⅜% income, at what rate of premium or discount were they purchased?
7. An electric light company with a capital stock of $50,000 earned above all expenses $3,212.50 the first half year. It passed $212.50 to the repair fund and declared a semi-annual dividend. What did the man receive who owned $2,150 of the stock?
8. Explain what you consider the best method of computing interest.
9. A merchant bought a bill of goods for $1,875.60 on 90 days' time, 5% off for cash. He hired at a bank at 8% enough money to pay cash. How much did he gain by so doing?
10. The wheels of my bicycle are 28 inches in diameter. The sprocket wheels have 26 and 9 sprockets respectively. If I pedal at the rate of 30 strokes per minute, how many miles am I going per hour?
11. Three men form a partnership. A puts into the business $3,000, B $5,000, and C his time worth $1,000 a year. If money is worth 6% per annum, how should their annual profit of $2,960 be divided among them?
12. A hollow brass sphere 4 in. in diameter weighs ⅛ as much as a solid sphere of the same size and material. How thick is the shell?
13. How many yards of duck will it take to line the carpet for a room 18 ft. by 12 ft., if the duck is ¾ yd. wide, and shrinks 10% in length and 5% in width?
14. A man left $10,000 for his three sons aged 12, 15 and 18 years respectively, to be invested at 4% compound interest, in such sums that each son should at 21 yrs. of age receive the same amount. How much was set aside for each son?
15. About a circular field 80 rods in diameter is a circular road of uniform width containing six acres. What is the width of the road?

Third Grade.

Class B.

1. Explain as to a class the significance of the terms of a fraction.
2. Show how the principles of division apply in operations on fractions.
3. What added to the sum of ½, ¼ and 5.25 will make 6.42?
4. Show how the value of a fraction is affected by adding the same number to both terms.
5. If ¾ of a load of hay is worth $15, what is the value of ½ of the load? Solve by cancellation.

Note. Examiners should accept no other solution.

6. How many square yards in 3 A. 5 sq. rd. 12 sq. yd.?
7. How many sq. yd., ft., and in. in the floor of a room 4 yd. 2 ft. 6 in. lond and 3 yd. 1 ft. 9 in. wide?
8. Write the following forms of commercial paper: (a) negotiable promissory note; (b) check upon bank; (c) receipt for interest on a note.

Note. Analyze in full the remaining problems.

9. A, having $240 more than B, bought with his money 7-11 of a piece of land, B buying the remainder. How much did the land cost?
10. When strawberries are worth ⅔ as much as raspberries and a quart and a pint of each cost 45 cents, how much is each per quart?

CLASS A.

1. Explain as to a class the significance of the terms of a fraction.
2. Show how the principles of division apply in operations on fractions.
3. Explain as to a class the units, tens, and hundreds in 542.
4. How would you explain to pupils the subtraction of 169 from 244?
5. Do you teach pupils the multiplication table? If so, how? In what grades?
6. (a) How do you explain cancellation to pupils?
   (b) Form a problem such as pupils ought to be taught to solve by cancellation.
7. What is the order in which you would present number-work in the first four grades?
8. (a) How do you introduce fractions?
   (b) Do you teach the "broken object" or the fractional form first? Why?
9. Explain as to a class the following problem: James had 4½ apples and gave his brother 2⅔ apples; how many had he left?
10. A man sold 20 acres less than ⅝ of his land. He then sold the remainder for $50 an acre, receiving for the same $4,000. How many acres had he at first? Analyze fully.

MENTAL ARITHMETIC.

All Grades.

NOTE—(1) Distribute these lists among all the applicants, placing them face down upon the desks.
(2) Each applicant write his number or name across the back of the list.
(3) At a signal from the commissioner, all reverse the papers and in the *right hand margin* write as many answers to the questions as possible in 15 *minutes*.
(4) At the second signal, all again reverse the papers when they will at once be collected by the examiners.
Give *one credit* for each correct answer written, making 20 credits for this part of the examination.

	ANSWER.
1. What is the sum of four 5's, five 4's, three 8's, and five 13's?	1
2. What is the difference between six dozen dozen and half a dozen dozen?	2
3. How many times can 16 be taken away from 320?	3
4. From the sum of 3⅔ and 3¼ take the product of ½ and 1½.	4
5. 12 is ⅔ of how many times 6?	5
6. Of what number is 22 eleven halves?	6
7. At what rate per day can 8 men earn $60 in 2½ days?	7
8. What is the interest on $120 for 6 days at 6%?	8
9. The interest on $600 for three months is $4.50. What is the rate per cent?	9
10. If a peck of cherries cost 40c, at what price per quart must they be sold to gain 50%?	10
11. If a man receives 10% from a grower for selling his fruit, at what price must he sell peaches that it cost the grower 40c per bushel to raise so that the grower may gain 12½%?	11
12. What per cent of 2½ bushels is 2½ pecks?	12
13. Sold for 30 cents, losing 50%. What was the cost?	13
14. Sold for 30 cents, gaining 50%. What was the cost?	14
15. How many rods around a "square 40" acres?	15
16. What is the square root of 4x25x9x49?	16
17. What per cent of apples is good when 2 apples out of every 5 are rotten?	17
18. What fraction increased by its 20% becomes 6-7?	18
19. What fraction is 25% less than 4-5?	19
20. Multiply 24 by 33⅓; 72 by 11 1-9.	20

BOTANY.

1. (a) State some facts in regard to the geographical distribution of plants.
   (b) What subjects are closely allied to botany?
2. Give several experiments to show important facts to be noted about germination of seeds.

3. Draw a section showing the structure of the tip of a root of a growing plant.
4. Describe root hairs, root fibers, root cap, root stock.
5. Describe the growth of an orchid.
6. Describe the habits of climbing and twining plants or stems.
7. Name the several kinds of plant tissue and describe each.
8. Describe the leaf arrangement of the oak, the horse chestnut, the birch, the willow, the pine.
9. Give the details of the work of the leaf.
10. Describe the parts of a flower, and explain the terms estivation, vernation, fertilization, fruits.

Second Grade.

1. Give the functions of roots.
2. Define stem, bud, node, perennial.
3. Name five wild plants that flower in the fall.
4. What bulbs may be planted in the fall for early spring flowers?
5. Explain the terms habitat, symmetrical, regular, perfect.
6. Name the native trees in your county.
7. Define calyx, corolla, receptacle, pistil, ovary.
8. Describe berry, akene, capsule, legume, nut.
9. What plants are suitable for window gardens?
10. Name the parts of a typical leaf, a typical flower.

CIVIL GOVERNMENT.

First and Second Grades.

Applicants for second grade answer the first ten questions; for first grade, the last ten.

1. (a) Who are the President's closest political advisers? (b) How are they chosen? (c) Salaries? (d) Mention three cases in each of which a different one of these officials would act.
2. What limits the powers of Congress? (b) What changes have been made in this instrument since it was first adopted? (c) Why is it sacred?
3. Explain as fully as you can how treaties are made.
4. (a) What constitutes a citizen of the United States?
   (b) Give the various steps by which an alien can become a citizen.
5. What is the constitutional provision with reference to "trial of all crimes"? Why this provision?
6. (a) When will the next State legislature meet in general session? (b) Mention three important measures enacted into laws by the last legislature. (c) Give the history of the "primary election law" legislation.
7. (a) Name three of the State boards or commissions. (b) How are the officers chosen? (c) Mention the duties of each of these boards.
8. (a) Give the definition of treason against the United States. (b) Discuss the crime of treason and its punishment. (c) What is "corruption of blood"?
9. State three facts relating to the constitutional convention authorized at the last session of our legislature.
10. Discuss extradition with reference to (a) what it is, (b) extraditable crimes, (c) method of operation, (d) reasons for.
11. Outline the Federal Judiciary with reference to (a) selection, (b) organization, (c) jurisdiction, (d) tenure of office and salary.
12 Discuss the territories of the United States with reference to (a) location, (b) government, (c) powers, (d) admission as state.
13. Does the United States make any distinction between its continental and its insular territory? If so, what?
14. City government.
    (a) Give the usual organization. (b) Discuss the evil effects of rapid growth. (c) Mention some of the common complaints against the ordinary city government.
15. Discuss the "spoils system" in both city and state government.

Third Grade.

BOTH CLASSES.

1. (a) Give some of the reasons for government.
   (b) Name the principal forms of government.
2. Name the departments of government. State three things with reference to each.
3. Mention five parallels between the United States Constitution and Michigan State Constitution.
4. Name the various cabinet offices, and state a case in which the head of one of these departments would act.
5. (a) Mention three things that Congress cannot legally do. (b) Give the language of the Constitution with reference to each.
6. The State legislature:
   (a) How many members, date of election, salary?
   (b) Who was your representative last winter?
   (c) In what legislation was he prominent or of what committee was he a member?
7. Give the ordinary steps in passing a law.
8. Is it always wrong to disobey a law? Discuss your answer.
9. (a) Who is the State Superintendent of Public Instruction?
   (b) Mention his principal duties.
10. The County Board of School Examiners:
    (a) Who are they in your county? (b) When elected? (c) Salaries?
    (b) Who is the secretary and what are his principal duties aside from acting as secretary of the board at its meetings?

COURSE OF STUDY.

All Grades.

NOTE. No person failing to pass in this subject can legally receive a certificate. Examiners please take notice.

1. (a) What do you understand to be the purpose of a course of study?
   (b) What is its special value in an ungraded school in contrast with a graded school?
   (c) How can it be used without injustice to a pupil who is slow in mechanical work but vigorous and active in thought work?
2. Give six of the principles of Pestalozzi given in the Course of Study.
3. (a) Discuss "Proceed from the known to the related unknown."
   "Never tell a child what he can discover for himself."
   How rigidly would you enforce this?
4. Give five of the suggestions under "government."
5. Give outline for nature study for Fall or Winter term in one of the primary grades.
6. Give the exercises with a string in second grade drawing, or draw three of the figures given in the same grade.
7. Mention the poems given in the third grade for memorizing.
8. What device is given in fifth grade for training pupils in deciding when to multiply and when to divide in the solution of problems?
9. What suggestions are given with reference to "alternation"?
10. What suggestion is made with reference to ninth grade work in the eighth grade subjects?

GENERAL HISTORY.

First Grade.

1. Who are Confucius, Lycurgus, Aeschylus, Solon, Richelieu, Garibaldi, Attila, Charles Martel, Robert Walpole, Count Cavour?
2. (a) What was the "Petition of Rights"? The "Bill of Rights"?
   (b) Explain the "Divine Right of Kings." What English rulers were firm believers in this?
3. Who was the first ruler to bear the title of German Emperor? How did he come to get it, and where and when was it bestowed?
4. (a) What was the Holy Alliance? Explain its significance.
   (b) What is meant by the "Hundred Days"?

5. What were the "Council of the North" the "Star Chamber" and the "Court of High Commission"? Why and by whom were they established?
6. What were the Wars of the Roses? Give causes and results.
7. (a) Who were the "Mayors of the Palace"?
   (b) What was the "New Model"?
   (c) Who was the Great Elector?
8. (a) Under whom and how did Russia come into political prominence?
   (b) What was the significance of the battle of Chalons?
9. When and by whom was the battle of Hastings fought? Discuss the results.
10. (a) What was the Inquisition? By whom established?
    (b) When was the States General created, and how?

Second Grade.

1. Characterize the Age of Pericles.
2. What were the causes and results of the Franco-Prussian War?
3. What was the Reform Bill of 1832? What led up to it, and what were the results?
4. (a) What was the Long Parliament?
   (b) What were the then existing political and social conditions in England?
5. What was the War of the Austrian Succession? Causes and results.
6. Discuss the rise of English power in India.
7. Who was Peter the Great and what did he do for his country?
8. (a) What was the Reign of Terror?
   (b) Give the principal men and events connected with this.
9. (a) What was the Edict of Nantes? By whom issued? When and by whom revoked?
   (b) What was the massacre of St. Bartholomew's Day? Who was responsible for it?
10. Name ten present day rulers and the countries they govern.

GEOGRAPHY.

First and Second Grades.

Applicants for second grade answer first ten; for first grade, last ten.

1. Give the effects that would be produced if the earth's axis were perpendicular to the plane of its orbit.
2. What is the value of ocean currents? Name and locate several.
3. With what countries do we compete in production of cotton, sugar, live stock, wheat, steel rails?
4. Name the plateaus and plains of Asia. What name is given to the great Arctic plain of Siberia?
5. Name and describe the river systems of Europe.
6. Give the political divisions of Asia. Name the seaports of eastern Asia including Japan.
7. Name the natural resources of Canada? What are the chief articles of trade between United States and Canada?
8. (a) Draw a map of Africa and sketch the location of the territory controlled by the several European powers. (b) What countries largely control the trade with South America?
9. (a) Name ten important cities west of the Mississippi.
   (b) Name the important wheat producing states.
10. (a) What is the present status of Manchuria and Korea?
    (b) What is the present status of Cuba? Locate the Isle of Pines.
11. What parts of Europe are most visited by American tourists? What would you desire to see in London?
12. Describe sinking and rising coasts and give theory of cause. Locate two.
13. (a) Define erosion, detritus, geyser, tides, reefs.
    (b) Give notable examples of the first three mentioned above.
14. Name the chief food plants of the temperate zone; of the torrid zone. What is the character of animal life in each?
15. Compare the Appalachian system with the Rocky system as to structure, area, character of peaks and valleys, and mining possibilities.

Third Grade.

BOTH CLASSES.

1. Describe the drainage systems of North America giving for each—chief rivers, slope, area drained, character of streams as to size, length, current.
2. Give the political divisions of Asia with capital and chief commercial city of each.
3. Name five cities of India and state the form of government, educational system, articles of commerce.
4. Name the islands of the Atlantic that are of commercial importance.
5. (a) Locate Java, Borneo, Philippines, New Zealand.
   (b) State to what country each belongs and why they are valuable possessions.
6. Define continental and oceanic islands. State to which class each mentioned in questions 4 and 5 belong.
7. Name the divisions of Canada. Locate 8 cities of Canada. Give the natural resources of Canada.
8. Compare the educational system of Ontario with that of Michigan.
9. (a) Give ten names of places, counties, or cities of Michigan given us by French occupants. Locate each.
   (b) To what countries has the territory of Michigan belonged?
10. For your own county give the following: Names of all postoffices, number of teachers employed, number of school districts, names of county officers, population, names of lakes and streams, agricultural products, manufacturers, and the nearest route to Chicago.

GEOMETRY.

First Grade.

NOTE. Applicants must use instruments in constructing figures. All theorems should be demonstrated; all constructions should be line-constructions and as exact as they can be made with ordinary instruments.

1. The straight lines drawn from the vertices of an obtuse-angled triangle perpendicular to the opposite sides are concurrent.
2. Define: symmetrical figures, centroid of a triangle, orthocentre, scalene triangle.
3. If a triangle is symmetrical with reference to a median, it is isosceles.
4. Draw the direct and the reverse common tangents to two unequal circles which are wholly external to each other. Explain.
5. The sides of a triangle are 6, 7, 8, respectively. Find the length of the segments made by the line that bisects the smallest angle. Give proof of solution.
6. In the same or equal circles the angles at the centre are in the same ratio as the arcs subtending them.
7. Prove the ratio of the circumference of a circle to its diameter.
8. Inscribe a regular decagon in a circle. Prove the work.
9. (a) Construct the square root of 3; of 5.
   (b) Construct a circle whose radius is ½ inch shorter than the side of its inscribed square. Give proof.
10. Construct a right triangle whose inscribed circle has a diameter of three-fourths inch. Give proof.

GRAMMAR.

First and Second Grades.

Applicants for second grade answer first ten; for first grade, last ten.

1. Explain the difference between the study of grammar and the study of English.
2. Classify sentences as to structure. Give examples.
3. Explain as to a class the conjunctive adverb, and the relative pronoun.
4. Explain and illustrate the infinitive in *ing*. How can we determine when the form in *ing* is a gerund, a participle, or an abstract noun?

5. Give sentences to illustrate the following uses of a noun: a predicate complement, term of address, an independent element, an object complement, subject of an infinitive, the equivalent of an adverbial phrase. Parse any two of them.
6. Define mode. State how many modes and give the functions of each.
7. What words usually introduce noun clauses, adverb clauses, adjective clauses?
8. Explain the constructions known as a direct object, indirect object, factitive object. Illustrate each.
9. Analyze,—We rode ten *miles* to give our *friends* a *view* of the falls *which* we believed to be the *finest* in the State.
10. (a) Give the construction of the italicized words in foregoing sentence.
(b) Give principal parts of all verbs in above sentence.
11. (a) What is the purpose of the use of complex sentences?
(b) To what forms may most clauses be reduced or condensed? Illustrate.
12. Explain and illustrate co-ordinate clauses, subordinate clauses. Give examples of conjunctions used in each.
13. (a) What is the regular order of the parts of speech or equivalent expressions in the English sentence?
(b) For what purposes is this order changed? Illustrate.
14. How may the teaching of grammar be brought into touch with actual life or made real and effective with students?
15. Explain the various uses of as, like, so, but, the.

Third Grade.

Both Classes.

1. Define pronoun, antecedent, declension.
2. (a) Why are certain pronouns called *personal* pronouns?
(b) Select one and decline.
3. Some authors give five classes of pronouns. Name them, define and give four examples of each.
4. Distinguish the meanings in the following:
(a) A king and a priest, a king and priest; a black and a white cat, a black and white cat.
(b) Give the various uses of *a*: in noun series, to distinguish, and with a series of adjectives; also state three uses of the word *the*.
5. Give three rules for comparing adjectives and adverbs. Compare pretty, cheerful, mellow, hot, noble.
6. Define and illustrate co-ordinate and subordinate conjunctions. Give lists of conjunctions used to introduce clauses of time, cause, condition, purpose.
7. (a) What is the purpose of sentence analysis?
(b) Define infinitive, participle, gerund.
8. Give sentences to illustrate the following uses of the infinitive: as a subject, as a part of a noun phrase used as the object of a verb, as an adverbial modifier.
9. Analyze—I like *to walk* in the *deep forest where no* sound comes *to disturb* the honesty of *my thoughts*.
10. Give the construction of the italicized words in the foregoing sentence.

ORTHOGRAPHY.

All Grades.

1. What are synonyms? Homonyms? Give examples of each.
2. What is accent? Give a general rule for accent.
3. What is meant by the literal meaning of a word? The figurative meaning? The technical meaning? Give examples of each.
4. Define penult, antepenult, ultima.
5. (a) Give a prefix meaning *not*, *before*, *from*.
(b) Give an adverb suffix meaning *direction*.
(c) Give an adjective suffix meaning *without*, *made of*.
6. Name six diacritical marks and illustrate.

LIST OF WORDS.

All Grades.

1. accede
2. changing
3. lilies
4. acknowledge
5. avoirdupois
6. neuralgia
7. Marseilles
8. judicial
9. diphthong
10. Cincinnati
11. apparition
12. distress
13. corpuscle
14. sergeant
15. osseous
16. coercion
17. allegiance
18. imagine
19. capsule
20. deciduous
21. forebode
22. surgeon
23. bilious
24. filial
25. Boise
26. essence
27. device
28. millionaire
29. accommodate
30. perennial
31. homely
32. disappearance
33. gorgeous
34. licorice
35. grandeur
36. desirable
37. abbreviation
38. exquisite
39. lieutenant
40. facilitate
41. announced
42. proxy
43. proctor
44. transient
45. Psyche
46. statute
47. miscellany
48. piebald
49. management
50. sophomore.

PENMANSHIP.

All Grades.

NOTE. This must be written with pen. Fifty credits should be given for answer, and fifty for the handwriting.

1. Describe the proper position for writing with reference to, (a) body, (b) arm, (c) hand and fingers.
2. (a) How often do you have a general exercise in penmanship? (b) Do you teach pupils to write the same hand as far as possible? Why?
3. Select three dissimilar capital letters and tell how you present them to a class in penmanship.
4. (a) Give some exercises in "movement" that you have found helpful in securing both legibility and speed.
   (b) How often do you use them and in what grades?
5. How can the study of penmanship as taught in schools be made of intellectual benefit?

PHYSICS.

First Grade.

1. Give the facts and theory of the osmose of liquids.
2. Define science, matter, physics, chemistry.
3. (a) Give the laws for accelerated motion.
   (b) Make and solve a problem under one of these laws.
4. Explain the hammer as a lever when used to draw nails. Solve a problem using 3 movable pulleys.
5. Discuss Archimedes' principle. Give practical applications.
6. What weight of water at 85° will just melt 15 lbs. of ice at 0° ?
7. (a) Discuss correlation of heat and mechanical energy.
   (b) Give Jouls's principle and practical applications.
8. Explain how the candle power of a given light is determined. Make and solve a problem using the photometer.
9. Draw figure and explain the action of a double convex lens on light. Explain chromatic aberration.
10. Explain the construction of an induction coil, a simple dynamo, a transformer.

Second Grade.

1. Name the properties of matter. Define solid, fluid, gas.
2. Explain and illustrate the three classes of levers.
3. Explain how to find the specific gravity of cork.
4. Give the general theory of sound.
5. Draw figure and explain the force pump.
6. Give the laws of evaporation.
7. Draw figure and explain action of plane mirror on light.
8. Define focus, virtual image, conjugate foci.
9. State several simple experiments to show opposite electrifications. What is the theory?
10. What is meant by "charging" a body? Define electrical field, induction, resistance.

PHYSIOLOGY.

First and Second Grades.

Applicants for second grade answer first ten questions; for first grade, last ten.

1. (a) What is the composition of air?
   (b) How is air purified?
2. (a) Describe a nerve.
   (b) What are the Haversian canals?
3. (a) Describe and locate hinge joints, ball and socket joints, pivot joints.
   (b) What are "blackheads"?
4. (a) Show how alcohol produces kidney diseases, and how sugar and sweets act in the same way.
   (b) How does the system throw off poisons?
5. (a) What is the ordinary temperature of the body?
   (b) Show how heat is distributed in the body.
6. Discuss bacteria—how they enter the body, and how they are destroyed.
7. Explain the healing of a cut.
8. (a) Describe the larynx.
   (b) How is the pitch of the voice changed?
9. Discuss the relative value of cotton, wool, silk, and fur for clothing for summer and winter.

11. How many teeth has an adult? Name them and state the purposes of each.

11. What is the sympathetic nervous system?

12. (a) What is mucous membrane? Where found in the body?
    (b) What is epithelium? Where found in the body?
13. (a) What is the cause of near-sightedness? Of far-sightedness? What is astigmatism?
    (b) What lenses should be used for each of the above?

Third Grade.

BOTH CLASSES.

1. Define anatomy, physiology, hygiene, an organ, a cell, a system.
2. Name the different fluids in the body and tell what each does.
3. (a) What is the tympanum?
   (b) What is the cause of "shortness of breath"?
4. (a) What is food? Its composition?
   (b) What is a ptomaine, an anti-toxin, an emulsion?
5. (a) What is the effect of a cold bath?
   (b) What is the effect of a hot bath?
6. (a) Why is the fur on an animal's head, neck, and feet not so thick as on the other parts of the body?
   (b) How is air purified?
7. (a) Describe the skin, derma, epidermis, subcutaneous tissue, and coloring matter.
   (b) What changes occur in the epidermis in the case of a callous spot? A corn?
8. (a) How many bones in the body?
   (b) Name and locate five.
9. (a) What are the sebaceous glands and of what use are they?
   (b) What causes freckles?

10. Make a drawing of the head and brain and locate and name the following: The three principal parts of the brain, the centers of hearing, sight, smell, speech, and motion.
    (b) How do the vocal chords produce sound?

READING.

Tennyson's Princess.

All Grades.

Answer any ten.

1. Give a sketch of the life of Tennyson.
2. Give the setting and the plan of the poem. Why is it a medley?
3. Give a brief sketch of the story.
4. Who were Melissa, Florian, Walter, Arac, Lady Psyche, Gama, Lilia and Cyril?
5. Who was Aglaia and what does she add to the poem?
6. Give a character sketch of the Prince.
7. Give a character sketch of the Princess.
8. How was Ida finally won over to the Prince?
9. What was the condition and belief regarding the higher education of women in England at this time? How then would such a work as this naturally be received?
10. What is the purpose and what the value of the lyrics introduced into the poem?
11. Give two quotations of at least five lines each from the poem.
12. Discuss the literary value of the poem as to style, language, and meter.
13. What can you say regarding the metrical devices resorted to by the poet in such passages as the following:

"I stood and seemed to hear,
As in a poplar grove when a light wind wakes
A lisping of innumerous leaf and dies,
Each hissing in his neighbor's ears."

"The moan of doves in immemorial elms
And murmuring of innumerable bees."

"And all the plain, brand, mace, and shaft and shield
Shocked, like iron-clanging anvil banged."

"Myriads of rivulets hurrying through the lawn."

SCHOOL LAW.

All Grades.

Answer any five.

1. Who is the legal librarian in a school district, in a township?
2. Specify the differences between a primary school district and a graded school district.
3. Give the procedure in organizing a township district.
4. Name the several kinds of teacher's certificates granted in Michigan and the authority granting each.
5. Why must a teacher hold a certificate covering at least the period of her contract?
6. Give the duties of the teacher in connection with the enforcement of the truancy law.
7. Give ten duties of a school director.
8. Give the substance of five amendments made in the school law by the legislature of 1907.

THEORY AND ART.

All Grades.

Applicants for second and third grades answer first ten; first grade, last ten.

1. Describe fully a "study lesson," a "recitation lesson."
2. Name five "good things" you have seen teachers do.
3. What books have you read to your pupils during the past year? If you have not taught, tell what books you will read to pupils during the coming year. State *why in each case.*

4. Show how you connect the subjects of division, fractions, and percentage in your teaching.
5. How do you seek to secure the interest of your pupils in teaching reading, arithmetic, language?
6. What is the relation of clear ideas to the will?
7. Why should a teacher be a director of the games and sports of the children as well as director of studies?
8. What is your idea of the proper results to be secured in teaching history, civics, writing?
9. Name five proper school incentives.
10. Name the representative faculties of the mind.
11. Which is of greater value to the child, the personality or the academic preparation of the teacher?
12. Explain the operation of the mind in forming a judgment.
13. In what ways may the moral faculties of the child be trained? Is this important? Why?
14. Name the mental faculties. At what ages are each predominant?
15. Name an author in psychology or pedagogy and state his classification of the subject.

UNITED STATES HISTORY.

First and Second Grades.

Applicants for second grade answer first ten questions; for first grade, last ten.

1. What were the Intolerable Acts of 1774?
2. What was the political significance of Shay's Rebellion?
3. Give the terms of the treaty which settled the Revolution.
4. (a) When, where, and by whom was the first national anti-slavery party formed?
   (b) What were the Lincoln-Douglas debates?
5. What were the causes and results of the Mexican War?
6. What can you say of America's naval power in the war of 1812?
7. (a) What was accomplished by the first Continental Congress? When was it held?
   (b) How many continental congresses were held?
8. What is meant by the Reconstruction Period? Why so called?
9. (a) What were the causes of the Spanish-American War?
   (b) Why was it that the war was carried over into the Philippines?
10. (a) Why is the battle of Gettysburg called a decisive battle?
    (b) What was the purpose of Sherman's march to the sea?
11. (a) What was the effect of Lincoln's election in 1860?
    (b) Discuss the differences between the North and the South in 1850-60.
12. (a) Give four provisions of the Ordinance of 1787?
    (b) How did it concern Michigan?
13. What territory has been acquired by the United States since 1890?
14. What is despotism, anarchy, a democracy, an oligarchy, a republic, a monarchy?

Third Grade.

Both Classes.

1. (a) What was the Stamp Act? Its effects?
   (b) What was the Stamp Act Congress and what did it do?
2. (a) What were the Committees of Correspondence?
   (b) What is the importance of the battle of Yorktown? State the results.
3. When, where, by whom, and under what circumstances were the following sentences uttered:
   "We have met the enemy and they are ours."
   "Don't give up the ship."
   "I propose to fight it out on this line if it takes all summer."
4. (a) What was the Compromise of 1850?
   (b) What was the Dred Scott decision? Its effects?
   (c) What was the "underground railway"?
5. What is known as the Critical Period in United States History? Why?
6. (a) What was the Ordinance of 1787?
   (b) Give four provisions of the same.

7. Name five of the most important battles of the Civil War and name the generals on each side.
8. What were the causes of the Mexican War?
9. (a) When and where was the treaty signed which closed the Spanish-American War?
   (b) What were its provisions?
10. (a) What is meant by the Reconstruction Period?
    (b) Explain under what conditions the Southern States were restored to civil and political rights.

III. Questions prepared by the Superintendent of Public Instruction for the regular examination, October 17–18, 1907.

ALGEBRA.

Second Grade.

1. What principles or axioms are involved in the following operations or equations:
   (a) transposing terms, (b) clearing of fractions, (c) dividing by coefficient of the unknown.
2. Explain as to a class the algebraic significance of the signs plus and minus in addition, subtraction, multiplication and division.
3. Simplify the following expressions: $17 - [45 - (9 - \overline{23 - 32})]$, $\frac{a^{\frac{2}{3}} - b^{\frac{2}{3}}}{a^{\frac{1}{3}} - b^{\frac{1}{3}}}$,
$(a + b + c)(-a + b + c)(a - b + c)(a + b - c.)$
4. Factor $(a^2 + 9)^2 - 36a^2$, $a^6 - a^4 - a^2 + 1$, $a^{10} - 1$.
5. Reduce to simplest form $\dfrac{\frac{1 - x^2}{1 + x^2} - \frac{1 + x^2}{1 - x^2}}{\frac{1 - x}{1 + x} - \frac{1 + x}{1 - x}}$
6. Solve the equations $\left\{\begin{array}{l} u + x + y = 6 \\ x + y + z = 7 \\ y + z + u = 8 \\ z + u + x = 9 \end{array}\right\}$
7. Solve for value of x, $\sqrt{x + 6} + \sqrt{x + 9} = \sqrt{4x + 29}$.
8. If the product of two numbers be added to their difference the result is 26; and the sum of their squares exceeds their difference by 50. What are the numbers?
9. If the product of three consecutive numbers be divided by each of them in turn, the sum of the three quotients is 74. What are the numbers?
10. Write the Binomial formula for $(a+x)^n$ to the sixth term and apply the same in expanding $(x+2y)^5$.

ARITHMETIC.

Second Grade.

1. Formulate and solve problems to illustrate three cases in percentage.
2. Show how the principles of division apply in the operations on fractions.
3. Show the relation of division, of fractions, and of ratio to one another.
4. If 25 hills of corn produce a basket of ears of corn, how many baskets will a square 40-acre field produce, the hills being 2½ ft. apart and the outside rows 5 ft. from the fence around the field?
5. Explain the effect of the following: (a) annexing two ciphers to a whole number, (b) to a decimal, (c) annexing two ciphers to a whole number then multiplying by 4 and dividing by 3, (d) cutting off 2 figures and multiplying by 4.
6. If 6% bonds pay annually 4⅔% income, at what rate of premium or discount were they purchased?

7. An electric light company with a capital stock of $50,000 earned above all expenses $3,212.50 the first half year. It passed $212.50 to the repair fund and declared a semi-annual dividend. What did a man receive who owned $2,150 of the stock?
8. Explain what you consider the best method of computing interest.
9. A merchant bought a bill of goods for $1,875.60 on 90 days' time, 5% off for cash. He hired at a bank at 8% enough money to pay cash. How much did he gain by so doing?
10. The wheels of my bicycle are 28 inches in diameter. The sprocket wheels have 26 and 9 sprockets respectively. If I pedal at the rate of 30 strokes per minute, how many miles am I going per hour?

Third Grade.

Both Classes.

1. (a) Given the subtrahend and the remainder, to find the minuend.
   (b) Given the quotient, remainder, and dividend, to find the divisor.
2. Classify the following with reference to being abstract or concrete: (a) the minuend, (b) the multiplicand, (c) the product, (d) the quotient, (e) the remainder in division. Explain your answers.
3. Illustrate some proofs for addition, for substraction, for division.
4. Examiner give test in addition, using *twenty* numbers of *four* figures each.

Note.—Allow but one addition, and have no figures put down except upon the paper containing the list of numbers. If any erasures or changes are shown on the paper, count the example wrong.

5. Define: (a) prime number, (b) composite number.
   (b) Give three sets of factors of 360, one of which shall be prime.
   (c) Explain as to a class finding the L. C. M. of 240, 72, and 96, using the factor method.
6. A could do a piece of work in 14 days. He and B did the work for $21.00, of which B took $12.00. How long did it take them together to do the work, providing that each received pay proportional to the work he did?
7. How many thousand shingles will it take to cover both sides of a roof 36 ft. long whose rafters are 18 ft. long, the shingles to average 4 in. wide and to lay 5 in. to the weather?
8. If goods cost 80 cents per yard, at what price must they be marked so that a reduction of 20% may be made from the marked price and still there be a profit of 30%?
9. How many bricks will be required to build the walls of a house 60x40x34 feet on the outside, allowing ½ for windows and doors, the walls to be three bricks thick?
10. Formulate and solve a problem in fractions showing, as to a class, the use of cancellation in the solution of such problems.

MENTAL ARITHMETIC.

All Grades.

Note—(1) Distribute these lists among all the applicants, placing them face down upon the desks.
(2) Each applicant write his number or name across the back of the list.
(3) At a signal from the commissioner, all reverse the papers and in the *right hand margin* write as many answers to the questions as possible in 15 *minutes*.
(4) At the second signal, all again reverse the papers when they will at once be collected by the examiners.
Give *one credit* for each correct answer written, making 20 credits for this part of the examination.

	ANSWERS.
1. What is the sum of four 5's, five 4's, three 8's, and five 13's?	1.
2. What is the difference between six dozen dozen and half a dozen dozen?	2.
3. How many times can 16 be taken away from 320?	3.
4. From the sum of 3⅔ and 3¼ take the product of ½ and 1½.	4.
5. 12 is ⅔ of how many times 6?	5.
6. Of what number is 22 eleven halves?	6.
7. At what rate per day can 8 men earn $60 in 2½ days?	7.
8. What is the interest on $120 for 6 days at 6%?	8.

ANSWERS.

9. The interest on $600 for three months is $4.50. What is the rate per cent? 9.
10. If a peck of cherries cost 40c, at what price per quart must they be sold to gain 50%? 10.
11. If a man receives 10% from a grower for selling his fruit, at what price must he sell peaches that it cost the grower 40c per bushel to raise so that the grower may gain 12½%? 11.
12. What per cent of 2½ bushels is 2½ pecks? 12.
13. Sold for 30 cents, losing 50%. What was the cost? 13.
14. Sold for 30 cents, gaining 50%. What was the cost? 14.
15. How many rods around a "square 40" acres? 15.
16. What is the square root of 4x25x9x49? 16.
17. What per cent of apples is good when 2 apples out of every 5 are rotten? 17.
18. What fraction increased by its 20% becomes six-sevenths? 18.
19. What fraction is 25% less than ⅘? 19.
20. Multiply 24 by 33⅓; 72 by 11⅓. 20.

BOTANY.

Second Grade.

1. Give the functions of roots.
2. Define stem, bud, node, perennial.
3. Name five wild plants that flower in the fall.
4. What bulbs may be planted in the fall for early spring flowers?
5. Explain the terms habitat, symmetrical, regular, perfect.
6. Name the native trees in your county.
7. Define calyx, corolla, receptacle, pistil, ovary.
8. Describe berry, akene, capsule, legume, nut.
9. What plants are suitable for window gardens?
10. Name the parts of a typical leaf, a typical flower.

CIVIL GOVERNMENT.

Second Grade.

1. (a) Who are the President's closest political advisers? (b) How are they chosen? (c) Salaries? (d) Mention three cases in each of which a different one of these officials would act.
2. What limits the powers of Congress? (b) What changes have been made in this instrument since it was first adopted? (c) Why is it sacred?
3. Explain as fully as you can how treaties are made.
4. (a) What constitutes a citizen of the United States?
   (b) Give the various steps by which an alien can become a citizen.
5. What is the constitutional provision with reference to "trial of all crimes"? Why this provision?
6. (a) When will the next State legislature meet in general session? (b) Mention three important measures enacted into laws by the last legislature. (c) Give the history of the "primary election law" legislation.
7. (a) Name three of the State boards or commissions. (b) How are the officers chosen? (c) Mention the duties of each of these boards.
8. (a) Give the definition of treason against the United States. (b) Discuss the crime of treason and its punishment. (c) What is "corruption of blood"?
9. State three facts relating to the constitutional convention authorized at the last session of our legislature.
10. Discuss extradition with reference to (a) what it is, (b) extraditable crimes, (c) method of operation, (d) reasons for.

Third Grade.

Both Classes.

1. (a) Name the State offices and the persons filling them.
   (b) From what county or representative district are the following officers: Governor, secretary of state, superintendent of public instruction.
2. Mention five distinct duties of the governor.
3. What relation does the superintendent of public instruction sustain to the State board of education? To the various colleges of the State?
4. Name five positions that the governor fills by appointment.
5. What are the duties of the governor with respect to legislation?

6-7. Give a complete outline of the public school system of Michigan.

8. What are the various life certificates for teaching in this State and how are they procured?
9. Give full plan by which teachers become qualified to teach in the various counties of the State, including: officers having to do with the matter, examinations, questions, grades of certificates, fees, renewals, transfers, indorsements, filing, etc.
10. School funds: What are they, (b) how procured, (c) the source of each fund. State fully with reference to the above.

COURSE OF STUDY.

All Grades.

NOTE. No person failing to pass in this subject can legally receive a certificate. Examiners please take notice.

1. (a) What do you understand to be the purpose of a course of study?
   (b) What is its special value in an ungraded school in contrast with a graded school?
   (c) How can it be used without injustice to a pupil who is slow in mechanical work but vigorous and active in thought work?
2. Give six of the principles of Pestalozzi given in the Course of Study.
3. (a) Discuss, "Proceed from the known to the related unknown."
   (b) "Never tell a child what he can discover for himself."
   How rigidly would you enforce this?
4. Give five of the suggestions under "government."
5. Give outline for nature-study for Fall or Winter term in one of the primary grades.
6. Give the exercises with a string in second grade drawing, or draw three of the figures given in the same grade.
7. Mention the poems given in third grade for memorizing.
8. What device is given in fifth grade for training pupils in deciding when to multiply and when to divide in the solution of problems?
9. What suggestions are given with reference to "alternation"?
10. What suggestion is made with reference to ninth grade work in the eighth grade subjects?

GENERAL HISTORY.

Second Grade.

1. Characterize the Age of Pericles.
2. What were the causes and results of the Franco-Prussian War?
3. What was the Reform Bill of 1832? What led up to it, and what were the results?
4. (a) What was the Long Parliament?
   (b) What were the then existing political and social conditions in England?
5. What was the War of the Austrian Succession? Causes and results.
6. Discuss the rise of English power in India.
7. Who was Peter the Great and what did he do for his country?
8. (a) What was the Reign of Terror?
   (b) Give the principal men and events connected with this.

9. (a) What was the Edict of Nantes? By whom issued? When and by whom revoked?
(b) What was the massacre of St. Bartholomew's Day? Who was responsible for it?
10. Name ten present day rulers and the countries they govern.

GEOGRAPHY.

Second Grade.

1. Give the effects that would be produced if the earth's axis were perpendicular to the plane of its orbit.
2. What is the value of ocean currents? Name and locate several.
3. With what countries do we compete in production of cotton, sugar, live stock, wheat, steel rails?
4. Name the plateaus and plains of Asia. What name is given to the great arctic plain of Siberia?
5. Name and describe the river systems of Europe.
6. Give the political divisions of Asia. Name the seaports of eastern Asia including Japan.
7. Name the natural resources of Canada. What are the chief articles of trade between United States and Canada?
8. (a) Draw a map of Africa and sketch the location of the territory controlled by the several European powers. (b) What countries largely control the trade with South America?
9. (a) Name ten important cities west of the Mississippi.
(b) Name the important wheat producing states.
10. (a) What is the present status of Manchuria and Korea?
(b) What is the present status of Cuba? Locate the Isle of Pines.

Third Grade.

Both Classes.

1. Compare the climate of Michigan with that of the country in the same latitude in South America. Why the difference?
2. Describe the distribution of animal life in North America, with reasons therefor.
3. Compare the climate of China with that of England.
4. Name the divisions of South America, indicating the correct pronunciation of each.
5. Name the resources, railroads, and chief cities of Mexico.
6. Locate and describe the territory in Africa controlled by England.
7. Name the articles of commerce between United States and South America.
8. Name and locate the chief cities of Africa.
9. Give the physiography of Mexico.
10. Give several statements in regard to the trouble between France and Morocco.

GRAMMAR.

Second Grade.

1. Explain the difference between the study of grammar and the study of English.
2. Classify sentences as to structure. Give examples.
3. Explain as to a class the conjunctive adverb, and the relative pronoun.
4. Explain and illustrate the infinitive in *ing*. How can we determine when the form in *ing* is a gerund, a participle, or an abstract noun?
5. Give sentences to illustrate the following uses of a noun: a predicate complement, a term of address, an independent element, an object complement, subject of an infinitive, the equivalent of an adverbial phrase. Parse any two of them.
6. Define mode. State how many modes and give the functions of each.
7. What words usually introduce noun clauses, adverb clauses, adjective clauses?

8. Explain the constructions known as a direct object, indirect object, factitive object. Illustrate each.
9. Analyze,—We rode ten *miles* to give our *friends* a *view* of the falls *which* we believed to be the *finest* in the state.
10. (a) Give the construction of italicized words in foregoing sentence.
 (b) Give principal parts of all verbs in above sentence.

Third Grade.

Both Classes.

1. Define sentence, clause, paragraph.
2. Give two rules for the use of the period, three for the comma, one for the semicolon.
3. Name all the modifications of verbs.
4. What is meant by giving the construction of a word? Illustrate.
5. What are idioms? How should they be treated in the analysis of sentences?
6. Punctuate the following sentences:
 (a) A man going to sea his wife requested the prayers of the people
 (b) What do you think I will shave you for nothing and give you a drink
 (c) O that I had the wings of a dove for then I should fly away and be at rest
7. Give the construction of the italicized words in the following sentence: Come *what* may, I shall *endeavor to serve* my country *faithfully* at all *times* and in all places.
8. Parse the italicized words in the foregoing sentence.
9-10. Write two paragraphs on the subject: "The Panama Canal."

Note—Examiners will mark on thought, neatness, punctuation, capitalization, use of words, arrangement and clearness of sentences.

ORTHOGRAPHY.

All Grades.

1. What are synonyms? Homonyms? Give examples of each.
2. What is accent? Give a general rule for accent.
3. What is meant by the literal meaning of a word? The figurative meaning? The technical meaning? Give examples of each.
4. Define penult, antepenult, ultima.
5. (a) Give a prefix meaning *not*, *before*, *from*.
 (b) Give an adverb suffix meaning *direction*.
 (c) Give an adjective suffix meaning *without*, *made of*.
6. Name six diacritical marks and illustrate.

LIST OF WORDS.

All Grades.

1. accede
2. changing
3. lilies
4. acknowledge
5. avoirdupois
6. neuralgia
7. Marseilles
8. judicial
9. diphthong
10. Cincinnati
11. apparition
12. distress
13. corpuscle
14. sergeant
15. osseous
16. coercion
17. allegiance
18. imagine
19. vermilion
20. deciduous
21. forebode
22. surgeon
23. bilious
24. filial
25. admissible
26. essence
27. device
28. millionaire
29. accommodate
30. perennial
31. homely
32. disappearance
33. gorgeous
34. licorice

35. grandeur
36. desirable
37. abbreviation
38. exquisite
39. lieutenant
40. facilitate
41. announced
42. proxy
43. consensus
44. transient
45. Psyche
46. statute
47. miscellany
48. piebald
49. management
50. sophomore

PENMANSHIP.

All Grades.

NOTE. This must be written with pen. Fifty credits should be given for answer, and fifty for the handwriting.

1. Describe the proper position for writing with reference to, (a) body, (b) arm, (c) hand and fingers.
2. (a) How often do you have a general exercise in penmanship? (b) Do you teach pupils to write the same hand as far as possible? Why?
3. Select three dissimilar capital letters and tell how you present them to a class in penmanship.
4. (a) Give some exercises in "movement" that you have found helpful in securing both legibility and speed.
   (b) How often do you use them and in what grades?
5. How can the study of penmanship as taught in schools be made of intellectual benefit?

PHYSICS.

Second Grade.

1. Name the properties of matter. Define solid, fluid, gas.
2. Explain and illustrate the three classes of levers.
3. Explain how to find the specific gravity of cork.
4. Give the general theory of sound.
5. Draw figure and explain the force pump.
6. Give the laws of evaporation.
7. Draw figure and explain action of plane mirror on light.
8. Define focus, virtual image, conjugate foci.
9. State several simple experiments to show opposite electrifications. What is the theory?
10. What is meant by "charging" a body? Define electrical field, induction, resistance.

PHYSIOLOGY.

Second Grade.

1. (a) What is the composition of air?
   (b) How is air purified?
2. (a) Describe a nerve.
   (b) What are the Haversian canals?
3. (a) Describe and locate hinge joints, ball and socket joints, pivot joints.
   (b) What are "blackheads"?
4. (a) Show how alcohol produces kidney diseases, and how sugar and sweets act in the same way.
   (b) How does the system throw off poisons?
5. (a) What is the ordinary temperature of the body?
   (b) Show how heat is distributed in the body.
6. Discuss bacteria—how they enter the body, and how they are destroyed.
7. Explain the healing of a cut.
8. (a) Describe the larynx.
   (b) How is the pitch of the voice changed?
9. Discuss the relative value of cotton, wool, silk, and fur for clothing for summer and winter.
10. How many teeth has an adult? Name them and state the purpose of each.

Third Grade.

BOTH CLASSES.

1. Define anatomy, physiology, hygiene, organ, cell, system.
2. Name the different fluids in the body and tell what each does.
3. (a) What is the tympanum?
   (b) What is the cause of "shortness of breath"?
4. (a) What is food? Its composition?
   (b) What is a ptomaine, an antitoxin, an emulsion?
5. (a) What is the effect of a cold bath?
   (b) What is the effect of a hot bath?
6. (a) Why is the fur on an animal's head, neck, and feet not so thick as on the other parts of the body?
   (b) How is air purified?
7. (a) Describe the skin, derma, epidermis, subcutaneous tissue, and coloring matter.
   (b) What changes occur in the epidermis in the case of a callous spot? A corn?
8. (a) How many bones in the body?
   (b) Name and locate five.
9. (a) What are the sebaceous glands and of what use are they?
   (b) What causes freckles?
10. Make a drawing of the head and brain and locate and name the following: The three principal parts of the brain, the centers of hearing, sight, smell, speech, and motion.
   (b) How do the vocal chords produce sound?

READING.

All Grades.

"To a Skylark."

1. (a) What is a lyric poem?
   (b) What is the rhyme scheme and meter of this poem?
2. Give a brief sketch of the life of the author. Name two of his other works.
3. (a) Why does the author address the bird as a spirit?
   (b) What is the central thought of the whole poem?
4. With what persons and creatures does the author compare the skylark? Are these visible or not, and why?
5. What are the meanings of the following words: aërial, chaunt, satiety, vernal, joyance, hymenæal?

6-7. Paraphrase the following stanzas:

All the earth and air
  With thy voice is loud,
As, when night is bare,
  From one lonely cloud
The moon rains out her beams, and Heaven is overflowed.

Teach me half the gladness
  That thy brain must know,
Such harmonious madness
  From my lips would flow,
The world should listen then—as I am listening now.

8. Quote one stanza not given here.

9-10. Explain the following stanzas:

Yet if we could scorn
  Hate and pride and fear,
If we were things born
  Not to shed a tear,
I know not how thy joy we ever should come near.

Keen as are the arrows
  Of that silver sphere,
Whose intense lamp narrows
  In the white dawn clear,
Until we hardly see—we feel that it is there.

SCHOOL LAW.

All Grades.

Answer any five.

1. Who is the legal librarian in a school district, in a township?
2. Specify the differences between a primary school district and a graded school district.
3. Give the procedure in organizing a township district.
4. Name the several kinds of teacher's certificates granted in Michigan and the authority granting each.
5. Why must a teacher hold a certificate covering at least the period of her contract?
6. Give the duties of the teacher in connection with the enforcement of the truancy law.
7. Give ten duties of a school director.
8. Give the substance of five amendments made in the school law by the legislature of 1907.

THEORY AND ART.

All Grades.

1. Describe fully a "study lesson," a "recitation lesson."
2. Name five "good things" you have seen teachers do.
3. What books have you read to your pupils during the past year? If you have not taught, tell what books you will read to pupils during the coming year. State *why* in each case.
4. Show how you connect the subjects of division, fractions, and percentage in your teaching.
5. How do you seek to secure the interest of your pupils in teaching reading, arithmetic, language?
6. What is the relation of clear ideas to the will?
7. Why should a teacher be a director of the games and sports of the children as well as director of studies?
8. What is your idea of the proper results to be secured in teaching history, civics, writing?
9. Name five proper school incentives.
10. Name the representative faculties of the mind.

UNITED STATES HISTORY.

Second Grade.

1. What were the Intolerable Acts of 1774?
2. What was the political significance of Shay's Rebellion?
3. Give the terms of the treaty which settled the Revolution.
4. (a) When, where, and by whom was the first national anti-slavery party formed?
   (b) What were the Lincoln-Douglas debates?
5. What were the causes and results of the Mexican War?
6. What can you say of America's naval power in the War of 1812?
7. (a) What was accomplished by the First Continental Congress? When was it held?
   (b) How many continental congresses were held?
8. What is meant by the Reconstruction Period? Why so called?
9. (a) What were the causes of the Spanish-American War?
   (b) Why was it that the war was carried over into the Philippines?
10. (a) Why is the battle of Gettysburg called a decisive battle?
    (b) What was the purpose of Sherman's march to the sea?

Third Grade.

Both Classes.

1. Name the thirteen original colonies.
2. What was the first permanent colony within the limits of the present United States? The second? The third? By whom was each made?
3. What were the effects of the American discoveries upon France? England? Spain?
4. (a) Compare the policies of the French and the English in their treatment of the colonists.
   (b) What conflicts ensued as the results of the territorial claims of these two nations?
5. What was the importance of the capture of forts Duquesne and Quebec in the French and Indian War?
6. Give a brief statement concerning each of the following: Roger Williams, John Harvard, King Philip, Braddock, Champlain.
7. Name ten early explorers, stating under what flag each travelled, and what part of America each visited or explored.
8. Give an acccount of the early settlement of Georgia. Of Rhode Island.
9. What was the West India Company? London Company? Plymouth Company? State the object of each.
10. (a) When, where, and by whom was the first settlement made in Michigan?
    (b) Mention three important events in Michigan history.

EIGHTH GRADE EXAMINATION.

Questions prepared by the Superintendent of Public Instruction for the regular examination, May 9—10, 1907.

ARITHMETIC.

1. Express in words $\frac{88}{1001}$, 5.05, .0083, 100.01.
2. Give illustration of a number that is a perfect cube, a compound number, an abstract number.
3. Make a problem that can be solved by cancellation and solve it.
4. Make out a receipted bill of not less than five articles bought at a general store.

NOTE.—Half the credit for correct form, capitals and punctuation; half the credit for correct computation.

5. What will it cost to fence 20 acres of land, the rectangular field being 80 rods long, at $2.50 per rod of fence?
6. What will four loads of hay cost, weighing with wagon 4,200 lbs., 3,980 lbs., 4,600 lbs., and 3,240 lbs., respectively, at $18 a ton; the empty wagon weighing 1,160 lbs.
7. Estimate or measure the size of the room in which you are writing this examination and find the number of square yards of plaster upon the walls and ceiling.
8. Give the following:

1 acre = ? sq. rods.	
1 sq. rod = ? sq. ft.	1 ton = ? cwt.
1 bbl. = ? gals.	1 qr. = ? oz.
1 gill = ? qt.	1 bu. = ? qts.
1 gross = ? doz.	1 lb. = ? pwt.

9. How much lumber will it take to cover the two gable ends of a barn 32 ft. wide having rafters 22 ft. long, provided the rafters project 2 ft.?

NOTE.—If pupils do not see the square root application in No. 9. the examiner may suggest it.

10. Show by a diagram the N. E. $\frac{1}{4}$ of the N. E. $\frac{1}{4}$ of sec. 16, and compute the value of the land at $50 an acre.
11. What is the interest on $240 for 3 years, 4 months, 15 days at $5\frac{1}{2}$ % per annum?
12. How many cubic feet in a cube 18 inches on the edge?
13. It costs $1.50 an acre to plow land, $0.75 an acre to fit it and plant it, and $0.60 for seed corn. It takes $1\frac{1}{2}$ days per acre to cultivate the corn at $1.75 per day for man and horse, 1 day to cut it at $1.50 per day, and 3 cents per bushel to husk and crib it. The crop averages 90 baskets of ears of corn per acre and sells for 24 cents per basket in the crib. How much does a man make or lose on 20 acres of corn?

SOLVE THE REMAINING PROBLEMS BY ANALYSIS.

14. I $\frac{3}{4}$ lb. of butter costs 18 cents, what will $2\frac{1}{2}$ lbs. cost?
15. What gain per cent do I make in buying at $24 and selling at $28?

CIVIL GOVERNMENT.

1. What particular things has the study of civil government emphasized in your mind?
2. (a) What are the three great branches of government?
   (b) Who discharge the duties in each?
3. Explain the steps necessary to take in a township to build a town hall.

4. (a) Where and how often does the State legislature meet?
   (b) What are the presiding officers called?
5. Who is the most influential State officer? Why?
6. (a) How are U. S. Senators chosen?
   (b) Who was last chosen in this State?
   (c) Where is his home?
7. What is the President's Cabinet? Of how many departments does it consist?
8. How does an alien become a citizen? Give steps.
9. How does a territory become a State?
10. State five facts with reference to the county board of school examiners.

GEOGRAPHY.

1. Name the zones and give the width of each in degrees.
2. What is meant by the sun "crossing the line"?
3. Define plain, valley, water shed, river system.
4. Name and locate the mountain ranges of Asia.
5. Name and locate two important cities in each of the following countries: Germany, South Africa, China, France, Russia.
6. Name the islands under the control of the United States, and name a city in each.
7. Name the countries from which the following are imported to the United States: Coffee, hides, rubber, ivory, lumber.
8. What articles manufactured in Michigan are exported to foreign countries?
9. Locate Yellowstone Park, Yosemite Valley, Mammoth Cave, Pictured Rocks, Canyons of the Colorado.
10. Name the river systems of South America.
11. What are the chief industries of the gulf states?
12. Name the different states that produce copper, gold, lead.
13. Name the productions and manufactures of your county.
14. What territories are about to become states?
15. For what are the states of Central America important?

GRAMMAR.

1. The language, arrangement of paragraphs, correctness of sentences, and neatness of paper will count for this number.
2. Name the essential parts of a sentence.
3. Define adjective, participle, pronoun, and give examples.
4. Define case, number, gender.
5. Define transitive verb, mode, voice.
6. State and illustrate three ways of forming the plurals of nouns.
7. Write the possessive forms of lady, women, teachers, attorney-at-law, Mr. Johnson.
8. Compare great, rapidly, beautiful, able, much.
9. Write a complex, declarative sentence, and state of what it is composed.
10. Give the principal parts of sit, sing, drink, eat.
11. Write sentences to illustrate each of the following:
    (a) A conjunctive adverb.
    (b) A relative clause.
    (c) An objective complement.
    (d) A clause used as an object.
12. Name the kinds of sentences according to use and illustrate each.
13. Analyze: This paper *should show your* ability to use good *language* and to express yourself *clearly*.
14. Parse the italicized words in the foregoing sentence.
15. Conjugate the verb *sing* in the present, past, perfect, and future tenses, active voice, indicative mode.

ORTHOGRAPHY.

1. Define vowel, consonant, articulation.
2. Indicate the sounds of a, i, and o by proper diacrit
3. Give the meaning of the following: Hon., Supt., lb., c Y., %, Pres.
4. Define accent, root, prefix, suffix.

5. Use the following words in sentences: root, route; sweet, suite; meed, mead; boy, buoy; principle, principal.
6. Indicate the pronunciation of the following words by using proper diacritical marks and accent: educator, exhaust, combatant, Singapore, Escanaba, Aconcagua, Tacoma.

SPELLING.

1. paragraph
2. superintendent
3. thistle
4. needles
5. potatoes
6. mottoes
7. envelope
8. pictures
9. promontory
10. priest
11. deceive
12. camphor
13. cultivate
14. quotation
15. notation
16. numeration
17. multiplication
18. subtract
19. subtrahend
20. crayon
21. composition
22. area
23. concrete
24. Leelanau
25. Keweenaw
26. perfumery
27. cemetery.
28. secretary
29. crease
30. rectangle
31. separate
32. require
33. partridge
34. squirrel
35. peaceable
36. biscuit
37. carriage
38. hygiene
39. picnic
40. eighth
41. bureau
42. engine
43. acre
44. genuine
45. illustrate
46. comparison
47. denominator
48. dividend
49. factor
50. Genesee.

PENMANSHIP.

1. Show your teacher the proper position at the desk and the correct position for holding the pen.
2. Assuming these positions as given by you, write with pen (a) the one space letters, (b) the capital letters embodying the oval.

3-5. Write as a specimen of your handwriting the first stanza of America.

PHYSIOLOGY.

1. Describe the epidermis.
2. Define secretion. Name five secretions of the body. Where is each secreted?
3. Why should one avoid sitting in a draft when over-heated?
4. Describe the inner ear.
5. Mention some common habits which injure the ear.
6. Describe reflex action. Why is it important?
7. Compare the veins and arteries.
8. Describe the lymphatic circulation.
9. Mention five foods especially good for this time of year. Why are they so?
10. (a) Name two exercises which develop certain muscles. Name the muscles which are so developed.
    (b) Name two games which will develop the chest.
11. Describe normal breathing.
12. What are the functions of the liver?
13. What is the composition of the bones? How are the bones nourished?
14. (a) How does alcohol affect the heart?
    (b) Name five drinks which contain alcohol.
15. (a) What is the purpose of ventilation?
    (b) How is your school room ventilated?

READING.

"Rip Van Winkle."

1. Give the setting of this legend.
2. Describe Rip Van Winkle's appearance.
3. What can you say of his character and ambitions? Why had he never succeeded?
4. Name seven other persons mentioned or described in this legend.
5. (a) What is satire? humor?
   (b) When does Irving use these?
6. Mention some characteristics of the Dutch homes of this period.
7. Tell in a paragraph how Rip Van Winkle came to take his long sleep.
8. What events in the history of the United States had taken place during Van Winkle's sleep? How do you know this from the story?

9–10. Describe the home coming.

11. What emotions does the story of the home-coming arouse in you.
12. (a) Who was Peter Stuyvesant?
    (b) Mention three other references to the history of New Netherlands.
13. Mention some things of the present day which would undoubtedly surprise one who had been asleep from 1886 to 1906.
14. (a) Name ten new words which you have added to your vocabulary by this study.
    (b) Mention some expressions which seem especially fitting.
15. What do you like best about this story? Why?

UNITED STATES HISTORY.

1. For what purpose were the following colonies founded: Georgia, Rhode Island, New Jersey, Maryland?
2. (a) What conditions in Europe caused the early explorations?
   (b) Name six great explorers and tell under what flag each sailed.
3. What constituted New France? Outline the steps in its overthrow.
4. (a) When and where was the first settlement in Michigan?
   (b) Tell of Pontiac's conspiracy.
5. (a) What text-book in United States history have you studied?
   (b) What history stories have you read and to what part of our history does each refer?
6. Describe the present United States flag.
7. Make statements regarding three of the following: The Japanese in California; the Panama Canal; Jamestown Exposition; Disaster in Jamaica; Elmer E. Brown; Andrew Carnegie.

8–9. Give an account of Burgoyne's campaign and state its importance and the results.

10. (a) Tell of Arnold's treason.
    (b) What lessons did you learn from this?
11. Name ten important events which took place between 1820 and 1850.
12. What territory has the United States secured by purchase?
13. What was the Emancipation Proclamation?
14. Tell of the life and services of William McKinley.
15. Name five inventions which have influenced our history.

EDUCATIONAL FUNDS

AND REPORT OF

UNIVERSITY OF MICHIGAN

19

EDUCATIONAL FUNDS.

PRIMARY SCHOOL FUNDS.

Seven per cent fund:		
Amount on which State pays interest, June 30, 1907	$4,258,766 04	
Due from purchasers of land, June 30, 1907	45,855 76	
Total seven per cent fund, June 30, 1907		$4,304,621 80
Five per cent fund:		
Amount on which State pays interest, June 30, 1907		963,790 57
Total school fund, June 30, 1907		$5,268,412 37

INCOME ON PRIMARY SCHOOL INTEREST FUND.

Interest paid by State on seven per cent fund during year ending June 30, 1907	$298,113 62	
Interest and penalty paid by holders of land on seven per cent fund during year ending June 30, 1907	3,815 95	
Interest paid by State on five per cent fund	48,189 53	
Total income from both funds		$350,119 10
Surplus of specific taxes transferred	$786,282 33	
Paid by trespassers on school land	29 00	
Total		786,311 33
Total income for year ending June 30, 1907		$1,136,430 43

UNIVERSITY FUND.

Amount on which State pays interest June 30, 1907	$544,244 40	
Interest paid by State (on land grant)		$38,081 00
Interest paid by State on deposit		50.00
Interest and penalty paid by holders of land.		404 46
Total income for year ending June 30, 1907		$38,535 46

AGRICULTURAL COLLEGE FUND.

Amount on which State pays interest June 30, 1907	$977,727 49	
Interest paid by State		$68,271 42
Interest and penalty paid by holders of land		1,927 33
Paid by trespassers on lands		....
Received from United States government		25,000 00
Total income for year ending June 30, 1907		$95,198 75

NORMAL SCHOOL FUND.

Amount on which State pays interest June 30, 1907	$68,811 79	
Interest paid by State		$4,300 26
Interest and penalty paid by holders of lands		40 06
Total income for year ending June 30, 1907		$4,340 32

UNIVERSITY OF MICHIGAN.

FINANCIAL STATEMENT OF THE UNIVERSITY OF MICHIGAN FOR THE FISCAL YEAR ENDING JUNE 30, 1907.

CONDENSED STATEMENT GENERAL, SPECIAL, AND BUILDING FUNDS.

	Receipts 1	Disbursements 2
Balance July 1, 1906	$85,652 29	
State Treasurer: ¼ Mill Tax, General Fund	342,920 00	Column 4
University Interest	38,524 59	Column 4
Special Appropriations	9,000 00	Column 8
Building Fund	44,375 00	Column 12
Miscellaneous Sources, General Fund	396,070 82	Column 4
	$916,542 70	
General Fund	Column 5	$814,025 71
Special Appropriation	Column 10	7,064 10
Building Fund	Column 14	22,622 74
Balance June 30, 1907	....	72,830 15
		$916,542 70

DETAILED STATEMENT GENERAL FUND.

	Student Fees 3	Receipts 4	Disbursements 5	Salaries 6	Refunds 7
Balance July 1, 1906		$97,011 78			
State Treasurer, ¼ Mill tax		342,920 00			
State Treasurer, University Interest		38,524 59			
Alumni Association			$1,900 00		
Appointment Committee			76 86		
Advertising and Printing			2,362 80		
Arboretum			507 68		
Barbour Gymnasium	$690 00	690 00	304 31		$6 00
Contingent		2,248 64	31,108 16		
Care of Teams			1,980 45		
Carpenter Shops			1,780 38		
Commencement		205 50	967 47		
Combined Course	1,044 00	1,044 00	10 00		10 00
Diplomas	9,000 00	9,000 00	1,664 80		70 00
Electrical Supplies		14 70	2,442 17		
Fuel		1,064 00	41,094 63		
General Library, Books			12,668 93		
General Library, Pay Roll			15,019 03	$15,019 03	
General Library, Contingent			2,500 36		
General Pay Roll			65,310 84	65,310 84	
Heating Supplies			1,399 27		
Hinsdale History		967 10	4,662 57		
Humanistic Series			292 00		
Interest		2,532 28			
Key Deposits	362 00	362 00	324 00		324 00
Laundry		700 74	8,810 19		
Lights		250 83	2,814 53		
Museum			451 32		
Observatory			1,558 70		
Oratorical Association			96 29		
Postage			2,126 51		
Psychopathic Ward Loan		2,000 00			
Printing Plant		422 52	2,367 55		
Repairs			16,258 58		
School Inspection			537 03		
Summer School, Literary	8, 00	8,	60 00		60 00
Summer School, Law	3,445 00	3,445 00			
Summer School, Medical	1,[illegible] 00	1,[illegible] 00	15 00		15 00
Summer School Expenses			829 71		
Summer School Pay Roll			15,466 00	15,466 00	
Summer School Gymnasium	00	57	1 00		1 00
Thesis	57 00	100 00	200 00		200 00
Waterman Gymnasium	3,[illegible] 00	3,028 00	219 32		14 00

	Student Fees 3	Receipts 4	Disbursements 5	Salaries 6	Refunds 7
Water Supply			$2,731 49		
Dental Department	$9,830 00	$9,830 00	5,861 33		$317 50
Dental Library			109 49		
Dental Pay Roll			12,338 05	$12,338 05	
Dental Supplies		6,123 93			
Dental Laboratory	465 00	465 00	6 00		6 00
Architecture			*2,084 61		
Civil Engineering	550 00	550 00	2,020 11		10 00
Drawing Boards	1,320 00	1,320 00	1,105 50		1,105 50
Engineering Shops		354 64	2,666 53		
Engineering Lockers	21 00	21 00	9 00		9 00
Engineering Department	65,342 50	65,342 50	4,038 02		2,022 50
Engineering Library			1,898 21		
Engineering Pay Roll			106,315 57	106,315 57	
Electrical Engineering	1,922 00	1,922 00	250 39		46 00
Mechanical Laboratory	6,235 00	6,235 00	1,319 32		43 00
Marine		50 00	206 01		
Physics			1,465 27		
Homeopathic College	3,870 00	3,870 00	453 45		
*Homeopathic College Pay Roll			8,937 10	*8,937 10	
Homeopathic Library			194 9[illegible]		
Homeopathic Hospital		23,795 35	17,349 26		
Homeopathic Hospital Pay Roll			8,416 85	8,416 85	
Law Department	44,874 00	44,874 00	1,997 83		1,235 00
Law Department Pay Roll			50,453 61	50,453 61	
Law Library		9 20	3,177 18		
American History			48 30		
Accounting Laboratory	29 50	29 50			
Botanical Laboratory	1,018 00	1,018 00	937 92		49 00
Botanical Garden			261 90		
English			106 61		
Forestry			473 67		
French			33 05		
Geology			417 40		
German			42 70		
Greek			183 84		
History			78 40		
Literary Department	68,840 00	68,840 00	159,229 26	159,229 26	
Literary Department Refunds			1,010 00		1,010 00
Latin			188 20		
Music			192 65		
Mineralogy	645 00	645 00	943 88		85 00
Political Economy	69 95	69 95	71 94		
Philosophy			309 57		
Rhetoric			20 88		
Zoology	561 00	561 00	800 07		2 00
Anatomical Laboratory			208 05		
Anatomical Material			2,293 28		
Dermatology			83 90		
Electrotherapeutics	696 00	696 00	705 59		182 45
Histology	1,165 00	1,165 00	867 80		40 00
Hygiene	4,699 34	4,699 34	5,922 60		610 93
Medical Department	19,115 00	19,115 00	1,458 77		895 00
Medical Pay Roll			54,468 31	54,468 31	
Medical Library			2,397 40		
Medical Demonstrations	4,450 00	4,450 00	5 00		5 00
Materia Medica			512 11		
Nervous Diseases			252 43		
Ophthalmology			467 87		
Otology			672 16		
Pasteur Institute		7,510 00	497 15		
Physiology	465 15	465 15	460 67		5 00
Pathology	1,250 00	1,250 00	1,250 79		254 22
Pharmacology	480 00	480 00	7 50		7 50
Practical anatomy	2,175 00	2,175 00	5 00		5 00
Roentgen Laboratory			514 63		
Surgical Department			527 31		
Theory and Practice			449 08		
University Hospital		59,047 68	41,630 08		
University Hospital Pay Roll			15,642 60	15,642 60	
Chemical Laboratory	15,534 27	15,534 27	12,041 31		1,625 28
Pharmacy and Chemical Pay Roll			29,549 80	29,549 80	
Pharmacy Department	5,465 00	5,465 00	190 00		190 00
Balance June 30, 1907			60,501 48		
Total Student Fees	$288,773 71			$541,147 02 Total salaries	$10,470 88 Fees refunded
Less Fees Refunded (Column 7)	10,470 88	$874,527 19	$874 527 19		
Student Fees Net	$278,302 83				

DETAILED STATEMENT SPECIAL APPROPRIATIONS.

HOMEOPATHIC MEDICAL COLLEGE.

	Receipts 8	Total 9	Disbursements 10	Total 11
Balance July 1, 1906		$1,463 14		
From State Treasurer	$6,000 00	6,000 00		
*Paid Vouchers			*$3,956 10	$3,956 10
Balance June 30, 1907				3,507 04
		$7,463 14		$7,463 14

Summer Hospitals.

	Receipts 8	Total 9	Disbursements 10	Total 11
From State Treasurer	$3,000 00	$3,000 00		
Paid Vouchers			$3,000 00	$3,000 00
		$3,000 00		$3,000 00

Psychopathic Ward.

	Receipts 8	Total 9	Disbursements 10	Total 11
Balance overdrawn July 1, 1906				$9,356 63
Paid Vouchers			$108 00	108 00
Balance overdrawn June 30, 1907		$9,464 63		
	$9,000 00	$9,464 63	$7,064 10	$9,464 63

DETAILED STATEMENT BUILDING ACCOUNT.

ACCUMULATION OF SAVINGS.

New Engineering Building.

	Receipts 12	Total 13	Disbursements 14	Total 15
From State Treasurer	$9,375 00	$9,375 00		
Balance overdrawn July 1, 1906				$7,629 10
Paid Vouchers			$1,718 15	
Returned to State Treas., to Bldg. Acct.			27 75	1,745 90
		$9,375 00		$9,375 00

New Medical Building.

	Receipts 12	Total 13	Disbursements 14	Total 15
Balance July 1, 1906		$4,066 81		
Returned to State Treas., to Bldg. Acct.			$4,066 81	$4,066 81
		$4,066 81		$4,066 81

Repairs to Woman's Gymnasium.

	Receipts 12	Total 13	Disbursements 14	Total 15
Balance July 1, 1906		$798 94		
Leturned to State Treas., to Bldg. Acct.			$798 94	$798 94
		$798 94		$798 94

Addition to Physical Laboratory.

From State Treasurer	$5,000 00	$5,000 00		
Balance overdrawn July 1, 1906				$866 78
Returned to State Treas., to Bldg. Acct			$4,133 22	4,133 22
		$5,000 00		$5,000 00

Addition and Repairs to Observatory.

	Receipts 12	Total 13	Disbursements 14	Total 15
Balance July 1, 1906		$164 13		
Returned to State Treas., to Bldg. Acct			$164 13	$164 13
		$164 13		$164 13

Equipment to Observatory.

From State Treasurer	$15,000 00	$15,000 00		
Paid Vouchers			$2,265 11	$2,265 11
Balance June 30, 1907				12,734 89
		$15,000 00		$15,000 00

Equipment to Engineering Laboratory.

From State Treasurer	$15,000 00	$15,000 00		
Paid Vouchers			$9,448 63	$9,448 63
Balance June 30, 1907				5,551 37
	$44,375 00	$15,000 00	$22,622 74	$15,000 00

SPECIAL AND BUILDING FUNDS.

SUMMARY OF BALANCES JUNE 30, 1907.

Psychopathic Ward overdraft	$9,464 63	
Balance on hand June 30, 1907	12,328 67	$21,793 30

Credit Balance.

Homeopathic Medical College	3,507 04	
Equipment to Observatory	12,734 89	
Equipment to Engineering Laboratory	5,551 37	21,793 30

*Pay Roll, Homeopathic College General Fund	8,937 10
*Pay Roll, Homeopathic Special Account	3,956 10
Total Pay Roll	$12,893 20

GIFT AND TRUST FUNDS.

Under this head are included gifts and other funds which the Regents have received from time to time from benefactors for special purposes. The new accounts opened during the year are:

Peter White Gift to Arboretum.
A. M. Todd, Prize Fund.
Peter White Gift to Humanistic Series, $1,000.00.
Franklin H. Walker Gift to Humanistic Series, $500.00

CONDENSED STATEMENT.

Total Funds July 1, 1906	$329,312 09
Interest, Rentals, etc	20,265 76
New Funds, Contributions, etc	24,506 54
	$374,084 39
Expenditures	$20,423 29
Balance in Funds June 30, 1907	353,661 10
	$374,084

TABULATED STATEMENT (DETAILED).

Name	Amount in Fund July 1, 1906	Income		Expenditures	Amount in Fund June 30, 1907
		Interest or Rentals	Contributions		
A. M. Todd Prize Fund			$500 00		$500 00
Alice Freeman Palmer Memorial	$1,081 48	$32 69	28 00		1,142 17
Allopathic Hospital Fund	2,246 86	127 81		$65 15	2,309 52
American School at Rome	5 45		25 00	30 00	45
A. B. Whittier Botany Fellowship	4,003 28	198 44		120 00	4,081 72
Ann Arbor Branch Coll. Alumnae	151 20	3 66	50 00		204 86
Bates Professorship Fund	116,393 86	9,192 48	4,500 00	6,757	123,328 61
Ben Greet Dramatic Fund	371 20		1,464 95	1,137	698 33
Buhl Classical Fellowship	55 43		500 00	375 72	180 43
Buhl Law Library Fund	352 47	10 24		45 [illegible]	317 71
Chas. A. Kent Fund, transferred to J. B. Angell Fund					
Class of '94 Scholarship	1,986 22	85 73			2,071 95
Class of '97 Scholarship	203 46	27 04			230 50
Class of '98 Scholarship	439 88	7 55			447 43
Class of '99 Law Scholarship	34 64	3 18			37 82
Class of '03 Memorial	147 73	4 46			152 19
Coyl Collection Library Fund	11,562 96	677 02		1,409 39	10,830 59
D. M. Ferry Botanical Fund			500 00	450 00	50 00
English Book Fund, transferred to Ben Greet Dramatic Fund					
Ford-Messer Fund	22,060 56	1,138 66		1,638 47	21,560 75
Fred'k Stearns & Co., Pharm. Fellowship			390 00	390 00	
Gas Asso. Fellowship	4 28		600 00	552 41	51 87
Geo. S. Morris Philos. Fellowship			400 00	350 00	50 00
Goethe Fund	218 60	6 49		28 43	196 66
Good Government Club	796 94	24 13			821 07
Helen H. Newberry Class. Fellowship			200 00	200 00	
Herbarium Expedition	200 00			200 00	
Humanistic Series Fund	24 01	4 24	1,500 00		1,528 25
James B. Angell Fund	848 11	768 05			1,616 16
L. H. Stone Supp. Loan Fund	5,438 79	174 20			5,612 99
Marine Biological Fellowship	50 00		50 00	100 00	
McMillan Shakespeare Fund	6 96	3 37		10 33	
Morris Alumni Fund	3,202 03	268 35			3,470 38
Museum Expedition	21 95		51 65	73 60	
Music Hall Fund	1,550 23	56 88			1,607 11
Newton Vander Veer Loan Fund	450 36	13 62			463 98
Palmer Memorial Free Bed Fund	15,587 45	433 53		812 45	15,208 53
Parke, Davis & Co. Fund	50 00		550 00	450 00	150 00
Peter White Fellowship American History	894 67	19 04	400 00	400 00	913 71
Peter White Classical Fellowship	300 00		300 00	300 00	300 00
Peter White Gift to Arboretum			300 00	300 00	
Phillips Scholarship Fund	929 03	149 41		100 00	978 44
Pittsburg Alumni Scholarship Fund	100 00	2 27			102 27
Philo Parsons Fund	132 94	4 02			136 96
Philosophy Library—Victoria Morris	4 41	28	50 00	49 61	5 08
Saginaw Valley Alumnae Association Scholarship Fund	160 60	1 23	40 00		201 83
Seth Harrison Scholarship Fund	29,818 18	1,552 21		1,600 00	29,770 39
Special Latin Fund	2 82				2 82
Students' Lecture Association	1,277 36	41 50			1,318 86
Treadwell Free Bed Fund	87	50 56			51 43
Walter Crane Fund	1,291 82	834 25		1,837 60	288 47
*Walter Crane Fund Property Account	4,692 01		4,694 94		9,386 95
Warner Fund	1 40	04	1 00		2 44
Williams Professorship Fund	4,653 44	220 55		50 00	4,823 99
*Williams Professorship Property	15,871 98	919 94			16,791 92
Wm. Wilson, Jr., Pharm. Fund	50 00	93		50 00	93
Woman's Gym. Fund—Peter White	100 75	3 10			103 85
Woman's Professorship Fund	13,267 93	788 88			14,056 81
Total	$263,096 00	$17,850 03	$17,095 54	$19,882 99	$278,159 18
Alumni Memorial Building Fund	66,215 49	2,415 73	7,411 00	540 30	75,501 92
Grand Total	$329,312 09	$20,265 76	$24,506 54	$20,423 29	$353,661 10

*The care of the Williams Professorship Property Account and the Walter Crane Property Account has been in the hands of Mr. George S. Field. A summary of the report of Mr. Field is in an appendix to the present report. (See Appendix.)

APPENDIX A.

WILLIAMS PROFESSORSHIP FUND (PROPERTY ACCOUNT.)

This is in the hands of Mr. George S. Field for management, and the summary of his report from June 15th, 1906, to June 15th, 1907, is as follows:

June 15th, 1907, Cash on hand	$900 24	
Real Estate Mortgages	14,125 00	
Land Contracts	200 00	
Real Estate	1,566 68	
		$16,791 92

Contra.

Total amount in valuation on hand at last report, June 15th, 1906	$15,871 98	
Net gain in value for the year ending June 15th, 1907	919 94	
		$16,791 92

APPENDIX B.

WALTER CRANE FUND (PROPERTY ACCOUNT).

This is in the hands of Mr. George S. Field for management, and the summary of his report from June 15th, 1906, to June 15th, 1907, is as follows:

Amount of land contracts on hand at this date, June 15th, 1907	$23,564 70	
Amount of cash in banks	418 27	
		$23,982 97

Contra.

Total amount in valuation on hand at last report, June 15, 1906		$11,453 56	
New contracts taken during year	$13,600 00		
Less payments made by Field	2,200 00		
		11,400 00	
Net gain in value for year ending June 15, 1907		1,129 41	
			$23,982 97
Total amount in valuation on hand June 15, 1907		$23,982 97	
Subject to loan of $14,596 02		14,596 02	
Total Walter Crane Fund Property Account		$9,386 95	

HENRY W. CAREY,
ARTHUR HILL,
Finance Committee.

STATISTICAL TABLES.

STATISTICAL TABLES.

TABLE I.

Comparative summary of statistics for the years 1906 and 1907.

Items.	1906.	1907.	Increase.	Decrease.
Districts and Schools.				
Number of townships and cities reporting	1,303	1,308	5	....
Number of graded school districts	573	578	5	....
Number of ungraded school districts	6,721	6,724	3	....
Total	7,294	7,302	8	....
Number of township unit districts	138	146	8	....
School census of graded school districts	430,586	437,183	6,597	....
School census of ungraded school districts	317,301	305,847	....	11,454
Total	747,887	743,030	....	4,857
Enrollment in graded school districts	303,930	305,668	1,738	....
Enrollment in ungraded school districts	226,413	218,301	....	8,112
Total	530,343	523,969	....	6,374
Enrollment in graded school districts:				
Resident pupils	303,930	305,668	1,738	....
Non-resident pupils	10,652	10,943	291	....
Total	314,582	316,611	2,029	....
Enrollment in ungraded school districts:				
Resident pupils	226,413	218,301	....	8,112
Non-resident pupils	9,098	7,839	....	1,259
Total	235,511	226,140	....	9,371

TABLE I.—CONTINUED.

Items.	1906.	1907.	Increase.	Decrease.
Enrollment in all school districts:				
Resident pupils	530,343	523,969		6,374
Non-resident pupils	19,750	18,782		968
Total	550,093	542,751		7,342
Enrollment in city school districts	228,699	249,134	20,435	
Percentage of attendance for the State	69	69		
Percentage of attendance in graded school districts	84	83		1
Number of districts reporting having maintained school	7,235	7,241	6	
Average duration in months in graded schools	9.5	9.5		
Average duration in months in ungraded schools	8.4	8.4		
Average for the State	8.4	8.5	0.1	
Number of private and parochial schools reported	484	465		19
Number of men teachers in such schools	335	341	6	
Number of women teachers in such schools	899	938	39	
Estimated number of pupils attending such schools	55,385	56,468	1,083	
Number of day schools for the deaf in the State	12	12		
Number of teachers employed in same	20	19		1
Number of pupils attending same	141	148	7	
Number of county normal training classes in the State	25	32	7	
Number of teachers employed in same	92	131	39	
Number of graduates	293	400	107	
Teachers and their employments.				
Number of teachers necessary to supply graded schools	7,796	8,256	460	
Number of teachers necessary to supply ungraded schools	7,464	7,426		38
Total	15,260	15,682	422	
Number of men teachers employed in graded schools	996	1,019	23	
Number of men teachers employed in ungraded schools	1,572	1,483		89
Total	2,568	2,502		66

TABLE I.—CONTINUED.

Items.	1906.	1907.	Increase.	Decrease.
Number of women teachers employed in graded schools	6,995	7,507	512	....
Number of women teachers employed in ungraded schools	7,361	7,277	....	84
Total	14,356	14,784	428	....
Whole number of different teachers employed in graded schools	7,991	8,526	535	....
Whole number of different teachers employed in ungraded schools	8,933	8,760	....	173
Total	16,924	17,286	362	....
Average number of months taught by men in graded schools	9.17	9.58	0.41	....
Average number of months taught by men in ungraded schools	7.17	7.22	0.05	....
General average	7.94	8.19	0.25	....
Average number of months taught by women in graded schools	9.53	9.46	....	0.07
Average number of months taught by women in ungraded schools	6.95	7.23	0.28	....
General average	8.21	8.36	....	0.15
Total wages of men teachers in graded schools	$834,021 46	$916,174 09	$82,152 63	....
Total wages of men teachers in ungraded schools	451,602 55	461,672 15	10,069 60	....
Total	$1,285,624 01	$1,377,846 24	$92,222 23	....
Total wages of women teachers in graded schools	$3,371,510 18	$3,839,655 36	$468,145 18	....
Total wages of women teachers in ungraded schools	1,700,037 53	1,870,087 96	170,050 43	....
Total	$5,071,547 71	$5,709,743 32	$638,195 61	....
Aggregate wages of all teachers in graded schools	$4,205,531 64	$4,755,829 45	$550,297 81	....
Aggregate wages of all teachers in ungraded schools	2,151,640 08	2,331,760 11	180,120 03	....
Total	$6,357,171 72	$7,087,589 56	$730,417 84	....
Aggregate wages of teachers in city school districts	$2,820,767 34	$3,391,484 89	$570,717 55	....
Average monthly wages of men teachers in graded schools	$91 31	$93 79	$2 48	....
Average monthly wages of men teachers in ungraded schools	40 07	43 08	3 01	....

TABLE I.—CONTINUED.

Items.	1906.	1907.	Increase.	Decrease.
Average monthly wages of men teachers in all schools	$63 01	$67 26	$4 25	
Average monthly wages of women teachers in graded schools	$50 57	$54 04	$3 47	
Average monthly wages of women teachers in ungraded schools	33 21	35 53	2 32	
Average monthly wages of women teachers in all schools	$43 03	$46 17	$3 14	
Examination and certification of teachers.				
Number of public examinations held	240	226		14
Number of applicants for regular certificates	9,992	9,621		371
Number of county first grade certificates granted	72	74	2	
Number of indorsed first grade certificates granted	50	47		3
Number of second grade certificates granted	1,860	2,089	229	
Number of third grade certificates granted	3,603	3,789	186	
Whole number of regular certificates granted	5,585	5,999	414	
Number of applicants for special certificates	1,344	1,086		258
Number of special certificates granted	1,133	913		220
Number holding certificates issued or indorsed by State board of education	622	610		12
Number holding Normal school certificates	1,412	1,905	493	
Number holding certificates issued by city boards of education	2,528	2,790	262	
Number holding county normal training class certificates	594	1,001	407	
Whole number of legally qualified teachers	17,049	17,842	793	
Number licensed without previous experience in teaching	1,827	1,957	130	
Number of applicants who had attended State normal	876	1,328	452	
Number of applicants who had attended institutes during the year	4,101	3,932		169
School property.				
Number of school houses	8,331	8,390	59	
Number of school houses to be built during year	175	148		27
Cost of same	$1,547,954 00	$1,581,907 19	$33,953 19	
Estimated value of property in graded school districts	$21,706,713 00	$24,704,667 00	$2,997,954 00	
Estimated value of property in ungraded school districts	5,886,877 00	6,239,367 00	352,490 00	
Total	$27,593,590 00	$30,944,034 00	$3,350,444 00	

TABLE I.—Continued.

Items.	1906.	1907.	Increase.	Decrease.
Financial.				
Amount of one mill tax received	$1,092,688 64	$1,058,866 43	....	$33,822 21
Amount of primary school interest fund received	2,706,165 10	8,803,794 67	$6,097,629 57	....
Amount received from non-resident tuition	110,495 58	120,112 81	9,617 23	....
Amount received from district taxes	5,591,319 75	4,223,343 58	....	1,367,976 17
Amount received from all other sources	739,606 07	1,053,777 15	314,171 08	....
Total net receipts	$10,240,275 14	$15,259,[illegible]94 64	$5,019,619 50	....
Amount received from loans	1,060,380 37	1,072,233 91	11,853 54	....
Balance on hand from preceding year	2,932,874 20	2,870,321 06	....	$62,553 14
Total resources, including amount on hand from preceding year	$14,233,529 71	$19,202,449 61	$4,968,919 90	....
Amount paid men teachers	$1,285,495 61	$1,378,430 54	$92,934 93	....
Amount paid women teachers	5,071,726 26	5,713,435 82	641,709 56	....
Amount paid for building, repairs and site	1,954,746 61	2,530,991 12	576,244 51	....
Amount paid for interest on loans	175,596 60	167,468 61	....	$8,127 99
Amount paid for all other purposes	2,116,338 87	2,295,556 83	179,217 96	....
Total net expenditures	$10,603,903 95	$12,085,8[illegible]2 92	$1,481,978 97	....
Amount paid on bonded indebtedness	740,504 41	781,496 72	40,992 31	....
Balance carried to next year	2,889 121 35	6,335,0[illegible]9 97	3,445,948 62	....
Total expenditures, including amount on hand	$14,233,529 71	$19,202,449 61	$4,968,919 90	....
Total expenditures in graded school districts	$7,584,396 01	$8,665,490 61	$1,081,094 60	....
Total expenditures in ungraded school districts	3,019,507 94	3,420,392 31	400,862 82	....
Total net expenditures	$10,603,903 95	$12,085,882 92	$1,481,957 42	....
Total bonded indebtedness of districts	$3,504,397 78	$3,636,184 41	$131,786 63	....
Total floating indebtedness of districts	103,557 91	234,773 53	71,215 62	....
Total indebtedness	$3,667,955 69	$3,870,957 94	$203,002 25	....
Total indebtedness in graded school districts	$3,323,507 81	$3,493,842 01	$170,334 20	....
Total indebtedness in ungraded school districts	344,447 88	377,115 93	32,668 05	....
Total indebtedness	$3,667,955 69	$3,870,957 94	$203,002 25	....
Total amount due the districts	$413,590 45	$406,793 25	....	$6,797 20
Amount received from non-resident tuition in graded school districts	$104,823 60	$113,650 51	$8,826 91	....
Amount received from non-resident tuition in ungraded school districts	5,071 98	6,462 30	790 32	....
Total	$110,495 58	$120,112 81	$9,6[illegible]	

21

TABLE I.—CONTINUED.

Items.	1906.	1907.	Increase.	Decrease.
School libraries.				
Number of townships reporting libraries	355	343		12
Number of districts reporting libraries	5,063	5,211	148	
Total number of libraries	5,418	5,554	136	
Number of volumes in township libraries	167,054	166,309		745
Number of volumes in district libraries	1,193,899	1,218,889	24,990	
Total number of volumes in all libraries	1,360,953	1,385,198	24,245	
Amount of taxes voted for township libraries	$3,380 39	$4,575 03	$1,194 64	
Amount received from county treasurers for township libraries	8,224 43	8,557 42	332 99	
Number of townships forfeiting library money	868	878	10	
Amount paid for support of township libraries	$11,457 17	$13,086 74	$1,629 57	
Amount paid for support of district libraries	158,521 40	174,359 97	15,838 57	
Teachers' Institutes.				
Number of State Institutes held	83	131	48	
Number of men enrolled at such institutes	2,433	5,391	2,958	
Number of women enrolled at such institutes	13,185	19,134	5,949	
Total enrollment	15,618	24,525	8,907	
Amount received from State Treasurer for such institutes	$2,993 30	$1,873 28		$1,120 02
Amount received from county treasurers for such institutes	10,509 08	11,471 45	$962 37	
Total amount expended	$13,502 38	$13,344 73		$157 65
Miscellaneous.				
Number of counties reporting county teachers' associations	65	66	1	
Amount per diem received by examiners	$19,826 40	$21,191 33	$1,364 93	
Amount paid commissioners of schools	83,920 00	86,200 00	2,280 00	
Total compensation	$103,746 40	$107,391 33	$3,644 93	

TABLE I.—Concluded.

Items.	1906.	1907.	Increase.	Decrease.
Amount allowed by supervisors for expenses of county boards	$14,155 69	$13,683 38		$472 31
Amount paid and due township inspectors for services	19,767 81	17,455 25		2,312 56
Amount paid chairmen of boards of inspectors	43,143 26	43,887 15	$743 89	
Total amount of primary school interest fund apportioned	$8,901,106 00	$3,735,274 00		$5,165,832 00
Rate per capita, May apportionment	$1 00	$1 00		
Rate per capita, November apportionment	11 00	4 00		$7 00
Rate per capita for year	$12 00	$5 00		$7 00
Number of eighth grade diplomas granted during year	5,209	6,286	1,077	
Number of pupils in eighth grade exclusive of graded schools	13,275	14,414	1,139	
Number of districts furnishing free text-books	966	1,006	40	
Number of districts reporting dictionaries in schools	7,178	6,894		284
Number of districts reporting globes in schools	6,310	6,224		86
Number of districts reporting maps in schools	6,885	6,773		112
Total number of U. S. flags in school districts	6,919	6,999	80	
Total number of children in the State blind or with defective vision		361		

TABLE II.

Forty-fourth and forty-fifth semi-annual apportionment of the primary school interest fund.

Counties.	Apportionment made May 10, 1907, rate per capita $1.00.			Apportionment made November 10, 1907, rate per capita $4.00.		
	Whole number of children.	Number children included in apportionment.	Amount apportioned.	Whole number of children.	Number children included in apportionment.	Amount apportioned.
Totals	747,857	746,910	$746,910 00	747,887	747,091	$29,883 64
Alcona	2,063	2,063	$2,063 00	2,093	2,093	k $8,402 00
Alger	1,998	1,998	1,998 00	1,998	1,998	7,992 00
Allegan	11,646	11,646	11,646 00	11,646	11,646	l 46,728 00
Alpena	6,661	6,661	6,661 00	6,661	6,661	26,644 00
Antrim	4,873	4,837	4,837 00	4,873	4,837	19,348 00
Arenac	3,744	3,744	3,744 00	3,744	3,744	14,976 00
Baraga	1,877	1,877	1,877 00	1,877	1,877	7,508 00
Barry	5,804	5,782	5,782 00	5,804	5,782	23,128 00
Bay	22,832	22,832	22,832 00	22,832	22,832	91,328 00
Benzie	3,273	3,269	3,269 00	3,273	3,269	13,076 00
Berrien	14,716	14,705	14,705 00	14,716	14,705	58,820 00
Branch	6,460	6,447	6,447 00	6,460	6,447	25,788 00
Calhoun	12,464	12,464	12,464 00	12,464	12,464	49,856 00
Cass	4,998	4,970	4,970 00	4,998	4,970	19,880 00
Charlevoix	5,462	5,460	5,460 00	5,462	5,460	21,840 00
Cheboygan	5,899	5,899	5,899 00	5,899	5,899	23,596 00
Chippewa	7,245	7,206	7,206 00	7,245	7,245	m 29,019 00
Clare	3,313	3,274	3,274 00	3,313	3,274	13,096 00
Clinton	6,593	6,593	6,593 00	6,593	6,593	26,372 00
Crawford	1,205	1,174	1,174 00	1,205	1,174	4,696 00
Delta	9,036	8,994	8,994 00	9,036	8,994	35,976 00
Dickinson	6,612	6,612	6,612 00	6,612	6,612	26,448 00
Eaton	7,271	7,271	a, b 7,271 00	7,271	7,271	29,084 00
Emmet	5,423	5,423	5,423 00	5,423	5,423	21,692 00
Genesee	10,698	10,683	c 10,731 00	10,698	10,683	42,732 00
Gladwin	3,087	2,967	2,967 00	3,087	3,079	n 12,428 00
Gogebic	6,080	6,080	6,080 00	6,080	6,080	24,320 00
Grand Traverse	6,316	6,316	6,316 00	6,316	6,316	25,264 00
Gratiot	8,523	8,523	d 9,063 00	8,523	8,523	34,092 00
Hillsdale	7,396	7,372	e 7,648 00	7,396	7,372	29,488 00
Houghton	24,514	24,514	24,514 00	24,514	24,514	o 99,196 00
Huron	12,339	12,339	12,339 00	12,339	12,339	49,356 00
Ingham	10,709	10,709	10,709 00	10,709	10,709	42,836 00
Ionia	8,809	8,809	8,809 00	8,809	8,809	35,236 00
Iosco	3,559	3,559	3,559 00	3,559	3,559	14,236 00
Iron	3,059	3,059	3,059 00	3,059	3,059	12,236 00
Isabella	7,345	7,345	f 7,465 00	7,345	7,345	29,380 00
Jackson	11,116	11,097	11,097 00	11,116	11,097	44,388 00
Kalamazoo	12,984	12,969	12,969 00	12,984	12,969	51,876 00
Kalkaska	2,263	2,263	2,263 00	2,263	2,263	9,052 00
Kent	39,833	39,769	39,769 00	39,833	39,769	159,076 00
Keweenaw	1,451	1,451	1,451 00	1,451	1,451	5,804 00
Lake	1,513	1,497	g 1,717 00	1,513	1,497	5,988 00
Lapeer	7,403	7,403	7,403 00	7,365	7,365	29,460 00
Leelanau	3,710	3,699	3,699 00	3,710	3,699	14,796 00

a Deficiency to dist. 4, Eaton Tp. $24.00.
b Less amount overpaid district 11 fr. Eaton Tp. $24.00.
c Includes $48 deficiency to district 4, Atlas, May and November, 1906.
d Includes $540 deficiency to district 8, Washington, May and November, 1906.
e Includes $276 deficiency to district 4, Somerset, May and November, 1906.
f Includes $120 deficiency to district 3, Coldwater, May and November, 1906.
g Includes $220 deficiency to district 2, Elk, November, 1906.
k Includes $30 deficiency May 10, 1907.
l Includes $144 deficiency May and November, 1906.
m Includes $39 deficiency May 10, 1907.
n *Includes $112 deficiency May 10, 1907.*
o *Includes $1,140 deficiency May and November, 1906.*

TABLE II.—Concluded.

Counties.	Apportionment made May 10, 1907, rate per capita $1.00.			Apportionment made November 10, 1907, rate per capita $4.00.		
	Whole number of children.	Number children included in apportionment.	Amount apportioned.	Whole number of children.	Number children included in apportionment.	Amount apportioned.
Lenawee	12,225	12,219	$12,219 00	12,225	12,219	$48,876 00
Livingston	4,801	4,794	h 4,950 00	4,801	4,794	19,176 00
Luce	939	928	928 00	939	928	3,712 00
Mackinac	2,648	2,620	i 3,496 00	2,648	2,620	10,480 00
Macomb	9,978	9,978	9,978 00	9,978	9,978	39,912 00
Manistee	9,142	9,142	9,142 00	9,142	9,142	36,568 00
Marquette	13,582	13,582	13,582 00	13,582	13,582	54,328 00
Mason	6,700	6,700	6,700 00	6,700	6,700	26,800 00
Mecosta	6,549	6,549	6,549 00	6,549	6,549	26,196 00
Menominee	9,789	9,707	9,707 00	9,789	9,707	38,828 00
Midland	4,787	4,781	4,781 00	4,787	4,781	19,124 00
Missaukee	3,687	3,647	3,647 00	3,687	3,647	14,588 00
Monroe	9,898	9,898	9,898 00	9,898	9,898	39,592 00
Montcalm	10,038	10,038	10,038 00	10,038	10,038	40,152 00
Montmorency	1,166	1,157	1,157 00	1,166	1,157	4,628 00
Muskegon	12,076	12,066	12,066 00	12,076	12,066	48,264 00
Newaygo	6,147	6,092	6,092 00	6,147	6,092	24,368 00
Oakland	10,942	10,907	10,907 00	10,942	10,907	43,628 00
Oceana	5,474	5,462	5,462 00	5,474	5,462	21,848 00
Ogemaw	3,144	3,140	3,140 00	3,144	3,140	12,560 00
Ontonagon	2,594	2,594	2,594 00	2,594	2,594	10,376 00
Osceola	6,092	6,092	6,092 00	6,092	6,092	24,368 00
Oscoda	714	698	698 00	714	698	2,792 09
Otsego	2,270	2,269	2,269 00	2,270	2,269	9,076 00
Ottawa	13,972	13,972	13,972 00	13,972	13,972	55,888 00
Presque Isle	3,478	3,478	3,478 00	3,478	3,478	13,912 00
Roscommon	584	579	j 759 00	584	579	2,316 00
Saginaw	26,890	26,890	26,890 00	26,890	26,890	107,560 00
St. Clair	16,261	16,261	16,261 00	16,261	16,261	65,044 00
St. Joseph	5,986	5,986	5,986 00	5,986	5,986	23,944 00
Sanilac	11,556	11,542	11,542 00	11,556	11,542	46,168 00
Schoolcraft	2,651	2,640	2,640 00	2,651	2,640	10,560 00
Shiawassee	8,555	8,545	8,545 00	8,555	8,545	34,180 00
Tuscola	10,540	10,540	10,540 00	10,578	10,578	42,312 00
Van Buren	9,756	9,756	9,756 00	9,756	9,756	39,024 00
Washtenaw	11,731	11,721	11,721 00	11,731	11,721	46,884 00
Wayne	110,217	110,217	110,217 00	110,217	110,217	440,868 00
Wexford	6,123	6,099	6,099 00	6,123	6,099	24,396 00

h Includes $156 deficiency to district 2, Hartland, May and November, 1906.
i Includes $876 deficiency to Bois Blanc Tp., May and November, 1906.
j Includes $180 deficiency to district 2, Denton, May and November, 1906.

TABLE III.

General school statistics as reported by school inspectors for the year ending July 8, 1907.

Counties.	Number of townships and cities reporting.	Whole number of school districts.	Number of districts that maintained school.	Number of graded school districts.	Number of township unit districts.	Number of children 5 years of age and under 20.	Number of children 5 years of age and under 20 that attended school during the year.	Whole number of days of school.	Percentage of attendance.	Number of schoolhouses.	Estimated value of school property.	Number of school houses to be built during ensuing year.	Average number months of school.
Totals	1,308	7,302	7,241	578	146	743,030	523,969	1,234,166	69	8,390	$30,944,034	148	8.5
Alcona	11	36	35	1	3	2,072	1,482	5,780	57	36	$31,800	....	8.2
Alger	8	8	8	3	8	1,981	1,682	1,415	76	32	50,191	1	9.0
Allegan	24	185	185	15	......	11,306	8,732	31,286	73	195	266,769	....	5.5
Alpena	8	19	18	2	5	6,370	3,712	3,227	64	69	120,710	....	8.9
Antrim	15	72	71	6	......	4,763	3,959	11,741	63	76	167,110	1	8.3
Arenac	11	42	41	7	......	3,560	2,612	7,300	67	42	68,350	2	8.9
Baraga	5	5	5	2	5	1,842	1,215	928	73	24	67,432	3	9.3
Barry	17	144	143	5	......	5,679	4,439	23,913	70	147	201,070	....	8.4
Bay	15	70	70	8	1	22,825	11,867	12,450	64	93	722,880	3	8.9
Benzie	12	53	52	6	......	3,227	2,831	8,110	66	54	91,475	1	7.8
Berrien	23	146	145	19	......	14,627	10,807	23,991	75	159	459,902	2	8.3
Branch	17	127	125	5	......	6,349	5,016	21,369	74	131	262,500	....	8.5
Calhoun	23	164	164	8	......	12,523	9,688	28,385	74	184	831,625	2	8.6
Cass	16	112	112	5	......	5,005	4,065	18,917	70	114	209,266	....	8.4
Charlevoix	15	67	67	4	......	5,370	4,447	10,670	66	75	165,203	....	8.0
Cheboygan	18	57	56	3	3	5,935	4,149	9,077	64	76	135,934	3	8.1
Chippewa	15	56	56	4	8	7,228	5,242	9,553	67	90	289,640	5	8.5
Clare	17	67	60	3	......	3,290	2,457	9,575	67	62	48,735	3	8.0
Clinton	17	29	129	7	......	6,335	4,617	21,880	70	130	193,849	1	8.5
Crawford	5	29	24	1	......	1,106	961	3,119	72	26	29,844	2	6.5
Delta	15	29	29	2	9	9,404	6,610	4,867	69	71	294,498	....	9.1
Dickinson	8	8	8	2	6	6,564	4,982	1,536	91	37	343,700	7	9.6
Eaton	18	44	144	9	......	7,156	5,724	24,728	70	152	285,025	....	8.6
Emmet	16	73	72	5	......	5,416	4,027	11,234	66	78	148,120	....	7.8
Genesee	20	57	157	13	......	10,509	8,516	27,667	71	167	542,318	2	8.8

Gladwin	13	52	50	3	2	2,878	2,245	8,414	65	52	70,025	1	8.4
Gogebic	8	8	8	3	6	6,394	4,845	1,429	82	37	343,725	5	8.9
Grand Traverse	14	67	67	3	......	6,290	5,452	10,588	70	73	245,930	5	7.9
Gratiot	19	132	132	11	......	8,256	6,669	22,107	71	135	228,100	2	8.4
Hillsdale	19	163	163	14	......	7,237	5,860	28,033	74	166	330,900	1	8.6
Houghton	15	35	35	7	8	24,639	17,398	6,799	79	108	1,062,329	1	9.7
Huron	27	121	119	20	......	11,922	8,301	21,674	63	121	235,690	6	9.1
Ingham	17	137	137	11	......	10,623	7,779	23,608	69	155	422,660	2	8.6
Ionia	18	141	141	12	......	8,631	6,403	24,597	75	148	271,091	1	8.7
Iosco	13	31	31	7	1	3,387	2,571	5,269	66	38	53,950	1	8.5
Iron	7	7	7	4	7	3,151	2,349	1,364	78	35	199,200	3	9.7
Isabella	17	106	106	3	......	6,965	4,707	17,845	63	108	140,825	......	8.4
Jackson	20	155	153	9	......	11,269	8,056	26,667	69	171	610,100	1	8.7
Kalamazoo	17	133	133	8	......	13,086	9,256	22,798	74	145	822,475	......	8.6
Kalkaska	11	51	50	3	......	2,264	1,820	7,976	60	52	76,150	2	8.0
Kent	25	205	204	17	......	39,629	24,831	35,887	69	244	2,048,850	2	8.8
Keweenaw	5	5	5	......	3	1,553	1,142	968	69	12	43,500	......	9.7
Lake	11	44	43	3	......	1,521	1,170	6,134	72	45	36,450	1	7.1
Lapeer	1[illegible]	134	134	11	......	7,051	5,447	23,867	72	135	184,300	......	8.9
Leelanau	11	58	58	3	......	3,538	2,531	8,412	64	58	62,627	......	7.2
Lenawee	24	196	194	12	......	11,883	9,076	33,777	76	209	520,805	1	8.7
Livingston	16	135	134	4	......	4,585	3,601	22,887	67	138	155,275	2	8.5
Luce	4	4	4	1	4	952	868	746	67	13	24,500	1	9.3
Mackinac	14	14	13	2	12	2,625	1,963	2,112	71	56	66,600	3	8.1
Macomb	15	113	113	14	......	9,814	6,188	20,262	68	120	315,056	1	8.9
Manistee	14	64	64	6	......	9,220	5,341	10,505	69	69	215,265	2	8.2
Marquette	21	21	21	6	18	13,526	9,794	3,961	72	77	735,962	6	9.4
Mason	15	64	64	3	......	6,566	4,625	10,655	67	73	245,070	1	8.3
Mecosta	17	108	108	7	......	6,208	4,769	17,322	66	111	500,338	1	8.0
Menominee	11	41	41	3	6	9,601	6,447	6,819	69	92	298,305	6	8.3
Midland	17	81	79	3	......	4,674	3,618	12,992	60	84	109,543	......	8.2
Missaukee	14	62	62	4	......	3,615	2,941	9,903	61	65	90,612	1	8.0
Monroe	16	138	138	4	......	9,[illegible]49	6,519	23,803	69	141	213,725	......	8.6
Montcalm	22	141	141	13	......	9,580	7,530	24,522	69	146	210,455	4	8.7
Montmorency	7	8	8	2	6	1,175	969	1,400	67	30	21,935	1	8.7
Muskegon	20	92	89	9	......	11,724	9,422	14,515	73	108	1,941,326	......	7.9
Newaygo	22	118	118	5	......	6,032	4,701	18,651	68	121	141,710	1	7.9
Oakland	26	201	197	15	......	10,835	8,232	34,521	68	210	572,225	2	8.7
Oceana	16	91	89	4	......	5,383	4,117	14,669	70	93	123,750	2	8.2
Ogemaw	13	49	49	3	1	3,154	2,425	8,022	62	52	60,150	4	8.2
Ontonagon	10	10	10	5	19	2,461	2,078	1,726	78	44	106,420	4	8.6
Osceola	16	93	93	7	......	6,003	4,518	15,261	66	94	122,750	1	8.2
Oscoda	4	18	16	......	1	759	572	2,219	61	25	22,985	2	7.5
Otsego	9	38	35	4	1	2,257	1,745	5,294	64	40	65,400	1	7.6
Ottawa	17	124	124	23	......	13,678	9,941	21,892	76	132	390,300	2	8.8

TABLE III.—Concluded.

Counties.	Number of townships and cities reporting.	Whole number of school districts.	Number of districts that maintained school.	Number of graded school districts.	Number of township unit districts.	Number of children 5 years of age and under 20.	Number of children 5 years of age and under 20 that attended school during the year.	Whole number of days of school.	Percentage of attendance.	Number of schoolhouses.	Estimated value of school property.	Number of school houses to be built during ensuing year.	Average number months of school.
Presque Isle	14	38	37	3	3	3,490	2,171	5,505	63	47	49,788	5	7.4
Roscommon	7	26	24	1	......	593	429	3,030	66	21	10,603	2	6.3
Saginaw	30	164	164	9	......	26,229	14,833	28,795	69	187	1,127,994	1	8.8
St. Clair	26	156	156	8	......	16,429	10,446	27,674	66	172	951,850	2	8.9
St. Joseph	18	123	123	8	......	5,937	4,930	20,894	73	130	332,375	......	8.5
Sanilac	27	155	154	24	......	11,160	9,060	28,012	61	156	220,293	2	9.0
Schoolcraft	10	10	10	1	9	2,619	1,922	1,783	77	33	90,785	2	8.9
Shiawassee	18	124	122	10	......	7,988	6,073	21,811	74	129	381,345	......	8.9
Tuscola	23	150	149	12	......	10,047	7,339	26,776	63	153	230,350	2	9.0
Van Buren	19	153	152	15	......	9,349	7,298	25,526	74	158	314,275	1	8.4
Washtenaw	22	166	165	8	......	11,496	7,896	28,906	73	177	715,860	......	8.7
Wayne	22	149	149	22	......	114,781	72,202	27,159	69	239	5,500,104	7	9.1
Wexford	17	80	80	6	......	6,166	4,699	12,705	68	87	230,527	3	7.9

TABLE IV.

Employment of teachers as reported by school inspectors for the year ending July 8, 1907.

Counties.	Number of teachers required.		Number of different teachers employed.		Aggregate number of months taught.		Total wages of teachers.			Average monthly wages.	
	Graded schools.	Ungraded schools.	Men.	Women.	Men.	Women.	Men.	Women.	Total.	Men.	Women.
Totals	8,256	7,426	2,502	14,784	20,484	123,673	$1,377,846 24	$5,709,743 32	$7,087,589 56	$67 26	$46 17
Alcona	4	37	11	34	89	254	$3,809 00	$9,453 75	$13,262 75	$42 80	$37 22
Alger	37	17	10	50	89	430	5,985 00	21,450 00	27,435 00	67 25	49 88
Allegan	86	182	59	255	431	1,890	23,495 35	70,319 56	93,814 91	54 51	37 21
Alpena	56	60	8	126	55	975	4,510 00	36,695 75	41,205 75	82 00	37 94
Antrim	55	68	24	121	178	887	10,971 00	35,831 25	46,802 25	61 64	40 40
Arenac	27	36	18	53	146	454	7,245 00	17,543 35	24,788 35	49 62	38 64
Baraga	29	9	8	33	65	303	5,475 00	14,156 25	19,631 25	84 23	46 72
Barry	48	142	48	166	369	1,291	18,531 00	48,997 82	67,528 82	50 22	37 95
Bay	212	82	36	265	337	2,506	26,859 67	113,327 09	140,186 76	79 70	45 24
Benzie	41	48	15	86	127	618	7,367 12	23,248 64	30,615 76	58 01	37 62
Berrien	181	143	60	272	498	2,297	33,120 21	96,962 09	130,082 30	66 71	42 21
Branch	68	123	50	176	371	1,303	20,196 40	51,926 55	72,122 95	54 44	39 85
Calhoun	194	160	44	338	369	2,922	28,043 21	124,315 73	152,358 94	78 71	42 55
Cass	56	109	34	154	288	1,173	15,756 00	44,985 38	60,741 38	54 01	38 34
Charlevoix	66	69	15	135	127	1,004	8,038 57	40,286 44	48,325 01	63 30	41 26
Cheboygan	41	73	16	107	143	862	9,422 50	35,918 05	45,340 55	65 90	40 51
Chippewa	83	14	28	138	250	1,163	17,576 00	53,734 07	71,310 07	70 30	46 20
Clare	20	60	21	87	125	535	6,114 25	18,797 13	24,911 38	48 91	35 13
Clinton	53	125	32	166	243	1,332	13,412 38	48,447 92	61,860 30	55 20	36 37
Crawford	11	27	4	46	31	265	1,935 25	10,101 50	12,036 75	62 43	38 12
Delta	81	85	15	161	138	1,397	11,346 75	62,392 60	73,739 35	82 22	44 66
Dickinson	74	41	18	123	146	962	15,191 15	62,210 92	77,402 07	104 11	64 67
Eaton	91	137	30	227	237	1,824	14,927 25	71,236 41	86,163 66	62 98	39 06
Emmet	59	69	27	133	185	889	11,514 25	35,981 12	47,495 37	62 24	40 47
Genesee	137	145	56	244	465	2,176	27,153 75	85,798 70	112,952 45	58 40	39 43

TABLE IV.—Concluded.

Counties.	Number of teachers required.		Number of different teachers employed.		Aggregate number of months taught.		Total wages of teachers.			Average monthly wages.	
	Graded schools.	Ungraded schools.	Men.	Women.	Men.	Women.	Men.	Women.	Total.	Men.	Women.
Gladwin	16	49	15	56	123	440	$5,157 00	$15,381 58	$20,538 58	$41 93	$34 96
Gogebic	14	23	10	125	97	1,244	10,550 00	64,532 25	75,082 25	108 76	51 87
Grand Traverse	69	70	24	128	196	1,020	12,360 53	45,526 70	57,887 23	63 06	44 71
Gratiot	76	24	46	205	295	1,427	14,959 54	55,114 25	70,073 79	50 71	38 62
Hillsdale	87	55	66	204	509	1,636	24,142 25	55,692 66	79,834 91	47 43	34 04
Houghton	93	88	48	462	442	4,269	46,442 20	237,355 20	283,797 40	105 07	50 91
Huron	75	12	51	137	486	1,233	25,859 00	46,155 00	72,014 00	53 20	37 43
Ingham	48	27	39	284	295	2,209	19,825 95	95,825 78	115,651 73	67 21	43 76
Ionia	105	31	37	232	272	1,878	14,899 50	70,814 69	85,714 19	54 78	37 12
Iosco	43	25	10	62	85	542	5,269 00	20,473 23	25,742 23	61 99	37 77
Iron	73	10	9	77	82	729	6,022 50	36,473 50	42,496 00	73 45	50 02
Isabella	28	103	23	134	190	958	10,949 39	37,387 85	48,337 24	57 60	39 03
Jackson	143	117	49	293	338	2,357	21,548 50	97,545 19	119,093 69	63 75	41 39
Kalamazoo	201	133	67	300	496	2,527	31,991 75	116,775 05	148,766 80	64 50	46 21
Kalkaska	17	47	8	66	59	471	2,866 50	18,979 00	21,845 50	48 58	40 29
Kent	59	98	72	697	615	6,387	48,815 00	373,678 72	422,493 72	79 37	58 51
Keweenaw		31	7	25	69	230	4,819 00	10,894 25	15,713 25	71 92	47 37
Lake	10	40	8	55	63	316	2,962 50	10,451 75	13,414 25	47 02	33 07
Lapeer	60	26	32	162	287	1,427	15,480 60	51,364 61	66,845 21	53 94	35 99
Leelanau	12	60	16	65	117	430	6,886 00	16,906 75	23,792 75	58 85	39 46
Lenawee	126	188	49	301	412	2,451	24,968 17	96,929 12	121,897 29	60 60	39 55
Livingston	37	133	42	159	291	1,207	12,723 50	37,953 04	50,676 54	43 62	31 44
Luce	17	12	4	30	33	246	2,860 50	11,260 05	14,120 55	86 68	45 61
Mackinac	15	52	16	69	104	473	5,902 50	20,456 50	26,359 00	56 75	43 25
Macomb	86	100	34	158	318	1,408	19,683 31	52,898 07	72,581 38	61 90	37 57
Manistee	87	74	23	154	186	1,299	12,989 00	56,672 62	69,661 62	69 83	43 63
Marquette	97	60	25	252	236	2,362	25,830 00	129,210 00	155,040 00	109 45	54 70
Mason	58	70	16	121	139	996	8,794 42	42,748 02	51,542 44	70 47	42 92
Mecosta	45	103	19	161	147	1,113	7,700 28	40,917 16	48,677 44	52 79	36 76
Menominee	98	85	20	155	185	1,386	14,023 33	62,547 51	76,573 84	75 82	45 13

Midland	28	79	17	04	31	92	6,219 74	27,778 65	33,998 39	47 48	35 07
Missaukee	23	62	22	96	54	47	7,775 50	20,284 00	28,050 50	50 49	37 08
Monroe	39	148	41	72	86	1,33	15,439 85	48,539 85	63,979 70	50 46	36 14
Montcalm	73	132	38	99	36	1,61	17,033 00	59,451 25	76,484 25	53 90	36 90
Montmorency	15	21	8	30	68	30	3,010 00	8,449 00	11,459 00	44 26	33 80
Muskegon	165	81	29	232	269	2,021	26,777 00	98,251 65	25 ,08 65	99 54	49 11
Newaygo	35	116	29	171	193	1,064	9,331 25	38,409 85	47,81 10	48 35	36 10
Oakland	133	188	31	297	287	2,662	19,609 90	97,571 16	17 ,81 06	68 33	36 63
Oceana	36	93	27	117	195	904	10,117 50	34,554 87	44,62 37	51 88	38 22
Ogemaw	16	48	8	59	68	474	3,542 50	16,554 90	20,07 40	52 19	34 93
Ontonagon	70	15	9	83	83	689	7,500 00	33,438 25	40,938 25	90 36	48 53
Osceola	48	90	31	131	230	954	12,171 70	36,239 10	48,410 80	52 92	37 99
Oscoda	....	27	5	27	31	161	1,165 00	5,076 50	6,241 50	37 58	31 53
Otsego	24	37	5	67	46	45	2,932 50	16,953 6?	19,886 18	63 75	40 85
Ottawa	136	108	43	217	374	1,890	23,125 79	74,770 75	97,896 54	61 83	39 51
Presque Isle	24	39	18	54	132	95	6,732 45	15,720 90	22,453 35	51 00	39 80
Roscommon	4	23	6	30	32	47	1,596 25	5,164 00	6,760 25	49 88	35 13
Saginaw	281	171	64	408	565	3,38	46,152 25	175,613 92	221,766 17	81 69	46 98
St. Clair	146	153	36	277	324	2,72	21,366 25	101,138 99	122,505 24	65 95	40 91
St. Joseph	87	116	48	188	355	1,45	18,845 49	52,986 30	71,831 79	53 09	36 67
Sanilac	66	33	77	33	663	1,54	33,83 55	43,692 06	76,875 61	50 05	36 66
Schoolcraft	31	30	9	59	65	88	5,43 75	23,435 71	28,849 46	83 29	44 39
Shiawassee	08	15	41	99	357	1,34	21,91 77	66,738 81	87,830 58	59 08	38 49
Tuscola	70	43	40	86	362	1,63	19,04 35	56,152 37	75,656 72	53 88	34 81
Van Buren	08	40	41	20	355	1,818	22,007 28	70,116 76	92,24 14	09	38 58
Washtenaw	80	59	38	97	340	2,618	30,154 90	103,326 10	33 .81 00	88 69	39 47
Wayne	1,88	45	151	1,57	1,400	14,753	162,202 34	1,068,273 10	1,20 ,35 44	115 76	72 41
Wexford	67	77	18	69	114	1,099	8,503 50	48,022 67	56,36 17	760	43 70

TABLE V.

Resources of school districts as reported by school inspectors for the year ending July 8, 1907.

Counties.	Ordinary receipts. One-mill tax.	Primary school interest fund.	Library moneys.	Tuition of non-resident pupils.	District taxes for all purposes.	Raised from all other sources.	Total net receipts.	Received from loans.	Money on hand July 9, 1906.	Total resources including amount on hand and loans.
Totals	$1,058,866 43	$8,803,794 67	$144,622 40	$120,112 81	$4,223,343 58	$909,154 75	$15,259,894 64	$1,072,233 91	$2,870,321 06	$19,202,449 61
Alcona	$552 79	$25,199 41	$30 25	$25 88	$6,129 58	$2,182 58	$34,120 49	$1,150 00	$9,710 97	$44,981 46
Alger	322 80	21,842 00	1,472 22	....	43,648 19	1,143 34	68,428 55	36,350 00	9,741 06	114,519 61
Allegan	20,393 87	139,980 35	1,734 19	2,895 50	40,410 97	5,431 54	210,846 42	2,344 90	39,423 82	252,615 14
Alpena	65 00	82,435 00	624 48	1 00	25,700 38	820 22	109,655 08	12,367 50	7,014 22	129,036 80
Antrim	4,773 91	58,395 96	230 52	85	31,443 65	2,894 30	98,273 19	6,483 18	26,200 17	130,956 54
Arenac	85 31	43,929 47	233 07	149 42	11,415 18	4,373 47	60,885 92	1,458 88	17,479 09	79,823 89
Baraga	1,825 52	21,507 00	715 58	....	20,110 62	5,176 48	49,035 20	22,000 00	8,134 68	79,169 88
Barry	13,91 72	69,731 43	688 09	2,051 76	27,735 19	2,403 20	116,501 39	14,043 90	17,432 28	147,977 57
Bay	63	269,119 00	418 42	1,285 55	92,710 54	8,173 39	375,707 83	3,681 80	50,312 65	429,702 28
Benzie	62	37,327 58	59 00	139 01	21,128 85	1,174 93	61,881 49	4,344 90	9,526 23	75,752 62
Berrien	15,469 64	171,417 20	2,648 60	4,084 77	72,600 22	8,415 82	274,636 25	54,813 88	47,854 54	377,304 67
Branch	19,575 89	76,647 58	601 70	2,068 40	39,100 38	2,904 35	140,898 30	1,988 45	25,671 02	168,557 77
Calhoun	21,994 21	148,132 00	3,157 81	4,077 46	139,963 42	24,159 99	341,484 89	5,646 87	81,999 49	429,131 25
Cass	12,875 90	59,639 26	637 98	1,400 48	31,928 60	2,028 19	108,510 41	5,553 41	16,682 94	130,746 76
Charlevoix	3,791 95	63,591 10	693 12	207 87	32,043 93	4,110 47	104,438 44	5,200 28	20,914 45	130,553 17
Cheboygan	5,349 03	43,943 24	1,348 53	501 49	34,467 68	40,987 21	126,597 18	11,500 00	20,708 91	158,806 09
Chippewa	11,360 83	83,514 00	717 79	15 85	74,361 74	4,218 07	174,188 28	1,973 00	37,038 26	213,199 54
Clare	564 38	36,143 84	87 69	344 06	15,202 68	6,206 34	58,548 99	8,605 00	14,938 64	82,092 63
Clinton	17,831 81	79,454 69	491 58	1,962 06	29,046 43	5,397 85	134,184 42	4,143 35	27,305 25	165,633 02
Crawford	590 07	13,646 00	55 20	....	10,498 13	1,524 20	26,313 60	2,000 00	8,099 47	36,413 07
Delta	2,076 36	102,101 00	451 93	365 72	85,505 15	8,318 61	198,818 77	28,000 00	40,466 92	267,285 69
Dickinson	9,233 21	78,046 00	750 15	1,806 07	81,183 79	3,504 34	174,523 56	914 00	66,442 23	241,879 79
Eaton	20,124 83	83,810 77	431 91	3,453 98	47,950 41	2,197 99	157,969 89	12,570 39	28,692 16	199,232 44
Emmet	4,872 10	59,235 14	349 12	265 98	41,925 95	2,851 56	109,499 85	2,615 72	18,759 12	130,874 69
Genesee	28,634 17	129,220 50	1,255 67	5,043 73	68,217 95	2,797 88	235,169 90	5,095 29	21,091 54	261,956 73
Gladwin	1,392 44	35,364 00	195 39	303 55	11,303 90	1,706 38	50,265 66	3,150 11	14,464 31	67,880 08
Gogebic	16,437 61	68,341 00	448 15	153 00	102,310 78	11,059 38	198,749 92	54,000 00	46,739 71	299,489 63
Grand Traverse	7,718 24	74,113 35	293 26	1,238 12	36,601 96	3,159 06	123,123 99	2,273 34	15,100 85	140,498 18
Gratiot	11,612 16	100,065 62	831 82	1,335 54	39,606 55	3,857 29	157,307 98	7,040 30	22,155 15	186,503 43
Hillsdale	21,536 12	87,841 70	615 54	3,455 91	40,864 67	2,670 80	156,984 80	21,301 32	28,344 03	206,630 15

Houghton	102,571 78	290,076 00	3,962 68	4,841 70	236,909 20	11,869 43	650,230 79	26,399 34	236,187 16	912,817 29
Huron	9,471 26	149,607 99	290 90	831 65	28,448 62	3,625 38	192,275 80	22,312 06	47,020 09	261,607 95
Ingham	26,076 52	130,203 77	2,348 70	2,814 48	79,134 45	3,681 48	244,259 40	10,632 50	40,186 79	295,078 69
Ionia	17,740 89	105,347 00	527 53	3,541 07	39,308 11	6,823 14	173,287 74	13,272 05	36,742 85	223,302 64
Iosco	1,187 39	42,930 60	44 01	55 50	9,320 73	5,143 83	58,682 06	3,806 51	20,833 52	83,324 09
Iron	2,571 43	34,026 80	630 73	46 88	77,871 12	7,633 64	122,780 60		12,482 35	135,262 95
Isabella	6,281 79	85,488 03	155 19	501 35	19,586 89	4,714 12	116,727 37	4,541 64	20,921 75	142,190 76
Jackson	31,820 08	133,454 68	1,459 77	2,220 35	42,750 84	2,548 04	214,254 36	17,024 85	31,729 56	263,008 77
Kalamazoo	27,971 70	147,690 12	1,797 79	2,981 75	122,947 22	5,583 50	306,972 08	110,521 63	22,027 22	441,520 93
Kalkaska	1,616 50	26,099 00	218 76	119 50	19,101 63	3,477 10	50,632 49	7,451 63	13,305 95	71,390 07
Kent	92,977 75	471,391 04	2,245 48	4,603 55	234,318 11	34,470 92	840,006 85	34,365 06	177,645 22	1,052,017 13
Keweenaw	7,776 43	15,852 00	347 29		12,806 24	1,163 85	37,945 81	81 67	16,039 83	54,327 31
Lake	372 38	17,342 68	205 63	2 50	9,241 63	1,314 83	28,479 65		8,991 83	37,471 48
Lapeer	15,399 55	88,664 56	812 75	2,451 71	22,263 04	1,104 69	130,696 30	10,142 04	29,187 86	170,026 20
Leelanau	2,199 81	43,720 69	30 44	154 06	8,824 07	3,275 02	58,204 09	707 27	9,108 21	68,019 57
Lenawee	35,677 33	144,934 04	2,255 61	4,648 71	68,010 97	2,871 68	258,398 34	27,01 32	36,194 19	321,593 85
Livingston	14,474 99	56,527 85	402 52	2,249 58	15,533 07	748 41	89,936 42	1,[illegible]0 13	14,495 36	106,181 91
Luce	149 51	10,609 00	252 82		18,421 04	1,075 09	30,507 46	75 00	8,047 99	38,930 45
Mackinac	2,248 21	31,197 25	379 37	65 93	22,897 70	2,208 77	59,057 23		15,510 93	74,568 13
Macomb	19,286 14	123,419 00	1,616 60	2,297 63	30,503 32	10,075 23	187,177 92	14,[illegible]	43,988 31	245,911 89
Manistee	8,094 35	111,809 10	137 13	952 01	25,983 92	8,013 95	54,[illegible]90 46	3,875 00	28,364 85	187,230 31
Marquette	24,296 41	159,101 00	1,511 99	67 50	155,206 13	5,948 67	3[illegible],31 70	8,400 00	59,153 52	413,685 22
Mason	5,548 65	76,603 15	505 67	746 40	31,854 66	6,028 53	121,287 06	14,125 00	14,883 66	150,295 72
Mecosta	2,483 55	76,598 59	893 49	383 24	24,747 50	5,091 34	110,797 71	4,800 46	35,162 75	150,760 92
Menominee	6,755 22	114,018 00	55 80	421 50	58,017 40	8,037 64	187,305 56	2,806 00	27,865 36	217,976 92
Midland	2,013 35	58,938 00	56 03	227 50	10,321 31	5,209 42	76,765 61	1,208 18	15,786 27	93,700 06
Missaukee	1,000 97	41,792 52	237 94	74 50	18,632 27	3,467 06	65,205 26	4,655 74	16,509 43	86,430 43
Monroe	18,216 48	119,118 88	827 78	1,484 35	18,841 89	1,979 94	160,469 32	7,584 31	25,591 62	193,645 25
Montcalm	9,340 70	118,048 99	790 03	2,322 23	31,909 45	2,894 75	105,306 15	5,290 55	31,694 02	202,290 72
Montmorency	441 77	13,426 00		125 00	8,531 33	1,540 69	24,064 79		7,930 58	31,995 37
Muskegon	14,434 01	146,381 32	1,81 86	1,374 65	63,022 23	49,663 42	276,657 49	543 96	51,992 68	329,194 13
Newaygo	3,828 45	71,345 58	47 18	876 60	21,669 38	6,093 42	103,960 61	4,863 15	25,020 08	133,843 84
Oakland	31,173 54	127,105 65	85 61	4,781 54	61,070 20	2,381 74	227,138 28	12,474 96	39,692 63	279,305 87
Oceana	4,745 55	65,309 00	83 90	905 19	22,613 39	5,830 52	99,707 55	2,661 41	21,452 54	123,821 50
Ogemaw	580 97	35,977 28	47 67	168 42	16,135 54	3,431 78	56,441 66	975 00	23,502 07	80,918 73
Ontonagon	2,384 16	25,866 00	80 76	242 20	55,755 61	2,601 42	87,380 15	15,500 00	15,556 06	118,436 21
Osceola	3,289 11	69,728 11	87 98	721 98	28,016 37	3,818 59	106,002 14	4,392 77	21,225 22	131,620 13
Oscoda	38 41	6,405 00	32 17	10 50	5,072 25	11,160 39	22,718 72	500 00	3,037 54	26,256 26
Otsego	1,709 57	25,966 73	91 19	121 12	17,037 83	2,460 27	47,586 71		9,429 62	57,016 33
Ottawa	15,068 76	162,450 80	44 91	1,565 19	46,327 64	5,531 52	231,408 82	38,315 03	43,945 75	313,669 60
Presque Isle	1,398 90	42,643 00	123 54	84 26	14,361 94	1,404 26	60,015 90	3,360 74	15,043 79	78,420 43
Roscommon	153 41	5,597 38	8 70		3,044 11	3,993 23	12,796 83	391 77	7,396 82	20,585 42
Saginaw	10,027 34	321,943 28	3,358 73	3,342 25	110,844 27	184,783 15	634,299 02	34,153 65	66,312 10	734,764 77
St. Clair	25,547 85	196,954 20	6,532 49	875 40	66,356 05	33,628 44	329,894 43	9,161 54	33,896 92	372,952 89
St. Joseph	16,936 46	71,528 00	936 02	2,416 01	52,535 04	2,236 46	146,587 99	35,473 67	17,596 45	199,658 11

TABLE V.—CONCLUDED.

Counties.	Ordinary receipts.							Received from loans.	Money on hand July 9, 1906.	Total resources including amount on hand and loans.
	One-mill tax.	Primary school interest fund.	Library moneys.	Tuition of non-resident pupils.	District taxes for all purposes.	Raised from all other sources.	Total net receipts.			
Sanilac	$12,894 27	$142,329 00	$179 23	$1,519 39	$35,020 36	$2,771 45	$194,713 70	$18,600 76	$29,631 92	$242,946 38
Schoolcraft	2,056 79	30,529 40	686 10	318 18	33,877 08	1,775 59	69,243 14	60 00	6,429 06	75,732 20
Shiawassee	22,777 33	101,836 00	777 31	2,067 35	39,327 82	2,989 92	169,775 73	4,520 00	24,173 73	198,469 46
Tuscola	12,713 96	127,223 56	281 94	2,902 28	31,985 79	2,878 89	177,986 41	10,176 73	41,395 97	229,559 11
Van Buren	14,739 35	113,315 42	767 65	4,982 67	51,597 95	4,325 00	189,728 04	17,247 23	29,927 87	236,903 14
Washtenaw	36,964 06	128,719 06	962 62	7,697 27	78,511 41	22,686 38	275,540 80	95,634 77	26,864 09	398,039 66
Wayne	42,264 66	1,316,146 69	77,442 88	2,413 47	467,023 32	210,015 76	2,115,306 78	50,299 00	378,451 59	2,544 057 37
Wexford	5,631 12	66,722 69	542 71	327 75	44,777 67	4,554 78	122,556 72	11,580 40	36,313 37	170,450 49

TABLE VI.

Expenditures of school districts as reported by school inspectors for the year ending July 8, 1907.

Counties.	Ordinary expenditures for maintaining the schools. Paid men teachers.	Paid women teachers.	Paid for building, repairs and site.	Paid for books and care of library.	Paid interest on loans.	Paid for all other purposes.	Total net expenses.	Paid on indebtedness (principal).	Amount on hand July 8, 1907.	Total expenditures including amount on hand and paid on indebtedness.
Totals	$1,378,430 54	$5,713,435 82	$2,530,991 12	$174,359 97	$167,468,61	$2,121,196,86	$12,085,882 92	$781,496 72	$6,335,009 97	$19,202,449 61
Alcona	$3,809 00	$9,523 75	$2,971 08	....	$300 57	$3,205 21	$19,869 61	$1,200 00	$23,911 85	$44,981 46
Alger	5,985 00	21,450 00	46,073 62	$489 32	1,317 26	15,508 91	90,824 11	10,447 19	13,248 31	114,519 61
Allegan	23,495 35	70,319 56	14,460 30	1,014 82	828 77	21,140 21	131,259 01	7,594 57	113,761 56	252,615 14
Alpena	4,510 00	36,812 50	8,206 95	724 81	217 84	11,030 98	61,503 08	13,272 25	54,261 47	129,036 80
Antrim	11,008 95	35,831 25	12,256 95	389 43	271 66	12,733 51	72,491 75	4,039 03	54,425 76	130,956 54
Arenac	7,302 00	17,543 25	7,619 55	220 59	640 41	7,352 35	40,678 25	2,066 86	37,078 78	79,823 89
Baraga	5,475 00	14,156 25	27,208 25	50 00	28 00	9,232 32	56,149 82	4,000 00	19,020 06	79,169 88
Barry	18,531 00	48,997 82	13,959 10	1,105 82	619 61	11,464 67	94,678 02	14,839 02	38,460 53	147,977 57
Bay	26,859 67	113,327 09	60,775 61	323 98	7,815 30	48,984 73	258,086 38	4,709 77	166,906 13	429,702 28
Benzie	7,367 12	23,318 64	10,584 71	301 61	754 75	8,041 79	50,368 62	3,724 95	21,659 05	75,752 62
Berrien	33,120 21	96,962 09	46,450 35	935 09	2,313 49	47,156 09	226,937 32	19,531 23	130,836,12	377,304 67
Branch	20,196 40	51,926 55	7,727 78	788 17	492 59	17,556 26	98,687 75	5,479 35	64,390 67	168,557 77
Calhoun	28,043 21	124,355 73	74,608 60	3,928 06	655 69	45,565 51	277,156 80	5,412 33	146,562 12	429,131 25
Cass	15,756 00	44,985 78	5,494 63	350 97	1,283 11	14,064 17	81,934 23	13,030 00	35,782 50	130,746 76
Charlevoix	8,038 57	40,303 94	10,513 98	750 37	2,848 06	13,282 67	75,737 59	11,311 47	43,504 11	130,553 17
Cheboygan	9,422 50	35,918 05	22,882 38	1,029 61	1,862 20	32,577 23	103,091 97	8,904 43	46,709 69	158,806 09
Chippewa	17,576 00	53,772 82	7,922 71	287 76	5,515 28	27,200 66	112,275 23	3,584 28	97,340 03	213,199 54
Clare	6,114 25	18,939 13	6,187 67	113 61	89 68	6,054 97	37,499 31	925 14	43,668 18	82,092 63
Clinton	13,412 38	48,447 92	11,306 16	1,548 28	365 92	16,581 44	91,662 10	4,594 41	69,376 51	165,633 02
Crawford	1,935 25	10,101 50	2,081 67	11 25	398 00	3,271 42	17,799 09	3,998 51	14,615 47	36,413 07
Delta	11,346 75	62,392 60	93,177 38	517 48	4,687 40	34,352 76	206,474 37	4,893 52	55,917 80	267,285 69
Dickinson	15,191 15	62,210 92	45,569 52	3,461 94	5,028 00	40,728 01	172,189 54	7,680 00	62,010 25	241,879 79
Eaton	14,927 25	71,236 41	18,440 74	718 24	469 95	20,199 17	125,991 76	10,203 89	63,036 79	199,232 44
Emmet	11,514 25	35,941 12	9,599 29	818 02	1,701 42	10,890 57	70,464 67	3,154 94	57,255 08	130,874 69
Genesee	27,153 75	85,798 70	14,623 47	6,029 53	3,199 47	32,124 60	168,929 52	11,815 87	81,211 34	261,956 73
Gladwin	5,282 00	15,381 58	6,908 84	180 00	1,533 49	4,947 47	34,233 38	2,377 25	31,269 45	67,880 08
Gogebic	10,550 00	64,532 25	41,777 68	640 47	4,390 00	45,435 18	167,325 58	2,750 00	129,414 05	299,489 63
Grand Traverse	12,360 53	45,526 70	14,939 90	1,023 03	1,633 80	19,090 66	94,574 12	11,773 20	34,150 80	140,498 18
Gratiot	14,959 54	54,834 25	17,606 00	856 39	1,235 28	23,474 66	112,966 12	3,436 19	70,101 12	186,503 43
Hillsdale	24,142 26	55,692 66	19,512 17	733 74	2,310 90	18,965 91	121,357 63	29,581 18	55,691 34	206,630 15

TABLE VI.—CONCLUDED.

Counties.	Ordinary expenditures for maintaining the schools.							Paid on indebtedness (principal).	Amount on hand July 8, 1907.	Total expenditures including amount on hand and paid on indebtedness.
	Paid men teachers.	Paid women teachers.	Paid for building, repairs and site.	Paid for books and care of library.	Paid interest on loans.	Paid for all other purposes.	Total net expenses.			
Houghton	$46,442 20	$237,355 20	$144,382 83	$4,226 71	$1,471 84	$114,095 55	$550,974 33	$15,648 81	$346,194 15	$912,817 29
Huron	25,859 00	46,155 00	31,318 29	350 81	3,154 17	19,440 33	126,277 60	11,971 52	123,358 83	261,607 95
Ingham	19,825 95	95,875 78	28,509 59	7,528 50	1,538 29	33,103 05	186,381 16	13,017 75	95,679 78	295,078 69
Ionia	14,899 50	70,814 69	25,675 30	346 25	954 52	20,149 31	132,839 57	7,490 55	82,972 52	223,302 64
Iosco	5,241 50	20,473 23	8,492 66	43 35	223 20	6,634 98	41,108 92	915 32	41,299 85	83,324 09
Iron	6,022 50	36,473 50	32,528 43	534 08	1,362 50	27,747 46	104,668 47	9,000 01	21,594 48	135,2 2 95
Isabella	10,949 39	37,387 85	7,634 96	627 27	1,302 72	13,840 33	71,742 52	3,374 00	67,074 24	142,190 76
Jackson	21,548 50	97,545 19	20,486 08	896 54	1,333 04	46,306 12	188,115 47	5,532 12	69,361 18	263,008 77
Kalamazoo	31,991 75	116,775 05	100,830 95	6,723 55	9,768 81	44,474 15	310,564 26	55,545 75	75,410 92	441,520 93
Kalkaska	2,866 50	18,961 50	8,013 79	188 20	611 16	6,152 87	36,794 02	7,281 96	27,314 09	71,390 07
Kent	48,815 00	373,788 72	84,740 62	1,567 68	8,323 54	104,008 29	621,243 65	74,900 25	355,873 03	1,052,017 13
Keweenaw	4,819 00	10,894 25	9,070 36	478 92	....	8,798 20	34,060 73	....	20,266 58	54,327 31
Lake	2,962 50	10,451 75	2,468 49	116 48	44 46	2,976 37	19,020 05	690 56	17,760 87	37,471 48
Lapeer	15,480 60	51,364 61	19,036 84	604 71	394 35	14,389 40	101,270 51	3,936 39	64,819 30	170,026 20
Leelanau	6,886 00	16,906 75	4,793 90	2 50	154 82	3,278 48	32,022 45	1,253 92	34,743 20	68,019 57
Lenawee	24,968 17	96,929 12	31,752 47	4,592 55	2,546 43	27,267 51	188,056 25	33,063 31	100,474 29	321,593 85
Livingston	12,723 50	37,953 04	7,072 02	279 11	223 24	9,595 47	67,846 38	2,284 25	36,051 28	106,181 91
Luce	2,860 50	11,260 05	2,694 93	127 02	....	5,830 53	22,773 03	562 83	15,594 59	38,930 45
Mackinac	5,902 50	20,456 50	7,914 15	106 07	644 87	11,203 26	46,227 35	303 00	28,037 81	74,568 16
Macomb	19,683 31	52,898 07	17,228 55	2,405 50	965 12	24,975 91	118,156 46	7,901 35	119,854 08	245,911 89
Manistee	12,989 00	56,672 62	13,630 30	334 44	848 05	25,252 52	109,726 93	4,772 85	72,730 53	187,230 31
Marquette	25,830 00	129,210 00	69,374 51	1,770 94	7,113 74	57,861 81	291,161 00	7,900 00	114,624 22	413,685 22
Mason	8,794 42	42,748 02	13,429 70	206 19	1,733 31	14,770 54	81,682 18	14,282 80	54,330 74	150,295 72
Mecosta	7,760 28	40,917 16	11,336 18	447 61	423 19	11,277 94	72,162 36	3,982 93	74,615 63	150,760 92
Menominee	14,430 33	64,074 51	20,828 42	343 44	2,506 83	27,918 07	130,101 60	6,774 49	81,100 83	217,976 92
Midland	6,219 74	27,828 65	5,998 63	....	303 97	8,726 70	49,077 69	1,984 67	42,697 70	93,760 06
Missaukee	7,775 50	20,284 00	9,853 39	50 02	742 40	7,432 05	46,137 36	3,967 53	36,325 54	86,430 43
Monroe	15,439 85	48,539 85	13,513 66	1,223 07	1,096 48	13,394 33	93,207 24	6,530 02	91,907 99	193,645 25
Montcalm	17,033 00	59,451 25	9,396 51	373 37	1,467 66	16,602 72	104,324 51	6,526 00	91,440 21	202,290 72
Montmorency	3,010 00	8,414 00	1,219 93	....	9 84	4,653 03	17,306 80	200 00	14,488 57	31,995 37
Muskegon	26,777 00	98,251 65	30,568 97	7,026 96	7,087 12	43,418 95	213,080 65	10,321 82	105,791 66	329,194 13
Newaygo	9,331 25	38,409 85	12,629 70	226 03	373 26	10,063 11	71,033 20	3,029 89	59,780 75	133,843 84
Oakland	19,609 90	97,609 16	10,908 24	850 57	4,818 31	33,281 00	167,077 18	10,020 09	102,208 60	279,305 87
Oceana	10,126 60	34,554 87	11,446 29	162 26	621 14	8,808 32	65,719 48	3,406 65	54,695 37	123,821 50
Ogemaw	3,542 50	16,470 90	6,928 74	210 60	1,150 06	5,331 38	33,634 18	1,480 03	45,804 52	80,918 73

Ontonagon	7,500 00	33,438 25	13,242 20	496 97	1,714 98	21,101 86	77,494 26	16,500 00	24,441 95	118,436 21
Osceola	12,171 70	36,239 10	16,815 02	324 36	330 87	12,429 90	78,310 95	3,325 00	49,984 18	131,620 13
Oscoda	1,040 00	5,076 50	2,450 27	....	44 02	2,754 35	11,365 14	580 50	14,310 62	26,256 26
Otsego	3,142 50	18,918 18	6,361 08	360 47	747 26	5,340 19	34,869 68	3,100 00	19,046 65	57,016 33
Ottawa	23,125 79	74,770 75	47,790 98	1,448 61	2,759 06	30,228 65	180,123 83	22,624 97	110,920 80	313,669 60
Presque Isle	6,732 45	15,720 90	4,467 89	57 86	699 65	6,057 22	33,735 97	3,488 10	41,196 36	78,420 43
Roscommon	1,308 75	5,108 00	1,461 71	27 20	150 25	1,261 85	9,317 76	300 08	10,967 58	20,585 42
Saginaw	46,152 25	175,613 92	242,840 53	5,187 71	3,094 56	67,470 21	540,359 18	16,568 83	177,837 26	734,764 77
St. Clair	21,366 25	101,138 99	50,174 33	5,965 50	1,661 66	39,069 45	219,394 18	8,922 96	144,633 75	372,952 89
St. Joseph	18,845 49	52,986 30	19,239 40	504 65	2,694 89	19,458 62	113,729 35	31,001 65	54,927 11	199,058 11
Sanilac	33,183 55	43,692 06	25,511 45	388 45	1,696 56	16,509 85	121,071 92	8,217 32	113,657 14	242,946 38
Schoolcraft	5,545 00	23,390 71	11,340 78	561 02	659 96	10,183 41	51,680 88	5,605 02	18,445 70	75,732 20
Shiawassee	21,091 77	66,738 81	12,258 11	488 37	1,745 31	23,090 82	125,413 19	12,380 55	60,675 72	198,469 46
Tuscola	19,504 35	56,152 37	19,682 91	438 12	1,384 06	16,903 16	114,064 97	7,912 74	107,581 40	229,559 11
Van Buren	22,007 38	70,116 76	34,042 27	1,004 63	1,619 94	19,891 55	148,682 53	21,211 76	67,008 85	236,903 14
Washtenaw	30,204 90	103,341 60	115,747 34	2,797 60	8,634 01	40,473 12	301,198 57	12,663 71	84,177 38	398,039 66
Wayne	162,202 34	1,068,273 10	364,227 34	79,711 50	13,702 54	318,169 45	2,006,286 27	24,044 77	513,726 33	2,544,057 37
Wexford	8,503 50	48,022 67	26,182 09	283 26	1,059 20	15,359 07	99,409 79	10,864 42	60,176 28	170,450 49

TABLE VII.

Miscellaneous statistics as reported by school inspectors for the year ending July 8, 1907.

Counties.	Bonded indebtedness of the districts.	Total indebtedness of the districts.	Amount due the districts.	Amount paid and due inspectors and members of school boards for services.	Amount paid and due township chairmen and other officers for services.
Totals	$3,636 184 41	$3,870,957 94	$406,793 25	$17,455 25	$43,887 15
Alcona	$5,700 00	$5,804 52	$1,618 00	$64 50	$58 00
Alger	31,200 00	40,049 33	3 00	638 00	924 00
Allegan	13,428 57	13,602 47	4,870 69	213 29	55 79
Alpena	125 00	125 00	2,070 54	343 25	374 85
Antrim	5,300 00	6,562 09	14,753 37	74 70	17 50
Arenac	14,395 00	14,945 18	3,645 25	73 25	21 30
Baraga	20,000 00	20,000 00	180 59	120 00	939 00
Barry	6,042 33	9,303 33	3,008 28	171 25	25 25
Bay	126,300 00	169,776 45	2,893 80	252 50	880 75
Benzie	13,487 37	13,724 42	10,308 42	69 75	7 50
Berrien	56,650 00	58,776 88	7,826 63	175 25	558,25
Branch	9,744 00	10,016 22	1,348 78	107 00	216 50
Calhoun	15,600 00	15,873 18	1,478 79	105 06	719 30
Cass	27,750 00	28,053 41	5,343 35	187 75	109 75
Charlevoix	49,600 00	50,494 25	5,879 84	112 75	21 00
Cheboygan	58,000 00	58,178 09	4,558 83	193 75	155 25
Chippewa	123,993 72	125,959 55	3,694 50	268 00	982 00
Clare	9,647 68	10,032 15	4,571 28	181 00	99 25
Clinton	27,200 00	33,483 60	2,314 57	129 85	33 50
Crawford	5,000 00	5,347 45	1,096 61	66 75	6 50
Delta	106,252 00	106,852 59	1,285 96	301 50	1,503 50
Dickinson	109,065 00	110,0[illegible]5 00	330 29	288 00	1,900 00
Eaton	7,295 00	9,630 89	4,720 31	106 95	348 35
Emmet	33,800 00	34,075 63	9,663 20	174 00	28 00
Genesee	71,490 00	72,791 37	2,476 09	276 28	430 32
Gladwin	28,353 77	29,110 42	2,905 40	141 00	115 75
Gogebic	130,500 00	130,500 00	1,729 00	546 25	1,875 00
Grand Traverse	700 00	976 15	7,181 49	99 00	27 25
Gratiot	40,400 00	41,341 19	8,682 01	118 25	109 75
Hillsdale	35,450 00	53,185 17	6,602 06	139 75	194 07
Houghton	109,200 00	109,399 34	604 38	337 50	619 50
Huron	62,202 80	72,132 72	4,665 80	245 50	78 75
Ingham	23,075 00	29,624 75	4,867 66	96 75	1,009 75
Ionia	14,815 00	14,942 88	1,240 92	89 50	178 00
Iosco	4,650 00	5,308 05	2,935 25	184 75	212 25
Iron	78,500 00	78,500 00	8,797 39	501 50	900 00
Isabella	26,275 00	26,448 14	9,349 03	158 50	230 50
Jackson	73,230 00	74,226 72	3,718 06	127 25	818 45
Kalamazoo	189,726 58	190,520 07	3,869 58	112 75	915 50
Kalkaska	10,250 00	11,742 13	3,175 13	....	....
Kent	201,100 00	203,900 35	7,882 87	212 70	58 15
Keweenaw	....	....	1,491 00	179 50	360 00
Lake	300 00	2,004 96	3,937 85	105 55	19 50
Lapeer	11,491 51	13,827 94	4,056 53	78 50	85 75
Leelanau	2,083 00	2,751 80	6,314 65	123 50	9 00
Lenawee	46,354 00	47,632 73	3,912 84	217 85	104 00
Livingston	3,616 68	4,020 69	2,154 92	114 75	9 75
Luce	....	....	1,130 00	299 00	710 00
Mackinac	9,775 00	9,775 00	2,580 62	427 00	1,583 50
Macomb	30,151 00	30,702 38	459 76	184 25	304 25
Manistee	12,650 00	13,712 33	8,455 59	121 75	216 50
Marquette	156,840 00	158,340 09	293 78	571 50	3,982 00
Mason	27,300 00	28,620 00	7,739 45	114 85	310 00
Mecosta	4,653 00	5,597 46	10,233 61	92 00	165 75
Menominee	27,206 80	34,481 86	8,570 26	662 10	1,331 30

TABLE VII.—CONCLUDED.

Counties.	Bonded indebtedness of the districts.	Total indebtedness of the districts.	Amount due the districts.	Amount paid and due inspectors and members of school boards for services.	Amount paid and due township chairmen and other officers for services.
Midland	$2,696 98	$3,649 92	$3,350 26	$131 50	$98 50
Missaukee	13,773 00	16,863 54	6,202 44	129 25	22 25
Monroe	12,181 20	20,317 29	1,449 40	140 65	52 26
Montcalm	25,458 00	30,602 00	16,494 97	209 75	138 00
Montmorency	100 00	135 00	357 55	531 18	260 09
Muskegon	136,330 00	136,966 73	17,407 70	164 75	52 50
Newaygo	6,924 00	7,851 54	15,747 28	175 50	27 25
Oakland	95,494 00	97,152 25	3,914 09	240 75	198 75
Oceana	14,875 75	14,877 16	9,544 74	247 00	66 25
Ogemaw	19,104 18	19,702 59	4,503 82	186 50	66 90
Ontonagon	25,300 00	26,579 47	2,006 00	534 00	1,680 00
Osceola	5,935 00	6,942 77	11,247 53	163 50	36 50
Oscoda	185 00	228 93	3,857 91	54 00	59 30
Otsego	10,000 00	10,000 00	4,205 85	131 25	54 50
Ottawa	60,007 75	66,786 52	5,106 25	244 50	225 50
Presque Isle	12,830 88	18,134 49	851 03	168 32	95 50
Roscommon	700 00	1,601 21	2,989 10	68 75	9 45
Saginaw	72,000 00	98,219 92	9,383 33	780 50	2,572 00
St. Clair	37,355 00	39,055 61	2,310 55	251 75	219 50
St. Joseph	53,600 00	61,508 48	1,241 64	102 25	241 00
Sanilac	36,030 76	37,729 79	2,540 56	229 50	96 25
Schoolcraft	4,800 00	6,843 12	3,309 39	395 30	1,308 50
Shiawassee	34,400 00	34,866 60	1,945 99	108 75	298 50
Tuscola	25,625 60	26,613 58	6,298 40	228 25	32 75
Van Buren	29,205 01	32,381 98	8,592 23	129 00	60 00
Washtenaw	261,375 00	263,605 23	2,858 15	177 75	223 75
Wayne	318,282 49	330,819 94	8,568 31	289 00	8,701 00
Wexford	13,700 00	14,574 00	10,430 92	164 63	21 02

TABLE VIII.

Cost per capita of public schools of the state for the year ending July 8, 1907.

Counties.	Number of pupils included in school census in—		Number of pupils enrolled in—		Cost per capita for instruction based on school census in—			Cost per capita for instruction based on enrollment in—			Total expenses per capita during year based on enrollment in—		
	Graded school districts.	Ungraded school districts.	Graded school districts.	Ungraded school districts.	Graded school districts.	Ungraded school districts.	All school districts.	Graded school districts.	Ungraded school districts.	All school districts.	Graded school districts.	Ungraded school districts.	All school districts.
Totals	437,183	305,847	305,668	218,301	$10 94	$7 55	$9 54	$15 64	$10 58	$13 53	$28 35	$15 67	$23 06
Alcona	202	1,870	168	1,314	$8 11	$6 25	$6 43	$9 74	$8 90	$8 99	$12 41	$13 53	$13 41
Alger	1,517	464	1,253	429	13 23	15 86	13 85	16 02	17 15	16 31	59 49	37 95	53 99
Allegan	3,458	7,848	2,906	5,826	10 51	7 32	8 21	12 58	9 86	10 74	19 51	12 79	15 03
Alpena	4,000	2,370	2,167	1,545	6 19	6 99	6 48	11 42	10 72	11 13	17 86	14 75	16 56
Antrim	2,125	2,638	1,965	1,994	11 70	8 32	9 83	12 65	11 02	11 83	19 28	17 35	18 31
Arenac	1,450	2,110	1,131	1,481	8 04	6 24	6 97	10 31	8 90	9 51	16 35	14 97	15 57
Baraga	1,541	301	1,016	199	10 23	12 84	10 65	15 51	19 43	16 15	48 71	33 48	46 21
Barry	1,553	4,126	1,343	3,096	15 85	10 40	11 89	18 32	13 86	15 21	31 78	17 22	21 32
Bay	15,517	7,308	7,749	4,118	6 97	4 37	6 14	13 96	7 51	11 81	26 71	12 40	21 75
Benzie	1,643	1,584	1,504	1,327	10 35	8 64	9 51	11 31	10 30	10 84	19 85	15 45	17 79
Berrien	8,103	6,524	6,388	4,419	10 56	6 82	8 89	13 40	10 07	12 03	25 88	13 94	20 91
Branch	2,406	3,943	2,069	2,947	13 62	9 97	11 35	15 84	13 35	14 37	23 67	16 87	19 67
Calhoun	8,101	4,422	6,429	3,259	13 34	10 02	12 17	16 81	13 59	15 73	34 45	17 06	28 71
Cass	1,961	3,044	1,782	2,283	13 57	11 21	12 13	14 93	14 95	14 94	22 45	18 37	20 15
Charlevoix	2,948	2,422	2,497	1,950	9 65	8 20	9 00	11 40	10 19	10 87	18 46	15 20	17 03
Cheboygan	2,775	3,160	1,752	2,397	7 23	7 99	7 64	11 45	11 54	10 92	36 85	16 32	24 99
Chippewa	4,461	2,767	3,252	1,990	10 86	8 27	9 87	14 90	11 49	13 61	24 78	15 92	21 41
Clare	1,034	2,256	856	1,601	8 31	7 29	7 61	10 04	10 27	10 20	16 10	14 81	15 26
Clinton	1,736	4,599	1,600	3,017	13 41	8 38	9 76	14 55	12 78	13 39	26 69	16 22	19 85
Crawford	532	574	457	504	9 77	11 91	10 88	11 38	13 56	12 52	18 18	18 83	18 52
Delta	5,301	4,103	3,703	2,907	7 97	7 66	7 84	11 41	10 82	11 15	41 52	18 13	31 23
Dickinson	4,879	1,685	3,696	1,286	11 41	12 28	11 80	15 07	16 87	15 53	33 74	36 92	34 56
Eaton	3,054	4,102	2,645	3,079	14 24	10 40	12 04	16 44	13 85	15 05	26 29	18 33	22 01
Emmet	2,930	2,486	2,284	1,743	9 67	7 68	8 76	12 41	10 95	11 78	18 30	16 45	17 49
Genesee	5,841	4,668	4,900	3,556	11 85	9 31	10 73	13 97	12 23	13 24	22 56	16 03	19 83
Gladwin	640	2,238	630	1,615	9 70	6 45	7 18	9 85	8 95	9 20	17 73	14 27	10 79
Gogebic	5,577	817	4,184	661	11 67	12 21	11 74	15 56	15 09	15 49	30 41	60 67	34 53
Grand Traverse	3,211	3,079	3,026	2,426	10 89	7 44	9 20	11 56	9 44	10 61	20 82	13 01	17 34
Gratiot	2,904	5,352	2,555	4,114	10 92	7 11	8 45	12 41	9 25	10 46	24 71	12 11	16 94
Hillsdale	2,838	4,399	2,591	3,269	13 23	9 61	11 03	14 53	12 93	13 62	26 34	16 24	20 70
Houghton	20,275	4,364	14,367	3,031	11 35	9 97	11 11	16 72	27 05	16 31	32 76	26 48	31 66
Huron	4,241	7,681	3,062	5,239	7 73	5 11	6 04	10 70	7 49	8 67	21 35	11 02	15 21
Ingham	7,002	3,621	5,060	2,719	11 13	10 41	10 89	15 41	13 88	14 87	27 15	19 84	23 96
Ionia	4,301	4,330	3,361	3,042	11 28	8 58	9 91	14 44	12 22	13 38	25 24	15 78	20 74
Iosco	2,176	1,211	1,710	861	8 52	5 51	7 59	10 84	8 33	10 00	16 70	14 44	15 99
Iron	2,836	315	2,138	211	13 40	14 28	13 48	17 77	21 32	18 09	45 47	35 23	44 55
Isabella	1,461	5,504	895	3,812	9 79	6 18	6 94	15 98	8 92	10 26	28 09	12 22	15 24
Jackson	6,914	4,355	4,933	3,123	11 49	9 09	10 56	16 11	12 68	14 78	27 78	16 35	23 35
Kalamazoo	9,261	3,825	6,478	2,778	11 82	10 26	11 36	16 90	14 12	16 07	40 15	18 16	33 55
Kalkaska	667	1,597	616	1,204	10 63	9 22	9 64	11 51	12 23	11 99	22 24	19 17	20 21
Kent	30,709	8,920	18,371	6,460	11 74	6 94	10 66	19 63	9 58	17 01	29 34	12 71	25 01
Keweenaw	......	1,553	......	1,142	......	10 19	10 19	....	13 75	13 75	......	29 82	29 82
Lake	511	1,010	427	743	7 89	9 28	8 82	9 44	12 62	11 46	13 01	18 12	16 25
Lapeer	2,089	4,962	1,765	3,682	14 04	7 55	9 48	16 73	10 18	12 27	30 19	13 03	18 59
Leelanau	657	2,881	514	2,017	8 24	6 38	6 72	10 55	9 11	9 40	18 28	11 21	12 65
Lenawee	5,279	6,604	4,200	4,876	11 80	9 02	10 26	14 83	12 21	13 43	26 57	15 68	20 72
Livingston	1,160	3,426	968	2,633	13 86	10 09	11 05	16 61	13 14	14 07	24 26	16 84	18 84
Luce	622	330	591	277	15 68	13 23	14 83	16 50	15 76	16 26	23 70	31 64	26 23
Mackinac	842	1,783	619	1,344	9 75	10 17	10 04	13 27	13 50	13 42	19 86	25 24	23 54
Macomb	4,584	5,230	3,012	3,176	9 08	5 91	7 39	13 83	9 73	11 72	24 54	13 96	19 09

TABLE VIII.—Concluded.

Counties.	Number of pupils included in school census in—		Number of pupils enrolled in—		Cost per capita for instruction based on school census in—			Cost per capita for instruction based on enrollment in—			Total expenses per capita during year based on enrollment in—		
	Graded school districts.	Ungraded school districts.	Graded school districts.	Ungraded school districts.	Graded school districts.	Ungraded school districts.	All school districts.	Graded school districts.	Ungraded school districts.	All school districts.	Graded school districts.	Ungraded school districts.	All school districts.
Manistee	4,920	4,300	2,541	2,800	$8	$6 13	$7 55	$17 03	$9 41	$13 04	$27 36	$14 35	$20 54
Marquette	11,132	2,394	8,121	1,673	11	11 07	11	15 82	15 85	15 83	29 30	31 80	29 72
Mason	2,966	3,600	1,884	2,741	9	6 37	7	15 19	8 37	11 14	23 19	13 85	17 66
Mecosta	2,117	4,151	1,094	3,075	9 79	6 76	7 46	12 16	9 13	10 20	18 24	13 41	15 13
Menominee	5,850	3,751	3,781	2,666	8 [illegible]	6 94	8 [illegible]	13 88	9 77	12 17	23 61	15 31	20 18
Midland	1,184	3,490	1,122	2,496	10	6 23	7 28	10 96	8	9 41	16 98	12 02	13 56
Missaukee	1,017	2,598	925	2,016	8	7 30	7 76	9 82	9	9 54	16 42	15 35	15 69
Monroe	2,398	7,251	1,357	5,162	7	6 35	6 63	13 18	8	9 81	19 12	13 02	14 29
Montcalm	3,388	6,192	2,951	4,579	10 39	6 43	7 98	12 42	8	10 15	17 78	11 32	13 85
Montmorency	583	592	537	452	8 [illegible]	10 50	9 72	9 69	14 [illegible]	11 79	15 35	20 98	17 86
Muskegon	8,270	3,454	7,024	2,398	12 22	6	10 66	14 25	9 98	13 26	25 77	13 37	22 61
Newaygo	1,369	4,663	1,269	3,432	10 66	7	7 91	11 51	9 65	10 15	19 18	13 C0	15 11
Oakland	5,374	5,461	4,454	3,778	12 25	9	10 82	14 79	13 59	14 24	22 78	17 35	20 29
Oceana	1,277	4,106	1,101	3,016	12 33	7 92	8 30	14 30	9 59	10 85	20 54	14 28	15 96
Ogemaw	1,025	2,119	866	1,559	6 43	6 [illegible]	6 34	7 68	8 56	8 25	14 37	13 59	13 87
Ontonagon	2,136	325	1,841	237	16 64	16 58	16 63	19 31	22 73	19 70	35 16	53 82	37 29
Osceola	1,925	4,078	1,510	3,008	11 11	6 62	8 06	14 17	8 97	10 71	22 93	14 52	17 33
Oscoda	....	759	....	572	....	8 06	8 06	....	10 69	10 69	.....	19 87	19 87
Otsego	1,080	1,177	885	860	11 81	7 90	9 77	14 41	10 82	12 64	23 76	16 09	19 98
Ottawa	7,721	5,957	5,723	4,218	8 04	6 01	7 15	10 85	8 49	9 84	20 44	14 95	18 12
Presque Isle	1,239	2,251	1,061	1,110	9 16	4 93	6 43	10 70	9 99	10 34	46	15 61	15 54
Roscommon	133	460	109	320	13 12	10 15	10 82	16 00	14 50	14 95	29	21 48	21 67
Saginaw	15,846	10,383	8,393	6,440	10 43	5 44	8 41	19 68	8 77	14 95	14	13 33	36 30
St. Clair	9,195	7,234	5,420	5,026	8 07	6 67	7 45	13 69	9 61	11 72	15 33	14 17	21 00
St. Joseph	2,945	2,902	2,569	2,361	13 62	10 59	12 09	15 61	13 43	14 57	[illegible] 72	16 91	23 07
Sanilac	3,429	7,731	2,868	6,192	8 46	6 19	6 88	10 12	7 72	8 48		12 19	13 36
Schoolcraft	1,505	1,114	1,005	917	11 18	10 86	11 04	16 75	13 19	15 05		21 06	26 88
Shiawassee	4,038	3,950	3,187	2,886	12 86	9 08	10 99	16 29	12 44	14 46	15 88	14 95	20 65
Tuscola	2,829	7,218	2,344	4,995	11 17	6 10	7 53	13 48	8 82	10 31	[illegible]	12 86	15 54
Van Buren	3,876	5,473	3,262	4,036	12 53	7 96	9 85	14 88	10 79	12 62	28	13 78	20 37
Washtenaw	6,609	4,887	4,607	3,289	13 38	9 22	11 61	19 20	13 70	16 91	52 52	17 58	38 14
Wayne	106,695	8,086	67,036	5,166	11 05	6 32	10 72	17 59	9 89	17 04	28 [illegible]	20 45	27 78
Wexford	3,277	2,889	2,576	2,123	10 32	7 85	9 17	13 13	10 68	12 03	23 75	18 01	21 16

TABLE IX.

Statistics of township and district libraries as reported by school inspectors for the year ending July 8, 1907.

Counties.	Number of townships forfeiting library money.	Number of townships maintaining libraries.	Number of volumes added to township libraries during the year.	Whole number of volumes in township libraries.	Amount of taxes voted for township libraries.	Amount of fines, etc., received from county treasurer for township libraries.	Amount paid for books and care of township libraries.	Amount of township library money on hand July 8, 1907.	Number of districts maintaining libraries.	Number of volumes added to district libraries during the year.	Whole number of volumes in district libraries.	Amount paid for the support of district libraries.	Amount of fines, etc., received from county treasurer for district libraries.
Totals	878	343	9,703	166,309	$4,575 03	$8,557 42	$13,086 74	$17,936 93	5,211	95,577	1,218,889	$174,359 97	$144,622 40
Alcona	10	1	32	298		$18 10	$30 09	$155 49	11	282	814		$30 25
Alger	6	2		516		660 24	100 00	637 38	8	342	1,847	$489 32	1,472 22
Allegan	16	8	1,186	9,520	$1,200 00	722 73	1,729 26	595 59	140	1,344	14,997	1,014 82	1,734 19
Alpena	6	1		300			10 00	152 73	7	372	4,990	724 81	624 48
Antrim	7	8	61	2,298		177 47	168 28	616 89	32	775	3,884	3[illegible] 43	230 52
Arenac	11								29	453	3,364	220 59	233 07
Baraga	5								4	23	1,259	50 00	715 58
Barry	12	4	74	1,286		99 40	94 41	72 57	111	1,9[illegible]9	14,516	1,105 82	688 09
Bay	6	8	299	4,598		327 61	285 78	464 23	54	618	6,728	323 98	418 42
Benzie	3	9	43	2,894		25 36	189 07	140 25	29	415	4,752	301 61	59 00
Berrien	16	4	243	5,341	200 00	504 56	416 21	628 49	143	1,557	22,710	935 09	2,648 60
Branch	12	4	245	4,782	350 00	154 00	618 47	720 52	123	1,541	9,606	788 17	601 70
Calhoun	17	3	49	1,378		8 96	116 11	138 46	160	2,675	36,009	3,928 06	3,157 81
Cass	9	6	107	3,361	467 67	157 08	265 56	650 42	70	1,050	7,992	350 97	637 98
Charlevoix	11	3	91	802	13 70	18 00	80 78	30 45	38	934	5,759	750 37	693 12
Cheboygan	13	4	25	885			2[illegible] 71	80 37	42	894	9,689	1,029 61	1,348 53
Chippewa	14								22	839	5,122	287 76	717 79
Clare	13	2	31	584			35 10	34 21	26	429	2,627	113 61	87 69
Clinton	12	4	140	2,198		78 65	122 16	106 32	92	643	5,380	1,548 28	491 58
Crawford	4	1		1,388	59 68	80 00		30 80	11	204	1,584	11 25	55 20
Delta	11	2	21	536		24 05	19 21	29 77	9	63	4,482	517 48	451 93
Dickinson	6								2	1,539	14,467	3,461 94	759 15
Eaton	8	8	308	6,651	200 00	159 30	531 89	471 35	110	1,062	14,614	718 24	431 91
Emmet	6	9	292	3,317		47 3[illegible]	223 4[illegible]	868 74	51	551	5,425	818 02	349 12
Genesee	17	1	104	1,263		36 80	61 00	36 80	152	2,268	25,390	6,029 53	1,255 67
Gladwin	10	2	62	740			35 58		30	383	2,501	180 00	195 39

Gogebic	5	1	282	369		2 18	25 00		2	130	4,057	640 47	448 15
Grand Traverse	4	9	162	4,545		412 80	309 77	625 03	29	256	4,268	1,023 03	293 26
Gratiot	17								126	981	15,448	856 39	831 82
Hillsdale	17	1		526		8 53	24	8 53	142	825	12,562	733 74	615 60
Houghton	11	3	4	2,883		451 33	369 63	708 30	13	2,856	25,001	4,226 71	3,962 68
Huron	20	7		2,151		119 28	120 00	203 72	100	785	8,555	350 81	290 90
Ingham	16								128	4,302	31,438	7,528 50	2,348 70
Ionia	15	1	283	1,700	1,000 00		331 58	668 42	109	466	9,675	346 25	527 53
Iosco	5	5	75	672		10 23	66 23	202 98	16	370	3,607	43 35	44 01
Iron	7									525	4,606	534 08	630 73
Isabella	13	3		480		16 95	11 00	101 88	81	786	5,406	627 27	155 19
Jackson	19								142	1,263	17,188	896 54	1,459 77
Kalamazoo	14	2	80	1,638		6 88	158 25½	148 11	100	2,515	48,371	6,723 55	1,797 79
Kalkaska	8	3							29	444	2,313	188 20	218 76
Kent	19	5	61	3,214	200 00	162 10	194 44	205 50	184	10398	110,160	1,567 68	2,245 48
Keweenaw	4	1	140	140	73 48	70 68	73 48	72 62	1	515	2,300	478 92	347 29
Lake	3	8	126	2,394		60 60	187 96	149 98	13	241	853	116 48	205 63
Lapeer	15	3	40	1,455	10 00	23 40	30 00	94 45	115	869	13,214	604 71	812 75
Leelanau	1	10	296	3,439	50 00	184 89	328 85	444 95	27	136	2,163	2 50	30 44
Lenawee	21	1		400		61 59	15 00	121 01	172	2,563	41,906	4,592 55	2,255 61
Livingston	14	2		810		9 47	5 00	179 83	54	377	6,039	279 11	402 52
Luce	4									7	1,446	127 02	252 82
Mackinac	8	3		517		57 70	15 00	57 78	2	45	1,735	106 07	379 37
Macomb	12	2		691		34 43	40 00	129 53	77	1,316	17,188	2,405 50	1,616 60
Manistee	6	7	353	4,225		74 84	253 13	275 71	45	508	6,192	334 44	137 13
Marquette	17	1		36			36 99		2	1,411	12,263	1,770 94	1,511 99
Mason	9	5	75	3,073	25 00	57 40	153 65	141 33	40	386	7,601	206 19	505 67
Mecosta	12	4	64	1,474		30 66	97 53	68 69	72	548	6,057	447 61	893 49
Menominee	8	2	100	1,440			50 00	11 36	23	354	6,339	343 44	55 80
Midland	12	4		200		18 70	43 14	11 67	34	124	3,231		56 03
Missaukee	8	6	51	1,443		128 31	105 90	247 43	27	185	2,379	50 02	237 94
Monroe	8	7	20	1,950		79 27	62 38	129 51	134	1,560	17,525	1,223 07	827 78
Montcalm	15	5	179	2,770		36 96	208 83	183 42	103	868	12,660	373 37	790 03
Montmorency	5	2	55	447			75 70	17 44			519		
Muskegon	3	14	140	5,946	84 50	148 89	495 72	533 54	45	1,165	46,225	7,026 96	1,781 86
Newaygo	12	10		1,967		24 62	88 25	159 89	91	684	8,990	226 03	147 18
Oakland	22	3	217	2,710		241 89	261 88	94 01	123	1,272	18,022	850 57	625 61
Oceana		16	734	7,974	215 00	677 21	455 65	1,138 83	56	722	5,181	162 26	303 90
Ogemaw	8	4	275	3,448		113 80	244 57	149 53	21	224	1,359	210 60	147 67
Ontonagon	10				100 00			3 82		584	2,787	496 97	530 76
Osceola	9	7	176	3,140		447 86	314 62	589 08	50	640	5,304	324 36	427 98
Oscoda	3	1		103		52	20 00	136 59	2		384		32 17
Otsego	2	7	547	4,457	50 00	517 14	665 09	843 34	26	437	2,694	360 47	291 19
Ottawa	7	8	350	6,609		205 49	280 13	265 45	75	1,866	11,826	1,448 61	464 91

TABLE IX.—Concluded.

Counties.	Number of townships forfeiting library money.	Number of townships maintaining libraries.	Number of volumes added to township libraries during the year.	Whole number of volumes in township libraries.	Amount of taxes voted for township libraries.	Amount of fines, etc., received from county treasurer for township libraries.	Amount paid for books and care of township libraries.	Amount of township library money on hand July 8, 1907.	Number of districts maintaining libraries.	Number of volumes added to district libraries during the year.	Whole number of volumes in district libraries.	Amount paid for the support of district libraries.	Amount of fines, etc., received from county treasurer for district libraries.
Presque Isle	13	1	....	16	....	....	....	....	9	200	1,162	$57 86	$123 54
Roscommon	4	3	108	828	....	$38 71	$61 54	$14 32	3	122	142	27 20	8 70
Saginaw	18	9	139	6,001	....	114 54	293 54	500 99	90	2,050	36,856	5,187 71	3,358 73
St. Clair	20	3	22	1,975	....	19 01	80 04	4 36	143	3,312	35,622	5,965 50	6,532 49
St. Joseph	12	4	319	2,392	$200 00	56 05	407 15	92 37	116	891	11,846	504 65	936 02
Sanilac	17	9	62	2,238	....	4 75	67 54	63 51	101	1,376	7,201	388 45	179 23
Schoolcraft	8	1	....	270	....	....	....	34 90	1	106	2,312	561 02	686 10
Shiawassee	15	1	....	800	15 00	40 50	13 61	76 53	117	676	11,628	488 37	777 31
Tuscola	13	10	156	2,853	25 00	104 75	164 20	379 67	79	753	9,093	438 12	281 94
Van Buren	12	6	100	3,337	....	48 30	227 00	176 36	123	1,914	16,660	1,004 63	767 65
Washtenaw	17	3	18	1,927	36 00	23 95	63 20	72 30	117	1,526	30,246	2,797 60	962 62
Wayne	17	3	12	1,988	....	95 93	53 00	212 64	133	12,658	251,604	79,711 50	77,442 88
Wexford	3	13	469	5,268	....	214 64	302 20	493 36	32	307	3,942	283 26	542 71

TABLE X.

Branches of instruction as reported by school inspectors for the year ending July 8, 1907.

Counties.	Number of districts in which instruction is given in—													
	Algebra.	Arithmetic.	Botany.	Civil government.	General history.	Geography.	Geometry.	Grammar.	Orthography.	Penmanship.	Physics.	Physiology.	Reading.	U. S. history.
Totals	1,394	7,184	745	5,849	1,494	7,093	517	7,018	4,612	5,164	563	6,940	7,080	6,835
Alcona	8	31	4	21	10	32	2	30	18	22	2	29	30	30
Alger	6	8	2	7	5	8	3	8	6	8	3	8	8	8
Allegan	27	184	15	175	30	184	10	180	147	155	10	181	181	177
Alpena	2	16	1	13	1	16	1	17	9	13	1	17	18	16
Antrim	12	68	7	48	27	69	5	67	44	42	5	67	67	66
Arenac	14	42	7	33	13	42	4	41	22	35	6	40	41	41
Baraga	2	5	2	5	2	5	2	5	5	5	2	5	5	5
Barry	22	139	12	116	20	141	7	139	54	89	7	141	135	136
Bay	18	70	5	68	23	70	5	68	32	60	2	68	68	54
Benzie	10	50	6	39	10	50	3	48	31	20	4	49	50	49
Berrien	33	142	18	112	22	140	15	139	129	86	18	140	139	188
Branch	18	121	6	97	10	122	7	110	51	77	7	117	121	111
Calhoun	48	164	15	148	30	162	10	156	117	129	10	156	162	142
Cass	18	108	8	77	17	109	7	108	66	78	8	106	107	103
Charlevoix	9	66	4	46	12	65	3	65	40	51	3	63	65	61
Cheboygan	14	56	14	35	13	56	5	55	53	46	5	55	57	55
Chippewa	5	53	3	40	14	51	1	49	32	40	2	49	52	48
Clare	8	60	4	42	20	60	3	60	40	36	4	53	59	55
Clinton	19	128	10	110	17	127	8	127	60	52	7	127	126	122
Crawford	5	22	3	12	3	21	1	21	13	19	1	20	21	17
Delta	9	28	3	16	9	27	2	27	20	21	3	27	28	26
Dickinson	6	8	3	8	5	8	3	8	8	7	2	8	8	8
Eaton	24	142	10	127	20	140	10	141	97	97	8	142	141	138
Emmet	10	72	7	46	11	75	5	71	35	57	3	72	71	64
Genesee	34	156	21	127	23	156	12	151	108	94	14	119	155	147
Gladwin	11	47	3	29	72	46	2	48	26	32	2	45	48	44
Gogebic	5	8	3	7	5	8	4	8	7	8	2	8	8	8
Grand Traverse	8	66	6	56	14	65	2	62	44	48	3	63	61	63
Gratiot	20	130	12	117	31	127	7	127	95	80	9	127	126	126
Hillsdale	30	158	16	123	23	158	14	157	76	109	15	153	158	155
Houghton	20	36	14	26	17	35	10	28	27	31	8	35	36	34
Huron	17	119	12	112	29	116	9	119	78	91	13	116	118	117
Ingham	19	134	11	114	25	135	8	132	88	90	11	134	134	128
Ionia	18	140	13	88	16	141	10	140	64	86	13	133	140	133
Iosco	8	31	7	25	16	30	8	31	13	24	5	30	31	27
Iron	4	7	3	6	4	7	4	7	6	7	4	7	7	7
Isabella	11	106	7	86	21	106	6	102	74	68	5	98	103	99
Jackson	34	151	13	126	36	149	10	151	114	129	13	148	151	133
Kalamazoo	40	133	21	101	39	133	13	133	77	100	10	134	134	133
Kalkaska	8	52	3	36	9	52	1	52	28	25	2	46	47	45
Kent	65	205	37	187	50	203	14	200	169	160	16	197	196	192
Keweenaw	0	5	0	5	2	5	0	5	2	3	0	5	5	5
Lake	3	45	3	31	5	41	1	42	35	30	2	39	42	35
Lapeer	27	147	14	128	26	146	12	146	84	108	14	142	146	142
Leelanau	10	57	7	44	16	56	7	55	28	45	8	49	54	51
Lenawee	51	188	17	164	38	189	11	187	125	155	12	195	195	194
Livingston	48	131	10	112	31	130	9	131	74	97	10	123	128	126
Luce	1	4	1	4	1	4	1	4	3	4	1	4	4	4
Mackinac	4	14	3	14	3	14	3	14	12	13	2	14	14	14
Macomb	27	110	18	86	29	110	11	112	64	111	14	110	111	102

TABLE X.—CONCLUDED.

Counties.	Number of districts in which instruction is given in—													
	Algebra.	Arithmetic.	Botany.	Civil government.	General history.	Geography.	Geometry.	Grammar.	Orthography.	Penmanship.	Physics.	Physiology.	Reading.	U. S. history.
Manistee	14	62	8	49	23	60	4	62	44	49	6	60	60	58
Marquette	9	21	6	18	7	21	6	21	17	20	6	20	20	21
Mason	6	65	4	53	14	64	3	63	44	46	2	63	63	59
Mecosta	14	107	12	93	19	107	6	107	80	69	9	106	107	106
Menominee	10	37	6	28	12	38	4	39	21	25	4	37	38	35
Midland	11	81	6	67	28	81	7	76	46	54	4	81	80	75
Missaukee	10	59	7	46	19	59	5	59	50	42	7	51	58	52
Monroe	18	134	6	122	11	135	5	135	110	96	4	136	135	133
Montcalm	25	139	18	115	26	137	8	139	71	77	14	137	138	134
Montmorency	3	8	3	7	4	8	1	8	7	6	1	8	8	8
Muskegon	22	89	10	73	23	87	9	88	65	57	11	85	85	84
Newaygo	9	114	6	80	15	113	5	111	40	45	5	110	112	104
Oakland	43	193	20	130	35	181	13	186	87	142	15	185	193	183
Oceana	9	88	10	65	14	86	8	86	39	55	7	85	86	79
Ogemaw	7	44	5	25	12	46	3	46	20	24	2	46	45	41
Ontonagon	6	10	5	8	6	10	4	10	9	10	4	10	10	10
Osceola	11	93	7	74	12	88	14	85	63	62	7	91	93	87
Oscoda	4	15	1	9	7	15	1	16	10	12	0	14	16	15
Otsego	7	34	3	24	9	34	3	34	20	26	4	33	34	33
Ottawa	23	124	16	108	26	125	8	114	102	82	13	123	122	119
Presque Isle	7	33	4	17	10	34	2	34	16	30	2	30	36	33
Roscommon	5	22	1	8	4	23	1	15	10	16	1	18	22	16
Saginaw	30	172	18	142	38	161	9	161	108	118	9	157	160	155
St. Clair	28	154	11	148	24	155	6	155	153	145	9	153	153	149
St. Joseph	15	122	8	97	11	122	8	122	95	116	10	122	122	116
Sanilac	60	162	28	147	31	149	7	150	144	108	9	162	161	161
Schoolcraft	4	10	3	8	4	10	2	10	7	10	2	9	10	8
Shiawassee	18	124	11	104	22	123	8	122	106	102	10	121	123	121
Tuscola	24	145	14	133	24	147	13	147	72	118	16	152	158	158
Van Buren	19	153	14	138	21	153	9	152	114	93	13	151	148	148
Washtenaw	19	173	10	132	19	157	10	157	64	130	9	154	157	151
Wayne	27	159	15	126	27	146	10	148	87	123	13	139	148	141
Wexford	7	75	5	60	12	78	4	76	60	54	4	77	77	68

TABLE XI.

Private or parochial schools for the year ending July 8, 1907.

Counties.	Number of private schools.	Number of parochial schools.	Number of teachers. Men.	Number of teachers. Women.	Estimated number of pupils.
Totals	78	387	341	938	56,468
Alcona	......	......	......	......	......
Alger	......	......	......	......	......
Allegan	......	3	1	4	102
Alpena	......	2	1	1	50
Antrim	......	......	......	......	......
Arenac	......	2	2	......	56
Baraga	......	......	......	......	......
Barry	1	......	......	1	15
Bay	2	26	28	51	5,062
Benzie	......	1	......	1	18
Berrien	......	7	5	3	495
Branch	......	1	......	3	175
Calhoun	......	3	1	12	380
Cass	......	1	......	1	12
Charlevoix	......	......	......	......	......
Cheboygan	1	3	......	9	400
Chippewa	3	1	......	8	400
Clare	......	......	......	......	......
Clinton	......	5	2	9	515
Crawford	......	......	......	......	......
Delta	......	2	......	14	850
Dickinson	......	1	1	4	160
Eaton	......	......	......	......	......
Emmet	2	1	......	7	285
Genesee	......	1	1	......	170
Gladwin	......	......	......	......	......
Gogebic	......	1	......	9	500
Grand Traverse	......	......	......	......	......
Gratiot	1	......	3	4	102
Hillsdale	1	......	......	1	15
Houghton	4	9	1	42	2,741
Huron	1	11	10	5	809
Ingham	......	4	2	6	468
Ionia	1	3	1	9	307
Iosco	......	2	2	1	165
Iron	1	......	1	......	13
Isabella	......	3	1	10	480
Jackson	......	......	......	......	......
Kalamazoo	2	4	3	14	1,000
Kalkaska	......	......	......	......	......
Kent	6	22	18	124	5,948
Keweenaw	......	......	......	......	......
Lake	......	......	......	......	......
Lapeer	1	......	1	......	14
Leelanau	1	4	2	10	450
Lenawee	1	3	4	2	143
Livingston	......	......	......	......	......
Luce	......	......	......	......	......
Mackinac	......	2	1	4	83
Macomb	1	19	18	13	1,526
Manistee	2	8	8	20	1,401
Marquette	......	3	......	24	1,175
Mason	......	5	5	9	520
Mecosta	1	4	2	6	365
Menominee	1	4	2	14	646
Midland	......	1	1	......	20
Missaukee	2	......	1	1	105
Monroe	4	14	10	15	921
Montcalm	......	2	2	......	48
Montmorency	......	1	2	......	100
Muskegon	1	7	5	17	1,000
Newaygo	......	1	......	1	15
Oakland	......	3	2	7	218
Oceana	2	1	......	2	110
Ogemaw	1	......	......	1	6
Ontonagon	......	......	......	......	......
Osceola	......	2	2	......	106
Oscoda	......	......	......	......	......
Otsego	......	1	......	2	60
Ottawa	1	7	6	14	794
Presque Isle	2	10	8	6	440
Roscommon	......	......	......	......	......
Saginaw	8	29	22	23	1,611
St. Clair	4	13	6	27	1,324
St. Joseph	......	5	4	4	125
Sanilac	......	1	1	......	15
Schoolcraft	......	1	......	5	225
Shiawassee	......	2	1	4	202
Tuscola	......	9	7	4	430
Van Buren	1	4	4	1	76
Washtenaw	......	17	15	10	728
Wayne	17	80	112	331	19,595
Wexford	1	5	3	8	178

TABLE XII.

Examination and certification of teachers as reported by the county commissioner for the year ending June 30, 1907.

Counties.	Number of public examinations held.	Number of applicants for regular certificates.	Number of applicants for special certificates.	Number of applicants receiving certificates. County first grade.	Indorsed first grade.	Second grade.	Third grade.	Special.	Number licensed without experience in teaching.	Number of applicants having received normal school instruction.	Number of applicants having attended institute during the year.	Number of teachers holding— State certificates.	State normal college certificates.	Central normal school certificates.	Northern normal school certificates.	Western normal school certificates.	County normal training class certificates.	Certificates issued by county board of examiners.	Certificates issued by city boards of education.	Number of legally qualified teachers in the county including city teachers.	Number of certificates suspended.	Number of certificates annulled.	Number of certificates transferred.	Number of districts hiring teachers by the year.	Number of new teachers added to teaching force during year.
Totals	226	9,621	1,086	74	47	2,080	3,789	913	1,957	1,328	3,932	610	1,283	426	144	52	1,001	10,198	2,790	17,842	3	3	398	5,963	2,459
Alcona	2	34	2	....	....	2	6	2	6	....	6	....	....	1	....	....	....	37	....	39	....	....	1	34	6
Alger	2	18	1	1	....	2	8	....	3	4	4	....	4	1	3	....	....	42	....	55	....	....	1	8	10
Allegan	3	311	25	4	2	65	111	25	44	88	106	3	17	2	....	3	12	212	....	308	....	....	10	150	50
Alpena	3	72	14	....	....	10	26	14	9	1	13	....	....	....	....	....	1	37	18	115	....	....	2	40	16
Antrim	3	27	5	....	....	19	13	3	7	1	13	11	18	5	....	....	3	67		....	....	....	9	58	17
Arenac	3	36	1	2	....	9	11	1	11	9	18	3	....	1	....	....	19	43	....	66	....	....	....	5	11
Baraga	2	20	12	....	....	4	12	10	7	12	12	4	3	....	6	....	....	34	....	47	....	....	....	5	4
Barry	3	170	10	1	1	50	51	10	22	52	54	3	14	....	....	1	56	165	6	28	....	....	12	125	44
Bay	3	135	5	....	....	13	50	5	21	21	35	....	4	....	....	....	7	9[illegible]	220	37	....	....	....	74	27
Benzie	3	22	8	2	....	16	35	8	15	3	15	21	9	6	....	....	....	90	....	18	....	....	2	28	15
Berrien	3	243	9	....	2	48	121	9	70	20	125	13	20	....	....	1	1	200	....	318	....	....	3	130	80
Branch	3	146	35	....	....	37	53	22	31	35	94	10	29	4	....	2	11	187	16	259	....	....	9	102	53
Calhoun	3	195	18	3	2	59	77	15	35	35	120	3	6	3	....	2	24	227	75	374	....	....	8	141	51
Cass	3	96	15	....	....	26	41	15	28	14	110	3	17	3	....	2	30	137	14	213	....	....	6	100	42
Charlevoix	3	93	9	....	....	23	34	9	17	10	33	2	16	20	....	....	42	120	....	180	....	....	4	55	24
Cheboygan	3	106	35	....	....	6	28	20	17	4	17	6	5	10	1	1	3	76	18	120	....	....	15	67	42
Chippewa	3	91	15	....	3	15	45	13	23	12	33	11	28	12	3		4	76	4	161	....	....	4	90	10
Clare	3	80	27	3	3	18	44	19	23	25	68	15	8	3	....	....	....	78	....	101	....	....	3	32	25
Clinton	3	116	7	1	....	32	49	7	20	11	65	6	17	8	....	....	32	125	6	195	....	....	5	75	30
Crawford	3	23	15	....	....	6	10	21	10	1	12	....	....	1	....	....	3	25	....	39	....	....	3	5	5
Delta	3	79	7	1	1	7	28	6	20	9	42	12	8	3	12	....	....	82	39	56	....	....	3	68	45
Dickinson	2	8	14	....	....	3	4	14	1	11	20	2	3	....	4	....	....	18	64	35	....	....	8	6	10
Eaton	3	184	4	....	....	56	127	4	95	23	39	....	34	26	1	2	2	183	27	25	....	....	13	120	100
Emmet	3	123	14	....	....	14	45	12	19	6	16	7	11	10	....	....	4	117	15	64	....	....	6	....	....
Genesee	3	205	12	6	2	62	81	9	40	75	105	1	5	....	....	....	....	250	70	30	....	....	6	100	50

Gladwin	2	64	1			16	19		8	12	32	1	2	2				61		66				30	8
Gogebic	2	36				7	21		17	3		1	12	7	10	5		32	67	134			1	7	10
Grand Traverse	2	87	4			7	39	4	14	4	21	1	25	16		2		51	8	143	1		6	61	30
Gratiot	3	124	25	2	2	32	48	9	24	23	72	9	10	40			40	160		266			2	100	67
Hillsdale	2	155	29	1		17	62	28	44	3	35	15	26	1				301	9	352			2	139	44
Houghton	2	127	78	3		88	47	68	30	45	155	76	82	4	12	1		270		450			2	28	10
Huron	2	191	12		1	41	59	12	27	10	41	3	24	11				168		203			1	119	30
Ingham	3	120	20	1	1	11	36	18	24	18	48	2	7	3			35	48	100	283			8	74	45
Ionia	3	168	20	2	2	44	86	15	46	28	43	1	9	12			22	184	55	333			4	100	50
Iosco	3	43	1			14	5	1	1	6	18	4	4	1			32	40		81			4	26	17
Iron	3	23	5			1	16	5	4	3	14	45	11	5	8			31		78				7	25
Isabella	3	173	8			29	46	6	24	22	65		2	43				75	15	135			3	78	30
Jackson	3	195	12			39	54	40	52	28	75		6	2				130	97	235			8	78	70
Kalamazoo	3	166	15			34	53	12	31	4	75	3	58	3	2	13		185	101	369			8	128	40
Kalkaska	2	35	19			9	7	9	2	2	7	13	4	9			25	27		75			12	41	20
Kent	3	258	4	5	4	34	89	4	62	3	82	24	11					391	444	835		1	4	200	50
Keweenaw	2	10	5		1	2	8	5	2	4	10	3	2		7		1	11		28				5	10
Lake	3	60	8			27	39	8	21		42									66		1	5	11	21
Lapeer	2	160	2	1		70	79	2	40		150	3	14					187	11	212			8	100	40
Leelanau	3	47	2			14	18	2	7	6	28	3	1	6				65		75			2		16
Lenawee	3	217	25			29	116	21	51	33	114	21	37	2			14	260	34	368			4	165	65
Livingston	3	213	7			25	123	7	56	40	57	3	35	1				280		351			3	71	
Luce	3	8	4				4	4	1				7				1	14		28			4	4	1
Mackinac	2	29	24			9	8	23	7	6	8	1	6	3	2		2	38		95	1		20	70	10
Macomb	3	120	3	2		15	26	6	20	10			29				46	69	11	222			2	113	28
Manistee	3	113	5			12	37	3	25	1	28	18	3	12			25	104	50	179			3	52	22
Marquette	2	60	14			4	33	14	15	35	17	20	26		60		1	86	101	310			2	21	25
Mason	3	67	1	1	1	15	32	1	20		20	6		4			37	75	36	127				60	25
Mecosta	3	230	3	1	1	39	62	3	23		35	3	1	1			35	102	26	212			19	78	20
Menominee	3	142	11	3		27	51	11	16	9	65	8		2	2			108	58	179			1		20
Midland	3	114	29		1	16	30	20	8	8	58	19	4	9			34	84	4	117			4	65	25
Missaukee	2	76	7			10	30	5	10	7	31	13	3	5			1	72		92			1	51	12
Monroe	3	172	25	1		47	84	20	34	86	125		14				1	212	11	242			3	130	35
Montcalm	3	202	4	3	3	29	78	4	45	47	33	2	2	12			5	277	27	231			2	75	35
Montmorency	3	78	4			10	30	3	15	2	35	4	3				1	48		52			2	28	10
Muskegon	3	121	5			30	65	3	35	15	42	13	7				4	143	149	292			8	75	35
Newaygo	3	143	25		1	28	61	25	21	16	74	4	6	3			14	154		199			9	84	46
Oakland	3	176	26	1	1	41	86	16	45	21	48	6	42	12			54	250	15	379			14	200	50
Oceana	3	123	16	1		15	50	16	26	6	21	1	7	1			27	200		250	1		4	80	25
Ogemaw	3	73	11	1		12	35	12	15	2	33	1						47		62			6	34	15
	3	75	21			12	29	19	17	25	12	2	10	2	4			62		80			4		12
	2	87	8			34	26	8	13	16	30	5	12	7	1		42	119		187			6	72	35
	3	19	6			2	7	3	2			1					1	16		17		1	2		2
	2	14	10			10	8	10	10	11	20		7	4			11	20		60			9	24	27
	3	200	3	2		58	75	3	30	24	80	9	20	4		1	11	212	30	290			7	124	40

TABLE XII.—CONCLUDED.

Counties.	Number of public examinations held.	Number of applicants for regular certificates.	Number of applicants for special certificates.	Number of applicants receiving certificates. County first grade.	Indorsed first grade.	Second grade.	Third grade.	Special.	Number licensed without experience in teaching.	Number of applicants having received normal school instruction.	Number of applicants having attended institute during the year.	Number of teachers holding— State certificates.	State normal college certificates.	Central normal school certificates.	Northern normal school certificates.	Western State normal school certificates.	County normal training class certificates.	Certificates issued by county board of examiners.	Certificates issued by city boards of education.	Number of legally qualified teachers in the county including city teachers.	Number of certificates suspended.	Number of certificates annulled.	Number of certificates transferred.	Number of districts hiring teachers by the year.	Number of new teachers added to teaching force during year.
Presque Isle	3	70	18	....	....	14	19	12	3	4	40	4	2	3	....	....	......	53	......	62	....	....	2	3	......
Roscommon	....	....	....	....	....	....	....	....	....	....	....	....	....	....	....	....	....	....	....	....	....	....	....	....	....
Saginaw	3	263	23	3	1	75	29	8	17	13	103	2	39	15	....	....	25	273	275	548	....	....	7	140	50
St. Clair	3	123	11	....	....	43	59	9	23	23	61	1	37	2	....	....	65	102	82	331	....	....	1	145	30
St. Joseph	5	163	37	1	....	24	59	33	16	15	28	17	14	1	....	3	......	190	......	222	....	....	2	109	71
Sanilac	3	254	11	3	3	32	82	11	39	12	113	28	15	3	....	....	1	221	......	239	....	....	3	154	39
Schoolcraft	2	19	2	....	....	8	10	2	4	14	18	1	9	2	6	2	24	24	29	65	....	....	3	26	6
Shiawassee	3	164	25	1	....	41	79	19	49	15	115	6	12	4	....	....	27	231	16	296	....	....	4	95	45
Tuscola	3	225	20	3	2	57	84	20	42	16	70	9	2	5	....	....	4	214	......	229	....	....	4	100	40
Van Buren	3	218	3	1	1	41	98	3	55	67	84	29	24	3	....	11	10	209	11	312	....	....	7	140	55
Washtenaw	3	164	8	1	1	35	53	8	33	5	50	......	10	....	....	....	......	217	76	357	....	....	6	125	33
Wayne	3	120	24	6	5	56	64	24	30	18	46	9	247	15	....	....	......	208	208	1,644	....	....	6	148	35
Wexford	2	73	18	....	....	8	26	13	12	......	30	1	5	5	....	....	48	54	42	154	....	....	1	52	35

TABLE XIII.

Miscellaneous statistics as reported by the county commissioner for the year ending June 30, 1907.

Counties.	Number of meetings of county teachers' associations.	Number of other teachers' meetings.	Number of days devoted to meetings of county board.	Amount allowed by board of supervisors for stationery, etc.	Amount of compensation received by members of the board, other than the commissioner.	Salary of the commissioner.	Amount of institute fees collected.	Number of districts visited by the commissioner during the year.	Number of visits made by commissioner and assistant visitor during the year.	Number of districts in which the compulsory attendance law is enforced.
Totals......	162	548	691	$13,683 38	$21,191 33	$86,200 00	$10,822 52	7,288	12,442	6,983
Alcona..........	2	2	8	$72 00	$68 00	$300 00	......	36	42	35
Alger..........	......	......	6	......	......	500 00	......	45	45	8
Allegan..........	3	8	6	350 00	486 00	1,400 00	$193 50	182	232	185
Alpena..........	......	......	30	150 00	240 00	700 00	62 50	28	28	60
Antrim..........	1	1	3	200 00	157 00	1,000 00	54 00	72	150	72
Arenac..........	2	......	14	......	112 00	750 00	39 00	43	120	43
Baraga..........	......	......	3	15 00	96 00	650 00	28 00	5	85	4
Barry..........	2	14	11	66 34	216 00	1,200 00	178 50	139	165	143
Bay..........	3	......	4	......	348 00	1,200 00	194 50	74	175	74
Benzie..........	2	3	6	199 96	216 00	700 00	60 50	53	90	53
Berrien..........	1	3	12	225 00	600 00	1,200 00	286 00	142	150	142
Branch..........	3	9	3	108 50	170 00	1,500 00	136 50	126	304	126
Calhoun..........	2	35	12	300 00	350 00	1,500 00	220 50	164	238	164
Cass..........	2	1	3	176 55	347 00	1,200 00	115 50	111	120	111
Charlevoix..........	2	......	3	175 00	200 00	1,200 00	89 50	63	200	67
Cheboygan..........	2	......	11	156 40	268 00	1,000 00	69 00	66	93	69
Chippewa..........	1	......	4	400 00	282 00	1,200 00	69 50	61	140	......
Clare..........	2	......	9	95 00	180 00	600 00	62 00	62	82	64
Clinton..........	5	1	6	200 00	285 50	1,350 00	114 00	129	200	129
Crawford..........	2	10	4	24 00	46 00	300 00	19 50	14	20	25
Delta..........	......	......	6	75 00	172 00	1,200 00	105 00	68	160	68
Dickinson..........	1	......	6	200 00	40 00	1,200 00	74 50	6	200	6
Eaton..........	2	......	4	526 95	346 00	1,500 00	167 50	136	250	136
Emmet..........	29	80	11	100 00	328 00	1,000 00	92 00	......	......	73
Genesee..........	4	5	7	200 00	526 00	1,200 00	227 50	120	170	158
Gladwin..........	1	1	3	95 82	165 00	500 00	42 00	40	45	50
Gogebic..........	......	......	3	60 00	48 00	600 00	......	7	160	7
Grand Traverse..	......	20	6	50 00	217 00	1,200 00	98 50	65	90	65
Gratiot..........	2	2	12	300 00	280 00	1,200 00	136 00	132	295	132
Hillsdale..........	2	48	4	59 04	312 00	1,200 00	147 50	163	211	163
Houghton..........	1	......	4	90 00	120 00	1,200 00	343 00	28	50	34
Huron..........	6	......	4	225 00	336 00	1,200 00	160 00	116	125	115
Ingham..........	1	......	32	168 57	250 00	1,350 00	165 00	134	231	136
Ionia..........	3	4	14	200 00	320 00	1,200 00	176 50	142	250	135
Iosco..........	1	18	9	200 00	......	800 00	40 50	31	105	31
Iron..........	......	1	3	100 00	64 00	600 00	43 00	25	28	4
Isabella..........	1	......	5	200 00	366 00	1,400 00	118 00	93	122	84
Jackson..........	1	......	4	250 00	352 00	1,500 00	186 50	156	312	......
Kalamazoo..........	1	......	6	200 00	381 25	1,350 00	186 50	133	241	133
Kalkaska..........	2	7	3	200 00	100 00	750 00	51 50	49	129	52
Kent..........	5	5	52	490 00	950 50	1,500 00	526 50	170	174	205
Keweenaw..........	1	10	11	9 00	44 00	250 00	18 50	5	11	2
Lake..........	......	......	3	50 00	288 00	550 00	46 00	78	45	40
Lapeer..........	3	40	6	200 40	448 00	1,200 00	223 50	134	190	100
Leelanau..........	3	2	3	47 50	160 00	700 00	53 50	58	97	58
Lenawee..........	2	66	10	256 43	348 00	1,500 00	243 00	168	174	196
Livingston..........	3	3	9	88 57	304 00	1,200 00	170 00	127	189	119
Luce..........	......	16	3	......	64 00	200 00	16 50	4	20	
Mackinac..........	......	......	6	15 00	140 00	600 00	33 00	30	50	
Macomb..........	1	......	6	......	304 00	1,600 00	[illegible]	112	[illegible]	

TABLE XIII.—Concluded.

Counties.	Number of meetings of county teachers' associations.	Number of other teachers' meetings.	Number of days devoted to meetings of county board.	Amount allowed by board of supervisors for stationery, etc.	Amount of compensation received by members of the board, other than the commissioner.	Salary of the commissioner.	Amount of institute fees collected.	Number of districts visited by the commissioner during the year.	Number of visits made by commissioner and assistant visitor during the year.	Number of districts in which the compulsory attendance law is enforced.
Manistee	3	8	6	$200 00	$352 00	$850 00	$120 00	69	123	69
Marquette	.....	6	2	421 91	132 00	1,600 00	153 00	48	209	48
Mason	1	25	10	245 00	230 00	1,200 00	77 50	66	170	66
Mecosta	2	2	4	200 00	278 00	1,000 00	150 50	108	165	108
Menominee	3	.....	9	....	100 00	1,500 00	108 50	82	200	82
Midland	1	2	3	180 00	253 60	1,000 00	66 00	80	119	80
Missaukee	1	1	5	....	180 00	800 00	50 50	62	92	....
Monroe	2	.....	36	200 00	388 00	1,200 00	159 50	125	130	137
Montcalm	1	.....	9	62 20	404 00	1,400 00	143 00	137	151	130
Montmorency	.....	2	15	20 00	120 00	300 00	35 50	30	40	28
Muskegon	2	3	6	110 00	322 00	1,200 00	105 00	97	300	90
Newaygo	3	5	19	214 68	382 00	1,200 00	114 00	116	203	118
Oakland	1	.....	10	400 00	350 00	1,400 00	190 50	200	250	200
Oceana	2	3	5	125 00	404 50	1,000 00	104 50	89	380	91
Ogemaw	1	1	4	32 81	152 00	500 00	48 50	48	85	48
Ontonagon	2	.....	8	35 04	176 00	750 00	60 50	79	155	79
Osceola	1	3	2	196 75	204 00	1,200 00	93 00	93	137	93
Oscoda	.....	.....	8	8 85	60 00	200 00	14 50	18	24	18
Otsego	1	.....	3	75 00	116 00	500 00	33 50	36	50	36
Ottawa	8	9	3	....	....	1,200 00	214 50	124	138	120
Presque Isle	2	.....	12	70 00	120 98	500 00	52 52	36	46	36
Roscommon	.....	.....	.....	....	....	....	....	.....	.....	.....
Saginaw	2	.....	25	1,000 00			417 50	165	400	165
St. Clair	1	.....	4	500 00	600 00	1,500 00	184 50	152	174	152
St. Joseph	.....	5	3	230 96	378 00	1,800 00	164 50	123	251	123
Sanilac	.....	20	21	200 00	691 00	1,500 00	226 50	154	212	154
Schoolcraft	.....	8	8	100 00	32 00	500 00	36 50	27	90	27
Shiawassee	3	12	3	....	432 00	1,200 00	160 50	122	235	122
Tuscola	1	2	4	380 70	250 00	1,500 00	159 50	141	160	149
Van Buren	1	12	3	190 00	356 00	1,400 00	186 00	151	241	152
Washtenaw	1	4	12	....	328 00	1,500 00	223 50	135	180	164
Wayne	2	.....	13	441 45	512 00	2,000 00	896 00	148	275	....
Wexford	1	.....	3	272 00	278 00	1,000 00	76 50	81	122	81

TABLE XIV.

Condition of schools and schoolhouses as reported by the county commissioner for the year ending June 30, 1907.

Counties.	Number of schools supplied with dictionaries.	Number of schools supplied with maps.	Number of schools supplied with globes.	Number of schoolhouses properly heated and ventilated.	Number of schools having uniform text-books in each branch.	Number of schools having a prescribed course of study.	Number of schools properly classified.	Number of schools in which physiology, etc., is taught.	Number of districts that have adopted text-books in physiology.	Number of districts that have taught communicable diseases according to law.	Number of townships organized as township districts.	Number of districts furnishing free text-books.	Number of pupils in 8th grade exclusive of graded schools.	Number of 8th grade diplomas granted.
Totals	6,894	6,773	6,224	3,379	6,226	3,427	6,278	7,597	6,502	6,669	128	1,006	14,414	6,286
Alcona	33	32	32	....	36	3	36	35	35	35	3	9	52	11
Alger	25	30	20	20	45	....	35	45	45	45	8	8	25	33
Allegan	185	175	165	170	185	10	150	185	185	160	....	7	450	136
Alpena	55	50	45	30	40	30	45	61	30	60	5	....	25	....
Antrim	72	70	70	60	65	65	72	72	60	72	....	26	63	30
Arenac	43	40	38	....	30	5	43	43	43	43	....	15	78	64
Baraga	30	30	30	12	35	25	18	35	5	5	5	5	8	5
Barry	131	125	120	130	135	5	132	143	143	143	....	4	295	171
Bay	74	74	70	37	74	2	74	74	74	74	1	32	200	149
Benzie	53	53	53	45	48	5	53	53	53	53	1	6	50	33
Berrien	120	116	110	20	85	20	....	142	....		....	5	....	175
Branch	97	81	73	25	117	11	98	118	120	75	....	2	175	70
Calhoun	164	155	148	100	145	50	130	164	164	164	....	8	220	136
Cass	104	95	96	89	91	104	109	112	112	112	....	....	281	44
Charlevoix	67	67	67	15	60	4	40	67	67	50	....	24	120	34
Cheboygan	65	65	56	10	65	14	60	70	69	59	....	47	130	30
Chippewa	48	77	60	1	42	90	65	90	90	90	8	45	....	29
Clare	35	47	38	1	20	5	50	64	....	25	....	22	58	35
Clinton	129	120	75	125	125	125	125	125	125	125	....	3	275	140
Crawford	25	20	20	16	25	2	12	25	25	25	....	....	15	5
Delta	60	70	60	51	51	4	82	69	69	69	9	4	40	26
Dickinson	6	6	6	6	6	6	6	6	6	6	....	....	19	....
Eaton	100	100	90	8	136	136	136	136	136	136	....	5	167	97
Emmet	70	70	....	6	70	....	....	73	73		....	....	71	....
Genesee	75	125	120	12	75	40	125	158	158	....		2	....	260
Gladwin	45	40	40	35	40	10	40	50	50	40	2	15	60	29
Gogebic	27	27	27	27	19	27	2	27	27	7	5	5	15	12
Grand Traverse	65	60	60	12	50	4	65	65	65	60	....	11	125	81
Gratiot	120	110	100	5	132	....	130	132	132	132	....	3	300	188
Hillsdale	147	137	142	107	154	109	157	163	163	163	....	....	219	85
Houghton	35	35	35	35	26	9	31	27	20	30	1	10	20	....
Huron	110	106	107	60	119	119	119	119	119	112	....	20	275	80
Ingham	134	122	103	5	130	10	48	136	136	136	....	....	406	27
Ionia	135	130	100	12	135	....	135	142	142	70	....	....	300	109
Iosco	30	22	22	16	24	7	20	31	31	31	1	14	38	7
Iron	31	20	26	25	26	4	26	32	32	26	7	19	22	5
Isabella	98	90	100	64	80	61	77	101	100	91	....	3	224	88
Jackson	130	125	110	75	....	150	140	156	....	156	....	....	213	73
Kalamazoo	115	115	90	20	130	....	133	133	133	133	....	3	224	132
Kalkaska	50	45	45	4	50	35	50	50	10	50	....	40	90	39
Kent	205	200	200	100	168	205	205	205	205	205	....	8	381	238
Keweenaw	4	4	4	2	4	3	2	4	4	4	3	....	16	10
Lake	40	40	3	40	3	25	45	45	20	45	....	8	60	40
Lapeer	80	80	60	80	80	....	80	80	100	100	....	....	190	104
Leelanau	53	51	43	7	41	28	9	58	28	58	....	3	66	47
Lenawee	187	186	183	165	191	170	187	196	196	175	....	2	552	149
Livingston	91	93	81	117	127	131	131	135	135	78	....	....	226	105
Luce	12	12	12	1	4	4	16	16	4	4	4	4	15	3
Mackinac	40	40	27	20	35	....	30	57	57	37	12	....	7	41
Macomb	56	56	56	....	....	56	15	113	113	113	....	1	112	

TABLE [illegible] (continued)

Counties	[illegible]	[illegible]	[illegible]	[illegible]	[illegible]	[illegible]	Number of ... school	Number of schools in which physiology ... is taught	Number of districts that have adopted text-books in place ...	Number of districts that have ... according to law	Number of townships organized as township districts	Number of districts furnishing free text-books	Number of pupils in 8th grade ... of graded schools	Number of 8th grade diplomas granted
[illegible]	[illegible]	[illegible]	[illegible]	[illegible]	[illegible]	[illegible]	[illegible]	[illegible]	[illegible]	[illegible]		[illegible]	[illegible]	[illegible]
[illegible]	[illegible]	[illegible]	[illegible]	[illegible]	[illegible]	[illegible]	[illegible]	[illegible]	[illegible]	[illegible]	[illegible]	[illegible]	[illegible]	[illegible]
[illegible]	[illegible]	[illegible]	[illegible]	[illegible]	[illegible]	[illegible]	[illegible]	[illegible]	[illegible]	[illegible]		[illegible]	[illegible]	[illegible]
[illegible]	[illegible]	[illegible]	[illegible]	[illegible]	[illegible]	[illegible]	[illegible]	[illegible]	[illegible]	[illegible]		[illegible]	[illegible]	[illegible]
[illegible]	[illegible]	[illegible]	[illegible]	[illegible]	[illegible]	[illegible]	[illegible]	[illegible]	[illegible]	[illegible]	[illegible]	[illegible]	[illegible]	[illegible]
[illegible]	[illegible]	[illegible]	[illegible]	[illegible]	[illegible]	[illegible]	[illegible]	[illegible]	[illegible]	[illegible]		30	150	[illegible]
[illegible]	[illegible]	[illegible]	[illegible]	[illegible]	[illegible]		[illegible]	[illegible]					[illegible]	[illegible]
[illegible]	[illegible]	[illegible]	[illegible]	[illegible]	[illegible]	[illegible]	[illegible]	[illegible]	[illegible]	[illegible]		[illegible]	[illegible]	[illegible]
[illegible]	[illegible]	[illegible]	[illegible]	[illegible]	[illegible]	[illegible]	[illegible]	[illegible]		[illegible]		[illegible]	[illegible]	[illegible]
[illegible]	[illegible]	[illegible]	[illegible]	[illegible]	[illegible]	[illegible]	[illegible]	[illegible]		30	[illegible]	[illegible]	[illegible]	[illegible]
[illegible]	[illegible]	[illegible]	[illegible]	[illegible]	[illegible]	[illegible]	[illegible]	[illegible]	[illegible]	[illegible]		[illegible]	[illegible]	[illegible]
[illegible]	[illegible]	[illegible]	[illegible]	[illegible]	[illegible]	[illegible]	[illegible]	[illegible]	[illegible]	[illegible]		[illegible]	[illegible]	[illegible]
[illegible]	[illegible]	[illegible]	[illegible]	[illegible]	[illegible]	[illegible]	200	200	200	200			[illegible]	[illegible]
[illegible]	[illegible]	[illegible]	[illegible]	[illegible]	[illegible]	[illegible]	[illegible]	[illegible]	[illegible]	[illegible]		[illegible]	205	[illegible]
[illegible]	[illegible]	[illegible]	[illegible]	[illegible]	[illegible]	[illegible]	[illegible]	[illegible]	[illegible]	[illegible]	[illegible]	[illegible]	[illegible]	[illegible]
[illegible]	[illegible]	[illegible]	[illegible]	[illegible]	[illegible]	[illegible]	[illegible]	[illegible]	[illegible]	[illegible]	[illegible]	[illegible]	45	[illegible]
[illegible]	[illegible]	[illegible]	[illegible]	[illegible]	[illegible]	[illegible]	[illegible]	[illegible]	[illegible]	[illegible]		[illegible]	[illegible]	[illegible]
[illegible]	[illegible]	[illegible]	[illegible]					[illegible]				[illegible]		[illegible]
[illegible]	[illegible]	[illegible]	[illegible]	[illegible]	[illegible]	[illegible]	[illegible]	[illegible]	[illegible]	[illegible]	[illegible]	[illegible]	30	[illegible]
[illegible]	[illegible]	[illegible]	[illegible]	[illegible]	[illegible]	[illegible]	[illegible]	[illegible]		130		[illegible]	300	175
Presque Isle	[illegible]	[illegible]	[illegible]	[illegible]	[illegible]	[illegible]	60	42	[illegible]	34	4	22	21	7
Roscommon														
Saginaw	[illegible]	[illegible]	[illegible]	[illegible]	[illegible]	[illegible]	160	[illegible]	145	[illegible]		47	794	250
St. Clair	[illegible]	[illegible]	[illegible]	[illegible]	[illegible]	[illegible]	152	152	152	152		22	290	130
St. Joseph	[illegible]	[illegible]	[illegible]	[illegible]	[illegible]	25	[illegible]	123		123			360	73
Sanilac	154	[illegible]	[illegible]	[illegible]	154	154	154	154	154	154		5	400	153
Schoolcraft	27	27	27	27	27	27	27	27	27	27	8	5	16	12
Shiawassee	114	110	106	[illegible]	[illegible]	12	25	122	122	122		1	379	148
Tuscola	[illegible]	110	115	[illegible]	140	12	100	140	140	140		5	450	90
Van Buren	[illegible]	147	145	117	[illegible]	19	122	151	151	151		2	237	132
Washtenaw	[illegible]	[illegible]	128	10	115	150	164	164	164	164		12	290	158
Wayne	137	115	120	[illegible]	115	[illegible]	[illegible]	[illegible]	[illegible]	[illegible]		10	275	149
Wexford	78	77	64	76	74	41	77	81	81	81		34	136	29

TABLE XV.

Showing the extent to which physiology was taught in the schools of the state during the year ending July 8, 1907, as compiled from director's reports.

Counties.	Number of districts in county.	Number of districts reporting physiology taught.	Number of districts reporting physiology not taught.	Number of districts not reporting.
Totals	7,302	6,444	170	688
Alcona	36	29	1	6
Alger	8	8	……	……
Allegan	185	168	3	14
Alpena	19	15	1	3
Antrim	72	69	1	2
Arenac	42	36	1	5
Baraga	5	5	……	……
Barry	144	125	2	17
Bay	70	61	5	4
Benzie	53	49	……	4
Berrien	146	116	6	24
Branch	127	122	3	2
Calhoun	164	153	2	9
Cass	112	108	2	2
Charlevoix	67	60	1	6
Cheboygan	57	52	2	3
Chippewa	56	50	2	4
Clare	67	53	2	12
Clinton	129	116	2	11
Crawford	29	18	3	8
Delta	29	23	1	5
Dickinson	8	8	……	……
Eaton	144	134	4	6
Emmet	73	65	1	7
Genesee	157	138	5	14
Gladwin	52	38	4	10
Gogebic	8	8	……	……
Grand Traverse	67	56	2	9
Gratiot	132	111	3	18
Hillsdale	163	132	3	28
Houghton	35	29	1	5
Huron	121	106	1	14
Ingham	137	117	4	16
Ionia	141	125	5	11
Iosco	31	26	……	5
Iron	7	7	……	……
Isabella	106	102	1	3
Jackson	155	130	5	20
Kalamazoo	133	114	2	17
Kalkaska	51	43	2	6
Kent	205	182	4	19
Keweenaw	5	3	……	2
Lake	44	35	2	7
Lapeer	134	124	5	5
Leelanau	58	39	4	15
Lenawee	196	190	3	3
Livingston	135	113	5	17
Luce	4	4	……	……
Mackinac	14	12	……	2
Macomb	113	101	1	11
Manistee	64	58	1	5
Marquette	21	21	……	……
Mason	64	58	1	5
Mecosta	108	97	……	11
Menominee	41	36	……	5
Midland	81	75	2	4
Missaukee	62	47	2	13
Monroe	138	119	4	15
Montcalm	141	127	3	11
Montmorency	8	8	……	……
Muskegon	92	76	5	11
Newaygo	118	97	4	17
Oakland	201	192	2	7
Oceana	91	82	2	7
Ogemaw	49	40	2	7
Ontonagon	10	9	……	1
Osceola	93	87	3	3
Oscoda	18	13	3	2
Otsego	38	28	……	10
Ottawa	124	117	2	5
Presque Isle	38	33	1	4
Roscommon	26	19	1	6
Saginaw	164	150	4	10
St. Clair	156	156	……	……
St. Joseph	123	111	1	11
Sanilac	155	133	4	18
Schoolcraft	10	8	……	2
Shiawassee	124	121	2	1
Tuscola	150	135	……	15
Van Buren	153	122	8	23
Washtenaw	166	138	4	24
Wayne	149	129	2	18
Wexford	80	74	……	6

TABLE XVI.

Graded school statistics compiled from inspectors'

Districts.	Counties.	Number of children between 5 and 20 years.	Number of children that attended school during the year.	Number of days' school.	Percentage of attendance.	Estimated valuation of school property.	Total indebtedness.	Number of teachers employed.	
								Men.	Women.
Totals............	....	437,183	305,668	109,238	83	$24,704,667	$3,493,842 01	1,019	7,507
Ada..............	Kent..........	109	105	180	74	$3,000	....	1	2
Addison...........	Lenawee.......	171	147	175	92	15,000	$9,700	4	3
Adrian............	Lenawee.......	2,498	1,805	200	95	15,000	....	3	47
Alabaster.........	Iosco.........	140	111	180	53	3,000	....	.....	2
Alanson...........	Emmet.........	226	224	180	83	7,000	900 00	1	4
Alba..............	Antrim........	145	167	180	58	6,000	....	2	2
Albert Tp.........	Montmorency...	304	303	200	80	6,000	....	1	7
Albion............	Calhoun.......	1,639	1,114	190	96	75,000	....	4	26
Alden.............	Antrim........	129	118	180	62	4,500	850 00	1	2
Algonac...........	St. Clair.....	477	390	180	90	20,000	800 00	1	9
Allegan...........	Allegan.......	785	660	190	86	5,000	1,428 57	2	19
Allen.............	Hillsdale.....	87	72	180	98	5,000	....	1	2
Alma..............	Gratiot.......	678	616	196	95	50,000	18,000 00	2	16
Almont............	Lapeer........	190	172	200	96	12,500	....	2	5
Alpena............	Alpena........	3,727	2,008	200	94	89,000	....	4	45
Ann Arbor.........	Washtenaw.....	3,326	2,171	200	95	415,000	242,000 00	10	66
Applegate.........	Sanilac.......	84	66	180	78	1,600	....	1	1
Arcadia...........	Manistee......	175	89	180	69	2,000	....	1	1
Armada............	Macomb........	206	160	190	93	12,000	....	1	6
Ashley............	Gratiot.......	193	166	190	69	3,000	....	2	3
Athens............	Calhoun.......	186	154	180	92	3,500	....	1	4
Atlantic Mine.....	Houghton......	2,087	1,484	200	78	97,000	....	7	31
Attica............	Lapeer........	99	94	200	68	1,200	....	1	1
Augusta...........	Kalamazoo.....	136	103	180	71	6,000	....	2	4
Au Sable..........	Iosco.........	486	391	200	92	8,000	....	2	8
Au Train Tp.......	Alger.........	107	89	174	73	3,300	....	2	4
Bad Axe...........	Huron.........	515	412	190	91	25,000	6,000 00	2	10
Bainbridge........	Berrien.......	124	87	160	79	1,800	....	1	2
Baldwin...........	Lake..........	168	124	200	80	1,200	1,557 52	1	2
Bancroft..........	Shiawassee....	147	111	200	94	9,000	....	1	5
Bangor............	Van Buren.....	398	374	190	89	25,000	9,000 00	3	8
Baraga............	Baraga........	959	591	200	82	17,500	....	2	14
Baroda............	Berrien.......	198	153	160	81	6,000	....	1	2
Barryton..........	Mecosta.......	174	154	190	77	8,000	....	1	4
Bath..............	Clinton.......	101	86	180	80	3,000	....	1	2
Battle Creek......	Calhoun.......	4,756	3,943	191	95	475,000	....	11	101
Bay City..........	Bay...........	14,599	7,303	200	98	600,000	147,000 00	19	182
Bay Port..........	Huron.........	97	78	200	87	2,000	....	1	1
Bear Lake.........	Manistee......	155	149	180	80	6,000	1,350 00	1	3
Beaverton.........	Gladwin.......	250	252	180	78	4,000	376 80	2	6
Belding...........	Ionia.........	821	698	197	91	26,000	8,500 00	1	20
Bellaire..........	Antrim........	365	332	180	90	8,000	....	1	9
Belleville........	Wayne.........	150	116	200	91	11,500	2,000 00	1	3
Bellevue..........	Eaton.........	272	241	190	97	15,000	1,900 00	1	7
Benton Harbor.....	Berrien.......	1,978	1,790	180	95	100,000	43,000 00	3	40
Benzonia..........	Benzie........	231	191	180	83	5,000	400 00	1	5
Berlamont.........	Van Buren.....	87	68	180	70	1,500	....	1	2
Berlin............	Ottawa........	116	109	180	85	2,500	....	1	2
Berlin Tp. 3 fr...	Ionia.........	82	60	180	63	700	....	....	1
Berrien Springs...	Berrien.......	225	190	175	93	7,000	....	1	6
Bessemer..........	Gogebic.......	1,249	992	200	96	43,000	45,000 00	3	27

TABLE XVI.

reports for the year ending July 8, 1907.

Aggregate number of months taught by all teachers.		Total wages of teachers for the year.		Average monthly wages of teachers.		Amount paid for superintendence and instruction.	Total cost of school.	Number of non-resident pupils.	Tuition of non-resident pupils.
Men.	Women.	Men.	Women.	Men.	Women.				
9,768.3	71,045.6	$916,174 09	$3,839,655 36	$93 79	$54 04	$4,783,112 73	$8,665,490 61	10,943	$113,650 51
9.	18.	$468 00	$576 00	$52 00	$32 00	$1,044 00	$1,526 27	14	$108 96
27.	18.	1,700 00	630 00	62 96	35 00	2,330 00	5,168 71	26	294 75
30.	465.	3,900 00	23,361 00	130 00	50 24	27,261 00	57,723 31	70	976 10
....	18.	....	735 00	....	40 83	735 00	939 00	3	....
9.	36.	495 00	1,350 00	55 00	37 50	1,845 00	3,070 96	2	16 63
18.	18.	1,071 00	720 00	59 50	40 00	1,791 00	2,388 14	4	1 00
10.	70.	700 00	2,300 00	70 00	32 86	3,000 00	4,796 13	5	....
28.	247.	4,000 00	14,112 31	105 26	57 13	18,112 31	50,802 01	47	575 00
9.	18.	540 00	665 00	60 00	36 94	1,205 00	2,570 82	11	29 00
9.	73.7	1,000 00	3,035 50	111 11	41 16	4,035 50	6,286 97	10	50 75
19.	166.	2,488 35	8,237 97	130 96	49 63	10,726 32	18,101 06	28	350 00
9.	18.	600 00	585 00	66 67	32 50	1,185 00	1,623 71	10	70 50
20.	100.	1,777 50	7,068 75	88 87	44 18	8,846 25	19,372 17	38	282 73
10.	50.	825 00	2,200 00	82 50	44 00	3,025 00	4,369 94	16	156 30
40.	450.	3,850 00	18,720 00	96 25	41 60	22,570 00	36,084 14	....	....
100.	660.	14,475 00	35,069 10	144 75	53 13	49,544 10	186,053 16	201	4,855 06
9.	7.	450 00	210 00	50 00	30 00	660 00	879 14	4	....
9.	9.	495 00	360 00	55 00	40 00	855 00	1,039 12	2	....
9.5	47.5	844 36	1,648 42	88 88	34 70	2,492 78	3,750 53	37	410 34
19.	25.	902 50	910 63	47 50	36 42	1,813 13	2,477 25	4	....
9.	36.	630 00	1,440 00	70 00	40 00	2,110 00	2,637 46	22	208 49
70.	289.7	6,900 00	17,111 00	98 57	59 12	24,011 00	51,879 78	14	....
10.	10.	500 00	280 00	50 00	28 00	780 00	974 96	4	26 00
18.	36.	1,065 00	1,494 00	59 17	41 50	2,559 00	3,974 89	34	241 25
20.	80.	1,300 00	2,864 75	65 00	35 81	4,164 75	5,038 89	1	6 00
18.	34.	900 00	1,620 00	53 30	47 65	2,580 00	4,321 51	....	....
20.	100.	1,600 00	3,925 00	80 00	39 25	5,525 00	8,061 92	21	273 20
8.	8.	400 00	320 00	50 00	40 00	720 00	857 42	1	....
10.	20.	557 50	670 00	55 75	33 50	1,227 50	1,551 52	12	....
10.	40.	800 00	1,500 00	80 00	37 50	2,300 00	4,077 03	20	148 78
28.5	67.5	1,975 00	2,899 00	69 30	42 95	4,874 00	6,938 57	58	506 45
20.	139.	1,900 00	6,325 00	95 00	45 50	8,225 00	12,021 90	....	....
8.	16.	560 00	640 00	70 00	40 00	1,200 00	2,026 16	6	35 90
9.5	28.5	570 00	1,140 00	60 00	40 00	1,710 00	2,348 41	7	17 00
9.	18.	540 00	630 00	60 00	35 00	1,170 00	1,841 25	7	36 40
110.	1010.	12,437 50	52,229 41	113 07	51 71	64,666 91	131,716 14	89	1,252 78
190.	1820.	18,958 67	84,434 33	99 78	46 40	103,393 00	198,014 95	133	1,211 00
10.	10.	550 00	380 00	55 00	38 00	930 00	1,098 04	....	....
9.	27.	630 00	1,150 00	70 00	42 59	1,780 00	3,704 26	8	67 25
17.8	49.5	1,004 00	1,610 00	56 40	32 53	2,614 00	4,585 43	4	36 55
10.	194.7	1,250 00	,179 38	125 00	42 00	9,429 38	25,536 59	22	369 60
9.	81.	900 00	3,217 50	100 00	39 72	4,117 50	5,637 73	9	79 02
10.	30.	750 00	1,200 00	75 00	40 00	1,950 00	2,834 13	27	188 98
9.5	66.5	900 00	,432 00	94 74	36 57	3,332 00	10,747 08	25	174 92
27.	360.	3,450 78	1 ,123 22	127 80	47 56	20,574 00	52,418 11	102	1,253 88
9.	45.	699 99	,800 00	77 78	40 00	2,499 99	3,383 87	7	12 45
5.	13.	237 50	452 25	47 50	34 79	689 75	847 47	4	17 00
9.	18.	540 00	630 00	60 00	35 00	1,170 00	1,439 36	15	144 50
....	9.	....	405 00	....	45 00	405 00	537 93	....	....
9.5	56.5	897 18	2,127 50	94 44	37 65	3,024 68	3,957 26	21	204 00
30.	270.	3,250 00	13,345 00	108 33	49 43	16,595 00	33,068 98	3	78 00

TABLE XVI.—Continued.

Districts.	Counties.	Number of children between 5 and 20 years.	Number of children that attended school during the year.	Number of days' school.	Percentage of attendance.	Estimated valuation of school property.	Total indebtedness.	Number of teachers employed.	
								Men.	Women.
Big Rapids	Mecosta	1,332	1,008	200	96	$400,000	....	2	25
Birmingham	Oakland	363	337	200	93	30,000	$3,000 00	1	10
Blissfield Tp. 1 fr	Lenawee	191	144	200	93	10,000	....	1	3
Blissfield Tp. 2 fr	Lenawee	243	254	200	92	35,000	22,000 00	1	8
Bloomingdale	Van Buren	141	135	180	90	6,500	231 25	1	5
Boardman	Kalkaska	202	185	176	70	5,000	1,200 00	1	3
Boyne	Charlevoix	1,267	1,096	180	92	45,000	19,331 81	2	25
Boyne Falls	Charlevoix	218	130	180	82	5,500	2,000 00	1	3
Breckenridge	Gratiot	167	172	180	70	3,500	2,000 00	1	4
Breedsville	Van Buren	105	75	180	75	9,000	3,600 00	1	1
Bridgehampton Tp. 1	Sanilac	67	47	200	00	600	....	.....	1
Bridgehampton Tp. 2	Sanilac	90	68	200	55	2,000	....	1	.....
Bridgehampton Tp. 5 fr	Sanilac	68	49	180	69	1,400	....	.....	1
Bridgeman	Berrien	171	109	160	72	1,500	450 00	.....	2
Bridgeport	Saginaw	114	88	180	68	5,000	....	1	1
Brighton	Livingston	184	166	200	96	19,000	2,500 00	1	5
Britton	Lenawee	118	113	187	82	9,000	2,150 00	.....	3
Bronson	Branch	272	230	190	93	15,000	3,000 00	2	9
Brooklyn	Jackson	154	130	185	96	6,000	....	2	4
Brown City	Sanilac	223	206	200	89	9,500	9,000 00	3	2
Buchanan	Berrien	405	351	190	93	6,000	....	2	11
Burden	Sanilac	162	79	200	60	2,000	120 88	1	.....
Burlington	Calhoun	96	90	180	65	3,500	....	1	2
Burnips Corners	Allegan	96	77	180	92	3,000	....	1	1
Burr Oak	St. Joseph	163	156	190	92	20,000	....	1	7
Burt Tp.	Alger	510	486	200	79	20,000	8,549 33	.....	12
Byron	Shiawassee	114	113	200	92	7,000	....	1	2
Cadillac	Wexford	2,247	1,731	180	94	115,000	4,000 00	3	41
Cady	Macomb	135	54	180	55	1,000	....	.....	1
Caledonia	Kent	149	135	200	84	6,000	....	3	3
Caledonia Tp. 3	Kent	51	37	180	70	2,000	....	1	.....
Calumet	Houghton	8,036	5,953	200	87	404,000	....	8	160
Calumet Tp. 2	Houghton	1,538	1,262	200	87	26,579	....	.....	28
Camden	Hillsdale	114	105	180	94	8,000	1,900 00	2	4
Cannon Tp. 2 fr	Kent	81	44	180	90	1,500	....	1	1
Capac	St. Clair	209	182	200	90	10,000	....	1	5
Caro	Tuscola	553	472	200	95	22,000	....	3	17
Carrollton Tp. 1	Saginaw	399	313	200	90	10,000	....	1	5
Carrollton Tp. 2	Saginaw	316	148	200	79	4,000	....	1	2
Carson City	Montcalm	264	205	190	87	15,000	6,144 70	1	7
Carsonville	Sanilac	200	171	200	63	4,000	....	1	3
Caseville	Huron	183	182	200	71	5,000	....	1	3
Casnovia	Muskegon	96	87	180	88	4,500	1,400 00	1	2
Cass City	Tuscola	417	353	200	93	10,525	2,575 00	2	9
Cassopolis	Cass	262	251	182	93	18,000	....	4	6
Cedar Springs	Kent	200	248	190	80	22,500	2,500 00	1	7
Central Lake	Antrim	350	300	180	78	40,000	....	1	9
Centreville	St. Joseph	167	174	180	45	15,000	....	1	5
Ceresco	Calhoun	68	54	180	38	1,200	....	.....	2
Champion Tp.	Marquette	517	393	200	72	13,000	....	2	8
Chandler Tp. 5 fr	Huron	197	127	200	50	1,600	39 15	1	1
Charlevoix	Charlevoix	763	664	180	82	42,000	23,000 00	2	20
Charlotte	Eaton	1,040	902	183	95	40,000	....	2	24
Charlton Tp	Otsego	153	115	160	77	6,500	2,000 00	.....	5
Chase	Lake	101	87	180	70	1,500	....	1	1
Cheboygan	Cheboygan	2,320	1,349	200	91	65,000	54,000 00	4	27
Chelsea	Washtenaw	512	425	200	95	15,000	....	1	15
Chesaning	Saginaw	324	209	194	93	15,000	....	2	6
Chief	Manistee	92	87	160	63	1,700	1,400 00	2	1
Chickaming Tp. 3	Berrien	92	49	180	80	1,500	....	1	1

TABLE XVI.—CONTINUED.

Aggregate number of months taught by all teachers.		Total wages of teachers for the year.		Average monthly wages of teachers.		Amount paid for superintendence and instruction.	Total cost of school.	Number of non-resident pupils.	Tuition of non-resident pupils.
Men.	Women.	Men.	Women.	Men.	Women.				
20.	250.	$1,950 00	$11,470 00	$97 50	$45 88	$13,420 00	$19,961 49	28	$210 53
10.	100.	1,200 00	4,306 25	120 00	43 06	5,506 25	8,132 91	55	901 00
10.	30.	800 00	1,010 00	80 00	33 67	1,810 00	2,649 67	6	41 00
10.	60.	1,000 00	2,600 00	100 00	43 37	3,600 00	6,233 15	41	371 53
9.	36.	700 00	1,235 00	77 78	34 30	1,935 00	3,401 52	16	124 75
9.	27.	585 00	1,080 00	65 00	40 00	1,665 00	2,265 57	9	18 00
18.	216.	1,694 91	9,270 00	94 16	42 91	10,964 91	17,859 38	10	77 00
9.	26.8	540 00	1,070 00	60 00	40 00	1,610 00	2,687 25	2	18 75
9.	34.	475 00	1,213 75	52 78	35 70	1,688 75	3,078 73	20	131 26
9.	9.	540 00	315 00	60 00	35 00	855 00	1,601 77	9	40 00
....	10.*	....	450 00	....	45 00	450 00	584 13	5	....
10.	....	455 00	....	45 50	....	455 00	564 74	3	....
....	9.	....	432 00	....	48 00	432 00	541 73	1	....
....	16.	....	600 00	....	37 50	600 00	868 75	....	....
9.	9.	500 00	315 00	55.56	35 00	815 00	1,050 87	1	1 00
10.	50.	850 00	1,660 00	85 00	33 20	2,510 00	3,936 44	23	232 30
....	28.	....	1,198 25	....	42 80	1,198 25	1,831 76	7	45 00
11.5	61.	887 50	2,675 00	77 17	43 85	3,562 50	5,473 17	17	204 93
10.2	37.	830 00	1,657 93	80 97	44 81	2,487 93	3,:93 73	28	190 25
29.	20.	1,615 00	800 00	55 69	40 00	2,415 00	5,341 21	52	328 93
19.	104.5	1,570 00	4,749 97	82 63	45 45	6,319 97	9,425 89	46	439 16
10.	....	550 00	....	55 00	....	550 00	850 43	....	....
9.	18.	450 00	585 00	50 00	32 50	1,035 00	1,317 13	7	19 50
9.	9.	540 00	360 00	60 00	40 00	900 00	1,113 75	12	82 07
9.5	55.	700 00	2,003 75	80 00	36 43	2,763 75	3,425 89	22	....
....	120.	....	6,350 00	....	52 92	6,350 00	14,321 23	....	....
10.	20.	700 00	700 00	70 00	35 00	1,400 00	2,303 43	18	179 82
27.	369.	3,950 00	20,898 93	146 30	56 64	24,848 93	41,113 13	3	28 00
....	9.	....	405 00	....	45 00	405 00	510 86	9	....
11.7	28.3	765 75	1,047 00	65 17	37 06	1,812 75	2,289 18	33	289 10
9.	....	405 00	....	45 00	....	405 00	554 53	....	....
80.	1,595.	11,800 00	93,378 27	147 50	58 54	105,178 27	186,395 58	66	2,442 56
....	234.7	....	14,304 62	....	60 95	14,304 62	24,402 55	....	....
18.	27.	909 93	943 64	50 55	34 95	1,853 57	2,593 18	20	68 00
9.	9.	450 00	270 00	50 00	30 00	720 00	791 98	10	51 27
10.	40.	750 00	1,775 00	75 00	44 37	2,525 00	3,322 19	27	232 88
30.	120.	2,550 00	5,059 37	85 00	42 16	7,009 37	10,118 78	89	776 45
10.	50.	800 00	1,750 00	80 00	35 00	2,550 00	3,963 51	4	5 80
10.	20.	550 00	835 00	55 00	41 75	1,385 00	2,166 92	....	....
9.5	66.5	800 00	2,903 75	84 21	43 67	3,703 75	5,192 56	31	388 89
10.	30.	650 00	1,150 00	65 00	38 33	1,800 00	2,988 52	10	53 69
10.	29.5	700 00	1,020 00	70 00	34 57	1,720 00	2,304 63	6	38 50
9.	18.	585 00	630 00	65 00	35 00	1,215 00	1,605 29	12	78 50
20.	90.	1,400 00	3,680 00	70 00	40 89	5,080 00	10,862 8ɜ	60	.632 24
28.5	57.	2,050 00	2,495 00	71 93	43 77	4,545 00	6,608 80	19	208 05
9.5	66.5	925 00	2,812 00	97 37	42 30	3,737 00	8,639 12	38	402 48
9.	76.	1,000 00	3,242 50	111 11	42 66	4,242 50	5,911 91	9	104 21
9.	45.	800 00	1,800 00	88 89	40 00	2,600 00	3,391 34	16	145 50
....	18.	....	630 00	....	35 00	630 00	829 69	....	....
20.	80.	2,200 00	4,500 00	110 00	56 25	6,700 00	10,227 64	....	....
10.	8.	500 00	240 00	50 00	30 00	740 00	1,053 47	....	....
18.	162.	1,527 66	7,574 54	84 87	46 76	9,102 20	15,304 27	17	60 50
18.3	219.6	2,250 00	11,397 64	122 95	51 90	13,647 64	21,119 84	61	1,083 95
....	42.	....	1,683 00	....	40 07	1,683 00	3,185 67	9	....
9.	9.	450 00	315 00	50 00	35 00	765 00	1,092 64	....	....
40.	270.	3,570 00	11,824 60	89 25	43 80	15,394 60	58,674 84	52	425 24
10.	138.	1,000 00	5,235 00	100 00	37 93	6,235 00	8,431 90	45	613 00
20.	60.	1,500 00	2,635 00	75 00	43 91	4,135 00	6,919 32	17	186 50
7.2	8.	387 50	280 00	53 45	35 00	667 50	2,464 32	5	14 75
8.	9.	360 00	315 00	45 00	35 00	675 00	865 60	....	

TABLE XVI.—Continued.

Districts.	Counties.	Number of children between 5 and 20 years.	Number of children that attended school during the year.	Number of days' school.	Percentage of attendance.	Estimated valuation of school property.	Total indebtedness.	Number of teachers employed. Men.	Women.
China Tp. 4	St. Clair	92	78	180	68	$1,500	...	1	1
Clare	Clare	472	440	196	91	2,600	...	2	10
Clarkston	Oakland	140	116	200	83	4,000	...	1	3
Clarksville	Ionia	103	89	180	88	4,000	...	1	2
Clayton	Lenawee	91	74	180	80	1,500	...	1	2
Climax	Kalamazoo	143	97	180	88	6,350	...	1	3
Clinton	Lenawee	229	195	199	91	20,000	$13,196 61	1	7
Clio	Genesee	172	153	200	85	6,000	...	1	5
Coldwater	Branch	1,342	1,184	185	95	100,000	...	5	29
Coleman	Midland	391	392	200	68	12,000	...	3	7
Coloma	Berrien	218	189	180	80	8,000	1,200 00	1	6
Colon	St. Joseph	211	174	180	96	15,000	18,750 00	2	6
Columbiaville	Lapeer	144	112	188	76	16,000	...	1	3
Commerce Tp. 10	Oakland	30	25	180	76	600	...	...	1
Comstock	Kalamazoo	264	197	180	78	3,000	...	2	5
Concord	Jackson	125	107	190	94	9,000	...	1	6
Conklin	Ottawa	80	71	180	92	1,200	...	1	1
Constantine	St. Joseph	262	211	180	80	25,000	...	1	7
Coopersville	Ottawa	202	171	190	92	5,000	...	1	5
Copemish	Manistee	139	118	180	81	2,100	...	1	2
Coral	Montcalm	143	95	180	85	3,000	...	1	3
Corunna	Shiawassee	382	372	200	94	35,000	1,000 00	1	13
Covert	Van Buren	190	169	180	86	3,000	...	2	3
Croswell	Sanilac	398	362	198	92	8,000	1,500 00	2	5
Crystal	Montcalm	115	90	180	90	4,000	...	1	1
Crystal Falls	Iron	1,327	1,094	186	80	110,000	47,000 00	1	35
Custer	Mason	125	107	180	75	2,500	...	1	2
Dansville	Ingham	100	79	200	85	4,500	...	1	3
Davison	Genesee	189	184	200	75	10,000	...	3	3
Dearborn	Wayne	353	255	200	81	30,000	...	1	8
Decatur	Van Buren	378	308	190	91	15,000	...	1	8
Deckerville	Sanilac	187	182	200	67	9,000	5,000 00	1	3
Deerfield	Lenawee	173	135	180	91	8,000	...	1	4
Detour	Chippewa	347	276	200	74	5,000	400 00	1	5
Detroit	Wayne	97,508	60,840	200	94	4,709,770	...	90	1,225
Dewitt	Clinton	119	99	180	90	3,500	...	1	1
Dexter	Washtenaw	257	231	180	97	21,000	...	1	8
Dimondale	Eaton	109	81	180	87	2,200	...	1	3
Dorr	Allegan	96	73	177	73	1,000	...	1	1
Douglas	Allegan	155	126	179	88	5,000	...	1	3
Dowagiac	Cass	1,202	1,095	196	97	75,000	27,700 00	4	28
Downington	Sanilac	87	71	200	65	1,200	200 00	...	1
Dryden	Lapeer	138	105	200	88	2,800	...	1	2
Dundee	Monroe	270	243	180	93	20,000	...	2	9
Durand	Shiawassee	461	382	200	93	25,000	1,200 00	4	10
East Grand Rapids	Kent	129	112	200	69	6,000	1,559 04	...	3
East Jordan	Charlevoix	700	607	180	92	19,500	3,000 00	3	13
East Tawas	Iosco	480	441	200	90	10,500	...	1	10
Eaton Rapids	Eaton	415	367	195	94	75,000	...	2	13
Eau Claire	Berrien	137	131	180	70	6,000	...	1	3
Ecorse Tp. 1	Wayne	409	222	200	90	20,000	5,119 00	1	7
Ecorse Tp. 3	Wayne	270	220	200	91	10,000	...	1	4
Ecorse Tp. 12	Wayne	199	154	200	65	12,000	11,000 00	1	4
Edenville	Midland	97	63	180	66	1,500	...	1	1
Edmore	Montcalm	284	221	190	92	4,000	...	1	4
Edwardsburg	Cass	125	111	180	93	3,000	...	1	3
Elk Rapids	Antrim	552	521	176	85	30,000	...	1	16
Elkton	Huron	284	219	200	80	8,000	5,000 00	1	5
Elk Tp. 4 fr.	Sanilac	98	78	200	83	800	...	1	...
Elm Hall	Gratiot	101	84	179	70	2,500	...	1	6

TABLE XVI.—CONTINUED.

Aggregate number of months taught by all teachers.		Total wages of teachers for the year.		Average monthly wages of teachers.		Amount paid for superintendence and instruction.	Total cost of school.	Number of non-resident pupils.	Tuition of non-resident pupils.
Men.	Women.	Men.	Women.	Men.	Women.				
9.	9.	$405 00	$288 00	$45 00	$32 00	$693 00	$1,004 48	1	$15 00
13.	97.	1,035 00	3,680 00	79 61	37 94	4,715 00	6,827 78	26	216 94
10.	30.	750 00	1,175 00	75 00	39 17	1,925 00	2,491 12	13	183 50
9.	18.	585 00	720 00	65 00	40 00	1,305 00	1,655 01	6	47 50
9.	18.	720 00	585 00	80 00	32 50	1,305 00	1,677 27	13	86 50
9.	27.	630 00	990 00	70 00	36 67	1,620 00	2,095 54	15	130 15
10.	60.	900 00	2,310 00	90 00	38 50	3,210 00	5,109 97	24	274 07
10.	50.	750 00	2,000 00	75 00	40 00	2,750 00	3,895 49	36	371 70
46.	267.	4,370 00	13,239 37	95 00	49 51	17,609 37	27,934 28	45	600 00
20.	70.	1,085 00	2,331 00	54 25	33 30	3,416 00	4,536 13	13	46 00
9.	54.	630 00	2,070 00	70 00	38 33	2,700 00	3,597 90	48	417 80
9.	54.	782 24	2,340 00	86 92	43 33	3,122 24	3,857 93	24	249 11
10.	20.	800 00	1,200 00	80 00	40 00	2,000 00	3,021 57	17	80 65
....	9.	....	360 00	....	40 00	360 00	468 47	1	9 00
11.8	28.7	663 75	1,243 25	56 49	43 24	1,907 00	3,680 45	....	....
9.5	47.6	800 00	1,907 50	84 21	40 07	2,707 50	3,603 91	23	226 00
9.	9.	405 00	270 00	45 00	30 00	675 00	881 49	9	72 61
9.	63.	950 00	2,810 00	105 56	44 60	3,760 00	4,880 06	26	310 00
9.5	38.	590 54	1,465 90	62 16	38 58	2,056 44	2,805 82	28	255 42
9.	18.	450 00	675 00	50 00	37 50	1,125 00	1,258 65	11	9 50
8.5	18.	437 50	585 00	51 47	32 50	1,022 50	1,416 26	8	41 00
10.	113.	1,200 00	4,884 75	120 00	43 22	6,084 75	8,973 82	44	356 42
18.	27.	1,080 00	1,080 00	60 00	40 00	2,160 00	2,960 82	19	64 18
20.	50.	1,450 00	2,075	72 50	41 50	3,525 00	4,821 91	23	150 32
9.	9.	495 00	270 00	55 00	30 00	765 00	1,081 71	7	71 00
10.	375.	1,600 00	16,450 00	160 00	49 10	18,050 00	51,152 97	....	....
9.	18.	450 00	675 00	50	37 50	1,125 00	2,013 56	1	....
10.	30.	700 00	1,050 00	70	35 00	1,750 00	2,167 66	14	93 40
30.	30.	1,375 00	1,050 00	45 83	35 00	2,425 00	3,127 95	28	315 95
10.	60.	800 00	2,007 00	80 00	33 45	2,807 00	4,319 33	5	30 00
9 5	76.	1,000 00	2,692 00	105 26	35 42	3,692 00	6,036 82	51	456 37
10.	30.	750	1,100 00	75 00	36 67	1,850 00	2,871 41	17	113 39
9.	36.	650	962,305 00	72 22	36 25	1,955 00	2,287 45	21	150 25
10.	50.	750	,069 00	75 00	41 78	2,839 00	4,220 14	1	....
900.	12,250.	130,983 30	,576 62	145 54	78 98	1,098,559 92	1,731,003 91	180	....
9.	9.	495 00	315 00	55 00	35 00	810 00	1,266 27	3	15 00
9.	63.	855 00	2,475 00	95 00	39 28	3,330 00	4,580 76	22	376 50
9.	18.	495 00	720 00	55 00	40 00	1,215 00	2,151 61	8	40 50
9.	9.	405 00	300 00	45 00	33 33	705 00	913 44	....	....
9.	27.	600 00	1,080 00	66 67	40 00	1,680 00	2,178 30	3	21 00
40.	280	3,475 00	11,813 75	86 87	42 19	15,288 75	23,212 68	73	494 86
....	10.	....	500 00	....	50 00	500 00	762 51	9	8 50
10.	20.	700 00	750 00	70 00	37 50	1,450 00	1,738 19	13	175 68
14.2	57.8	1,046 25	2,113 25	73 42	36 60	3,159 50	4,038 96	14	205 00
34.5	100.	2,155 75	3,885 00	62 48	38 85	6,040 75	10,280 27	24	129 75
....	30.	....	1,250 00	....	41 67	1,250 00	2,046 99	....	....
27.	117.	1,950 00	4,837 50	72 22	41 35	6,787 50	10,241 76	6	42 62
10.	100.	775 00	4,239 25	77 50	42 39	5,014 25	6,977 57	....	....
20.	130.	1,800 00	5,470 00	90 00	42 08	7,270 00	9,916 60	43	594 48
9.	27.	675 00	1,080 00	75 00	40 00	1,755 00	2,397 20	25	110 33
10.	60.	750 00	2,500 00	75 00	41 67	3,250 00	7,834 86	....	....
10.	40.	750 00	1,600 00	75 00	40 00	2,350 00	3,254 92	....	....
10.	30.	650 00	805 00	65 00	26 83	1,455 00	3,478 98	....	....
9.	9.	405 00	315 00	45 00	35 00	720 00	1,249 78	....	....
9.5	38.	750 00	1,539 00	78 95	40 50	2,289 00	3,456 68	32	182 60
9.	27.	675 00	1,012 50	75 00	37 50	1,687 50	2,414 81	25	166 00
9.	130.4	1,300 00	5,757 50	144 44	44 15	7,057 50	10,825 82	16	149 72
10.	50.	850 00	1,755 00	85 00	35 00	2,605 00	3,967 74	17	128 68
10.	....	500 00	....	50 00	....	500 00	821 30	....	....
9.	13.9	402 75	497 57	44 75	35 80	900 32	1,216 43	8	34 55

TABLE XVI.—Continued.

Districts.	Counties.	Number of children between 5 and 20 years.	Number of children that attended school during the year	Number of days school.	Percentage of attendance.	Estimated valuation of school property.	Total indebtedness.	Number of teachers employed. Men.	Women.
Elmira	Otsego	148	134	170	73	$1,500	....	3	1
Elsie	Clinton	204	144	190	89	25,000	$10,000 00	2	4
Empire	Leelanau	201	168	180	83	5,000	....	1	3
Erie	Monroe	174	152	180	76	4,800	89 81	.....	3
Escanaba	Delta	4,237	2,793	200	94	189,282	73,500 00	4	61
Essexville	Bay	578	141	200	89	6,000	....	1	5
Estey	Gladwin	99	90	180	71	1,500	....	1	1
Evart	Osceola	452	341	200	95	15,000	3,000 00	2	10
Fairgrove	Tuscola	140	125	200	71	4,500	1,800 00	1	3
Farmington	Oakland	156	156	200	83	5,500	2 40	1	4
Farwell	Clare	320	223	180	91	3,000	8,100 00	1	5
Fennville	Allegan	237	201	180	89	5,000	....	1	4
Fenton	Genesee	524	547	200	94	75,000	....	3	12
Fife Lake	Grand Traverse	134	126	180	86	5,000	....	1	2
Filion	Huron	82	51	189	70	1,500	....	....	1
Fillmore Tp. 1	Allegan	145	99	180	83	2,000	....	1	1
Fillmore Tp. 2	Allegan	170	130	180	89	2,400	....	.....	2
Flat Rock	Wayne	138	100	200	91	12,000	....	1	3
Flint	Genesee	3,789	3,080	200	94	300,000	69,000 00	4	75
Flushing	Genesee	191	160	190	95	15,000	....	2	4
Forest Grove	Ottawa	100	73	180	81	1,500	....	1	1
Forestville	Sanilac	90	72	180	60	1,200	70 89	1	1
Fostoria	Tuscola	118	117	200	89	3,000	230 85	1	2
Fowlerville	Livingston	292	154	200	91	10,000	....	1	8
Frankfort	Benzie	637	589	192	94	30,000	9,035 00	1	15
Freeport	Barry	154	159	180	92	4,000	....	2	3
Fremont	Newaygo	387	389	200	84	15,000	....	2	10
Frontier	Hillsdale	81	74	180	95	4,000	....	1	2
Fruitport	Muskegon	109	99	200	87	1,400	....	1	2
Gagetown	Tuscola	205	93	200	74	3,000	....	1	2
Gaines	Genesee	97	93	200	88	4,000	....	1	2
Galesburg	Kalamazoo	149	118	180	94	12,000	....	1	7
Galien	Berrien	175	143	180	92	5,000	....	1	4
Gaylord	Otsego	574	454	200	91	30,000	8,000 00	1	10
Gladstone	Delta	1,064	910	200	96	50,000	30,000 00	2	17
Gladwin	Gladwin	291	288	200	84	21,000	15,000 00	1	6
Gobleville	Van Buren	168	141	190	88	8,000	....	1	4
Goodrich	Genesee	71	66	200	92	2,000	....	1	1
Graafschap	Allegan	142	101	180	70	1,400	....	.....	2
Grand Blanc	Genesee	106	100	200	82	7,000	2,000 00	2	2
Grand Haven	Ottawa	1,047	1,138	200	97	90,000	30,000 00	1	30
Grand Junction	Van Buren	93	67	175	86	3,500	....	1	1
Grand Ledge	Eaton	603	534	198	88	25,000	4,000 00	3	14
Grand Rapids	Kent	27,325	15,650	200	95	1,736,200	167,000 00	24	428
Grandville	Kent	309	245	200	80	10,000	600	1	5
Grant	Newaygo	133	101	180	78	5,000	2,400 00	1	2
Grass Lake	Jackson	192	189	200	86	12,000	....	1	9
Grattan	Kent	97	74	175	55	1,400	....	3	1
Grayling	Crawford	532	457	200	87	15,000	5,000 00	2	9
Greenland Tp.	Ontonagon	636	613	198	90	17,920	9,000 00	2	14
Greenville	Montcalm	845	904	200	94	33,000	....	1	22
Grindstone City	Huron	160	152	200	70	1,500	....	1	3
Grosse Isle	Wayne	192	131	200	54	9,000	23 63	1	3
Grosse Pointe Tp. 1	Wayne	260	172	200	58	34,000	30,000 00	1	5
Hadley	Lapeer	98	85	190	90	3,000	....	1	2
Hale	Iosco	123	84	180	70	2,500	800 00	.....	2
Halfway	Macomb	162	85	200	93	3,200	....	.....	3
Hamilton	Allegan	99	94	180	88	6,000	....	1	1
Hamtramck	Wayne	935	555	200	91	40,000	27,000 00	1	11
Hamtramck Tp. 3	Wayne	128	75	200	66	2,500	1,000 00	.....	2

TABLE XVI.—Continued.

Aggregate number of months taught by all teachers.		Total wages of teachers for the year.		Average monthly wages of teachers.		Amount paid for superintendence and instruction.	Total cost of school.	Number of non-resident pupils.	Tuition of non-resident pupils.
Men.	Women.	Men.	Women.	Men.	Women.				
25.5	8.2	$1,232 50	$330 00	$48 33	$40 00	$1,562 50	$1,785 00	7	$16 62
19.	38.	1,045 00	1,330 00	55 00	35 00	2,375 00	3,875 31	27	229 25
9.	27.	900 00	23,125 00	100 00	41 67	2,025 00	2,342 83	2	10 00
......	27.	......	,055 00	......	39 07	1,055 00	1,420 47	9	17 50
40.	576.	4,700 00	,332 85	117 50	49 19	33,032 85	114,842 53	19	365 72
10.	39.	750 00	1,530 00	75 00	39 23	2,280 00	4,467 58	......	......
9.	9.	315 00	360 00	35 00	40 00	675 00	972 39	......	......
15.	100.	1,325 88	4,400 00	88 39	44 00	5,725 88	10,398 77	15	171 00
10.	27.8	600 00	890 00	60 00	32 07	1,490 00	2,487 30	26	117 42
10.	40.	650 00	1,300 00	65 00	32 50	1,950 00	2,714 75	8	120 40
9.	45.	600 00	1,629 00	66 67	36 20	2,229 00	4,378 85	8	2 50
9.	36.	765 00	1,620 00	85 00	45 00	2,385 00	3,180 24	23	175 59
30.	120.	2,660 00	4,775 00	88 67	39 79	7,435 00	13,739 95	60	753 21
9.	18.	585 00	720 00	65 00	40 00	1,305 00	3,087 97	9	46 25
......	10.	......	480 00	......	48 00	480 00	579 50	1	......
9.	9.	414 00	270 00	46 00	30 00	684 00	845 23	3	......
......	18.	......	792 00	......	44 00	792 00	1,034 91	5	......
10.	30.	750 00	1,290 00	75 00	43 00	2,040 00	2,665 54	28	224 79
40.	750.	6,150 00	36,545 57	153 75	48 73	42,695 57	69,917 24	97	1,879 93
20.	40.	1,400 00	1,450 00	70 00	36 25	2,850 00	4,455 27	27	386 90
9.	9.	495 00	315 00	55 00	35 00	810 00	1,006 64	......	......
9.	6.	450 00	180 00	50 00	30 00	630 00	1,047 94	1	......
10.	20.	650 00	700 00	65 00	35 00	1,350 00	1,630 46	16	49 60
10.	70.	800 00	2,600 00	80 00	37 14	3,400 00	4,080 56	48	657 63
10.	135.	1,100 00	5,470 00	110 00	40 52	6,570 00	10,980 56	8	61 75
18.	27.	1,080 00	990 00	60 00	36 67	2,070 00	2,659 48	13	100 20
20.	90.	1,300 00	3,586 40	65 00	39 85	4,886 40	7,779 70	57	460 24
9.	18.	450 00	585	50 00	32 50	1,035 00	1,283 62	31	132 25
10.	20.	700 00	800	70 00	40 00	1,500 00	2,162 78	......	......
10.	20.	600 00	600	60 00	30 00	1,200 00	1,443 92	9	20 75
10.	20.	650 00	700 00	65 00	35 00	1,350 00	2,370 53	20	216 77
9.	49.5	750 00	1,899 00	83 33	38 36	2,649 00	3,350 42	46	475 00
9.	27.	675 00	1,170 00	75 00	43 33	1,845 00	2,359 85	14	170 25
9.5	95.	1,100 00	,488 31	115 79	4 24	7,712 81	13,164 38	19	101 00
20.	165.	1,950 00	,305 00	95 00	27	9,255 00	38,923 68	11	......
10.	59.	650 00	2,270 00	65 00	38 47	2,920 00	5,616 02	22	259 00
9.5	38.	620 00	1,472 50	65 26	38 75	2,092 50	3,307 95	20	190 00
10.	10.	700 00	350 00	70 00	35 00	1,050 00	1,443 89	21	114 75
......	18.	......	810 00	......	45 00	810 00	1,053 46	12	......
20.	10.	1,000 00	400 00	50 00	40 00	1,400 00	2,343 55	20	198 95
10.	300.	1,795 00	13,894 75	179 50	46 31	15,689 75	25,427 31	25	388 25
9.	9.	468 00	300 00	52 00	40 00	828 00	1,390 90	16	44 75
30.	139.5	2,400 00	5,797 50	80 00	41 56	8,197 50	11,405 23	56	572 75
240.	4,280.	29,585 00	298,850 37	123 27	69 82	328,435 37	487,173 86	92	2,055 91
10.	50.	840 00	1,850 00	84 00	37 00	2,090 00	4,407 05	37	310 46
9.	18.	550 00	630 00	61 11	35 00	1,180 00	5,108 17	8	20 50
10.	60.	825 00	2,400 00	82 50	40 00	3,225 00	4,232 66	22	263 08
9.	9.	450 00	270 00	50 00	30 00	720 00	895 26	1	5 00
20.	90.	1,500 00	3,700 00	75 00	41 11	5,200 00	8,309 77	8	......
20.	140.	2,000 00	7,000 00	100 00	50 00	9,000 00	16,289 21	......	......
10.	220.	1,200 00	9,540 00	120 00	43 36	10,740 00	14,105 47	39	580 33
10.	30.	600 00	950 00	60	31 67	1,550 00	8,759 49	......	......
10.	30.	650 00	1,425 00	65	47 50	2,075 00	3,693 56	......	......
5.	44.	300 00	2,080 00	60	47 27	2,380 00	24,960 43	......	......
9.5	19.	600 00	688 75	63 16	36 25	1,288 75	1,559 88	30	280 40
......	18.	......	720 00	......	40 00	720 00	1,355 71	4	......
......	20.	......	800 00	......	40 00	800 00	1,096 90	4	......
9.	9.	450 00	315 00	50 00	35 00	765 00	1,995 36	2	3 00
10.	100.	1,000 00	4,336 25	100 00	43 36	5,336 25	9,758 03	5	28 49
......	20.	......	850 00	......	42 50	850 00	1,109 68	7	13 80

TABLE XVI.—CONTINUED.

Districts.	Counties.	Number of children between 5 and 20 years.	Number of children that attended school during the year.	Number of days' school.	Percentage of attendance.	Estimated valuation of school property.	Total indebtedness.	Number of teachers employed.	
								Men.	Women.
Hamtramck Tp. 5	Wayne	274	144	190	74	$10,000	$9,228 67	1	2
Hancock	Houghton	2,070	1,525	194	96	151,297	12,000 00	4	26
Hanover	Jackson	116	94	200	91	6,000	....	1	3
Harbor Beach	Huron	435	324	195	93	30,000	16,000 00	1	8
Harbor Springs	Emmet	701	431	180	91	20,000	8,000 00	1	12
Harrietta	Wexford	129	121	180	86	3,500	....	1	2
Harrison	Clare	242	190	180	75	2,500	....	2	2
Harrisville	Alcona	202	160	180	72	5,000	....	1	3
Hart	Oceana	463	383	180	91	20,000	1,000 00	1	14
Hartford	Van Buren	364	300	180	90	15,000	8,500 00	1	12
Haslett	Ingham	105	96	180	73	3,000	....	1	1
Hastings	Barry	808	650	200	94	45,000	....	5	18
Hematite Tp.	Iron	175	163	200	81	9,000	....	1	5
Hersey	Osceola	146	136	188	79	5,000	200 00	1	3
Hesperia	Newaygo	142	160	180	74	6,000	....	1	4
Highland Park	Wayne	371	237	200	87	20,000	18,000 00	1	7
Hillman	Montmorency	279	234	180	61	3,575	....	1	6
Hillsdale	Hillsdale	1,122	1,064	190	95	110,000	43,960 00	3	28
Holland	Ottawa	2,846	2,153	200	96	125,000	19,000 00	2	43
Holland Tp. 3	Ottawa	130	95	200	75	2,000	....	1	1
Holland Tp. 4	Ottawa	108	52	180	73	1,700	....	1	....
Holland Tp. 6	Ottawa	139	85	180	80	2,000	750 00	....	2
Holland Tp. 9	Ottawa	185	118	177	52	10,000	8,000 00	....	3
Holland Tp. 11 fr.	Ottawa	101	70	172	83	3,000	972 91	1	1
Holly	Oakland	360	322	189	94	18,500	....	1	8
Holt	Ingham	110	90	180	82	3,000	....	1	2
Holton	Muskegon	104	80	180	87	2,000	....	....	2
Homer	Calhoun	219	213	176	94	25,000	3,846 87	1	8
Honor	Benzie	196	190	180	69	3,500	....	1	4
Horton	Jackson	71	58	190	93	5,000	....	1	2
Houghton	Houghton	1,955	1,206	200	92	160,000	70,000 00	11	53
Howard City	Montcalm	372	332	190	91	5,000	....	1	10
Howell	Livingston	552	521	200	94	35,000	....	1	20
Hubbardston	Ionia	127	71	180	86	4,500	....	1	3
Hudson	Lenawee	586	514	190	94	25,000	....	3	13
Hudsonville	Ottawa	189	140	180	70	2,500	....	1	2
Hume Tp. 1	Huron	74	48	200	68	800	....	....	1
Imlay City	Lapeer	382	300	200	92	20,000	8,500 00	1	7
Ionia	Ionia	1,652	1,142	200	98	65,000	....	3	28
Iron Mountain	Dickinson	3,230	2,591	180	95	200,000	32,500 00	7	58
Iron River	Iron	645	394	198	82	40,000	17,500 00	2	14
Ironwood	Gogebic	3,678	2,697	199	93	225,000	57,000 00	3	66
Ishpeming	Marquette	4,015	3,230	188	88	250,000	45,000 00	4	73
Ithaca	Gratiot	590	464	190	96	35,000	6,000 00	2	14
Jackson	Jackson	5,855	3,990	194	95	425,000	73,000 00	7	96
Jamestown	Ottawa	154	128	180	88	2,000	....	1	2
Jennings	Missaukee	359	318	180	88	10,000	....	1	11
Jerome	Hillsdale	73	73	180	80	1,000	....	1	3
Jonesville	Hillsdale	320	300	200	94	30,000	....	2	8
Kalamazoo	Kalamazoo	7,987	5,452	188	93	650,000	189,000 00	13	146
Kalkaska	Kalkaska	347	343	178	70	25,000	5,000 00	1	10
Kendall	Van Buren	54	46	180	80	1,000	....	....	2
Kent City	Kent	167	108	180	81	7,700	3,000 00	1	3
Kilmanagh	Huron	198	127	200	54	2,000	....	1	1
Kingsley	Grand Traverse	198	160	180	85	5,000	....	1	3
Kingston	Tuscola	137	140	200	82	7,000	3,000 00	1	2
Kochville Tp. 6	Saginaw	113	65	180	81	1,600	....	1	2
Laingsburg	Shiawassee	137	91	200	93	5,000	....	1	4
Lake Ann	Benzie	92	61	160	75	3,500	....	1	1
Lake City	Missaukee	275	276	180	70	18,000	9,000 00	1	7

TABLE XVI.—Continued.

Aggregate number of months taught by all teachers.		Total wages of teachers for the year.		Average monthly wages of teachers.		Amount paid for superintendence and instruction.	Total cost of school.	Number of non-resident pupils.	Tuition of non-resident pupils.
Men.	Women.	Men.	Women.	Men.	Women.				
10.	20.	$675 00	$850 00	$67 50	$42 50	$1,525 00	$5,836 03	2	$5 00
40.	258.	4,655 00	13,672 50	116 37	53 00	18,327 50	42,829 79	19	777 14
10.	30.	600 00	1,125 00	60 00	37 50	1,725 00	2,379 61	39	347 90
10.	80.	850 00	3,400 00	85 00	42 50	4,250 00	10,209 54	10	73 00
9.	108.	1,100 00	4,706 50	122 22	43 58	5,806 50	8,814 68	4	41 81
9.	18.	540 00	675 00	60 00	37 50	1,215 00	1,730 70	....	....
18.	18.	935 00	720 00	51 94	40 00	1,655 00	2,577 90	8	74 75
9.	27.	540 00	1,098 00	60 00	40 67	1,638 00	2,085 30	7	5 00
9.	132.	1,200 00	6,075 00	133 33	46 02	7,275 00	10,664 70	30	288 00
9.	90.3	850 00	[illegible],199 63	94 44	46 53	5,049 63	7,436 69	58	652 39
9.	9.	450 00	315 00	50 00	35 00	765 00	1,190 23	9	48 70
50.	180.	4,075 00	9,255 23	81 50	51 42	13,330 23	24,227 21	55	868 16
10.	40.	900 00	2,244 00	90 00	56 10	3,144 00	10,063 99	....	....
9.5	28.5	570 00	1,140 00	60 00	40 00	1,710 00	3,751 26	15	99 58
9.	36.	585 00	1,305 00	65 00	36 25	1,890 00	2,592 00	23	223 25
10.	55.	1,100 00	3,070 00	110 00	55 82	4,170 00	9,914 87	13	97 50
9.	51.	540 00	1,665 00	60 00	32 64	2,205 00	3,447 62	4	....
28.5	266.	3,075 00	11,992 50	107 90	45 08	15,067 50	25,918 70	102	1,248 75
20.	409.	3,657 75	18,612 50	182 89	45 50	22,270 25	53,725 73	30	355 24
9.	10.	450 00	350 00	50 00	35 00	800 00	1,100 82	....	....
9.	....	540 00	....	60 00	....	540 00	1,211 01	....	....
....	18.	....	585 00	....	32 50	585 00	2,060 48	....	....
....	27.	....	963 00	....	35 67	963 00	9,655 02	....	....
9.	9.	405 00	243 00	45 00	27 00	648 00	1,950 17	6	20 19
9.5	75.	1,000 00	3,034 00	105 26	40 45	4,034 00	5,132 86	49	557 41
9.	18.	499 95	540 00	55 56	30 00	1,039 95	1,785 67	11	96 89
....	18.	....	697 50	....	38 75	697 50	860 67	8	33 00
9.2	74.	900 00	3,275 00	97 30	44 25	4,175 00	10,996 33	36	363 95
9.	36.	675 00	1,355 00	45 00	37 64	2,030 00	3,160 25	8	27 50
9.5	19.	600 00	608 00	63 16	32 00	1,208 00	1,492 91	9	68 10
85.7	376.3	7,331 75	20,473 75	85 55	54 41	27,805 50	86,074 74	14	713 00
9.5	85.5	900 00	3,848 25	94 74	45 01	4,748 25	6,022 54	17	104 00
10.	164.7	1,400 00	6,367 20	140 00	38 64	7,767 20	12,042 26	84	1,120 20
9.	18.	585 00	720 00	65 00	40 00	1,305 00	1,682 82	15	138 50
28 5	123 5	2,305 00	5,580 46	82 98	45 23	7,951 46	11,473 74	66	811 73
9.	18.	540 00	630 00	60 00	35 00	1,170 00	1,520 19	4	24 50
....	10.	....	400 00	....	40 00	400 00	523 33	5	....
10.	70.	1,000 00	2,775 00	100 00	39 64	3,775 00	15,763 96	23	285 51
30.	280.	2,700 00	1[illegible],162 71	90 00	50 58	16,862 71	25,118 93	96	1,001 73
66.5	377.	7,797 50	3[illegible],231 87	117 26	85 50	40,029 37	66,096 18	3	40 00
14.	139.	862 50	7,845 00	61 60	56 44	8,707 50	19,897 78	4	45 00
30.	660.	4,700 00	35,312 25	156 67	53 50	40,012 25	73,205 04	6	75 00
38.	693.5	5,500 00	43,440 00	144 74	62 64	48,940 00	81,733 07	....	....
10.	115.	948 04	4,975 00	94 80	43 26	5,923 04	16,798 61	49	498 75
70.	960.	9,000 00	52,839 85	128 57	55 04	61,839 85	112,676 29	52	625 45
9.	13.5	450 00	427 50	50 00	31 66	877 50	1,173 45	....	....
9.	55.2	580 00	2,253 75	64 44	40 79	2,833 75	5,573 27	3	....
9.	9.	375 00	[illegible]277 50	41 67	30 83	652 50	1,218 91	....	....
20.	80.	1,100 00	[illegible],910 00	55 00	36 37	4,010 00	6,115 66	39	297 50
123.5	1,387.	14,675 00	7[illegible]953 58	118 82	55 48	91,628 58	234,342 60	48	681 49
9.	90.	500 00	4,105 00	55 56	45 61	4,605 00	8,141 90	14	96 50
....	18.	....	630 00	....	35 00	630 00	883 53	....	....
9.	18.	585 00	585 00	65 00	32 50	1,170 00	1,888 06	15	122 50
9.	10.	510 00	350 00	56 67	35 00	860 00	1,049 06	5	5 41
9.	26.	600 00	854 00	66 67	32 85	1,454 00	1,992 79	4	41 10
10.	20.	575 00	650 00	57 50	32 50	1,225 00	2,395 91	22	82 69
4.	14.	180 00	520 00	45 00	37 14	700 00	1,115 50	....	....
10.	40.	675 00	1,600 00	67 50	40 00	2,275 00	2,897 24	19	212 33
8.	8.	322 13	396 95	40 27	49 62	719 08	920 97	....	....
9.	54.	600 00	2,205 00	66 67	40 83	2,805 00	4,945 66	14	42 60

TABLE XVI.—Continued.

Districts.	Counties.	Number of children between 5 and 20 years.	Number of children that attend school during the year.	Number of days school.	Percentage of attendance.	Estimated valuation of school property.	Total indebtedness.	Number of teachers employed. Men.	Women.
Lake Linden	Houghton	1,882	833	200	98	$44,300	....	1	29
Lake Odessa	Ionia	354	328	186	93	15,000	....	1	9
Lakeview	Montcalm	315	277	190	92	3,000	....	3	8
L'Anse	Baraga	582	425	198	80	42,032	$20,000 00	3	11
Lansing	Ingham	5,191	3,461	190	95	230,000	....	6	89
Lapeer	Lapeer	567	506	200	90	30,000	....	1	19
Lawrence	Van Buren	190	179	180	90	10,000	375 00	1	7
Lawton	Van Buren	237	198	180	89	13,000	4,000 00	1	6
Leitch	Sanilac	63	62	200	53	900	....	......	1
Lennon	Shiawassee	94	82	200	86	2,500	....	1	1
Lenox Included in Richmond.	Macomb.								
Leonard	Oakland	134	106	200	79	4,000	....	1	2
LeRoy	Osceola	181	107	180	82	5,000	....	1	3
Leslie	Ingham	262	230	198	92	10,000	....	1	5
Levering	Emmet	113	117	200	61	3,500	2,500 00	1	3
Lexington	Sanilac	156	152	200	95	10,000	....	1	4
Lincoln Tp. 2	Huron	94	78	200	53	1,000	....	1	1
Lincoln Tp. 4	Berrien	107	53	160	79	4,000	....	1	1
Linden	Genesee	172	143	194	83	7,000	....	1	4
Lisbon	Ottawa	82	59	179	83	2,500	....	1	1
Litchfield	Hillsdale	159	145	180	85	10,000	....	1	4
Lowell	Kent	443	394	200	85	18,000	200 00	3	12
Lucas	Missaukee	128	101	178	88	1,100	....	1	2
Ludington	Mason	2,606	1,551	190	96	150,000	17,000 00	3	45
Luther	Lake	242	216	190	70	5,500	....	1	6
Lyons	Ionia	161	131	180	94	3,000	....	1	5
Mackinac Island	Mackinac	202	150	180	93	10,000	....	1	3
Mackinaw City	Cheboygan	216	203	180	72	6,500	....	1	4
Macomb Tp. 2 fr.	Macomb	102	42	180	42	650	....	1	....
Mancelona	Antrim	584	527	178	93	15,000	1,000 00	3	11
Manchester	Washtenaw	349	270	200	95	20,000	....	1	8
Manistee	Manistee	4,216	1,967	200	95	136,500	6,500 00	5	68
Manistique	Schoolcraft	1,505	1,005	200	93	70,000	4,000 00	3	28
Manton	Wexford	440	341	180	81	30,000	8,000 00	1	9
Maple Rapids	Clinton	150	123	200	80	3,000	....	1	3
Maple Ridge	Arenac	91	62	180	84	3,000	201 00	2	1
Maple Ridge Tp	Alpena	273	159	180	57	3,000	....	......	10
Marcellus	Cass	240	211	180	97	18,000	....	1	6
Marine City	St. Clair	1,314	690	200	92	59,000	16,000 00	3	15
Marion	Osceola	303	256	175	87	6,000	....	1	5
Marlette	Sanilac	363	293	200	92	20,000	7,000 00	1	10
Marquette	Marquette	3,209	2,187	193	94	292,500	90,000 00	8	54
Marshall	Calhoun	976	722	197	96	125,000	11,000 00	3	26
Martin	Allegan	111	93	190	80	4,000	....	1	3
Marysville	St. Clair	144	92	180	69	1,000	....	1	1
Mason	Ingham	411	354	200	93	40,000	24,500 00	1	15
Matchwood Tp	Ontonagon	176	138	180	78	12,000	2,000 00	1	6
Mattawan	Van Buren	108	101	172	91	6,000	....	......	2
Mayville	Tuscola	235	199	200	85	10,000	5,000 00	2	4
McBain	Missaukee	255	230	180	68	5,000	....	1	5
McBride	Montcalm	135	117	190	71	3,000	....	1	2
McMillan Tp.	Luce	622	591	200	65	15,000	....	3	15
McMillan Tp.	Ontonagon	145	116	180	77	6,600	....	1	5
Mecosta	Mecosta	137	135	200	65	2,500	....	1	2
Memphis	Macomb	183	158	200	84	5,000	....	1	4
Mendon	St. Joseph	217	183	180	90	25,000	20,046 48	1	8
Menominee	Menominee	3,821	2,252	187	95	160,000	20,000 00	6	56
Mesick	Wexford	174	139	180	91	3,500	....	1	3
Metamora	Lapeer	106	93	200	90	2,000	....	1	3
Michigamme	Marquette	246	218	200	83	9,000	....	1	9

TABLE XVI.—Continued.

Aggregate number of months taught by all teachers.		Total wages of teachers for the year.		Average monthly wages of teachers.		Amount paid for superintendence and instruction.	Total cost of school.	Number of non-resident pupils.	Tuition of non-resident pupils.
Men.	Women.	Men.	Women.	Men.	Women.				
10.	260.	$1,805 00	$15,791 00	$180 50	$60 73	$17,596 00	$27,264 40	23	$899 00
9.5	85.5	900 00	3,324 10	94 73	38 88	4,224 10	10,051 39	40	376 65
28.5	47.5	1,926 25	1,729 00	67 59	36 40	3,655 25	4,622 04	34	273 95
30.	99.5	2,700 00	4,838 75	90 00	48 63	7,538 75	37,464 10	2	....
57.	845.5	7,200 00	46,443 18	128 28	54 93	53,643 18	101,357 72	70	685 05
10.	190.	1,200 00	9,542 21	126 00	50 22	10,802 21	15,526 07	35	547 02
9.	63.	900 00	2,520 00	100 00	40 00	3,420 00	5,735 89	35	402 34
9.	54.	850 00	,102 00	94 44	38 93	2,952 00	9,010 63	65	475 14
....	10.	....	450 00	....	45 00	450 00	551 88	2	....
10.	10.	520 00	370 00	52 00	37 00	890 00	1,034 47	9	81 00
10.	20.	500 00	640 00	50 00	32 00	1,140 00	1,463 05	3	16 13
9.	27.	540 00	1,080 00	60 00	40 00	1,620 00	2,754 29	10	36 75
10.	50.	1,100 00	2,050 00	110 00	41 00	3,150 00	4,281 46	44	456 05
10.	21.2	600 00	891 05	60 00	43 44	1,491 05	2,418 86	1	5 00
10.	40.	700 00	1,650 00	70 00	41 25	2,350 00	3,065 73	12	95 50
10.	7.	450 00	206 25	45 00	29 46	656 25	792 98	7	8 00
6.	8.	390 00	320 00	65 00	40 00	710 00	924 64	....	....
10.	40.	650 00	1,400 00	65 00	35 00	2,050 00	2,878 67	20	116 50
9.	8.7	630 00	348 00	70 00	40 00	978 00	1,368 42	5	29 00
9.	36.	800 00	1,479 00	88 89	41 08	2,279 00	2,869 48	35	402 00
30.	110.	2,050 00	3,240 00	68 33	29 45	5,290 00	8,814 93	29	369 60
9.	15.	540 00	525 00	60 00	35 00	1,065 00	1,498 83	3	....
28.5	427.5	3,367 50	20,908 02	118 16	48 91	24,275 52	37,152 77	26	345 28
9.5	41.5	650 00	1,390 25	68 42	33 50	2,040 25	2,911 50	....	....
9.	36.	810 00	1,465 00	90 00	40 69	2,275 00	2,864 52	30	125 60
9.	27.	900 00	1,575 00	100 00	58 33	2,475 00	3,436 47	2	....
9.	27.	675 00	1,200 00	75 00	44 44	1,875 00	2,295 23	....	....
9.	....	414 00	....	46 00	....	414 00	491 70	....	....
27.	99.	2,140 00	4,320 00	79 26	43 64	6,460 00	10,553 24	15	171 90
10.	80.	1,000 00	3,272 00	100 00	40 90	4,272 00	5,950 94	33	418 00
50.	680.	5,584 50	32,802 24	111 69	48 24	38,386 74	58,985 76	46	790 13
30.	280.	3,600 00	13,235 00	120 00	47 27	16,835 00	32,867 41	16	160 94
9.	78.	800 00	3,002 75	88 89	38 50	3,802 75	11,300 36	19	213 36
10.	30.	750 00	1,150 00	75 00	38 33	1,900 00	2,502 09	22	176 49
9.	9.	450 00	270 00	50 00	30 00	720 00	1,109 11	....	....
....	63.	....	2,190 00	....	34 76	2,190 00	2,626 41	....	....
9.	54.	845 00	2,610 00	93 89	48 33	3,455 00	4,858 13	45	421 67
30.	150.	2,550 00	6,291 65	85 00	41 94	8,841 65	15,019 21	15	124 50
10.	50.	888 82	2,050 00	88 88	41 00	2,938 82	4,840 86	6	83 90
10.	85.	850 00	3,725 00	85 00	43 82	4,575 00	7,942 22	41	574 10
80.	540.	8,910 00	29,363 00	111 37	54 38	38,273 00	66,502 31	3	....
30.	253.	3,500 00	11,641 25	116 67	46 01	15,141 25	20,140 16	83	1,372 01
9.5	28.5	712 50	1,258 75	75 00	44 17	1,971 25	2,849 16	12	112 00
9.	9.	450 00	270 00	50 00	30 00	720 00	885 45	....	....
10.	130.	1,200 00	5,990 00	120 00	46 06	7,190 00	10,550 86	45	405 09
9.	54.	720 00	2,520 00	80 00	46 67	3,240 00	7,426 17	....	....
....	18.	....	720 00	....	40 00	720 00	1,005 66	2	....
9.7	40.	682 50	1,665 00	70 00	41 62	2,347 50	3,322 60	27	142 24
9.	45.	585 00	1,800 00	65 00	40 00	2,385 00	3,171 61	6	26 00
9.5	19.	650 00	663 75	68 42	34 93	1,313 75	2,311 10	13	99 88
30.	140.	2,762 50	6,991 75	92 08	49 94	9,754 25	14,008 92	1	....
9.	45.	720 00	2,070 00	80 00	46 00	2,790 00	4,547 30	....	....
10.	20.	650 00	750 00	65 00	37 50	1,400 00	1,726 58	8	40 13
10.	40.	700 00	1,577 00	70 00	39 42	2,277 00	3,355 87	38	275 51
9.	54.	850 00	2,097 00	94 44	38 83	2,947 00	19,177 09	32	301 24
57.	532.	6,437 43	28,046 98	112 94	52 72	34,484 41	60,104 17	9	....
9.	27.	540 00	945 00	60 00	35 00	1,485 00	2,776 94	7	27 00
10.	30.	750 00	1,200 00	75 00	40 00	1,950 00	2,483 49	20	199 56
10.	50.	1,000 00	2,500 00	100 00	50 00	3,500 00	6,390 06	[illegible]	[illegible]

TABLE XVI.—CONTINUED.

Districts.	Counties.	Number of children between 5 and 20 years.	Number of children that attended school during the year.	Number of days school.	Percentage of attendance.	Estimated valuation of school property.	Total indebtedness.	Number of teachers employed.	
								Men.	Women.
Middleton	Gratiot	126	117	180	69	$2,500	$7 04	1	1
Middleville	Barry	198	173	200	93	20,000		2	5
Midland	Midland	696	667	196	78	45,000		2	15
Milan	Washtenaw	332	283	180	82	20,000	10,500 00	2	9
Milford	Oakland	241	179	200	89	16,000	500 00	1	7
Millbrook	Mecosta	88	80	180	69	800		1	2
Millburg	Berrien	135	125	180	81	2,500		1	2
Millersburg	Presque Isle	227	207	200	64	5,000	400 00	1	4
Millington	Tuscola	199	163	200	93	7,000		1	4
Minden City	Sanilac	166	133	200	61	5,000		1	2
Monroe	Monroe	1,732	774	185	93	38,000	7,500 00	3	19
Montague	Muskegon	263	231	175	83	25,000	213 61	2	6
Montgomery	Hillsdale	104	105	180	75	5,000	900 00	1	2
Montrose	Genesee	140	135	200	89	2,000	1,500 00	2	2
Morenci	Lenawee	347	310	180	90	5,500		1	8
Morley	Mecosta	121	108	180	91	4,500		1	2
Morrice	Shiawassee	119	104	197	93	5,000		1	4
Moscow	Hillsdale	91	80	180	60	1,000		1	1
Mt. Clemens	Macomb	2,251	1,328	200	93	125,000	18,000 00	4	26
Mt. Morris	Genesee	196	156	200	83	6,000		1	3
Mt. Pleasant	Isabella	972	502	190	91	30,000	9,000 00	4	14
Muir	Ionia	102	89	177	87	5,700		1	3
Munising Tp	Alger	900	678	198	85	12,200	30,000 00	6	16
Muskegon	Muskegon	6,618	5,670	200	94	1,766,500	134,000 00	14	111
Muskegon Heights	Muskegon	365	299	200	90	24,000		1	8
Napoleon	Jackson	109	101	190	85	7,000	950 00	1	3
Nashville	Barry	303	277	200	90	28,000	7,100 00	3	7
Negaunee	Marquette	2,287	1,470	200	95	90,453	12,000 00	3	33
Newaygo	Newaygo	466	393	200	91	15,000		2	9
New Baltimore	Macomb	231	163	200	91	20,000		1	9
New Buffalo	Berrien	180	149	180	87	3,000		1	5
New Era	Oceana	160	116	180	82	4,000	1,300 00	1	1
New Haven	Macomb	150	119	180	78	4,000		2	1
New Holland	Ottawa	148	110	200	80	2,000		1	1
New Hudson	Oakland	55	47	180	93	3,000		1	1
New Troy	Berrien	195	175	175	81	3,000		1	2
Niles	Berrien	1,330	1,020	189	95	65,000		2	25
Noordeloos	Ottawa	91	68	200	75	1,800	100 00	1	1
North Adams	Hillsdale	115	99	190	87	10,000		2	4
North Branch	Lapeer	222	195	180	94	10,000		1	5
North Muskegon	Muskegon	124	97	187	88	12,000			3
Northport	Leelanau	256	245	180	75	6,500	600 00	1	5
North Star	Gratiot	97	79	180	79	2,000			3
Northville	Wayne	461	382	200	91	32,000	7,000 00	2	12
Norway	Dickinson	1,649	1,105	180	96	88,000	71,225 00	3	27
Nunica	Ottawa	125	105	180	86	3,500		1	2
Oakley	Saginaw	64	64	180	83	1,200		1	2
Okemos	Ingham	120	105	180	91	3,000		1	2
Olivet	Eaton	180	139	200	96	9,000		1	9
Omer	Arenac	190	161	200	74	6,000	1,451 05	1	3
Onaway	Presque Isle	696	630	200	87	12,000	9,500 00	2	14
Onekama	Manistee	143	131	180	80	1,500		1	3
Onondaga	Ingham	75	74	180	67	3,500	1,000 00	1	2
Ontonagon Tp	Ontonagon	643	552	183	89	28,000		1	22
Orion	Oakland	198	159	200	89	12,000	706 40	1	5
Ortonville	Oakland	109	111	195	70	1,500		1	3
Osceola Tp	Houghton	2,707	2,044	200	94	25,500	14,000 00	3	59
Oscoda	Iosco	345	283	198	93	500		2	5
Osseo	Hillsdale	83	82	180	94	1,800		1	1
Otisville	Genesee	131	100	200	77	2,000		1	2

TABLE XVI.—Continued.

*Aggregate number of months taught by all teachers.		Total wages of teachers for the year.		Average monthly wages of teachers.		Amount paid for superintendence and instruction.	Total cost of school.	Number of non-resident pupils.	Tuition of non-resident pupils.
Men.	Women.	Men.	Women.	Men.	Women.				
9.	9.	$540 00	$315 00	$60 00	$35 00	$855 00	$1,033 92	4	$24 75
20.	50.	1,350 00	1,950 00	67 50	39 00	3,300 00	5,518 81	36	349 16
15.	147.	1,561 04	6,607 80	104 07	44 95	8,168 84	13,276 55	30	100 50
9.	72.	870 90	2,678 75	96 77	37 20	3,549 65	5,346 59	23	301 50
10.	70.	1,000 00	2,610 00	100 00	37 29	3,610 00	4,746 88	63	553 38
9.	9.	495 00	281 [illegible]	55 00	31 25	776 25	945 61	8	36 98
9.	18.	585 00	630	65 00	35 00	1,215 00	1,661 05	4	51 95
10.	38.5	650 00	1,530 00	65 00	39 74	2,180 00	2,892 13	....	....
10.	40.	850 00	1,450 00	85 00	36 25	2,300 00	3,694 74	61	464 49
10.	18.	600 00	585 00	60 00	32 50	1,185 00	1,872 57	9	....
30.	190.	3,350 00	8,226 75	111 67	43 30	11,576 75	17,908 90	54	754 97
18.	54.	1,050 00	2,250 00	58 33	41 67	3,300 00	4,907 05	23	119 65
9.	18.	630 00	603 65	70 00	33 54	1,233 65	1,751 31	25	117 75
20.	20.	875 00	700 00	48 75	35 00	1,575 00	2,440 85	27	178 30
9.	63.	1,166 67	2,376 00	129 63	37 71	3,542 67	4,554 88	45	327 40
9.	18.	450 00	639 00	50 00	35 50	1,089 00	1,366 40	8	45 00
10.	40.	750 00	1,150 00	75 00	28 75	1,900 00	2,818 87	13	72 50
9.	9.	450 00	270 00	50 00	30 00	720 00	971 00	....	....
40.	260.	4,350 00	12,048 00	108 75	46 34	16,398 00	37,758 09	35	336 60
10.	30.	800 00	1,225 00	80 00	40.83	2,025 00	3,028 15	37	288 95
40.	140.	3,388 64	6,750 00	84 [illegible]	48 21	10,138 64	18,606 45	25	278 30
9.	27.	540 00	900 00	60 00	33 33	1,440 00	2,262 76	8	63 00
53.	139.5	3,935 00	7,210 00	74 24	51 68	11,145 00	55,898 41	....	....
140.	1,110.	19,362 00	64,197 53	138 30	57 83	83,559 53	145,533 76	55	924 25
10.	80.	900 00	3,071 93	90	38 40	3,971 93	13,530 49	8	40 50
9.5	28.5	550 00	1,122 50	57 90	39 38	1,672 50	3,202 67	16	90 90
30.	70.	1,900 00	2,752 00	63 33	39 31	4,652 00	7,076 82	19	311 10
30.	330.	3,500 00	19,112 50	116 67	57 91	22,612 50	60,610 09	....	....
14.	90.	1,040 00	3,505 00	74 29	38 94	4,545 00	5,995 41	13	90 50
10.	66.	940 30	2,990 00	94 03	45 30	3,930 30	5,108 64	27	161 05
9.	27.	675 00	1,080 00	75 00	40 00	1,755 00	2,411 89	6	56 25
9.	9.	432 00	315 00	48 00	35 00	747 00	1,424 03	....	....
18.	9.	967 50	315 00	53 75	35 00	1,282 50	1,759 28	8	58 50
10.	10.	600 00	330 00	60 00	33 00	930 00	1,241 84	....	....
9.	8.8	495 00	306 25	55 00	35 00	801 25	1,049 07	12	69 84
8.	18.	520 00	720 00	65 00	40 00	1,240 00	2,054 89	8	43 00
19.	237.	2,500 00	10,748 00	131 58	45 35	13,248 00	18,269 65	51	583 50
9.	10.	495 00	400 00	55 00	40 00	895 00	1,134 25	2	6 00
9.	37.5	665 81	1,423 20	73 98	37 95	2,089 01	4,384 99	31	210 75
10.	50.	900 00	1,900 00	90 00	38 00	2,800 00	4,589 27	46	607 89
....	28.	....	1,048 60	....	37 45	1,048 60	2,315 66	2	9 00
9.	35.8	675 00	1,504 00	75 00	42 07	2,179 00	2,716 65	17	85 75
....	26.8	....	1,124 50	....	42 04	1,124 50	1,519 10	10	34 50
20.	110.	1,700 50	4,234 15	85 02	38 49	5,934 65	11,415 38	31	342 36
28.5	229.8	3,304 90	12,304 75	118 07	53 56	15,609 65	58,613 53	12	1,296 07
9.	15.	540 00	470 25	60 00	31 35	1,010 25	1,406 81	6	48 75
9.	9.	540 00	225 00	60 00	25 00	765 00	883 65	4	3 50
9.	18.	500 00	585 00	55 56	32 50	1,085 00	1,538 40	16	111 50
10.	70.	900 00	2,385 25	90 00	34 07	3,285 25	5,434 62	25	232 75
10.	29.7	600 00	1,098 75	60 00	36 93	1,698 75	3,204 53	2	....
20.	123.5	1,400 00	5,409 00	70 00	43 80	6,809 00	10,488 21	8	84 26
9.	18.	540 00	655 00	60 00	36 39	1,195 00	2,071 72	8	35 03
9.	18.	495 00	585 00	55 00	32 50	1,080 00	1,532 15	19	61 66
10.	214.	1,500 00	10,175 00	150 00	47 55	11,675 00	21,531 57	9	242 20
10.	50.	750 00	1,775 00	75 00	35 50	2,525 00	3,437 61	7	61 60
10.	20.	675 00	650 00	67 50	32 50	1,325 00	,660 03	22	150 25
30.	546.	4,000 00	29,044 31	133 33	53 20	33,044 31	51,850 63	1	....
19.7	46.4	1,184 00	1,683 75	60 10	36 29	2,867 75	3,504 90	....	....
9.	9.	540 00	360 00	60 00	40 00	900 00	1,146 54	5	[illegible]
10.	20.	650 00	700 00	65 00	35 00	1,350 00	[illegible]	24	

TABLE XVI.—CONTINUED.

Districts.	Counties.	Number of children between 5 and 20 years.	Number of children that attended school during the year.	Number of days school.	Percentage of attendance.	Estimated valuation of school property.	Total indebtedness.	Number of teachers employed. Men.	Women.
Otsego	Allegan	604	556	180	92	$37,500	$10,750 00	1	20
Otter Lake	Lapeer	73	56	180	70	1,100	....	1	1
Otto	Sanilac	87	68	200	51	800	....	1	....
Overisel	Allegan	108	77	180	94	2,000	....	1	1
Ovid	Clinton	301	243	180	92	....	22,000 00	2	10
Owosso	Shiawassee	2,291	1,674	188	96	175,000	28,000 00	4	46
Oxford	Oakland	290	235	200	93	20,000	....	2	6
Palmyra	Lenawee	102	82	180	84	2,500	....	1	1
Palo	Ionia	80	72	178	80	4,000	....	1	3
Paris Tp. 1	Kent	150	105	197	67	2,000	....	....	2
Parma	Jackson	168	150	200	84	14,000	....	1	5
Paw Paw	Van Buren	360	305	185	97	15,000	2,000 00	3	7
Pellston	Emmet	328	279	180	78	5,000	2,500 00	1	6
Pentwater	Oceana	305	280	180	94	10,000	....	1	9
Perry	Shiawassee	178	169	200	93	10,000	4,067 50	1	5
Petersburg	Monroe	222	188	180	91	8,000	....	2	4
Petoskey	Emmet	1,502	1,233	190	95	60,500	18,000 00	5	27
Pewamo	Ionia	124	94	180	76	8,000	2,000 00	1	2
Pickford	Chippewa	169	133	200	85	5,000	3,000 00	1	2
Pierson	Montcalm	103	66	180	80	1,000	....	1	1
Pigeon	Huron	327	221	200	64	7,000	1,808 00	1	4
Pinckney	Livingston	132	127	200	90	10,000	....	1	4
Pinconning	Bay	340	305	200	92	20,000	12,000 00	....	7
Pine Run	Genesee	63	43	180	90	800	....	....	1
Pinnebog	Huron	136	115	200	63	2,000	....	1	1
Pittsford	Hillsdale	116	102	190	89	10,000	....	2	2
Plainwell	Allegan	306	272	190	95	25,000	....	1	9
Plymouth	Wayne	495	438	200	93	25,000	....	1	12
Pontiac	Oakland	2,408	1,978	195	95	281,000	75,000 00	3	51
Port Austin	Huron	244	196	200	89	6,500	3,000 00	1	5
Port Hope	Huron	154	79	200	90	1,500	....	1	2
Port Huron	St. Clair	5,825	3,235	190	96	670,000	....	4	85
Portland	Ionia	453	385	190	93	25,000	4,000 00	1	13
Port Sanilac	Sanilac	96	86	180	75	2,000	....	....	3
Potterville	Eaton	141	121	180	86	7,000	....	1	5
Prescott	Ogemaw	145	98	180	70	1,000	....	1	1
Quincy	Branch	307	240	191	95	16,000	5,200 00	1	11
Rapid City	Kalkaska	118	88	180	77	6,500	3,500 00	1	3
Ravenna	Muskegon	155	142	180	87	5,500	....	1	2
Reading	Hillsdale	252	214	188	96	15,000	....	2	6
Reed City	Osceola	544	421	190	87	26,000	....	2	15
Remus	Mecosta	152	105	180	73	6,000	1,650 00	1	2
Republic Tp	Marquette	858	623	200	78	17,000	....	1	15
Richland	Kalamazoo	87	69	180	90	4,500	....	1	4
Richmond	Macomb	325	223	200	90	9,500	....	1	7
Riverdale	Gratiot	89	95	175	80	2,000	....	2	1
River Rouge	Wayne	1,111	896	200	92	166,199	62,600 00	2	20
Rochester	Oakland	309	271	200	90	15,000	6,090 00	1	6
Rockford	Kent	201	173	200	90	25,000	1,040 00	1	5
Rockland Tp	Ontonagon	536	422	174	81	27,000	12,500 00	3	17
Rockwood	Wayne	107	81	200	70	4,000	....	1	1
Rogers	Presque Isle	316	224	200	89	7,500	4,328 67	3	2
Romeo	Macomb	373	312	200	97	31,599	....	1	11
Romulus	Wayne	107	69	180	58	3,000	....	1	1
Roscommon	Roscommon	133	109	180	65	3,500	....	1	3
Rose City	Ogemaw	322	254	190	83	5,000	2,500 00	1	4
Royal Oak	Oakland	348	268	200	91	15,000	10,000 00	1	6
Saganing	Arenac	137	103	180	74	1,800	....	1	1
Saginaw	Saginaw	8,236	3,923	190	94	657,953	30,000 00	17	148
Saginaw, W. S.	Saginaw	5,681	3,001	200	76	266,803	60,000 00	6	77

TABLE XVI.—Continued.

Aggregate number of months taught by all teachers		Total wages of teachers for the year.		Average monthly wages of teachers.		Amount paid for superintendence and instruction.	Total cost of school.	Number of non-resident pupils.	Tuition of non-resident pupils.
Men.	Women.	Men.	Women.	Men.	Women.				
9.	150.5	$1,250 00	$5,745 53	$138 89	$38 17	$6,995 53	$10,383 23	36	$530 49
9.	9.	450 00	315 00	50 00	35 00	765 00	866 17	15	47 00
10.	....	550 00	....	55 00	....	550 00	700 45	....	....
9.	9.	423 00	225 00	47 00	25 00	648 00	815 50	7	24 00
20.	80.	1,500 00	2,870 00	75 00	35 87	4,370 00	8,971 81	44	446 65
40.	400.	4,800 00	22,757 06	120 00	49 47	27,557 06	43,145 04	43	525 16
20.	60.	1,500 00	2,355 00	75 00	45 92	4,255 00	5,498 79	22	218 35
9.	9.	450 00	15 00	50 00	35 00	765 00	1,209 27	7	42 00
9.	27.	585 00	47 00	65 00	27 67	1,332 00	1,786 20	35	354 25
....	20.	....	800 00	....	40 00	800 00	1,351 42	1	10 00
10.	50.	700 00	1,730 00	70 00	34 60	2,430 00	3,306 94	23	169 65
28.5	66.5	2,350 00	3,197 50	82 45	48 06	5,547 50	9,447 54	66	673 16
9.	41.	630 00	1,685 00	70 00	41 10	2,315 00	3,209 36	6	....
9.	65.2	900 00	2,408 32	100 00	36 91	3,308 32	4,712 25	11	64 00
10.	50.	800 00	1,746 50	80 00	34 93	2,546 50	3,960 20	14	88 75
18.	36.	877 50	1,215 00	48 75	33 75	2,092 50	2,584 39	15	172 13
47.5	256.5	4,700 00	12,195 82	98 95	47 55	16,895 82	24,208 19	20	197 04
9.	18.	540 00	648 00	60 00	36 00	1,188 00	1,839 12	15	23 21
10.	20.	525 00	750 00	52 50	37 50	1,275 00	1,798 60	....	....
9.	9.	405 00	288 00	45 00	32 00	693 00	1,067 34	10	32 50
10.	40.	750 00	1,400 00	75 00	35 00	2,150 00	7,037 36	5	40 00
10.	40.	800 00	2,600 00	80 00	40 00	2,400 00	3,431 18	10	96 00
....	60.2	....	,566 00	....	42 62	2,566 00	4,531 80	10	49 00
....	9.	....	310 00	....	34 40	310 00	393 48	3	....
10.	10.	500 00	450 00	50 00	45 00	950 00	1,066 35	4	30 00
19.	19.	950 00	665 00	50 00	35 00	1,615 00	2,171 80	23	....
9.5	85.5	1,150 00	3,317 48	128 05	38 80	4,467 48	6,203 55	43	623 36
10.	120.	1,150 00	4,615 00	11 00	38 46	5,765 00	8,809 98	47	495 05
30.	510.	3,550 00	26,374 36	11 33	51 71	29,924 36	52,429 19	50	855 98
10.	48.5	750 00	2,047 50	7 00	42 22	2,797 50	6,324 71	15	20 00
10.	20.	600 00	650 00	60 00	32 50	1,250 00	1,765 41	3	46 75
38.	807.5	5,700 00	39,455 47	150 00	48 85	45,155 47	99,010 24	16	70 00
9.5	114.	325 00	5,405 00	34 21	47 41	5,730 00	7,663 08	42	584 20
....	27.	....	,080 00	....	40 00	1,080 00	1,310 57	3	19 00
9.	27.	540 00	,080 00	60 00	40 00	1,620 00	2,300 64	10	66 00
9.	9.	360 00	315 00	40 00	35 00	675 00	797 30	1	....
10.	80.	1,050 00	3,031 50	105 00	37 90	4,081 50	5,844 86	52	613 64
7.	11.	387 50	435 00	55 37	39 55	822 50	3,294 25	1	2 00
9.	18.	675 00	765 00	75 00	42 50	1,440 00	2,709 72	7	37 25
19.	47.5	1,600 00	1,834 25	84 21	38 62	3,434 25	5,588 11	50	620 94
19.	130.5	1,800 00	5,336 75	94 74	40 90	7,136 75	9,588 56	35	232 75
9.	18.	540 00	630 00	60 00	35 00	1,170 00	1,782 19	1	11 00
10.	150.	1,300 00	7,200 00	130 00	48 00	8,500 00	12,489 18	....	....
4.	32.	260 00	1,394 00	65 00	43 56	1,654 00	2,276 33	....	....
10.	65.	950 00	2,825 00	95 00	43 46	3,775 00	5,078 52	18	209 38
9.	9.	485 00	360 00	53 89	40 00	845 00	1,051 22	2	7 50
20.	200.	1,900 00	9,625 00	95 00	48 12	11,525 00	19,754 00	....	....
10.	60.	1,000 00	2,375 00	100 00	39 58	3,375 00	5,146 19	40	259 75
10.	50.	800 00	1,775 00	80 00	35 50	2,685 00	4,087 08	24	146 25
26.	125.	2,020 00	6,825 00	77 69	54 60	8,845 00	14,944 10	....	....
10.	10.	550 00	300 00	55 00	30 00	850 00	1,141 21	2	9 00
30.	20.	1,565 00	800 00	52 17	40 00	2,365 00	3,027 84	....	....
10.	98.7	1,350 00	3,581 25	135 00	36 26	4,931 25	7,337 66	43	528 20
9.	9.	585 00	315 00	65 00	35 00	900 00	1,267 95	6	17 50
9.	27.	700 00	1,045 00	77 78	38 70	1,745 00	2,430 15	7	....
9.5	40.5	617 50	1,330 00	65 00	32 84	1,947 50	2,682 99	4	....
10.	60.	750 00	2,200 00	75 00	36 67	2,950 00	4,297 31	25	222 00
9.	9.	430 00	270 00	47 78	30 00	700 00	1,080 72	....	....
170.	1,480	22,000 00	79,333 98	129 41	53 60	101,333 98	324,488 42	100	2,610 18
60.	770.	7,120 00	40,273 87	118 67	52 30	47,393 87	104,425 40	28	[illegible]

TABLE XVI.—Continued.

Districts.	Counties.	Number of children between 5 and 20 years.	Number of children that attended school during the year.	Number of days school.	Percentage of attendance.	Estimated valuation of school property.	Total indebtedness.	Number of teachers employed.	
								Men.	Women.
St. Charles	Saginaw	599	522	200	93	$16,000	....	1	10
St. Clair	St. Clair	759	429	190	94	35,000	....	1	14
St. Ignace	Mackinac	640	469	176	93	25,000	$8,875 00	3	8
St. Johns	Clinton	784	841	200	96	60,000	....	2	24
St. Joseph	Berrien	1,537	993	180	96	80,000	10,000 00	3	30
St. Louis	Gratiot	667	600	200	76	32,000	13,000 00	1	16
Salem	Washtenaw	68	59	180	80	1,100	....	1	1
Saline	Washtenaw	210	163	200	84	30,000	75 00	1	6
Sand Lake	Kent	137	128	180	83	2,800	....	1	3
Sandusky	Sanilac	325	287	190	78	12,000	6,000 00	1	5
Sanilac Tp. 3	Sanilac	65	56	180	62	1,000	....	......	1
Sanilac Tp. 8 fr.	Sanilac	67	51	200	60	700	....	......	1
Saranac	Ionia	242	202	200	94	12,000	....	1	7
Saugatuck	Allegan	220	168	170	70	12,500	....	1	5
Sault Ste. Marie	Chippewa	3,522	2,468	192	95	240,000	119,000 00	12	50
Schoolcraft	Kalamazoo	187	167	180	96	24,000	....	1	7
Scottville	Mason	235	226	190	94	15,000	4,800 00	2	5
Sebewaing	Huron	578	295	192	90	27,000	16,574 27	1	6
Shelby	Oceana	349	322	190	93	7,500	....	1	9
Shepherd	Isabella	272	228	180	93	20,000	13,000 00	1	6
Sheridan	Montcalm	148	113	180	96	5,200	600 00	1	3
Sherman	Wexford	187	171	180	80	4,000	....	1	4
Sherman Tp. 2	Osceola	142	108	172	65	1,700	....	1	3
Sherwood	Branch	131	101	180	79	6,000	....	1	3
Soule	Huron	109	101	200	83	1,500	258 52	1	1
South Frankfort	Benzie	191	187	195	78	8,600	2,060 00	2	4
South Haven	Van Buren	1,003	796	190	96	60,000	1,250 00	3	25
South Lyon	Oakland	173	144	190	97	3,000	....	1	4
Spalding Tp.	Menominee	709	527	183	66	7,200	3,500 00	1	13
Sparta	Kent	310	279	200	93	10,000	3,000 00	1	10
Spring Lake	Ottawa	229	163	190	94	6,000	....	1	4
Springport	Jackson	124	114	200	95	8,000	....	1	4
Springwells Tp. 3	Wayne	271	161	200	89	12,000	16,000 00	1	3
Stambaugh Tp.	Iron	689	487	180	70	30,000	14,000 00	4	14
Standish	Arenac	452	338	200	76	12,000	7,500 00	2	8
Stanton	Montcalm	378	314	190	90	25,000	20,434 18	1	7
Stanwood	Mecosta	113	104	176	70	2,500	800 00	1	3
Stephenson Tp.	Menominee	1,320	1,002	178	80	20,300	2,787 72	3	24
Sterling	Arenac	212	153	200	81	4,000	....	......	4
Stevensville	Berrien	262	144	180	80	5,500	....	1	4
Stockbridge	Ingham	177	190	197	96	5,000	....	1	4
Sturgis	St. Joseph	749	695	190	93	50,000	....	2	16
Sumner Tp. 4 fr.	Gratiot	98	83	180	62	3,600	....	1	1
Sunfield	Eaton	119	104	190	85	5,000	....	1	4
Superior Tp	Chippewa	423	375	187	65	6,600	....	2	11
									4
Sutton's Bay	Leelanau	200	101	180	72	5,000	....	1	2
Tallmadge Tp. 1 fr.	Ottawa	110	94	180	60	1,500	....	1	1
Tawas City	Iosco	462	316	200	95	6,000	....	1	8
Tecumseh	Lenawee	530	427	187	96	53,000	....	1	16
Tekonsha	Calhoun	161	139	190	90	5,000	....	1	4
Thompsonville	Benzie	296	286	180	80	4,000	....	1	6
Thornville	Lapeer	61	47	180	77	2,000	....	1	1
Three Oaks	Berrien	389	290	180	93	5,000	1,000 00	1	9
Three Rivers	St. Joseph	1,033	848	190	95	80,000	22,477 00	4	28
Traverse City	Grand Traverse	2,879	2,740	188	92	175,000	....	7	55
Trenton	Wayne	434	318	200	91	22,000	20,000 00	2	8
Trufant	Montcalm	173	132	180	61	4,000	350 00	1	2
Turner	Arenac	192	106	200	81	2,000	....	1	2
Tuscola	Tuscola	89	78	180	79	1,500	....	1	1
Tustin	Osceola	157	141	180	82	5,500	....	1	3

TABLE XVI.—Continued.

Aggregate number of months taught by all teachers.		Total wages of teachers for the year.		Average monthly wages of teachers.		Amount paid for superintendence and instruction.	Total cost of school.	Number of non-resident pupils.	Tuition of non-resident pupils.
Men.	Women.	Men.	Women.	Men.	Women.				
10.	88.	$1,000 00	$3,660 00	$100 00	$41 70	$4,669 00	$7,195 50	2	$30 00
10.	140.	1,300 00	6,430 00	130 00	45 93	7,730 00	14,640 95	10	90 13
27.	72.	2,025 00	3,715 00	75 00	51 60	5,740 00	8,859 60	6	54 00
20.	240.	2,250 00	9,521 90	112 50	39 67	11,771 90	22,799 00	41	805 50
27.	270.	3,795 00	14,975 00	140 56	55 46	18,770 00	43,265 58	19	202 00
10.	160.	1,100 00	7,100 00	110 00	44 38	8,200 00	14,555 43	34	289 50
9.	9.	425 00	270 00	47 22	30 00	695 00	1,010 79	12	45 00
10.	60.	1,000 00	2,600	100 00	43 34	3,600 00	6,273 09	39	403 62
9.	27.	450 00	855 00	50 00	31 67	1,305 00	1,958 01	13	92 50
9.5	47.5	700 00	2,023 50	73 68	42 60	2,723 50	4,267 97	17	91 25
....	9.	....	360 00	....	40 00	360 00	670 17	10	....
....	10.	....	400 00	....	40 00	400 00	551 45	5	....
10.	59.	750 00	2,290 00	75 00	38 81	3,040 00	3,840 80	54	439 03
9.	45.	900 00	21,530 00	100 00	34 00	2,430 00	3,148 18	12	163 08
120.	500.	11,200 00	,578 32	93 33	55 16	38,778 32	66,320 57	....	....
9.	54.	1,000 00	2,403 00	111 11	44 50	3,403 00	4,631 97	27	356 16
19.	47.5	1,266 67	1,947 50	66 67	41 00	3,214 17	4,530 25	35	372 62
10.	60.	800 00	2,450 00	80 00	40 83	3,250 00	5,975 39	8	....
9.5	85.5	950 00	3,467 50	100 00	40 55	4,417 50	5,818 74	45	421 74
9.	54.	700 00	2,115 00	77 78	39 17	2,815 00	4,594 46	15	200 05
0.	27.	630 00	990 00	70 00	36 67	1,620 00	2,248 93	34	232 26
9.	27.	600 00	1,080 00	66 67	40 00	1,680 00	2,237 48	2	26 75
3.	14.1	150 00	501 50	50 00	41 95	741 50	999 05	....	....
9.	27.	495 00	1,080 00	55 00	40 00	1,575 00	1,920 56	23	108 00
10.	10.	500 00	300 00	50 00	30 00	800 00	1,230 22	4	14 25
20.	40.	1,075 00	1,329 00	53 75	33 22	2,474 00	6,844 10	6	24 75
28.5	237.5	3,019 75	10,956 16	105 95	46 13	13,975 91	31,891 92	147	1,264 01
9.5	38.	725 00	1,464 50	76 32	38 54	2,189 50	2,834 04	30	364 00
10.	122.	888 90	5,374 00	88 89	44 05	6,262 90	12,669 01	17	....
10.	79.	900 00	3,255 00	90 00	41 20	4,155 00	5,785 93	20	296 12
9.5	38.	760 00	1,520 00	80 00	40 00	2,280 00	3,549 49	1	95
10.	40.	650 00	1,525 00	65 00	38 12	2,175 00	2,762 84	31	199 00
10.	30.	350 00	1,850 00	35 00	61 67	2,200 00	6,874 30	1	4 00
38.	125.	2,260 00	5,834 50	59 47	46 68	8,094 50	16,118 67	5	1 88
20.	80.	930 00	3,150 00	46 50	39 37	4,080 00	6,605 25	15	106 25
9.5	67.5	925 00	2,876 61	97 37	42 61	3,801 61	7,967 96	15	193 50
9.	18.	297 00	734 51	33 00	40 80	1,031 51	2,771 54	5	....
27.	213.8	1,710 00	8,072 40	63 33	33 08	11,713 40	16,492 74	5	....
....	28.3	....	1,351 10	....	47 74	1,351 10	1,767 58	2	....
8.	34.	560 00	1,360 00	70 00	40 00	1,920 00	2,449 46	12	89 50
10.	40.	800 00	1,600 00	80 00	40 00	2,400 00	3,668 79	39	322 74
19.	150.	1,530 00	6,108 50	80 53	40 72	7,638 50	10,895 26	31	404 81
9.	9.	405 00	337 50	45 00	37 50	742 50	1,144 98	....	....
9.5	28.5	570 00	1,140 00	60 00	40 00	1,710 00	2,468 42	22	169 00
19.	104.	1,264 00	4,307 55	66 53	41 41	5,571 55	8,242 33	5	....
9.	18.	540 00	675 00	60 00	37 50	1,215 00	4,334 11	4	....
9.	9.	450 00	360 00	50 00	40 00	810 00	1,678 69	1	9 00
10.	80.	800 00	3,367 48	80 00	42 09	4,107 48	5,741 81	5	39 50
9.5	133.	600 00	6,798 94	63 16	51 12	7,398 94	10,483 34	61	858 24
9.5	38.	686 11	1,520 00	72 22	40 00	2,206 11	3,039 69	22	250 23
9.	54.	675 00	2,040 00	75 00	37 78	2,715 00	4,576 22	7	....
9.	9.	450 00	270 00	50 00	30 00	720 00	907 54	1	3 75
9.	78.	1,000 00	3,151 25	111 11	40 40	4,151 25	10,418 25	24	180 00
38.	241.5	3,650 00	10,711 50	96 05	44 35	14,361 50	24,214 38	24	381 50
66.5	522.5	6,056 91	26,163 60	91 08	50 07	32,220 51	57,936 77	111	1,137 70
10.	59.8	850 00	2,540 00	85 00	42 59	3,390 00	6,201 00	11	54 50
9.	18.	540 00	630 00	60 00	35 00	1,170 00	1,577 44	[illegible]	17 60
10.	20.	700 00	800 00	70 00	40 00	1,500 00	2,14[illegible]		11 00
9.	9.	468 75	270 00	52 08	30 00	738 75	[illegible]		46 00
9.	27.	540 00	990 00	60 00	36 67	1,530 00	2,3[illegible]		[illegible]3 75

TABLE XVI.—Concluded.

Districts.	Counties.	Number of children between 5 and 20 years.	Number of children that attended school during the year.	Number of days school.	Percentage of attendance.	Estimated valuation of school property.	Total indebtedness.	Number of teachers employed. Men.	Women.
Twining	Arenac	176	148	200	88	$6,000	$907 80	1	3
Tyre	Sanilac	152	128	170	40	1,600	1,400 00	1	1
Union City	Branch	354	314	200	93	25,000	......	2	10
Unionville	Tuscola	211	178	200	70	16,000	4,000 00	1	3
Utica	Macomb	204	153	200	76	3,000	10,235 00	1	4
Vandalia	Cass	132	114	180	89	6,000	......	1	7
Vanderbilt	Otsego	205	182	200	80	3,000	......	1	3
Vassar	Tuscola	444	362	200	95	25,000	......	1	12
Vermontville	Eaton	175	156	190	93	10,000	......	1	7
Vernon	Shiawassee	115	80	200	92	8,000	......	2	3
Vestaburg	Montcalm	113	85	180	72	1,500	......	1	2
Vicksburg	Kalamazoo	308	275	180	94	10,000	......	2	8
Vriesland	Ottawa	142	102	190	93	3,000	......	1	1
Wacousta	Clinton	77	64	179	75	1,100	......	1	1
Wakefield	Gogebic	690	495	200	90	29,000	13,000 00	2	13
Waldron	Hillsdale	121	106	171	91	8,300	5,600 00	2	3
Warren	Macomb	100	81	180	75	2,500	......	1	1
Warren Tp. 1 fr	Macomb	85	66	180	71	1,500	15 22	1	1
Washington Tp. 4 fr.	Sanilac	86	70	200	67	1,000	......	1	......
Washington Tp. 12 fr.	Macomb	77	68	200	83	1,500	......	1	1
Watervliet	Berrien	245	247	180	80	1,000	......	1	6
Watrousville	Tuscola	81	64	200	80	2,500	......	1	3
Wayland	Allegan	184	179	180	91	8,000	......	2	3
Wayne	Wayne	335	314	200	77	15,000	......	2	14
Webberville	Ingham	138	116	180	88	4,000	......	1	4
Weideman	Isabella	217	165	180	70	3,000	......	1	2
West Branch	Ogemaw	568	514	180	94	15,000	12,000 00	1	8
Wheeler	Gratiot	98	79	177	75	1,200	......	......	2
White Cloud	Newaygo	241	226	180	77	7,500	......	1	5
Whitehall	Muskegon	436	319	190	93	30,000	......	1	9
White Pigeon	St. Joseph	143	128	190	90	18,000	......	2	5
White Rock	Huron	41	37	160	58	600	......	......	1
Whittemore	Iosco	140	104	200	61	5,000	2,627 50	2	1
Williamston	Ingham	313	265	200	87	25,000	1,000 00	1	10
Winsor Tp. 1	Huron	191	128	200	83	3,000	......	1	1
Winsor Tp. 2	Huron	142	92	200	46	2,000	1,000 00	......	2
Wolverine	Cheboygan	239	200	190	68	7,500	......	1	5
Woodland	Barry	90	84	180	92	3,000	......	1	2
Worth Tp. 12 fr.	Sanilac	49	31	180	70	600	......	1	......
Wyandotte	Wayne	2,187	1,156	196	93	120,000	72,380 00	1	34
Wyoming Tp. 7	Kent	314	182	200	70	5,000	3,000 00	1	1
Wyoming Tp. 9 fr.	Kent	477	352	200	85	15,000	12,100 00	1	7
Yale	St. Clair	375	324	200	92	30,500	17,634 35	1	12
Ypsilanti	Washtenaw	1,555	1,005	200	96	70,000	8,000 00	5	28
Yuma	Wexford	100	73	175	75	2,000	......	......	2
Zeeland	Ottawa	563	458	200	91	20,000	......	1	12
Zeeland Tp. 4 fr.	Ottawa	108	70	200	80	2,500	......	1	1
Zutphen	Ottawa	126	91	180	73	1,200	......	1	1

TABLE XVI.—CONCLUDED.

Aggregate number of months taught by all teachers.		Total wages of teachers for the year.		Average monthly wages of teachers.		Amount paid for superintendence and instruction.	Total cost of school.	Number of non-resident pupils.	Tuition of non-resident pupils.
Men.	Women.	Men.	Women.	Men.	Women.				
10.	21.	$700 00	$910 50	$70 00	$43 36	$1,610 50	$2,594 33	4	$24 31
8.5	7.	449 80	184 00	52 92	26 28	633 80	1,466 19	......	......
20.	100.	1,750 00	4,200 00	87 50	42 00	5,950 00	7,799 31	44	408 50
10.	30.	650 00	1,070 00	65 00	35 67	1,720 00	2,767 02	13	82 30
10.	40.	900 00	,550 00	90 00	38 75	2,450 00	4,416 93	10	114 19
9.	30.7	630 00	1,002 50	70 00	32 65	1,632 50	2,900 56	9	94 65
10.	29.9	600 00	[illegible],196 00	60 00	40 00	1,796 00	2,894 72	1	......
10.	120.	1,100 00	[illegible]18 00	110 00	38 42	5,710 00	8,444 65	31	292 80
9.5	57.	800 00	[illegible]1 50	84 21	42 43	3,218 50	3,934 33	33	410 58
20.	20.	1,150 00	800 00	57 50	26 67	1,950 00	2,763 60	17	178 07
9.	18.	405 00	720 00	45 00	40 00	1,125 00	1,414 40	3	23 50
18.	72.	1,395 00	2,718	77 50	37 75	4,113 00	5,773 88	41	562 47
9.5	9.5	475 00	304	50 00	32 00	779 00	1,160 75	......	......
9.	9.	537 00	358 00	59 67	39 78	895 00	1,462 51	20	151 25
20.	126.	1,500 00	7,000	75 00	55 55	8,500 00	20,946 52	......	......
18.	27.	776 38	703 00	43 13	26 04	1,479 38	10,605 07	10	60 56
9.	9.	450 00	315 00	50 00	35 00	765 00	1,096 28	8	3 00
9.	9.	450 00	315 00	50 00	35 00	765 00	860 95	1	8 00
10.	......	550 00	......	55 00	......	550 00	590 65	6	......
10.	10.	600 00	400 00	60 00	40 00	1,000 00	1,186 94	11	74 75
9.	54.	900 00	2,250 00	100 00	41 67	3,150 00	5,110 16	22	126 91
10.	10.	500 00	332 50	50 00	33 25	832 50	1,050 48	8	43 00
18.	27.	1,170 00	900 00	65 00	33 33	2,070 00	2,901 49	61	570 00
10.	90.1	1,010 00	4,041 00	101 00	44 85	5,051 00	6,373 83	44	521 50
9.	18.	540 00	634 00	60 00	35 22	1,174 00	1,670 01	10	61 00
9.	18.	540 00	810 00	60 00	45 00	1,350 00	1,948 39	4	2 75
9.5	76.	900 00	3,135 00	94 74	41 25	4,035 00	8,947 66	28	122 27
......	18.	......	778 50	......	43 25	778 50	889 82	......	......
9.	41.	630 00	1,472 00	70 00	35 90	2,102 00	2,872 58	9	54 75
9.5	85.5	900 00	3,468 50	94 74	40 56	4,368 50	7,394 69	10	122 50
12.8	47.5	1,195 00	1,731 25	93 72	36 44	2,926 25	3,943 38	53	578 73
......	8.	......	280 00	......	35 00	280 00	348 85	......	......
10.	10.	550 00	250 00	55 00	35 00	872 50	5,011 88	8	10 00
10.	90.2	1,000 00	3,714 75	100 00	41 16	4,714 75	7,685 30	46	381 05
10.	10.	540 00	360 00	54 00	36 00	900 00	1,087 35	......	......
......	18.	......	690 00	......	38 33	690 00	2,137 78	2	......
9.5	47.5	712 50	2,090 00	75 00	44 00	2,802 50	3,588 85	6	75 50
9.	18.	540 00	720 00	60	40 00	1,260 00	1,855 52	26	231 20
9.	......	405 00	......	45	......	405 00	487 16	......	......
10.	340.	1,300 00	14,793 21	130	43 51	16,093 21	31,090 35	19	341 00
10.	10.	550 00	500 00	55 00	50 00	1,050 00	1,519 12	......	......
10.	68.5	800 00	2,637 50	80 00	38 50	3,437 50	5,348 87	29	239 50
10.	94.5	850 00	3,664 12	85 00	38 77	4,514 12	7,986 06	22	256 39
50.	280.	4,925 00	12,316 00	98 50	44 00	17,241 00	25,727 11	47	662 52
......	18.	......	810 00	......	45 00	810 00	2,014 82	......	......
10.	116.	800 00	4,400 00	80 00	37 93	5,200 00	7,381 78	8	62 54
10.	10.	600 00	350 00	60 00	35 00	950 00	1,175 35	2	......
8.	9.	384 00	297 00	48 00	33 00	681 00	929 18	1	3 50

TABLE XVII.

Census, enrollment attendance, etc., of city and graded village

Incorporated cities.	School population from inspectors' report.	Enrollment.				Average number belonging.				
		High school department.	Grammar department.	Primary department.	Whole school.	High school department.	Grammar department.	Primary department.	Whole school.	High school department.
Totals for cities	314,731	24,515	77,434	147,185	249,134	20,296	52,869	89,684	162,849	19,618
Adrian	2,498	319	633	1,051	2,003	259	497	742	1,498	253
Albion	1,639	208	373	580	1,161	185	313	418	916	179
Allegan	785	185	232	243	660	163	218	218	599	156
Alma	678	99	204	541	844	80	147	286	513	77
Alpena	3,727	145	595	1,268	2,008	129	519	977	1,625	126
Ann Arbor	3,326	634	863	947	2,444	537	*1,531	....	2,068	510
†Au Gres	....	....	....	....	....	....	....	....	....	....
Au Sable	486	63	146	182	391	60	129	160	349	56
Bad Axe	515	79	154	179	412	65	148	164	377	61
Battle Creek	4,756	466	1,173	2,393	4,032	429	1,013	1,887	3,329	422
Bay City	14,599	931	2,922	6,141	9,994	620	1,727	3,526	5,873	602
Beaverton	250	37	52	142	231	33	35	120	188	29
Belding	821	101	227	313	641	90	223	294	607	93
Benton Harbor	1,978	285	589	916	1,790	258	461	586	1,305	248
Bessemer	1,249	105	296	594	995	102	288	518	908	99
Big Rapids	1,332	153	317	566	1,036	133	221	422	776	130
Boyne City	1,267	76	262	565	903	63	200	407	670	59
Brown City	223	72	52	134	258	56	46	106	208	50
Cadillac	2,247	217	650	1,302	2,169	200	477	1,021	1,698	211
Charlevoix	763	150	214	300	664	139	184	246	569	133
Charlotte	1,040	201	302	463	966	170	260	334	773	174
Cheboygan	2,320	126	398	918	1,442	103	325	688	1,116	98
Clare	472	76	156	208	440	71	134	159	364	64
Coldwater	1,342	185	395	723	1,303	172	334	531	1,037	165
Coleman	391	52	131	195	378	46	111	157	314	41
Corunna	382	75	137	204	416	70	97	149	316	67
Croswell	398	62	96	236	394	53	73	162	288	58
Crystal Falls	1,327	109	474	1,136	1,719	96	265	571	932	93
Detroit	97,508	4,689	22,762	51,223	78,674	3,599	12,150	24,014	39,763	3,446
Dowagiac	1,202	148	426	745	1,319	132	332	507	971	129
†East Lansing	....	....	....	....	....	....	....	....	....	....
East Tawas	480	56	152	233	441	50	148	191	389	47
Eaton Rapids	415	131	105	165	401	128	97	121	344	124
Escanaba	4,237	306	907	1,580	2,793	277	645	1,167	2,089	269
Flint	3,789	470	1,533	2,248	4,251	379	843	1,216	2,438	368
Gladstone	1,064	103	244	482	829	96	213	406	715	92
Gladwin	291	54	92	142	288	48	81	115	244	45
Grand Haven	1,647	156	471	652	1,279	148	372	512	1,032	146
Grand Ledge	603	100	170	210	480	96	156	184	436	90
Grand Rapids	27,325	1,941	7,511	13,760	23,212	1,359	4,205	7,575	13,139	1,319
Greenville	845	172	503	618	1,293	160	273	280	713	152
Hancock	2,070	165	579	1,299	2,043	128	310	620	1,058	124
Harrison	242	33	81	46	160	28	68	37	133	26
Harrisville	202	19	68	83	170	18	65	75	158	17
Hastings	808	148	191	311	650	140	180	300	620	130
Hillsdale	1,122	268	338	500	1,106	234	271	387	892	227
Holland	2,846	143	801	1,448	2,392	119	587	915	1,621	118
Hudson	586	155	169	243	567	133	140	194	467	125
Ionia	1,652	129	275	511	915	117	227	394	738	111
Iron Mountain	3,230	160	820	1,911	2,891	145	709	1,454	2,308	137

*Includes grammar and primary departments.
†Not legally graded.

TABLE XVII.

schools as reported by superintendents for the school year 1906-7.

Average daily attendance.			Percentage of attendance.				Number of regular teachers employed.								Portion of superintendent's time devoted to supervision.	No. of special teachers.
							High school department.		Grammar department.		Primary department.		Whole school.			
Grammar department.	Primary department.	Whole school.	High school department.	Grammar department.	Primary department.	Whole school.	Men.	Women.	Men.	Women.	Men.	Women.	Men.	Women.		
50,483	84,179	154,280	95	92	94	92	271.6	610.4	69.3	1,585.2	26.4	2,528.4	432.	4,724		203
461	691	1,405	97	93	93	94	3.	8.	....	13.	....	21	3	42	All	5
294	385	858	97	94	91	96	3.2	5.	....	8.	....	11	4	24	5-6	2
210	201	567	95	90	92	91	1.5	4	....	5	....	8	2	17	1-2	....
141	265	483	98	96	92	94	1.4	2.5	....	5	....	8.5	2	16	5-8	1
505	923	1,554	97	97	94	96	3	3	....	15	....	24	4	42	All	3
*1,473	....	1,983	96	*96	....	96	8	12	....	23.5	....	24.5	9	60	All	5
....	....	....	....	....	....	....	......	......	....	....	....	....	....	....	......	....
120	127	303	98	93	87	92	.8	1	1	3	....	4	2	8	1-5	....
128	153	342	90	94	91	91	1.5	2	....	4	....	4	2	10	1-2	1
974	1,790	3,186	98	96	94	96	5	12	3	27	....	59	9	98	All	5
1,703	3,467	5,772	96	98	98	98	12	17	2	61.4	2	99.6	18	178	All	5
31	99	159	88	89	82	86	1	1	....	1	1	2	2	4	......	....
206	258	557	95	90	84	90	.5	4	....	6	....	8	1	18	1-2	2
439	553	1,240	96	95	94	95	2	7	....	14	....	18	3	39	All	1
279	501	879	96	97	95	96	1.5	3	....	8	....	14	2	25	1-2	1
217	404	751	97	98	95	96	1	5	....	7.5	....	12.5	2	25	All	1
192	363	614	94	95	89	93	.3	4	....	7	....	10	1	21	2-3	....
43	91	184	89	93	79	87	2	......	1	....	....	2	3	2	......	....
461	918	1,590	95	94	92	94	2	5	....	14	....	22	3	41	All	1
176	234	543	96	92	94	94	1	5	....	5	....	8	1	18	All	2
247	331	752	97	95	93	95	2.4	4	....	7	....	10	3	21	3 5	2
299	625	1,022	94	92	91	91	2	2	1	7.7	....	16.3	4	26	All	1
119	142	325	84	76	68	76	.8	2	....	4	....	4	1	10	1-4	....
320	503	988	95	95	94	95	4.2	2	1	9.5	....	15.5	6	27	7-8	2
97	133	271	89	88	87	88	.8	1	1	2	....	4	2	7	1-5	4
99	148	314	96	95	93	94	.5	2	....	4	....	5	1	11	1-2	2
67	146	271	97	91	90	92	1.6	......	....	2	....	3	.2	5	1-3	....
253	528	874	96	95	93	94	.2	4	....	7	....	23	1	34	4-5	1
11,676	22,635	37,757	95	96	92	94	49	111	20	429	17	680	87	1,220	All	9
321	462	912	97	96	92	93	1.3	4	1	10	....	13	3	27	5-7	1
....	....	....	....	....	....	....	......	......	....	....	....	....	....	....	......	....
140	152	339	83	92	65	80	.5	1	....	4	....	5	1	10	1-2	....
83	111	318	98	83	92	91	1.5	4	....	3	....	4	2	11	1 2	4
616	1,148	2,033	97	95	93	95	3	7	....	18	....	26	4	51	All	3
778	994	2,140	97	94	93	94	1	13	....	24	....	35	2	72	All	4
209	401	702	97	98	98	98	1.5	2	....	5	....	8	2	15	1-2	2
72	91	208	83	88	82	84	.8	1	....	2	....	3	1	6	1-5	....
364	493	1,003	98	97	97	97	.2	5	....	9	....	15	1	29	5-6	1
143	167	400	93	91	91	92	2.5	4	....	5	....	4	3	13	1-2	1
4,024	7,166	12,509	97	94	93	95	14	39	6	153.9	2	213.1	23	406	All	5
258	262	672	95	94	93	94	.5	6	....	6.5	....	8.5	1	21	1-2	2
298	602	1,024	98	96	97	96	3.1	4	....	8	....	14	4	26	6-7	....
63	34	123	92	93	91	92	.1	......	1	1	....	1	2	2	......	....
64	72	153	89	94	82	86	.8	......	....	1.5	....	1.5	1	3	1-6	....
175	295	600	98	94	90	94	2.3	3	2	3	....	9	5	15	5-7	3
261	363	851	97	96	94	95	2.2	6	....	8	....	11	3	26	3-4	3
565	867	1,550	98	95	94	95	1	4	....	15	....	22	2	41	All	2
130	183	438	95	92	94	94	2.6	2	1	3	....	7	4	12	3-7	1
223	372	706	98	98	96	97	1.3	6	....	10	....	14	2	30	5-7	....
670	1,376	2,183	94	94	94	94	2	1.2	2	17	....	35.7	6	54	All	5

TABLE XVII.—CONTINUED.

Incorporated cities.	School population from inspectors' report.	Enrollment.				Average number belonging.				
		High school department.	Grammar department.	Primary department.	Whole school.	High school department.	Grammar department.	Primary department.	Whole school.	High school department.
Ironwood	3,638	147	983	1,067	2,197	140	914	992	2,046	135
Ishpeming	4,015	360	1,000	1,870	3,230	301	864	1,657	2,822	293
Jackson	5,855	402	1,384	2,800	4,586	332	1,078	1,959	3,369	322
Kalamazoo	7,987	662	3,086	4,990	8,738	543	1,830	2,697	5,070	527
Lansing	5,191	432	1,170	2,099	3,701	376	933	1,527	2,836	365
Lapeer	567	122	165	219	506	120	151	190	461	112
Ludington	2,606	167	516	993	1,676	153	443	801	1,397	146
Mackinac Island	202	61	47	41	149	48	36	34	118	44
Manistee	4,216	268	804	1,399	2,471	205	604	1,126	1,935	182
Manistique	1,505	....	....	....	....	....	....	....	....	....
Marine City	1,314	80	204	382	666	66	173	286	525	62
Marquette	3,209	233	698	1,278	2,209	204	568	952	1,724	198
Marshall	976	233	249	323	805	195	217	264	676	187
Mason	411	95	132	172	399	85	120	119	324	80
McBain	255	18	58	162	238	13	51	141	205	12
Menominee	3,821	219	1,021	2,042	3,282	170	623	1,354	2,147	162
Midland	696	131	186	428	745	114	140	314	568	107
Monroe	1,732	122	242	453	817	110	225	397	732	106
Mt. Clemens	2,251	139	501	688	1,328	109	343	568	1,020	105
Mt. Pleasant	972	220	128	135	483	202	125	120	447	198
Muskegon	6,618	617	2,021	3,032	5,670	480	1,079	1,828	3,387	465
Muskegon Heights	365	13	101	185	299	12	85	139	236	12
Negaunee	2,287	166	429	1,047	1,642	128	328	750	1,216	123
Niles	1,330	143	432	621	1,196	135	284	481	900	132
North Muskegon	124	....	87	49	136	....	55	35	90	....
Norway	1,049	67	315	735	1,117	64	276	657	997	63
Omer	190	34	76	48	158	27	67	39	133	26
Onaway	696	28	131	471	630	22	104	326	452	20
Owosso	2,291	231	611	1,058	1,900	209	469	801	1,479	246
Petoskey	1,502	151	398	711	1,260	124	259	506	889	118
Pontiac	2,408	254	616	1,158	2,028	234	536	814	1,584	224
Port Huron	5,825	421	1,087	1,902	3,410	337	1,040	1,593	2,970	326
Rose City	322	43	82	129	254	33	68	111	212	25
Saginaw	8,236	758	1,838	2,438	5,034	661	1,484	1,778	3,923	633
Saginaw, W. S.	5,681	285	1,288	1,702	3,275	235	966	1,199	2,400	230
St. Clair	759	97	155	403	655	92	114	208	414	89
St. Ignace	640	61	126	282	469	55	100	275	430	52
St. Johns	784	142	271	428	841	124	224	282	630	121
St. Joseph	1,537	131	381	606	1,118	123	326	485	934	117
St. Louis	667	82	175	376	633	70	151	264	485	69
Sandusky	325	52	87	151	290	44	65	104	213	44
Sault Ste. Marie	3,522	243	744	1,483	2,470	226	731	1,463	2,420	223
Scottville	235	64	87	121	272	55	73	106	234	53
South Haven	1,003	162	365	643	1,170	142	248	392	782	140
Standish	452	40	185	128	353	40	166	126	332	37
Stanton	378	47	89	192	328	44	81	134	259	42
Sturgis	749	92	235	385	712	82	162	282	526	79
Tawas City	462	39	90	187	316	35	75	148	258	34
Three Rivers	1,033	‡248	....	758	1,006	‡242	....	724	966	‡236
Traverse City	2,879	392	951	1,397	2,740	330	750	912	1,992	333
West Branch	568	70	80	290	440	60	75	270	405	60
Whittemore	140	....	68	44	112	....	63	39	102	....
Wyandotte	2,187	112	362	682	1,156	102	317	629	1,048	98
Yale	375	66	132	229	427	55	87	147	289	53
Ypsilanti	1,555	240	350	505	1,095	211	293	408	912	205
Zeeland	563	56	174	218	448	54	172	218	444	51

‡Includes high school and grammar department.

TABLE XVII.—Continued.

Average daily attendance.			Percentage of attendance.				Number of regular teachers employed.								Portion of superintendent's time devoted to supervision.	No. of special teachers.
							High school department.		Grammar department.		Primary department.		Whole school.			
Grammar department.	Primary department.	Whole school.	High school department.	Grammar department.	Primary department.	Whole school.	Men.	Women.	Men.	Women.	Men.	Women.	Men.	Women.		
900	950	1,985	96	93	93	94	2	3	....	17	....	41	3	61	All	6
859	1,649	2,801	97	98	98	97	3	15	....	19	....	35	4	69	All	7
1,029	1,860	3,211	96	95	94	95	4	10	2	29	....	55	7	94	All	2
1,730	2,466	4,723	97	94	90	93	5	19	2	51	2	67	10	137	All	12
890	1,411	2,666	97	95	94	95	5	10	....	39	....	40	6	89	All	4
140	176	428	90	91	90	90	.3	6	....	4	....	8	1	18	2-3	1
430	771	1,347	95	96	96	96	2	4	....	14	....	23	3	41	All	4
34	31	109	92	94	91	93	.8	1	....	1	....	1	1	3	1-6	....
560	1,095	1,837	89	93	97	95	3	9	....	19.5	....	36.5	4	65	All	4
......	......	......	....	....	....	....	....	....	....	......	....	......	....	......	......	....
157	261	480	92	92	92	92	2.2	1	....	5	....	8	3	14	3-4	1
529	893	1,620	96	93	93	94	5	4	....	16	1	29	7	49	All	6
210	252	649	96	96	95	96	2.7	6	....	7	....	10	3	23	2-3	3
115	118	313	84	87	69	80	.4	5	....	3	....	4	1	12	4-7	1
43	111	166	87	84	78	80	1	1	....	1	....	3	1	5	......	....
594	1,259	2,015	95	94	93	94	4	4.4	1	17	....	34.6	6	56	All	3
126	287	520	94	90	91	91	1.4	3	....	4.5	....	7.5	2	15	4-7	....
211	349	666	97	94	88	93	2.2	3	....	5	....	9	3	17	3-4	2
324	477	906	96	94	91	93	3	4	....	8	....	14	4	26	All	2
121	117	436	90	95	87	91	2.3	5	1	4	....	5	4	14	5-7	2
1,040	1,719	3,224	96	96	92	95	4	14	....	36	....	52	5	102	All	5
81	130	223	93	92	86	90	.7	1.2	....	2.8	....	4	1	8	1-3	....
317	662	1,102	96	93	94	95	2	5	....	8	....	19	3	32	All	1
264	433	829	95	95	95	95	1.2	4	....	7	....	13	2	24	5-6	1
48	30	78	....	55	61	58	....	......	....	2	....	1	......	3	......	....
265	630	958	98	96	94	96	2.7	2	....	7.5	...	14.5	3	24	2-3	2
62	30	118	78	93	76	82	1	......	....	2	....	1	1	3	......	....
90	267	377	95	85	82	87	.5	2	....	3.1	....	7.9	2	13	1-2	....
446	751	1,443	98	96	94	96	3	6	....	15	....	22	4	43	All	3
244	476	838	95	94	94	94	4	3	....	7	...	16	5	26	All	1
512	773	1,509	95	95	94	95	3	7	....	14	....	26	4	47	All	3
994	1,499	2,819	96	95	95	95	3	11	....	30	....	41	4	82	All	1
53	76	154	58	64	58	60	1	......	....	2	....	2	1	4	......	....
1,443	1,665	3,741	95	97	93	95	11	29	6	43	....	67	18	139	All	8
928	1,136	2,294	80	72	66	72	2	9	2	26	....	36	5	71	All	6
108	193	390	96	94	92	94	.4	3	....	3.5	....	6.5	1	13	4-7	1
115	247	414	91	93	92	93	1.5	......	1	3	....	5	3	8	1-2	....
216	268	605	97	96	95	96	1.3	4	....	7.3	....	10.7	2	22	2-3	2
320	465	902	95	97	95	96	2.2	4	....	10	....	16	3	30	4-5	2
137	216	422	98	80	91	89	.5	4	....	4.5	....	5.5	1	14	1-2	1
65	104	213	83	78	80	80	.9	1	....	2	....	2	1	5	1-8	....
701	1,403	2,327	96	97	92	95	4.3	5	5.3	16	1.4	29	12	50	All	4
68	100	221	96	93	94	94	1.8	1	....	2	....	2	2	5	1-6	1
241	372	753	98	96	93	96	1.3	4	1	7	....	12	3	23	5-7	1
110	123	270	90	60	81	77	.8	2	1	2	....	3	2	7	1-4	....
70	112	224	94	90	89	91	.5	2	....	2	....	3	1	7	1-2	....
148	265	492	95	92	93	93	.5	3	1	4	....	8	2	15	1-2	1
50	125	219	97	90	91	93	.6	1	....	3	....	3	1	7	2-5	1
......	693	929	97	....	96	96	3.1	7	....	......	....	17	4	24	7-8	1
709	830	1,872	97	91	91	94	2	6	1	17	....	36	3	59	All	2
75	270	405	....	....	....	....	.8	1	....	1	....	6	1	8	1-5	....
46	18	64	....	84	95	89	....	......	1	......	....	1	1	1	......	....
299	595	992	96	91	94	94	1	6	....	8	....	18	1	32	All	2
83	138	274	96	95	94	95	.6	2	....	4	....	4	1	10	3-7	....
276	382	863	97	94	93	94	2.1	5	....	9	....	12	3	26	6-7	3
170	215	436	95	94	93	94	.7	2	....	4	....	5	1	11	[illegible]	[illegible]

TABLE XVII.—CONTINUED.

Incorporated villages.	School population from inspectors' report.	Enrollment.				Average number belonging.				
		High school department.	Grammar department.	Primary department.	Whole school.	High school department.	Grammar department.	Primary department.	Whole school.	High school department.
Addison	171	59	42	82	183	50	35	64	149	56
Alanson	226	18	61	118	197	16	58	101	175	14
Algonac	477	41	108	248	397	31	85	186	302	30
Almont	199	41	53	106	200	37	43	91	171	36
Applegate	84	....	66	....	....	....	....	....	....	....
Armada	206	62	60	90	212	58	56	78	192	56
Ashley	193	52	46	68	166	32	35	48	115	20
Athens	186	39	58	80	177	35	51	68	154	33
†Atlanta	....	....	....	....	....	....	....	....	....	....
Attica	99	10	31	54	95	9	24	50	83	7
Augusta	136	46	56	50	152	38	50	40	128	38
Baldwin	168	43	55	60	158	39	33	39	111	30
Bancroft	147	22	59	50	131	20	38	35	93	19
Bangor	398	135	121	176	432	125	108	152	385	118
Baraga	959	40	225	326	591	26	198	250	474	21
Baroda	198	40	46	73	159	36	42	60	138	32
Barryton	174	23	33	99	155	14	30	83	127	11
Bear Lake	155	20	44	93	157	20	44	93	157	17
Bellaire	365	47	96	157	300	45	90	146	281	44
Belleville	150	40	36	67	143	38	32	60	130	35
Bellevue	272	86	90	90	266	79	84	81	244	71
Bensonia	231	18	73	107	198	15	62	86	163	13
Berrien Springs	225	47	70	94	211	44	64	77	185	43
Birmingham	363	115	104	166	385	100	84	119	303	95
Blissfield No. 1 fr	191	41	51	73	165	37	40	52	129	36
Blissfield No. 2 fr	243	56	91	148	295	42	70	103	215	41
Bloomingdale	141	71	35	38	144	66	35	38	139	59
Boardman	202	30	43	138	211	18	29	40	87	18
Boyne Falls	218	24	27	47	98	22	25	35	82	20
Breedsville	105	....	44	40	84	....	39	38	77	....
Brighton	184	46	68	66	180	44	63	53	160	43
Britton	118	31	38	44	113	26	34	39	99	25
Bronson	272	60	106	63	76	54	100	58	71	50
Brooklyn	154	41	54	61	156	40	50	57	147	39
Buchanan	405	74	142	194	410	63	104	132	299	61
†Buckley	....	....	....	....	....	....	....	....	....	....
Burlington	96	30	27	33	90	27	16	21	64	23
Burr Oak	103	38	52	66	156	33	49	65	147	50
Byron	114	39	40	53	132	36	35	47	118	34
Caledonia	149	66	55	47	168	60	51	43	154	53
Calumet	8,036	401	1,740	3,140	6,019	342	1,655	3,861	5,858	327
Camden	114	27	18	36	80	24	17	34	75	24
Capac	209	53	40	122	215	49	32	102	183	46
Caro	553	288	144	148	580	226	125	130	481	213
Carson City	264	75	71	90	236	70	65	80	215	....
Carsonville	200	66	65	59	190	50	52	42	144	44
Caseville	183	54	63	65	182	46	53	40	139	41
Casnovia	96	21	26	51	98	17	23	45	85	16
Cass City	417	106	111	159	376	91	99	135	325	88
Cassopolis	262	62	108	90	260	51	96	68	215	50
Cedar Springs	200	40	74	125	248	46	72	120	238	45
Central Lake	350	44	130	157	331	40	86	119	245	37
Centreville	167	45	42	87	174	37	41	77	155	37
Chelsea	512	120	145	205	470	114	124	179	417	112
Chesaning	324	40	88	156	284	37	75	111	223	36

†Not legally graded.

TABLE XVII.—Continued.

Average daily attendance.			Percentage of attendance.				Number of regular teachers employed.								Portion of superintendent's time devoted to supervision.	No. of special teachers.
							High school department.		Grammar department.		Primary department.		Whole school.			
Grammar department.	Primary department.	Whole school.	High school department.	Grammar department.	Primary department.	Whole school.	Men.	Women.	Men.	Women.	Men.	Women.	Men.	Women.		
40	75	171	95	96	92	94	2	....	1	....	....	2	3	2	....	....
53	97	164	78	86	82	82	.8	....	....	2	....	2	1	4	1 5	....
76	162	268	93	90	88	90	.9	1	....	2	....	5	1	8	1-8	....
42	86	164	98	96	95	96	.9	1	....	2	....	2	1	5	1-9	....
66	....	....	....	....	....	....	....	....	1	1	....	....	1	1	....	....
53	71	180	97	92	89	93	1	1	....	2	....	2	1	5	....	....
27	30	77	65	77	62	68	2	....	....	1	....	2	2	3	....	....
48	62	143	94	94	91	92	1	1	....	1	....	2	1	4	....	....
....	....	....	....	....	....	....	....	....	....	....	....	....	....	....	....	....
19	38	64	66	79	76	73	.6	....	.4	.8	....	.2	1	1	....	....
46	35	119	90	92	90	90	.9	1	1	1	....	2	2	4	1 8	....
40	37	107	68	60	65	64	1	....	1	....	....	1	1	2	....	....
35	33	87	97	91	93	94	.8	1	....	2	....	1	1	4	1-5	....
98	128	344	94	90	84	89	2.8	2	....	2	....	3	3	7	1-4	....
198	210	441	80	88	84	82	.8	1	1	5	....	7	2	13	1-4	....
38	51	121	90	82	69	80	1	....	....	1	....	1	1	2	....	....
22	65	98	79	74	78	77	1	....	1	....	....	2	1	3	....	....
36	74	127	85	82	80	80	1	....	....	1	....	2	1	3	....	1
90	143	277	94	92	93	93	1	1	....	2	....	4	1	7	....	2
28	55	118	94	87	92	91	1	....	....	1	....	2	1	3	....	....
74	59	204	90	88	72	83	.7	2	....	2	....	2	1	6	1-3	1
51	67	131	88	82	79	83	.8	1	....	2	....	2	1	5	1-4	....
51	66	160	98	90	93	93	.8	1	....	2	....	2	1	5	1-6	1
80	111	286	95	95	93	94	.5	2	....	3	....	5	1	10	1-2	1
36	47	119	97	90	92	93	1	1	....	1	....	1	1	3	....	....
66	92	199	97	94	90	92	.8	2	....	2	....	2	1	6	1-4	....
29	20	108	83	80	51	72	1	2	....	1	....	1	1	4	....	....
29	40	88	60	70	93	75	1	....	....	1	....	2	1	3	....	....
21	28	69	91	87	80	83	.8	....	....	2	....	1	1	3	1·4	..
80	26	56	....	70	80	75	....	....	1	....	....	1	1	1	....	....
61	50	154	97	96	94	96	.9	1	....	2	....	2	1	5	1 10	....
32	75	92	91	94	90	82	....	1	....	1	....	1	....	3	....	....
75	56	181	90	95	94	93	.7	2	....	3	....	2	1	7	1-3	....
48	55	142	95	88	90	91	.9	1	....	1.3	....	1.7	1	4	1 10	....
92	123	276	95	93	92	93	1.5	2	....	4	....	4	2	10	1 2	1
....	....	....	....	....	....	....	....	....	....	....	....	....	....	....	....	....
17	18	58	87	77	85	83	1	....	....	1	....	1	1	2	....	....
49	48	147	90	94	73	86	1.5	2	....	2	....	2	1	6	1 2	....
32	41	107	95	91	89	92	1	....	....	1	....	1	1	2	....	....
47	39	139	80	85	83	83	1	....	....	1.7	....	1.3	1	3	....	....
1,455	3,394	5,176	95	88	88	88	5	10	1	48	....	100	6	158	All	5
17	34	75	90	96	95	93	.8	1	1	....	....	2	2	3	1-6	....
37	86	169	97	89	81	89	.9	1	....	1	....	1	1	3	1 8	....
122	125	460	94	97	96	95	2.5	2	....	4	....	5	3	11	1-2	1
....	....	....	....	....	....	87	.9	2	....	2	....	3	1	7	1-8	....
36	33	113	67	80	56	67	1	1	....	1	....	1	1	3	....	....
50	31	122	79	86	49	71	1	1	....	1	....	1	1	3	....	....
21	40	77	93	90	90	91	1	....	....	1	....	1	1	2	....	....
92	121	301	96	90	89	91	1.8	2	....	2	....	5	2	9	1-6	....
88	62	200	95	92	91	93	1.3	1.6	1.3	1.4	....	3	3	6	3-7	....
70	105	230	42	59	95	65	.8	2	....	2	....	2	1	6	1 6	1
72	106	215	92	83	89	88	.7	2	....	2	....	4	1	8	1·3	1
36	76	149	93	86	76	84	.8	1	....	2	....	2	1	5	1-5	....
121	163	396	98	97	91	95	.7	4	....	4	....	5	1			1
71	101	208	97	94	91	94	1.7	1.5	....	2	....	2.5	2			.

TABLE XVII.—Continued.

Incorporated villages.	School population from inspectors' report.	Enrollment.				Average number belonging.				
		High school department.	Grammar department.	Primary department.	Whole school.	High school department.	Grammar department.	Primary department.	Whole school.	High school department.
Clarkston	140	29	55	45	129	28	48	45	121	25
Clayton	91	37	42	51	130	31	30	40	101	26
†Clifford	......	......	......	......	......	......	......	......	......	......
Climax	143	32	45	49	126	31	43	48	122	27
Clinton	229	56	79	65	200	55	75	62	192	54
Clio	172	39	63	94	196	35	55	80	170	31
Coloma	218	43	69	120	232	40	67	112	219	35
Colon	211	58	84	67	209	49	70	57	176	46
Columbiaville	144	56	35	38	129	38	27	30	95	35
Concord	125	36	39	55	130	28	36	44	108	25
Constantine	262	64	107	100	271	57	89	74	220	56
Coopersville	202	43	71	98	212	40	68	83	191	37
Copemish	139	14	52	52	118	14	52	52	118	13
†Croton	......	......	......	......	......	......	......	......	......	......
Custer	125	32	35	30	97	30	32	18	80	22
†Daggett	......	......	......	......	......	......	......	......	......	......
Dansville	100	31	29	43	103	28	26	35	89	26
Davison	189	43	79	90	212	28	67	89	184	24
Dearborn	353	25	102	133	260	20	83	117	220	16
Decatur	378	86	89	200	375	75	85	168	328	73
Deckerville	187	45	33	84	162	45	33	70	147	27
Deerfield	173	44	69	55	168	38	58	35	131	35
Detour	347	25	54	176	255	24	51	169	244	20
Dexter	257	77	93	100	270	72	82	89	243	71
Douglas	155	23	46	60	128	20	43	41	104	20
Dryden	138	......	60	45	105	......	60	45	105	......
Dundee	270	35	79	129	243	31	72	117	220	29
Durand	461	55	192	249	496	49	147	166	362	46
†Eagle	......	......	......	......	......	......	......	......	......	......
East Grand Rapids	129	32	32	48	112	25	26	35	86	23
East Jordan	700	104	178	325	607	76	125	226	427	73
Eau Claire	137	21	84	48	153	20	60	35	115	13
Ecorse	270	7	60	153	220	7	47	39	93	6
Edmore	284	43	109	101	253	41	80	84	205	37
Elk Rapids	552	91	178	278	547	80	155	237	472	77
Elkton	284	52	41	143	236	52	41	143	236	43
Elsie	204	60	70	80	220	45	58	65	168	43
†Emmet	......	......	......	......	......	......	......	......	......	......
Empire	201	35	71	98	204	31	66	89	185	31
Essexville	578	......	49	81	130	......	43	75	118	......
Evart	452	85	110	161	356	80	107	150	337	80
†Fairgrove	......	......	......	......	......	......	......	......	......	......
**Fairview	......	......	......	......	......	......	......	......	......	......
Farmington	156	......	......	......	......	......	......	......	......	......
Farwell	320	47	69	123	239	40	56	85	181	37
Fennville	237	63	66	95	224	55	63	86	204	51
Fenton	524	143	178	286	607	130	148	203	481	126
Fife Lake	134	47	37	54	46	46	31	47	124	45
Flushing	191	61	86	82	229	55	79	71	205	53
Ford	409	......	71	151	222	......	65	150	215	......
Forestville	90	......	......	......	......	......	......	......	......	......
†Fowler	......	......	......	......	......	......	......	......	......	......
Fowlerville	292	74	67	67	208	67	57	51	175	64
†Frankenmuth	......	......	......	......	......	......	......	......	......	......
Frankfort	637	53	197	360	610	50	188	327	565	49

†Not legally graded.
**Now part of Detroit.

TABLE XVII.—CONTINUED.

Average daily attendance.			Percentage of attendance.				Number of regular teachers employed.								Portion of superintendent's time devoted to supervision.	No. of special teachers.
							High school department.		Grammar department.		Primary department.		Whole school.			
Grammar department.	Primary department.	Whole school.	High school department.	Grammar department.	Primary department.	Whole school.	Men.	Women.	Men.	Women.	Men.	Women.	Men.	Women.		
48	34	107	88	87	88	87	1	1	....	1	....	1	1	3	......	....
34	15	75	84	95	87	74	1	......	....	1	....	1	1	3	......	....
....	....	....	....	....	....	....	....	....	....	....	....	....	....	....	......	....
86	38	101	90	87	86	88	1	1	....	1	....	1	1	3	......	....
73	61	188	96	92	93	93	.7	2	....	2	....	2	1	6	1-3	....
49	71	151	91	90	75	85	.9	1	....	1	....	2	1	4	1-8	1
61	84	180	90	90	84	88	.8	1	....	3	....	2	1	6	1-4	....
66	54	166	93	95	94	94	.9	1	....	3	....	2	1	6	1-8	....
24	24	73	90	82	88	87	1	1	....	1	....	1	1	3	......	....
35	41	101	89	97	92	94	1	1	....	1.4	....	1.6	1	4	1-10	1
85	67	208	96	96	90	94	.7	3	....	3	....	2	1	8	1-3	....
62	77	176	91	91	92	92	.9	1	....	1	....	2	1	4	1-8	....
47	45	105	93	90	86	89	.8	......	....	1	....	1	1	2	1-6	....
....	....	....	....	....	....	....	....	....	....	....	....	....	....	....	......	....
28	25	75	68	80	83	77	1	......	....	1	....	1	1	2	......	....
....	....	....	....	....	....	....	....	....	....	....	....	....	....	....	......	....
23	83	76	92	88	94	91	1	3	....	1.3	....	1.3	1	3	......	....
51	74	149	74	75	79	76	2	......	....	2	....	2	2	4	......	....
70	95	181	80	84	81	81	1	.5	....	1.5	....	3	1	5	......	1
80	146	300	96	94	87	91	.9	2	....	2	....	3	1	7	......	....
18	50	95	61	57	72	63	1	......	....	1	....	2	1	3	......	....
61	36	132	87	89	94	93	1	2	....	1	....	1	1	4	......	....
45	146	211	80	83	82	81	1	......	....	1	....	4	1	5	......	....
74	80	225	98	97	95	97	.7	2	....	2	....	2	1	6	2-7	1
38	35	93	90	89	86	88	.8	.3	....	.7	....	2	1	3	1-5	....
85	86	171	....	86	86	86	......	......	1	1	....	1	1	2	......	....
69	107	205	94	95	91	93	1	2	....	2	....	3	1	7	1-4	....
139	153	338	95	95	92	93	2.4	1	1	3	....	5	4	9	3-7	1
....	....	....	....	....	....	....	....	....	....	....	....	....	....	....	......	....
24	30	77	92	92	86	90	......	1	....	1	....	1	......	3	......	....
110	198	381	94	92	90	92	1.7	2	....	5	....	6	2	13	1-3	1
30	29	72	62	76	59	65	1	......	....	2	....	1	1	3	......	....
42	34	84	85	89	88	91	.8	......	....	2	....	2	1	4	1-5	....
74	78	189	90	73	83	78	1	......	....	1.7	....	2.3	1	4	......	....
148	221	446	83	83	85	83	.5	3	....	4.5	....	7.5	1	15	1-2	....
28	143	214	80	66	64	70	1	1	....	1	....	3	1	5	......	....
49	60	152	95	85	92	90	1.9	......	....	2	....	2	2	4	1-10	....
....	....	....	....	....	....	....	....	....	....	....	....	....	....	....	......	....
65	88	184	96	96	91	92	1	......	....	1.4	....	1.6	1	3	......	....
42	73	115	....	85	90	87	......	......	1	1	....	2	1	3	......	1
101	151	332	95	97	93	95	1.5	3	....	2	....	6	2	11	1-2	....
....	....	....	....	....	....	....	....	....	....	....	....	....	....	....	......	....
....	....	....	....	....	....	....	....	....	....	....	....	....	....	....	......	....
....	....	....	....	....	....	....	....	....	....	....	....	....	....	....	......	....
51	77	165	93	91	89	91	1	1	....	2	....	2	1	5	......	....
56	81	188	92	88	94	91	1	1	....	1	....	2	1	4	......	....
139	183	448	97	96	91	94	3	1	....	4	....	6	3	11	......	1
27	40	112	91	80	89	86	1	......	....	1	....	1	1	2	......	....
71	66	190	96	90	92	92	1.9	......	....	2	....	2	2	4	1-8	....
56	105	161	....	86	70	74	......	......	1	1	....	4	1	5	......	1
....	....	....	....	....	....	....	....	....	....	....	....	....	....	....	......	....
....	....	....	....	....	....	....	....	....	....	....	....	....	....	....	......	....
56	46	166	96	92	91	93	.8	2	....	2	....	2	1	6	1-6	1
....	....	....	....	....	....	....	....	....	....	....	....	....	....	....	......	....
151	298	498	95	95	91	93	.5	2	....	4	....	7	1	13	1-2	1

TABLE XVII.—Continued.

Incorporated villages.	School population from inspectors' report.	Enrollment.				Average number belonging.				
		High school department.	Grammar department.	Primary department.	Whole school.	High school department.	Grammar department.	Primary department.	Whole school.	High school department.
†Fraser										
Freeport	154	47	38	87	172	45	36	71	153	38
Fremont	387	118	103	205	426	104	100	201	405	98
Fruitport	109	18	39	60	117	14	33	52	99	11
Gagetown	205	37	30	33	100	30	29	32	91	26
Gaines	97	21	50	57	128	19	46	53	118	18
Galesburg	149	55	49	65	169	47	47	49	143	45
Galien	175	34	48	75	157	32	45	62	139	26
†Garden										
Gaylord	574	42	158	226	426	42	106	175	323	34
a Glenwood										
Gobleville	168	60	48	63	171	57	45	21	163	54
Grandville	309	53	74	155	282	48	65	117	230	45
Grant	133	15	47	49	111	13	38	39	90	10
Grass Lake	192	51	72	88	211	42	63	68	173	40
Grayling	532	45	148	264	457	40	120	225	385	34
Grosse Pointe	260		62	126	188		41	100		
†Grosse Pointe Farms										
†Grosse Pointe Park										
Hamtramck	935		100	460	560		98	307	405	
Hanover	116	36	35	76	147	30	30	70	130	25
Harbor Beach	435	46	110	239	395	40	96	151	287	43
Harbor Springs	761	74	182	175	431	70	168	116	354	65
Harietta	129	25	35	61	121	25	35	61	121	20
Hart	463	105	107	204	416	100	100	200	400	95
Hartford	364									
Hersey	146	28	58	64	150	25	49	44	118	24
Hesperia	142	43	51	68	162	35	41	56	132	31
Highland Park	371		72	155	227		70	144	214	
Hillman	279									
Holly	380	71	136	165	372	67	107	130	304	62
Homer	219	65	91	107	213	60	89	105	254	58
Houghton	1,955	167	471	922	1,560	154	387	735	1,276	146
Howard City	372	53	114	182	349	45	90	127	262	45
Howell	552	154	206	263	623	138	194	249	581	132
Hubbardston	127	25	23	38	86	23	21	34	78	22
¶Hubbell										
Imlay City	382	69	129	100	298	68	123	94	285	67
Iron River	645	55	119	238	412	49	93	194	336	47
Ithaca	590	106	186	221	513	92	146	184	422	89
Jerome	73		23	52	85		19	38	57	
Jonesville	320	66	101	155	322	47	105	123	275	47
Kalkaska	347	40	116	192	357	44	89	145	278	42
†Kinde										
Kingsley	198	15	65	67	147	15	65	67	147	13
Kingston	137	56	49	56	161	45	37	40	122	32
Laingsburg	137	32	58	40	130	32	54	35	121	30
Lake Ann	92		31	51	82		29	43	72	
Lake City	275	35	26	215	276	30	35	189	254	25
Lake Linden	1,882	164	203	466	833	152	173	360	685	152
Lake Odessa	354	70	132	165	367	59	109	131	299	52
Lakeview	315	97	90	120	307	84	64	90	238	80
L'Anse	582	37	142	257	436	34	135	240	409	32
§Laurium										
Lawrence	190	79	103	53	235	75	76	46	197	75

†Not legally graded.
§Report included in Calumet.
¶Report included in Lake Linden.
a Report included in Wyandotte.

TABLE XVII.—CONTINUED.

Average daily attendance.			Percentage of attendance.				Number of regular teachers employed.								Portion of superintendent's time devoted to supervision.	No. of special teachers.
							High school department.		Grammar department.		Primary department.		Whole school.			
Grammar department.	Primary department.	Whole school.	High school department.	Grammar department.	Primary department.	Whole school.	Men.	Women.	Men.	Women.	Men.	Women.	Men.	Women.		
33	63	134	95	94	90	93	1	1	1	...	...	2	2	3	...	...
96	170	366	94	96	84	90	2	2	...	3	...	4	2	9	...	...
30	45	86	78	91	86	85	1	...	...	1	...	1	1	2	...	...
24	25	75	70	80	75	75	1	...	...	1	...	1	1	2	...	...
43	52	113	88	86	91	88	1	...	...	1	...	1	1	2	...	...
45	45	135	96	95	92	94	.8	2	...	1.5	...	1.5	1	5	1-4	1
41	54	121	81	91	87	87	.7	1	.3	1	...	1	1	3	...	...
103	155	292	92	89	90	91	.7	2	...	3	...	5	1	10	1-3	...
38	55	147	91	70	80	82	.9	1	...	1.5	...	1.5	1	4	1-9	...
61	120	226	94	94	87	92	.7	1	...	2	...	2	1	5	1-3	...
34	35	79	81	88	86	85	1	...	...	1	...	1	1	2	...	...
59	65	164	95	94	95	95	.8	2	...	1	...	1	1	5	1-6	1
110	190	234	91	93	94	93	2	...	...	4	...	4	2	8	...	1
...	82	...	...	...	81	...	...	...	1	1	...	3	1	4	...	...
...	...	...	...	...	...	...	...	...	...	...	...	...	...	...	...	...
91	271	362	...	90	91	91	...	...	1	3	...	7	1	10	...	2
26	49	100	69	74	92	78	1	...	...	1	...	2	1	3	...	...
85	131	259	96	94	92	94	.8	1.5	...	2.5	...	4	1	8	1-4	1
158	92	315	93	94	79	89	.5	3	...	4	...	5	1	12	1-2	1
29	47	96	80	82	77	79	1	...	...	1	...	1	1	2	All	...
96	186	377	95	86	94	91	.7	3	...	1	...	8	1	12	1-3	1
...	...	...	...	...	...	...	.8	3	...	2	...	2	1	8	1-4	1
45	40	108	96	90	89	91	.8	.5	...	1.2	...	1.3	1	3	...	...
37	48	116	88	90	77	85	.8	1	...	1	...	2	1	4	1-6	...
57	121	178	...	87	83	85	...	...	.8	2	...	4	1	6	1-4	1
...	...	...	...	...	...	...	...	...	...	...	...	...	...	...	...	...
93	112	267	92	94	87	91	1	2	...	2	...	3	1	7	...	1
68	77	203	94	74	71	79	1	2	...	2	...	3	1	7	...	1
375	710	1,231	96	90	84	90	4	4	1	10.3	1	22.7	7	37	All	1
81	115	231	99	90	88	93	.5	2	...	2	...	4	1	8	1-2	1
182	236	550	96	94	95	95	.7	4	...	5	...	6	1	15	1-3	2
19	32	73	93	93	93	93	1	...	...	1	...	1	1	2	...	...
119	91	277	96	94	91	93	.8	2	...	2	...	3	1	7	1-5	...
85	191	323	95	91	99	95	.4	2	...	3	...	5	1	10	5-8	1
142	174	405	96	97	94	96	.7	3	...	3	...	5	1	11	1-3	1
15	31	46	...	88	90	89	...	...	1	...	...	1	1	1	...	...
84	116	247	99	80	95	89	1	2	...	2	...	3	1	7	...	1
83	124	249	86	71	70	72	.8	2.5	...	2.5	...	5	1	10	1-5	...
60	55	128	86	92	82	86	.8	...	...	2	...	1	1	3	1-5	...
36	31	99	72	92	79	82	1	...	...	1	...	1	1	2	...	...
50	35	115	94	93	90	92	.9	1	...	1	...	1	1	3	1-8	...
25	32	57	...	87	64	76	...	...	1	...	...	1	1	1	...	...
30	159	214	72	70	71	71	1	...	...	1	...	5	1	6	...	...
171	348	671	90	98	97	98	1	6	...	7	...	11	1	24	All	2
101	126	279	89	92	96	93	.8	1.5	...	3.5	...	4	1	9	1-4	...
58	80	218	95	90	89	91	1.8	1	1	1	...	3	3	5	1-5	...
130	232	394	95	96	96	95	1.8	1	1	3	...	6	3	10	1-4	...
77	42	194	95	74	88	85	.7	2	...	3	...	1	1	6	1-3	1

TABLE XVII.—Continued.

Incorporated villages.	School population from inspectors' report.	Enrollment.				Average number belonging.				
		High school department.	Grammar department.	Primary department.	Whole school.	High school department.	Grammar department.	Primary department.	Whole school.	High school department.
North Adams	115	58	45	37	140	53	39	33	145	52
North Branch	222	72	65	104	241	66	55	81	202	64
Northport	256	26	95	118	239	19	78	104	201	16
Northville	461	65	187	130	382	51	140	135	326	50
Oakley	64	...	25	40	65	...	23	38	61	...
Olivet	180	55	65	54	174	55	65	54	174	54
Onekama	143	...	...	...	...	...	...	...	...	...
Ontonagon	643	77	223	252	552	73	208	209	490	73
Orion	198	35	59	68	162	31	54	58	143	27
Ortonville	109	34	34	51	119	30	31	37	98	23
Oscoda	345	42	31	160	233	42	31	154	224	42
Otisville	131	50	33	51	134	46	29	45	120	41
Otsego	604	116	186	310	612	102	172	295	569	93
Otter Lake	73	...	18	50	68	...	16	44	60	...
Ovid	301	81	89	113	283	75	89	97	261	75
†Owendale	...	...	...	...	...	...	...	...	...	...
Oxford	290	59	87	111	257	52	83	75	210	50
Parma	168	49	30	96	175	42	27	88	157	40
Paw Paw	360	129	106	133	368	114	93	110	317	113
†Peck	...	...	...	...	...	...	...	...	...	...
Pellston	328	15	74	225	314	15	64	180	259	12
Pentwater	305	44	105	114	263	40	93	97	230	33
†Perrinton	...	...	...	...	...	...	...	...	...	...
Perry	178	32	74	63	169	27	68	59	154	26
Petersburg	222	37	72	76	185	35	67	73	175	33
Pewamo	124	42	33	27	102	34	27	16	77	22
Pierson	103	...	37	38	75	...	37	38	75	...
Pigeon	327	21	90	110	221	36	139	152	327	16
Pinckney	132	35	48	38	121	29	22	28	79	27
Pinconning	340	70	60	100	230	60	52	89	201	55
Plainwell	306	88	78	149	315	80	74	128	282	74
Plymouth	495	90	153	242	485	81	127	189	397	77
Port Austin	244	26	24	146	196	22	22	120	164	20
Port Hope	154	20	23	22	65	19	20	21	60	18
Portland	453	70	146	211	427	70	138	150	358	67
Port Sanilac	96	23	31	35	89	22	30	34	86	17
†Posen	...	...	...	...	...	...	...	...	...	...
Potterville	141	30	41	50	121	28	40	45	113	23
Quincy	307	113	71	110	294	101	66	92	259	104
Reading	252	96	87	81	264	81	78	67	226	80
†Redford	...	...	...	...	...	...	...	...	...	...
§Red Jacket	...	...	...	...	...	...	...	...	...	...
Reed City	544	76	158	222	456	70	152	174	396	63
†Reese	...	...	...	...	...	...	...	...	...	...
Richland	87	38	31	19	88	36	30	15	81	35
b Richmond	325	34	98	91	223	29	92	87	208	28
River Rouge	1,111	28	219	655	902	24	194	611	829	23
Rochester	369	79	91	141	311	78	80	120	278	67
Rockford	201	44	71	82	197	41	58	74	173	38
Rogers	316	15	66	104	185	8	51	86	145	7
Romeo	373	86	113	156	355	78	97	116	291	78
Roscommon	133	31	28	50	109	26	24	35	85	22
Royal Oak	348	30	61	177	268	23	56	109	188	28
St. Charles	599	22	130	235	387	25	96	262	383	24
†St. Clair Heights	...	...	...	...	...	...	...	...	...	...

†Not legally graded.
§*Report included in Calumet.*
b *Lenox school district united with this.*

TABLE XVII.—CONTINUED.

Average daily attendance.			Percentage of attendance.				Number of regular teachers employed.								Portion of superintendent's time devoted to supervision.	No. of special teachers.
							High school department.		Grammar department.		Primary department.		Whole school.			
Grammar department.	Primary department.	Whole school.	High school department.	Grammar department.	Primary department.	Whole school.	Men.	Women.	Men.	Women.	Men.	Women.	Men.	Women.		
36	31	119	95	92	97	91	1	1	....	2	....	1	1	4	....	....
51	75	190	96	93	92	94	1	1	....	2	....	2	1	5	....	....
69	87	172	86	89	84	86	1	....	....	1.5	....	2.5	1	4	....	....
127	126	303	98	90	93	91	1.7	1	....	5	....	4	2	10	1-3	1
15	25	40	....	80	83	81	....	....	1	....	....	1	1	1	....	....
62	51	167	97	96	94	96	.8	2	....	2	....	2	1	6	1-6	....
....	....	....	....	....	....	....	1	....	....	1	....	1	1	2	....	....
208	209	490	98	88	83	89	.5	3	....	12	....	6	1	21	1-2	....
47	56	130	85	84	81	83	.8	1	....	2	....	2	1	5	1-4	....
26	29	78	76	86	78	80	1	....	....	1	....	1	1	2	....	....
31	149	222	96	95	94	95	.8	1	1	1	....	2	2	4	1-6	....
24	31	96	89	83	61	77	1	....	....	1	....	1	1	2	....	....
163	268	524	91	94	91	92	.7	3.5	....	5	....	7	1	15.5	2-7	1.5
13	35	48	....	91	80	86	....	....	....	1	....	1	....	2	....	....
84	87	246	92	96	98	95	1.7	1	....	2.5	....	3.5	2	7	3-8	1
....	....	....	....	....	....	....	....	....	....	....	....	....	....	....	....	....
77	69	196	96	92	92	93	.8	2	1	2	....	2	2	6	1-5	....
26	77	143	90	86	88	88	.8	1	....	1	....	2	1	4	1-6	1
89	101	303	99	96	95	96	1.7	2	1	1.5	....	2.5	3	6	2-7	1
....	....	....	....	....	....	....	....	....	....	....	....	....	....	....	....	....
59	140	211	80	93	77	83	1	....	....	2	....	3	1	5	....	....
82	88	203	95	93	94	94	.5	1.2	....	2.3	....	2.5	1	6	1 2	....
....	....	....	....	....	....	....	....	....	....	....	....	....	....	....	....	....
64	53	143	81	86	84	83	.2	1	....	2	....	2	1	5	3 4	....
65	71	169	95	98	96	96	.9	1	1	.5	....	2.5	2	4	1 9	....
28	13	63	81	80	60	75	1	....	....	1	....	1	1	2	....	....
31	26	57	....	84	67	75	....	....	1	....	....	1	1	1	....	....
53	80	149	76	59	72	63	1	....	....	2	....	2	1	4	....	....
21	26	74	95	96	92	94	1	1	....	2	....	1	1	4	....	....
48	83	186	78	80	83	80	....	1.8	....	2	....	2	....	6	1 5	....
55	120	249	98	98	88	95	.7	3	....	2	....	3	1	8	1 3	1
120	171	368	95	93	89	93	.6	2.5	....	3.5	....	4	1	10	3 7	2
21	106	147	92	90	87	89	.8	1	....	1	....	3	1	8	1-6	....
15	21	55	92	91	92	91	1	....	....	1	....	1	1	2	....	....
131	150	348	96	95	90	93	....	4.5	....	4	....	4	....	13	1 2	....
22	18	57	....	....	....	65	....	1	....	1	....	1	....	3	....	....
36	40	99	76	87	80	81	1	....	....	1.5	....	1.5	1	3	....	....
68	11	263	96	95	96	95	.8	4	....	2	....	2	1	8	1 4	1
72	65	217	98	96	98	98	1.8	1	....	2	....	2	2	5	1-4	....
....	....	....	....	....	....	....	....	....	....	....	....	....	....	....	....	....
146	159	368	82	92	71	81	1.6	2	....	4	....	6	2	12	4 7	2
27	13	75	97	90	87	91	.8	1	....	1	....	1	1	3	1 6	....
87	86	201	82	89	85	90	1	2	....	2	....	3	1	7	....	....
188	596	707	97	92	88	92	1	2	1	5	....	12	2	19	All	2
69	84	220	88	90	90	90	.8	1.5	....	2.5	....	2	1	6	1 5	....
56	65	159	96	94	94	95	.9	1	....	2	....	2	1	5	1-8	....
48	73	128	87	94	85	88	.6	....	1.4	....	....	2	2	2	....	....
94	111	283	99	97	95	97	.5	3	....	3	....	3	1	9	1-2	1
18	31	71	85	94	84	88	.8	1	....	1	....	1	1	4	1-6	....
35	147	230	94	89	88	90	1	2	....	1	....	3	1	6	....	....
89	244	357	91	93	92	92	.8	1	....	3	....	5	1	9	1-4	....
....	....	....	....	....	....	....	....	....	....	....	....	....	....	....	....	....

TABLE XVII.—Concluded.

Incorporated villages.	School population from inspectors' report.	Enrollment.				Average number belonging.				
		High school department.	Grammar department.	Primary department.	Whole school.	High school department.	Grammar department.	Primary department.	Whole school.	High school department.
Saline	210	62	83	62	207	54	71	53	178	51
Sand Lake	137	......	......	......	......	......	......	......	......	......
Saranac	242	49	102	102	253	44	85	78	207	42
Saugatuck	220	51	29	106	186	46	28	86	160	43
S hoolcraft	187	47	70	77	194	41	64	68	173	40
Sebewaing	578	32	114	139	285	28	81	123	232	24
Shelby	349	88	117	163	368	78	95	125	298	74
Shepherd	272	31	64	109	204	25	55	101	181	24
Sheridan	148	28	74	70	172	28	74	70	172	24
Sherman	187	28	43	103	174	27	33	82	142	27
Sherwood	131	31	25	80	136	22	25	73	118	20
†Sibley	......	......	......	......	......	......	......	......	......	......
South Frankfort	191	51	43	88	182	44	40	83	167	......
South Lyon	173	59	41	74	174	56	40	74	170	55
Sparta	310	63	116	113	292	58	112	110	280	53
Spring Lake	229	14	55	92	161	13	45	82	140	12
Springport	124	50	74	36	160	46	59	31	137	46
Stambaugh	689	32	146	309	487	28	130	281	439	25
Stanwood	113	......	......	......	......	......	......	......	......	......
†Stephenson	......	......	......	......	......	......	......	......	......	......
Stevensville	262	23	41	92	156	21	37	76	134	20
Stockbridge	177	44	80	66	190	38	68	59	165	36
Sunfield	119	45	42	67	154	36	38	56	130	34
Sutton's Bay	200	29	33	33	95	20	28	25	73	20
Tecumseh	530	151	163	232	546	135	139	166	440	131
Tekonsha	161	41	37	83	161	35	30	74	139	30
Thompsonville	296	20	90	183	293	17	75	142	234	15
Three Oaks	389	57	133	124	314	51	114	107	272	49
Trenton	434	21	105	204	330	17	99	191	307	16
Tustin	157	25	42	80	147	21	39	73	133	18
Twining	176	34	52	70	156	30	45	63	138	26
†Ubly	......	......	......	......	......	......	......	......	......	......
Union City	354	79	112	168	359	70	92	138	300	69
Unionville	211	41	93	60	194	35	74	40	149	29
Utica	204	31	52	80	163	26	40	63	130	25
Vandalia	132	50	31	40	121	48	28	39	115	46
Vanderbilt	205	62	56	64	182	54	50	56	160	41
Vassar	444	75	123	195	393	72	113	176	361	69
Vermontville	175	63	54	63	180	58	47	52	157	57
Vernon	115	30	29	36	95	25	28	32	85	23
Vicksburg	308	72	120	124	316	63	98	97	258	58
Wakefield	690	15	114	406	535	13	98	382	493	......
Waldron	121	36	46	38	120	32	33	30	95	29
Warren	100	......	......	......	......	......	......	......	......	......
Watervliet	245	50	76	139	265	48	69	119	236	45
Wayland	184	......	......	......	......	98	60	75	233	90
Wayne	335	85	120	153	358	78	99	119	296	74
Webberville	138	37	43	46	126	30	39	32	101	28
†Westphalia	......	......	......	......	......	......	......	......	......	......
White Cloud	241	52	49	134	235	40	48	130	218	34
Whitehall	436	78	133	149	360	70	116	127	313	67
White Pigeon	143	74	48	84	206	66	44	68	179	56
Williamston	313	96	86	139	321	84	82	139	305	76
Wolverine	239	28	70	108	206	28	70	108	206	18
Woodland	90	35	18	39	92	34	18	35	87	34
‡Woodmere	......	......	......	......	......	......	......	......	......	......

†Not legally graded.
‡*Included in* Detroit.

TABLE XVII.—Concluded.

Average daily attendance.			Percentage of attendance.				Number of regular teachers employed.								Portion of superintendent's time devoted to supervision.	No. of special teachers.
							High school department.		Grammar department.		Primary department.		Whole school.			
Grammar department.	Primary department.	Whole school.	High school department.	Grammar department.	Primary department.	Whole school.	Men.	Women.	Men.	Women.	Men.	Women.	Men.	Women.		
68	52	171	94	95	97	95	.7	2	....	2	....	2	1	6	1-3	1
....	....	....	....	....	....	....	....	....	....	....	....	....	....	....	....	....
81	75	198	94	95	95	95	1	1	....	3	....	2	1	6	....	....
26	75	144	93	91	91	91	1	1	....	1	....	3	1	5	....	....
62	65	167	97	97	96	96	.8	2	....	2	....	2	1	6	1-4	....
69	98	191	90	91	90	90	1	1	....	2	....	3	1	6	....	....
89	116	279	94	94	93	93	.6	2	....	4	....	3	1	9	2-5	....
47	98	169	77	73	92	80	.5	1	.5	2	....	3	1	6	....	....
56	43	123	89	74	61	75	1	....	....	2	....	1	1	3	....	....
31	77	135	98	94	94	95	1	....	....	1.5	....	1.5	1	3	....	....
22	58	100	88	88	79	85	1	....	....	1	....	2	1	3	....	....
....	....	....	....	....	....	....	....	....	....	....	....	....	....	....	....	....
....	....	....	37	37	78	60	1	1	....	2	....	2	1	5	All	....
36	64	156	98	91	87	92	.8	1	....	1	....	2	1	4	1-5	....
92	93	238	92	94	93	93	.8	1	....	3	....	3	1	7	1-6	1
41	77	130	94	92	94	93	.8	....	....	2	....	2	1	4	1-6	....
67	32	145	92	90	88	90	.8	1	....	2	....	1	1	4	1-4	....
112	240	377	90	83	85	86	.8	1	2	3	1	8	4	12	1-4	2
....	....	....	....	....	....	....	....	....	....	....	....	....	....	....	....	....
....	....	....	....	....	....	....	....	....	....	....	....	....	....	....	....	....
33	63	116	95	89	83	89	1	1	....	1	....	2	1	4	....	....
65	56	157	95	96	95	95	.8	.2	....	1.8	....	2	1	4	1-5	....
32	45	111	95	83	80	86	.8	.3	....	1.3	....	1.4	1	3	1-6	....
28	25	73	71	86	76	77	1	....	....	1	....	1	1	2	....	....
135	163	429	96	97	97	97	.3	4	....	4	....	5	1	13	5-7	1
29	69	126	90	89	91	90	.8	1	....	1	....	2	1	4	1-6	....
68	119	202	93	90	83	89	.9	....	....	3	....	3	1	6	1-8	....
107	93	249	95	93	91	93	.5	2	....	3	....	3	1	8	1-2	1
91	184	291	93	91	90	91	1	....	....	2	....	4	1	6	....	....
34	62	114	92	90	92	92	1	....	....	1	....	2	1	3	....	....
40	56	122	76	76	80	77	1	....	....	1	....	1	1	2	....	....
....	....	....	....	....	....	....	....	....	....	....	....	....	....	....	....	....
86	131	286	87	76	79	80	1.5	2	....	4	....	4	2	10	1-2	....
64	31	124	72	70	52	70	1	....	....	2	....	1	1	3	....	....
36	56	117	92	93	87	91	1	1	....	1.4	....	1.6	1	4	....	....
26	33	105	92	90	97	93	1	1	....	1	....	1	1	3	....	....
37	43	121	66	66	67	66	1	1	....	1	....	1	1	3	....	....
108	167	344	95	95	95	95	.5	3	....	3	....	5	1	11	1-2	1
47	46	150	91	85	73	83	.8	2	....	2	....	2	1	6	1-5	....
26	30	79	90	93	94	92	1	....	1	1	....	1	2	2	....	1
92	92	242	91	94	94	93	2	1.5	....	2.5	....	3	2	7	....	1
....	....	....	....	....	....	90	.5	2	1	3	....	8	2	13	1-2	1
30	28	87	94	92	80	89	1.8	1	....	1	....	1	2	3	1-6	....
....	....	....	....	....	....	....	....	....	....	....	....	....	....	....	....	....
62	96	203	94	90	80	88	.9	1	....	2	....	3	1	6	1-8	....
52	63	205	92	87	85	88	2	....	....	1	....	1	2	3	....	....
96	109	279	95	95	92	94	.7	2	....	2	....	4	1	8	3-8	1
32	30	90	90	82	93	88	1	....	....	1	....	1	1	2	....	....
....	....	....	....	....	....	....	....	....	....	....	....	....	....	....	....	....
38	104	176	65	78	78	77	1	1	....	1	....	2	1	4	1-6	1
113	116	296	85	84	85	84	1	1	....	4	....	4	1	9	....	1
41	65	164	86	93	95	91	.8	2	....	1	....	2	1	5	1-4	....
60	97	233	96	81	87	88	.7	3	....	2	....	3	1	8	1-3	1
31	37	86	79	66	72	73	1	1	....	2	....	2	1	5	....	1
16	31	81	97	90	83	90	1	....	....	1	....	1	1	2	....	1
....	....	....	....	....	....	....	....	....	....	....	....	....	....	....	....	....

TABLE XVIII.

Miscellaneous statistics of city and graded village schools as

Incorporated cities.	Average number pupils to each teacher.				Number of non-resident pupils.				Rate of tuition per year.			Average age of class.		
	High school department.	Grammar department.	Primary department.	Whole school.	High school department.	Grammar department.	Primary department.	Whole school.	High school department.	Grammar department.	Primary department.	Graduated.	Promoted to high school.	Promoted to grammar department.
Adrian	23	38	35	33	65	5	....	70	$20 00	$16 00	$12 00	18.8	14.6	10.5
Albion	22	39	38	32	40	6	1	47	15 20	15 20	13 20	18	14	9
Allegan	29	43	27	31	28	....	....	28	19 00	....	....	....	....	17.2
Alma	20	30	32	28	30	6	2	38	10 00	10 00	10 00	18	....	....
Alpena	18	34	40	35	....	....	....	....	....	....	....	18	15.2	11.4
Ann Arbor	26	*32	....	30	183	*18	....	201	30 00	13 50	9 00	19.3	14.2	10.5
†Au Gres	....	....	....	....	....	....	....	....	....	....	....	....	....	....
Au Sable	33	32	40	34	1	....	....	....	6 00	....	....	17	....	....
Bad Axe	18	37	41	31	19	1	1	21	20 00	17 50	15 00	17	14	11
Battle Creek	26	34	36	34	52	13	24	89	24 00	18 00	12 00	18	....	....
Bay City	21	27	34	30	69	30	34	133	25 00	13 50	10 00	18.3	15.1	11.3
Beaverton	17	35	40	31	1	2	1	4	13 50	6 75	6 75	15	11	8
Belding	21	35	35	31	22	2	....	24	16 00	16 00	16 00	17	13	9
Benton Harbor	29	33	33	32	70	14	18	102	18 00	14 40	14 40	18	14	10
Bessemer	18	36	37	32	3	....	....	3	26 00	26 00	26 00	17	13	9
Big Rapids	21	31	32	28	6	7	15	28	18 00	15 00	12 00	18.5	14.2	10.3
Boyne City	15	28	40	30	6	1	....	7	18 00	13 50	13 50	16	14.8	10.5
Brown City	28	46	53	42	38	4	10	52	10 00	10 00	7 50	....	15	11
Cadillac	25	36	21	38	3	....	....	3	9 00	....	....	17.5	....	....
Charlevoix	19	36	30	28	14	1	....	15	13 50	12 08	....	18	....	....
Charlotte	29	36	33	33	50	10	1	61	4 75	3 80	3 32	18	....	....
Cheboygan	24	37	40	37	27	9	17	52	15 00	15 00	10 00	18	....	....
Clare	25	33	39	33	26	....	....	26	10 00	....	....	17	14	11
Coldwater	20	30	35	31	36	6	3	45	20 00	16 00	12 00	18.9	15.5	11.5
Coleman	25	37	39	35	5	3	3	11	10 00	10 00	10 00	17	15	12
Corunna	23	24	30	26	26	10	8	44	10 00	7 50	7 50	18	13	....
Croswell	40	34	58	41	17	2	4	23	10 00	10 00	10 00	18	14	9
Crystal Falls	22	35	24	26	....	....	....	....	....	....	....	18	14	10
Detroit	22	27	35	30	130	....	....	130	40 00	14 00	14 00	18.4	14.6	....
Dowagiac	23	30	39	32	36	14	8	58	16 00	12 00	10 00	19.1	14.6	10.7
†East Lansing	....	....	....	....	....	....	....	....	....	....	....	....	....	....
East Tawas	33	37	38	35	....	....	....	....	12 00	....	....	18	....	....
Eaton Rapids	23	32	30	26	34	7	1	42	16 00	12 00	12 00	17	13	10
Escanaba	25	36	45	38	12	3	2	17	30 00	20 00	15 00	18	14	10
Flint	25	35	35	32	86	13	15	114	....	....	....	18	14	10
Gladstone	27	40	49	42	4	7	....	11	....	....	....	18	13	10
Gladwin	24	40	38	35	22	2	....	24	12 50	7 50	5 00	....	13	....
Grand Haven	28	41	34	34	16	5	4	25	20 00	15 00	10 00	18	....	....
Grand Ledge	15	31	46	27	36	14	6	56	14 00	10 00	10 00	18	14	9.5
Grand Rapids	26	33	36	33	54	18	20	92	50 00	30 00	20 00	18	14.7	11.1
Greenville	24	42	32	34	19	19	1	39	25 00	12 00	10 00	18	14	10
Hancock	17	37	43	36	18	....	1	19	48 00	20 00	20 00	17.3	13.8	11
Harrison	28	34	37	33	7	3	....	10	9 00	9 00	9 00	16	12	8
Harrisville	24	37	50	39	6	1	2	9	5 00	5 00	5 00	17	14.2	11
Hastings	23	36	33	31	50	3	2	55	16 00	14 00	14 00	18	14	10
Hillsdale	28	34	34	31	80	19	3	102	15 00	12 00	9 00	18.4	....	....
Holland	20	39	41	38	12	20	8	40	12 00	12 00	12 00	18.5	14.5	10.5
Hudson	30	35	27	29	58	7	....	65	15 20	15 54	9 50	18	....	....
Ionia	16	23	21	23	42	82	14	138	20 00	15 00	10 00	19.3	16.5	12.4
Iron Mountain	43	35	41	37	2	....	....	2	15 00	10 00	10 00	19	14.5	10.5
Ironwood	23	53	34	31	5	....	....	5	25 00	15 00	15 00	16	14	10
Ishpeming	15	45	47	38	....	....	....	....	....	....	....	17.5	13	9
Jackson	23	35	36	34	33	9	5	47	20 00	16 00	12 00	19	15	11
Kalamazoo	22	34	41	34	20	17	11	48	38 00	19 00	12 16	18.9	14.6	....
Lansing	25	31	38	31	35	15	20	70	9 00	9 50	9 50	17.4	14.5	....

*Includes grammar and primary departments.
†Not legally graded.

TABLE XVIII.

reported by superintendents for the school year 1906-7.

Number of graduates.	Number of U. S. flags.	Has school kindergarten below primary grade?	Portion of time in first primary devoted to kindergarten work.	Number of grades in the school.	Number of pupils studying— Latin.	Greek.	French.	German.	Does school give special instruction in— Vocal music?	Drawing?	Penmanship?	Manual training?	Domestic science?	Has school a commercial course?	Is the compulsory attendance law enforced?	Has school an ungraded department?	Has school a day school for the deaf?
36	7	Yes	1-3	12	100	....	6	61	Yes	Yes	No	Yes	Yes	No	Yes	No	No
36	5	No	1-2	12	60	....	....	60	Yes	Yes	No	Yes	No	No	Yes	No	No
21	5	No	1-5	12	24	....	....	40	Yes	Yes	No	No	No	Yes	Yes	No	No
11	2	Yes	1-3	12	42	....	....	21	Yes	Yes	....	....	....	Yes	Yes	No	No
23	8	....	....	12	68	....	....	22	Yes	Yes	Yes	No	No	Yes	Yes	No	No
84	7	No	1-8	12	261	7	93	143	Yes	Yes	No	Yes	Yes	Yes	Yes	No	No
....	....	....	....	....	....	....	....	....	....	....	....	....	....	....	....	....	....
11	2	Yes	1-6	11	30	....	....	21	No	No	No	No	No	Yes	No	No	No
7	1	No	1-4	12	18	....	....	10	Yes	No	No	No	No	Yes	Yes	No	No
46	11	Yes	....	13	241	8	42	85	Yes	Yes	No	Yes	Yes	Yes	Yes	Yes	No
80	18	Yes	....	12	281	6	100	172	Yes	Yes	Yes	Yes	Yes	Yes	Yes	No	Yes
3	2	No	....	12	....	....	....	4	....	....	....	....	....	No	Yes	No	No
14	1	Yes	1-2	12	28	....	....	18	Yes	Yes	Yes	No	No	Yes	Yes	No	No
46	5	No	....	12	110	....	....	127	Yes	Yes	Yes	No	No	Yes	Yes	No	No
25	4	No	1-4	12	61	....	....	20	Yes	Yes	No	No	No	No	Yes	No	No
26	4	Yes	1-2	12	40	....	....	29	Yes	Yes	Yes	No	No	Yes	Yes	No	No
6	1	No	1-2	12	....	....	....	....	No	No	No	No	No	No	Yes	No	No
....	1	No	....	12	....	....	....	....	....	....	....	....	....	....	Yes	No	No
22	4	Yes	1-5	12	65	....	....	40	Yes	Yes	No	No	No	No	Yes	No	....
23	1	No	1-6	12	24	....	....	18	Yes	Yes	Yes	Yes	No	Yes	Yes	No	No
32	....	No	1-5	12	35	....	....	28	Yes	Yes	No	Yes	No	Yes	Yes	No	No
15	7	No	....	12	43	....	....	31	Yes	Yes	No	No	No	Yes	Yes	Yes	No
15	1	No	....	12	24	....	....	20	No	No	Yes	No	No	No	Yes	No	No
20	4	Yes	5-6	12	77	....	....	44	Yes	Yes	No	Yes	No	Yes	Yes	No	No
7	1	No	1-2	12	10	....	....	....	....	....	....	....	....	Yes	No	No	No
15	1	Yes	All	12	32	....	....	6	Yes	Yes	No	No	No	No	Yes	No	No
5	1	No	1-2	12	45	....	....	7	No	No	No	No	No	No	Yes	No	No
18	11	Yes	....	12	62	....	....	33	Yes	Yes	No	No	No	No	Yes	No	No
437	82	Yes	....	12	1634	58	473	1153	Yes	Yes	No	Yes	Yes	Yes	Yes	Yes	Yes
22	3	Yes	....	12	63	....	....	38	Yes	Yes	Yes	No	No	Yes	Yes	No	....
....	....	....	....	12	....	....	....	....	....	....	....	....	....	....	....	....	....
8	1	No	....	12	9	....	....	....	No	No	Yes	No	No	Yes	Yes	No	No
7	1	No	1-5	12	27	....	....	14	Yes	Yes	No	Yes	....	No	Yes	No	....
38	4	Yes	1-6	12	92	....	40	49	Yes	Yes	Yes	No	No	Yes	Yes	No	No
57	....	Yes	1-5	12	184	11	15	67	Yes	Yes	Yes	Yes	Yes	Yes	Yes	No	No
13	1	Yes	....	12	29	....	....	9	No	No	No	No	No	No	....	No	No
....	1	No	1-4	11	10	....	....	8	No	No	No	No	No	No	Yes	No	No
25	4	Yes	....	12	75	....	....	66	Yes	Yes	Yes	No	No	Yes	Yes	No	No
12	1	No	1-4	12	47	....	....	21	Yes	No	No	No	No	No	Yes	No	No
169	....	Yes	....	12	636	....	95	467	Yes	Yes	No	Yes	Yes	Yes	Yes	Yes	Yes
18	1	No	1-3	12	46	....	50	42	Yes	Yes	No	No	No	Yes	Yes	No	....
19	3	No	....	12	33	....	19	23	No	Yes	Yes	No	No	Yes	Yes	No	No
6	1	No	....	12	....	....	....	....	....	....	....	....	....	No	Yes	....	....
....	1	No	1-3	11	3	....	....	....	No	No	Yes	No	No	Yes	Yes	No	No
14	4	Yes	1-6	12	50	....	....	40	Yes	Yes	Yes	Yes	No	Yes	Yes	No	No
47	3	Yes	....	12	116	....	....	70	Yes	Yes	No	Yes	No	No	Yes	No	No
22	4	Yes	1-4	12	25	....	....	33	Yes	Yes	No	Yes	No	No	Yes	Yes	No
17	3	Yes	1-4	12	....	....	....	....	Yes	Yes	No	No	No	No	Yes	No	....
21	4	Yes	1-2	12	38	....	....	46	Yes	Yes	Yes	No	No	Yes	Yes	No	No
12	9	No	1-3	12	66	....	....	153	Yes	Yes	No	Yes	Yes	Yes	Yes	No	Yes
20	8	Yes	....	12	50	....	....	90	Yes	Yes	Yes	No	Yes	No	Yes	No	Yes
48	8	Yes	....	12	120	....	52	78	Yes	Yes	Yes	Yes	Yes	Yes	Yes	No	Yes
34	16	No	1-2	13	....	....	....	....	Yes	Yes	No	No	No	Yes	Yes	No	No
56	13	Yes	1-4	12	204	....	19	113	Yes	Yes	No	Yes	Yes	Yes	Yes	Yes	Yes
55	14	No	1-5	12	117	13	....	176	Yes	Yes	No	Yes	Yes	No	Yes	No	No

TABLE XVIII.—Continued.

Incorporated cities.	Average number pupils to each teacher.				Number of non-resident pupils.				Rate of tuition per year.			Average age of class.		
	High school department.	Grammar department.	Primary department.	Whole school.	High school department.	Grammar department.	Primary department.	Whole school.	High school department.	Grammar department.	Primary department.	Graduated.	Promoted to high school.	Promoted to grammar department.
Lapeer	19	37	23	24	33	2	....	35	$20 00	$16 00	$12 00	18	14	10
Ludington	22	32	35	34	24	1	1	26	15 00	12 00	12 00	18	14	10
Mackinac Island	27	36	34	37	2	....	....	2	......	......	......	15	13	11
Manistee	16	30	30	28	33	10	3	46	20 00	14 00	10 00	18	14	10
Manistique	......	......	......	......					......	......	......	......	......	......
Marine City	20	34	35	30	....	....		....	20 00	10 00	10 00	18	14	11
Marquette	22	35	31	31	1	....	2	3	......	......	......	17.1	15.6	10.3
Marshall	23	31	29	27	63	15	5	83	20 00	16 00	10 00	18.5	14.2	9.8
Mason	15	40	29	24	27	15	2	44	12 00	8 00	8 00	18	......	......
McBain	6	51	47	34	4	....	1	5	9 00	......	9 00	......	15	......
Menominee	21	38	39	37	4	2	3	9	19 00	15 00	10 00	19	15	11
Midland	28	30	40	33	30	....	....	30	15 00	10 00	7 50	18	14	10
Monroe	21	45	44	36	28	18	11	57	16 00	12 00	8 00	18	14	11
Mt. Clemens	14	43	40	34	21	12	2	35	12 00	10 00	10 00	18.5	......	......
Mt. Pleasant	25	25	24	25	25	....	....	25	13 00	......	......	18	14	......
Muskegon	26	30	34	32	32	9	4	45	36 00	20 00	16 00	18.5	......	......
Muskegon Heights	6	31	35	26	1	4	3	8	10 00	7 50	6 50	15	14	9
Negaunee	16	42	39	35	....	....	....	....	......	......	......	18	14	......
Niles	25	40	37	34	33	12	5	50	15 20	11 40	7 60	18	14	11
North Muskegon	......	27	35	30	....	2	....	2	......	10 00	......	......	15	......
Norway	15	32	42	34	9	3	....	12	35 00	20 00	20 00	17	14.3	11.3
Omer	27	33	39	33	2	....	....	2	......	......	......	......	14	10
Onaway	9	29	39	30	6	2	....	8	20 00	15 00	10 00	18	14	10
Owosso	38	17	13	18	....	....	....	..	16 00	12 00	10 00	18	......	......
Petoskey	17	37	31	29	14	1	5	20	14 25	......	9 50	......	......	......
Pontiac	21	38	31	31	31	15	4	50	20 00	18 00	14 00	19.3	15.2	11.3
Port Huron	24	35	39	33	7	8	5	20	20 00	14 00	9 00	18	14	10
Rose City	33	34	55	42	....	....	....	....	10 00	......	......	......	16	......
Saginaw	16	30	26	24	70	20	10	100	28 00	20 00	16 00	18.9	14.6	9.9
Saginaw W. S.	20	34	33	31	10	6	12	28	25 00	12 00	9 00	18.5	......	......
St. Clair	25	33	32	29	7	3	....	10	15 00	10 00	7 50	18.2	15	10.4
St. Ignace	30	35	43	36	6	1	....	7	9 00	......	......	17	......	......
St. Johns	22	28	27	27	41	10	....	51	20 00	12 50	12 50	17.7	14.7	11.5
St. Joseph	20	32	30	28	7	11	1	19	18 00	14 40	14 40	......	14.5	11.7
St. Louis	15	31	37	32	16	9	9	34	12 50	10 00	10 00	18	14	9
Sandusky	23	32	51	35	16	1	....	17	9 50	9 50	9 50	19	13	......
Sault Ste. Marie	24	35	48	40	....	....	....	....	......	......	......	19	14.5	......
Scottville	20	36	53	38	32	4	2	38	11 87	11 87	11 87	19	14	10
South Haven	27	31	33	30	72	37	38	147	15 20	8 50	5 70	18.5	14.5	10.5
Standish	14	55	42	36	11	4	....	15	12 50	10 00	10 00	17.6	14.2	10
Stanton	16	36	41	93	14	1	....	15	13 50	9 50	9 50	18	14	12
Sturgis	23	30	33	30	18	6	7	31	16 00	13 00	10 00	18.7	14.5	10.8
Tawas City	18	38	37	32	4	1	....	5	10 00	......	......	17	14	11
Three Rivers	......	‡23	42	34	....	‡21	3	24	......	‡16 00	14 00	18.3	......	......
Traverse City	30	41	25	32	40	21	4	65	19 00	15 20	15 20	18	......	......
West Branch	33	75	45	45	14	8	10	32	7 50	......	......	17	......	......
Whittemore	......	63	39	51	....	8	....	....	......	......	......	......	......	......
Wyandotte	14	39	34	31	16	3	....	19	15 00	10 00	10 00	18	14	10
Yale	21	22	36	26	18	1	....	19	15 00	10 00	10 00	18	14	10.6
Ypsilanti	26	39	34	35	38	3	6	47	16 00	10 00	10 00	19	14	10
Zeeland	20	43	43	37	5	2	1	8	16 00	10 00	8 00	......	13	9

‡Includes high school and grammar departments.

TABLE XVIII.—Continued.

Number of graduates.	Number of U. S. flags.	Has school kindergarten below primary grade?	Portion of time in first primary devoted to kindergarten work.	Number of grades in the school.	Number of pupils studying— Latin.	Greek.	French.	German.	Does school give special instruction in— Vocal music?	Drawing?	Penmanship?	Manual training?	Domestic science?	Has school a commercial course?	Is the compulsory attendance law enforced?	Has school an ungraded department?	Has school a day school for the deaf?
21	1	No	1-6	12	22	....	8	21	Yes	Yes	No	No	No	Yes	Yes	....	....
33	7	Yes	....	12	112	....	....	70	Yes	Yes	Yes	Yes	Yes	No	Yes	No	No
....	1	No	....	12	7	....	8	....	No	No	Yes	No	No	No	Yes	No	No
53	6	Yes	....	12	57	....	21	28	Yes	Yes	No	Yes	Yes	Yes	Yes	No	Yes
....	....	....	....	....	....	....	....	....	....	....	....	....	....	....	....	....	....
1	3	Yes	1-3	12	27	....	....	19	Yes	Yes	No	No	No	Yes	Yes	No	No
24	11	Yes	....	12	61	....	36	56	Yes	Yes	No	Yes	Yes	Yes	Yes	No	No
31	5	No	1-3	12	....	....	....	....	Yes	Yes	No	Yes	No	Yes	Yes	No	No
16	1	....	....	12	50	....	....	33	Yes	Yes	No	No	No	No	Yes	No	....
....	1	No	2-3	12	....	....	....	....	No	No	No	No	No	No	Yes	No	No
21	1	Yes	All	12	89	....	....	60	Yes	Yes	No	Yes	Yes	No	Yes	No	Yes
20	5	No	2-3	12	72	....	....	32	No	No	No	No	No	Yes	Yes	No	No
10	3	No	1-3	12	44	....	5	28	Yes	Yes	Yes	Yes	No	No	Yes	No	No
14	4	Yes	1-2	12	59	....	....	20	Yes	Yes	No	No	No	Yes	No	Yes	No
23	4	No	1-4	13	18	....	....	13	Yes	Yes	No	No	No	Yes	Yes	No	No
56	15	Yes	....	12	141	....	40	49	Yes	Yes	Yes	Yes	Yes	Yes	Yes	No	No
4	1	Yes	1-3	10	....	....	....	4	No	No	Yes	No	No	Yes	Yes	No	....
12	3	Yes	....	12	39	....	17	15	Yes	Yes	Yes	No	No	Yes	Yes	No	No
20	7	No	1-4	12	77	....	....	36	Yes	Yes	No	No	No	No	Yes	No	No
....	1	No	....	8	....	....	....	....	No	No	No	No	No	No	Yes	No	No
13	5	No	....	12	33	....	....	15	Yes	Yes	Yes	No	No	Yes	Yes	No	No
9	1	No	....	....	....	....	....	....	No	No	No	No	No	Yes	Yes	No	No
4	2	Yes	1-2	12	8	....	....	7	No	No	No	No	No	Yes	Yes	No	No
38	4	No	1-4	12	84	....	....	154	Yes	Yes	No	Yes	No	No	Yes	No	No
9	4	No	1-2	12	30	....	....	30	Yes	Yes	Yes	No	No	Yes	Yes	Yes	No
33	6	Yes	....	12	115	4	20	70	Yes	Yes	No	Yes	Yes	No	Yes	No	No
53	14	No	1-4	12	140	....	60	75	Yes	Yes	....	....	....	Yes	Yes	No	....
....	1	No	1-2	10	10	....	....	....	....	....	....	....	....	....	Yes	....	....
107	10	No	....	12	110	9	76	404	Yes	Yes	Yes	Yes	Yes	Yes	Yes	Yes	Yes
19	9	No	....	12	51	....	22	840	Yes	Yes	Yes	Yes	Yes	Yes	Yes	No	No
15	2	Yes	....	12	36	....	....	33	Yes	Yes	No	No	No	No	Yes	No	No
12	3	Yes	....	12	25	....	....	....	No	No	No	No	....	No	Yes	No	No
12	3	No	1-2	13	40	....	....	22	Yes	Yes	Yes	Yes	....	Yes	Yes	No	No
23	3	Yes	....	12	59	....	....	42	Yes	Yes	....	Yes	....	Yes	Yes	No	No
15	2	Yes	....	12	28	....	....	16	Yes	Yes	No	No	No	Yes	Yes	No	No
4	1	No	1-3	12	....	....	....	10	No	No	No	No	No	No	Yes	No	No
26	7	Yes	1-2	12	85	....	32	28	Yes	Yes	Yes	Yes	Yes	Yes	Yes	No	Yes
7	1	No	1-2	12	36	....	....	20	Yes	Yes	....	....	....	Yes	Yes	No	No
13	3	No	1-2	12	65	....	....	55	Yes	Yes	Yes	No	No	Yes	Yes	No	No
3	1	No	....	12	5	....	....	25	No	No	No	No	No	Yes	No	No	No
6	1	Yes	1-3	12	14	....	....	....	No	No	No	No	No	Yes	Yes	No	No
11	1	Yes	....	12	40	....	....	23	Yes	Yes	No	No	No	No	Yes	No	....
6	2	No	1-8	12	16	....	....	....	No	No	No	No	No	Yes	Yes	No	No
20	5	Yes	....	12	30	....	15	25	Yes	Yes	Yes	Yes	No	Yes	Yes	No	No
50	6	Yes	All	12	100	....	....	131	Yes	Yes	Yes	Yes	....	Yes	Yes	Yes	Yes
8	1	No	1-3	12	12	....	....	12	No	No	No	No	No	No	Yes	No	No
....	1	No	....	10	....	....	....	....	No	No	No	No	No	No	Yes	No	No
14	3	Yes	....	12	15	....	....	36	Yes	Yes	Yes	No	No	No	Yes	No	No
7	1	No	1-2	12	27	....	....	6	No	No	No	No	No	No	Yes	No	....
46	4	No	1-5	12	122	....	12	59	Yes	Yes	No	Yes	Yes	No	Yes	No	No
....	1	Yes	1-2	12	19	....	....	14	Yes	Yes	Yes	No	No	Yes	Yes	No	No

TABLE XVIII.—Continued.

Incorporated villages.	Average number pupils to each teacher.				Number of non-resident pupils.				Rate of tuition per year.			Average age of class.		
	High school department.	Grammar department.	Primary department.	Whole school.	High school department.	Grammar department.	Primary department.	Whole school.	High school department.	Grammar department.	Primary department.	Graduated.	Promoted to high school.	Promoted to Grammar department.
Addison	25	35	32	32	26	5	......	31	$12 60	$10 80	$9 00	19	14.5	10
Alanson	20	29	50	35	2	......	......	2	11 25	......	......	18	14	11
Algonac	16	42	37	33	5	3	2	10	9 00	6 75	6 75	18	14	10
Almont	19	21	53	28	11	5	......	16	13 60	10 00	10 00	19	15	8.5
Applegate	......	66	......	......	......	4	......	......	......	......	......	......	......	......
Armada	29	28	39	32	32	4	1	37	14 25	14 25	4 75	18.1	14.5	11
Ashley	16	35	24	23	2	......	2	4	9 50	7 12	7 12	......	15	......
Athens	18	51	34	31	14	7	1	22	11 25	9 00	9 00	18.1	15.1	11
†Atlanta	......	......	......	......	......	......	......	......	......	......	......	......	......	......
Attica	28	30	62	41	......	4	......	4	10 00	10 00	5 00	......	12	9
Augusta	20	25	20	21	25	7	2	34	9 00	9 00	9 00	17.8	15	10.1
Baldwin	39	33	39	37	12	......	......	12	......	......	......	16	......	......
Bancroft	11	19	35	18	6	7	7	20	10 00	10 00	10 00	17	14	11
Bangor	21	54	50	38	40	9	9	58	13 30	9 50	3 80	17	......	......
Baraga	15	33	35	32	......	......	......	......	......	......	......	18	14	9
Baroda	36	42	60	46	6	......	......	6	10 00	......	......	16	......	......
Barryton	14	30	41	32	4	......	3	7	9 50	9 50	9 50	16	14	11
Bear Lake	20	44	31	31	6	2	......	8	13 50	12 25	......	......	14	10
Bellaire	15	30	36	28	7	3	......	10	11 25	9 00	......	17	......	......
Belleville	38	32	30	32	15	6	6	27	10 00	7 50	5 00	17	......	......
Bellevue	29	42	41	30	20	4	......	24	12 50	12 50	12 50	15	12	7
Benzonia	8	32	42	27	5	2	......	7	12 60	12 60	9 00	16.5	......	......
Berrien Springs	24	32	38	26	16	4	1	21	12 00	12 00	10 00	17	14	10
Birmingham	40	28	19	25	50	4	......	......	20 00	10 00	......	17	14	10
Blissfield No. 1 fr	18	40	52	32	6	......	......	......	10 00	......	......	18	......	......
Blissfield No. 2 fr	14	35	51	31	31	9	1	41	15 00	15 00	15 00	18	14	11
Bloomingdale	22	35	38	28	16	......	......	......	9 00	......	......	17	12	9
Boardman	18	18	20	29	4	......	......	......	9 00	......	......	16	14	9
Boyne Falls	27	12	35	20	2	......	......	......	9 00	......	......	......	......	......
Breedsville	......	39	38	38	......	9	......	9	......	9 00	6 75	......	......	......
Brighton	22	31	26	26	14	4	2	20	14 00	10 00	10 00	19	14	12
Britton	26	34	39	33	6	......	......	......	9 00	9 00	9 00	......	16	......
Bronson	20	33	29	18	10	3	2	......	13 30	9 50	9 50	14	11	8
Brooklyn	21	31	33	28	17	4	5	26	10 00	10 00	7 50	17	13	10
Buchanan	18	26	33	23	31	14	1	46	12 66	9 50	7 60	17	15	9
†Buckley	......	......	......	......	......	......	......	......	......	......	......	......	......	......
Burlington	27	16	21	21	5	......	......	......	9 00	......	......	......	......	......
Burr Oak	13	24	32	21	17	5	......	22	17 10	14 25	10 45	17	12	8
Byron	36	35	47	39	13	3	2	18	12 50	10 00	10 00	14	11	7
Caledonia	60	29	34	38	30	......	1	31	10 00	10 00	10 00	16	13	9
Calumet	20	32	38	35	65	1	......	66	40 00	20 00	20 00	19.1	14.5	11.2
Camden	13	17	17	15	......	......	......	......	......	......	......	......	......	......
Capac	25	32	102	45	19	3	5	27	15 00	15 00	12 00	18	14	[illegible]
Caro	30	31	26	34	77	7	5	89	13 00	10 00	7 80	17.5	13	10
Carson City	24	32	26	26	31	......	......	......	14 25	11 87	9 50	18	14	10
Carsonville	25	52	42	36	10	......	......	......	10 00	......	......	......	......	......
Caseville	23	53	40	34	4	2	......	6	10 00	10 00	......	16.3	......	......
Casnovia	17	23	45	28	8	3	1	12	13 50	9 00	4 50	......	13	10
Cass City	22	49	27	29	56	4	......	......	15 00	12 50	......	17	14	10
Cassopolis	18	35	22	23	13	9	2	24	13 30	11 40	9 50	17.6	14	10.5
Cedar Springs	16	36	60	34	8	8	22	38	14 25	11 40	6 33	18	14	11
Central Lake	11	33	26	24	8	1	......	9	13 50	9 00	9 00	18	13.3	10.8
Centreville	21	22	38	26	16	......	......	16	13 00	......	......	17	......	......
Chelsea	24	27	32	27	44	1	......	45	15 00	12 00	9 00	17.5	14	10
Chesaning	11	37	44	27	14	......	......	......	10 00	10 00	10 90	18	15	11

†Not legally graded.

TABLE XVIII.—CONTINUED.

Number of graduates.	Number of U. S. flags.	Has school kindergarten below primary grade?	Portion of time in first primary devoted to kindergarten work.	Number of grades in the school.	Number of pupils studying— Latin.	Greek.	French.	German.	Does school give special instruction in— Vocal music?	Drawing?	Penmanship?	Manual training?	Domestic science?	Has school a commercial course?	Is the compulsory attendance law enforced?	Has school an ungraded department?	Has school a day school for the deaf?
8	1	No	......	12	15	....	....	14	No	No	Yes	No	No	No	No	......	......
5	1	No	1-2	11	......	....	....	......	......	......	......	......	......	No	Yes	No	No
4	1	No	1-2	12	4	....	....	......	No	No	No	No	No	No	Yes	No	No
4	1	Yes	1-4	12	25	....	....	......	......	......	......	......	......	......	Yes	No	No
....	1	......	......	......	......	....	....	......	......	......	......	......	......	......	......	......	......
11	1	No	......	12	24	....	....	......	......	......	......	......	......		Yes	No	......
2	2	No	......	10	3	....	....	......	No	Yes	No	No	No	No	Yes	No	No
6	1	Yes	1-3	......	......	....	....	14	No	No	No	No	No	No	Yes	No	No
....	....	......	......	......	......	....	....	......	......	......	......	......	......	......	......	......	......
8	1	No	......	10	......	....	....	2	No	No	Yes	No	No	Yes	Yes	No	No
5	1	Yes	1-4	12	8	....	....	9	......	......	......	......	......	......	Yes	No	No
4	1	No	......	10	......	....	....	......	Yes	......	Yes	......	......	......	......	......	......
2	1	No	1-2	12	7	....	....	......	No	No	No	No	No	No	Yes	No	No
9	1	Yes	1-2	12	10	....	....	15	Yes	Yes	......	......	......	Yes	Yes	......	......
2	8	Yes	......	12	......	....	....	......	No	......	......	......	......	Yes	......	No	No
5	1	No	......	10	......	....	....	......	No	No	Yes	No	Yes	No	No	No	......
4	....	No	1-6	10	......	....	....	......	Yes	Yes	Yes	No	No	No	Yes	No	No
....	1	......	......	......	11	....	....	......	No	No	Yes	No	No	Yes	Yes	No	No
4	1	Yes	......	12	15	....	....	......	Yes	Yes	No	No	No	No	Yes	No	No
8	1	No	1-5	12	......	....	....	......	No	Yes	Yes	No	No	Yes	Yes	No	No
....	1	No	......	12	24	....	....	12	Yes	No	Yes	No	No	No	Yes	No	No
2	1	No	1-4	12	14	....	....	......	Yes	Yes	......	......	......	No	Yes	No	No
7	1	No	......	12	27	....	....	......	Yes	No	No	No	No	No	Yes	No	No
10	1	Yes	......	12	25	....	....	35	Yes	Yes	Yes	No	No	Yes	Yes	No	No
6	1	No	1-6	12	11	....	....	15	......	......	......	......	......	......	Yes	......	......
5	1	No	1-10	12	29	....	....	......	Yes	No	No	No	No	Yes	Yes	No	No
10	1	......	......	12	......	....	....	......	......	......	......	......	......	......	Yes	......	......
3	1	No	......	12	......	....	....	......	......	......	......	......	......	......	Yes	......	......
12	1	No	......	10	......	....	....	......	No	No	No	No	No	......	Yes	No	No
....	1	No	......	9	......	....	....	......	No	No	No	No	No	No	Yes	No	No
10	2	No	1-5	12	4	....	....	15	......	......	......	......	......	......	No	......	......
6	1	......	......	10	......	....	....	......	......	......	Yes	......	......	No	Yes	No	No
12	1	Yes	1-3	12	10	....	....	15	No	Yes	Yes	No	No	Yes	Yes	No	No
5	1	Yes	......	12	16	....	....	12	No	No	No	No	No	No	No	No	No
11	2	No	......	12	38	....	....	20	Yes	Yes	......	......	......	Yes	Yes	No	No
....	....	......	......	......	......	....	....	......	......	......	......	......	......	......	......	......	......
....	....	......	......	11	2	....	....	......	......	......	Yes	......	......	Yes	Yes	......	......
6	1	No	1-2	12	20	....	....	15	No	No	No	No	No	No	Yes	No	No
5	1	No	1-4	10	......	....	....	......	......	......	......	......	......	No	Yes	No	......
7	1	No	......	......	......	....	....	......	No	No	No	No	No	......	Yes	......	......
37	18	Yes	......	12	197	....	....	51	Yes	Yes	No	Yes	Yes	Yes	Yes	Yes	Yes
....	1	No	......	12	6	....	....	......	......	......	......	......	......	Yes	Yes	......	......
12	1	No	......	12	11	....	....	......	No	No	No	No	No	No	Yes	No	No
27	2	Yes	......	12	40	....	....	30	Yes	Yes	Yes	No	No	Yes	Yes	......	......
7	1	No	1-3	12	20	....	....	......	No	No	No	No	No	......	Yes	No	......
11	1	No	......	10	5	....	....	......	No	No	Yes	No	No	No	Yes	No	No
3	1	No	......	10	2	....	....	......	No	No	No	No	No	No	Yes	No	No
....	1	No	1-4	12	......	....	....	......	No	No	Yes	No	No	No	Yes	No	No
11	1	Yes	......	12	......	....	....	......	No	No	No	No	No	No	Yes	No	No
6	....	Yes	1-4	12	35	....	....	15	No	No	No	No	No	No	Yes	No	No
9	1	No	1-2	12	5	....	....	6	Yes	Yes	Yes	No	No	Yes	Yes	No	No
9	1	Yes	......	12	20	....	....	15	Yes	Yes	......	Yes	......	Yes	Yes	No	......
3	1	No	1-6	12	9	....	....	......	No	No	No	No	No	......	Yes	No	No
15	1	Yes	......	12	34	....	....	30	Yes	Yes	No	No	No	No	Yes	No	No
2	1	Yes	......	12	27	....	....	26	......	......	......	......	......	Yes	Yes	No	No

TABLE XVIII.—Continued.

Incorporated villages.	Average number pupils to each teacher.				Number of non-resident pupils.				Rate of tuition per year.			Average age of class.		
	High school department.	Grammar department.	Primary department.	Whole school.	High school department.	Grammar department.	Primary department.	Whole school.	High school department.	Grammar department.	Primary department.	Graduated.	Promoted to high school.	Promoted to grammar department.
Clarkston	15	48	34	97	15				$13 00	$10 00	$10 00	17.4		
Clayton	31	36	40	33	13				9 00	9 00	9 00	17		
†Clifford														
Climax	15	43	48	30	8	5	2	15	12 60	12 60	10 80	17		
Clinton	20	37	31	27	19	2		21	14 00	10 00	18 00	18		
Clio	18	55	40	28	18	14	4	36	14 00	12 00	10 00	17	14	10
Coloma	20	22	56	31	15	17	16	48	13 50	13 50	13 50	17	15	11
Colon	25	23	28	25	24				12 15			17		
Columbiaville	19	27	30	21	15	2		17	10 00	7 50	5 00	17	11.9	8
Concord	14	27	26	18	15	6	2	23	12 00	10 50	7 50	17.6	14	8
Constantine	15	29	37	24	26				10 00	12 00	9 00			
Coopersville	27	45	41	36	25	3		28	11 87	9 50	9 50	16	14	10
Copemish	17	52	52	39	11				4 50			16		
†Croton														
Custer	30	32	18	26	1			1						
†Daggett														
Dansville	23	19	26	29	14	3	3	20	10 00	8 00	8 00	17	13	9.6
Davison	14	33	44	44	14	12	2	28	15 00	15 00	12 00	15	13.5	11.5
Dearborn	13	55	39	36	5			5	10 00	7 50	7 50	17		
Decatur	26	42	56	41	42	13	9	64	13 00	10 00	7 00	18	15	11
Deckerville	45	32	35	36					15 00	10 00	7 50			
Deerfield	12	58	35	26	21				9 00					
Delray														
Detour	24	51	42	40	1			1						
Dexter	26	41	44	34	24	6	2	32	14 40	12 60	10 80	17.6	13.5	9.3
Douglas	13	43	20	26	3			3	9 00	9 00	9 00	17.6	14.6	10
Dryden		60	45	35		12	4	16		12 50	10 00		15.5	9
Dundee	10	36	39	27	14			14	5 00			18	14	11
Durand	12	37	33	27	12	9	3	24	12 00	12 00	10 00	17.7	14.7	10.4
†Eagle														
East Grand Rapids	25	26	35	29										
East Jordan	19	25	38	28		6		6	9 00	4 50	2 25	18	15	10
Eau Claire	20	30	35	28	25				9 00				12	
Ecorse	7	24	20	18										
Edmore	41	45	37	41	20	7	5	32	9 50	7 12	4 75	17	13	10
Elk Rapids	21	38	34	30	15		1	16	10 00	10 00	10 00			
Elkton	26	41	48	35	12	1	4	17	10 00	12 50	7 50	18	14	11
Elsie	23	29	32	28	27				11 81	11 81	11 81			
†Emmet														
Empire	31	47	55	46	3	1		4	9 00			17	13	9
Essexville		21	37	29			2	2		6 00			13	8
Evart	17	53	24	25	12	1	2	15	10 00	10 00	7 50	17	14	10
†Fairgrove														
**Fairview														
Farmington														
Farwell	19	28	43	30	5	3		8	9 00	6 30	6 30	18	14	11
Fennville	27	63	43	41	21	2		23	11 25	11 25	11 25	17	14	9
Fenton	32	37	34	34	42	12	6	60	20 00	16 00	12 00	18	15	10
Fife Lake	46	31	47	41	9				9 00				14	
Flushing	29	39	35	34	27	4		31	14 00	12 00	10 00	17.6	14.1	9.6
Ford		32	37	35									14	
Forestville														
†Fowler														
Fowlerville	23	28	25	25	42	9		51	15 00	12 00	12 00	18		
†Frankenmuth														

†Not legally graded.
**Now a part of Detroit.

TABLE XVIII.—Continued.

Number of graduates.	Number of U. S. flags.	Has school kindergarten below primary grade?	Portion of time in first primary devoted to kindergarten work.	Number of grades in the school.	Number of pupils studying— Latin.	Greek.	French.	German.	Does school give special instruction in— Vocal music?	Drawing?	Penmanship?	Manual training?	Domestic science?	Has school a commercial course?	Is the compulsory attendance law enforced?	Has school an ungraded department?	Has school a day school for the deaf?
7	1	No	......	12	12	....	....	......	No	No	Yes	No	No	No	Yes	No	No
5	....	No	......	10	......	....	....	......	No	Yes	Yes	No	No	No	Yes	No	No
....	....	......	......	......	......	....	....	......	......	......	......	......	......	......	......	......	......
6	1	No	1-3	12	9	....	....	......	No	No	No	No	No	No	Yes	......	......
10	1	No	1-2	12	23	....	....	14	No	No	No	No	No	No	Yes	No	No
2	1	No	1-5	12	19	....	....	10	Yes	Yes	No	No	No	No	Yes	No	No
1	1	Yes	1-2	12	12	....	....	......	No	No	No	No	No	......	Yes	......	......
5	1	No	......	12	11	....	....	12	......	......	No	No	No	No	Yes	No	......
2	1	No	......	11	......	....	....	......	......	......	......	......	......	No	Yes	No	No
6	1	No	1·5	12	1	....	....	......	Yes	Yes	Yes	No	No	No	Yes	No	No
16	1	......	......	12	35	....	....	......	......	......	......	......	......	......	Yes	No	No
12	....	Yes	1-3	11	......	....	....	......	No	No	No	No	No	......	Yes	No	No
5	1	No	......	......	......	....	....	......	......	......	......	......	......	......	Yes	No	No
....	....	......	......	......	......	....	....	......	......	......	......	......	......	......	......	......	......
....	1	Yes	1-3	10	3	....	....	......	Yes	Yes	Yes	Yes	No	No	Yes	No	......
....	....	......	......	......	......	....	....	......	......	......	......	......	......	......	......	......	......
4	....	No	......	12	......	....	....	......	......	......	......	......	......	Yes	Yes	......	......
....	1	Yes	1·3	11	17	....	....	......	No	No	No	No	No	......	Yes	No	......
4	1	No	1·3	12	......	....	....	......	Yes	Yes	No	No	No	No	Yes	No	No
12	1	No	......	12	26	....	....	26	No	......	......	......	......	No	Yes	No	No
....	1	No	1-3	10	......	....	....	......	No	Yes	......	......	......	No	No	No	No
....	....	No	1-2	12	......	....	....	......	No	No	Yes	No	No	Yes	Yes	No	No
....	....	......	......	......	......	....	....	......	......	......	......	......	......	......	......	......	......
2	1	No	......	10	......	....	....	......	No	......	......	......	......	No	No	Yes	No
5	1	No	1-3	12	31	....	....	15	Yes	No	No	No	No	No	Yes	No	No
3	1	No	......	11	10	....	....	......	No	......	Yes	No	No	No	Yes	No	No
6	1	Yes	1-3	10	......	....	....	......	No	Yes	Yes	No	No	No	Yes	No	No
3	1	......	......	12	......	....	....	......	......	......	......	......	......	Yes	Yes	......	......
6	1	Yes	1-3	12	15	....	....	......	Yes	Yes	Yes	Yes	No	Yes	Yes	No	No
....	....	......	......	......	......	....	....	......	......	......	......	......	......	......	......	......	......
8	1	No	......	9	......	....	....	......	......	No	Yes	No	No	No	No	No	No
7	3	Yes	1-5	12	25	....	....	20	Yes	Yes	Yes	No	No	Yes	Yes	Yes	No
....	1	No	......	12	20	....	....	......	No	No	No	No	No	No	Yes	No	No
2	1	No	......	10	......	....	....	......	No	......	......	......	......	......	Yes	......	No
12	1	Yes	1-2	11	......	....	....	......	No	No	No	No	No	No	Yes	No	......
9	2	Yes	2-3	12	32	....	....	......	No	Yes	Yes	No	No	No	Yes	No	No
9	....	......	......	11	18	....	....	......	No	No	No	No	No	Yes	Yes	......	......
5	1	No	......	12	10	....	....	1	......	......	......	......	......	No	Yes	......	......
....	....	......	......	......	......	....	....	......	......	......	......	......	......	......	......	......	......
6	1	Yes	1-3	12	5	....	....	......	No	No	No	No	No	No	Yes	......	......
....	....	No	......	8	......	....	....	......	Yes	No	No	No	No	No	Yes	No	......
13	1	Yes	......	13	11	....	....	......	No	No	Yes	Yes	No	No	Yes	No	No
....	....	......	......	......	......	....	....	......	......	......	......	......	......	......	......	......	......
....	....	......	......	......	......	....	....	......	......	......	......	......	......	......	......	......	......
....	....	......	......	......	......	....	....	......	......	......	......	......	......	......	......	......	......
4	1	No	1-10	12	14	....	....	10	No	No	Yes	No	No	Yes	Yes	No	No
9	1	No	......	12	26	....	....	......	......	......	......	......	......	Yes	Yes	No	No
30	3	No	1-3	12	10	....	....	55	Yes	Yes	Yes	No	No	No	Yes	No	No
10	1	......	......	10	......	....	....	......	......	......	......	......	......	......	Yes	......	......
6	1	No	1-4	12	23	....	....	......	No	No	No	No	No	No	Yes	No	No
....	2	Yes	1-5	8	......	....	....	......	Yes	......	......	......	......	No	Yes	No	No
....	....	......	......	......	......	....	....	......	......	......	......	......	......	......	......	......	......
17	1	Yes	1-2	12	......	....	....	......	Yes	......	......	......	......	Yes	Yes	......	......
....	....	......	......	......	......	....	....	......	......	......	......	......	......	......	......	......	......

TABLE XVIII.—CONTINUED.

Incorporated villages.	Average number pupils to each teacher.				Number of non-resident pupils.				Rate of tuition per year.			Average age of class.		
	High school department.	Grammar department.	Primary department.	Whole school.	High school department.	Grammar department.	Primary department.	Whole school.	High school department.	Grammar department.	Primary department.	Graduated.	Promoted to high school.	Promoted to grammar department.
Frankfort	16	47	51	40					$10 00	$10 00	$5 00	18		
†Fraser														
Freeport	22	36	35	37	10	1	2	13	10 80	9 00	9 00		13	8
Fremont	26	33	50	36	23	3	2	28	15 00	10 00	10 00	18	14	9
Fruitport	14	33	52	33									14	
Gagetown	30	29	32	30	7	1	1	9	10 00	10 00	10 00	17	12	8
Gaines	19	46	53	39	21	3	2	26	12 50	10 00	10 00	17		
Galesburg	17	31	33	24	33	7	6	46	12 60	10 80	7 20	17	13.7	10.1
Galien	32	30	49	35	12	4		16	13 50	13 50		18	14	
†Garden														
Gaylord	15	35	35	29	7	8	4	19	10 00	8 00	6 00	17	12.5	8.1
a Glenwood														
Gobleville	30	30	40	32	19			19	10 00	7 00	7 00	16		
Grandville	27	32	58	38	33	4		37	12 50	12 50	12 50	17	14	10
Grant	12	38	39	30	8			8	9 00	9 00	9 00			
Grasslake	15	63	34	28	18	3	1	22	12 00	9 00	9 00	17		
Grayling	20	30	56	38	5	2		7				18	12	8
Grosse Point		20	33	28									13	
†Grosse Pointe Farms														
†Grosse Pointe Park														
Hamtramck		24	43	34		4	1	5		7 50	7 50		14.1	10.6
Hanover	30	30	35	32	39			39	12 00	9 00	9 00			
Harbor Beach	18	38	38	32	7	3		10	11 50	10 00	7 00	18	14	10
Harbor Springs	17	42	23	27	4			4				18	15	
Harietta	25	35	61	40									16	
Hart	27	100	25	30	24	10		34	12 00	9 00	6 00	17		
Hartford			34	29					13 50	6 75	4 50			
Hersey	16	42	33	29	10	4	1	15	9 50			17	13	9
Hesperia	19	41	28	26	19	2	2	23	12 00	8 00	8 00	18	14	10.3
Highland Park		25	36	31		7	6	13		12 00	12 00		15	
Hillman														
Holly	22	53	43	38	33	17	1	51	14 00	10 00	10 00	19	14.8	10.6
Homer	20	44	35	31	36			36	13 00	10 00	6 50	18		
Houghton	20	32	28	30	14				50 00			18.3	14.9	11.1
Howard City	18	45	32	29	16			16	9 50			18	14	10
Howell	29	39	41	36	72	10	2	84	16 00	13 00	13 00	18.3	14	10
Hubbardston	23	20	34	26	11	3	1	15	9 00	9 00	9 00		13.2	11
¶Hubbell														
Imlay City	22	61	31	35	19			19	15 00			17	13	9
Iron River	19	31	38	30	3	1		4	20 00	17 50	15 00	18		
Ithaca	25	49	37	35	41	6	2	49	11 88	9 50	9 50	19	14	12
Jerome		19	38	20									12	
Jonesville	16	50	41	34	21	14	4	39	10 00	10 00	10 00	18	14	9
Kalkaska	13	35	29	25	9	5		14	13 50	9 00		17	11.7	8.5
†Kinde														
Kingsley	18	34	67	36	6			6	10 80			15	11	7
Kingston	45	37	39	40	18	2	2	22	10 00	7 50	5 00			
Laingsburg	16	54	35	30	14	4	1	19	12 50	10 00	5 00	18		9
Lake Ann		29	43	36					12 00					
Lake City	30	35	37	36	14			14	9 00			17		
Lake Linden	25	24	32	28	23			23	40 00			17.8		
Lake Odessa	25	31	32	29	23	16	1	40	13 30	12 35	9 50	18.2	14	11
Lakeview	40	27	30	29	30	4	1	35	11 87	7 12	7 12	18		
L'Anse	12	34	40	31	2			2				18	14	12
§Laurium														

†Not legally graded.
¶Report included in Linden.
§Report included in Calumet.
a Report included in Wyandotte.

TABLE XVIII.—Continued.

Number of graduates.	Number of U. S. flags.	Has school kindergarten below primary grade?	Portion of time in first primary devoted to kindergarten work.	Number of grades in the school.	Number of pupils studying— Latin.	Greek.	French.	German.	Does school give special instruction in— Vocal music?	Drawing?	Penmanship?	Manual training?	Domestic science?	Has school a commercial course?	Is the compulsory attendance law enforced?	Has school an ungraded department?	Has school a day school for the deaf?
9	1	Yes	1-4	12	...			...	Yes	Yes	Yes	No	...	No	Yes	No	...
...	...	...	...	...	...			...	...	...	...	...	...	...	...	...	...
...	...	No	...	12	...			...	No	No	Yes	No	No	No	Yes	No	...
14	1	Yes	1-2	12	26			9	No	No	No	No	No	Yes	Yes	No	No
3	1	No	...	10	...			...	No	No	No	No	No	No	Yes	No	No
1	1	No	1-4	10	...			...	...	Yes	Yes	Yes	No	No	No	...	...
6	1	No	1-5	10	...			...	...	...	...	...	...	No	Yes	...	...
3	1	No	1-3	12	7			...	Yes	Yes	Yes	No	No	Yes	No	No	No
8	1	No	...	12	1			...	No	No	No	No	No	...	Yes	No	No
...	...	...	...	...	...			...	...	...	...	...	...	...	...	...	...
4	1	Yes	...	12	15			18	No	No	No	No	No	No	Yes	No	No
...	...	...	...	...	...			...	...	...	...	...	...	...	...	...	...
8	1	No	1-4	12	10			16	...	...	...	...	...	No	Yes	No	No
4	1	No	1-4	12	10			...	No	No	No	No	No	Yes	Yes	No	No
...	1	No	...	11	...			...	No	No	No	No	No	No	Yes	No	No
5	1	No	1-2	12	18			16	Yes	No	Yes	No	No	No	Yes	No	No
1	1	No..	1-4	12	5			16	Yes	Yes	Yes	No	No	Yes	Yes	No	No
...	2	No	...	8	...			...	No	No	No	No	No	No	No	No	No
...	...	...	...	...	...			...	...	...	...	...	...	...	...	...	...
...	...	...	...	...	...			...	...	...	...	...	...	...	...	...	...
...	1	Yes	...	8	...			...	Yes	Yes	No	No	No	...	Yes	No	No
8	1	No	1-2	11	...			...	No	No	No	No	No	No	Yes	No	No
3	1	No	1-2	12	...			...	Yes	No	No	Yes	No	No	Yes	No	No
9	...	Yes	...	...	30			15	Yes	Yes	Yes	...	...	No	Yes	No	No
...	1	...	...	10	...			...	No	No	...	...	No	No	Yes	...	...
15	1	Yes	...	12	30			22	Yes	...	...	...	...	Yes	Yes	...	...
15	1	Yes	1-4	11	...			...	Yes	Yes	Yes	Yes	Yes	No	Yes	...	...
3	1	No..	1-2	12	4			...	No	No	No	No	No	Yes	Yes	No	No
...	1	...	1-4	...	...			8	Yes	No	Yes	No	No	No	Yes	No	No
...	1	...	3-5	8	...			...	Yes	Yes	Yes	Yes	...	No	Yes	No	...
...	...	...	...	...	...			...	...	...	...	...	...	...	...	...	...
7	2	No	...	12	60			19	Yes	Yes	...	No	No	No	Yes	No	No
11	1	No	...	12	20			20	Yes	Yes	...	...	...	...	Yes	No	...
15	9	Yes	...	12	45			43	Yes	Yes	Yes	Yes	No	Yes	Yes	No	No
9	9	Yes	1-5	12	32			...	Yes	Yes	No	No	No	...	Yes	No	No
24	...	No	1-4	12	91			39	Yes	Yes	Yes	Yes	No	No	Yes	No	No
...	1	No	1-3	11	...			...	No	No	No	No	No	No	Yes	No	No
...	...	...	...	...	...			...	...	...	...	...	...	...	...	...	...
9	1	Yes	1-5	12	18			8	...	...	...	...	...	...	Yes	...	...
8	1	Yes	1-4	12	35			6	Yes	Yes	Yes	No	No	...	Yes	Yes	No
15	1	Yes	...	12	45			23	Yes	Yes	No	No	No	No	Yes	No	No
...	...	No	...	12	2			...	No	No	No	...	...	Yes	Yes	No	No
4	...	Yes	1-2	12	25			14	Yes	Yes	...	...	...	No	Yes	No	...
5	1	Yes	1-3	12	...			...	No	No	No	No	No	No	Yes	No	No
...	...	...	...	...	...			...	...	...	...	...	...	...	...	...	...
2	1	No	1-5	10	...			...	No	No	Yes	No	No	No	Yes	No	No
...	1	No	...	10	...			...	No	No	Yes	No	No	Yes	Yes	No	No
4	1	Yes	1-6	12	4			...	Yes	Yes	Yes	No	No	Yes	Yes	No	No
...	1	No	...	10	...			...	...	...	...	...	...	...	No	No	...
4	1	...	...	12	4			...	...	Yes	Yes	...	...	...	Yes	...	...
22	5	No	...	12	63			27	Yes	Yes	No	No	No	Yes	Yes	No	No
4	1	No	...	12	7			...	No	No	No	No	No	No	Yes	No	No
8	...	Yes	...	12	7			...	No	No	No	No	No	...	Yes	...	...
5	6	No	1-4	12	14			6	No	No	No	No	No	Yes	Yes	No	...
...	...	...	...	...	...			...	...	...	...	...	...	...	...	...	...

TABLE XVIII.—Continued.

Incorporated villages.	Average number pupils to each teacher.				Number of non-resident pupils.				Rate of tuition per year.			Average age of class.		
	High school department.	Grammar department.	Primary department.	Whole school.	High school department.	Grammar department.	Primary department.	Whole school.	High school department.	Grammar department.	Primary department.	Graduated.	Promoted to high school.	Promoted to grammar department.
Lawrence	27	25	46	29	35			35	$12 00			18		
Lawton	26	40	51	37	38	17	10	65	12 00	$10 00	$8 00	18	12	8
Leonard	31	29	39	25	2	1			10 00	7 50	5 00	17		
Le Roy	18	35	39	32	9	1		10	4 50			17		
Leslie	39	42	45	40	32	11	1	44	16 00	10 00	8 00	18	14	10
Lexington	21	20	21	20	10	1	1	12	10 00	8 00	6 50	18	14	10
†Lincoln														
Linden	21	26	17	21	16	4		20	10 00	8 00	8 00	17		
Lisbon		35	35	30		3				9 00			16	
Litchfield	24	37	36	34	35			35	12 00	12 00	9 00	17	14	11
Lowell	22	32	18	20	28			28	16 00	10 00	7 00	16	14	10
Luther	23	27	45	35					7 50	6 00	3 00	16	14	9
Lyons	20	29	47	30	13	15	2	30	6 00	6 00	6 00	18	15	10
Mackinaw City	20	40	79	44								16.7		
Mancelona	25	32	30	29	14	1		15	10 80	9 00	6 75	18	14.5	10
Manchester	23	34	32	28	29	2		31	15 00	12 00	9 00	18.5	14	
Manton	18	51	56	36	10	7	2	19	13 95	12 15	12 15	18	15	11
Maple Rapids	28	25	44	31	20	1	1	22	12 00	10 00	10 00			
Marcellus	21	31	41	30	34	7	4	45	11 70	11 70	11 70	17	14	10
Marion	26	20	48	38	6			6	15 00	10 00	5 00			
†Marlborough														
Marlette	21	40	36	32	36	5		41	17 50	10 00	10 00	18.5	14	10.5
†Maybee														
Mayville	31	43	43	39	26	1		27	10 00	8 00	8 00	16	13	9
McBride	28	45	44	39	8	2	1	11	9 50	7 12	4 75	16	13	9
Mecosta	47	55	33	45	8			8	7 50					
†Melvin														
Memphis	42	23	48	35	36	2		38	12 50	12 50	10 00	17	13	10
Mendon	21	27	41	29	20	8	4	32	12 60	11 25	11 25	17	14	9.2
†Merrill														
Mesick	22	30	47	38					9 00	6 75	4 50			
Metamora	14	28	31	21	12	3	5	20	15 00	10 00	10 00	17	13	8
Middleville	16	33	31	79	26	5	5	36	12 00	5 25	4 50	17	14	10
†Mikado														
Milan	19	33	52	34	22	1		23				18	14	
Milford	17	37	28	26	47	9	7	63	14 00	10 00	10 00	18	13	10
Millersburg											5 00	17		
Millington		25	88		58	3		61	10 00	10 00	10 00	17		
Minden		41	65	41	7	1	1	9					13	11
Montague	28	31	30	[illegible]	13	6	4	23	9 00	4 50	4 50	18	13	10
Montrose														
Morenci				43	40	3	2	45	14 00	12 50	11 00	17.5	13.5	10
Morley				52	8			8	7 20			17		
Morrice	27	47		25	5	9		14	10 00	10 00	7 50	17	13	9
Mt. Morris	30	32	[illegible]	33	35	1	1	37	12 50	10 00	10 00	17	13	8
Muir	11	26	27	23	4	4	1	9	9 00			18	13	9
†Mulliken														
Munising			37	20								19	14.5	10
Nashville	23	23	37	26	18		1	19	16 00		12 00			
†Naubinway	15	29												
Newaygo	18	30	38	29	6	2		8	13 00	10 00	7 50	18	14	10
New Baltimore	17	33	34	26	19	8		27	10 00	8 00	8 00	17	14	11
Newberry														
†New Boston														
New Buffalo	22	29	47	34	5				12 00	8 00	8 00			

†Not legally graded.

TABLE XVIII.—CONTINUED.

Number of graduates.	Number of U. S. flags.	Has school a kindergarten below primary grade?	Portion of time in first primary devoted to kindergarten work.	Number of grades in the school.	Number of pupils studying—				Does school give special instruction in—					Has school a commercial course?	Is the compulsory attendance law enforced?	Has school an ungraded department?	Has school a day school for the deaf?
					Latin.	Greek.	French.	German.	Vocal music?	Drawing?	Penmanship?	Manual training?	Domestic science?				
10	1	No	...	12	45	...	...	...	Yes	Yes	...	...	...	...	Yes	No	...
10	...	Yes	1-2	12	17	...	...	4	...	...	...	...	...	Yes	...	...	...
5	1	No	...	10	...	...	...	...	No	No	No	No	No	No	No	No	No
4	1	Yes	1-4	12	...	...	...	...	...	...	...	...	...	...	Yes	No	...
11	1	No	1-4	12	34	...	...	9	No	Yes	Yes	No	No	Yes	Yes	No	No
5	1	No	1-4	12	...	...	...	6	No	No	No	No	No	Yes	Yes	No	No
...	...	...	...	...	...	...	...	...	...	...	...	...	...	...	...	...	...
2	...	No	1-4	11	5	...	...	...	No	No	No	No	No	No	Yes	No	No
4	1	No	1-2	10	...	...	...	...	No	No	Yes	No	No	No	Yes	No	No
8	...	Yes	...	12	22	...	...	...	Yes	No	No	No	No	...	Yes	...	...
23	...	Yes	...	12	11	...	...	8	No	Yes	Yes	No	No	Yes	Yes	No	No
5	1	Yes	...	11	...	...	...	...	No	No	No	No	No	...	Yes	No	No
7	...	Yes	1-3	12	9	...	...	...	No	No	Yes	No	No	No	Yes	...	...
5	1	No	1-2	10	...	...	...	...	No	...	...	...	No	...	No	No	...
10	3	Yes	...	25	...	...	...	15	Yes	Yes	...	Yes	No	Yes	Yes	No	...
19	1	No	1-3	12	18	...	...	24	Yes	No	Yes	No	No	Yes	Yes	No	No
6	1	Yes	...	12	7	...	...	12	Yes	No	No	No	No	No	Yes	No	No
11	1	No	...	...	...	...	...	...	...	...	...	...	...	No	Yes	No	...
11	1	No	...	12	23	...	...	14	No	No	No	No	No	Yes	Yes	No	No
...	1	Yes	...	12	...	...	...	...	No	No	No	No	No	Yes	Yes	No	No
...	...	...	...	...	...	...	...	...	...	...	...	...	...	...	...	...	...
8	1	Yes	...	12	39	...	...	...	No	Yes	...	No	No	...	Yes	No	No
...	...	...	...	...	...	...	...	...	...	...	...	...	...	...	...	...	...
10	1	No	1-2	12	9	...	...	12	No	No	No	No	No	No	Yes	No	No
7	1	Yes	1-2	11	...	...	...	...	No	Yes	Yes	No	No	No	Yes	No	No
5	1	No..	...	10	...	...	...	...	...	...	...	...	...	No	Yes	...	...
...	...	...	...	...	...	...	...	...	...	...	...	...	...	...	...	...	...
2	1	No	...	12	10	...	...	...	No	No	Yes	No	No	No	Yes	No	No
7	1	No	...	12	17	...	...	...	No	Yes	Yes	No	No	Yes	Yes	No	No
...	...	...	...	...	...	...	...	...	...	...	...	...	...	...	...	...	...
...	1	Yes	...	12	...	...	...	...	No	Yes	Yes	No	No	No	Yes	No	No
5	...	No	1-4	12	5	...	...	6	No	No	No	No	No	...	...	...	...
8	1	No	...	12	25	...	...	...	No	No	No	No	No	Yes	Yes	No	No
...	...	...	...	...	...	...	...	...	...	...	...	...	...	...	...	...	...
12	1	No	...	12	18	...	...	13	...	...	...	...	...	...	...	...	...
15	2	No	1-6	12	35	...	...	21	Yes	Yes	No	No	No	No	Yes	...	...
4	1	No	1-2	10	...	...	...	...	Yes	Yes	Yes	No	...	No	Yes	No	No
10	1	Yes	1-2	12	...	...	...	...	No	No	No	No	No	Yes	Yes	No	No
8	1	No	...	...	...	...	...	...	No	No	No	No	No	...	Yes	No	No
12	1	No	1-6	12	17	...	...	11	Yes	No	No	No	No	...	Yes	...	...
...	...	...	...	...	...	...	...	...	...	...	...	...	...	...	...	...	...
16	1	No	...	12	31	...	...	23	No	No	No	No	...	No	Yes	No	No
2	1	No	1-3	10	...	...	...	...	...	...	...	...	...	...	Yes	No	No
4	...	No	...	...	...	...	...	...	Yes	...	...	...	...	...	No	No	No
6	1	Yes	1-2	12	24	...	...	...	No	No	No	No	No	Yes	Yes	...	No
3	1	Yes	...	11	...	...	...	...	No	...	...	...	...	Yes	Yes	No	...
...	...	...	...	...	...	...	...	...	...	...	...	...	...	...	...	...	...
6	...	Yes	1-2	12	51	...	...	14	Yes	Yes	No	No	No	No	Yes	No	No
13	1	Yes	1-2	12	...	...	...	...	No	No	No	No	No	No	Yes	No	No
...	...	...	...	...	...	...	...	...	...	...	...	...	...	...	...	...	...
10	1	No	1-4	12	7	...	...	6	No	No	No	No	No	No	Yes	No	No
6	1	Yes	1-3	12	...	...	...	10	Yes	No	No	Yes	No	No	Yes	No	...
...	...	...	...	...	...	...	...	...	...	...	...	...	...	...	...	...	...
...	...	...	...	...	...	...	...	...	...	...	...	...	...	...	...	...	...
...	1	No	1-5	12	6	...	...	...	Yes	Yes	Yes	No	No	Yes	Yes	No	No

TABLE XVIII.—Continued.

Incorporated villages.	Average number pupils to each teacher.				Number of non-resident pupils.				Rate of tuition per year.			Average age of class.		
	High school department.	Grammar department.	Primary department.	Whole school.	High school department.	Grammar department.	Primary department.	Whole school.	High school department.	Grammar department.	Primary department.	Graduated.	Promoted to high school.	Promoted to grammar department.
New Haven	23	59	40	39	5	1	1	7	$9 00	$6 75	$4 50	17		
North Adams	27	17	34	29	27			27	9 50	9 50		18		
North Branch	33	27	40	33	37	7	2	46	15 00	15 00	15 00	17.5	13.5	12
Northport	18	52	42	40	4	12	1	17	9 00	9 00	9 00	18	14	11
Northville	18	28	33	27	31			31	16 00			18		
Oakley		23	38	30		2	2	4		9 00				
Olivet	19	32	27	24	16	9		25	12 00	10 00	10 00	18	14	10
Onekama					6	1		7	9 00	9 00	9 00	16	13	
Ontonagon	21	17	34	22	2			2				18	12	7
Orion	17	27	29	23					10 00			19		
Ortonville	30	30	37	32	15	7		22	10 00		7 50	16.8	13.6	9.5
Oscoda	23	15	77	37								18	14	11
Otisville	46	29	45	40	23	1		24	10 00	8 00	6 00	17	13	9
Otsego	30	33	38	37	25	10	1	36	18 00	14 40	14 40	18	14.5	11
Otter Lake		16	44	30					6 00		6 00			
Ovid	29	33	25	30	32	7	3	42	15 00	12 00	12 00	18	14	10
Owendale	18	28	37	26	18	3	1	22				18		
Oxford														
Parma	23	28	44	31	15	3	1	19	12 00	9 00	7 50		13	12
Paw Paw	28	37	44	35	56	8	2	66	13 00	13 00	10 00	18.5	14.2	10
†Peck														
Pellston	15	32	60	43	4			4	13 50					
Pentwater	22	37	36	36	10	1		11	9 00	6 00	3 00	17	14	10
†Perrinton														
Perry	22	34	29	25	8	4	2	14	10 00	10 00	10 00	17	14	10
Petersburg	18	44	20	29	10	5		15	13 50	9 00		17.6	14	10
Pewamo	34	26	16	25	9	4	2	15	9 00	9 00	9 00	17	13	9
Pierson		37	38	37	24			24	6 00					
Pigeon	36	69	76	65	5			5	12 50			19		
Pinckney	14	11	28	15	9	1		10	15 00	12 50	10 00	17.1		
Pinconning	30	26	44	33	5			5	10 00			16	12	10
Plainwell	21	39	42	31	40	3		43	19 00	15 20	11 40	17	14	
Plymouth	27	36	47	36	38	9		47	14 00	14 00	8 00	18	14	10
Port Austin	12	22	40	27			18	18				19	15	8
Port Hope	19	20	21	20	4	2	2	8	10 00	5 00	3 50	15.3	13	10
Portland	16	34	37	27	23	9	10	42	15 20	11 40	11 40	18	14	10
Port Sanilac	22	30	34	29	3			3	7 20				15	
†Posen														
Potterville	30	26	30	28	6			6	9 00			16		
Quincy	21	33	46	28	44	6	2	52	14 00	10 00	7 50	17	12	8
Reading	29	39	33	32	45	9	4	58	14 25	14 25	11 87	18.2	15.1	10.5
§Red Jacket														
†Redford														
Reed City	19	38	30	28	19	10	13	42	12 00	12 00	10 00			
†Reese														
Richland	20	30	15	20	11	3	1	15	14 40	9 00	9 00	17	14	10
b Richmond	9	46	29	26	18			18	15 00			18	13	10
River Rouge	8	32	50	38								15	12	8
Rochester	33	32	60	39	32	5	3	40	13 00	10 00	8 00	17	14	10
Rockford	21	29	37	29	16	4	4	24	14 00	11 00	10 00	18	14	10
Rogers	12	38	43									15	14	10
Romeo	22	26	35	29	37	3	3	43	16 00	13 00	8 00	17.5	14	10
Roscommon	14	24	35	17	1	3	3	7					15	11
Royal Oak	7	56	36	26	25			25	12 00	9 00	6 00	17		
St. Charles	14	32	52	38	2	1	1	4	10 00	10 00	10 00	17.8		

†Not legally graded.
§Report included in Calumet.
b *Lenox school district* united with this.

TABLE XVIII.—CONTINUED.

Number of graduates.	Number of U. S. flags.	Has school kindergarten below primary grade?	Portion of time in first primary devoted to kindergarten work.	Number of grades in the school.	Number of pupils studying— Latin.	Greek.	French.	German.	Does school give special instruction in— Vocal music?	Drawing?	Penmanship?	Manual training?	Domestic science?	Has school a commercial course?	Is the compulsory attendance law enforced?	Has school an ungraded department?	Has school a day school for the deaf?
1	1	No	...	11	...	...	...	...	No	No	No	No	No	Yes	Yes	No	...
7	...	No	...	12	25	...	...	...	No	No	Yes	No	No	...	...	...	...
14	1	No	1-8	12	32	...	...	...	No	No	No	No	No	...	Yes	No	No
3	...	No	1-4	12	...	...	...	...	No	No	No	No	No	Yes	Yes	No	No
10	1	Yes	...	12	...	...	...	...	Yes	No	No	No	No	No	Yes	No	No
...	1	No	...	...	...	...	...	...	No	No	No	No	No	No	Yes	No	No
7	...	Yes	...	12	26	...	...	16	Yes	Yes	Yes	No	No	No	No	No	No
1	1	No	...	12	22	...	...	...	...	...	Yes	...	...	...	Yes	No	No
9	10	No	...	12	...	...	...	...	No	No	No	No	No	Yes	Yes	No	No
4	1	No	...	12	4	...	...	11	No	No	No	No	No	No	Yes	No	No
6	1	No	...	12	...	...	...	...	No	No	No	No	No	No	Yes	No	No
9	2	Yes	1-2	11	...	...	...	...	No	No	Yes	...	...	No	Yes	Yes	No
...	1	...	...	...	...	...	...	...	...	...	...	...	...	No	Yes	No	No
14	1	Yes	2-3	12	27	...	...	18	Yes	Yes	...	...	...	Yes	Yes	No	No
3	1	No	...	10	...	...	...	...	...	...	...	...	...	No	Yes	...	...
13	...	No	1-4	12	40	...	...	24	Yes	No	No	No	No	No	Yes	No	No
8	1	No	1-3	12	39	...	...	...	Yes	...	Yes	...	...	No	...	No	No
10	1	No	1-3,	12	...	...	...	...	Yes	...	Yes	...	...	No	Yes	No	No
14	1	Yes	1-4	12	55	...	...	30	Yes	Yes	...	...	...	...	...	...	...
...	1	No	...	10	...	...	...	...	No	No	Yes	No	No	No	...	No	...
6	1	Yes	...	12	...	...	...	3	No	No	No	No	No	...	Yes	No	No
10	...	No	1-2	12	10	...	...	3	No	No	Yes	No	No	Yes	Yes	No	No
7	1	No	1-3	12	7	...	...	22	No	No	Yes	No	No	No	Yes	No	No
...	1	No	...	11	...	...	...	...	No	No	No	No	No	No	Yes	No	No
...	1	No	...	10	...	...	...	...	No	No	Yes	No	No	Yes	Yes	No	No
2	1	No	...	12	2	...	...	...	No	Yes	Yes	No	No	Yes	Yes	No	No
6	1	No	...	12	6	...	...	8	No	No	No	No	No	No	Yes	No	No
12	1	No	1-4	10	...	...	...	...	No	No	No	No	No	No	Yes	No	No
19	2	No	1-3	12	30	...	...	12	Yes	Yes	Yes	No	No	Yes	Yes	No	No
14	1	Yes	...	12	28	...	...	27	No	Yes	No	No	No	No	Yes	No	No
2	1	Yes	1-4	12	3	...	...	18	No	No	No	No	...	Yes	Yes	...	...
...	1	Yes	...	10	...	...	...	...	No	No	No	No	No	Yes	Yes	No	No
11	2	No	1-3	12	23	...	...	16	Yes	Yes	No	No	No	No	Yes	No	No
5	1	No	...	11	...	...	...	...	...	...	...	...	...	No	Yes	No	No
6	1	...	...	...	20	...	...	...	...	Yes	Yes	Yes	No	No	Yes	No	No
10	1	Yes	...	12	11	...	...	20	Yes	No	Yes	No	No	Yes	Yes	No	No
7	1	Yes	...	12	29	...	...	20	No	No	No	No	No	No	Yes	No	...
7	2	Yes	...	12	50	...	...	15	Yes	Yes	Yes	Yes	No	No	Yes	No	No
10	1	No	1-6	12	4	...	...	...	...	...	...	...	...	Yes	Yes	No	No
11	2	No	...	12	21	...	...	1	No	No	Yes	No	No	Yes	Yes	No	No
5	2	Yes	...	10	18	...	...	...	Yes	Yes	No	No	No	No	Yes	No	No
11	1	Yes	1-2	12	3	...	...	3	No	No	No	No	No	No	Yes	No	No
5	1	No	3-10	12	34	...	...	...	No	No	No	No	No	Yes	Yes	No	...
2	1	No	1-8	...	...	...	...	...	No	No	Yes	No	No	No	Yes	No	No
12	3	Yes	1-2	12	20	1	...	24	No	Yes	No	No	No	Yes	Yes	No	No
...	...	Yes	1-6	12	...	...	...	...	No	No	Yes	No	No	Yes	No	No	No
...	...	No	1-3	12	12	...	...	3	...	...	...	...	...	...	No	...	...
5	1	Yes	...	12	6	...	...	...	No	No	No	No	No	No	Yes	No	No

TABLE XVIII.—Concluded.

Incorporated cities.	Average number pupils to each teacher.				Number of non-resident pupils.				Rate of tuition per year.			Average age of class.		
	High school department.	Grammar department.	Primary department.	Whole school.	High school department.	Grammar department.	Primary department.	Whole school.	High school department.	Grammar department.	Primary department.	Graduated.	Promoted to high school.	Promoted to grammar department.
†St. Clair Heights														
Saline	20	35	26	25	27	11	1	39	$16 00	$13 00	$10 00	18	14	10
Sand Lake														
Saranac	22	28	39	29	25	21	8	54	13 00	10 00	10 00	16	14	10
Saugatuck	23	28	28	26	12			12	12 00			17	14	9
Schoolcraft	14	32	34	25	12	11	4	27	18 00	16 00	14 40	18	14	11
Sebewaing	28	40	41	33		3	4	7				18	14	11
Shelby	26	24	42	30	39	5	1	45	12 00	12 00	12 00	18	15	10
Shepherd	16	22	33	24	15			15	18 00	13 50	13 50	16.6	11.9	8
Sheridan	28	37	70	43	11	17	3	31	9 00	9 00	4 50	18		
Sherman	27	23	46	35	1	2		3	9 00			17	14	10
Sherwood	22	23	36	25	21			21	9 00			19		
†Sibley														
South Frankfort	22	20	41	27	2			2	10 00			16		
South Lyon	31	41	37	35	29	1		30	12 00	12 00	12 00	17	14	11
Sparta	32	37	37	35	14	4		18	20 00	12 00	12 00	18		
Spring Lake	13	22	41	28			1	1	9 50	7 22			16	13
Springport	25	29	31	27	28			28	10 00			18		
Stambaugh	14	22	31	22		2	2	4	7 22	7 22	7 22		14	11
Stamwood														
†Stephenson														
Stevensville	11	37	38	27	8	1	3	12	10 00	6 00		18	14.5	11
Stockbridge	24	52	28	33	21	14	4	39	12 50	10 00	9 00	17	13	10.5
Sunfield	33	30	43	33	21	1		22	9 50	9 50	9 50	18	13.5	10
Sutton's Bay	20	28	25	73	1			1	9 00				14.4	10.5
Tecumseh	27	34	33	31	50	10	1	61	16 67	13 33	11 67	18	13	9
Tekonsha	19	30	74	27	19	2	1	22	4 00	3 50		18	14	10
Thompsonville	18	25	47	33	2	3		5					14	10
Three Oaks	16	36	54	30	14	8	2	24	13 50	11 25	9 00	17	12	7.3
Trenton	17	53	47	43	5	4	2	11	10 00	8 00	6 00	19	15	
Tustin	21	39	36	33	6			6	9 00	9 00	9 00	16.2		13
Twining	30	45	63	46					7 50	5 00	3 50			
†Ubly														
Union City	20	23	34	25	45			45	15 00	12 00	9 00	17.5		
Unionville	35	37	40	38	12	2		14	10 00			18	13	7
Utica	13	30	38	26	10			10	13 00			19	14	10
Vandalia	24	28	39	28	9			9	9 00			18		
Vanderbilt	27	50	56	40	1			1	5 00			18.5		
Vassar	13	37	35	30	20	11		31	12 00	10 00	8 00	18		
Vermontville	20	26	26	22	33	3	1	37	13 30	9 50		18	14	9.2
Vernon	25	14	32	21					12 00	9 00	9 00	16	14	10
Vicksburg	18	39	32	28	25	16		41	16 00	14 00	12 00	17.5	13.5	9
Wakefield	5	24	45	43								16		
Waldron	11	33	30	19	7	3		10	11 25			18.7		
Warren														
Watervliet	25	34	39	33	14	4	4	22	11 25	9 00	6 75	17	14	11.6
Wayland	49	59	73	46	54	4	3	61	11 00	11 00	7 00	17		
Wayne	25	49	29	32	37	9	1	47	14 00	10 00	8 00			
Webberville	30	39	32	33	10			10	9 00	9 00	9 00	16.5	13.3	11
†Westphalia														
White Cloud	20	48	65	43	7	1	1	9	9 00	9 00	6 75			
Whitehall	35	29	31	31	10			10	9 50			17		
White Pigeon	23	44	34	29	44	3	6	53	15 00	12 00	10 00	18	14	10
Williamston	17	41	46	33	37	7	2	46	14 00	10 00	8 00	19	15	11
Wolverine	14	35	54	34	5	1		6						12
Woodland	34	18	35	29	24	2		26	10 80	10 80	7 20	16	13	11
‡Woodmere														

†Not legally graded.
‡Included in Detroit.

TABLE XVIII.—Concluded.

Number of graduates.	Number of U. S. flags.	Has school kindergarten below primary grade?	Portion of time in first primary devoted to kindergarten work.	Number of grades in the school.	Number of pupils studying— Latin.	Greek.	French.	German.	Does school give special instruction in— Vocal music?	Drawing?	Penmanship?	Manual training?	Domestic science?	Has school a commercial course?	Is the compulsory attendance law enforced?	Has school an ungraded department?	Has school a day school for the deaf?
....																	
11	1	Yes	1-4	12	28			20	Yes	Yes	Yes	No	No	Yes	Yes		
....																	
3	1	No	1-10	12	13				No	No	No	No	No	No	Yes	No	No
10	2	No		11	12			22							Yes	No	
7	1	No	1-4	12	14			16	No	No	No	No	No	No	Yes	No	No
5	1	No	1-2	12	12				No	No	No	No	No	Yes		No	No
10	1				41				No	No	No	No	No	No	Yes		
6	1	Yes		12	6				No	Yes	Yes	Yes		No	Yes	No	No
2	1	No		12					No	No	No	No	No	No	Yes	No	No
9	1		1-5	11					Yes					Yes	Yes	No	
1	1	No	1-3	12	5				No	No	Yes	No	No	No	Yes	No	No
....																	
5		Yes		12					No	Yes	Yes	Yes	No	No	Yes	No	
6	1	Yes	1-4	12	25				Yes	Yes	Yes	No	No	Yes	Yes	No	No
9	1	Yes	1-2	12	5			7	Yes	Yes		Yes		No	Yes	No	No
3		No	1-6	10					No	No	No	No	No	No	Yes	No	No
8	1	Yes	1-3	12	18				No	No	No	No	No		Yes	No	
....	2	Yes	All	11	11				Yes	Yes	Yes	No	No	Yes	Yes	No	No
....																	
....																	
1	1	Yes	1-4	12	19			4	No	No	No	No	No	No	Yes	No	No
1	1	Yes	1-2	12					Yes	Yes	Yes	No	No	Yes	Yes	No	No
3	1	No	1-2	12					No	No	Yes	No	No	No	No	No	No
....	1	No	1-5	11					No	No	No	No	No	No	Yes		
19	2	No	1-4	12	53			37	Yes	Yes	Yes	No	No	No	Yes	No	No
6	1	No		12	19				No	No	No	No	No	Yes	Yes		
....	1	No			15									No	Yes	No	No
12	2	No	1-3	12	17			27	Yes	No	No	No	No	No	Yes	No	No
1	1	Yes	1-2	12	3				No	Yes	Yes			Yes	Yes	No	No
4	1	No	1-4	11					No	No	Yes	No	No	Yes	Yes	No	No
....	1	No		10	8				No	Yes	Yes	No	No	Yes	Yes	No	No
....																	
9	1	Yes		12	25			14	No	No	No	No	No	No	Yes	No	No
4	1		1-4	12	1									Yes	Yes		
2	1	No		12	15				No	No	No	No	No	No	Yes	No	No
4	1	No			10				No	Yes	Yes	No	No	No	Yes	No	
4	1	No		12							Yes			Yes	No	No	
11	3	No	1-3	12	17			13	Yes	No	No	No	No	Yes	Yes	No	No
7		No	1-4	12	36			14		Yes		Yes		No	Yes	No	
....	1	No	1-4	12	2										Yes	No	No
11	1	Yes		12	40			28	Yes	Yes	No	No	No	Yes	Yes	No	No
4	5	Yes	All	10					No	No	Yes	No	No	Yes	Yes	No	No
8	1	No		12	5				No	No	Yes	No	No	Yes	Yes	No	No
....																	
5	1	Yes	All	12	12				No	No	No	No	No	Yes	Yes		
9	1	No		12					No	No	No	No	No	No	Yes	No	No
15	1	No		12	31			24	Yes	No	No	No	No	Yes	Yes	No	No
4	1	No	1 2	10					No	No	No	No	No	Yes	Yes	No	No
....																	
....	1	No	1-3	11	9				Yes		Yes			Yes	Yes		
10	1	No	1-4	12	7			30	Yes	No	No	No	No	Yes	Yes		
11	1	Yes	1-9	12	15			7	No	Yes	Yes	No	No	No	Yes	No	No
18	1	No	1-2	12	24			19	Yes	No	No	No	No	No	Yes	No	No
....	1	No		12	3			4	No	No	No	No	No	No	Yes	No	No
17	1	No	1-2	10											Yes		
....																	

TABLE XIX.

Financial statistics of city schools as reported by superintendents for the year 1903-7.

Incorporated cities.	Amount paid superintendent.	Amount paid regular teachers.	Amount paid special teachers.	Total amount paid for instruction.	Cost of education per capita in—											
					High school.			Grammar department.			Primary department.			Whole school.		
					Instruction.	Incidentals.	Total.	Instruction.	Incidentals.	Total.	Instruction.	Incidentals.	Total.	Instruction.	Incidentals.	Total.
Adrian	$1,800 00	$22,061 00	$3,400 00	$27,261 00	$30 30	$12 01	$42 31	$14 63	$12 01	$26 64	$16 35	$12 01	$28 36	$18 19	$12 01	$30 20
Albion	1,600 00	15,565 50	978 00	18,143 50	30 61	3 88	34 49	14 14	3 88	18 02	10 94	3 88	14 82	19 80	3 88	23 68
Allegan	1,700 00	8,776 32	....	10,476 32	27 73	2 30	30 03	10 47	2 30	12 77	16 38	2 30	18 68	17 48	2 30	19 78
Alma	1,300 00	8,346 25	500 00	10,146 25	29 33	7 73	37 06	17 31	7 73	25 04	18 38	7 73	26 11	19 78	7 73	27 51
Alpena	1,500 00	19,270 00	1,800 00	22,570 00	36 43	8 31	44 74	14 24	8 31	22 55	10 72	8 31	19 03	13 88	8 31	22 19
Ann Arbor	2,500 00	42,894 10	4,150 00	84, 10	41 17	9 52	50 69	17 92	9 52	27 44	*	9 52	*	23 95	9 52	33 47
†Au Gres	....	....	....	....	....	....	....	....	....	....	....	....	....	....	....	....
Au Sable	800 00	3,364 75	....	4,164 75	10 63	2 50	13 13	14 65	2 50	17 15	10 23	2 50	12 73	11 93	2 50	14 43
Bad Axe	1,000 00	4,125 00	400 00	5,525 00	27 17	6 72	33 89	12 78	6 72	19 50	11 37	6 72	18 09	14 65	6 72	21 37
Battle Creek	2,400 00	57,226 88	4,075 00	63,701 88	37 40	10 43	47 83	17 03	10 43	27 46	16 11	10 43	26 54	19 13	10 43	29 57
Bay City	2,800 00	96,585 72	4,000 00	103,385 72	40 78	7 36	48 14	17 97	7 36	25 33	13 34	7 36	20 70	17 60	7 36	24 96
Beaverton	650 00	1,514 00	....	2,164 00	23 63	3 17	26 80	12 71	3 17	15 88	7 82	3 17	10 99	11 51	3 17	14 68
Belding	1,250 00	7,354 38	825 00	9,429 38	34 16	3 23	37 39	15 24	3 23	18 47	10 04	3 23	13 27	15 53	3 23	18 76
Benton Harbor	1,750 00	18,274 00	550 00	20,574 00	23 16	6 00	29 16	14 16	6 00	20 16	13 77	6 00	19 77	15 76	6 00	21 76
Bessemer	1,500 00	15,095 00	650 00	17,245 00	52 45	18 14	70 59	16 26	18 14	34 40	13 33	18 14	31 47	18 98	18 14	37 12
Big Rapids	1,400 00	11,220 00	400 00	13,270 00	31 85	8 09	39 94	18 40	8 09	26 49	11 17	8 09	19 26	17 10	8 09	25 19
Boyne City	1,200 00	8,190 00	....	9,390 00	42 07	5 57	47 64	34 29	5 57	39 86	9 50	5 57	15 07	13 85	5 57	19 42
Brown City	700 00	1,715 00	....	2,415 00	18 12	4 23	22 36	13 04	4 23	17 27	7 54	4 23	11 77	11 61	4 23	15 84
Cadillac	1,600 00	22,673 90	559 03	24,848 93	23 39	7 00	30 39	9 46	7 00	16 46	15 33	7 00	22 33	14 63	7 00	21 63
Charlevoix	1,100 16	5,858 65	2,143 39	9,102 20	25 50	25 04	50 54	18 09	25 04	43 13	9 05	25 04	34 09	15 99	25 04	41 03
Charlotte	1,500 00	11,147 64	1,000 00	13,647 64	28 42	9 62	38 04	17 16	9 62	26 78	12 26	9 62	21 88	17 59	9 62	27 21
Cheboygan	1,350 00	13,384 60	660 00	15,394 60	32 42	4 55	36 97	11 21	4 55	15 76	10 76	4 55	15 37	13 79	4 55	18 34
Clare	900 00	3,815 00	....	4,715 00	23 26	5 80	29 06	11 48	5 80	17 28	9 58	5 80	15 38	12 95	5 80	18 75
Coldwater	1,600 00	15,559 37	1,100 00	18,259 37	32 47	9 65	42 12	16 40	9 65	26 05	13 54	9 65	23 19	17 69	9 65	27 34
Coleman	700 00	2,700 00	....	3,400 00	22 97	3 94	26 91	9 43	3 94	13 37	8 25	3 94	12 19	10 82	3 94	14 76
Corunna	1,200 00	4,549 75	235 00	5,984 75	26 00	9 11	35 11	19 58	9 11	28 69	15 10	9 11	24 21	18 88	9 11	27 99
Croswell	850 00	3,525 00	....	4,375 00	39 64	4 14	43 78	12 86	4 14	17 00	8 14	4 14	12 28	15 15	4 14	19 29
Crystal Falls	1,600 00	15,800 00	650 00	18,050 00	33 82	37 66	71 48	15 24	37 66	52 90	18 84	37 66	56 50	19 36	37 66	57 03
Detroit	4,000 00	1,075,317 44	23,242 48	1,102,559 92	49 86	7 70	57 56	30 80	7 70	38 50	28 23	7 70	35 93	27 72	7 70	35 42
Dowagiac	1,500 00	12,288 75	397 00	14,185 75	30 39	6 85	37 24	14 82	6 85	21 67	10 45	6 85	17 30	14 60	6 85	21 45

†East Lansing																
East Tawas	775 00	4,239 25		5,014 25	22 33	3 86	26 19	11 97	3 86	15 83	11 12	3 86	14 98	12 89	3,86	16 75
Eaton Rapids	1,200 00	6,070 00		7,270 00	24 75	2 50	27 25	19 58	2 50	22 08	18 59	2 50	21 09	21 13	2 50	23 63
Escanaba	2,250 00	32,982 85	1,900 00	37,132 85	32 67	4 18	36 85	14 69	4 18	18 87	15 95	4 18	20 08	17 77	4 18	21 95
Flint	2,000 00	38,513 07	2,182 50	42,695 57	32 14	9 96	42 10	19 06	9 96	29 02	11 87	9 96	21 83	17 51	9 96	27 47
Gladstone	1,200 00	7,580 00		8,780 00	25 60	3 37	28 97	12 65	3 37	16 02	8 92	3 37	12 27	12 26	3 37	15 63
Gladwin	800 00	2,120 00		2,920 00	21 73	11 04	32 77	13 62	11 04	24 66	6 72	11 04	17 76	11 55	11 04	22 59
Grand Haven	1,545 00	12,415 00	438 75	14,398 75	23 58	6 54	30 12	12 40	6 54	18 94	10 33	6 54	16 87	13 95	6 54	20 49
Grand Ledge	950 00	7,047 50	200 00	8,197 50	41 92	6 80	48 72	14 51	6 80	21 36	10 32	6 80	17 12	18 80	6 80	25 60
Grand Rapids	50,140 00	282,795 37	5,500 00	338,435 37	45 88	8 15	54 03	27 97	8 15	36 12	20 91	8 15	29 06	25 75	8 15	33 90
Greenville	1,200 00	8,900 00	600 00	10,700 00	24 68	19 63	44 31	11 90	19 63	31 53	12 50	19 63	32 13	15 00	19 63	34 63
Hancock	1,800 00	16,527 50		18,327 50	45 12	7 73	52 85	15 49	7 73	23 22	12 54	7 73	20 27	17 32	7 73	25 05
Harrison	575 00	1,080 00		1,655 00	20 53	1 75	22 28	10 50	1 75	12 25	9 70	1 75	11 45	12 44	1 75	14 19
Harrisville	540 00	1,098 00		1,638 00	21 31	2 83	24 14	10 20	2 83	13 03	6 51	2 83	9 34	10 36	2 83	13 19
Hastings	1,000 00	11,030 23		12,030 23	29 99	32 57	62 56	13 82	32 57	46 39	17 81	32 57	50 38	19 40	32 57	51 97
Hillsdale	1,400 00	12,025 00	1,750 00	15,175 00	25 56	8 93	34 49	15 71	8 93	24 64	12 74	8 93	21 67	17 01	8 93	25 94
Holland	1,680 00	19,304 00	996 25	21,980 25	34 98	4 88	39 86	11 76	4 88	16 64	11 92	4 88	16 80	13 55	4 88	18 43
Hudson	1,300 00	6,651 46		7,951 46	24 43	7 54	31 97	14 02	7 54	21 56	14 13	7 54	21 67	17 02	7 54	24 56
Ionia	1,450 00	15,412 71		16,862 71	46 19	6 91	53 10	24 84	6 91	53 10	14 70	6 91	21 61	22 82	6 91	29 73
Iron Mountain	3,100 00	33,784 87	3,875 85	40,760 72	39 05	6 93	45 98	18 60	6 93	25 53	15 07	6 93	22 00	17 66	6 93	24 59
Ironwood	2,500 00	33,642 00	3,870 00	40,012 00	50 84	16 22	67 06	14 95	16 22	31 17	19 36	16 22	35 58	19 55	16 22	35 77
Ishpeming	3,000 00	45,940 00	5,150 00	54,090 00	48 89	11 33	60 22	21 91	11 33	33 24	12 33	11 33	23 66	19 16	11 33	30 49
Jackson	2,500 00	57,614 00	1,725 00	61,839 00	38 97	7 93	46 90	17 70	7 93	25 63	15 21	7 93	23 14	18 35	7 93	26 28
Kalamazoo	2,600 00	79,953 58	9,075 00	91,628 58	42 53	8 46	50 99	18 24	8 46	26 70	13 03	8 46	21 49	18 07	8 46	26 53
Lansing	2,000 00	49,093 18	2,550 00	53,643 18	34 88	8 75	43 63	19 29	8 75	28 04	14 74	8 75	23 49	18 91	8 75	27 66
Lapeer	1,300 00	8,050 00	600 00	9,950 00	32 12	10 24	42 36	17 03	10 24	27 27	18 53	10 24	28 77	21 58	10 24	31 82
Ludington	4,880 00	16,525 50	1,970 02	23,375 52	31 06	7 17	38 23	15 77	7 17	22 94	14 38	7 17	21 55	16 86	7 17	24 03
Mackinac Island	900 00	1,575 00		2,475 00	30 72	5 50	36 22	13 88	5 50	19 38	14 70	5 50	20 20	20 97	5 50	26 47
Manistee	1,900 00	34,247 49	2,239 25	38,386 74	45 82	8 46	54 28	19 33	8 46	27 79	15 37	8 46	23 83	19 83	8 46	28 29
Manistique																
Marine City	1,250 00	7,205 00	450 00	8,905 00	37 50	11 76	49 26	15 24	11 76	27 00	13 26	11 76	25 02	16 96	11 76	28 72
Marquette	3,868 00	30,472 00	4,150 00	38,490 00	49 58	8 62	58 20	19 51	8 62	28 13	18 16	8 62	26 78	22 33	8 62	30 95
Marshall	1,300 00	12,841 25	1,000 00	15,141 25	29 50	6 65	36 15	18 11	6 65	24 76	20 65	6 65	27 30	22 38	6 65	29 03
Mason	1,200 00	4,875 00	400 00	6,475 00	31 77	6 75	38 52	14 05	6 75	20 80	17 53	6 75	24 28	19 98	6 75	26 73
McBain	585 00	1,800 00		2,385 00	54 56	8 47	63 03	11 13	8 47	19 60	7 82	8 47	16 29	11 60	8 47	20 07
Menominee	3,200 14	29,277 84	2,066 43	34,484 41	33 01	7 33	40 34	14 77	7 33	22 10	14 52	7 33	21 85	16 06	7 33	23 39
Midland	1,100 00	70,850 00		8,180 00	23 86	5 39	29 25	15 92	5 39	21 31	10 28	5 39	15 67	14 40	5 39	19 79
Monroe	1,600 00	9,050 00	925 00	11,576 00	40 00	9 25	49 25	12 88	9 25	22 13	10 76	9 25	20 01	15 81	9 25	25 06
Mt. Clemens	1,600 00	14,298 00	500 00	16,398 00	47 73	7 35	55 08	15 47	7 35	22 82	10 30	7 35	17 65	16 06	7 35	23 41
Mt. Pleasant	2,325 00	8,250 00	588 64	11,163 64	27 54	9 33	36 87	20 80	9 33	30 13	25 00	9 33	34 33	24 95	9 33	34 28
Muskegon	2,700 00	60,623 15	3,850 00	67,173 15	35 58	10 64	46 22	19 18	10 64	29 82	16 70	10 64	27 34	19 82	10 64	30 46
Muskegon Heights	900 00	3,071 93		3,971 93	114 75	31 30	146 05	14 01	31 30	45 31	9 87	31 30	41 17	16 77	31 30	48 07
Negaunee	1,800 00	19,812 50	1,000 50	22,613 00	46 68	3 87	50 55	14 95	3 87	18 82	15 41	3 87	19 28	18 58	3 87	22 45
Niles	1,600 00	16,297 00	450 00	18,347 00	28 88	5 57	34 45	24 98	5 57	30 55	15 05	5 57	20 62	20 38	5 57	25 95

*Not legally graded.
†Included in Grammar department.

TABLE XIX.—CONTINUED.

Incorporated cities.	Amount paid superintendent.	Amount paid regular teachers.	Amount paid special teachers.	Total amount paid for instruction.	Cost of education per capita in— High school. Instruction.	High school. Incidentals.	High school. Total.	Grammar department. Instruction.	Grammar department. Incidentals.	Grammar department. Total.	Primary department. Instruction.	Primary department. Incidentals.	Primary department. Total.	Whole school. Instruction.	Whole school. Incidentals.	Whole school. Total.
North Muskegon	$418 60	$330 00	....	$1,048 60	....	....	....	$12 70	$22 42	$35 12	$10 00	$22 42	$32 42	$11 65	$22 42	$44 07
Norway	1,700 00	13,569 65	$400 00	15,669 65	$46 40	$20 33	$66 79	15 05	20 33	35 38	13 00	20 33	33 33	15 71	20 33	36 04
Omer	600 00	1,100 00	....	1,700 00	22 22	10 52	32 74	11 19	10 52	21 71	8 97	10 52	19 49	12 77	10 52	23 29
Onaway	1,000 00	5,384 00	....	6,384 00	80 30	8 12	88 42	76 38	8 12	24 50	8 39	8 12	17 01	14 09	8 12	22 21
Owosso	1,500 00	23,677 06	1,130 00	26,307 06	37 64	12 57	50 21	17 19	12 57	29 76	12 95	12 57	25 52	17 79	12 57	30 36
Petoskey	1,400 00	14,845 82	650 00	16,895 82	30 24	6 99	37 23	17 47	6 99	24 46	14 27	6 99	21 26	19 00	6 99	25 99
Pontiac	1,600 00	24,155 00	1,850 00	27,605 00	32 92	9 88	41 80	14 44	9 88	24 32	14 93	9 88	24 81	17 42	9 88	27 30
Port Huron	2,000 00	40,730 00	625 00	43,355 00	33 97	6 17	40 14	14 12	6 17	20 29	10 80	6 17	16 97	14 59	6 17	20 76
Rose City	617 50	1,330 00	....	1,947 50	18 71	3 46	22 17	9 80	3 46	13 26	5 98	3 46	9 44	9 18	3 46	12 64
Saginaw	2,500 00	93,633 98	5200 00	101,333 98	52 62	14 16	66 78	24 59	14 16	38 75	16 90	14 16	31 06	25 83	14 16	39 99
Saginaw, W. S.	2,000 00	40,653 87	4,740 00	47,393 87	45 30	9 90	55 20	19 11	9 90	29 01	15 24	9 90	25 14	19 74	9 90	29 64
St. Clair	1,300 00	5,930 00	500 00	7,730 00	26 75	9 44	36 19	16 58	9 44	26 02	16 23	9 44	25 67	18 67	9 44	28 11
St. Ignace	900 00	4,840 00	....	5,740 00	23 18	6 02	29 20	20 40	6 02	26 42	8 81	6 02	14 83	13 44	6 02	19 46
St. Johns	1,400 00	10,108 50	493 40	12,001 90	31 81	10 49	42 30	14 98	10 49	25 47	16 59	10 49	27 08	19 05	10 49	29 54
St. Joseph	1,650 00	16,070 00	1,050 00	18,770 00	40 24	11 97	52 21	5 98	11 97	17 05	24 41	11 97	36 36	20 09	11 97	32 06
St. Louis	1,100 00	5,900 00	500 00	7,500 00	39 29	4 98	44 27	12 87	4 98	17 85	10 61	4 99	15 59	8 47	4 98	13 45
Sandusky	1,555 00	1,168 50	....	2,723 00	25 57	7 25	32 82	12 03	7 25	19 28	7 83	7 25	15 08	12 78	7 25	20 03
Sault Ste. Marie	2,400 00	33,328 00	3,050 00	38,778 00	32 85	7 96	40 81	19 91	7 96	27 87	11 48	7 96	19 44	16 02	7 96	23 98
Scottville	790 00	2,042 00	380 00	3,212 00	23 13	5 62	28 75	12 86	5 62	18 48	9 81	5 62	15 43	13 72	5 62	19 34
South Haven	1,400 00	10,946 16	505 26	12,851 42	32 53	3 70	36 23	14 88	3 70	18 58	11 50	3 70	15 20	16 43	3 70	20 13
Standish	1,050 00	2,800 00	....	3,850 00	29 37	7 60	36 97	8 30	7 60	15 90	10 21	7 60	17 81	11 59	7 60	19 19
Stanton	925 00	2,876 61	....	3,801 61	34 09	4 21	38 30	11 85	4 21	16 06	10 00	4 21	14 21	14 67	4 21	18 88
Sturgis	1,150 00	6,061 00	427 50	7,638 50	25 97	9 99	35 91	13 65	9 99	23 64	11 68	9 99	11 67	14 52	9 99	24 51
Tawas City	800 00	2,725 00	650 00	4,175 00	26 04	6 07	32 11	26 75	6 07	32 82	8 49	6 07	14 56	16 18	6 07	22 25
Three Rivers	1,400 00	12,391 50	570 00	14,361 50	....	....	....	....	....	....	....	....	....	19 81	6 73	26 54
Traverse City	2,000 00	31,033 01	1,187 51	34,220 51	27 63	3 29	30 92	15 09	3 29	18 38	‡	‡	‡	16 16	3 29	19 45
West Branch	900 00	3,135 00	....	4,035 00	20 92	12 03	32 95	5 87	12 08	17 90	8 67	12 08	20 70	9 96	12 03	21 99
Whittemore	550 00	350 00	....	850 00	8 73	2 16	10 89	....	....	....	8 97	2 16	11 13	8 33	2 16	10 49
Wyandotte	1,200 00	13,918 21	875 00	16,093 21	38 11	6 05	44 16	16 23	6 05	22 28	11 06	6 05	17 11	15 35	6 05	21 40
Yale	850 00	3,664 12	....	4,514 12	27 38	9 26	36 64	15 59	9 26	24 85	11 23	9 26	20 49	15 61	9 26	24 87
Ypsilanti	1,549 00	14,442 00	1,250 00	17,241 00	29 68	8 13	37 81	16 47	8 13	24 60	15 07	8 13	23 20	18 90	8 13	27 03
Zeeland	800 00	3,960 00	450 00	5,200 00	27 22	4 25	31 47	10 23	4 25	14 48	9 03	4 25	13 28	11 71	4 25	15 96

‡Included in the grammar department.

TABLE XIX.

Financial statistics of graded village schools as reported by superintendents for the year 1906-7.

Incorporated villages.	Amount paid superintendent.	Amount paid regular teachers.	Amount paid special teachers.	Total amount paid for instruction.	Cost of education per capita in— High school. Instruction.	Incidentals.	Total.	Grammar department. Instruction.	Incidentals.	Total.	Primary department. Instruction.	Incidentals.	Total.	Whole school. Instruction.	Incidentals.	Total.
Addison	$800 00	$1,530 00	....	$2,330 00	$25 00	$15 89	$40 89	$12 86	$15 89	$28 75	$9 84	$15 89	$25 73	$15 64	$15 89	$31 53
Alanson	495 00	1,350 00	....	1,845 00	26 81	4 54	31 35	12 21	4 54	16 75	7 01	4 54	11 55	10 54	4 54	15 08
Algonac	1,000 00	2,244 33	....	3,244 33	33 06	7 45	20 51	9 31	7 45	16 76	23	7 45	7 68	10 74	7 45	18 19
Almont	825 00	2,200 00	....	3,025 00	34 84	10 17	45 01	18 73	10 17	28 90	10 22	10 17	20 39	15 12	10 17	27 85
Applegate	450 00	210 00	....	....	....	....	....	....	....	....	....	....	....	....	....	....
Armada	844 36	1,648 42	....	2,492 78	21 68	6 74	28 42	11 16	6 87	18 03	7 68	4 98	12 66	13 83	6 19	20 02
Ashley	570 00	1,248 75	....	1,818 75	28 20	4 79	32 99	10 85	4 79	32 99	7 00	4 79	11 79	15 81	4 79	20 60
Athens	630 00	1,440 00	....	2,070 00	27 88	3 41	31 29	7 94	3 41	11 35	9 91	3 41	13 32	13 47	3 41	16 88
†Atlanta	....	....	....	....	....	....	....	....	....	....	....	....	....	....	....	....
Attica	500 00	280 00	....	780 00	22 22	222 28	244 50	14 83	222 28	237 11	4 48	222 28	226 76	9 39	222 28	231 67
Augusta	750 00	1,809 00	....	2,559 00	34 47	10 93	45 40	13 06	10 93	23 99	13 95	10 93	24 88	19 93	10 93	30 92
Baldwin	567 50	670 00	....	1,237 50	14 55	2 83	17 38	10 60	2 83	13 43	8 21	2 83	11 04	11 15	2 83	13 98
Bancroft	800 00	1,500 00	....	2,300 00	54 74	18 91	73 65	11 89	18 91	30 80	20 98	18 91	39 89	24 47	18 91	43 38
Bangor	1,000 00	3,589 00	$285 00	4,874 00	19 02	9 25	28 27	9 12	9 25	18 38	9 93	9 25	19 18	12 65	9 25	11 90
Baraga	1,200 00	8,025 00	....	9,225 00	59 61	4 81	64 42	20 70	4 81	25 51	14 30	4 81	19 11	19 46	4 81	24 27
Baroda	560 00	640 00	....	1,200 00	15 55	5 98	21 53	7 61	5 98	13 59	5 33	5 98	11 31	8 69	5 98	14 67
Barryton	....	1,710 00	....	1,710 00	40 00	4 10	44 10	12 66	4 10	16 76	9 16	4 10	13 26	13 50	4 10	17 60
Bear Lake	630 00	1,080 00	70 00	1,780 00	31 50	3 29	34 79	8 18	3 29	11 48	7 74	3 29	11 03	11 33	3 29	14 62
Bellaire	900 00	2,970 00	247 50	4,117 50	20 68	4 23	24 91	11 18	4 23	15 41	14 93	4 23	19 16	14 50	4 23	18 73
Belleville	750 00	1,200 00	....	1,950 00	1 98	6 80	8 78	12 50	6 80	18 80	13 33	6 80	20 13	15 00	6 80	21 80
Bellevue	900 00	2,270 00	152 00	2,322 00	20 32	139 96	160 28	10 84	139 96	150 80	9 94	139 96	149 90	13 61	139 96	153 57
Bensonia	699 99	1,800 00	....	2,499 99	62 88	3 57	66 45	12 55	3 57	16 12	9 15	3 57	12 72	15 33	3 57	18 90
Berrien Springs	897 18	1,947 50	180 00	2,844 68	31 93	5 04	36 97	12 65	5 04	17 69	10 51	5 04	15 55	15 37	5 04	20 41
Birmingham	1,200 00	4,100 00	250 00	5,550 00	19 00	3 30	22 30	14 58	3 30	17 88	20 37	3 30	23 67	3 96	3 30	7 26
Blissfield No. 1 fr	800 00	1,010 00	....	1,810 00	29 21	6 26	35 47	9 11	6 26	15 37	7 00	6 26	13 26	11 00	6 26	17 26
Blissfield No. 2 fr	1,000 00	2,600 00	....	3,600 00	43 65	6 32	49 97	13 38	6 32	19 70	8 66	6 32	14 98	16 74	6 32	23 06
Bloomingdale	700 00	1,235 00	....	1,935 00	19 77	10 47	30 24	10 28	10 47	20 75	7 10	10 47	17 57	13 91	10 47	24 38
Boardman	585 00	1,080 00	....	1,665 00	32 50	30 73	63 23	12 41	30 73	43 14	17 75	30 73	48 48	19 13	30 73	49 86
Boyne Falls	540 00	1,070 00	....	1,610 00	2 72	22 71	25 43	28 40	22 71	51 11	10 28	22 71	32 99	51 93	22 71	74 64

†Not legally graded.

TABLE XIX.—Continued.

Incorporated villages.	Amount paid superintendent.	Amount paid regular teachers.	Amount paid special teachers.	Total amount paid for instruction.	Cost of education per capita in— High school. Instruction.	High school. Incidentals.	High school. Total.	Grammar department. Instruction.	Grammar department. Incidentals.	Grammar department. Total.	Primary department. Instruction.	Primary department. Incidentals.	Primary department. Total.	Whole school. Instruction.	Whole school. Incidentals.	Whole school. Total.
Breedsville	$540 00	$315 00	....	$855 00	....	....	....	$13 84	$6 24	$20 08	$8 28	$6 24	$14 52	$11 10	$6 24	$17 34
Brighton	850 00	1,660 00	....	2,510 00	$27 12	$12 74	$39 86	9 65	12 74	22 39	13 36	12 74	26 10	15 68	12 74	28 42
Britton	489 50	708 75	....	1,198 25	18 82	3 54	22 36	11 11	3 54	14 65	8 48	3 54	12 02	12 10	3 54	15 64
Bronson	812 50	2,755 00	....	3,567 00	29 73	8 86	38 59	16 40	8 86	25 26	15 18	8 86	24 04	19 70	8 86	28 56
Brooklyn	800 00	2,500 00	....	3,300 00	51 16	6 16	57 32	12 53	6 16	18 69	10 99	6 16	17 15	22 44	6 16	28 60
Buchanan	1,000 00	4,283 75	$380 00	6,233 75	35 83	3 27	39 10	18 35	3 27	21 62	15 65	3 27	18 92	20 84	3 27	24 11
†Buckley	....	....	....	....	....	....	....	....	....	....	....	....	....	....	....	....
Burlington	450 00	585 00	....	1,035 00	16 66	4 40	21 06	16 08	4 40	20 48	15 00	4 40	19 40	19 29	4 40	23 69
Burr Oak	760 00	1,995 00	....	2,755 00	36 83	3 23	40 06	15 53	3 23	18 16	11 89	3 23	15 12	18 70	3 23	21 93
Byron	700 00	700 00	....	1,400 00	19 44	3 81	23 25	10 00	3 81	11 25	7 44	3 81	11 25	11 86	3 81	15 67
Caledonia	697 50	1,115 25	....	1,812 75	11 62	3 09	14 71	12 06	3 09	15 45	11 63	3 09	14 72	11 77	3 09	14 86
Calumet	3,500 00	96,078 27	5,600 00	105,178 27	39 05	5 99	45 04	17 27	5 99	23 26	16 38	5 99	22 37	17 95	5 99	23 94
Camden	600 00	1,272 00	....	1,872 00	35 40	9 70	45 10	20 15	9 70	29 85	19 30	9 70	29 00	24 70	9 70	34 40
Capac	750 00	1,775 00	....	2,525 00	23 21	4 35	27 56	75 03	4 35	79 38	4 71	4 35	9 06	13 79	4 35	18 14
Caro	1,200 00	5,959 37	450 00	7,609 37	14 38	5 21	19 59	15 80	5 21	21 01	17 57	5 21	22 78	15 81	5 21	21 02
Carson City	800 00	1,903 75	....	3,703 75	27 69	5 31	33 00	12 22	5 31	17 53	12 14	5 31	17 45	12 57	5 31	17 88
Carsonville	650 00	1,200 00	....	1,850 00	22 00	8 04	30 04	7 69	8 04	15 73	8 33	8 04	16 37	12 84	8 04	20 88
Caseville	700 00	1,020 00	....	1,720 00	23 47	4 92	28 39	6 03	4 92	10 95	8 00	4 92	12 92	12 37	4 92	17 29
Casnovia	585 00	630 00	....	1,215 00	34 41	3 01	37 42	13 70	3 01	16 71	7 00	3 01	10 01	14 30	3 01	17 31
Cass City	900 00	2,744 50	....	3,644 50	10 04	6 94	16 98	8 26	6 94	15 20	14 14	6 94	21 08	11 21	6 94	18 15
Cassopolis	1,100 00	3,445 00	....	4,545 00	43 27	9 60	52 87	1 57	9 60	11 17	19 16	9 60	28 76	21 14	9 60	30 74
Cedar Springs	925 00	2,432 00	380 00	3,737 00	39 21	9 33	48 54	13 69	9 33	23 02	7 90	9 33	17 23	15 70	9 33	25 03
Central Lake	1,000 00	2,783 75	447 50	4,231 25	38 43	6 74	45 17	11 30	6 74	18 04	12 78	6 74	19 52	17 27	6 74	24 01
Centreville	800 00	1,800 00	....	2,600 00	30 90	8 20	39 10	17 76	8 20	25 96	9 46	8 20	17 66	16 77	8 20	24 97
Chelsea	1,000 00	4,925 00	310 00	6,235 00	21 51	5 26	26 77	12 91	5 26	18 17	10 39	5 26	15 65	14 95	5 26	20 21
Chesaning	500 00	3,648 00	....	4,148 00	38 08	3 27	41 35	16 61	3 27	19 88	13 36	3 27	16 63	18 60	3 27	21 87
Clarkston	750 00	1,175 00	....	1,925 00	26 70	4 53	31 23	16 66	4 53	21 19	8 33	4 53	11 86	15 90	4 53	20 43
Clayton	720 00	585 00	....	1,305 00	23 22	3 59	26 81	8 75	3 59	12 34	6 75	3 59	10 34	12 92	3 59	16 51
†Clifford	....	....	....	....	....	....	....	....	....	....	....	....	....	....	....	....
Climax	630 00	990 00	....	1,620 00	30 48	3 86	34 34	7 32	3 86	11 18	7 50	3 86	11 36	13 27	3 86	17 13
Clinton	900 00	2,310 00	....	3,210 00	29 09	5 63	34 72	11 06	5 63	16 69	12 58	5 63	18 21	16 71	5 63	20 34

Clio	750 00	1,650 00	350 00	2,750 00	33 92	5 64	39 56	11 02	5 64	16 66	11 95	5 64	17 59	16 17	5 64	21 81
Coloma	630 00	2,070 00	....	2,700 00	23 25	3 60	26 85	15 55	3 60	19 15	6 49	3 60	10 09	12 32	3 60	15 92
Colon	782 24	2,340 00	....	3,122 24	24 58	3 63	28 21	16 51	3 63	20 14	13 17	3 63	16 80	17 68	3 63	21 31
Columbiaville	800 00	1,200 00	....	2,000 00	3 12	10 70	13 82	14 81	10 70	24 51	13 33	10 70	24 03	20 96	10 70	31 66
Concord	800 00	2,490 00	225 00	2,715 00	74 88	8 23	83 11	18 46	8 23	26 69	17 10	8 23	25 33	25 13	8 23	33 46
Constantine	950 00	2,800 00	....	7,80 00	27 87	5 14	33 02	27	5 14	32 16	23 04	5 14	28 18	34 09	5 14	39 23
Coopersville	600 00	1,473 75	....	2,073 75	16 99	2 59	198	8 41	2 59	11 00	9 45	2 59	12 04	10 82	2 59	13 41
Copemish	450 00	1,340 00	....	1,790 00	75 00	149 74	2247 4	7 40	149 74	157 14	6 53	149 74	156 27	15 16	149 74	164 90
†Croton	....	....	....	....	....	....	....	....	....	....	....	....	....	....	....	....
Custer	450 00	675 00	....	25 0	15 00	25	15	10 54	2 55	13 09	18 75	2 55	21 30	13 94	2 55	16 49
†Daggett	....	....	....	....	....	....	....	....	....	....	....	....	....	....	....	....
Dansville	700 00	1,050 00	....	1,750 00	29 16	4 69	33 85	17 99	4 69	22 68	13 33	4 69	18 02	19 66	4 69	24 35
Davison	650 00	1,775 00	....	2,425 00	36 60	4 43	41 03	10 44	4 43	14 87	7 86	4 43	12 29	13 17	4 43	17 60
Dearborn	800 00	1,924 50	62 50	2,787 00	53 12	6 87	59 99	8 13	6 87	15 00	8 97	6 87	15 84	12 66	6 87	19 53
Decatur	1,000 00	2,692 00	....	3,692 00	23 84	7 44	31 28	9 45	7 44	15 93	6 48	7 44	13 92	11 24	7 44	18 68
Deckerville	750 00	1,100 00	....	1,850 00	16 66	5 44	22 10	12 50	5 44	17 94	10 00	5 44	15 44	12 57	5 44	18 01
Deerfield	650 00	1,955 00	....	2,605 00	43 84	11 35	55 19	10 86	11 35	22 21	9 00	11 35	20 35	19 88	11 35	31 23
Delray	....	....	....	....	....	....	....	....	....	....	....	....	....	....	....	....
Detour	800 00	2,039 00	....	2,839 00	33 33	5 66	38 99	8 82	5 66	14 48	9 40	5 66	15 06	11 63	5 66	17 29
Dexter	855 00	2,340 00	135 00	3,330 00	21 86	3 12	24 85	10 99	3 12	14 11	9 67	3 12	12 79	13 68	3 12	16 80
Douglas	600 00	1,080 00	....	1,680 00	30 49	4 78	35 27	6 51	4 78	11 29	18 53	4 78	23 31	161 02	4 78	165 80
Dryden	700 00	750 00	....	1,450 00	11 60	41 20	52 80	....	....	....	8 88	41 20	50 08	13 80	41 20	17 92
Dundee	810 00	3,159 50	....	3,969 50	72 25	3 43	75 68	10 41	3 43	13 84	8 37	3 43	12 80	18 04	3 43	21 47
Durand	1,000 00	4,860 75	180 00	6,040 75	53 47	15 02	68 49	18 92	15 02	33 94	3 89	15 02	18 91	16 68	15 02	31 70
†Eagle	....	....	....	....	....	....	....	....	....	....	....	....	....	....	....	....
East Grand Rapids	450 00	800 00	....	1,250 00	18 00	15 94	33 94	15 38	15 94	31 32	11 42	15 94	27 36	14 54	15 94	30 48
East Jordan	1,060 00	4,972 50	405 00	6,427 50	28 50	17 26	45 76	16 77	17 26	34 03	9 58	17 26	26 84	15 05	17 26	32 31
Eau Claire	675 00	1,080 00	....	1,755 00	33 75	5 58	39 33	12 00	5 58	17 58	10 28	5 58	15 86	15 26	5 58	20 84
Ecorse	750 00	1,100 00	....	1,850 00	92 85	9 73	102 58	15 95	9 73	25 68	11 53	9 73	21 26	19 89	9 73	29 62
Edmore	750 00	1,539 00	....	2,289 00	18 29	8 87	27 16	9 73	8 87	18 60	9 04	8 87	17 91	11 16	8 87	20 03
Elk Rapids	1,300 00	5,757 50	....	7,057 50	29 02	11 16	40 18	12 35	11 16	23 51	11 90	11 16	23 06	14 74	11 16	25 90
Elkton	850 00	1,755 00	....	2,605 00	25 00	4 13	29 13	9 75	4 13	13 88	6 32	4 13	10 45	11 03	4 13	15 16
Elsie	665 00	1,710 00	....	2,375 00	22 12	7 60	29 72	11 89	7 60	19 49	10 60	7 60	18 20	14 13	7 60	21 73
†Emmet	....	....	....	....	....	....	....	....	....	....	....	....	....	....	....	....
Empire	900 00	1,125 00	....	2,025 00	293	71	30 74	8 86	1 71	10 57	6 06	171	7 77	10 94	1 71	2165
Essexville	750 00	1,350 00	180 00	2,280 00	....	....	....	25 50	18 45	43 95	12 00	18 45	30 45	19 29	18 45	37 74
Evart	525 80	5,200 00	....	5,725 00	30 65	1 70	32 35	13 69	1 70	15 39	11 93	1 70	13 63	16 97	1 70	18 67
†Fairgrove	....	....	....	....	....	....	....	....	....	....	....	....	....	....	....	....
‡Fairview	....	....	....	....	....	....	....	....	....	....	....	....	....	....	....	....
Farmington	650 00	650 00	650 00	1,950 00	....	....	....	....	....	....	....	....	....	....	....	....
Farwell	600 00	1,629 00	....	2,229 00	25 37	2 70	28 07	11 21	2 70	13 91	6 93	2 70	9 63	12 28	2 70	14 98
Fennville	765 00	1,620 00	....	2,385 00	22 09	3 89	25 98	8 57	3 89	12 46	7 32	3 89	11 21	11 60	3 89	15 49
Fenton	1,200 00	5,835 00	400 00	7,435 00	25 18	13 10	38 28	12 28	13 10	25 38	11 54	13 10	24 64	15 45	13 10	28 55
Fife Lake	585 00	720 00	....	1,305 00	12 71	15 94	28 65	11 61	15 94	27 55	7 65	15 94	23 59	10 52	15 94	26 46

†Not legally graded.
‡Now a part of Detroit.

TABLE XIX.—Continued.

Incorporated villages.	Amount paid superintendent.	Amount paid regular teachers.	Amount paid special teachers.	Total amount paid for instruction.	Cost of education per capita in—											
					High school.			Grammar department.			Primary department.			Whole school.		
					Instruction.	Incidentals.	Total.	Instruction.	Incidentals.	Total.	Instruction.	Incidentals.	Total.	Instruction.	Incidentals.	Total.
Flushing	$1,400 00	$1,450 00		$2,850 00	$23 18	$9 76	$32 94	$9 91	$9 76	$19 67	$11 04	$9 76	$20 80	$13 88	$9 76	$25 64
Ford	750 00	2,200 00	$300 00	3,250 00				16 15	20 04	52 19	13 00	20 04	33 04	15 11	20 04	35 15
Forestville	450 00	180 00		630 00												
†Fowler																
Fowlerville	800 00	2,400 00	200 00	3,400 00	23 47	3 88	27 35	14 42	3 88	18 30	15 81	3 88	19 69	19 41	3 88	23 29
†Frankenmuth																
Frankfort	1,80	5,60	400 00	6,570 00	33 16	2 86	36 02	11 07	2 86	13 93	8 64	2 86	11 50	11 62	2 86	14 48
†Fraser																
Freeport	675 00	1,395 00		2,070 00	23 00	3 84	26 84	11 25	3 84	15 09	8 57	3 84	12 41	13 52	3 84	17 36
Fremont	800 00	4,086 40		4,885 40	19 71	3 76	13 47	5 31	3 76	9 07	11 47	3 76	15 23	12 06	3 76	15 82
Fruitport	700 00	800 00		1,500 00	50 00	4 24	54 24	10 60	4 24	14 84	8 65	4 24	12 89	15 15	4 24	19 39
Gagetown	1,325 00			1,325 00	22 50	2 68	25 18	12 60	2 68	15 28	9 37	2 68	12 05	14 50	2 68	17 18
Gaines	650 00	700 00		1,350 00	34 21	8 64	42 85	7 60	8 64	16 24	6 60	8 64	15 24	11 44	8 64	20 08
Galesburg	750 00	1,836 00	63 00	2,649 00	30 96	4 42	35 38	12 61	4 42	17 03	12 17	4 42	16 59	18 52	4 42	22 94
Galien	675 00	1,170 00		1,845 00	18 59	4 65	23 24	16 80	4 65	21 45	7 98	4 65	12 63	13 27	4 65	17 92
†Garden																
Gaylord	1,100 00	4,088 31		5,188 31	47 86	27 74	75 60	13 22	27 74	40 96	10 13	27 74	37 87	16 03	27 74	43 77
a Glenwood																
Gobleville	620 00	1,472 52		2,092 52	28 44	7 45	35 89	11 46	7 45	18 91	9 40	7 45	16 85	12 83	7 45	20 28
Grandville	840 00	1,850 00		2,690 00	21 42	7 46	28 88	12 58	7 46	20 04	7 20	7 46	14 66	11 69	7 46	19 15
Grant	550 00	630 00		1,180 00	42 96	3 91	46 87	8 28	3 91	12 19	7 91	3 91	11 82	13 02	3 91	16 93
Grass Lake	825 00	2,000 00	400 00	3,225 00	40 87	5 82	46 69	9 98	5 82	15 80	12 92	5 82	18 72	18 64	5 82	24 46
Grayling	1,000 00	3,800 00	400 00	5,200 00	37 50	4 94	42 44	13 33	4 94	18 27	7 55	4 94	12 49	13 50	4 94	18 44
Grosse Pointe	550 00	1,830 00		2,380 00												
†Grosse Pointe Farms																
†Grosse Pointe Park																
Hamtramck	1,000 00	85	65 40	81 65				23 14	15 65	38 79	10 15	15 65	25 80	13 30	15 65	28 95
Hanover	600 00	1,128 00		1,725 00	20 00	5 03	25 03	12 50	5 03	17 53	10 71	5 03	15 74	14 03	5 03	19 05
Harbor Beach	850 00	3,350 00	50 00	4,250 00	41 87	22 85	64 72	13 41	22 85	36 26	8 52	22 85	31 37	14 80	22 85	37 65
Harbor Springs	1,100 00	4,701 00	450 00	6,251 00	25 79	7 21	33 00	13 26	7 21	20 47	19 11	7 21	26 32	17 65	7 21	24 86
Harietta	540 00	675 00		1,215 00	21 60	4 40	26 00	10 28	4 40	14 68	5 16	4 40	9 56	10 04	4 40	14 44
Hart	1,200 00	5,137 50	237 50	6,575 00	26 83	10 96	37 79	17 72	10 96	28 68	10 59	10 96	21 55	16 43	10 96	27 39

Hartford	650 00	2,874 63	275 00	2,799 63	....	....	....	....	....	....	....	....	....	12 66	12 96	25 62
Hersey	570 00	1,140 00	2 80	1,712 80	36 10	3 67	39 77	8 72	3 67	12 39	8 63	3 67	12 30	14 51	3 67	18 18
Hesperia	585 00	1,305 00	....	1,890 00	25 14	5 31	30 45	8 47	5 31	13 78	11 83	5 31	17 14	14 32	5 31	19 63
Highland Park	1,100 00	3,257 50	30 00	4,387 50	....	....	....	16 02	17 50	33 52	12 74	17 50	30 24	20 50	17 50	38 00
Hillman	....	....	....	....	....	....	....	....	....	....	....	....	....	....	....	....
Holly	1,000 00	3,200 00	....	4,200 00	29 19	3 71	32 90	10 30	3 71	14 01	8 79	3 71	12 50	13 79	3 71	17 50
Homer	900 00	2,925 00	400 00	4,225 00	32 46	6 40	38 86	7 03	6 40	13 43	15 72	6 40	22 12	16 63	6 40	23 03
Houghton	1,700 00	25,425 00	680 50	27,805 50	45 90	16 15	62 05	20 91	16 15	37 09	16 72	16 15	32 87	21 78	16 15	37 93
Howard City	900 00	3,444 50	403 75	4,748 25	32 94	4 71	37 65	19 15	4 71	23 86	12 14	4 71	16 85	18 12	4 71	22 83
Howell	1,400 00	5,887 20	480 00	7,767 20	25 35	1 36	26 71	15 49	1 36	16 85	9 08	1 36	10 44	13 36	1 36	14 72
Hubbardston	585 00	720 00	....	1,305 00	24 89	4 84	29 73	17 42	4 84	22 26	10 58	4 84	15 42	16 73	4 84	21 57
¶Hubbell	....	....	....	....	....	....	....	....	....	....	....	....	....	....	....	....
Imlay City	1,000 00	2,775 00	....	3,775 00	25 98	11 32	37 30	6 63	11 32	17 95	12 67	11 32	23 99	13 24	11 32	24 56
Iron River	1,500 00	5,650 00	200 00	7,350 00	41 66	18 08	59 74	25 58	18 08	43 66	15 09	18 08	33 17	21 87	18 08	39 95
Ithaca	948 04	4,675 00	300 00	5,923 04	24 71	8 95	33 66	10 27	8 95	19 22	11 68	8 95	20 63	14 04	8 95	22 99
Jerome	652 50	....	....	652 50	....	....	....	19 73	9 93	29 66	5 33	9 93	15 26	11 45	9 93	21 38
Jonesville	850 00	2,910 00	750 00	4,510 00	43 04	5 76	48 80	10 27	5 76	16 03	11 45	5 76	17 21	16 40	5 76	22 16
Kalkaska	500 00	4,105 00	....	4,605 00	32 68	4 98	37 66	13 29	4 98	18 27	13 67	4 98	18 65	16 56	4 98	21 54
†Kinde	....	....	....	....	....	....	....	....	....	....	....	....	....	....	....	....
Kingsley	600 00	720 00	160 00	1,480 00	34 66	9 47	44 13	6 15	9 47	15 62	8 35	9 47	17 82	10 07	9 47	19 54
Kingston	575 00	650 00	....	1,225 00	12 69	7 51	20 20	9 33	7 51	16 84	7 52	7 51	15 03	9 98	7 51	17 49
Laingsburg	675 00	2,275 00	....	2,950 00	55 27	5 14	60 41	14 78	5 14	19 92	11 48	5 14	16 62	24 38	5 14	29 52
Lake Ann	460 00	258 40	....	718 40	....	....	....	15 86	2 80	18 66	6 01	2 80	8 81	9 98	2 80	12 78
Lake City	600 00	2,205 00	....	2,805 00	20 00	6 04	26 04	12 57	6 04	18 61	9 28	6 04	15 32	11 43	6 04	17 47
Lake Linden	1,805 00	14,539 25	1,251 75	17,596 00	35 19	14 11	49 30	32 26	14 11	46 37	18 47	14 11	32 58	25 67	14 11	39 78
Lake Odessa	900 00	3,324 10	....	4,224 10	23 61	5 13	28 74	12 33	5 13	17 46	10 79	5 13	15 92	14 12	5 13	19 25
Lakeview	1,000 00	2,655 25	....	3,655 25	21 62	4 06	25 68	12 54	4 06	16 60	11 50	4 06	15 56	15 35	4 06	19 43
L'Anse	1,200 00	6,338 75	....	7,538 95	66 17	8 38	74 55	19 58	8 38	27 96	11 02	8 38	19 40	18 43	8 38	26 82
§Laurium	....	....	....	....	....	....	....	....	....	....	....	....	....	....	....	....
Lawrence	900 00	2,250 00	270 00	3,420 00	23 71	11 71	35 42	15 48	11 71	27 19	9 86	11 71	21 57	17 38	11 71	29 09
Lawton	850 00	2,101 00	....	2,951 00	20 00	7 66	27 66	8 60	7 66	16 26	6 35	7 66	14 01	11 22	7 66	18 88
Leonard	500 00	640 00	....	1,140 00	16 12	3 24	19 36	11 03	3 24	14 27	8 20	3 24	11 44	50 00	3 24	14 74
Le Roy	540 00	1,080 00	....	1,620 00	23 33	8 65	31 98	10 98	8 65	19 63	10 77	8 65	19 42	12 65	8 65	21 30
Leslie	1,100 00	2,050 00	....	3,150 00	19 76	4 63	24 39	10 58	4 63	15 15	9 70	4 63	14 33	12 91	4 63	17 54
Lexington	700 00	1,650 00	....	2,350 00	28 21	5 96	34 17	10 97	5 96	16 93	19 97	5 96	25 93	19 58	5 96	25 54
†Lincoln	....	....	....	....	....	....	....	....	....	....	....	....	....	....	....	....
Linden	1,000 00	1,050 00	....	2,050 00	21 26	7 67	28 93	8 01	7 67	15 68	20 90	7 67	28 57	18 98	7 67	26 65
Lisbon	630 00	360 00	....	990 00	....	....	....	22 50	6 25	28 75	10 90	6 25	17 15	16 22	6 25	22 47
Litchfield	1,160 09	1,119 00	....	2,279 00	24 00	3 76	27 76	10 94	3 76	14 70	10 00	3 76	13 76	14 51	3 76	18 27
Lowell	1,000 00	4,670 00	....	5,670 00	27 71	11 10	38 81	14 05	11 10	25 15	23 45	11 10	34 55	21 39	11 10	32 49

¶Report included in Lake Linden.
§Report included in Calumet.
†Not legally graded.
a Report included in Wyandotte.

TABLE XIX.—Continued.

Incorporated villages.	Amount paid superintendent.	Amount paid regular teachers.	Amount paid special teachers.	Total amount paid for instruction.	Cost of education per capita in— High school. Instruction.	High school. Incidentals.	High school. Total.	Grammar department. Instruction.	Grammar department. Incidentals.	Grammar department. Total.	Primary department. Instruction.	Primary department. Incidentals.	Primary department. Total.	Whole school. Instruction.	Whole school. Incidentals.	Whole school. Total.
Luther	$650 00	$1,390 25		$2,040 25	$25 12	$5 18	$30 30	$13 28	$5 18	$18 46	$8 18	$5 18	$13 36	$12 14	$5 18	$17 52
Lyons	810 00	1,465 00		2,275 00	29 44	3 92	33 36	14 12	3 92	18 04	8 55	3 92	12 47	15 16	3 92	19 08
Mackinaw City	675 00	1,200 00		1,875 00	33 75	2 35	36 10	9 37	2 35	11 72	5 69	2 35	8 04	10 47	2 35	12 82
Mancelona	1,150 00	5,310 00		6,460 00	25 04	92	25 96	13 74	92	14 66	13 30	92	14 22	15 56	92	16 48
Manchester	1,000 00	3,105 00	$500 00	4,605 00	27 92	4 23	32 15	13 04	4 23	17 27	11 29	4 23	15 52	17 71	4 23	21 94
Manton	800 00	2,520 00	405 00	3,725 00	30 43	6 96	37 39	9 92	6 96	16 88	7 05	6 96	14 01	11 60	6 96	18 56
Maple Rapids	750 00	1,150 00		1,900 00	19 96	4 29	24 25	13 56	4 29	17 85	9 00	4 29	13 29	14 82	4 29	19 11
Marcellus	845 00	2,610 00		3,455 00	25 52	6 61	32 18	13 61	6 61	20 22	11 05	6 61	17 66	16 29	6 61	22 90
Marion	888 82	2,050 00		2,938 82	34 18	7 18	41 36	22 50	7 18	29 68	8 64	7 18	15 82	12 72	7 18	19 90
†Marlborough																
Marlette	850 00	3,725 00		4,575 00	23 62	3 44	27 06	10 45	3 44	13 89	12 89	3 44	16 33	11 61	3 44	15 05
†Maybee																
Mayville	700 00	2,365 00		3,065 00	30 08	3 77	33 85	9 30	3 77	13 07	8 98	3 77	12 75	15 96	3 77	19 73
McBride	650 00	563 75		1,213 75	23 21	8 52	31 73	7 69	8 52	16 21	7 24	8 52	15 73	10 37	8 52	18 89
Mecosta	650 00	750 00		1,400 00	13 82	2 41	16 23	7 27	2 41	9 68	10 60	2 41	13 01	10 37	2 41	12 78
†Melvin																
Memphis	700 00	1,577 00		2,277 00	12 94	5 83	18 77	16 88	5 83	22 71	8 33	5 83	14 16	12 16	5 82	17 99
Mendon	850 00	2,097 00		2,947 00	25 92	9 93	35 85	13 47	9 93	23 40	8 14	9 93	18 07	15 01	9 93	24 94
†Merrill																
Mesick	540 00	945 00		1,485 00	24 54	16 60	41 14	10 50	16 60	27 10	6 70	16 60	23 30	10 17	16 60	26 77
Metamora	750 00	1,200 00		1,950 00	35 11	5 80	40 91	17 26	5 80	23 06	15 59	5 80	21 39	22 41	5 80	28 21
Middleville	950 00	2,350 00		3,300 00	25 90	10 67	36 57	18 34	10 67	29 01	13 95	10 67	24 62	18 75	10 67	29 42
†Mikado																
Milan	950 00	2,700 00		3,650 00	30 08	5 72	35 80	9 90	5 72	15 62	6 01	5 72	11 73	11 62	5 72	17 34
Milford	1,000 00	680 00	450 00	2,130 00	28 43	5 43	33 86	5 40	5 43	10 83	3 33	5 43	8 76	10 19	5 43	15 62
Millersburg	650 00	1,530 00		2,180 00										10 53	4 57	15 10
Millington	850 00	1,450 00		2,300 00	16 25	6 70	22 95	10 64	6 70	17 34	7 67	6 70	14 37	11 66	6 70	18 36
Minden	600 00	585 00		1,185 00	15 78	4 77	20 56	7 68	4 77	12 45	4 14	4 77	8 91	8 23	4 77	13 00
Montague	950 00	2,250 00	100 00	3,300 00	30 10	12 34	42 44	12 46	12 34	24 40	12 58	12 34	24 92	16 92	12 34	29 26
Montrose																
Morenci	1,167 00	2,386 00		3,553 00	23 68	3 34	27 02	7 48	3 34	10 82	7 64	3 34	10 98	11 72	3 34	15 06

	1	2	3	4	5	6	7	8	9	10	11	12	13	14	15	16
Morley	450 00	639 00	..	1,089 00	11 14	2 66	13 80	12 77	2 66	15 43	8 42	2 66	11 08	10 46	2 66	13 12
Morrice	750 00	1,050 00	100 00	1,900 00	52 22	8 92	61 14	11 63	8 92	20 55	13 95	8 92	22 87	18 44	8 92	27 38
Mt. Morris	800 00	1,225 00	..	2,025 00	30 62	7 71	38 33	6 25	7 71	13 96	15 38	7 71	23 09	15 57	7 71	23 28
Muir	540 00	900 00	..	1,440 00	49 09	8 94	58 03	12 11	8 94	21 05	10 64	8 94	19 58	15 65	8 94	24 59
†Mulliken	..	..	..	..	..	..	..	..	..	..	..	..	..	..	..	..
Munising	1,300 00	9,270 00	500 00	11,070 00	31 70	76 37	108 07	21 01	76 37	97 38	14 79	76 37	91 16	18 8	76 37	15 22
Nashville	900 00	4,625 00	27 00	5,552 00	52 50	8 06	60 56	14 06	8 06	22 12	10 02	8 06	18 08	21 10	8 06	29 16
†Naubinway	..	..	..	..	..	..	..	..	..	..	..	..	..	..	..	..
Newaygo	90 00	8,	140 00	4,545 00	32 60	4 41	87	7 60	4 47	12 07	13 08	4 47	35	14 07	4 47	18 54
New Baltimore	80 00	2,90 00	..	3,240 00	29 20	1 90	31 10	11 66	1 90	13 56	13 30	1 90	15 20	17 19	1 90	19 09
Newberry	..	..	..	..	..	..	..	..	..	..	..	..	..	..	..	..
†New Boston	..	..	..	..	..	..	..	..	..	..	..	..	..	..	..	..
New Buffalo	675 00	1,080 00	..	1,755 00	30 68	4 83	35 51	12 42	4 83	27 25	7 65	4 83	12 48	12 90	4 83	17 73
New Haven	562 50	720 00	..	1,282 50	23 12	4 00	32 12	6 86	4 00	10 86	7 87	4 00	11 87	10 77	4 00	14 77
North Adams	665 81	1,423 20	..	2,089 01	19 51	15 82	35 33	18 26	15 82	34 08	10 07	15 82	25 89	16 57	15 82	32 39
North Branch	900 00	1,900 00	..	2,800 00	20 37	1 04	21 41	13 53	1 04	14 51	8 61	1 04	9 65	13 70	1 04	14 74
Northport	675 00	1,520 00	..	2,195 00	36 38	2 32	38 70	7 93	2 32	10 25	8 60	2 32	10 92	10 90	2 32	13 22
Northville	1,100 00	4,834 65	250 00	6,184 65	48 14	3 82	51 96	15 76	3 82	19 58	11 27	3 82	15 09	18 94	3 82	22 76
Oakley	540 00	225 00	..	765 00	..	..	..	23 47	1 92	25 39	5 92	1 92	7 84	12 54	1 92	14 48
Olivet	900 00	2,235 25	150 00	3,285 25	30 93	16 37	47 30	12 00	16 37	28 37	14 80	16 37	31 17	18 88	16 37	35 25
Onekama	540 00	655 00	..	1,195 00	..	..	..	..	..	..	..	..	..	..	..	..
Ontonagon	1,500 00	9,475 00	..	11,675 00	39 72	19 60	59 32	14 42	19 60	34 02	27 60	19 60	47 20	23 80	19 60	43 40
Orion	750 00	1,775 00	..	2,525 00	34 34	17 41	51 75	13 19	17 41	30 60	12 65	17 41	30 06	17 51	17 41	34 92
Ortonville	675 00	650 00	..	1,325 00	22 50	3 41	25 91	11 26	3 41	14 67	8 10	3 41	11 51	13 52	3 41	16 93
Oscoda	792 00	1,96 00	..	2,768 00	28 54	2 79	31 33	14 06	2 79	16 85	7 29	2 79	10 08	12 19	2 79	14 98
Otisville	650 00	90 00	..	1,250 00	14 13	15 57	29 70	12 06	15 57	27 63	7 77	15 57	23 34	11 25	15 57	26 82
Otsego	1,250 00	5,63 53	132 00	6,995 53	27 69	5 05	32 74	8 55	5 05	13 60	9 15	5 05	14 20	12 29	5 05	17 34
Otter Lake	450 00	35 00	..	765 00	..	..	..	28 12	1 25	29 37	7 16	1 25	8 41	12 75	1 25	14 00
Ovid	900 00	3,30 00	120 00	4,370 00	17 90	11 48	29 38	15 30	11 48	26 78	17 16	11 48	28 64	16 74	11 48	28 22
†Owendale	..	..	..	..	..	..	..	..	..	..	..	..	..	..	..	..
Oxford	1,000 00	4,255 00	..	5,255 00	98 49	5 58	104 07	80	5 58	6 38	88	5 58	6 46	25 02	5 58	30 60
Parma	700 00	1,550 00	180 00	2,430 00	24 57	5 55	30 12	17 88	5 55	23 43	10 21	5 55	15 76	15 38	5 55	20 93
Paw Paw	1,200 00	3,825 00	522 50	5,547 50	25 64	15 45	41 09	12 33	15 45	27 78	13 42	15 45	28 87	17 50	15 45	32 95
†Peck	..	..	..	..	..	..	..	..	..	..	..	..	..	..	..	..
Pellston	630 00	1,685 00	..	2,315 00	42 00	53	42 53	11 95	53	12 48	5 11	53	5 64	8 93	53	9 46
Pentwater	900 00	500 00	..	1,400 00	26 25	6 10	32 35	2 15	6 10	8 25	1 54	6 10	7 64	6 08	6 10	12 18
†Perrinton	..	..	..	..	..	..	..	..	..	..	..	..	..	..	..	..
Perry	800 00	1,750 00	..	2,550 00	27 77	8 15	35 92	13 97	8 15	22 12	14 40	8 15	22 55	16 56	8 15	24 71
Petersburg	540 00	1,683 00	..	2,223 00	24 00	2 81	26 81	8 15	2 81	10 96	11 18	2 81	13 99	12 70	2 81	15 51
Pewamo	540 00	648 00	..	1,188 00	15 77	5 64	21 41	12 27	5 64	17 91	19 69	5 64	25 33	15 41	5 64	21 05
Pierson	405 00	315 00	..	720 00	..	..	..	10 94	3 73	14 67	8 28	3 73	12 01	9 60	3 73	13 33
Pigeon	750 00	1,400 00	..	2,150 00	20 83	14 94	35 77	5 03	14 94	19 97	4 60	14 94	19 54	6 57	14 94	21 51
Pinckney	1,350 00	1,050 00	..	2,400 00	46 96	13 01	59 97	15 71	13 01	28 72	24 84	13 01	37 85	30 29	13 01	43 30
Pinconning	600 00	2,050 00	..	2,650 00	16 16	1 99	18 15	16 15	1 99	18 14	9 43	1 99	11 42	13 18	1 99	15 17

†Not legally graded

TABLE XIX.—Continued.

Incorporated villages.	Amount paid superintendent.	Amount paid regular teachers.	Amount paid special teachers.	Total amount paid for instruction.	Cost of education per capita in— High school. Instruction.	High school. Incidentals.	High school. Total.	Grammar department. Instruction.	Grammar department. Incidentals.	Grammar department. Total.	Primary department. Instruction.	Primary department. Incidentals.	Primary department. Total.	Whole school. Instruction.	Whole school. Incidentals.	Whole school. Total.
Plainwell	$1,150 00	$3,182 50	$135 00	$4,467 50	$28 96	$5 35	$40 34	$13 42	$5 35	$10 70	$9 04	$5 35	$14 39	$15 84	$5 35	$21 19
Plymouth	1,150 00	4,325 00	250 00	5,725 00	28 32	6 40	34 72	12 29	6 40	18 69	9 87	6 40	16 27	14 42	6 40	20 82
Port Austin	750 00	2,047 50	....	2,797 50	52 08	7 51	59 59	24 55	7 51	32 06	9 06	7 51	16 57	16 99	7 51	24 50
Port Hope	600 00	700 00	....	1,300 00	31 57	10 42	41 99	17 50	10 42	27 92	16 66	10 42	27 08	21 66	10 42	32 08
Portland	950 00	4,780 00	....	5,730 00	38 40	8 19	46 59	11 47	8 19	19 66	9 72	8 19	17 91	16 00	8 19	24 19
Port Sanilac	495 00	585 00	....	1,080 00	22 05	2 67	24 72	10 50	2 67	13 17	7 94	2 67	10 61	12 55	2 67	15 22
†Posen																
Potterville	540 00	1,080 00	....	1,620 00	19 28	60	19 88	13 50	60	14 10	12 00	60	12 60	14 33	60	14 93
Quincy	1,050 00	2,732 50	299 00	4,081 50	18 31	6 35	24 66	15 33	6 35	21 68	13 25	6 35	19 60	15 75	6 35	22 10
Reading	1,000 00	2,414 50	....	3,414 50	22 46	9 51	31 97	10 37	9 51	19 88	11 64	9 51	21 15	15 08	9 51	24 59
†Redford																
§Red Jacket																
Reed City	1,[illegible]0	[illegible]0	504 00	7,159 00	33 95	6 18	30 13	14 95	6 18	21 13	14 41	6 18	30 59	18 07	6 18	24 25
†Reese																
Richland	610 00	1,[illegible]0	....	1,654 00	26 94	7 60	34 54	11 40	7 60	19 00	22 80	7 60	30 40	20 41	7 60	28 01
b Richmond	950 00	2,825 00	....	3,775 00	57 75	6 17	63 92	9 51	6 17	15 68	14 08	6 17	20 25	18 14	6 17	24 31
River Rouge	1,100 00	9,325 00	1,000 00	11,425 00	50 91	9 85	60 76	19 54	9 85	29 39	10 49	9 85	20 34	13 78	9 85	23 63
Rochester	1,000 00	2,375 00	....	3,375 00	23 28	3 87	27 15	9 89	3 87	13 76	6 38	3 87	10 25	12 14	3 87	16 02
Rockford	800 00	1,775 00	....	2,575 00	29 26	8 10	37 36	12 06	8 10	20 16	2 12	8 10	17 22	14 88	8 10	22 98
Rogers	400 00	1,500 00	....	1,900 00	50 00	4 57	54 57	13 92	4 57	18 49	9 30	4 57	13 87	13 10	4 57	17 67
Romeo	1,350 00	3,325 00	56 25	5,031 25	26 52	7 91	34 43	15 93	7 91	23 84	12 13	7 91	20 04	17 25	7 91	25 16
Roscommon	700 00	1,045 00	....	1,745 00	36 42	6 29	42 71	16 62	6 29	22 91	11 39	6 29	17 68	20 52	6 29	26 81
Royal Oak	750 00	2,200 00	....	2,950 00	67 34	8 84	76 18	6 25	8 84	15 09	9 63	8 84	18 47	15 69	8 84	24 53
St. Charles	1,000 00	3,669 00	....	4,669 00	52 93	6 58	59 51	13 00	6 58	19 67	7 87	6 58	14 45	12 16	6 58	18 74
†St. Clair Heights																
Saline	1,00	[illegible]0	[illegible] 75	3,708 75	28 70	5 55	36 10	15 42	5 55	20 97	19 78	5 55	25 33	20 73	5 55	26 28
Sand Lake																
Saranac	750 00	2,290 00	....	3,040 00	29 61	3 81	33 42	12 85	3 81	16 66	9 24	3 82	13 06	14 48	3 81	18 29
Saugatuck	900 00	630 00	585 00	2,115 00	19 56	11 77	31 33	20 89	11 77	32 66	7 32	11 77	19 09	13 21	11 77	26 40
Schoolcraft	1,000 00	2,403 00	....	3,403 00	43 65	6 80	50 44	13 23	6 80	20 03	11 26	6 80	18 06	19 67	6 80	26 47

Sebewaing	800 00	2,050 00		2,850 00	44 64	11 74	56 38	4 93	11 74	16 67	9 75	11 74	21 49	12 28	11 74	24 02
Shelby	950 00	3,467 50		4,417 50	19 59	4 70	24 29	17 07	4 70	21 77	10 13	4 70	14 38	14 82	4 70	19 52
Shepherd	1,105 00	1,710 00		2,815 00	44 20	13 35	57 55	13 09	13 35	26 44	9 80	15 35	25 15	15 55	15 35	30 90
Sheridan	630 00	990 00		1,620 00	22 50	2 92	25 42	8 81	2 92	11 73	4 82	2 92	7 74	9 41	2 92	12 33
Sherman	600 00	1,080 00		1,680 00	21 81	3 91	25 72	14 54	3 91	18 45	7 32	3 91	11 23	11 83	3 91	15 74
Sherwood	495 00	1,080 00		1,575 00	22 50	2 65	25 15	23 47	2 65	26 12	7 39	2 65	10 04	13 34	2 65	15 99
†Sibley																
South Frankfort	700 00	1,400 00	350 00	2,450 00	18 18	40 83	59 01	20 00	40 83	60 83	10 24	40 83	51 07	14 67	40 83	55 50
South Lyon	725 00	1,520 00		2,245 00	18 00	5 68	23 68	10 70	5 68	16 38	10 92	5 68	16 60	13 20	5 68	18 88
Sparta	900 00	2,880 00	375 00	4,155 00	23 27	9 39	32 66	12 99	9 39	22 38	12 27	9 39	21 66	14 89	9 39	24 28
Spring Lake	760 00	1,520 00		2,280 00	51 96	8 17	60 13	17 82	8 17	25 99	9 78	8 17	17 95	16 28	8 17	24 45
Springport	800 00	1,650 00		2,450 00	24 27	4 28	28 55	7 83	4 28	12 11	14 74	4 28	19 02	17 80	4 28	22 08
Stambaugh	900 00	6,479 50	715 00	8,094 50	48 39	18 27	66 66	22 17	18 27	40 44	13 72	18 27	31 99	18 43	18 27	36 70
Stanwood																
†Stephenson																
Stevensville	560 00	1,360 00		1,920 00	41 90	3 70	45 60	8 65	3 70	12 35	9 47	3 70	13 17	14 33	3 70	18 03
Stockbridge	800 00	1,600 00		2,400 00	28 77	10 11	38 88	6 66	10 11	16 77	14 46	10 11	24 57	14 54	10 11	24 65
Sunfield	570 00	1,150 00		1,770 00	21 02	5 21	26 23	13 33	5 21	18 54	8 15	5 21	13 36	13 23	5 21	18 44
Sutton's Bay	540 00	675 00		1,215 00	27 00	5 32	32 32	12 85	5 32	18 17	12 60	5 32	17 92	16 64	5 32	21 96
Tecumseh	821 43	6,177 51	400 00	7,398 94	20 25	5 14	25 39	15 25	5 14	20 39	15 26	5 14	20 40	16 79	5 14	21 93
Tekonsha	686 11	1,520 00		2,206 11	28 28	6 71	34 99	13 90	6 71	20 61	10 78	6 71	17 49	15 89	6 71	22 60
Thompsonville	675 00	2,040 00		2,715 00	37 50	7 95	45 45	14 14	7 95	22 09	6 96	7 95	14 91	11 60	7 95	19 55
Three Oaks	1,000 00	2,880 00	135 00	4,015 00	33 36	23 04	56 40	11 33	23 04	34 37	9 54	23 04	32 58	14 70	23 04	37 74
Trenton	850 00	2,540 00		3,390 00	50 00	8 93	58 93	9 09	8 93	18 02	8 58	8 93	17 51	11 04	8 93	19 97
Tustin	540 00	990 00		1,530 00	25 71	5 79	21 50	9 23	5 79	15 02	8 63	5 79	14 42	11 50	5 79	17 29
Twining	700 00	1,950 00		2,650 00	58 33	7 21	65 54	10 00	7 21	17 21	7 14	7 21	14 36	19 18	7 21	26 39
†Ubly																
Union City	1,100 00	2,650 00		3,750 00	10 47	6 16	16 65	14 49	6 16	20 65	12 12	6 16	18 28	12 50	6 16	18 66
Unionville	650 00	1,070 00		1,720 00	18 54	5 19	23 73	9 62	5 19	14 81	8 76	5 19	13 95	11 48	5 19	16 67
Utica	900 00	1,550 00		2,450 00	49 31	13 39	62 70	12 80	13 39	26 19	9 92	13 39	23 31	24 01	13 39	37 40
Vandalia	630 00	1,000 00		1,630 00	29 16	4 56	33 72	11 25	4 56	15 81	8 07	4 56	12 63	14 17	4 56	18 73
Vanderbilt	600 00	1,200 00		1,800 00	18 51	4 84	23 35	8 00	4 84	12 84	7 14	4 84	11 98	11 25	4 84	16 09
Vassar	1,100 00	4,210 00	400 00	5,710 00	31 01	8 31	39 42	12 34	8 31	20 65	11 83	8 31	20 14	15 80	8 31	24 11
Vermontville	800 00	2,418 50		3,218 50	53 63	4 60	58 23	1 13	4 60	5 73	1 03	4 60	5 63	20 50	4 60	25 10
Vernon	800 00	1,050 00	100 00	1,950 00	36 00	9 57	45 57	18 75	9 57	28 32	16 40	9 57	25 97	22 94	9 57	32 51
Vicksburg	900 00	2,898 00	315 00	4,113 00	30 47	9 09	39 56	9 36	9 09	18 45	23 08	9 09	32 17	15 91	9 09	25 80
Wakefield	1,000 00	8,025 00		9,025 00	143 58	43 57	187 15	18 53	43 57	62 10	13 98	43 57	57 55	18 30	43 57	61 87
W[illegible]	1,253 00	226 38		1,479 38	27 38	37 04	64 42	8 72	37 04	45 76	10 50	37 04	47 54	15 57	37 04	52 61
	900 00	2,250 00		3,750 00	28 43	7 50	35 93	10 32	7 50	17 82	9 01	7 50	16 53	13 30	7 50	20 80

ded.
1 in Calumet.
listrict united with this.

TABLE XIX.—Concluded.

Incorporated villages.	Amount paid superintendent.	Amount paid regular teachers.	Amount paid special teachers.	Total amount paid for instruction.	Cost of education per capita in—											
					High school.			Grammar department.			Primary department.			Whole school.		
					Instruction.	Incidentals.	Total.	Instruction.	Incidentals.	Total.	Instruction.	Incidentals.	Total.	Instruction.	Incidentals.	Total.
Wayland	$720 00	$1,350 00	....	$2,070 00	$11 93	$3 56	$15 48	$6 89	$3 56	$10 45	$6 73	$3 56	$10 29	$8 88	$3 56	$12 44
Wayne	1,010 00	3,891 00	$150 00	5,051 00	26 12	4 45	30 57	14 81	4 45	19 26	11 67	4 45	16 12	17 03	4 45	21 48
Webberville	540 00	634 00	....	1,174 00	18 00	4 91	22 91	8 53	4 91	13 44	9 41	4 91	14 32	11 62	4 91	16 53
†Westphalia	....	....	....	....	....	....	....	....	....	....	....	....	....	....	....	....
White Cloud	630 00	1,422 00	50 00	2,102 00	23 41	3 53	26 94	8 57	3 53	12 10	5 78	3 53	9 31	9 64	3 53	13 17
Whitehall	900 00	3,47 50	114 00	4,481 50	20 18	9 30	29 48	13 22	9 30	22 52	12 08	9 30	21 38	14 31	9 30	23 61
White Pigeon	1,000 00	1,9[illegible] [illegible]5	....	2,936 25	24 21	5 67	29 88	13 99	5 67	19 66	10 61	5 67	16 28	16 40	5 67	22 07
Williamston	1,600 00	300 00	200 00	4,830 00	25 52	13 42	38 94	10 70	13 42	24 12	13 50	13 42	26 92	15 73	13 42	29 15
Wolverine	712 50	290 00	700 00	2,809 50	42 41	3 37	45 78	11 53	3 37	14 90	7 54	3 37	10 91	13 63	3 37	17 00
Woodland	540 00	20 00	....	1,260 00	15 85	6 84	22 69	20 00	6 84	26 84	10 28	6 84	17 12	14 48	6 84	21 32
‡Woodmere	....	....	....	....	....	....	....	....	....	....	....	....	....	....	....	....

†Not legally graded.
‡Included in Detroit.

TABLE XX.

Special report of the superintendents of schools.

Incorporated cities.	No. of teachers employed in all the schools under your supervision, including superintendent and special teachers.	No. of special teachers employed.	No. of instructors in manual training.	No. of instructors in penmanship.	No. of instructors in drawing.	No. of instructors in music.	No. of instructors in kindergarten.	No. of instructors in physical culture.	No. of instructors in commercial course.	No. of instructors in domestic science.	How many of your teachers of kindergarten, music and drawing are holders of certificates according to Act 24 of 1905?	How many other special teachers are holders of certificates other than city certificates?	If not, how many have been granted city certificates?	Are all your regular teachers holders of legal certificates of qualification?	No. holding certificates granted by State University under provisions of section 4804 of compiled laws.	No. holding college certificates granted according to section 4805 of compiled laws.	No. holding certificates granted upon examination by the State Board or indorsed by it.	No. holding State normal College certificate.	No. holding central normal school certificates.	No. holding northern normal school certificates.	No. holding western normal school certificates.	No. holding city certificates of first grade.	No. holding city certificates of second grade.	No. holding city certificates of third grade.	No. holding county certificates.	Portion of superintendent's time given to supervision.
Adrian	51	5	1	....	1	1	....	1	....	1	2	2	1	Yes	6	7	....	11	....	....	....	3	2	11	6	All
Albion	31	2	....	....	1	1	1	....	....	....	2	....	....	Yes	1	4	1	12	2	....	2	1	1	2	3	5-6
Allegan	22	2	....	....	.5	.5	....	....	1	....	1	....	....	Yes	1	1	....	6	1	....	3	....	....	....	9	1-2
Alma	19	2	....	....	.5	.5	1	....	....	....	1	....	....	Yes	....	4	....	5	3	....	....	....	....	....	6	3-4
Alpena	49	3	....	.5	.5	1	....	....	1	....	....	....	....	......	5	1	....	1	....	....	....	2	16	24	....	All
Ann Arbor	82	8	2	....	1	1	....	1	2	1	....	....	....	Yes	....	....	....	....	....	....	....	26	28	28	....	All
Au Gres	3	....	....	....	....	....	....	....	....	....	....	....	....	Yes	....	....	....	....	....	....	....	....	....	....	3	....
Au Sable	10	....	....	....	....	....	....	....	....	....	....	....	....	Yes	....	....	1	1	....	....	....	....	....	....	8	1-4
Bad Axe	14	2	....	....	.5	.5	1	....	....	....	....	....	....	Yes	1	....	....	6	....	....	....	....	....	....	6	3-5
Battle Creek	113	5	2	....	1	1	....	....	....	1	....	....	5	Yes	13	....	....	8	3	....	4	7	46	....	27	All
Bay City	204	15	2	....	1	1	6	....	4	1	8	....	....	Yes	16	....	....	6	3	....	....	150	[illegible]	18	3	All
Beaverton	6	....	....	....	....	....	....	....	....	....	....	....	....	Yes	....	1	....	....	1	....	....	....	....	....	4	....
Belding	21	4	....	.5	.5	.5	2	....	.5	....	....	....	....	Yes	1	....	2	8	3	1	....	1	2	....	3	1-2
Benton Harbor	46	1	....	.4	.3	.3	....	....	....	....	....	....	....	Yes	....	2	1	17	4	....	3	6	3	2	8	All
Bessemer	32	1	....	....	.5	.5	....	....	....	....	....	....	....	Yes	4	....	1	3	....	5	....	....	....	....	19	1-2
Big Rapids	28	1	....	....	.5	.5	....	....	....	....	....	....	1	Yes	3	....	1	1	....	....	....	2	5	10	5	7-8
Boyne City	30	....	....	....	....	....	....	....	....	....	....	....	....	Yes	....	....	1	6	6	....	....	....	....	....	17	5-7
Brown City	....	....	....	....	....	....	....	....	....	....	....	....	....	......	....	....	....	....	....	....	....	....	....	....	....	....
Cadillac	47	1	....	....	.5	.5	....	....	....	....	1	2	....	Yes	3	....	....	22	8	....	....	5	2	....	4	All
Charlevoix	20	2	....	....	.5	.5	....	....	1	....	1	1	....	Yes	2	2	....	6	4	....	....	....	1	....	3	All
Charlotte	28	3	1	....	.5	.5	....	....	1	....	3	....	....	Yes	3	....	....	14	1	....	....	....	4	3	....	4-5
Cheboygan	31	1	....	....	.5	.5	....	....	....	....	1	....	....	Yes	....	1	2	5	2	....	....	2	8	10	....	All
Clare	11	....	....	....	....	....	....	....	....	....	....	....	....	Yes	....	1	....	3	2	....	....	....	....	....	5	3-8
Coldwater	38	5	1	....	.5	.5	2	....	1	....	1	....	....	Yes	....	....	....	....	....	....	....	25	7	6	....	6-7
Coleman	9	....	....	....	....	....	....	....	....	....	....	....	....	Yes	....	....	....	....	2	....	....	....	....	....	7	2-9
unna	13	1	....	....	....	....	1	....	....	....	....	....	....	......	3	....	....	3	....	....	....	....	....	3	4	3-7
well	9	....	....	....	....	....	....	....	....	....	....	....	....	Yes	1	....	1	....	1	....	....	....	....	....	6	1-3
tal Falls	37	5	....	....	.5	.5	4	....	....	....	3	2	....	Yes	4	....	2	3	1	8	....	....	....	....	14	5-6
oit	1,348	8	1	....	2	1	4	....	....	....	130	2	5	Yes	34	....	14	186	6	....	....	109	....	....	38	All
agiac	30	4	....	....	.5	.5	2	....	1	....	2	....	2	Yes	3	1	....	4	3	....	2	1	10	2	....	5-6

TABLE XX.—Concluded.

Incorporated cities.	No. of teachers employed in all the schools under your supervision, including superintendent and special teachers.	No. of special teachers employed.	No. of instructors in manual training.	No. of instructors in penmanship.	No. of instructors in drawing.	No. of instructors in music.	No. of instructors in kindergarten.	No. of instructors in physical culture.	No. of instructors in commercial course.	No. of instructors in domestic science.	How many of your teachers of kindergarten, music and drawing are holders of certificates according to Act 24 of 1905?	How many other special teachers are holders of certificates other than city certificates?	If not, how many have been granted city certificates?	Are all your regular teachers holders of legal certificates of qualification?	No. holding certificates granted by State University under provisions of section 4804 of compiled laws.	No. holding college certificates granted according to section 4805 of compiled laws.	No. holding certificates granted upon examination by the State Board or indorsed by it.	No. holding state normal college certificates.	No. holding central normal school certificates.	No. holding northern normal school certificates.	No. holding western normal school certificates.	No. holding city certificates of first grade.	No. holding city certificates of second grade.	No. holding city certificates of third grade.	No. holding county certificates.	Portion of superintendent's time given to supervision.
East Lansing	3													Yes					3							
East Tawas	11	1					1				1			Yes		3		1	1						5	1-3
Eaton Rapids	15	2	1		.5	.5					2			Yes				5	2			1	4	1		
Escanaba	65	7			1	1	3		2		3		2	Yes	4		2	7	1	21		9	6	10		All
Flint	82	10	1	1	1	1	5		1		6	2	1	Yes	3	9		18	1			6	13	18	5	All
Gladstone	19	2					2				1		1	Yes				3	1	5		2	2	1	3	1-2
Gladwin	7													Yes			1	1	2						3	
Grand Haven	34	5			.5	.5	3		1		2	1	2	Yes	2			10				1	11		5	6-7
Grand Ledge, 9 fr.	16	1			.5	.5					1			Yes		1		8	3						3	1-2
Grand Ledge, 11 fr.																										
Grand Rapids	475	81	16		4	1	47		6	7	35		All	Yes								113	217	85		All
Greenville	24	3			1	1			1				3	Yes	1	1		5	1			3	2	6	2	3-5
Hancock	31	3				1			2					Yes	4		1	7	1	7		5			6	All
Harrison																										
Harrisville																										
Hastings	25	3	.5	.5	1	.5			1		1	2		Yes	2	1	1	9				1	3		5	6-7
Hillsdale	31	4	.5		.5	1	2				3		1	Yes	2	2		13					4	6		4-5
Holland	47	7			1	1	5				3	4		Yes		5		26	2				2	2	3	All
Hudson	18	1			.5	.5					1			Yes		1		4			1			7	4	1-2
Ionia	32	2		.5	.5	.5			.5				2	Yes	6		3	5				3	10	1	2	5-7
Iron Mountain	67	5	1		1	1			1	1			5	Yes	2	1		13		5		8	31	2		All
Ironwood	70	19	1		1	1	13			3	3		9	Yes	1			3	4	6	2	11	14	17		All
Ishpeming	73	11	2	1	1	1			1		11		2	Yes	4			5		22		15	10	16	1	All
Jackson	103	2			1	1	5						2	Yes								17	31	55		All
Kalamazoo	181	31	3		2	1	18		1	6	21	3	1	Yes	20	19		29	1	3	15	2	44	13	8	All
Lansing	99	8	.1		1	1	4			1	8			Yes	7	3		19	3			40	7		3	All
Lapeer	20	2			.5	.5			1		1		1	Yes	2			7					7		2	5-7
Ludington	47	4	1		1	1				1		1	2	Yes	3	2		17	1		1	1	6	12		All
Mackinac Island	4													Yes											4	1-6
Manistee	71	13	1	1	1	1	6		2	1	8	3	2	Yes			1	9	1			5	19	22	1	All
Manistique	30	5			.5	.5	3		1		1	2	2	Yes		4		8		4	1	2	5	1		7-8

Marine City	18				.5	.5					1			Yes			1	8							8	1-2
Marquette	64	11	2		1	1			1	2		1	10	Yes	5		2	1		38		4		2		All
Marshall	29	2	.5		.5	1					2			Yes	6	1		5	2		2	3	3	5		3-4
Mason	14	1			.5	.5					1			Yes		3		10								4-7
McBain	6	1					1				1			Yes			1								4	1-5
Menominee	64	11	1	1	.5	.5	6		1	1			11	Yes								12	18	34		All
Midland	17													Yes			1	3	4			1	2		6	2-3
Monroe	24	3	.5	1	.5	.5				.5	1	1	1	Yes	4	1		6					8			4-5
Mt. Clemens	34	5			.5	.5	3		1		1	1	3	Yes	6			13				2	3	2	3	All
Mt. Pleasant	20	4	1		1	1			1				1	Yes	4	3			10						2	5-7
Muskegon	130	22	9	1	4	1	10	3	2	2	1	2	33	Yes	6			4				12	43	31	1	All
Muskegon Heights	9	1					1							Yes				1	2						6	1-5
Negaunee	37	5			.5	.5	3		1		3			Yes	1	1		2		26		3				All
Niles	29	1			.5	.5					1			Yes	3	4		3	5			1		6	6	5-6
North Muskegon	2													Yes											2	....
Norway	32	1			.5	.5					1			Yes	4			6	1	7	2	1	5	5		2-3
Omer	4													Yes			1								3	1-20
Onaway	15										1			Yes		1		1	5						7	1-2
Owosso	49	4	1		1	1				1	2	2		Yes	5	2	1	15	3			1	16		2	6-7
Petoskey	32	3			1	1				1	1		2	Yes	1	3		3	6	2		3	5	5		All
Pontiac																										....
Port Huron	87	4			1	1			2			2		Yes	10	2	1	5	4			3	27	33		All
Rose City	5													Yes											5	1-12
Saginaw, E. S.	165	23	14	1	1	1			3	3			23	Yes								165				All
Saginaw, W. S.	83	5	1		1	1			1	1	2	4		Yes	6	9	2	7				40			4	All
St. Clair	15	2	1		.5	.5							2	Yes	1			3				3	3	3	1	4-7
St. Ignace	13	1					1				1			Yes	1		1	2		2		1		2	4	5-7
St. Johns	27	2	.5		.5	1					2			Yes		2	1	10	2			3	1		6	2-3
St. Joseph	34	6	.5		.5	1	4				2		4	Yes	2		1	10	4		2	3	5			All
St. Louis	17	3			.5	.5	1		1		3			Yes	2			3	4				4			1-17
Sandusky	6													Yes		2		2							2	1-8
Sault Ste. Marie	61	8	1	.5	.5	1	3		1	1	6		3	Yes	3	1	3	20	7		2	10	6			All
Scottville	7	1			.5	.5								Yes			1								6	1-6
South Haven	28	1			.5	.5					1			Yes	2	3	1	6				1	9	4		6-7
Standish	10													Yes				5							5	1-3
Stanton	10	3			1	1	1				1					1		5							3	1-3
Sturgis	18	2			.5	.5	1				2			Yes		2	2	4			2				6	4-7
Tawas City	8													Yes	1		1	2	2						2	2-5
Three Rivers	33	4			.5	.5	2		1			2	2	Yes	2	2	2	6					2	5	9	3-4
Traverse City	62	9	.5		.5	1	6		1		8	1		Yes	3	4	1	20	11			2	6	5		All
West Branch	9													Yes											9	....
Whittemore	3													Yes											3	1-4
Wyandotte	34	5			1	1	3				5				3	3	1	15				1	1		5	All
[illegible]	11													Yes				2							8	1-4
[illegible]nti	33	3	.5		.5	1				1	1		1	Yes	4			17				3	5		1	6-7
[illegible]d	17													Yes			1	3	4			1	2		6	2-3

TABLE XXI.

Receipts and disbursements at teachers' institutes for the calendar year 1907.

Counties.	Location.	Date.	Receipts.		Expenditures.			
			County.	State.	Compensation of instructors and local committee.	Expenses of instructors.	Other expenses.	Total.
Totals			$11,471 45	$1,873 28	$9,636 00	$1,596 19	$2,112 54	$13,344 73
Alcona	Harrisville	Mar. 21-23	$42 00	$52 48	$63 00	$27 73	$3 75	$94 48
Allegan	Allegan and county	Jan. 7-12	66 34		62 00	4 34		66 34
	A[illegible]gan and county	Jan. 14-17	46 98		43 00	3 98		46 98
	Saugatuck	April 5-6	66 58		49 00	11 33	6 25	66 58
	Kalamazoo	June 24-Aug. 2.	70 15		60 00		10 15	70 15
	Allegan	Oct. 12	23 25		18 00	1 25	4 00	23 25
	Allegan	Dec. 14	16 00		13 00	1 00	2 00	16 00
Antrim	Bel [illegible]re	July 22-Aug. 2	55 50	100 00	125 00	13 40	7 10	155 50
Baraga	Marquette	June 24-Aug. 2	37 00	2 80	26 00		13 80	39 80
Barry	Hastings	Jan. 3-5	62 79		51 00	11 79		62 79
	Hastings and county	Jan. 7-12	38 09		27 00	11 09		38 09
	Hastings	Feb. 15-16	24 73	44 25	45 00	9 98	14 00	68 98
	[illegible]oo	June 24-Aug. 2	100 10		74 00		26 10	100 10
Bay	Pinconning	Feb. 14-15	81 46		40 00	17 86	14 60	81 46
	Bay City and county	Nov. 18-23	129 79		72 00	12 10	45 69	129 79
Benzie	Frankfort	Mar. 7-9	81 00	23 06	68 00	27 06	9 00	104 06
Berrien	St. Joseph	Mar. 8-9	154 27		137 00	17 27		154 27
Branch	Coldwater	Jan. 21-25	114 30		67 00	21 05	26 25	114 30
	Kalamazoo	June 24-Aug. 2	35 00	76 23	74 00		37 23	111 23
Calhoun	Marshall	Jan. 26	27 82		18 00	2 82	7 00	27 82
	[illegible]o	June 24-Aug. 2	88 35		66 00		22 35	88 35
Cass	[illegible]c	April 27	44 97		27 00	14 22	3 75	44 97
	Kalamazoo	June 24-Aug. 2	45 93	50 75	69 93		26 75	96 68
Charlevoix	[illegible]x	July 22-Aug. 2	89 50	73 72	125 00	32 80	5 42	163 22
Cheboygan	Cheboygan	Aug. 19-30	104 00	33 28	125 00	8 43	3 85	137 28
	Cheboygan	Dec. 13-14	59 00	27 63	52 00	31 13	3 50	86 63
Chippewa	Sault Ste. Marie	April 8-10	75 00	70 02	83 00	62 02		145 02
	Sault Ste. Marie	Nov. 1-3	78 00	46 35	83 00	39 85	1 50	124 35
Clare	Mt. Pleasant	June 24-Aug. 2	35 30	4 00	35 00		4 30	39 30
	Clare	Oct. 9-11	56 64	50 37	68 00	10 51	28 50	107 01
Clinton	St. [illegible]ns	Aug. 30-31	23 50		12 00	1 50	10 00	23 50
Delta	Marquette	June 24-Aug. 2	50 60	17 50	30 00		38 10	68 10
	Escanaba	Oct. 31-Nov. 2	6 31		5 00		1 31	6 31
Dickinson	Marquette	June 24-Aug. 2						
	Escanaba	[illegible]v. 2	29 55		25 00		4 55	29 55

34

Eaton	Charlotte	Aug. 26-30	171 16		135 00	21 51	14 65	171 16
Emmet	Petoskey	Aug. 26-30	75 00	41 44	85 00	23 44	8 90	116 44
Genesee	Flint	July 15-Aug. 2	331 57		280 00	21 07	30 50	331 57
	Flint and county	Nov. 18-22	116 00		82 00	26 96	7 04	116 00
Gladwin	Gladwin	Jan. 25-27	54 00	14 40	47 00	15 70	5 70	68 40
	Mt. Pleasant	June 24-Aug. 2	25 00	34 50	49 00		10 50	59 50
Gogebic	Ironwood	Oct. 17-19	81 99		48 00	31 24	2 75	81 99
Grand Traverse	Traverse City	Feb. 15-16	66 68		49 00	8 92	8 76	66 68
Gratiot	Alma	Jan. 11	46 66		24 00	5 86	16 80	46 66
	Ithaca	May 17	42 84		17 00	11 34	14 50	42 84
	Mt. Pleasant	June 24-Aug. 2	83 12	11 25	85 25		9 12	94 37
Hillsdale	Hillsdale	May 10-11	32 28		21 00	11 28		32 28
	Hillsdale	July 22-Aug. 7	254 07		226 00	3 15	24 92	254 07
Houghton and Keweenaw	Houghton and Keweenaw	Oct. 18-19	234 32		108 00	93 29	33 03	234 32
Huron	Bad Axe	Oct. 10-12	114 06		73 00	19 31	21 75	114 06
Ingham	Mason	July 15-Aug. 2	147 05	75 00	205 00	60	16 45	222 05
Ionia	Ionia and county	Sept. 23-28	102 36		82 00	8 96	11 40	102 36
Iosco	Tawas City and county	Nov. 4-8	64 00	31 03	65 00	13 03	17 00	95 03
Iron	Marquette	June 24-Aug. 2	15 00	4 18	12 00		7 18	19 18
Isabella	Mt. Pleasant	June 24-Aug. 2	150 00	74 05	213 75	9 80	50	224 05
Jackson	Jackson and county	Feb. 5-8	44 93		28 00	6 39	10 54	44 93
	Ypsilanti	June 24-Aug. 2	137 63		76 00		61 63	137 63
	Jackson and county	Dec. 16-21	86 68		63 00	3 48	20 20	86 68
Kalamazoo	Kalamazoo	June 24-Aug. 2	125 50		124 00		1 50	125 50
Kalkaska	Kalkaska	Jan. 25-26	25 12		15 00	7 62	2 50	25 12
	Kalkaska	Dec. 14	52 43		18 00	16 10	18 33	52 43
Kent	Grand Rapids	Feb. 1-2	118 00		105 00		13 00	118 00
	Kent City	Mar. 8	57 58		32 00	19 08	6 50	57 58
	Grand Rapids	Mar. 20	78 60		54 00	19 60	5 00	78 60
	Grand Rapids	April 11	90 00		80 00		10 00	90 00
	Grandville	April 12	59 45		32 00	16 70	10 75	59 45
	Grand Rapids	May 10-11	125 00		105 00		20 00	125 00
	Grand Rapids	Aug. 19-23	147 07		115 00	27 07	5 00	147 07
	Grand Rapids	Nov. 23	25 36		20 00	5 36		25 36
Keweenaw	See Houghton Co							
Lapeer	Lapeer	July 22-Aug. 7	200 01		170 00	5 01	25 00	200 01
	Lapeer	Oct. 5	31 84		16 00	7 01	8 83	31 84
Leelanau	Sutton's Bay	Nov. 11-15	70 50	59 79	85 00	26 19	19 10	130 29
Lenawee	Blissfield	Mar. 22-23	175 39		107 00	52 94	15 45	175 39
	Ypsilanti	June 24-Aug. 2	135 37		76 00		59 37	135 37
Livingston	Ypsilanti	June 24-Aug. 2	132 53		80 00		52 53	132 53
Mackinac	St. Ignace	Dec. 2-6	63 50	58 47	86 00	26 82	9 15	121 97
Manistee	Manistee	Feb. 13-16	72 50	8 16	48 00	13 61	19 05	80 66
	Onekama and Bear Lake	Sept. 10	15 50	27 32	17 00	17 17	8 65	42 82
Marquette	Marquette	June 24-Aug. 2	144 40	85 00	209 00		20 40	229 40
	Marquette, Ishpeming, Negaunee	Dec. 2-6	115 07		62 00	43 32	9 75	115 07
—n.	Ludington	Aug. 19-23	37 00	68 73	80 00	13 00	12 73	105 73
ta.	Big Rapids	July 1-Aug. 7	230 50		230 00		50	230 50
inee.	Marquette	June 24-Aug. 2	54 18		33 00		21 18	54 18
d.	Mt. Pleasant	June 24-Aug. 2	25 00		25 00			25 00
ikee.	Missaukee, Butterfield, Jennings	Dec. 9-13	77 27	23 68	77 00	14 00	9 95	100 95

TABLE XXI.—Concluded.

Counties.	Location.	Date.	Receipts.		Expenditures.			
			County.	State.	Compensation of instructors and local committee.	Expenses of instructors.	Other expenses.	Total.
	Monroe	Mar. 8-10	$73 11	$8 31	$52 00	$21 92	$7 50	$81 42
Monroe	Ypsilanti	June 24-Aug. 2	70 50	23 75	74 00		20 25	94 25
	Monroe	Aug. 31	24 40		16 00	3 05	5 35	24 40
Montcalm	Mt. Pleasant	June 24-Aug. 2	50 00	20 00	70 00			70 00
Montmorency	Atlanta	Nov. 6-8	46 50	74 68	76 00	40 68	4 50	121 18
Muskegon	Muskegon	Nov. 21-23	142 88		116 00	14 33	12 55	142 88
	[illegible]o	Feb 1416	50 75		41 00	9 75		50 75
	White Cloud							
Newaygo	Big Prairie, Wooster	Feb. 18-19	19 25	16 00	29 00		6 25	35 25
	Grant	[illegible] 17		30 48	19 00	11 48		30 48
	Fremont	Oct. 3-5	89 06		68 00	19 06	2 00	89 06
Oakland	Pontiac	Jan. 1418	128 05		72 00	13 22	42 83	128 05
	Ypsilanti	June 24-Aug. 2	140 80		76 00		64 80	140 80
Oceana	Shelby and county	Feb. 18-22	103 10		50 00	19 90	33 20	103 10
	Pentwater	May 17-18	28 71	4 00	29 00	3 71		32 71
Osceola	Evart	[illegible] 15-16	93 37		59 00	26 09	8 28	93 37
	Mt. Pleasant	June 24-Aug. 2	83 50	25 00	99 00		9 50	108 50
Saginaw	Saginaw	Jan. 14- 15	144 07		30 00	9 37	104 70	144 07
	Saginaw and county	Mar. 11-12	263 32	75 00	120 00	23 52	194 80	338 22
Oscoda	Mio	July [illegible]g. 9	106 79	100 00	165 00	38 66	3 13	206 79
Otsego	Ga[illegible]rd	April 25-27	28 50	65 15	63 00	28 76	1 89	93 65
Ottawa	Holland	Mar. 22-23	82 80		49 00	17 73	16 07	82 80
	Grand [illegible]aven	July 15-Aug. 7	262 43		240 00	5 74	16 69	262 43
St. Clair	[illegible]rt [illegible]n	[illegible] 11-22	181 51	96 13	210 00	40 18	27 46	277 64
St. Joseph	Kalamazoo	June 24-Aug. 2	109 78		74 00		35 78	109 78
	Three Rivers and county	Oct. 7-12	115 01		82 00	9 01	24 00	115 01
Sanilac	Sandusky	[illegible]uly 22-[illegible]g. 7	304 14		264 00	24 34	15 80	304 14
Shiawassee	[illegible]runna	[illegible] 17-18	43 99		25 00	4 84	14 15	43 99
Tuscola	Caro	July 22-Aug. 1	224 21		164 00	16 69	43 52	224 21
Van Buren	Hartford	A[illegible]il 19-20	82 74		24 00	35 22	23 52	82 74
	Kalamazoo	June 24-Aug. 2	99 32	4 07	78 07		25 32	103 39

Washtenaw	Manchester	Jan. 19	24 68		17 00	2 18	5 50	24 68
	Dexter	Jan. 26	17 70		17 00	70		17 70
	Ann Arbor	Mar. 2	45 00		37 00		8 00	45 00
	Ypsilanti	June 24–Aug. 2	154 53		132 00		22 53	154 53
	Chelsea	Oct. 5	20 00		18 00	50	1 50	20 00
	Milan	Nov. 9	25 13		18 00	3 00	4 13	25 13
	Dexter	Nov. 23	22 98		18 00	1 20	3 78	22 98
	Manchester	Dec. 7	25 52		18 00	2 96	4 56	25 52
Wayne	Plymouth and county	Feb. 18–23	203 26		87 00	34 23	82 03	203 26
	Detroit	Mar. 18–19	85 00		60 00	25 00		85 00
	Sand Hill	April 27	47 76		25 00	7 21	15 55	47 76
	Detroit	May 29	110 10		105 00		5 10	110 10
	Ypsilanti	June 24–Aug. 2	174 38		126 00		48 38	174 38
	Detroit	Nov. 11–13	134 00		134 00			134 00
	Wayne	Dec. 7	94 45		82 00		12 45	94 45
Wexford	Harrietta, Sherman, Manton	Nov. 25–27	73 50	41 27	76 00	21 52	17 25	114 77

TABLE XXII.

Local committees, conductors, and instructors at

Counties.	Term.	Local committees.
Alcona	3 days	W. H. Sanborn
Alger (with Marquette).		
Allegan	5 days.	Ira G. Thorpe
	3 days	Ira G. Thorpe
	2 days	Ira G. Thorpe
	30 days	Ira G. Thorpe
	1 days	Ira G. Thorpe
	1 day	Ira G. Thorpe
Antrim	30 days	H. M. Coldren
Baraga	30 days	S. O. Clinton
Barry	2 days	J. C. Ketcham
	5 days	J. C. Ketcham
	2 days	J. C. Ketcham
	30 days	E. J. Edger
Bay	2 days	J. B. Laing
	5 days	J. B. Laing
Benzie	3 days	W. E. Daines
Berrien	2 days	C. D. Jennings
Branch	5 days	J. Swain
	30 days.	J. Swain
Calhoun	1 day	F. D. Miller
	30 days	F. D. Miller
Cass	1 day	W. H. C. Hale
	30 days	W. H. C. Hale
Charlevoix	10 days	J. H. Milford
Cheboygan	10 days	E. W. Baker
	2 days	E. W. Baker
Chippewa	3 days	T. R. Easterday
	4 days	T. R. Easterday
Clare	30 days	E. G. Welch
	3 days	E. G. Welch
Clinton	2 days	T. Townsend
Delta	30 days	P. R. Legg
	3 days	P. R. Legg
Dickinson	30 days	E. L. Parmenter
	3 days.	E. L. Parmenter
Eaton	5 days	Cynthia Green
Emmet	5 days.	H. S. Babcock
Genesee	15 days	F. J. Johnson
	5 days	F. J. Johnson
Gladwin	3 days	F. E. Armstrong
	30 days	F. E. Armstrong
Gogebic	3 days	Laura Bowden
Grand Traverse	2 days	G. L. Crispe
Gratiot	1 day	C. F. Pike
	30 days	C. F. Pike
	1 day	C. F. Pike
Hillsdale	2 days	H. McClave
	15 days	H. McClave
Houghton and Keweenaw	2 days	W. Bath. F. M. Bradshaw
Huron	3 days	C. F. Hey
Ingham	15 days	F. E. Searl
Ionia	5 days	H. H. Lowry
Iosco	5 days	J. A. Campbell
Iron	30 days	J. F. Mason
Isabella	30 days	K. T. Cameron
Jackson	4 days	T. M. Sattler
	30 days	T. M. Sattler
	5 days	T. M. Sattler
Kalamazoo	30 days	J. W. Hazard Sheridan Mapes
Kalkaska	2 days	Irene L. Getty
	1 day	Irene L. Getty

TABLE XXII.

teachers' institutes for the calendar year 1907.

Conductors.	Instructors.	Instructors.	Instructors.
A. H. Smith	A. H. Smith	Fannie I. Allen.	
D. B. Waldo	D. B. Waldo.		
J. C. Ketcham	J. C. Ketcham.		
J. C. Ketcham	Lois Wilson.		
D. B. Waldo	Emilie Townsend.		
I. G. Thorpe	L. H. Wood.		
I. G. Thorpe	E. Burnham.		
P. F. McCormick	P. F. McCormick	H. M. Coldren	Anna Hazard.
J. H. Kaye	E. L. Parmenter.		
J. C. Ketcham	E. Burnham.		
J. C. Ketcham	F. L. Keeler	W. J. McKone.	
J. C. Ketcham	Abbie Roe.		
D. B. Waldo	C. B. Williams	C. S. Larzelere.	
S. B. Laird	S. B. Laird.		
J. C. Ketcham	J. C. Ketcham	C. S. Larzelere.	
C. O. Hoyt	C. O. Hoyt	R. D. Calkins.	
E. P. Clark	E. E. Sparks	H. H. Barrows	Florence Fox.
D. B. Waldo	D. B. Waldo	J. C. Ketcham	Martha Sherwood.
D. B. Waldo	E. M. McElroy.		
R. S. Garwood	W. D. Henderson.		
D. B. Waldo	Emilie Townsend.		
F. L. Keeler	F. L. Keeler	Anna Hazard	W. E. Conklin.
D. B. Waldo	E. A. Aseltine	Emilie Townsend.	
W. H. Woodley	W. H. Woodley	Alice Reed	J. H. Milford.
Cora Willsey	Cora Willsey	A. F. Wood	E. W. Baker.
S. B. Laird	S. B. Laird	Lucy A. Sloan.	
W. H. Cheever	W. H. Cheever	R. D. Calkins.	
J. H. Kaye	J. H. Kaye	S. B. Laird.	
C. T. Grawn	Flora R. Linn	H. A. Graham.	
E. Burnham	E. Burnham	W. D. Miller.	
T. Townsend	C. D. Smith.		
J. H. Kaye	E. L. Parmenter.		
P. R. Legg.			
J. H. Kaye	J. H. Kaye.		
C. T. Grawn	Sara M. Nicholson.		
W. N. Ferris	W. N. Ferris	H. C. Lott	Martha Sherwood.
E. H. Burnham	E. H. Burnham	Lucy Bettes.	
A. N. Cody	A. N. Cody	Viola Marshall	{ F. J. Johnson. Sarah Greeley.
H. R. Pattengill	H. R. Pattengill	J. L. Hughes.	
H. R. Pattengill	H. R. Pattengill	R. D. Calkins.	
C. T. Grawn	Flora Linn.		
W. N. Ferris	W. N. Ferris.		
R. D. Calkins	R. D. Calkins	I. B. Gilbert.	
H. R. Pattengill	H. R. Pattengill	H. A. Graham.	
C. T. Grawn	Flora Linn.		
D. B. Waldo	D. B. Waldo.		
H. McClave	F. L. Keeler.		
J. F. Rieman	J. F. Rieman	Hazel Ackley	H. McClave.
J. H. Kaye	J. H. Kaye	E. G. Lancaster	D. B. Waldo.
A. H. Smith	A. H. Smith	Margaret Wise.	
F. Fullerton	F. Fullerton	Ida Huston	F. E. Searl.
H. R. Pattengill	H. R. Pattengill	R. D. Calkins.	
H. R. Pattengill	H. R. Pattengill	C. B. Chaffee.	
J. H. Kaye	E. L. Parmenter.		
C. T. Grawn	E. H. Ryder	G. F. Roxburgh	Flora Linn.
T. M. Sattler	D. E. McClure.		
N. A. Harvey	Mildred Gapen.		
T. M. Sattler	J. C. Ketcham	E. Burnham.	
D. B. Waldo	Lillie Robinson	H. D. Lee	E. McElroy.
F. L. Keeler	F. L. Keeler.		
Irene L. Getty	C. O. Hoyt.		

TABLE XXII.—Concluded.

Counties.	Term.	Local committees.
Kent	2 days	A. R. Zimmer
	1 day	A. R. Zimmer
	1 day	W. A. Greeson
	1 day	W. A. Greeson
	1 day	A. R. Zimmer
	2 days	A. R. Zimmer
	5 days	A. M. Freeland
	1 day	A. M. Freeland
Keweenaw (with Houghton.)		
Lapeer	15 days	C. H. Naylor
	1 day	C. H. Naylor
Leelanau	5 days	E. F. Carr
Lenawee	2 days	M. W. Hensel
	30 days	M. W. Hensel
Livingston	30 days	J. A. Woodruff
Mackinac	5 days	E. J. Lachance
Manistee	4 days	H. J. Leighton
	1 day	H. J. Leighton
Marquette and Alger	30 days	A. E. Sterne
	5 days	A. E. Sterne
Mason	5 days	C. A. Rinehart
Mecosta	28 days	B. J. Ford
Menominee	30 days	J. Hubbard
Midland	30 days	J. Mustard
Missaukee	5 days	E. S. Hall
Monroe	3 days	A. C. Marvin
	30 days	J. J. Kelly
	1 day	J. J. Kelly
Montcalm	30 days	E. D. Straight
Montmorency	3 days	B. J. Watters
Muskegon	3 days	Nellie B. Chisholm
Newaygo	3 days	Isabella M. Becker
	2 days	Isabelle M. Becker
	1 day	Isabelle M. Becker
	3 days	Isabelle M. Becker
Oakland	5 days	H. S. Elliott
	30 days	H. S. Elliott
Oceana	5 days	E. Fleming
	2 days	E. Fleming
Osceola	2 days	G. F. Roxburgh
	30 days	G. F. Roxburgh
Oscoda	15 days	Leah Young
Otsego	3 days	R. D. Bailey
Ottawa	2 days	M. M. DeGraff
	20 days	M. M. DeGraff
Saginaw	2 days	J. C. Nafe
	10 days	J. C. Nafe
St. Clair	10 days	E. T. Blackney
St. Joseph	30 days	L. E. Miller
	5 days	L. E. Miller
Sanilac	15 days	C. G. Putney
Shiawassee	2 days	H. E. Slocum
Tuscola	15 days	H. P. Bush
Van Buren	2 days	E. A. Aseltine
	30 days	V. R. Hungerford
Washtenaw	1 day	C. E. Foster
	1 day	C. E. Foster
	1 day	C. E. Foster
	30 days	E. Essery
	1 day	E. Essery
	1 day	E. Essery
	1 day	E. Essery
	1 day	E. Essery
Wayne	5 days	E. W. Yost
	2 days	W. C. Martindale
	1 day	E. W. Yost
	1 day	W. C. Martindale
	30 days	E. W. Yost
	3 days	W. C. Martindale
	1 day	E. W. Yost
Wexford	3 days	W. H. Faunce

TABLE XXII.—Concluded.

Conductors.	Instructors.	Instructors.	Instructors.
A. R. Zimmer	N. C. Schaeffer.		
H. R. Pattengill	H. R. Pattengill	C. T. Grawn.	
W. A. Greeson	Patty Hill.		
W. A. Greeson	G. E. Vincent.		
H. R. Pattengill	H. R. Pattengill	F. L. Keeler.	
A. R. Zimmer	G. E. Vincent.		
F. L. Keeler	F. L. Keeler	A. H. Benson	Martha Sherwood.
A. M. Freeland	N. A. Harvey.		
E. J. Quackenbush	E. J. Quackenbush	C. H. Naylor	Emma R. O'Connor.
D. Fall	D. Fall.		
H. C. Lott	H. C. Lott	Lucy A. Sloan.	
C. W. Mickens	H. R. Pattengill	C. B. Gilbert.	
N. A. Harvey	Kate Van Cleve.		
N. A. Harvey	Lida Clark	Kate Van Cleve.	
J. H. Kaye	L. F. Anderson.		
C. T. Grawn	C. T. Grawn.		
F. L. Keeler	F. L. Keeler.		
A. E. Sterne	E. L. Parmenter	Sarah M. Nicholson.	
S. B. Laird	S. B. Laird	J. H. Kaye.	
G. D. Smith	G. D. Smith	Lulu B. Chase	C. A. Rinehart.
W. N. Ferris	W. N. Ferris.		
J. H. Kaye	E. L. Parmenter.		
C. T. Grawn	G. F. Roxburgh.		
C. E. Holmes	C. E. Holmes	C. T. Grawn	E. S. Hall.
F. L. Keeler	F. L. Keeler	Lois Wilson.	
N. A. Harvey	Mildred Gapen.		
C. O. Hoyt	C. O. Hoyt.		
C. T. Grawn	G. F. Roxburg	Flora Linn.	
C. O. Hoyt	C. O. Hoyt	Irene L. Getty.	
C. T. Grawn	C. T. Grawn	C. E. Holmes	J. M. Frost.
D. Fall	D. Fall.		
F. L. Keeler	F. L. Keeler.		
C. T. Grawn	C. T. Grawn.		
D. B. Waldo	D. B. Waldo	J. C. Stone.	
H. R. Pattengill	H. R. Pattengill	S. B. Laird.	
N. A. Harvey	G. Bates.		
D. E. McClure	D. E. McClure.		
D. Fall	D. Fall.		
C. T. Grawn	C. T. Grawn	C. D. Smith	A. G. Slocum.
C. T. Grawn	H. A. Graham	G. F. Roxburgh	
C. G. Wade	C. G. Wade	Lulu McCreery.	
C. S. Larzelere	C. S. Larzelere	Lucy A. Sloan.	
L. H. Vandenburg	W. D. Henderson	R. C. Ford.	
R. C. Ford	L. H. Vanden Burg	Louise Kilbourne	M. M. DeGraff.
J. C. Nafe	F. L. Keeler.		
J. C. Nafe	L. H. Jones	H. R. Pattengill.	
W. F. Lewis	W. F. Lewis	{E. T. Blackney. Jessie R. Doty.}	Alice P. Kimball.
D. B. Waldo	H. D. Lee.		
H. R. Pattengill	H. R. Pattengill	Florence Marsh.	
J. K. Osgerby	J. K. Osgerby	J. M. Tice	Martha McArthur.
H. E. Slocum	S. B. Laird.		
E. E. Fell	E. E. Fell	Agnes L. Gilbert	H. P. Bush.
E. A. Asseltine	O. J. Kern.		
D. B. Waldo	H. D. Lee	E. A. Asseltine.	
C. O. Hoyt	C. O. Hoyt.		
S. B. Laird	S. B. Laird.		
L. H. Jones	F. A. Barbour	L. H. Jones	D. H. Roberts.
N. A. Harvey	W. B. Arbaugh.		
E. Essery	W. D. Henderson.		
E. Essery	N. A. Harvey.		
E. Essery	C. O. Hoyt.		
E. Essery	R. C. Ford.		
E. W. Yost	O. J. Kern.		
W. C. Martindale	Patty Hill.		
E. W. Yost	W. D. Henderson	D. Fall.	
W. C. Martindale	E. E. Brown.		
N. A. Harvey	Lida Clark.		
W. C. Martindale	Patty Hill.		
T. O. Sweetland	J. W. Cook.		
A. H. Smith	A. H. Smith	Minnie I. Tennant.	

TABLE XXIII.

Enrollment at teachers' institutes for the calendar year 1903.

Counties.	Number of teachers required to supply schools.	Number enrolled.			Kinds and grades of certificates held by members.										Number without experience in teaching.	Number having received normal instruction.	Average attendance each half day.	Number of legally qualified teachers in the county.	Percentage of teachers in county attending institute.
		Men.	Women.	Total.	State.	University.	Normal.	First.	Second.	Third.	Special.	College.	City.	County normal.					
Totals	15,682	5,391	19,134	24,525	162	107	84	118	2,379	2,054	116	97	458	339	1,139	2,014	6,057	17,842	56
*Alcona	41																	39	
Alger (with Marquette)	54	3	7	10														55	
		230	481	711															
		322	664	986															
Allegan	268	17	55	72			1		29	19	1	1			21	23	57	308	17
		12	65	77	1				28	17					29				15
		21	89	110		1	12	1	36	34	1	1		7	17	49	.110		30
		7	31	38			5		7	8		1		2	15				8
†Alpena	116																	115	
Antrim	123	3	28	31			1		10	8				6	1	1	22		
†Arenac	63																	66	
Baraga	38		13	13					2	3	4				4			47	21
		†1121	2,256	3,377															
Barry	190	81	194	275														248	
		2	22	24					10	4				2	7				6
Bay	294	*20	77	97			4	2	36	25	1	2		6	25	24	92	337	22
Benzie	89	15	89	104	1	1	8	2	31	22	1	2		1	30	27	100	118	50
Berrien	324	97	192	289	5	5	39	8	57	67		5				55	240	318	59
Branch	191	45	131	176	3		32		70	47	6	2	15	1			155	259	68
		16	31	47			3		12	17	1				11		45		12
		26	102	128	2	13	21	6	33	22		1	5		10	45			28
Calhoun	354	‡12	26	38	3	4	4	1	5	8	1	2	1	7	2	5	70	374	10
		¶777	3,271	4,048															
Cass	165	8	80	88	3	2	9	1	20	14	3	3	14	10	9	28	100	213	37
		3	24	27					11	7			1	2	6				10
Charlevoix	135	8	47	55					22	16		1		8	10		38	180	26
Cheboygan	114	4	35	39			1		15	9			6	1	8	5	22		27
		14	110	124	3		17	1	33	16	3	3	17	12	19	37	112	120	88
Chippewa	97	19	109	128	5	2	30	5	27	25	1	1		3		57	108	161	62
		18	122	140													129		

		4	17	21														101	72
Clare	80	15	70	85	2		7	2	27	32	1	2			6	43	82		
Clinton	178	17	113	130	1	1	10	2	41	27		1		37	17	20	130	195	62
†Crawford	38																	39	
		10	73	83			2	1	42	33	3					27	81	156	52
Delta	166	*																	
Dickinson	115		13	13					2	3					8	13	12	135	4
Eaton	228	14	102	116	2		2	1	34	57	1	1		3	32	25	78	275	40
Emmet	128	11	52	63	3		1		19	39	1			1	18	7		164	37
Genesee	282	* 4	81	85			1		22	38				2	20	6	54	320	20
Gladwin	65	*																66	
		51	6	11															
Gogebic	137	7	133	140	44	1		4	33	28	1	1				64	133	134	51
Grand Traverse	139	11	30	50			6		23	18	2				1	7	47	143	34
*Gratiot	200																	266	
		31	113	144	4		2	1	60	32	8	1	3	9	24	33	48	352	34
Hillsdale	242	20	132	152			3	5	56	57	1				57	21	85		35
Houghton and Keweenaw	481	130	420	550														450	
*Huron	187																	203	
Ingham¶	275	8	71	79					17	26	1			8	27		59	283	18
Ionia	236																	333	
Iosco	68	7	56	63	2	1	4		17	9		5		9	18	13	65	81	58
Iron	83		7	7														78	
Isabella	131	12	51	63		6			7	15								135	21
		5	18	23			4	1	8	9	1				3	5			10
Jackson	290	2	36	38				1	10	17	2				8	2	30	235	13
		16	71	87			1	2	39	22	3				10		87		39
Kalamazoo	334	7	75	82														369	
Kalkaska	64	* 2	44	46			9		12					13	5	12	45	75	45
*Kent	727																	835	
Keweenaw (see Houghton)	31																	28	
†Lake	50																	66	
		*															3		
Lapeer	186	1	65	66			1		24	20			1	10	13	5	28	212	27
Leelanau	72	15	48	63			2	1	33	18					6	12	47	75	73
		32	238	270	2	6	30	2	78	70	7	8	25		42	114	225		62
Lenawee	314	2	30	32					7	14					10	1	29	368	6
Livingston	170		21	21					3	12	1				6	3	17	351	5
†Luce	29																	28	
Mackinac	67	12	62	74		1	5	2	25	17	1	1	4	1	18	15	62	95	60
†Macomb	186																	222	

*No report received. †No institute held. ¶All counties; held in connection with State association.

35

TABLE XXIII.—Concluded.

Counties.	Number of teachers required to supply schools.	Number enrolled.			Kinds and grades of certificates held by members.										Number without experience in teaching.	Number having received normal instruction.	Average attendance each half day.	Number of legally qualified teachers in the county.	Percentage of teachers in county attending institute.
		Men.	Women.	Total.	State.	University.	Normal.	First.	Second.	Third.	Special.	College.	City.	County normal.					
Manistee	161	15	135	150														179	
		7	30	37															
Marquette	267	5	161	166			4		7	16			10					310	12
		28	245	273	8	14	106	2	13	17	17	2	22		10	243	273		65
Mason	128	3	61	64	1		2	1	14	29				15	21	9	49	127	49
Mecosta	148	4	70	74				1	9	22	2			9	23	4	48	212	20
Menominee	183	1	33	34					6	18	1		1		8	25		179	15
Midland	107	11	100	111			12		26	33	5	1	3	14	17	41	83	117	80
Missaukee	85	6	30	36	4		7		11	15						5	28	92	40
		33	148	181		2	11		77	52	1	2	11		19	82	168		64
Monroe	187	4	17	21			1		2	10	1				9	2	16	242	6
		13	66	79															
*Montcalm	205																	231	
Montmorency	36	8	50	58			1	1	21	20					17	7	57	52	83
Muskegon	246	17	249	266		6	12	3	57	56	3	1	94		9	41	204	292	80
Newaygo	151	14	64	78	2		4		27	17	3	3	4		17	16	78	199	30
		9	109	118	4		9	1	44	25	6	1		20	7	30	116		60
Oakland	321	31	169	200	1	4	45	6	60	48	3	2	6	25			200	379	53
			30	30					15	12			1	2	1	6	26		8
Oceana	129	24	83	107			9	2	27	22	1	1			20	20	100	250	25
		5	24	29			8	1	8	3	1	2			2	9	29		9
†Ogemaw	64																	62	
†Ontonagon	85																	80	
		26	111	137			21	4	49	22				10		41	132		57
Osceola	138	27	125	152			22	3	46	24	1	2		18	10	52	136	187	62
		9	36	45															
Oscoda	27	4	17	21					1	6					13	1	17	17	41
Otsego	61	2	48	50		1	6	2	9	11	1	1			9	13	39	60	52
Ottawa	244	34	157	191	36	2	29	5	69	53	3	5	8		18	58	174	290	72
		7	40	47				1	7	25	1				12	1			12
†Presque Isle	63																	62	
†Roscommon	27																		

		60	139	199															
Saginaw	452	1,200	2,176	3,376	4	25	40	15	200	100	3	25	200	25	100	200	450	548	114
St. Clair	299	21	145	166			2		48	47				23	41	22	117	331	36
St. Joseph	203	* 4	35	39				1	3	17			1		10			222	10
Sanilac	199	23	102	125	2			2	24	68		1			44	5	74	239	40
†Schoolcraft	61																	65	
Shiawassee	228	19	108	127	2	5	13	1	47	30	4		5	14	6	46	100	296	41
*Tuscola	213																	229	
Van Buren	248	24	87	111	3	1	5	2	43	22		3			21	44	86	312	22
		9	87	96															
		6	52	58	1	1	5		18	16					17	34	58		12
		15	49	64															
		2	109	111			5	1	17	36					52	19	89		17
		2	82	84	2	1	8	1	38	26					7		84		21
Washtenaw	309	4	42	46	1		6		15	15				3	4	33		357	11
		4	45	49					22	15					4	38	49		10
		6	49	55			8	1	27	19					1	39	55		17
		3	27	30	1	1	4		15	8						16	30		8
		7	40	47															
		90	1,225	1,315															
		13	30	43			12	1	18		1								2
Wayne	1,633	94	32	126	4		16	4	34	21								1,644	5
		90	1,225	1,315															
		2	39	41			3		18	11	1				7	8	38		2
		45	193	238			41	4	54	36									8
*Wexford	144																	154	

†No institute held. *No report received.

TABLE XXIV.

County boards of school examiners for 1903-07.

County.	Name.	Address.	Occupation.
Alcona	W. H. Sanborn	Harrisville	Teacher.
	Franklin Webb	Harrisville	Teacher.
	W. R. Barber	Harrisville	Teacher.
Alger	Orvice LaBounty	Munising	Teacher.
	Melvin E. Shippey	Chatham	Teacher.
Allegan	Ira G. Thorpe	Allegan	Teacher.
	Volney Stuck	Hopkins Station	Teacher.
	R. M. Sprague	Ypsilanti	Teacher.
Alpena	Harry V. Knight	Alpena	Farmer.
	E. H. Fox	Long Rapids	Teacher.
	E. L. Little	Alpena	Preacher.
Antrim	H. M. Coldren	Bellaire	Teacher.
	Geo. E. Cabanis	Bellaire	Farmer.
	L. A. Butler	Central Lake	Teacher.
Arenac	Geo. H. Glasure	Au Gres	Teacher.
	E. N. Durfee	Standish	Teacher.
	F. B. Hamilton	Standish	Teacher.
Baraga	S. O. Clinton	Baraga	Teacher.
	Kate Curry	L'Anse	Teacher.
	Helen O'Connor	L'Anse	Teacher.
Barry	Ernest J. Edger	Hastings	Teacher.
	Don D. Putnam	Prairieville	
	O. E. Balyeat	Freeport	Teacher.
Bay	J. B. Laing	Bay City	Teacher.
	James Cotter	Essexville	Teacher.
	Otto J. Manary	West Bay City	Teacher.
Benzie	O. L. Bristol	Benzonia	
	Lizzie Tillie	South Frankfort	Teacher.
	Lillian Jaquith	Benzonia	Teacher.
Berrien	G. N. Otwell	St. Joseph	Teacher.
	E. C. Harner	Benton Harbor	Real Estate.
	Edward English	Hinchman	Teacher.
Branch	James Swain	Coldwater	Teacher.
	F. E. Knapp	Quincy	Teacher.
	A. W. Russell	Coldwater	Teacher.
Calhoun	Frank D. Miller	Marshall	Teacher.
	E. L. McPherson	Battle Creek	Teacher.
	B. J. Rivett	Homer	Teacher.
Cass	W. H. C. Hale	Cassopolis	Teacher.
	John Finley	Dowagiac	Teacher.
	H. S. East	Vandalia	Merchant.
Charlevoix	J. H. Milford	South Arm	Teacher.
	Hubert E. Bell	Boyne	Teacher.
	W. H. Woodley	Charlevoix	Teacher.
Cheboygan	E. W. Baker	Cheboygan	Teacher.
	W. L. Coffey	Wolverine	Teacher.
	C. J. Severance	Cheboygan	Teacher.
Chippewa	T. R. Easterday	Sault Ste. Marie	Preacher.
	T. B. Aldrich	Brimley	Teacher.
	D. W. McLean	Detour	Teacher.
Clare	E. G. Welch	Clare	Editor.
	John F. Brown	Temple	Teacher.
	Richard J. Woods	Harrison	Teacher.
Clinton	T. H. Townsend	St. Johns	
	B. A. Burnes	St. Johns	Teacher.
	E. J. Leddick	Fowler	Teacher.

TABLE XXIV.—CONTINUED.

County.	Name.	Address.	Occupation.
Crawford	J. E. Bradley	Grayling	Teacher.
	Mrs. Isabel Cobb	Frederick	Teacher.
	Julia Inglis	Frederick	Teacher.
Delta	P. R. Legg	Gladstone	
	Charles U. Woolpert	Wells	Teacher.
	F. D. Davis	Escanaba	Teacher.
Dickinson	E. L. Parmenter	Iron Mountain	
	E. P. Frost	Norway	Teacher.
	L. E. Amidon	Iron Mountain	Teacher.
Eaton	Cynthia Green	Charlotte	Teacher.
	A. A. Worcester	Eaton Rapids	Teacher.
	Garfield Inwood	Vermontville	Teacher.
Emmet	H. S. Babcock	Harbor Springs	
	Carl Worden	Petoskey	Teacher.
	J. E. Kennedy	Pellston	Teacher.
Genesee	F. J. Johnson	Flint	
	E. A. Branch	Otisville	Teacher.
	A. E. Potter	Grand Blanc	Teacher.
Gladwin	F. E. Armstrong	Gladwin	Teacher.
	Charlotte Ferrell	Beaverton	Teacher.
	Mervin Early	Beaverton	Teacher.
Gogebic	Laura Bowden	Ironwood	Teacher.
	Amelia F. Olcott	Bessemer	Teacher.
	L. W. Brice	Wakefield	Teacher.
Grand Traverse	Geo. Crisp	Traverse City	Teacher.
	E. O. Ladd	Old Mission	Farmer.
	Lee Hornsby	Traverse City	Teacher.
Gratiot	C. F. Pike	Ithaca	Teacher.
	W. E. Swope	Breckenridge	Teacher.
	M. L. Hull	St. Louis	Teacher.
Hillsdale	H. P. McClave	Hillsdale	Teacher.
	C. L. Poor	Waldron	Teacher.
	C. L. Chamberlain	Osseo	Teacher.
Houghton	Wm. Bath	Houghton	Clerk.
	A. E. Peterman	Calumet	Lawyer.
	F. W. Jeffers	Atlantic Mine	Teacher.
Huron	Chas. F. Hey	Sebewaing	Teacher.
	Geo. F. Manning	Elkton	Teacher.
	Geo. H. Hall	Elkton	Teacher.
Ingham	F. E. Searl	Mason	Farmer.
	Geo. W. Harvey	Lansing	Teacher.
Ionia	Harvey H. Lowrey	Ionia	
	Geo. E. Downs	Lake Odessa	Teacher.
	Chas. Reasoner	Pewamo	Teacher.
Iosco	J. A. Campbell	Whittemore	Teacher.
	B. G. Sutton	Au Sable	Teacher.
	B. Clancey	Au Sable	Teacher.
Iron	John F. Mason	Amasa	Teacher.
	A. L. Flewelling	Crystal Falls	Teacher.
	E. E. Allen	Stambaugh	Teacher.
Isabella	Ernest T. Cameron	Sherman City	Teacher.
	A. W. Lynch	Rosebush	Teacher.
	F. E. Morrison	Loomis	Teacher.
Jackson	Thos. M. Sattler	Jackson	Teacher.
	F. H. Brown	Brooklyn	Teacher.
	J. Ray Fisher	Rives Junction	Butcher.

TABLE XXIV.—CONTINUED.

County.	Name.	Address.	Occupation.
Kalamazoo	Sheridan F. Mapes	Kalamazoo	Teacher.
	Arthur Stannard	Galesburg	
	Clarence Hanes	Schoolcraft	Teacher.
Kalkaska	Irene L. Getty	Kalkaska	Teacher.
	Eugene Phelps	Darragh	Farmer.
	Frank Jensen	Kalkaska	Teacher.
Kent	A. M. Freeland	Grand Rapids	Teacher.
	C. M. Ferner	Grandville	Teacher.
	P. N. Sawyer	Sparta	Teacher.
Keweenaw	F. M. Bradshaw	Gay	Teacher.
	James Hamilton	Allouez	Teacher.
	Clarence Chrysler	Copper Falls Mine	Teacher.
Lake	W. C. Giberson	Baldwin	Insurance.
	Eugene Robertson	Bristol	Teacher.
Lapeer	C. H. Naylor	Lapeer	Teacher.
	R. V. Langdon	Clifford	Lawyer.
	O. M. Gass	Imlay City	Teacher.
Leelanau	J. O. Duncan	Sutton's Bay	Attorney.
	E. F. Carr	Empire	Teacher.
	S. E. Blackwood	Leland	Teacher.
Lenawee	M. W. Hensel	Blissfield	Teacher.
	Mae Hathaway	Blissfield	Teacher.
	John C. Howell	Macon	Student.
Livingston	J. A. Woodruff	Fowlerville	Teacher.
	Harry Durfee	Oak Grove	Teacher.
	T. J. Gaul	Pinckney	Teacher.
Luce	H. G. Warne	Newberry	Teacher.
	Eva E. Buermann	Newberry	Teacher.
	Edward Seymour	Newberry	Minister.
Mackinac	E. J. LaChance	St. Ignace	Bookkeeper.
	Lloyd Walker	St. Ignace	Teacher.
	J. L. Barnhart	Engardine	Teacher.
Macomb	O. D. Thompson	Mt. Clemens	Teacher.
	E. E. Crook	New Baltimore	Teacher.
	A. E. Millett	Armada	Undertaker.
Manistee	H. J. Leighton	Bear Lake	Teacher.
	E. M. Gerred	Filer City	Teacher.
	C. I. Richer	East Lake	Teacher.
Marquette	A. E. Sterne	Ishpeming	Teacher.
	T. W. Clemo	Republic	Teacher.
	Jas. H. Kaye	Marquette	Teacher.
Mason	C. A. Rinehart	Scottville	Editor.
	Pauline Smith	Ludington	Teacher.
	Gertrude L. Darr	Freesoil	Teacher.
Mecosta	Burt J. Ford	Big Rapids	Teacher.
	J. R. Miller	Big Rapids	Teacher.
	G. E. McCloskey	Barryton	Teacher.
Menominee	Jesse Hubbard	Menominee	Teacher.
	B. W. Weenink	Spalding	Teacher.
	J. O. Prosser	Stephenson	Teacher.
Midland	John Mustard	Midland	
	Agnes Menerey	Coleman	Teacher.
	Delila Lee	Midland	Teacher.
Missaukee	Ezra Hall	Lake City	
	O. J. Jackson	Lake City	Teacher.
	M. L. Wolverton	Lake City	Teacher.

TABLE XXIV.—Continued.

County.	Name.	Address.	Occupation.
Monroe	J. J. Kelley	Monroe	Teacher.
	Frank Partlem	Newport	Teacher.
	Theo. Drinkhahn	Scofield	Teacher.
Montcalm	E. D. Straight	Stanton	Teacher.
	F. E. Schall	Lakeview	Teacher.
	J. E. McClosky	Howard City	Teacher.
Montmorency	B. J. Watters	Lewiston	Teacher.
	Mrs. W. D. Rice	Big Rock	Teacher.
	Dave Farrier	Royston	Teacher.
Muskegon	Nellie B. Chisholm	Montague	Teacher.
	R. W. Brock	Muskegon	Teacher.
Newaygo	Isabella M. Becker	Fremont	
	John Harwood	White Cloud	Teacher.
	Carrie L. Carter	Newaygo	Teacher.
Oakland	H. S. Elliott	Oxford	Teacher.
	A. L. Craft	Rochester	Teacher.
	Theo. Goodfellow	Royal Oak	Teacher.
Oceana	Marguerite Lux	Hart	Editor.
	W. O. Cole	Shelby	Teacher.
	J. L. Walker	Crystal Valley	Teacher.
Ogemaw	Ben Bennett	West Branch	Teacher.
	Archie McMillan	Prescott	Teacher.
	H. S. Kercher	Rose City	
Ontonagon	A. C. Adair	Rockland	Hotel keeper.
	Mrs. Clara Omans	Rockland	Teacher.
	J. L. Wagner	Ontonagon	Teacher.
Osceola	Geo. F. Roxburg	Reed City	Teacher.
	F. C. Smith	Tustin	Teacher.
	M. D. Jerome	Evart	Teacher.
Oscoda	Mrs. J. A. Young	Mio	Teacher.
Otsego	R. D. Bailey	Gaylord	Teacher.
	Sim J. Lewis	Johannesburg	
	A. J. Armstrong	Vanderbilt	Teacher.
Ottawa	Martin DeGraff	Grand Haven	Teacher.
	Nelson Stanton	Holland	Teacher.
	L. Rens	Borculo	Teacher.
Presque Isle	M. H. Nester	Metz	Physician.
	Nettie Tower	Onaway	Teacher.
	C. S. Covey	Rogers	Teacher.
Roscommon	Ellen McRae	Roscommon	Druggist.
	Adelia McCrea	Roscommon	Teacher.
	Verna Gibbons	Roscommon	Housekeeper.
Saginaw	B. S. Teft	Saginaw, W. S	Teacher.
	J. B. Griffin	Carrollton	Teacher.
	A. C. Leach	Birch Run	Teacher.
St. Clair	E. T. Blackney	Port Huron	Teacher.
	W. J. Tripp	St. Clair	Teacher.
	W. F. Lewis	Port Huron	Teacher.
St. Joseph	L. E. Miller	Centerville	Teacher.
	Jas. J. Dock	Leonidas	Teacher.
	Geo. DeLong	Three Rivers	Teacher.
Sanilac	Chas. G. Putney	Sandusky	Teacher.
	Geo. E. Meredith	Speaker	Teacher.
	F. Dunn	Sandusky	Teacher.

TABLE XXIV.—CONCLUDED.

County.	Name.	Address.	Occupation.
Schoolcraft	W. T. S. Cornell	Manistique	Teacher.
	Dr. Hackwell	Blaney	Physician.
	Carey W. Dunton		Teacher.
Shiawassee	H. E. Slocum	Corunna	Teacher.
	T. A. Mears	Byron	Teacher.
	C. B. Jordan	Morrice	Teacher.
Tuscola	H. P. Bush	Caro	Teacher.
	C. L. Coffen	Unionville	Teacher.
	R. J. Smith	Kingston	Teacher.
Van Buren	V. R. Hungerford	Paw Paw	Teacher.
	R. B. Taylor	Paw Paw	Teacher.
	A. L. Hyames	Gobleville	Teacher.
Washtenaw	Evan Essery	Ann Arbor	Teacher.
	Josephine Hoppe	Chelsea	Teacher.
	M. J. Cavanaugh	Ann Arbor	Lawyer.
Wayne	E. W. Yost	Detroit	Teacher.
	W. Lightbody	Detroit	Teacher.
	W. Harris	Highland Park	Teacher.
Wexford	W. H. Faunce	Cadillac	Teacher.
	E. E. Irwin	Sherman	Teacher.
	R. J. Josenhans	Manton	Teacher.

TABLE XXV.

General statistics of educational institutions compiled from reports of officers for the academic year 1906--1907.

Name of institution.	Location.	Name of president, superintendent, or principal.	Date of organization.	Number of instructors.	Number of students or inmates during the year.	Number of students from Michigan.	Number of graduates at last commencement.	Whole number of graduates since founded.	Number of volumes in library.	Number of volumes added to library during year.
ESTABLISHED BY ACTS OF LEGISLATURE.										
Educational:										
Central Michigan Normal School	Mt. Pleasant	Charles T. Grawn	1895	39	968	961	163	1,277	9,750	1,771
Michigan Agricultural College	East Lansing	Jonathan L. Snyder	1857	80	1,001	937	96	1,279	28,177	1,484
Michigan College of Mines	Houghton	Fred W. McNair	1885	34	239	142	47	425	21,539	829
Michigan State Normal College	Ypsilanti	Lewis H. Jones	1852	76	2,501	2,233	424	5,892	30,000	1,000
Northern State Normal School	Marquette	James H. B. Kaye	1899	24	448	441	115	397	12,948	946
University of Michigan	Ann Arbor	James B. Angell	1837	336	4,746	2,573	902	24,206	222,609	12,696
Western Michigan Normal School	Kalamazoo	Dwight B. Waldo	1904	26	813	794	93	177	3,000	1,000
Totals			....	615	10,716	8,081	1,840	33,653	328,023	19,726
Charitable:										
Industrial Home for Girls	Adrian	Lucy M. Sickels	1881	36	350	350	....	....	1,586	....
Industrial School for Boys	Lansing	E. M. Lawson	1857	14	1,054	1,054	....	....	3,000	200
Michigan School for the Blind	Lansing	Clarence E. Holmes	1881	15	114	114	5	....	36,400	50
Michigan School for the Deaf	Flint	Francis D. Clarke	1854	46	325	324	17	1,729	5,561	247
State Public School	Coldwater	J. B. Montgomery	1874	6	184	184	....	....	2,280	....
Totals	....	....	....	117	2,027	2,026	22	1,729	48,827	497
INCORPORATED UNDER ACT 39, LAWS OF 1885.										
...minational:										
...n College	Adrian	B. W. Anthony	1859	16	172	57	13	594	7,000	300
... College	Albion	Samuel Dickie	1861	25	450	431	36	764	18,000	350
College	Alma	August F. Bruske	1886	22	273	257	7	126	20,142	282
...t College	Detroit	Richard D. Slevin	1881	15	250	250	23	339	13,325	275
...el Missionary College	Berrien Springs	Nelson W. Kanble	1899	12	169	124	....	3	3,000	....

TABLE XXV.—CONCLUDED.

Name of institution.	Location.	Name of president, superintendent, or principal.	Date of organization.	Number of instructors.	Number of students or inmates during the year.	Number of students from Michigan.	Number of graduates at last commencement.	Whole number of graduates since founded.	Number of volumes in library.	Number of volumes added to library during year.
Denominational. Con:										
Hillsdale College	Hillsdale	Joseph W. Mauck	1855	23	313		32	1,050	15,000	3,000
Hope College	Holland	G. J. Kollen	1866	21	309	211	19	359	15,000	125
Kalamazoo College	Kalamazoo	A. Gaylord Slocum	1855	13	229	198	31	463	11,051	600
Olivet College	Olivet	Ellsworth G. Lancaster	1844	30	255	220	20	661	31,500	1,000
Totals				177	2,420	1,748	181	4,359	134,018	5,932
Academies and Seminaries:										
Academy of the Ladies of the Loretto	Sault Ste. Marie	Mother M. Bride	1898	8	126	115	4	27	1,020	15
Academy of the Sacred Heart	Grosse Pointe Farms	Madame O'Keefe	1885	17	70	40	2	67	2,000	100
Academy of the Sacred Heart	Detroit	Madame L. Gerardin	1850	12	92	92			2,743	156
Benzonia Academy	Benzonia	G. R. Catton	1900	4	48	47	4	24	4,000	
Detroit Home and Day School	Detroit	Miss Ella M. Leggett	1882	36	320	308	22	368	3,650	150
Detroit University School	Detroit	Frederick L. Bliss		23	260	233	33	214	2,200	
Holy Rosary Academy	Bay City			8	50	50	1	1	340	70
Michigan Military Academy	Orchard Lake	Lawrence Cameron Hull	1877	12	108	29	18	500	5,000	125
Nazareth Academy	Nazareth	Sister M. Gertrude Keenan	1897	18	93	63	2	11	6,200	200
Raisin Valley Seminary	Adrian	Charles W. Obee	1855	4	51	50	9	202	750	
St. Mary's Academy	Monroe	Mother M. Mechtildis	1890	32	321	248	21	179	9,448	196
St. Mary's School	Sault Ste. Marie	Rev. Alex. A. Gagnieur		8	480	480			500	
Seminary of the Felician Sisters	Detroit	Cajetana Jankiewiss	1882	5	72	14	19	257	2,005	
Spring Arbor Seminary	Spring Arbor	Burton J. Vincent		9	164	136	4	202	600	20
Theological School of the Christian Ref. Church	Grand Rapids	Rev. W. Heyns	1878	10	159	108	10	125	3,800	700
Ursuline Academy	St. Ignace	Mother M. Angela	1899	9	100	97	1	11	850	20
Totals				215	2,514	2,110	150	2,188	45,106	1,752

Professional Schools:										
Detroit College of Law	Detroit	Philip T. Van Zile	1893	23	202	180	45	553	14,612	509
Detroit College of Medicine	Detroit	Theodore A. McGraw	1868							
Department of Dental Surgery				33	85	55	24	316		
Medicine				98	158	104	68	1,755	1,200	
Detroit Homeopathic College	Detroit	C. C. Miller	1871	38	29	22	9	74	1,000	1,000
Michigan College of Medicine	Detroit	Hal C. Wyman	1888	36	12	10		475	5,000	400
Sprague Correspondence School of Law	Detroit	William C. Sprague	1891	4	806					
Totals				232	1,292	371	146	3,173	21,812	1,909
Schools with Normal and Business Course:										
Benton Harbor College	Benton Harbor	G. J. Edgcumbe	1892	16	319	307	36	421	1,215	100
Cedar Lake Industrial Academy	Cedar Lake	S. M. Buttler	1902	4	61	60	2		200	
Cleary Business College	Ypsilanti	P. R. Cleary								
Ferris Institute	Big Rapids	Woodbridge N. Ferris	1894	22	1,962	1,884	123	850	1,988	21
International Business College	Saginaw	S. W. Pearcy	1896	5	229	229	14			
Jackson Business University	Jackson	B. J. Campbell	1901	4	151	149	28			
Ludington Business College	Ludington	W. H. Martindill	1898	2	91	89	37		110	12
Michigan Business and Normal College	Battle Creek	C. J. Argubright	1896	4	263	240	60		110	20
Valley City Commercial School	Grand Rapids	A. S. Parish		3	169	169				
Totals				60	3,245	3,127	390	1,271	3,623	153

TABLE XXVI.

Financial statistics of educational institutions compiled from reports of officers for the academic year 1906-1907.

Name of institution.	Annual cost of tuition per student.	Average cost of board per week	Total average annual cost to each student.	Total average annual cost of each student to the State.	Estimated value of grounds, buildings, library, apparatus, etc.	Amount of productive funds.	Income from productive funds.	Amount of legislative appropriation for 1906.	Receipts from tuition fees during the year.	Receipts from all other sources.	Current expenses for the year.	Expenses for permanent improvements.	Liabilities.
ESTABLISHED BY ACTS OF LEGISLATURE.													
Educational:													
Central Michigan Normal School	$12 00	$2 50	$150 00	$94 23	$177,500 00	....	....	$66,564 96	$1,884 00	$345 00	$68,000 00	....	....
Michigan Agricultural College	†15 00	2 58	225 00	....	860,869 85	$978,187 49	$10,155 22	188,310 00	970 00	230,709 78	225,265 21	$139,646 01	....
Michigan College of Mines	{ 25 00 / †150 00 }	5 00	{ †450 00 / †600 00 }	209 20	538,561 51	....	....	60,000 00	26,183 00	9,123 79	95,306 29	....	....
Michigan State Normal College	10 00	2 50	175 00	46 43	463,500 43	....	4,127 00	112,000 00	14,166 00	2,239 70	132,116 37	....	....
Northern State Normal School	12 00	3 75	174 00	91 52	169,701 30	....	....	41,000 00	2,781 50	....	43,781 50	40,133 20	....
University of Michigan	58 00	5 00	400 00	79 85	3,012,000 00	545,946 00	85,500 00	650,287 50	278,000 00	147,000 00	791,000 00	37,300 00	$10,350 00
Western Michigan Normal School	9 00	2 40	170 00	72 00	175,000 00	....	....	35,000 00	....	2,399 00	37,399 00	60,000 00	....
Charitable:													
Industrial Home for Girls	....	87	....	121 60	238,802 90	....	....	68,000 00	....	4,287 95	67,707 70	10,976 40	....
Industrial School for Boys	....	....	....	120 73	387,295 75	....	....	80,000 00	....	8,899 90	89,097 65	1,250 00	....
School for the Blind	....	....	....	304 84	178,196 32	....	....	35,000 00	....	871 57	34,752 12	440 89	....
School for the Deaf	73 62	1 10	....	253 22	525,877 30	....	....	85,000 00	250 00	....	94,410 02	1,559 95	....
State Public School	....	2 66	....	31 92	281,190 35	1,000 00	50 00	37,500 00	....	....	37,500 00	6,123 50	....
INCORPORATED UNDER ACT 39, LAWS OF 1885.													
Denominational:													
Adrian College	45 00	3 00	198 00	....	200,000 00	20,000 00	1,200 00	....	7,740 00	15,260 00	23,000 00	4,000 00	21,000 00
Albion College	30 00	2 35	200 00	....	250,000 00	275,000 00	14,500 00	....	17,274 95	22,353 00	41,159 03	16,193 03	....
Alma College	32 00	2 50	187 00	....	180 482 32	263,109 02	15,263 57	....	6,210 66	5,876 16	26,128 59	503 25	....
Detroit College	60 00	....	60 00	....	170 000 00	....	....	....	11,538 30	....	15,267 35	....	25,786 48
Emanuel Missionary College	90 00	1 25	150 00	....	59,043 50	....	....	....	1,250 00	3,886 00	4,206 09	1,800 00	17,816 83
Hillsdale College	23 50	2 50	175 00	....	120,000 00	250,007 36	12,221 14	....	2,162 40	6,028 77	20,412 31	1,500 00	22,169 35
Hope College	24 00	2 50	180 00	....	260,000 00	300,000 00	20,000 00	....	3,000 00	71,635 74	34,947 49	41,749 30	9,382 54
Kalamazoo College	30 00	2 75	250 00	....	135,000 00	436,190 22	17,358 65	....	6,140 50	2,939 76	24,944 41	1,009 15	1,996 50
Olivet College	50 00	2 50	225 00	....	400,000 00	117,166 00	5,746 06	....	17,065 03	22,268 84	47,000 00	1,000 00	78,954 56

Academies and Seminaries:													
Academy of the Ladies of the Loretto	20 00	3 50	130 00						4,000 00		4,000 00	270 00	5,500 00
Academy of the Sacred Heart	60 00		350 00									1,250 00	
Academy of the Sacred Heart	40 00								3,638 00		3,638 00	700 00	
Benzonia Academy	25 00	2 50	150 00		25,000 00	10,000 00	525 00		1,125 00	750 00	2,400 00		500 00
Detroit Home and Day School	70 00 to 200 00	5 00	50 00		90,000 00				54,000 00		51,000 00	3,000 00	
Detroit University School					155,002 44				48,095 66	4,422 77	58,693 85	115,993 62	98,708 72
Holy Rosary Academy	40 00	1 50			80,000 00				3,000 00		6,000 00		
Michigan Military Academy	‡500 00		750 00		250,000 00								
Nazareth Academy	150 00	3 75			125,000 00								50,000 00
Raisin Valley Seminary	20 00	2 25	155 00		6,000 00	10,600 00	733 00		858 00	549 00	1,912 00	57 00	350 00
St. Mary's Academy	40 00		160 00		250,000 00				42,907 73	6,623 30	38,195 38	8,000 00	110,626 00
St. Mary's School	5 00		5 00		30,000 00						2,500 00		9,000 00
Seminary of the Felician Sisters	80 00	1 75	140 00		91,000 00				774 25	978 00		98 00	
Spring Arbor Seminary	24 00	1 75	115 00		30,000 00	6,000 00	200 00		2,740 00	1,990 02	4,877 31	200 00	6,000 00
Theological School, Christian Reformed Church	26 00	3 50	250 00		40,000 00				3,524 00	9,223 02	12,768 81		
Ursuline Academy	5 00	3 00	120 00		13,000 00				800 00	2,400 00	3,000 00	500 00	400 00
Professional Schools:													
Detroit College of Law	75 00								13,900 71	526 30	14,143 07		
Detroit College of Medicine:													
Department of Dental Surgery	90 00	4 00	250 00		150,000 00		1,595 00		7,090 00				
Medicine	110 00	4 00	250 00						17,800	7,757 34	32,233 60		40,000 00
Detroit Homeopathic College	60 00	4 00			75,000 00				2,300 00	1,000 00	3,000 00	600 00	11,000 00
Michigan College of Medicine and Surgery	25 00		58 00		100,000 00				720 00	6,000 00	6,720 00	2,000 00	
Sprague Correspondence School of Law													
Schools with Normal and Business Courses:													
Benton Harbor College	32 00 to 60 00	2 75	130 00		60,000 00				6,850 00		5,325 00	200 00	450 00
Cedar Lake Industrial Academy	36 00	1 75	135 00		10,468 52								1,770 00
Cleary Business College													
Ferris Institute	30 00 to 60 00	2 50	210 00		75,000 00		40,904 39		4,750 00	39,000 00	25,000 00	4,845 00	
ernational Business College	75 00	3 50	275 00						5,233 72		4,985 98		
kson Business University	90 00	3 50	265 00						4,852 50	704 60	4,850 00	200 00	
ington Business College	45 00	3 00	150 00		3,500 00				1,409 20		300 00	200 00	
igan Business and Normal College	60 00	3 00	225 00		6,000 00				8,525 00	1,247 97	7,360 00	350 00	540 00
ey City Commercial School	84 00	4 00	312 00						8,166 82		8,062 91		

o non-residents of State.
Includes board, etc.

TABLE XXVII.

Special statistics compiled from commissioners' reports.

Counties.	Parochial schools.							
	Number of schools.	Number of children enrolled.	Age of same.	Branches taught.	Character of instruction.	Number of instructors.	Regularity of attendance.	Length of time of school.
Allegan	4	190	6 to 16	Religious doctrine, Bible history, English and German grammar, English and German spelling, reading, writing, geography, U. S. history, drawing, physiology, civics, and arithmetic	Fair	6	Good	9 to 10 mos.
Alpena	6	950	6 to 18	Same as in the public schools with religious instruction added. State course of study followed in some	Fair	18	Good	10 mos.
Arenac	2	35	1 to 16	Common branches, Bible study, German	Good	2	Good	6 or 7 mos.
Baraga	1	100	5 to 16	Arithmetic, reading, spelling, geography, language, history, and physiology	Good	6	Good	10 mos.
Barry	2	16	5 to 18	English branches, with Bible study		2	Fair	8 mos.
Bay	18							
Benzie	1							
Berrien	6	e 400	5 to 14	German and a little English	Poor			
Branch	1	174	8 to 17	Same as public schools up to 7th grade, also music, drawing, sewing and German	Fair	3	Good	8½ mos.
Calhoun	3	550	5 to 15	Common school branches	Good	20	Excellent	9 mos.
Cass	1	25	5 to 20	Arithmetic, grammar, civil govt., U. S. history, physiology, spelling and orthography and Adventist's creed	Good	1	Good	8 mos.
Cheboygan	4	400	7 to 16	Common school branches, music, drawing, needlework, religious instruction	Good	10	Very good	10 mos.
Chippewa	2	600	5 to 20	Common school and high school branches	Fair	14	Fair	10 mos.
Clinton	4	292	5 to 16	Common school branches with German	Good	9	Good	5 to 10 mos.
Delta	2	625	5 to 18	Common school and high school branches	Good	16	Good	10 mos.
Dickinson	1	300	6 to 14	Reading, writing, arithmetic, spelling, language, grammar, composition, Bible history, music	Good			
Eaton	2	34						
Emmet	3	400	5 to 16	Common school branches	Fair	12	Good	9 to 10 mos.
Genesee	1	150	5 to 14	Public school subjects through 8 grades	Fair	4	Good	9 to 10 mos.
Gogebic	1	506	5 to 18	Same as in the public schools	Good	12	Good	10 mos.
Grand Traverse	4	e 80	9 to 16	Common English branches and catechism	Good	11	Good	5 to 9 mos.
Gratiot	2	32	5 to 18	Common school branches and Bible	Good	2	Good	5 to 8 mos.
Houghton	12	2,740	9 to 20	Same as in public schools	Fair	68	Good	10 mos.
Huron	12	800	6 to 14	Common English branches, German and Polish languages, church history, doctrines, etc.	Fair	15	Fair	10 mos.
Ingham	3	460	6 to 19	Reading, mathematics, geography, grammar, history, physiology, civics, writing, music, catechism	Good	11	Good	10 mos.

Ionia	4	510	5 to 20	Catechism, English, grammar, U. S. history, civil government, reading, writing, arithmetic, algebra, geography, spelling, physics, physiology, music, drawing, Latin, German	Good	13	Good	7 to 10 mos.
Iosco	2	119	6 to 15	Common school branches through 7 grades	Excellent	3	Fair	9½ mos.
Iron	1	16	6 to 14	Com. branches as outlined in the Michigan Manual and course of study, with catechism	Good	1	Good	4 mos.
Isabella	2	425	6to 15	Common school branches, with catechism	Fair	7	Good	8 to 10 mos.
Jackson	4	700	....	Com. school branches and catechism	Fine	17	Good	9 mos.
Kalamazoo	5	1,160	5 to 20	Common school and high school subjects	Good	32	Good	9 mos.
Kent	30	6,100	5 to 16	Common school branches, religious doctrine	Good	6	Very good	9 mos.
Leelanau	2	225	5 to 20	English and commercial subjects, 12 grades	Fair	7	Good	9 to 10 mos.
Lenawee	7	400	5 to 16	Common school branches with church history	Good	7	Fair	6 to 10 mos.
Mackinac	2	50	6 to 20	All common school branches	Excellent	5	Good	10 mos.
Macomb	18	438	5 to 15	Common school subjects, church history, Bible	In some schools fine	27	Good	10 mos.
Manistee	9	1,500	7 to 14	Common branches and religious doctrine	Fair	15	Fair	9 to 10 mos.
Marquette	3	1,082	6 to 20	Christian doctrine, orthography, writing, reading, civics, drawing, grammar, geography, arithmetic, U. S. history, music, physiology, algebra, English, geometry, physics, rhetoric, literature, Latin, French, botany, astronomy	Catholic	24	Good	10 mos.
Mason	4	544	5 to 20	Same as public schools and religious doctrine	Good	13	Fair	9½ to 10 mos.
Menominee	3	582	....	English branches through 8 grades	....	15	....	9 mos.
Monroe	13	800	6 to 14	Arithmetic, geography, history, language, reading, writing	Good	20	Good	10 mos.
Montcalm	1	59	6 to 20	English branches, with science and languages	Fair	6	Good	8 mos.
Montmorency	1	45	5 to 14	Reading, writing, arithmetic, geography, church history, catechism	Poor	1	Fair	2 mos.
Muskegon	7	980	5 to 16	All grades, English, French, German, Holland	Good	25	Very good	9 to 11 mos.
Newaygo	1	13	5 to 17	Reading, orthography, spelling, writing, arithmetic, grammar, physiology, geography, U. S. history, language, and Bible study	Very good	1	Very good	8 mos.
Oakland	1	225	5 to 20	Full English course with Latin	Fair	6	Excellent	10 mos.
Oceana	2	150	5 to 20	Common school subjects	Good	3	Good	8 mos.
Osceola	1	70	6 to 15	English, German, religious doctrine	Fair	1	Fair	10½ mos.
Otsego	1	145	6 to 14	Common school branches through 6 grades, catechism, and reading in Polish	Fair	2	Good	10 mos.
Ottawa	7	850	5 to 20	Common subjects through 12 grades	Good	20	Fair	....
Presque Isle	6	310	8 to 15	Common branches, half in English, Polish, German	Fair	9	Very good	2 to 10 mos.
Saginaw	24	1,800	5 to 15	Common school branches and parochial subjects	Good	....	Fair	4 to 10 mos.
St. Clair	11	750	5 to 18	Common school branches through eight grades		21	....	5 to 7½ mos.
St. Joseph	1	50	5 to 17	Common school branches through eight grades	Very good	1	Good	9 mos.
Sanilac	5	....			....	....	....	....
Schoolcraft	1	250	5 to 19	Arithmetic, reading, writing, geography, spelling, grammar, physiology, English, U. S. history, general history, rhetoric, physical geography, algebra, physics, civics, Bible history	....	6	Good	10 mos.
Shiawassee	2	300	7 to 16	Common school branches and religious instruction	Catholic and Adventist	4	Good	9 to 10 mos.
Tuscola	6	....			....	....	....	....
Van Buren	3	60	6 to 16	Common school English branches, German, catechism, and Bible history	....	3	Good	6 to 8 mos.
Washtenaw	19	900	7 to 16	....	Mostly religious	26	Very good	2 to 9 mos.
Wayne	*6	....		English taught part of the day	....	....	....	....
Wexford	2	30	7 to 17	Common school branches	....	2	Good	9 mos.

*Outside city.

TABLE XXVII.—Continued.

Special statistics compiled from commissioners' reports.

Counties.	Commercial schools.						
	Number of schools.	Number of students	Branches taught.	Character of instruction.	Number of instructors.	Length of time of school	Name and location of each school.
Alpena	1	150	Branches usually taught in commercial schools of best class	Good	5	Whole year	Alpena Business College, Alpena.
Charlevoix							
Che'boygan	1	75	Commercial branches, stenography and typewriting	Excellent	1	11 mos	Cheboygan Business College, Cheboygan.
Chippewa	1	250	Book-keeping, shorthand, typewriting, telegraphy, music		3	12 mos.	Reid's College of Business.
Delta	1	45	Commercial branches	Fair	1	12 mos	Gordon's Business College.
Genesee	1	50	Commercial branches, music		2	12 mos.	Bliss Business College.
Gratiot	1	100	Book-keeping, writing, shorthand, music, typewriting				
Grand Traverse	1	100	Commercial branches, typewriting, stenography, English, with normal course during summer	Good	4 to 6	12 mos.	The Needham Business College, Traverse City.
Hillsdale	1	45	Commercial branches, with shorthand	Very good	2	9½ mos.	Hillsdale Business College, Hillsdale.
Jackson	1	300	Commercial branches	Fine	3	12 mos.	Jackson Business University, Jackson.
Kalamazoo	2	250	Commercial branches with shorthand and typewriting	Good	8	12 mos.	Parson's Business College, Kalamazoo. The Rowe Business College, Kalamazoo.
Manistee	1	200	Business subjects and English	Fair	4	11 mos.	Manistee Business College, Manistee.
Marquette	2	174	Book-keeping, banking, writing, commercial arithmetic, rapid calculations, shorthand, typewriting, letter writing, spelling, commercial law, English			12 mos. 50 wks.	Ishpeming Business College, Ishpeming. Marquette Business College, Marquette.
Oakland	1	40	Full commercial course		3	12 mos.	Pontiac Commercial school, Pontiac.
Ottawa	2						
Saginaw	2						Saginaw Business College, Saginaw, E. S. International Business College, Saginaw, E. S.
St. Clair	3	175	All common branches and commercial law		6	40 wks.	Port Huron Business University, Port Huron. International Business College, Port Huron. Sullivan's Shorthand School, Port Huron.
St. Joseph	1	40	Usual commercial subjects, arithmetic, spelling, commercial geography, book-keeping, writing, commercial law	Very good	2	9 mos.	Three Rivers Business College, Three Rivers.
Shiawassee	1	75	Commercial branches		2	9 mos.	Owosso Business College, Owosso.
Washtenaw	2	300	All branches			12 mos. 12 mos.	Cleary Business College, Ypsilanti. Moran Business College, Ann Arbor.

TABLE XXVII.—CONCLUDED.

Special statistics compiled from commissioners' reports.

Counties.	Private schools.						
	Number of schools.	Number of students.	Branches taught.	Character of instruction.	Number of instructors.	Length of time of school.	Name and location of each school.
Alger	1	3	Common school branches	Good	1	8 mos.	McKinnon.
Emmet	1	60	Common school branches				
Ionia	1	4	Studies outlined in State course of study, with Bible study	Very good	1	7 mos.	Odessa Christian School, Odessa Township.
Lenawee	1	250	Public school course through 12 grades, with music, art, and commercial courses	Good		38 wks.	St. Joseph's Academy, Adrian.
St. Clair	1	40	Common school subjects through eight grades	Fair	2	9½ mos.	Miss Coyle's, Port Huron.

TABLE XCVIII.

Special report of day schools for the deaf for the school year 1916–17.

Location.	Number of schools [illegible]	Number of pupils enrolled.	Total days attendance.	Average number [illegible]	Amount [illegible]
Totals	10	148	22,225	123.4682	$15,[illegible]
Bay City	1	10	1,490	9.1111	$1,0[illegible]
Calumet	1	10	1,[illegible]	10.2222	1,2[illegible]
Detroit	7	51	7,700	42.7777	5,[illegible]
Grand Rapids	2	19	2,761	15.3[illegible]	1,5[illegible]
Ironwood	1	7	1,140	6.3333	7[illegible]
Ishpeming	1	8	1,102	6.6194	[illegible]
Kalamazoo	1	8	991	5.5055	[illegible]
Manistee	1	8	1,224	6.8	[illegible]
Menominee	1	5	464	3.[illegible]	71[illegible]
Saginaw [illegible]	1	7	1,128	6.2555	[illegible]
Sault Ste. Marie	1	6	1,117	6.2027	70[illegible]
Traverse City	1	9	1,000	5.5583	910 [illegible]

TABLE XXIX.

Special report of the county normal training classes for the school year 1906-07.

Counties.	Number of teachers.	Amount paid teachers.	Number of graduates.	Average age of graduates.	Average number hours of practice teaching by graduates.
Totals	131	$45,666 00	400	19.1	57.1
Allegan	3	$1,500 00	12	18.4	54.9
Antrim	4	1,287 45	9	18.6	56.2
Arenac	3	1,200 00	12	18.2	40.0
Barry	9	1,250 00	22	19.3	52.3
Branch	6	1,300 00	8	20.6	50.0
Calhoun	4	1,350 00	10	......	56.5
Cass	4	1,100 00	16	19.2	51.0
Charlevoix	3	1,350 00	10	19.8	69.8
Clinton	4	1,400 00	14	19.3	53.2
Gratiot	4	1,200 00	6	18.5	50.0
Ingham	3	1,400 00	12	19.3	45.5
Ionia	5	1,500 00	12	18.1	34.0
Iosco	3	1,900 00	13	18.1	85.0
Kalkaska	2	1,100 00	10	18.1	53.3
Lapeer	7	2,143 55	14	19.1	70.0
Lenawee	3	2,250 00	14	19.3	69.1
Macomb	3	1,550 00	11	17.6	59.5
Manistee	6	1,350 00	9	18.9	57.7
Mason	5	1,460 00	11	20.2	69.0
Mecosta	3	1,250 00	15	18.3	50.0
Midland	4	1,400 00	11	19.4	50.0
Newaygo	4	1,200 00	12	19.1	54.8
Oakland	2	1,300 00	16	20.2	50.0
Oceana	6	1,200 00	8	18.1	90.0
Osceola	3	1,600 00	10	19.7	56.3
Otsego	3	1,150 00	7	19.4	52.0
Ottawa	4	1,300 00	12	20.5	90.0
St. Clair	2	1,500 00	21	19.0	69.0
Saginaw	8	1,100 00	20	18.8	50.0
Shiawassee	4	1,250 00	6	18.8	35.0
Van Buren	4	2,545 00	9	19.7	61.3
Wexford	3	1,300 00	19	19.5	80.0

TABLE XXX.

Summary of census of children blind or with defective vision under Act 116, 1907.

Counties.	Number of children blind or with defective vision.		
	Rural and village districts.	City districts.	Total.
Totals	268	93	361
Alcona	2		2
Alger			
Allegan	7		7
Alpena	1		1
Antrim	2		2
Arenac	4		4
Baraga			
Barry	12		12
Bay	2	2	4
Benzie	5		5
Berrien	3		3
Branch	5		5
Calhoun	12		12
Cass	5		5
Charlevoix	6		6
Cheboygan	4	3	7
Chippewa	1	1	2
Clare			
Clinton	3		3
Crawford	5		5
Delta			
Dickinson			
Eaton	1		1
Emmet	1		1
Genesee	2	1	3
Gladwin			
Gogebic	4	1	5
Grand Traverse	4		4
Gratiot	4		4
Hillsdale	3	1	4
Houghton	3	2	5
Huron	5		5
Ingham	4	7	11
Ionia	5		5
Iosco	1		1
Iron	1		1
Isabella	5		5
Jackson	1	1	2
Kalamazoo	3		3
Kalkaska	4		4
Kent	5	7	12
Keweenaw			
Lake	2		2
Lapeer			
Leelanau	1		1
Lenawee	9		9
Livingston	1		1
Luce			
Mackinac			
Macomb	2	1	3
Manistee	4	9	13
Marquette	2	3	5
Mason	2	2	4
Mecosta	1		1
Menominee	3		3
Midland	6		6
Missaukee			
Monroe	1	2	3
Montcalm	9	1	10
Montmorency			
Muskegon		1	1
Newaygo	9		9
Oakland	5		5
Oceana	8		8
Ogemaw	2		2
Ontonagon			
Osceola	1		1
Oscoda	1		1
Otsego			
Ottawa	8	2	10
Presque Isle	1		1
Roscommon			
Saginaw	8	10	18
St. Clair	6	9	15
St. Joseph	4	8	12
Sanilac	11		11
Schoolcraft			
Shiawassee	5		5
Tuscola	8		8
Van Buren	4		4
Washtenaw	6	1	7
Wayne		14	14
Wexford	3	4	7

INDEX.

INDEX.

Page.
Academies and seminaries, general and financial statistics of........282, 285
Academies of the Sacred Heart, general and financial statistics of........282, 285
Academy of the Ladies of the Loretto, general and financial statistics of........282, 285
Adrian College, general and financial statistics of........281, 284
Agricultural college (see Michigan Agricultural college).
Agriculture, county schools of........2, 35
Bulletin No. 24 on........36
Courses of study........39
Library and reference books........40
Organization........37
Qualifications of instructors........38
Agriculture in rural high schools........24
Suggestions for work in........28–32
Agriculture in the public schools........58
A short course in seeds and grains........61
An elementary laboratory study in crops........60
Bulletin No. 26 on........59
Corn........76
Corn judging........74
Laboratory equipment........61
Outline for scoring dent corn........77
Table of contents........60
The study of the seed:
A study in seed germination........62
Effect of age upon the vitality of seed........65
freezing upon the vitality of seed corn........70
temperature on the germination of seed........72
Germination of corn at different temperatures........73
in different soils........72
frozen corn........70
poor and of good seed oats........67
seeds at various depths........65
sprouted and unsprouted seeds........68
tip, middle, and butt kernels of corn........69
How the young plants appear above ground........63
Necessity for air in the germination of seeds........71
Practical seed corn testing........73
Quantity of food stored in seed........63
The depth to which seed should be planted........64
The importance of early saving and drying of seed corn........70
Vitality of bin grains........66
kernels from different parts of the ear........68
old seed corn........66
sprouted grain........67
Albion college, general and financial statistics of........281, 284
Algebra, number of districts giving instruction in........185
Alma college, general and financial statistics of........281, 284
Amount due the districts........161, 178
of township library money on hand July 8, 1907........182
paid and due inspectors........163, 178
commissioners........162, 191

Page.
examiners ... 162, 191
township chairmen and other officers ... 163, 178
Apportionment of the primary school interest fund ... 163, 164
Arithmetic, number of districts giving instruction in ... 185
Associations, county teachers', number held ... 191
township, number held ... 191
Attendance, percentage of, for State ... 158, 166
in city and graded village schools ... 217-231
graded school districts ... 158, 196-215

Benton Harbor college, general and financial statistics of ... 283, 285
Benzonia academy, general and financial statistics of ... 282, 285
Blind, School for the, general and financial statistics of ... 281, 284
statement regarding ... 5
summary of census of ... 292
Boards of examiners, expenses and compensation, amount of ... 163, 191
list of ... 276
number of days devoted to meetings of ... 191
Bonded indebtedness of the districts, amount of ... 161, 178
paid on ... 161, 175
Botany, number of districts giving instruction in ... 185
Branches of instruction, statistics of ... 185
Building and repairs, expenditures for ... 161, 175
Bulletin No. 16 on teachers' examinations ... 46, 47
24 on county schools of agriculture ... 36-42
25 on rural high schools ... 21-35
26 on agriculture in the public schools ... 59-77
Bulletins published, Superintendent's introduction ... 5

Cedar Lake Industrial academy, general and financial statistics of ... 283, 285
Central Michigan Normal school, attendance for academic year and summer session of 1907 ... 18
general and financial statistics of ... 281, 284
graduates from in 1907 ... 18
Certificates, city, granted according to the provisions of Sec. 20, Act No. 147 ... 160, 188, 261
college life, number holding ... 261
county normal training class, number holding ... 160, 188
different grades, number receiving ... 160, 188
kindergarten, music and drawing ... 48, 49
Normal, number of teachers holding ... 160, 188
number of applicants for, having received normal instruction ... 160, 188
regular and special ... 160, 188
receiving, who had attended institutes during year ... 160, 188
without previous experience in teaching ... 160, 188
revoked or suspended ... 188
State, number holding ... 160, 188
Charitable institutions, general and financial statistics of ... 281, 284
Children attending public school, number of ... 157, 166, 180
between 5 and 20, number of ... 157, 166, 180
enrolled in city school districts ... 158, 216
day schools for the deaf ... 158, 290
graded school districts ... 157, 180, 196
parochial schools ... 286
ungraded school districts ... 157, 180
summary of census of those blind or with defective vision ... 292
City and village schools;
Amount paid for instruction ... 248-259
regular teachers ... 248-259
special teachers ... 248-259
Attendance, average daily ... 217-230
Children between 5 and 20, number of ... 216-230
Commercial course, schools having ... 233-247
Compulsory attendance law, schools enforcing ... 233-247
Cost per capita by departments for instruction and incidentals ... 248-259
Day schools for the deaf, schools having ... 233-247
Domestic science, schools giving instruction in ... 233-247

Page.

Drawing, schools giving instruction in.......... 233-247
Enrollment by departments.......... 216-230
Flags, U. S., number having.......... 233-247
French, number studying.......... 233-247
German, number studying.......... 233-247
Graduates, average age of class.......... 232-246
number of.......... 233-247
Greek, number studying.......... 233-247
Instructors, number of, in commercial course.......... 261
domestic science.......... 261
drawing.......... 261
kindergarten.......... 261
manual training.......... 261
music.......... 261
penmanship.......... 261
physical culture.......... 261
Kindergarten below primary grade, schools having.......... 233-247
work, portion of time in first primary devoted to.......... 233-247
Latin, number studying.......... 233-247
Manual training, schools giving instruction in.......... 233-247
Music, vocal, schools giving instruction in.......... 233-247
Non-resident pupils, number of.......... 232-246
Number pupils belonging, average.......... 216-230
to each teacher.......... 232-246
Penmanship, schools giving instruction in.......... 233-247
Superintendents' time given to supervision.......... 217-231
Teachers, number employed.......... 217-231
special, number of.......... 217-231
Ungraded department, schools maintaining.......... 233-247

City teachers:
Certificates, college, number holding.......... 261
different grades held by.......... 261
granted by State board of education, number holding.......... 261
normal, number holding.......... 261
Number employed.......... 261
Civil government, number of districts giving instruction in.......... 185
Colleges, statistics of (see State and educational institutions).
Commercial course, schools having.......... 233-247
Commercial schools, not incorporated:
Branches taught.......... 288
Character of instruction.......... 288
Instructors, number of.......... 288
Name and location of schools.......... 288
Students enrolled, number of.......... 288
Commissioners for 1906-7.......... 276
number of schools visited by.......... 191
salaries of.......... 191
Comparative summary of statistics.......... 157
Compulsory attendance, Superintendent's introduction.......... 5
law, number districts in which enforced.......... 191
schools enforcing.......... 233-247
Consolidation.......... 12-15
Limitations.......... 13
Rearrangement on township basis.......... 13
Special conditions.......... 12
Consolidation, larger.......... 14
Economy of administration.......... 15
buildings.......... 15
child's time.......... 14
expense.......... 15
Cost per capita of schools.......... 180
County boards of school examiners.......... 276
County normal training classes.......... 4, 42-44
Average number hours of practice teaching by each graduate.......... 291
Counties maintaining.......... 42, 291

Page

Graduates.... 42, 43
average age of.... 291
number of.... 158, 291
Summer sessions.... 43
Teachers, amount paid.... 291
number employed.... 158, 291
Visitations.... 43
County schools of agriculture:
Bulletin No. 24.... 35-42
Course of study for.... 39, 40
Library for.... 40-42
Organization of.... 37, 38
Qualifications of instructors.... 38

Day schools for the deaf:
Cities maintaining.... 233-247, 290
Cost of school.... 290
Day schools and State institutions.... 81
Location of.... 82, 290
Pupils, average number belonging.... 290
number enrolled.... 158, 290
Teachers, number employed.... 158, 290
Teaching trades in.... 81
Deaf, Michigan School for the, general and financial statistics of.... 281, 284
statement regarding.... 5
Decisions of the Supreme Court (see Supreme Court decisions).
Denominational colleges, general and financial statistics of.... 281, 282, 284
Detroit college, general and financial statistics of.... 281, 284
Detroit College of Law, general and financial statistics of.... 283, 285
Detroit College of Medicine, general and financial statistics of.... 283, 285
Detroit Home and Day school, general and financial statistics of.... 282, 285
Detroit Homeopathic college, general and financial statistics of.... 283, 285
Detroit University school, general and financial statistics of.... 282, 285
Dictionaries, number of schools supplied with.... 163, 193
Diplomas, eighth grade, number granted.... 193
District libraries (see libraries).
taxes, amount received from.... 161, 172
Districts, expenditures of.... 161, 175
furnishing free text-books, number of.... 163, 193
graded, number of.... 157, 166
number supplied with flag and flagstaff.... 163
that have adopted text-books on physiology.... 193
taught communicable diseases according to law.... 193
visited by commissioners during the year.... 191
resources of.... 161, 172
township unit, number of.... 157, 166
ungraded school, number of.... 157
whole number of.... 157, 166
Domestic science, schools giving instruction in.... 233-247
Domestic science and art in rural high schools.... 25, 26
Drawing, schools giving instruction in.... 233-247

Educational funds.... 147
Educational institutions, general and financial statistics of.... 281-285
Eighth grade diplomas, number granted.... 193
number of pupils in exclusive of graded schools.... 193
Elementary laboratory study in crops.... 60-77
Emmanuel Missionary college, general and financial statistics of.... 281, 284
Examination questions for county certificates.... 107-139
eighth grade diplomas.... 140-143
State certificates.... 91-106
Examinations of teachers, public, number held.... 168, 188
statistics of.... 160, 188
Examiners, boards of, expenses and compensation, amount of.... 163, 191
list of.... 276

Page.

number of days devoted to meetings of.......... 191
Expenses of schools, total net.......... 161, 175

Ferris Institute, general and financial statistics of.......... 283, 285
Financial report of the University of Michigan.......... 148
statistics, miscellaneous.......... 248-259
Flag and flagstaff, number of districts supplied with.......... 163
Free text-books, number of districts furnishing.......... 163, 193
French, schools giving instruction in.......... 233-247
Funds, educational.......... 145

General history, number of districts giving instruction in.......... 185
General school statistics as reported by school inspectors.......... 166
Geography, number of districts giving instruction in.......... 185
Geometry, number of districts giving instruction in.......... 185
German, schools giving instruction in.......... 233-247
Globes, number of schools supplied with.......... 163, 193
Graded school districts:
Aggregate number of months taught in.......... 197
Children attending school in, number of.......... 157, 180, 196
between 5 and 20, number of.......... 157, 180, 196
Cost of, per capita.......... 180
Indebtedness of, total.......... 161, 196
Instruction and superintendence, amount paid for.......... 197
Non-resident pupils attending.......... 157, 197
tuition paid by.......... 161, 197
Number of.......... 157, 166
Percentage of attendance.......... 158, 196
Property, estimated valuation of.......... 160, 196
School, number of days taught in.......... 196
Teachers, number employed.......... 158, 159, 196
wages of, average monthly.......... 159, 160, 197
total.......... 159, 197
Grammar, number of districts giving instruction in.......... 185
school department statistics (see city and village schools).
Grand Rapids Business university (see Valley City Commercial school).
Greek, schools giving instruction in.......... 233-247

High schools, list of, on accredited list of the University.......... 10
Hillsdale college, general and financial statistics of.......... 282, 284
Holy Rosary academy, general and financial statistics of.......... 282, 285
Hope college, general and financial statistics of.......... 282, 284

Indebtedness of districts, amount paid on.......... 161, 175
bonded and total.......... 161, 178
Industrial education.......... 78, 79
Continuation schools.......... 78
Trade school.......... 78
Why pupils leave school.......... 78
Industrial Home for Girls, general and financial statistics of.......... 281, 284
statement regarding.......... 5
Industrial School for Boys, general and financial statistics of.......... 281, 284
statement regarding.......... 5
Inspectors and members of school boards, amount paid.......... 162, 163, 178
Institute fees, amount collected.......... 191
Institutes, average attendance at.......... 272
conductors and instructors at.......... 268
enrollment at.......... 162, 272
kinds and grades of certificates held by members.......... 272
location and date of.......... 264
number in attendance having received normal instruction.......... 272
without experience in teaching.......... 272
of, held.......... 162
percentage of whole number of teachers that attended.......... 272
receipts and disbursements at.......... 284

Page.
International Business college, general and financial statistics of.....283, 285
Investigation of school records, Superintendent's introduction..... 3

Jackson Business university, general and financial statistics of.....283, 285

Kalamazoo college, general and financial statistics of.....282, 824
Kelley, Patrick Henry, biographical sketch of..... 82, 83
Kindergarten, number of schools having..... 233-247
work, portion of time in first primary devoted to..... 233-247
Kindergarten, music, and drawing certificates, list of approved schools..... 48, 49
number issued..... 48

Latin, schools giving instruction in..... 233-247
Legally qualified teachers, number of.....160, 188
Legislation, enactments of Legislature of 1907..... 1, 2
proposed..... 7, 8
Libraries, district and township, amount of fines received from county treasurers for..... 182
taxes voted for.....162, 182
paid for support of.....162, 175, 182
general and financial statistics of.....162, 182
number of.....162, 182
volumes added to, during year..... 182
whole, in.....161, 182
Library books and care of library, expenditures for.....162, 175, 182
list of, for county schools of agriculture..... 40
rural high schools..... 33
moneys, amount received.....172, 182
number of townships forfeiting.....162, 182
townships, amount on hand July 8, 1907..... 182
List of high schools on accredited list of the University..... 10
Loans, amount of interest paid on.....161, 175
received from.....161, 172
Ludington Business College, general and financial statistics of.....283, 285

Manual training in rural high schools.....25, 27, 32
suggestions for work in..... 32
schools giving instruction in..... 233-247
Maps, number of schools supplied with.....163, 193
Michigan Agricultural college, control and management of..... 9
general and financial statistics of.....281, 284
Michigan Business and Normal college, general and financial statistics of.....283, 285
Michigan College of Medicine and Surgery, general and financial statistics of.....283, 285
Michigan College of Mines, general and financial statistics of.....281, 284
Michigan Military academy, general and financial statistics of.....282, 285
Michigan State Normal college, attendance for academic year and summer session of 1907... 18
general and financial statistics of.....281, 284
graduates from, in 1907..... 19
Moneys on hand, amount of..... 175

Nazareth academy, general and financial statistics of.....282, 285
Needed legislation, Superintendent's introduction..... 7, 8
Needed reform in school curriculum, Superintendent's introduction..... 11
Net receipts of all districts.....161, 172
New legislation, Superintendent's introduction..... 1, 2
Non-resident pupils, number in graded schools.....157, 197
ungraded schools..... 157
tuition from, amount received in graded school districts.....161, 197
ungraded school districts..... 161
Normal school system of Michigan..... 17-19
Executive council of..... 17
Enrollment in..... 18
Graduates from..... 18
Normal training classes (see county normal training classes).
Northern State Normal school, attendance for academic year and summer session of 1907. 18

Page.

general and financial statistics of 281, 284
graduates from, in 1907 18

Olivet college, general and financial statistics of 282, 284
One mill tax, receipts from 161, 172
Orthography, number of districts giving instruction in 185

Penmanship, number of districts giving instruction in 185
schools giving instruction in 233–247
Percentage of attendance for the State 156, 166
in city and graded village schools 217–231
graded school districts 158, 196
Physics, number of districts giving instruction in 185
Physiology, number of districts giving instruction in 185
having adopted text-books on 193
Primary school interest fund, apportionment of 163, 164
Private or parochial schools:
Attendance, regularity of 286
Branches taught 286
Character of instruction 286
Children enrolled, ages of 286
number of 286
Instructors, number of 286
Statistics of 158, 187
Professional schools, general and financial statistics of (see State and educational institutions).
Public examinations, number held 160, 188
Pupils, number enrolled in city school districts 158, 216
day schools for the deaf 158, 290
eighth grade, exclusive of graded schools 193
graded school districts 157, 180, 196
normal training classes 291
private or parochial schools 158, 187, 286
ungraded school districts 157, 180

Questions, examination, for county certificates 107–139
eighth grade diplomas 140–143
State certificates 91–106

Raisin Valley seminary, general and financial statistics of 282, 285
Reading, number of districts giving instruction in 185
Reforms needed, Superintendent's introduction 5
Report on auditing district accounts 53–58
Rural high schools, Superintendent's introduction 3, 20–35
Rural schools:
Consolidation 12–14
Problem of 11
Solution of 12
Statement concerning 8

St. Mary's academy, general and financial statistics of 282, 285
St. Mary's school, general and financial statistics of 282, 285
School, average number of months 158, 166
number of days in graded districts 196
whole 166
School board and inspectors, amount paid for services 163, 178
commissioners for 1907 276
number of schools visited by 191
salaries of 191
districts, statistics of (see districts).
for the Blind, general and financial statistics of 281, 284
Deaf, general and financial statistics of 281, 284
houses, number of 160, 166
properly ventilated 193
to be built during year 180
statistics, general .... [illegible]

Page.
School funds, uses of........ 51
library........ 52
primary........ 52
School moneys, care of........ 51
School officers' meetings, Superintendent's introduction........ 3,50
plan of organization........ 50
purpose of meetings........ 50
School savings banks, Superintendent's introduction........ 5
School system of Michigan;
Agricultural college........ 9
Graded and city schools........8, 9, 16, 17
Course of study........ 16
Number of........ 8, 16
Weak points........ 16, 17
High schools on accredited list of the University........ 10
Normal schools........9, 17–19
Executive council of........ 17
Number of graduates from........ 18
students enrolled in........ 18
Relation between normal and public schools........ 9
Rural schools........ 8, 11
Consolidation........ 12
Limitations........ 13
Rearrangement on township basis........ 13
Special conditions........ 12
Larger consolidation........ 14
Administration........ 15
Economy of buildings........ 15
expense........ 15
the child's time........ 14
Reform courses........ 14
State University........ 9, 19
Degrees conferred........ 19
Income........ 19
Purpose of higher education........ 19
Taxes........ 19
The rural high school........ 20–35
Township unit system........ 9
Schools and school houses, statistics as to conditions........ 193
centralized........ 12–15
commercial, not incorporated, special statistics........ 288
cost per capita........ 180
number having uniform text-books in each branch........ 193
in which physiology and hygiene is taught........ 193
properly classified........ 193
with prescribed course of study........ 193
private or parochial, number of........158, 187
rural........ 8, 11
special statistics of........286, 289
teachers employed in........158, 159, 169
with normal and business course, general and financial statistics of........283, 285
Seminary of the Felician Sisters, general and financial statistics of........283, 285
Sisters of the Order of St. Dominic (see Holy Rosary academy).
Special educational institutions, Superintendent's instruction........ 5
Special report of county normal training classes........ 291
day schools for the deaf........ 290
superintendents of schools........ 261
Special statistics compiled from commissioners' reports........ 286
Sprague Correspondence School of Law, general and financial statistics of........283, 285
Spring Arbor seminary, general and financial statistics of........282, 285
State Agricultural college (see Michigan Agricultural college).
State and educational institutions:
Amount of legislative appropriation........ 284
Cost per student........ 284
Current expenses for the year........ 284